National Poetry, Empires and War

Nationalism has given the world a genre of poetry bright with ideals of justice, freedom and the brotherhood of man but also, at times, burning with humiliation and grievance, hatred and lust for revenge, driving human kind, as the Austrian poet Grillparzer put it, 'From humanity via nationality to bestiality'. *National Poetry, Empires and War* considers national poetry and its glorification of war, from ancient to modern times, in a series of historical, social and political perspectives.

Starting with the Hebrew Bible and Homer and moving through the Crusades and examples of subsequent empires, this book has much on pre-modern national poetry. But it focuses chiefly on post-1789 poetry which emerged from the weakening and collapse of empires, as the idealistic liberalism of nationalism in the age of Byron was replaced by darker purposes culminating in World War I and the rise of fascism. Some poets associated with this transformation – including Whitman, D'Annunzio, Yeats, Bialik, and Kipling – are prominent in this book. Many national poets are the subject of countless critical and biographical studies, but this book aims to give a panoramic view of national poetry as a whole. It will be of great interest to any scholars of nationalism, Jewish Studies, history, comparative literature and general cultural studies.

David Aberbach is Professor of Hebrew and Comparative Literature, McGill University, Montreal. He has held visiting positions at Oxford, the LSE, UCL and Harvard. His work bridges the arts and social sciences, as seen in his current book on national poetry and also in previous books on loss and on charisma.

Routledge Interdisciplinary Perspectives on Literature

1. The Gothic in Contemporary Literature and Popular Culture
 Pop Goth
 Edited by Justin D. Edwards and Agnieszka Soltysik Monnet

2. Wallace Stevens and Pre-Socratic Philosophy
 Metaphysics and the *Play* of Violence
 Daniel Tompsett

3. Modern Orthodoxies
 Judaic Imaginative Journeys of the Twentieth Century
 Lisa Mulman

4. Eugenics, Literature, and Culture in Post-war Britain
 Clare Hanson

5. Postcolonial Readings of Music in World Literature
 Turning Empire on Its Ear
 Cameron Fae Bushnell

6. Stanley Cavell, Literature, and Film: The Idea of America
 Edited by Andrew Taylor and Áine Kelly

7. William Blake and the Digital Humanities
 Collaboration, Participation, and Social Media
 Jason Whittaker and Roger Whitson

8. American Studies, Ecocriticism, and Citizenship
 Thinking and Acting in the Local and Global Commons
 Edited by Joni Adamson and Kimberly N. Ruffin

9. International Perspectives on Feminist Ecocriticism
 Edited by Greta Gaard, Simon C. Estok and Serpil Oppermann

10. Feminist Theory across Disciplines
 Feminist Community and American Women's Poetry
 Shira Wolosky

11. Mobile Narratives
 Travel, Migration, and Transculturation
 Edited by Eleftheria Arapoglou, Mónika Fodor and Jopi Nyman

12. Shipwreck in Art and Literature
 Images and Interpretations from Antiquity to the Present Day
 Edited by Carl Thompson

13. Literature, Speech Disorders, and Disability
 Talking Normal
 Edited by Chris Eagle

14. The Unnameable Monster in Literature and Film
 Maria Beville

15. Cognition, Literature and History
 Edited by Mark J. Bruhn and Donald R. Wehrs

16. Community and Culture in Post-Soviet Cuba
 Guillermina De Ferrari

17 Class and the Making of American Literature
Created Unequal
Edited by Andrew Lawson

18 Narrative Space and Time
Representing Impossible Topologies in Literature
Elana Gomel

19 Trauma in Contemporary Literature
Narrative and Representation
Edited by Marita Nadal and Mónica Calvo

20 Contemporary Trauma Narratives
Liminality and the Ethics of Form
Edited by Susana Onega and Jean-Michel Ganteau

21 The Future of Testimony
Interdisciplinary Perspectives on Witnessing
Edited by Jane Kilby and Antony Rowland

22 Literature and the Glocal City
Reshaping the English Canadian Imaginary
Edited by Ana María Fraile-Marcos

23 Apocalyptic Discourse in Contemporary Culture
Post-Millennial Perspectives of the End of the World
Edited by Monica Germanà and Aris Mousoutzanis

24 Rethinking Empathy through Literature
Edited by Meghan Marie Hammond and Sue J. Kim

25 Music and Identity in Postcolonial British South-Asian Literature
Christin Hoene

26 Representations of War, Migration, and Refugeehood
Interdisciplinary Perspectives
Edited by Daniel H. Rellstab and Christiane Schlote

27 Liminality and the Short Story
Boundary Crossings in American, Canadian, and British Writing
Edited by Jochen Achilles and Ina Bergmann

28 Asian American Literature and the Environment
Edited by Lorna Fitzsimmons, Youngsuk Chae and Bella Adams

29 Transnational Feminist Perspectives on Terror in Literature and Culture
Basuli Deb

30 Children's Literature, Domestication, and Social Foundation
Narratives of Civilization and Wilderness
Layla AbdelRahim

31 Singularity and Transnational Poetics
Edited by Birgit Mara Kaiser

32 National Poetry, Empires and War
David Aberbach

National Poetry, Empires and War

David Aberbach

LONDON AND NEW YORK

First published 2015 by Routledge

2 Park Square, Milton Park, Abingdon, Oxfordshire OX14 4RN
52 Vanderbilt Avenue, New York, NY 10017

Routledge is an imprint of the Taylor & Francis Group, an informa business

First issued in paperback 2019

Copyright © 2015 Taylor & Francis

The right of David Aberbach to be identified as author of this work has been asserted by him in accordance with sections 77 and 78 of the Copyright, Designs and Patents Act 1988.

All rights reserved. No part of this book may be reprinted or reproduced or utilised in any form or by any electronic, mechanical, or other means, now known or hereafter invented, including photocopying and recording, or in any information storage or retrieval system, without permission in writing from the publishers.

Notice:
Product or corporate names may be trademarks or registered trademarks, and are used only for identification and explanation without intent to infringe.

Library of Congress Cataloging in Publication Data

Aberbach, David, 1953- author.
National poetry, empires and war / David Aberbach.
   pages cm. — (Routledge interdisciplinary perspectives on literature)
Includes bibliographical references and index.
   1. Poetry—History and criticism. 2. Nationalism in literature.
   3. War and literature. I. Title.
PN1080.A34 2014
809.1'93581—dc23   2014032734

ISBN: 978-1-138-80534-7 (hbk)
ISBN: 978-0-367-87019-5 (pbk)

Typeset in Sabon
by codeMantra

To Mimi, Gabriella, Shushu and Jessica

Contents

Acknowledgements — xi

Introduction: Unacknowledged Legislators: National Poets, Prophets and Revolution — 1

1 National Poetry and the Hebrew Bible: War and the Messianic Age — 35

2 Mythical History in National Poetry — 63

3 European National Poetry, Islam and the Defeat of the Medieval Church — 90

4 Medieval Spanish Hebrew National Poetry — 110

5 Poetry of the British Isles: History, Myth and Nationalism — 133

6 The Greek War of Independence and Its Poetry — 145

7 National Poetry and Russian-Ottoman Imperial Conflict — 166

8 Byron to D'Annunzio: From Liberalism to Fascism in National Poetry, 1789–1933 — 186

9 Walt Whitman, American Nationalism and the Revolutions of 1848–49 — 203

10 The Artist as Nation-Builder: Yeats and Bialik — 226

11 Defeat and Independence Struggles in National Poetry — 248

12 The British Empire and Revolutionary National Poetry — 267

Conclusion: National Poetry, Morality and Individual Creativity 292

Appendices 298
Bibliography 325
Index 349

Acknowledgements

This book builds on previous articles and books spanning over nearly 40 years. The Acknowledgements there apply here too, particularly in *Bialik* (1988); *Surviving Trauma: loss, literature and psychoanalysis* (1989); *Imperialism and Biblical Prophecy* (1993); *Charisma in Politics, Religion and the Media* (1996) and *Jewish Cultural Nationalism* (2008).

An article in *Encounter* (1981), the kernel of this book, is reprinted as Appendix (f), and I thank my editors, the late Mel Lasky and Margot Walmsley, who took the time and trouble to help me with it when I was young and out of work. A version of chapter 4 on medieval Spanish Hebrew poetry was first published as a working paper by the Department of Sociology, London School of Economics (1995). Chapter 5 on British national poetry first appeared in a *Festschrift* for Anthony D. Smith (2007). Chapter 8 on Byron and D'Annunzio evolved from a talk given at a conference of the American Byron Society. Appendix (b) on national poetry and Poor Law from Shakespeare to Wordsworth is based on a talk given at Harvard University and published by the Weatherhead Center for International Affairs at Harvard (2014).

Sometimes the study of national poetry has seemed like a form of archaeology, revealing layers of culture and meaning buried and largely forgotten.

I am grateful to the following people for various forms of advice and help: Linda Bree, Ardis Butterfield, John A. Hall, Stefka Iorgova, Susan Irvine, Cynthia Liu, Panagiotis Roilos, Jonathan Sacks, Elizabeth Sotir and Nicholas Watson. I am especially grateful to Anthony D. Smith for his encouragement and advice as editor of *Nations and Nationalism* where much of this book was published between 1999–2012 (for details see the Bibliography). From my colleagues and collaborators John Hutchinson and Athena Leoussi, I learned much about Irish and Greek national poetry, respectively. I thank the editors and readers of *Nations and Nationalism* and the editors at Routledge who prepared the book for publication.

*

I am indebted, too, to University College, London, English Department, and to various departments at the London School of Economics, Sociology,

Government and International Development, as well as to Harvard University, where I held visiting positions in the years 2000–2014. I thank the librarians of the various libraries I used at McGill University, Harvard University, London University (University College, Senate House, the London School of Economics and the School of East European Studies) and above all, the British Library.

I thank David Elmer and Peter McMurray for introducing me to the Milman Parry collection of Balkan oral literature at the Widener Library, Harvard University; Homi Bhabha, director of the Humanities Centre at Harvard, where I was a research associate in 2010–12; and Steve Bloomfield, director of The Weatherhead Center for International Affairs at Harvard, where I was a visiting scholar, 2012–14.

Several chapters in this book evolved as lectures at the universities of McGill, London and Harvard, in response to valued criticism by students and colleagues there.

As the book grew, ranging widely in poetry of many countries, I felt that it could serve as a bridge between the arts and the social sciences, for it shows that poetry is inseparable from the study of nationalism, and that history, political science and religion are essential in the study of national poetry.

I wrote much of this book in Quebec in the English ghetto of McGill University. Life in Quebec is itself an education in nationalism, strong enough to affect the entire character of the province, but milder than in 19th century Europe.

*

To my colleagues at McGill, I owe an incalculable debt for providing a stimulating collegial environment and much support over the years. From 2003, I taught a course on the poetry of nationalism at McGill, a testing ground for the book as it was written. I reckon this course might be the only one of its kind; and I have felt more and more the truth of Rabbi Akiba's saying, 'From all my teachers I have learned, and from my students more than the lot of them'.

To Mimi, Gabriella, Shushu and Jessica, who have made this a labor of love, this book is dedicated, with love.

4 August 2014

Introduction
Unacknowledged Legislators: National Poets, Prophets and Revolution

> *I see him from the crag-tops,*
> *I watch him from the hills –*
> *a people alone, thought nothing by the nations.*
> *Who can count Jacob's dust,*
>   *or the sand-clouds of Israel?*
>   (Hebrew Bible, Book of Numbers 23: 9–10;
>   12th century BCE?)

> *Sons of Greece, forward!*
> *Free the children and the women!*
> *Free the temples of your fathers' gods ...*
> *Now the struggle starts –*
>   *defend what belongs to you!*
>   (battle cry of the Greeks, Salamis, 480 BCE;
>   Aeschylus, *The Persians*)

Poets and their poetry are 'national' if believed to be so: if they write in the national language and speak to national concerns – above all the militant desire for independence from a foreign power; if they are ready to fight and die for the national cause; if they inspire; if they are read and sung, studied and discussed, and if extensive biographical and critical studies are made of them; if towns, streets, squares, and public buildings, mountains, learned societies – even football clubs – are named after them; if their statues, with statutory pigeon and droppings, grace city squares; if their picture is on bank notes and public holidays are associated with their names; and especially if their poetry is recited and sung by children in school.

As a child in Public School 234 in Baltimore in 1962–3, I was taken on a class trip to Fort McHenry by the harbor, where in 1814 the Americans fought off a British night attack from the sea. The poet Francis Scott Key witnessed the battle and saw the flag of stars and stripes still flying over the fort at dawn. On the spot he wrote the stirring doggerel that became the American national anthem, 'The Star Spangled Banner' – 'And the rockets' red glare, the bombs bursting in air/ Gave proof through the night that our flag was still there'. The story had heroic glamor and drama to us 9 and 10 year olds, though we (like many adults) had no idea why the British had taken Washington and were bombarding the Americans thirty years after independence was won. We knew, though, that America was threatened again in the 1960s. The school trip was at the height of the Cold War, when the Cuban crisis brought the world to the brink of nuclear war, and the basement of PS 234 was a nuclear shelter.

Children all over the world go on similar school trips, perhaps not always in such dramatic circumstances, but also with the general aim of teaching them their country's history, spirit and national identity through their poets. Italian children go to D'Annunzio's villa on Lake Garda, a national museum, the Vittoriale. Greek children go to Solomos' shrine on the island of Zakynthos where they are told, perhaps, how in 1824 Lord Byron died for Greek independence in the siege of Missolonghi on the mainland, visible a few miles away. Serbian children get the most exercise from the long climb up an enclosed stairway on Mount Lovćen near Cetinje to Njegoš' burial place, with a magnificent view on a clear day over much of the Balkans. English children are taken to Shakespeare's house in Stratford upon Avon or the equally-crowded Dove Cottage of the Wordsworths in Grasmere. Israeli children go to Bialik's purpose-built home in Tel Aviv; Egyptian children go to Shawqi's palace in Cairo; Russian children go to various houses associated with Pushkin and so on. Some houses commemorate poets in exile, for example, Mickiewicz's in Paris or Hugo's in Guernsey.

The quality of the poetry varies from poet to poet, but this is not usually of great concern to children, who at least have the poets to thank for being out of school. Nor do children care that different people have different ideas and expectations of a national poet. To Poles, for example, the poetry of Mickiewicz helped to preserve Polish national identity and the hope of independence from Russia. To Americans, Whitman's poetry catches the spirit of democracy of an emerging America. Pushkin to Russians expresses a distinct Russianness, or Kipling to his many admirers communicates a spirit of British identity as few politicians have done. To many Indians, Tagore is the quintessential Indian poet, though some also admire the dissident Tamil poet Bharati, who inspired by Shelley – particularly Shelley's conviction that poets can decide a nation's fate – adopted the name Shelley and became one of India's leading anti-British spokespersons in the early 20th century.

Some children are lucky to experience more than one national culture. In Bounds Green Primary School in London, where I went in 1960–61, the year before we moved to Baltimore, I drew the British Union Jack, sang 'God Save the Queen' in assembly and was taught about Churchill and the London Blitz, an education supplemented by my mother who had survived the bombing of the East End of London in 1940. Among my mother's precious relics of a patriotic education cut short (as English education generally was then) at 14 was 'This royal throne of kings' from *Richard II*. Like many of her generation, she could recite this by heart, with the added feeling of someone whose life had depended on England's survival. Among poems I learned as a child was the Jewish national anthem and the 'Hatikva' by Naphtali

Herz Imber, recalling the biblical longing of the Jews 'to be a free nation in our land/ In the land of Zion and Jerusalem'. I came early to an awareness of the exhilarating variety and destructive potential of national differences. My father, whose own father had served in the Austro-Hungarian army in World War I, was a multi-lingual, Viennese-born historian and Hebrew scholar who came to England in 1938 in a *Kindertransport* and who lived the rest of his life in Jewish communities with many refugees, immigrants and survivors from all over Europe. For a child in the American school system in the early 1960s, I was unusually well-travelled. Unlike any of my schoolmates, I was British, spoke Hebrew at home, had sailed across the Mediterranean and the Atlantic, been to France, Italy, Switzerland and Israel and heard different languages in each country. A childhood open to multiple influences was the gateway to this book. As a university student, I gravitated naturally to Hebrew and Comparative Literature. At Linacre College, Oxford (one of the most cosmopolitan of the Oxford colleges) I organized poetry, wine and cheese evenings (with the enthusiastic participation of the Principal, John Bamborough) in which students from all over the world read poetry in the original languages.

Hebrew for all its religious content is an education in nationalism, in the Bible, in the prayerbook, in the language itself, and in its extraordinary modern revival. Prior to 1881 Hebrew was not normally spoken as a daily vernacular. There were no schools with Hebrew as the language of instruction, and no parents raised their children speaking Hebrew as their first language. Spoken Hebrew was neglected for nearly two millennia. However, the Hebrew Bible's translation into a multitude of languages after the invention of printing in the 15th century has had immense, unparalleled influence on the growth of national languages, cultures and identities. Chapters 1, 4 and 10 cover biblical, medieval and modern Hebrew poetry, respectively. Other chapters (e.g., Chapter 2) refer to the long history of Hebrew and the Jewish people. A prelude to the poets and empires in this book is *Imperialism and Biblical Prophecy 750–500 BCE* (1993). It argued that the biblical prophets – in some ways, archetypal national poets – responded to imperial conquest and were deeply political. The three waves of prophecy, in the times of Isaiah ben Amotz, Jeremiah and the anonymous prophet known as Second Isaiah, coincided with waves of imperial expansion by Assyria, Babylonia and Persia, when the Middle East was still the center of civilization. To the prophets, true power, of a nation as of an empire, is spiritual and moral and contained in literature, and it would long outlast the cruel empires of their time. Yet the Hebrew Bible also includes much superb war poetry, with incalculable consequences in the rise of monotheist religions and the history of nationalism.[1]

>Blessed the Lord my Rock
>who teaches my hands for the fight,
>my fingers for war ...
>
>   (Psalms 144: 1)[2]

NATIONAL POETRY: A FORCE OF EXTREMES

Most of this book is on national poetry from the French Revolution to World War II (1789–1939). The French Revolution, widely justified in the name of universal revolutionary ideals, set off fierce national rivalries and hatreds lasting for generations. The growth of cities, industry and population; the advance of compulsory education and literacy and the rise of capitalism, democracy and print culture brought an expansion of national cultures. National poetry ranges from idealistic hope to violent brutality in the name of the Nation. Poets – 'unacknowledged legislators of the world' – determined the meaning of nationalism, as a force of morality and progress, as well as of corruption and ruin. Their authority came from the people; their poetry united masses of people with common territory, history and culture. After 1789, national poetry carried the spirit of revolt throughout Europe, starting with Greece, which unexpectedly won its War of Independence (1821–29) against the Ottoman Turks.[3] This was the first time a modern European people fought for and won independence from an imperial oppressor. Greece encouraged later wars of independence. Byron's intervention in the war defined the poet internationally as celebrity, champion of liberty and martyr for the Nation.[4]

Since the age of Byron, national poets are usually admired in their own countries as a force for the good, as nation builders, as national symbols and icons. At times, they are held up as models for idealistic fervor and hope, even as semi-prophetic figures, divinely inspired. They and their poetry enter the religion or secular religion of the nation. Literary memories are inscribed in the nation's calendar.[5] Finland celebrates Kalevala Day on 28 February, the date of Lönnrot's 1835 Preface to the first edition of *The Kalevala*. Bulgaria commemorates those who died fighting for freedom in World War II on 2 June, the day Hristo Botev, Bulgaria's national poet, died fighting for Bulgarian independence in 1876. Slovenians commemorate 8 February, the date of the death of France Prešeren, the Slovenian national poet, as Prešeren Day; some also celebrate on 3 December, Prešeren's birthday. Scotsmen throughout the world gather on 25 January to celebrate the birth of Robert Burns in 1759. Even those who do not know his poetry (or like poetry, for that matter) recite his poems and sing his songs, and certainly toast his memory.[6]

Until 1918, European empires dominated much of the world as well as the minorities they ruled and their cultures. National poetry helped political independence struggles but had a creative life of its own. This poetry, embedded in diverse cultures and educational systems of newly-emerging modern secular states, proclaimed national singularity and independence as moral imperatives. National poetry in its splendid variety is a cultural outcome of the pluralism articulated by Herder, who saw the Hebrew Bible as a model of national distinctiveness: each age, culture and nation is unique, it should be free to be itself and must be valued on its own terms; a nation's poetry reflects its deepest traits, its highest hopes and its spirit.[7] Yet, nationalism itself is amoral. It is a force of extremes, both creative and destructive, expressing the most admirable and despicable in human nature: pride and hope on the one hand; shame, hatred and despair on the other. Human nature is rarely so split as in national poetry. Nationalism has inspired – and been inspired by – secular ideals of liberty and justice, but has also engulfed the world in wars and genocides – including the Holocaust. Nationalism has given the world a genre of poetry bright with ideals of justice, freedom and the brotherhood of man, but also, at times, burning with humiliation and grievance, hatred and lust for revenge: 'From humanity via nationality to bestiality' (*Von der Humanität durch Nationalität zur Bestialität*), as the Austrian poet Grillparzer put it.[8] National poetry, most politically committed of all art forms,[9] with martyrs such as Velestinlis, Petőfi and Marti, is part of the most profound, tragic and incomprehensible metamorphosis in the history of civilization. It ranges from Petőfi's idealistic declaration in 1847 of 'Liberty and Love' (*Szabadság és Szerelem*) (1973: 172) to Stefan George's prophecy of mass slaughter on the eve of World War I in *The Star of the Covenant* (1913): 'Ten thousand must the holy madness strike' (*Zehntausend muss der heilige wahnsinn schlagen*) (1968: 361).

NATIONAL POETRY, WAR AND EMPIRE

National poetry thrives on war: in the Hebrew Bible and Homer; in reaction to the medieval Islamic conquests and the Crusades; in myth and legend and as a reflection of defeat and the desire for revenge. It thrives on war in the history of empires, particularly the Ottoman, Tsarist and British – the 'Other' in national poetry of the peoples they conquered – who also create significant, often-subversive, national poetry of their own. It thrives on war in response to the French Revolution, the Napoleonic wars and the rise of the secular nation state; in the independence struggles of countries under foreign rule; and in the failed revolutions of 1848–49 and the American Civil War (1861–65) in the poetry of Whitman. It thrives on war in the shift in national poetry from liberalism in one militant age to fascism in another. Even its cultural forms – through education and the preservation of tradition and ritual – are often preparation for war.

Much of this book is built around clusters of poets in three empires: the Tsarist Russian, the Ottoman Turkish and the British.[10] European poets from the Napoleonic era until World War I harried empires. As the empires weakened and collapsed in the 19th and early 20th centuries, the idealistic liberalism of nationalism in the age of Byron was replaced by darker purposes culminating in World War I and the rise of fascism.[11] Poets associated with this transformation include Byron, Whitman, D'Annunzio, Yeats, Bialik and Kipling. Poetry often asserts cultural independence as a prelude to political independence. Though national poetry grew strikingly during and after the French Revolution and the Napoleonic wars, its ancient roots

6 *Introduction*

often show, above all, in the Hebrew Bible.[12] The Bible, immersed in nations and war, imagines a world beyond nations and war, most famously in Isaiah's prediction of the messianic age:

> ... and they shall beat their swords into ploughshares,
> and their spears into pruninghooks:
> nation shall not lift up sword against nation,
> neither shall they learn war any more.
>
> (2:4)

This, the motto of the United Nations, inscribed on its cornerstone, has done little to prevent the wars which frequently break out among its member states.[13] Much national poetry, from the Bible on, is full of swords, spears and bloodshed, particularly in the centuries-long conflict between Islam and Christianity. Muslim poets such as Shawqi or Rusafi under British rule or East European Christian poets such as Botev or Eminescu under Ottoman rule, agitate for national independence while loathing not just the ruling empire but also the 'infidel' rival religion.[14] The chronic nature of this conflict is best expressed, perhaps, by Njegoš in *The Mountain Wreath*, the Serbian national epic, published in 1847, set c. 1700 but reaching back to the origins of the conflict in the Serb defeat by the Ottomans at Kosovo in 1389. An Orthodox Serb declares to his Muslim enemy over 300 years after Serbia came under Ottoman rule, 'Weren't we both on the field of Kosovo?/ I fought then and I am still fighting now' (Njegoš 1989: 16).[15] This idea of eternal religious-national conflict, its typological renewal inevitable, God-decreed by Scripture and frozen in song and oral poetry, admitting no prospect of change except through death or conversion, is lethal.[16]

NATIONAL POETRY: A BUNDLE OF CONTRADICTIONS

Prior to the emergence of modern nationalism, literature – particularly the 'classics' – was valued largely because it seemed to transcend the limitations of national identity.[17] Much post-1789 national poetry, too, was fostered by universalist ideals of the Enlightenment and German Romanticism – by Kant and Schelling, Goethe and Schiller – by the decline of faith and the Church and the rise of rationalism and the secular state. This intellectual ferment reacted in some ways *against* nationalism and the divisions among nations and peoples as dangerous provokers of violent social upheaval, international conflict and threats to individual freedom. Nationalism, then, could be seen as artistically limiting: a work of art ideally existed for its own sake, a fortress of the self.

National poets are often exceptionally alive to the conflict between individuality and universal values on the one hand and national identity and aspirations on the other. As nationalists they seem at times less concerned with creating enduring art than with national and universal goals. They are closer to Romanticism than to Modernism[18] and more often vindicated by history in their hope for national regeneration than in their call for revenge against enemies and oppressors. Often neglected in their lifetimes, and seldom known widely abroad even in good translations (Lönnrot is an exception), their influence begins mostly after their deaths.[19] In the original, their poetry is often hugely popular – Shevchenko in Ukraine, Solomos in Greece, Mickiewicz in Poland, Petőfi in Hungary, Botev in Bulgaria, Eminescu in Romania and so on. They teach love for and dedication to their country, their people and landscape, their customs and traditions, their language and literature.[20] As they inspire and justify the nation and the state, they are honored and read. To those who love these poets, their poetry helps make sense of the world, of that which is both basic and complex, irrational yet fundamental in human nature.

Yet national poetry is a dynamic art, with ever-present inner contradictions: its extremism and conservatism, its moral idealism and brutality, its psychology both outgoing and inturned, its politics of solidarity yet often prizing solitude, its use and abuse of history and myth, its triumphal individualism and frequent proximity to crisis, defeat and failure. Many poets are political leaders, with fruitful interaction of contradictory qualities: aesthetic versus social activistic, introversion versus extroversion, idealism versus compromise, elitism versus populism, provincialism versus internationalism.[21]

How can poetry be both personal and national, internal and external, lyrical and programmatic, regional and universalistic, liberal and fanatical, creative and destructive, spurred by hope and tormented by despair?[22] Was Plato right to attack poets such as Homer and Hesiod for their 'lies' and ban poets from the ideal state in *The Republic*? How can the paradoxes of modern national identity be reconciled: between the individual and the group, the narrowly national and the broadly universal, the moral ideals and violent depravity? 'Les grands artists', wrote de Musset, 'n'ont pas de patrie.' Can national poetry express both a public voice and mission and a purely inner artistic vision? Can it drive a nation to independence or merely follow a road already mapped out? How does poetry form and maintain national identity? What are the roles of history and myth in the poetry of nation-building? To what extent is the idea of a nation invented? What defines national poetry? Why is Browning not usually considered to be a 'national poet' while the Ukrainian Shevchenko is? Why Mickiewicz and Botev rather than Emily Dickinson or Mallarmé? Is there not also a matter of political conviction and intensity? Many national poems are by non-national poets, and many national poets can be deeply personal, even confessional, with scarcely a trace of public concern.[23] Is the commitment of poets who died fighting for their countries different from that of poets such as Yeats, who in the last years of his life seemed dedicated more to art than to Irish nationalism? If a poet is distinctive by being creatively original and apart from the group, how then can he or she be representative of that group? Is the notion of 'national poet' not a contradiction in terms?

POETRY AND THE INTERSECTION OF NATIONAL AND PERSONAL

These and other questions have baffled me since my Oxford graduate thesis on the Hebrew poet Bialik (1873–1934).[24] National poetry can be seen to conflict with individual creativity but there is much evidence for the reverse: that nationalism can heighten individual creativity while personal factors can give unexpected conviction to national aspirations. Bialik in his poetry suggests that the childhood loss of his father and consequent separation from his mother drove him creatively as a Romantic confessional poet, yet trauma also gave force to his conviction that the exiled Jewish people were spiritually orphaned.[25] Are there similar correspondences in other cultures between the inner world of the poet and external social and political reality? I took up this question in *Imperialism and Biblical Prophecy* (1993) and *Charisma: Politics, Religion and the Media* (1996), which look at the biblical prophets as poets, charismatics and nationalists. The present book continues the exploration of history and social change in relation to the national poet's inner life, the mainspring of his creativity. Some of the greatest national poets rebel against the nation and their national role. The individuality thereby expressed becomes paradoxically emblematic of the nation and its own struggle for independence.

The psychology of the national poet may be compared with that of political and religious charismatics who overcome personal disabilities and inner divisions by becoming one with the nation.[26] Individuals with similar family background, or life crises or comparable emotional problems, may be drawn to one another, even in the absence of verbal communication. Is this principle applicable to the relationship between individuals – including national poets – and groups? The intersection of personal and national pain may stimulate creative instinct, wedded to national hopes. The wounded Self can be regenerated through the Nation. Nationalism can give a damaged personality a sense of belonging to a wider family and, in a few, the gift of transforming mass trauma, alienation and weakness into a feeling of community and power. Nationalism, Anthony D. Smith observes, often involves 'the natural response of human beings whose social world, with its stable groupings, has collapsed; yearning to belong to a durable community, they turn to the transhistorical nation as the only available replacement for the extended family, neighbourhood and religious community' (1998: 97). National poets communicate power and unity, warning of the danger of weakness, disintegration and betrayal of national ideals precisely by those (the religious and political leaders) who should make the nation strong. Loss is no prerequisite for national identification and creativity. Yet many of the poets in this book suffered severe loss in childhood.[27] They identify strongly with a wounded, humiliated nation, long for it to be healed and revived and work to rediscover (or invent) lost national unity.

In some cases, poets find their relations with women to be uncannily like the national condition: 'To love all, first love one,' writes Ibsen in *Brand*. In the Bible, marriage (of the prophets Hosea and Ezekiel, for example) can represent the troubled 'marriage' of God and Israel.[28] In modern times, Kollar's life model for his lament for the Slavs in his sonnet collection *Daughter of Slava* (1824) was the daughter of a German Lutheran pastor whom he met while studying at Jena. Petőfi idealizes his wife in his poetry as symbol of the Hungarian nation. Prešeren in his sonnets mixes his unhappy love for Julija Primic with his ill-fated homeland, Slovenia, under Habsburg rule. Yeats' ambivalent romanticization of Ireland drew on the poet's unrequited passion for Maud Gonne, actress and revolutionary nationalist. Bialik, too, portrays the woman yearned for but emotionally out of reach as an overriding image for the poet's private failures and those of the Jewish people *vis-à-vis* their motherland and for the lofty biblical ideals beyond human reach.[29]

NATIONAL POETRY: POLITICAL-HISTORICAL PERSPECTIVES

Nationalism, old as the oldest poetry, has electrified modern poetry and politics. Poets have kept the past alive, or revived or invented the past, in history and myth. In the panorama of national poetry spanning over three thousand years, the Hebrew Bible stands out as the chief literary model for European nationalism, and the starkest warning of dangers of nationalism: loss of moral direction, incessant war, defeat and exile. The curses of the nation in the Book of Deuteronomy (ch. 28) start with moral failure and end with cannibalism. The poetry of Homer, too, warns of human weakness and immorality – lust, rape, kidnapping, rage, war, killing, destruction – leading to national disaster. Like the Hebrew Bible, it also shows how an ancient culture can be reborn in modern nationalism. Homer was chiefly responsible for the survival of the Greek language and Greek identity into modern times, as an essential part of European education.[30] The Hebrew Bible and Homer can be seen as foundations of national poetry, aesthetically and politically, and in their evocation of the distinctive history and myths of the nation, its oral and musical traditions. Yet the influence of the Bible goes far deeper. In the monotheist religions, and even among many secularists, it follows daily life from birth to death. It has largely survived as popular culture, even in translation. Homer's epics were not put in every parish church in England as the Bible was, by law; nor was Homer recited once a month as was Coverdale's translation of the Psalms, also by law.

Much national poetry evolved, as did the Bible and Homer, from oral sources,[31] and this poetry proved potent in politics. If not for Homer and the Bible, it is hard to imagine the creation of the modern Greek and Jewish states, both from fragments of once-powerful modern empires.[32] The biblical age ended with the rise of the Roman empire, but events following

10   *Introduction*

the empire's collapse a half-millennium later set the course of nationalism and national cultures. The following ten dates underlie much national poetry and outline the close links between this poetry and the history of war:

1. 638: Muslim conquest of Jerusalem
2. 1066: Norman invasion of England
3. 1099: First Crusade, conquest of the Holy Land
4. 1187: Muslim reconquest of Jerusalem by Saladin
5. 1453: Ottoman conquest of Constantinople
6. 1492: Spanish conquest of the kingdom of Granada
7. 1588: Spanish Armada
8. 1789: French Revolution
9. 1815: Napoleon's defeat at Waterloo
10. 1848: European revolutions

The Muslim conquest of the Holy Land from Christendom, the invasion of southwestern Europe in the 8th century and the Christian struggle, ultimately unsuccessful, to regain the Holy Land from Islamic rule in the Crusades dominated European culture, particularly its poetry, for centuries, from the Old French epic *The Song of Roland* (c. 1100) to the Albanian epic *The Highland Lute* (early 20th century). Throughout this time, the Hebrew Bible was a working blueprint for national identity, amid conflict both with Islam and among emerging European Christian countries and their separate languages and cultures. From the medieval period until the fall of the Ottoman empire, poetry was instrumental in the rise of European national identities, partly in reaction to centuries of Islamic ascendancy which undermined papal authority, the universal Church, the Gospel and Latin. The defeat of the medieval Church opened the way to narrower, more national and cultural concerns, reflected in a cluster of vernacular European poetic traditions. As languages grew, so did national identities.

In the two centuries after the invention of printing in the 1450s, vernacular Bible translations were the shining triumph of European culture.[33] The Bible was the chief text by which European nationalism evolved, particularly in Britain, whose poets (e.g., Spenser, Milton) tended to be staunch nationalists on the biblical model, and in Germany, where Luther's Bible translation united Germans by giving them a standard German language to read and speak. Biblical motifs suffused European national poetry and overseas as European empires grew. The Bible teaches hope for moral regeneration, it attacks enemies of the Nation and it can unite disparate groups despite geographic dislocation. Nations had biblical authority and the inspiration of progressive secular humanism for their chosenness and sense of moral integrity. Most national poets from 1789–1914 belonged to peoples who fought to be free.

NATIONAL POETRY AND THE HEBREW BIBLE

The Bible has many ingredients of modern national poetry: for example, the idea of the chosenness of the nation, its militarism and exclusiveness, and a universalist messianic vision and a common morality linking all humanity. Paradoxically, the Bible – not considered as profane 'literature' but as the Word of God, granted not just to one nation but to all humanity – had unparalleled influence on national identities.[34] Interpretations of modern nationalism often fit the world of the Hebrew Bible:[35] for example, the idea that nationalism has religious and historic roots; a loyalty to a 'high' literate culture, a language, an educational system, and a national 'will'; a stress on growth of capital cities, industry, armies, and political-military states with extended bureaucratic administration; the centrality of culture as a moral force; the ideology, identity and the split between state and society and the idea that alien rule is wrong. Even the idea of 'invented tradition' has biblical precedents.[36]

As we shall see in Chapter 1, the Hebrew Bible largely defined national poetry: aimed not at an elite but at humanity at large, whose responsibility it is to know the Law, and including complex, ironic and ambivalent prophets – undermining the nation if it fails to reach the highest moral standards. For in the Hebrew Bible, not the nation is paramount, but the divine moral ideals for which the nation is an often-inadequate vessel. The Hebrew Bible prefigures some of the great pre-modern epics – Virgil's *Aeneid*, Ferdowsi's *Shahnameh*, Tiruvalluvar's *Tirukural*, Camões' *The Lusiads*, Milton's *Paradise Lost*– which express forms of national identity in poetry.[37] In each case, as in the Hebrew Bible, an 'Other' stimulates awareness of national identity through the experience of exile, expansion through international trade and increased travel abroad, conquest of others or being conquered. The Hebrew Bible, confined at first to the Jews, was adopted as sacred in Christianity and Islam and became the most potent literary force of change in the history of civilization. As the literature of a largely impoverished minority, the Hebrew Bible makes nonsense of Marx's claim in *The German Ideology* (1845–6) that 'The ideas of the ruling class are in every epoch the ruling ideas: i.e., the class which is the ruling *material* force of society, is at the same time its ruling *intellectual* force' (Marx 1972: 172).[38] Above all, the Bible reminds us that even when nations lose political and territorial links with their ancient past, they are not totally cut off. If they preserve their culture, the links can be renewed.

The Hebrew Bible, preserved by the exiled Jews, spread internationally via Christianity among far larger numbers who were not Jewish. The Bible is the best selling and most widely circulated book of all time, with billions of copies sold or distributed free in countless translations throughout the world. Biblical notions of chosenness, equality in the eyes of God and the right to rebel against injustice were ideological underpinnings both of the English Revolution in the 1640s and the American

12 *Introduction*

Revolution of 1776. The Hebrew prophets inspired poets as diverse as Blake, Pushkin, Petőfi, Whitman and Yeats, as well as the neo-prophetic Hebrew poets Bialik and Greenberg. Even poets of nations committed to the separation of Church and State (Whitman, for instance) often speak in biblical tones as semi-religious leaders. Contrary to Machiavelli in *The Prince*, power is not defined by politics alone; often the unarmed prophet prevails. The modern perception of the poet as inspired prophet expressing strong emotion – not merely imitating, as in Aristotelian poetics – comes from the Hebrew Bible (Abrams 1975: 76–78) as does the concept of the divinely granted uniqueness of the poet as microcosm of the nation, independent and original. Prior to the modern age, wherever the vernacular Bible went, particularly in English-speaking countries, it was adopted as the sovereign and unique source of divine wisdom in practically every aspect of life. The Bible was the basis for much pre-modern education. Many non-Jewish poets used it as part of their own culture, defining the nation as an instrument of morality. The popular nature of the Bible, its sympathy for the poor and its aesthetic power, are among the reasons it was universally loved and believed. Its moral force and beauty had the stamp of truth.[39] Since its canonization around 100 CE, the Bible has repeatedly shown its power to unite highly disparate groups, regardless of religion, not only in major European countries such as Germany and Italy but also in small countries such as Serbia, whose literature was part of its struggle for independence and its creation of a modern national identity.

Printed translations of the Bible to most European languages in the 16th and 17th centuries revolutionized the vernacular, opening the way both to widespread literacy and, via the example of ancient Israel, to heightened national self-consciousness. Biblical prophets such as Hosea and Jeremiah anticipate modern poets (Byron, Shevchenko and Bialik, for example) who speak out of the depth of their inner life for a wounded, weak, humiliated nation. The Hebrew Bible is a blueprint for the survival of nations on the basis of ancient rather than more recent history and culture. Even when edited and canonized, much of the Bible was already ancient. Some countries, such as Albania, are too divided for poets to speak for all their different ethnic and religious groups. Ancient poetry, in the Bible and elsewhere, can inspire independence struggles and the creation of modern national identity.[40]

NATIONAL POETRY, TRADITION AND RITUAL

National poetry from the Hebrew Bible onward preserves tradition and daily ritual as forces of national unity and survival. In the Bible, the festivals and the Sabbath frame national identity, though the prophets warn against ritual replacing morality.[41] Especially in moments of radical change and fragmentation, the memory of tradition can steel a nation to the task of self-preservation. Poetry can record a vanished or vanishing world, kept alive in the imagination and, therefore, capable of revival in some form. Scott's *The Lay of the Last Minstrel* (1805) is a compendium of Scottish Highland customs. Italian national identity in Leopardi's 'Sabbath in the Village' (1829) is defined in the customs of ordinary Italians. Pushkin's *Eugene Onegin* (1831) was described by the pre-eminent Russian critic Belinsky as an encyclopedia of Russian life. Mickiewicz's *Pan Taduesz* (1834), filled with details of traditional Polish life in different social strata, extols Polish customs and virtues such as courtesy, hospitality and respect. Ibsen's *The Feast at Solhaug* (1856) describes a traditional Norwegian wedding.[42] Eino Leino portrays ordinary Finnish people in poems such as 'Kouta', 'Tuuri' and 'Ylermi'. Especially at moments of threat to survival, poetry of ceremony and ritual can help keep alive a national consciousness that might otherwise die. During the Anglo-Irish war in 1919–21, when Irish tradition seemed especially vulnerable, Yeats imagined in 'A Prayer for My Daughter' (1919) his infant daughter's wedding in the distant future as the force of tradition defeating arrogance and hatred: 'How but in custom and in ceremony/ Are innocence and beauty born?' Similarly, during the Russian civil war after World War I when, as Yeats put it, 'mere anarchy is loosed upon the world' ('The Second Coming'), the Hebrew poet Saul Tchernichowsky (though notorious for his attacks on Judaism, a fiercely secular Jew married outside the faith) returned to the security of custom and tradition.[43] His long narrative poem, *Elka's Wedding* (1920) set in Ukraine, celebrates Jewish marriage at a time when Judaism (and religion generally) was banned as counter-revolutionary in Soviet Russia. As in *Pan Tadeusz*, the rituals of a destroyed world might be recreated from this poem. At the poem's climax, the rabbi presents the bride with her marriage contract (*ketubah*) and makes the traditional seven blessings, and the groom smashes the wine-glass in memory of the Temple's destruction in Jerusalem. The poet affirms tradition as a living force in a secular world, and the past as a guide to human endeavor.

POLITICS AND NATIONAL POETS

Nation building is not usually associated with poets and poetry as much as with political and social processes, national liberation movements, charismatic leaders and liberators, wars of national independence and the struggle of national entities to emerge to independence from relative powerlessness and subservience to a dominant power. In truth, nations are as much cultural as political entities. Shelley was right to thunder at the end of his 'A Defence of Poetry' (1821) that 'Poets are the unacknowledged legislators of the world'. The nation is tested: can it create a unique high culture of world significance?[44]

The politically aware prophet-poet is first found in the Hebrew Bible. The idea expressed by Ho Chi Minh, 'Today we should make poems including iron and steel,/ And the poet also should know how to lead an attack'[45], is also not new. It goes back to the Hebrew Bible, to Moses, Deborah and King David. In their furious ambition to renew their people morally, national poets are often ready – as were Hebrew prophets such as Elijah and Jeremiah – for self-sacrifice, and even to give up their lives for the Nation. The poetry of the Hebrew Bible is the salient revolt in the ancient world against imperialism.[46]

True, the effects of culture are harder to measure than those of politics. Whereas Napoleon conquered territory, Byron conquered souls when he fought for Greek independence and wrote of liberty in his poetry. Verdi's impact on Italian nationalism is hardly as clear-cut as that of Cavour; and Wagner's impact on German nationalism is amorphous alongside the concrete political achievement of Bismarck. William Butler Yeats' influence on Irish nationalism is undefinable alongside that of Collins or De Valera. The inspiration of Bialik on Jewish nationalism is diffuse in comparison with that of Herzl. National poets rarely have a clear impact on the nation; the changes they bring are usually invisible and long-term. Most of the great national poets – Petőfi, Mickiewicz, Shevchenko, Lönnrot, Bialik – died before independence. Yet artists can have equal if not greater importance as exemplars of the nation's distinctiveness. Their creativity is part of the acceleration to independence. They are themselves symbols and icons of the nation's unique creative power, They regenerate their nation morally and speak for its heart and conscience. Though national poets are cultural aristocrats, and some well-born, others have humble backgrounds: Lomonosov, for example, was the son of a fisherman; Shevchenko was born a serf; Whitman's father was a carpenter; Bialik's father, a tavern keeper.

The poetry of nationalism often aims openly to bring political change, even violent struggle, leading to independence from a ruling power. To W.H. Auden, 'art is a product of history, not a cause' (Pritchard 1970: 142), a view echoed in his poem 'In Memory of W.B. Yeats' (1939): 'poetry makes nothing happen'. In fact, poets and poetry can make a great deal happen. At times, they transform a nation and its history.[47] It is not unusual for books of poetry to be described as declarations of independence from foreign rule, for example, Lönnrot's *The Kalevala* (1835) or Shevchenko's *The Kobzar* (1840).[48] Petőfi was not far wrong when he wrote that 'When the people are prominent in poetry, they are very near to power in politics'.[49] In their own countries, the political commitment of poets is often remarkable, though generally unrecognized elsewhere.

- Mihaly Vorosmarty was a member of the Hungarian parliament.
- Petar II Petrovic-Njegoš was the first Montenegrin head of state and the central figure in the emergence of modern Serbia/Montenegro.
- Alphonse de Lamartine was a French statesman who effectively served as head of government during the 1848 revolution.
- Aristotle Valaorites represented the island of Leucas in the Ionian parliament and, after union with Greece, in the Greek parliament.

- Allesandro Manzoni was a Senator in the Italian Parliament at the time of Italy's unification.
- Victor Hugo was a Senator of the French Third Republic.
- Yeats was a Senator in the Irish Free State.
- José Marti was a leader of Cuba's struggle for independence.
- Barudi, the Arabic poet, was an Egyptian statesman.
- Sayyid Maḥammad 'Abdille Ḥasan' (the 'Mad Mullah'), the Somali poet, was an important Muslim leader and warrior.
- Gjergi Fishta was vice president of the Albanian parliament.
- Saunders Lewis was a founder of the Welsh Nationalist Party (Plaid Cymru) in 1925.
- Muhammed Iqbal, the Urdu poet, was influential in Indian (and, ultimately, Pakistani) politics.
- Uri Zvi Greenberg, the Hebrew poet, was a member of the Israeli Knesset.
- Pablo Neruda was a Senator in the Chilean parliament.
- Aimé Césaire was Martinique's representative in the French government.
- Ernesto Cardenal, the Nicaraguan poet, was Minister of Culture in the revolutionary Sandinista government after the overthrow of the dictator Samoza.
- Dennis Chukwude Osadebay was Premier of the Midwestern Region of Nigeria.
- Antonio Jacinto was a member of the Angolan parliament.
- Leopold Sedar Senghor, the French poet, was the first president of Senegal (1960–80).
- Augustinho Neto, the Portuguese poet, was the first president of Angola (1975–79).

Other political leaders (Mao Zedong, Ho Chi Minh, and Che Guevara, for example) also wrote poetry.

NATIONAL POETS AS EDUCATORS

National poets are teachers. Kollar, Mickiewicz, Lönnrot, Wergeland, Njegoš, Tagore, Yeats, Bialik, Fishta, Rusafi and Senghor, among others, helped create a national curriculum – including their own poetry. National poets understand, perhaps best of all, the importance of education, of language, legend and folklore, as a binding force of the nation.

- Lönnrot, an inspector of Finnish schools, discovered Finnish myth on his journeys.
- Goethe, who was close to Herder, collected German folklore and song, which he adapted in his poetry.[50]

16 *Introduction*

- Burns, also a classical scholar, did the same for Scottish culture as Ibsen did for Norway.
- Kollar, a professor at the University of Vienna, studied the archaeology, ethnography, philology and history of the Slavs.
- Mickiewicz, a professor in Lausanne and later in Paris, did much research on Polish history and archaeology.
- Shevchenko, similarly, was a student of the history and culture of Ukraine.
- Yeats edited a number of works from Irish legend and folklore.[51]
- Gökalp collected Anatolian folk poems and folklore.
- Bialik, a brilliant talmudist, co-edited myths and legends of the Talmud and Midrash.[52]
- Tagore was a major educational force in India.

All had a surprisingly practical poetic vision.

National poets, starting from the biblical prophets, make the vernacular a tool of education and national identity. The prophets did not speak an esoteric language aimed at an elite. They spoke the language of the people, to the people. Bible translation in the two centuries after the invention of printing in the 1450s was a model for the vernacular and, through its sacred authority, for the assertion of national feeling and aspirations. The French Revolution hastened the growth of vernacular languages as part of the rise of modern nations. Macpherson, Leopardi, Soutsos, Kollar, Lönnrot, Eminescu, Yeats and Bialik are among many poets who set out to create a Herderian world of nations defined by the vernacular. They helped revive common idiomatic speech and traditional forms attuned to needs of modern nationalism. The Ukrainian poet Kotliarevsky, in *Aeneid* (1798), the first major poetry in the Ukrainian of the Poltava region, encouraged the growth of the Ukrainian language and nationalism under Russian rule and the rejection of Russian by younger Ukrainian writers, notably Shevchenko. Pushkin created a modern Russian language after the Napoleonic wars.[53] Leopardi, a contemporary of Pushkin, called for the regeneration of the Italian language and literature while keeping its ancient character, so that 'the fine, living Italian language should be a true derivation of the old, indeed a continuation of it' (Leopardi 1966: 90). Soutsos' use of demotic Greek helped free Greek poetry from 15-syllabic verse. The Egyptian poet Shawqi led a revolution against the traditional Arabic *qasida*, signalling a turn to nationalism and free verse after centuries of 'enslavement' to medieval Arabic verse and metrical forms. Eminescu contributed greatly in the creation of modern Romanian. In poems such as 'I am of Ireland', Yeats used Irish common speech. In the first decade of the 20th century, Bialik wrote the first folk poems in modern Hebrew – creating the ghost of the vernacular in the absence of native Hebrew speakers – and brought free verse back to Hebrew after a millennium of quantitative, rhymed verse.[54] Yehuda Amichai wrote of the creative challenge in adapting an ancient language 'torn blinded from biblical sleep' to a modern vernacular[55]'in words that spoke of miracles and God/ to say now: car, bomb, God' (Amichai 1975: 38).

The smaller and more vulnerable the country, the more vigorously its national poets react to threats to its language and its need for protection. Small nations, notably the Jews and Greeks, have produced some of the most powerful and enduring cultures. Language and culture can shore up weak nations, giving stability amid flux, integration amid chaos and value amid insecurity.[56]

Poets often have to fight hard for the cultural survival of the nation, against heavy odds. They struggle to raise the nation's status and its culture. For example:

- medieval Italian in relation to Latin in the age of Dante (early 14th century)
- medieval English in relation to French in the age of Chaucer (late 14th century)
- Irish, Scottish and Welsh in relation to English
- German and Russian in relation to French in the age of Herder (late 18th century–early 19th century)
- Ukrainian and Polish in relation to Russian in the age of the Romanov Tsars
- Finnish in relation to Swedish when Finland was part of the Tsarist empire
- Turkish in relation to Persian and Arabic
- Norwegian in relation to Danish
- Hebrew in relation to a series of cultures and languages, most importantly, in ancient Mesopotamia and Egypt in the time of the prophets Jeremiah and Ezekiel and in the Muslim empire in the time of Judah Halevi (11th–12th century) all major European languages, especially Russian and German, from 1789 to 1939

Many poets choose the less travelled road. Solomos, for instance, wrote in Greek, though his native Italian was easier. Other national poets – the Albanian Jeronim de Rada and the Maltese Dun Karm Psaila, for example – abandoned Italian for a vernacular of lesser status.[57] Shevchenko chose Ukrainian, which the Russian critic Belinsky mocked as a dead language, a view in turn mocked in living Ukrainian by Shevchenko: 'He is a fool who tells these tales/ in dead Ukrainian' ('The Haydamaks'). The Norwegian poet Wergeland had to contend with Danish cultural dominance (promoted by his foe, Welhaven) in early 19th century Norway. Lönnrot published *The Kalevala* (1835) in Finnish at a time when Swedish was the language of high culture in Finland. Hebrew writers in the 19th century encountered ignorance, perplexity and hostility as Yiddish was the language of most East European Jews, while West European Jews preferred the language of the country in which they lived. Tchernichowsky chose to write Hebrew though

18 *Introduction*

until the 1920s his readership was small. Had he written in Russian, his native language, he would have had a potential readership in the millions. (The Russian translations of Bialik's poems sold far more than the Hebrew originals.) In each case, the poet took a gamble, throwing his lot in with a cultural revival that might have guttered. Despite the risk of being dismissed as being narrow, pedantic, second-rate and, especially in translation, largely irrelevant beyond their country, national poets bravely assert historical and cultural distinctiveness in the conviction that their culture will prevail. Even their doggerel, mocked or ignored is sincere. Diplomacy is not a strong point of national poetry. This poetry often speaks plainly from a common pool of wisdom, myth, superstition and prejudice and expresses what ordinary people feel – even if wrongly.

NATIONAL POETS AND THE 'OTHER'

Poets are often haunted by a persecutory 'Other', usually an imperial power. Prophets such as Isaiah, Jeremiah and Ezekiel attack the powerful pagan Mesopotamian empires which destroyed the monotheist kingdoms. The poets of European countries under Islamic rule, including Greece, Bulgaria, Romania, Albania and Serbia, tended to see Islam as the hated Other that had defeated and enslaved them. In the writings of modern national poets, heroic struggles are often shadowed by political defeat and alienation. Many poets, repulsed by a dominant, often oppressive culture, console themselves with their crushed 'home' culture. In a sense, Schiller's concluding lines in the poem '*Die Götter Griechenlands*' (The Greek Gods, 1788), '*Was unsterblich im Gesang soll leben/ Muss im Leben untergehen*' (Whatever wants to live in song/ must die), are literally true. Defeat can steel national identity among subjugated peoples who treat the Hebrew Bible as their true heritage, their licence of chosenness as the 'new Israel'. Following the Hebrew prophets, national poetry – Macpherson's *Fingal* (1761), Mickiewicz's *Pan Tadeusz* (1834) or Shevchenko's 'The Haydamaks' (1841) – declares and represents cultural victory after political defeat by an oppressive Other. To Solomos, Botev and Toumanian, the Other is Ottoman Turkey; to Mickiewicz, Shevchenko, Petőfi, Lönnrot and Bialik, it is Tsarist Russia. To Yeats, Pearse, Greenberg and p'Bitek, the Other is the British empire; to Senghor and Césaire, it is France and to Neto, it is Portugal.[58] Among independent nations, national poets might feel their otherness when national liberal ideals are betrayed: for example, Pushkin reacting to the totalitarianism of Nicholas I;[59] Heine to the petty divisions and xenophobia in German society; Hugo to the suppression of liberty by Napoleon III;[60] Whitman to American slavery in the 1850s, when the nation was sliding to civil war, and his poetry asserted American Union under the banner of democracy. More recently, poets such as Mandelstam and Pasternak felt their otherness in reaction to Soviet totalitarianism.[61]

POETS AND ZEITGEIST

Most national movements have poets who catch the so-called 'spirit' of the nation, defining its identity and goals in clear speech of the national language: to gain independence, to educate its young, to develop its language and laws, to love its landscape and customs, to fight its enemies.[62] Chapter 2 explores national poets as agents of moral regeneration, reviving memories of a heroic past, real or imaginary,[63] and myths and legends unique to the nation. Poets often live in awe of mythical figures – especially warriors such as King Arthur in England, Arjuna in India, Cuchulain in Ireland, Vainamoinen in Finland, Wotan in Germany or Skanderbeg in Albania – who rouse the nation to action and freedom. Poets gather fragments of the past into new unity and recreate in their poetry the history and myths of the nation, adapting them to present needs. They shape history into myth and myth into history.

Much national poetry is uncompromising, with a vein of pride or grievance which, even when historically inaccurate or fabricated, can stir a nation to action.[64] Modern Greeks are not, for the most part, lineal descendants of the heroes of Marathon and Thermopylae. Yet this lineage was widely believed when Greece fought its war of independence against Turkey (1821–28). Similarly, most modern Jews are not descendants of the Maccabees. Yet when Bialik, in *The City of Slaughter*, in Hebrew worthy of the diatribes of Isaiah, taunted survivors of the Kishinev pogrom in 1903 as cowardly descendants of the heroic Maccabees, the shot hit home (Aberbach 1988). Within a few months, the Russian Jews began to organize self-defense groups to fight back in pogroms, evidently the first time Jews had done so since the Bar-Kokhba revolt in Judaea against Rome in 132–35 CE.

The importance of history and mythical history in national poetry is especially clear when considering the clash of Islam with Christian Europe. Chapter 3 shows that much European poetry over a thousand years, from the medieval French poem *The Song of Roland* to Njegoš's Serbian epic *The Mountain Wreath* (1847), is set against this conflict, as is the Hebrew poetry in medieval Spain, as seen in Chapter 4. In England, too, national poetry is interwoven with history and, at times (Coverdale's translation of the Hebrew Psalms, for example) makes history. In Chapter 5, we see that the poetry of the British isles reached artistic peaks in moments of heightened national self-awareness, when independence was threatened or lost, whether because of foreign invasion or internal wars or disasters.

Much national poetry, as mentioned earlier, came from the breakup of empires between 1789 and 1914. The rival Tsarist and Ottoman empires were challenged internally by clusters of national movements and their poetic cultures. Poets of these empires are explored in Chapters 6 and 7, for example, Soutsos (Greece) and Fishta (Albania) in the Ottoman-ruled Balkans and Shevchenko (Ukraine) and Lönnrot (Finland) in Tsarist Russia. Peoples scattered among the empires rediscovered their national identity through

20 *Introduction*

their poets after the French Revolution, notably the pan-Slavs (Kollar) and the Jews (Bialik). Zionism, the last European national movement of the 19th century, with grassroots mainly in violently anti-Semitic Tsarist Russia, aimed to renew Jewish life in Ottoman Palestine.

FROM LIBERALISM TO FASCISM

National poetry, as shown in Chapter 8, charts the shift from liberalism in the age of the French Revolution to fascism in the early 20th century. Nationalism might begin as a force of idealism, harmony and unity, but it often ends in violence. Poets within living memory of the French Revolution – Burns, Byron, Leopardi, Mickiewicz, Shevchenko and Petőfi – believed on the whole that the world was becoming a better place. Even after the French Reign of Terror, Burns could write in 1795:

> It's comin' yet for a' that
> That man to man the world o'er
> Shall brothers be for a' that.
>   'For A' That'

The late 18th century and early 19th century poets tended to be more idealistic, even innocent, in their nationalism than later national poets, such as Ibsen, Yeats, Bialik and Cavafi. To the earlier poets, civilization was moving, or capable of moving, towards universal goals. The Romantic ideal of individual creative independence and genius was often seen as a microcosm of a national and universal ideal. Poetry, too, could be part of a national movement, of creative birth, an essential part of independence struggles. Many nations salvaged in their poetry the memories of heroic struggle, strengthening the people's sense of unity, distinctiveness and the resolve to hold tight to national hopes. National poets often raged against external oppressors and against the nation itself, and the traitors within.[65]

Byron embodied the idealism of early 19th century national poetry triggered largely by the French Revolution. Byron's poetry inspired nationalism among forgotten or despised peoples [notably the Greeks in 'The Isles of Greece' (1810) and the Jews in *Hebrew Melodies* (1815)] who, in an era of dawning nationalism, stood a chance of revival. His imitations of biblical 'songs of Zion' made real the prospect of a Jewish national revival before political Zionism began.[66] Byron's involvement in the Greek War of Independence against Turkey was a major event in the history of nationalism.[67] His death at Missolonghi in 1824, depicted in the European press as a heroic sacrifice, was a factor in the Great Power intervention ensuring Greece's victory. Byron's idealism greatly influenced 19th and early 20th century national poets, including Petőfi, Mameli, Botev, Marti and Pearse; all died fighting for liberty.

From Byron's death to D'Annunzio's capture of Fiume for Italy in 1919, the nationalism of universal liberalism and independence struggles changed, in literature as in politics, to cruel dictatorial fascism. In particular, poetry changed after 1848–49, the year of failed revolutions throughout Europe, which led to chronic national rivalries and fears of despotism. 'Shame on it!' declared Petőfi expressing his disgust with reactionary Europe in 1849.[68] The upheavals exposed the violent incompatibility of universal revolutionary ideals and nationalist particularity. The Prussian-Danish war of 1864 and the Franco-Prussian war of 1870–71 also marked this change. Poetry reflected a growing uncertainty, a disillusionment and horror at the rise of violent national rivalry, the increase of state control on people's lives, and the decline in the expectations and value attached to human life, culminating in World War I. The changing view of nationalism is felt in Ibsen's verse dramas, *Brand* (1866) and *Peer Gynt* (1867), written in anger at Norway's betrayal of Denmark during the Prussian invasion in 1864. In contrast, in the 1820s the Great Powers had given Greece crucial aid in the War of Independence against the Ottoman Turks. National poetry followed nationalism itself in its turn from universalist liberalism to xenophobia, exclusiveness, racism, anti-Semitism and growing militancy.[69]

In the increasingly nationalistic 19th century, as seen in Chapter 9, Walt Whitman was practically the only major national poet who welcomed foreigners. Whitman, at the time of the first publication of *Leaves of Grass* (1855) almost totally unknown as a poet, observed America in the making as boatloads of immigrants arrived in New York in the 1840s and 1850s. After the failure of the 1848–49 European revolutions, Whitman wrote a new kind of poetry, portraying an ideal America of unique and growing diversity and individualism – in contrast with European xenophobia and intolerance – and despite the bitter conflict over slavery, the last outpost of liberal hopes. In contrast, as the British empire reached the height of its power in the 19th century, some prominent English poets, including Tennyson and Kipling, expressed fear of corruption as imperial power declined.[70] International tensions culminating in World War I exposed fully the intolerant, brutal side of nationalism.

The destructive nationalism of the West provoked recoil in poetry in the East. The Bengali poet Rabindranath Tagore and the Urdu and Persian poet Mohammed Iqbal, both poets of India under colonial rule, went against the grain of early 20th century Western poetry in their idealistic universalism, recalling early 19th century national poets such as Byron and Shelley. In 'National Song of India' (*Tarana-I-Hindi*, 1904), Iqbal merged national and universal feeling. True religion, he wrote, does not teach discord: 'Strung on a single thread, we are one./ We are Indians' (Burney 1987: 8).[71] Tagore, similarly, believed in an India of tolerance and inclusiveness, as in the Whitmanesque 'Pilgrimage to India' (1910) which defines national identity in international terms.[72] The poet recalls the peoples who, from ancient to modern times created India: Aryan and non-Aryan, Scythian, Hun, Mughal, Pathan and peoples from West, all bringing their bounty, 'Give and receive, merge and be merged:/ From India's ocean-shore of great humanity ...' (Tagore 2004: 200–1).[73] Such visions of harmony in the poetry of Tagore and Iqbal were punctured, as in the West, by the reality of religious hatred and war. Iqbal, 'the chief force behind the creation of Pakistan' (Rahman 1979: 225), did not live to see India's partition and the massacre that accompanied it. If he had, 'he would surely have recanted and admitted his mistake of arousing communal passion among his co-religionists' (Sud 1969: 43).

The most remarkable poetry of World War I was national in its hatred of war. Yet, most poetry written in response to the war was militant and nationalistic, and after 1918 some poets, notably Gabriele D'Annunzio, sought revenge. D'Annunzio (like Byron both a major literary figure and charismatic war leader) was pivotal in the rise of Italian fascism, glorifying violence and scorning democratic nationalism. The poet's annexation and 'lyrical dictatorship' of Fiume in 1919–20 foreshadowed Mussolini's seizure of power in 1922 and Hitler's failed *Putsch* in Munich in 1923.

POETRY AND NATIONAL DEFEAT

From the age of Byron, defeat is a chief motive and theme in national poetry. National poets have learned from the Hebrew prophets that spiritual defiance in defeat can bring rewards more lasting than military victory. Defeat can call up remarkable poetry among peoples struggling to survive and remain culturally independent of the ruling power, for example, Poland, Finland and the Ukraine under Russian rule; Greece and Bulgaria under Turkish rule; Italy and Hungary under Austrian rule; Scotland, Ireland, India and pre-State Israel under British rule; and the countries of Africa and Latin America under colonial rule. Among independent nations, too, major crises and conflict can inspire national poetry, whether as crude propaganda for the nation or transcending national boundaries, the barriers of translation and the age in which it is written. Much depends on how defeat is taken. The memory of defeat festering in the nation's psyche is often a more powerful stimulant than victory. A nation defeated, persecuted, weak and chaotic can learn through its poetry to treasure liberty and its own history and creative culture. The poet knows best, perhaps, that a weak nation that remembers its defeats survives better than a strong nation that forgets its victories.

Victory in war often stimulates national cultural achievement and ethnic identity. Victory – of ancient Greece over Persia, for example, or of Rome and later Islamic armies over most of the civilised world, of the Italian city-states over their enemies, of the English over the Spanish Armada and Napoleon, of the Allied powers over Germany in the two world wars – heralded cultural victory of various forms and degrees. Yet defeat too can trigger cultural nationalism. It did so in the Middle Ages and, as seen in Chapter 11, also in modern times. Armenians and Finns, Irish and Poles, Ukrainians and Bosnian

Muslims, Basques and Kurds, and Tamils and Palestinians are among many peoples whose identity has been galvanized and shaped by the frustration and humiliation of defeat.[74] At times, the music of defeat, as by the waters of Babylon, is sweeter than the drums of victory. Even Whitman, poet of a proud, independent America, sings of defeat, in solidarity not rancor, 'marches for conquer'd and slain persons .../ it is good to fall .../ Vivas to those who have fail'd' (*Song of Myself*, 18).

Many defeated peoples in modern times have taken strength from their religious-cultural heritage, making it a powerful force of nationalism. Cultural nationalism, even when rooted in defeat and grievance, can sometimes transcend these as a moral value of its own. In Ireland, for example, defeats by Cromwell in 1649 and William of Orange in 1690 heightened Irish national identity in Irish literature both Gaelic and English, culminating in the poetry of Yeats. (Yeats and Bialik are compared in Chapter 10 as poets of defeated peoples.) The French defeat by the British at Quebec in 1759 was a continual spur in Quebec nationalism with its slogan '*Je me souviens*'. Defeat and partition of Poland in the late 18th century and the failure of its revolts against Tsarist Russia in 1830 and 1863 led, again, to enhanced Polish national feeling and creative activity, notably the writings of Mickiewicz. The Finns, Ukrainians and other subject peoples produced equally significant works during the same period. Russia's military disaster in the Crimean War of 1854–6 and the reforms which followed triggered what is, arguably, the most creative period of literary fiction in history. Indian literature developed remarkably after the failed mutiny of 1857, notably in the writings of Tagore, as the sense of Indian identity was enhanced by oppressive British colonial rule. The French defeat by Prussia in 1870–1 (seen by many Germans as revenge for the Prussian defeat by the French at Jena in 1806) and the German defeat in World War I led, in each case, to heightened nationalism and a flowering of the arts.

At times, defeat can bring cultural advantages, promoting otherwise-impossible national identities. The British empire, though created and sustained by conquest, brought relative freedom of the press and greatly expanded literacy, and it set off an explosion of national poetry, in English and native languages, particularly in India, Africa and the Middle East. Colonial rule, as seen in Chapter 12, galvanized the poetry of the ruled. Poets, though often neglected in the scholarship on nationalism, were revolutionary, both aesthetically and politically, expressing a spirit of cultural independence. Among them: Shawqi of Egypt, Tagore of India, Rusafi of Iraq, Yeats of Ireland, Iqbal of Pakistan and Greenberg of pre-State Israel. In contrast with other empires, the British empire inspired poets to create revolutionary art and seek political independence. Most strikingly, British rule was instrumental in the revival of vernacular Hebrew poetry after 1917 as the centre of Hebrew literature shifted from Odessa to Tel Aviv. Long after independence, poets of former empires and slave-cultures (e.g., Césaire, Soyinka) probed psychological wounds left by slavery and colonialism.[75]

24 *Introduction*

Defeat leading to a sense of inferiority toward more successful nations spurs national identity. From the time of the French Revolution, relatively undeveloped countries of Eastern Slavs, Latin Americans and Africans, became increasingly and painfully aware of their shortcomings, disabilities and failings in comparison with more 'advanced' countries, France in particular. Their inherited skills, ideas and customs fell behind the West. Nationalism was then stimulated by their desire to overcome inferiority and catch up, technologically, economically, culturally and militarily. The memory of slavery was often a factor in this sense of inferiority, though some poets – notably Neruda – emphasize the power of the human spirit to endure slavery and colonization. While nations that won independence tended to be liberal, defeated and disappointed nations were often illiberal. Yet independence is not always a cure, as memory of defeat and failure can linger. Nationalism, imitative and hostile to that which it imitates, is reflected in national poetry: in Shevchenko and Petőfi among 19th century Slavic poets and in p'Bitek, Osadebay and David Diop among 20th century African poets.[76]

REVENGE IN NATIONAL POETRY

Defeated nations think of revenge. Poetry, like diplomacy, can continue war without bloodshed. The idealism in national poetry is rarely without a destructive element, even in the more liberal period of 1789–1848 when poets still believed that national rivalries could be overcome through universal brotherhood. In the ancient world, the Greeks and Jews reacted to defeat with the desire for revenge. In the early Middle Ages, the Islamic invasion of Europe triggered a cycle of wars of revenge, in the Crusades and after.[77] National poetry is not often politically correct or diplomatically disguised. It voices hatred and resentment, even threatens war. Vengeful rage and violence fill the poetry of defeated peoples, such as the Irish, the Scots, the Greeks, the Poles and the Ukrainians, dominated by powerful, ruthless empires.[78] Many poets write in the shadow of a hated oppressor or defeat, or in exile from their oppressed homeland. They rarely write for art's sake alone. They choose to soar, not grovel. Rational negotiated compromise may be foreign to most of them, but not fanaticism – All or Nothing. 'Use their corpses to dam the Rhine', wrote the German poet Theodor Körner about the hated French in 1813. Mickiewicz in the Epilogue to *Pan Tadeusz* (1835) imagines Poland victorious over Russia 'gorged with corpses, drunk with blood'. Shevchenko in 'The Haydamaks' (1841) elevates marauding Cossacks as Ukrainian national heroes who 'lit their pipes from Polish towns they set ablaze'. Petőfi, inflamed by the Hungarian revolt in 1848–49, glorifies poetry as herald of stormy revolution. Bialik, enraged by anti-Jewish violence in Russia, calls for revenge: 'With cruel fury/ we'll drink your blood./ We'll have no pity'.[79] National poetry may be beautiful and moving to readers at different times and places. But by definition it puts the nation first. Impediments to the national cause – apathy, corruption and materialism, especially that of their religious leaders; cowardice, lack of dedication to liberty and betrayal of the nation – must be overcome, generally through struggle, the redress of grievance and bloody revenge. Yet the early 19th century Romantics, for all the violence and hatred in their poetry, rarely imagined that nationalism could lead, not to universal brotherhood and love, but to persistent hatred and war, even genocide, which their poetry, nevertheless, foreshadows. Heine, a fervent German nationalist, was unusual in exposing with sober cynicism and cutting satire the dangers of nationalism.[80]

POETRY AS LEGISLATION AND LIBERATION

Common elements of humiliation, grievance, violence and the longing for freedom make for strange bedfellows among poets. For example, Mickiewicz of Poland, Shevchenko of Ukraine and Lönnrot of Finland share a hatred of Russian rule; while Pearse of Ireland, Rusafi of Iraq, Shawqi of Egypt and Greenberg of pre-State Israel have in common a militant repugnance to British colonial rule. Yet these poets totally differ from one another. This book aims at both at a broad picture of national poetry in a variety of authors, themes and settings and – particularly with Byron, Whitman, D'Annunzio, Yeats and Bialik – to explore the individuality of national poets and poetry. Differences are shaped by geography and history. European poets speak of nationalism in relation to country, while African and South American poets do so more in relation to continent than country, and Arab poets *vis-à-vis* Islam or pan-Arab identity. Balkan countries under Islamic rule were generally supported by other Christian countries in their independence struggles, in which religion and nation were explosively mixed. As countries change, so does their poetry and the response to it. Some poets, such as Petőfi or Shevchenko, seem born to the role of national poet. Others, including Mickiewicz and Yeats, achieve it despite the opposition of their countrymen.[81] Some national poets, such as Bialik, may hide, only to have the role thrust upon them. Yet others apply when there are no apparent vacancies:

> I want to be your national symbol of life
> because my heart is heavy country and exile calls
> Syl Cheney-Coker, 'On Being a Poet in Sierra Leone' (1980: 51)

Other complications arise: what of poets – including Mickiewicz, Yeats, Cavafy, Hugo and Bialik – exiled from their national territory or gripped with hatred for their own people? What of those, especially in former colonies in Africa and South America, writing in languages associated with colonial exploitation: English, Spanish, French and Portuguese?[82] Poetry has detractors from Plato to Peacock who, in 'Four Ages of Poetry' (1820), rejected poetry as trivial alongside 'real' knowledge – science, politics and

26 *Introduction*

philosophy. Shelley's riposte in *A Defence of Poetry* (1821) that 'Poets are the unacknowledged legislators of the world', is closer to the reality. As we have seen, many poets are politically and educationally active and influential. Children read or sing national poetry, not Plato, at school.

From the Hebrew Bible on, defiance of defeat in national poetry heralds ultimate political victory: 'there can be no political liberation without cultural liberation', wrote Leopold Senghor.[83] Poetry fights for a nation's inner independence through its vital originality, its proud and confident expression of a national character. At times, poets are acknowledged legislators. Asserting moral ideals, warning of the inhuman consequences of the corruption of those ideals – even at times when part of this corruption – they speak to people everywhere. What they legislate is too important to be confined to the nation.

NOTES

1. On war poetry in the Bible, see pp. 41–3.
2. The Hebrew reads:

    ברוך יהוה צורי
    המלמד ידי לקרב
    אצבעותי למלחמה

    Examples of the original texts are given throughout this book as a reminder of the enormous variety of languages in national poetry. This is one of many areas in which the writing of this book has exposed the author's woeful ignorance.
3. On the Greek War of Independence and its poetry, see Chapter 6.
4. Politically committed poet-martyrs such as Byron implicitly challenge critics such as Barthes and Derrida, who see the meaning of a text as out of the author's control. In national poetry, martyrdom can be seen as the ultimate affirmation of authorial control and unambiguous meaning. Yet, even a fanatical political commitment does not exclude other meanings.
5. Perhaps the oldest literary memorial is in the Jewish tradition, the Ninth of Av in the Hebrew calendar, commemorating the destruction of both temples in Jerusalem, marked by the reading of the scroll of Lamentations, attributed to the prophet Jeremiah.
6. Burns' Dedication to the Edinburgh Edition of 1787 is the basis for the inscription on the Burns statue on the Thames Embankment, London, expressing mutual identification of the divinely called poet-prophet and his nation: 'The Poetic Genius of my Country found me as the prophetic bard Elijah did Elisha – at the plough – and threw her inspiring mantle over me. She bade me sing the loves, the joys, the rural scenes and rural pleasures of my natal Soil, in my native land: I tuned my wild, artless notes, as she inspired.'
7. On Herder's influence on cultural nationalism, see pp. 67–9.
8. National poetry is, perhaps, unusual in the extreme reactions which it is capable of provoking. National poets are honored and remembered for expressing a

spirit of national individuality, defiance and independence, and also execrated for allegedly encouraging genocide. On genocidal elements in the poetry of Njegoš of Serbia and Gökalp of Turkey, see pp. 102–03, 171, 201 note 19, 255.
9. On poets actively involved in politics and government, see pp. 14–15.
10. These poets include, for example, in the Turkish empire: Solomos (Greece), Njegoš (Serbia/Montenegro), Botev (Bulgaria), Eminescu (Romania), Siamanto (Armenia) and Fishta (Albania). In the Russian empire they included Pushkin and Lermontov, Shevchenko (Ukraine), Mickiewicz (Poland), Lönnrot (Finland) and Bialik (pre-state Israel). In the British empire they include Burns (Scotland), Yeats (Ireland), Tagore (India), Iqbal (Pakistan), Shawqi (Egypt), Soyinka (Nigeria), Greenberg (pre-state Israel) and Kipling. For detailed accounts of national poetry in these empires, see Chapters 3, 4, 6, 7, 10, 11 and 12. For a list of the poets discussed in this book and their dates, see Index of Poets. These and many other national poets are often treated in individual critical and biographical studies. Yet they rarely figure in the broader context of nationalism and national poetry, though historians agree that this topic is of central importance in the study of civilization. Boundaries between fields of knowledge can be as artificial as borders dividing countries. For a critique in the *Times Higher Education Supplement* of compartmentalization in the universities, see Aberbach (2013a). As national poetry bridges the Arts and Social Sciences, it tends to be neglected both among scholars of nationalism and literary scholars. The indexes of most major studies of nationalism [e.g., Gellner (1964), Seton-Watson (1977), Armstrong (1982), Hroch (1985), Hobsbawm (1990), Breuilly (1993), Balakrishnan (1996), Hutchinson and Smith (2000), Guibernau and Hutchinson (2004), Roshwald (2006), Smith (2008), Hirschi (2012)] have no entry on the poetry of nationalism and rarely refer to poets. Literary scholarship has also neglected national poetry as a genre. For example, *The Princeton Encyclopedia of Poetry and Poetics* does not yet have an entry on national poetry or poetry in nationalism. (In contrast, national music is a recognized category.) See Aberbach (2003) on the general neglect of poetry in studies of nationalism and for an overview of national poetry.
11. On the turn from liberalism to fascism in 19th and early 20th century national poetry, see Chapter 8.
12. Poetry supports both the claim that nations and nationalism are a modern creation and that they are rooted in history and myth. On balance, poetry, especially that in the Hebrew Bible, gives most credence to the view that nations have pre-modern origins. On the Hebrew Bible, see Chapter 1; on history and myth, see Chapter 2; on the conflict between Islam and Christianity as a spur to national poetry, see Chapter 3. On nationalism as a modern phenomenon, see for example Kedourie (1960), Gellner (1983), Deutsch (1966), Hobsbawm (1990) and Anderson (1991). Even after the French Revolution, writes Hobsbawm (2001: 175), 'Outside Europe it is difficult to speak of nationalism at all'. Much of the terminology is modern: according to the OED, the word 'nation' in the sense of a people dates from 1818, 'nationalism' from 1844 and 'nationhood' from 1850. The opposing view, that nations do, indeed, have ancient 'navels', is argued among others by Seton-Watson (1977), Armstrong (1982), Hutchinson (1987) and Smith (1991). Also see Aberbach and Aberbach (2000: 4). On the debate 'Do nations have a navel?', see Smith (1996) and Gellner (1996). Distinctions between types of nationalism include: 'Western' as opposed to the 'Eastern' (Kohn 1946);

nations based on common descent against those based on shared institutions (Francis 1968); the 19th century unification movements of countries with well-established cultures versus the nationalism of those that had to create a national culture (Plamenatz 1976); 'new' in contrast to 'old' nations (Seton-Watson 1977). These distinctions appear to have only limited application to national poets. [On nationalism and the historians, see Smith's essay in Balakrishnan (1996).] As cultural nationalists, these poets often 'act as moral innovators who establish ideological movements at times of social crisis in order to transform existing belief systems from within and thereby enable socio-political development on indigenous lines' (Hutchinson 1994: 48). On difficulties in determining the origins of nationalism see, for example, Armstrong (1982), Taylor (1998), Hutchinson and Smith (2000) and Hirschi (2012). The present book aims at a panoramic view of national poetry as a genre, in which a variety of disciplines – literature, history, sociology, religion, war studies, political science – are combined. Individual national poets are, in effect, chapters in an ongoing story. Readers looking for 'my national poet' can easily find individual critical studies and biographies, many of which are listed in the Bibliography.

13. Already in 1919, at the time of the founding of the League of Nations, the precursor of the United Nations, W.B. Yeats saw the irony that 'no cannon had been turned/ Into a ploughshare' ('Nineteen Hundred and Nineteen').
14. On Shawqi's opposition to the rule of the British 'infidel' in Egypt, see pp. 274–5; on Njegoš' hatred of Muslim 'infidel' rule of Serbia, see p. 255. The role of religious conflict in nationalism and national poetry is seen especially in Chapters 3, 6, 7, 11 and 12.
15. The Serbian reads 'Какву сабљу кажеш и косово?/ да л' на њему заједно не бјесмо'.
16. In *Three Elegies for Kosovo*, Ismail Kadare (2000) gives a moving reconstruction of the Battle of Kosovo Fields in 1389 and the shocked and disoriented Albanian and Serbian minstrels caught up in the magnitude of defeat, yet unable to break the mould of their conflict to unite against a common foe, and continuing to hurl lamentations and violent curses against one another: 'what they declared in their songs was inevitably done, and what was done was then added to their songs, as poison is added to poison' (86).
17. On the concept of literature as a transcendence of national borders, see Corse (1997: 8).
18. In its eclectic, international allusiveness, elitism and modernist obscurity, and in its horrified recoil at the effects of World War I, T.S. Eliot's *The Waste Land* (1921) might be described as the quintessential un-national or anti-nationalist poem [but see Appendix (c)]. Yet Romantics are not necessarily overt nationalists. In most of their greatest poetry, Wordsworth, Coleridge and Keats were not nationalistic, and the emphasis on purely personal experience and feeling might even be seen as anti-nationalistic in a nationalistic age.
19. Some national poets are honored in their lifetimes. The street where Bialik lived in Tel Aviv in the 1920s and 1930s was named for him while he was still living there. In a charming story, two boys pass him in a barber's shop having his hair cut. One boy says to the other, 'Look, there's Bialik!' The other replies, 'Don't be silly, Bialik is a street'. See Aberbach (1988).
20. See the note on landscape, Appendix (d), pp. 309–10.
21. On poets as political leaders, see pp. 14–15.

22. The internal contradictions of national poets are exemplified above all by Byron, described in Chapter 8 (p. 189) as 'a serial national poet'. Byron's biographer Edna O'Brien writes: 'Everything about him was a paradox, insider and outsider, beautiful and deformed, serious and facetious, profligate but on occasion miserly, and possessed of a fierce intelligence trapped however in a child's magic and malices' (2009: 1).
23. Even Whitman, most public and optimistic of national poets, has moments of stabbing inner torment and self-doubt: 'Is it the prophet's thought I speak, or am I raving?/ What do I know of life? What of myself?' ('Prayer of Columbus'). On Whitman, see Chapter 9.
24. Published by Peter Halban in his Jewish Thinkers series, 1988. This book developed from an article in *Encounter* in 1981, on the paradox that Bialik, though a 'national poet', was obsessed by personal tragedies, particularly his orphanhood and childlessness. The original article appears as Appendix (f).
25. See my study of Bialik (1988) and bilingual anthology of Bialik's poems (2004) as well as my book on charisma (1996). 'Bialik's private agonies and hopes mirrored national trauma and revival in such an extraordinary way that the two became intertwined and inextricably linked in the poetry' (Aberbach 1988: 119).
26. On charismatic homogamy, see Aberbach (1995, 1996), and on the attraction of like to like, see Lieberman *et al.* (1973) and Skynner (1976).
27. Among poets with experience of childhood loss are Burns, Solomos, Shevchenko, Byron, Kölcsey, Leopardi, Fikret, Prešeren, Bialik and Neruda. For further remarks on loss and national poetry, see the Conclusion.
28. On Hosea, see p. 44; on Ezekiel, pp. 45–6. On both prophets, see p. 295.
29. On Yeats and Bialik, see Chapter 10. Among other poets, too, love for one's country is analogous to the love of women. For example, the Senegalese poet Senghor in *Chants pour Naëtt* (1949) depicts Africa symbolically as the woman the poet loves.
30. On Homer's influence on modern Greek nationalism, see Chapter 6.
31. Many of the great European epics (e.g., *The Song of Roland*) had oral sources. On oral poetry in Scandinavia, see p. 75ff; on Eastern European oral poetry, see p. 67. The oral tradition in Icelandic poetry survived to modern times in unusually harsh conditions, often in rural isolation and privation. In Laxness' Icelandic novel *Independent People* (1934–35) set in the early 20th century, the impoverished crofter, Bjartur, clings fiercely to a crippling independence while enduring, Job-like, one disaster after another. In a powerful scene, he nearly dies in a blizzard while his wife gives birth at home. Tempted to give up and lie down in the snow, he suddenly fixes on the saga of Prince Grimur the Noble who resisted the seductive charms of his step-mother, the Queen: 'Never should it be said of Bjartur of Summerhouses that on the field of battle he turned his back on his foes to go and lie with a trollopy slut of a queen'. At this moment, Icelandic verse, which he knows by heart, steels him to survive in the wild: 'Lustful thou art as a swine,/ Little honour can be thine' (1946: 92, 94). When Bjartur returns home, he finds his wife dead. He saves his newborn child and raises her himself, immersing her in old Icelandic poetry.
32. The Greeks and Jews have preserved from their ancient history, from Homer and the Bible, a veneration for poets and poetry. The death of Solomos, the Greek national poet, in 1857 occasioned national mourning in Greece. Much of

30 *Introduction*

the population of Corfu, where he died, attended his funeral. Bialik's death in 1934 was, similarly, a time of mourning throughout the Jewish world. A large part of the Jewish population of Palestine, tens of thousands, came specially to the funeral in Tel Aviv to pay tribute to their national poet. Both Solomos and Bialik lived and died under British rule, which more than any other empire valued and nourished the literary cultures of its subject peoples. On the stimulus to national poetry in the British empire, see Chapter 12.

33. On poetry and politics in the 15th century, see Scattergood (1971).
34. On biblical influence on modern nationalism, see Smith (1991, 1998, 2003), Grosby (1991, 1999), Greenfeld (1992) and Aberbach (2005).
35. For a variety of interpretations of nationalism, see Kedourie (1971), Gellner (1983), Hobsbawm and Ranger (1983), Giddens (1985), Anderson (1991), Breuilly (1993), Connor (1994) and Smith (2008).
36. Examples of 'invented tradition' in the Bible include the revival of the Passover festival by the Judean King Josiah (late 7th century BCE) and the establishment of the reading of the Torah by Ezra (mid-5th century BCE). The very idea of *Torah le-Moshe mi-Sinai* (Torah – i.e., the Five Books of Moses given to Moses on Mount Sinai) would be classed as 'invented tradition' by most scholars (and not a few rabbis) who claim that the Pentateuch in the form that has come down to us is no more contemporaneous with Moses than the *Odyssey* is with Homer. Print culture, a vital element in modern nationalism, has an ancient precedent in the tradition of the Hebrew scribes (*sofrim*) who preserved and disseminated the sacred texts generation after generation, and whose limitations were compensated by the Oral Tradition, by ritual weekly public readings of the Torah in synagogue and by an unusually high level of literacy among the Jews. Hastings (1997: 186) describes the Jews as 'the true proto-nation … the people who gave the world the model of nationhood and even nation-statehood'.
37. The ancient Tamil poet Tiruvalluvar (1st century BCE), like the modern Armenian poet Toumanian (1869–1923), reminds us that poetry with national significance can be created by peoples who fail to achieve statehood.
38. The young Karl Marx thought of himself primarily as a poet and was encouraged by his father to write a poem which 'should glorify Prussia and afford an opportunity of praising the genius of the Monarch … patriotic, emotional and composed in a Germanic manner' (McLellan 1973: 21–2). Nationalism, however, does not appear in Marx's sixty or so surviving poems. This evidently intentional omission might be seen to anticipate the thrust of Marx's later work, emphasizing phenomena such as class which cut across national boundaries.
39. When English poetry expresses strong sympathy for the poor, as in *King Lear* or *Lyrical Ballads*, for example, it seems to come closest to the biblical spirit. See Appendix (b).
40. On the use of ancient myth to unify divided nations, see p. 72.
41. See p. 39.
42. On *Peer Gynt* as a turning point in Ibsen's career, see p. 78.
43. On Judaism as an atrophied religion in Tchernichowsky's poetry, see p. 181.
44. On the importance of high culture in nationalism, see Gellner (1983) and Smith (1991). National anthems, however, tend to belong to popular culture. See Appendix (a). Some poets (e.g., T.S. Eliot, Paul Valéry) have thought deeply about the meaning of culture and national culture.

Introduction 31

45. 'On reading "Anthology of a Thousand Poets"' (Bold 1970: 150).
46. On anti-imperialism in biblical prophecy, see Aberbach (1993). Empires, however, can also be seen as 'the rod of [God's] wrath'. See p. 43.
47. Schiller, in *The Robbers* (1781), expressed the longing for action and freedom from restraint characteristic of many national movements and their poets: 'I want to breathe the air of freedom' (1995: 39).
48. Wilson (1976: x) describes the importance of *The Kalevala* to the Finns as 'their book of independence, their passport into the family of civilized nations'. Subtelny (1988: 234) affirms Shevchenko's book of poems, *The Kobzar* (1840) as 'a literary and intellectual declaration of Ukrainian independence'.
49. See Czigany (1984:191). Petőfi's juxtaposition of poetry and power may be compared with the Irish nationalist O'Grady's declaration in 1899: 'We have now a literary movement, it is not very important; it will be followed by a political movement, that will not be very important; then must come a military movement, that will be important indeed' (in Thompson 1967: 62).
50. The most famous collection of German folk songs was *Des Knaben Wunderhorn* (The Boy's Magic Horn), edited by Ludwig Achim von Arnim and Clemens Bretano between 1805 and 1808. From Schubert on, its 200 odd songs were set to music countless times. In some countries, the collecting of folk poetry and song began prior to the French Revolution. Bishop Percy's ballad collection *Reliques of Ancient English Poetry* first appeared in 1765. In Russia, Mikhail Chulkov published books of Russian folk songs and stories (later drawn on and made widely known by Pushkin) in the 1760s and 1770s (Neuhäuser 1975: 200).
51. Among the anthologies which Yeats edited are *Fairy and Folk Tales of the Irish Peasantry* (1888), *Stories from Careleton* (1889) and *Representative Irish Tales* (1890). On Yeats' use of myth, see ch. 10.
52. Bialik's *Sefer ha-Aggadah* (Book of Legends), edited with J.H. Ravnitzky, was first published in 1908. For an English translation, see Bialik (1992).
53. 'The creation of a national language seemed to the veterans of 1812 a means of fostering the spirit of the battlefield and of forging a new nation with the common man. "To know our people," wrote the Decembrist poet Alexander Bestuzhev, "one has to live with them and talk with them in their language, one has to eat with them and celebrate with them on their feast days, go bear-hunting with them in the woods, or travel to the market on a peasant cart." Pushkin's verse was the first to make this link. It spoke to the widest readership, to the literate peasant and the prince, in a common Russian tongue. It was Pushkin's achievement to complete this creation of the national language through his verse, and to use it with extraordinary grace' (Figes 2002: 83).
54. The adoption of free verse in national poetry, for example in the poetry of Whitman, Rusafi and Césaire, is often indicative of revolutionary social change. In *The Use of Poetry and the Use of Criticism* (1933), T.S. Eliot summed up this view: 'Any radical change in poetic form is likely to be the symptom of some very much deeper change in society and in the individual' (Eliot 1970: 75). See p. 214.
55. Hobsbawm's statement (1990: 54) that modern Hebrew is 'virtually invented' is untenable in view of the linguistic evidence:

> 'The [Hebrew] language has remained substantially the same down the years, undergoing changes that have appreciably affected its vocabulary but not, on the whole, its essential morphological, phonological or even syntactic

32 *Introduction*

structure. The truth of this statement even extends to Hebrew spoken and written today, following a fascinating process of revival. The fundamental unity of Hebrew, both its language and its literature, is beyond doubt. Not only have the basic structures of the language, its morphological system and especially its verbal morphology, been preserved without major changes over the centuries, but it is also possible to claim that the vocabulary of the Bible has been the basis for all later periods, despite the numerous innovations of each era' (Sáenz-Badillos, 1993: 50).

56. On the language as a tool of national identity, see for example, Hroch (1985), Anderson (1991), Sáenz-Badillos (1993), Smith (2008) and Bilenki (2012).
57. In the 14th century, Dante showed similar daring, abandoning Latin, the language of higher status, to write in Italian.
58. Poets of empires (Pushkin of Tsarist Russia, Fikret of Ottoman Turkey and Kipling of the British empire at its height) can be as critical and subversive as the poets of subjugated groups.
59. Pushkin was exiled as his poetry, envisaging a Russian awakening to freedom on 'the ruins of despotism' (Figes 2002: 88), helped to inspire the Decembrist uprising in 1825. Lermontov, similarly, condemns the Russian empire, for example in *Ismail Bey* (1832), his first major poem in which he describes the destruction of Chechen villages by Tsarist troops as 'A beast of prey with bayonet' (*ibid.*, 388). The poet's disillusionment with Russia and identification with Caucasus appears in his novel *A Hero of Our Times* (1837). For another indictment of Russian treatment of the Caucasus, see Shevchenko's 'The Caucasus'.
60. In *Les Chatiments* (Punishments, 1853), Hugo, like a modern Jeremiah 'in sackcloth and ashes', attacked Napoleon III for his 1851 coup: 'I show you the prison door'.
61. Not accidentally, after the collapse of the Soviet Union, the Bible became the best-selling book of the newly independent states.
62. Subtelny's encomium for Shevchenko is typical among historians who have learned to value the originality and commitment of 'their' national poet: '... it is difficult to find another example of an individual whose poetry and personality so completely embodied a national ethos as did Shevchenko for the Ukrainians' (Subtelny 1988: 233).
63. Imaginative distortion characterizes much national poetry, going back to the Hebrew Bible. Heine described 'true' history as poetry, not naked fact (Heine 1961: iii 209). See p. 71.
64. On the view of nationalism as a modern fabrication, see Hobsbawm and Ranger (1983), among others. On distortions of history in national poetry, see pp. 71–5.
65. For examples of traitors in national poetry, see pp. 253–9.
66. On Jewish national poetry, see the Index of Poets, s.v. 'Israel'.
67. On Byron, see pp. 156–9.
68. For the full quote from Petőfi, see p. 203.
69. The word 'nationalism' was first used in the mid-19th century as its negative associations became increasingly widespread (Baycroft 1998: 54).
70. On national self-doubt in British poetry, see pp. 141, 272.
71. Iqbal's poem moved Gandhi to tears and inspired his nonviolent protests against British rule. He sang it many times in jail: 'what could be sweeter than that religion never taught mutual hatred?' (Burney 1987: 9).
72. On Whitman's internationalism, see p. 205.

73. In a 1909 letter, Tagore wrote that 'India in different periods of her history received with open arms the medley of races that poured in on her without any attempt at shutting out undesirable elements. ... It is not manifestly her destiny that East and West should find their meeting place in her ever-hospitable bosom' (Tagore 2004: 407).
74. Religious defeat, too, can stir up national poetry. John Donne (1572–1631), born a Catholic in Protestant England which had suppressed Catholicism and was at war with Catholic Spain, was outspoken in his loyalty to 'England, to whom we owe, what we be, and have' (*The Storm*). Donne insisted that national loyalty was greater than religious affiliation and saw militant Roman Catholicism as a threat to England. In the 1590s, he fought for England against Spain and later became a pillar of the Protestant Church as Dean of St. Paul's (Stubbs 2006).
75. See Appendix (e), pp. 311–14.
76. Poetry often communicates post-independence disillusionment, a chronic sense of inferiority, *vis-à-vis* the West, exacerbated by the adoption of Western languages and cultural forms, or an awareness (especially in Africa) that 'the nation cannot be anything but an imagined, and very recent, community, one that is being quite deliberately engineered in often polyethnic societies' (Smith 1999: 166).
77. On revenge in the Bible, see pp. 43–4. On the conflict between Islam and the West, see Chapter 3.
78. On the vengeful poetry of defeated peoples, see General Index s.v. 'nationalism', 'revenge'.
79. On violence in the writings of Körner, Mickiewicz, Shevchenko, Petőfi and Bialik, see pp. 191, 237, 261–2.
80. See Bieber (1956: 131). In 1835, Heine recalled sitting in a Göttingen beer cellar sardonically admiring the thoroughness with which his Teutonic friends made lists of their enemies for the day they would come to power: 'Anyone descended (even unto the seventh generation) from a Frenchman, a Jew, or a Slav, was condemned to exile ...' (in Prawer 1983: 344). Though a radical, Heine opposed the coming Revolution, convinced that a mass uprising in Germany would lead to wanton violence, particularly against Jews: '... a victory of the demagogues would mean that some thousands of Jewish throats – and those precisely the best – would be slit'. In his original draft of *Germany: A Winter's Tale* (1844), Heine attacks German anti-Semites who continue the stupid, malicious hatred of the Middle Ages, though for publication, Heine changed 'hatred of Jews' (*Judenhass*) to 'sectarian intolerance' (*Glaubenshass*) (Prawer 1983: 454): 'Like dogs in an alley / evil couples with folly; / you can tell the pack they let loose – / they all hate the Jews.' The pain of being a German poet is itself a theme in Heine's poetry, for example in the poems *In der Fremde* and *Ich bin ein Deutscher dichter*.
81. Mickiewicz and Yeats were among national poets subjected to hostility by their own people. The Polish poet Cyprian Norwid reacted to Mickiewicz's epic *Pan Tadeusz* (1834) with sarcasm: 'An exceedingly national poem indeed, in which [everyone] eats, drinks, gathers mushrooms, and waits for the French to make a Fatherland for them' (Koropeckyj 2008: 220). Yeats, an English Protestant who spent much of his life out of Ireland, was a target of suspicion by Irish Catholic 'natives'. On Irish hostility to Yeats, see p. 228.
82. Among the peculiar ironies of national poetry and song is the fact that, in World War I the German Jewish poet Ernst Lissauer wrote the super-chauvinistic *Hassgesang* (Hate Song against England') – '*Wir haben alle nur einen Feind: England*'

(Albanis 2002: 215). This was the most popular song in Germany during the war, distributed to all regiments. In the 1930s, the Nazi poet Eberhard Wolfgang Möller (Hitler's 'muse') encountered vitriolic criticism for his commissioned poem, *Der Führer* (1938) – which within a few months had a half million copies in circulation – for not going far enough in praise of Hitler (Baird 2008: 188f). The Nazi ideologue and anti-Semite Alfred Rosenberg mocked the poem for its 'Old Testament cherubs' wringing their hands over the martyrs of the Munich *Putsch*.
83. See Senghor (1976: 71). Frantz Fanon, in contrast, put independence before culture: 'To fight for national culture means in the first place to fight for the liberation of the nation' (1983: 187).

1 National Poetry and the Hebrew Bible
War and the Messianic Age

והלכו גויים לאורך
and nations shall walk at thy light...

Isaiah 60: 3

As a dominant driving force in civilization and the main root of Judaism, Christianity and Islam, the Hebrew Bible has authored and nourished national identity and religious-cultural nationalism:

- belief in the chosenness of the nation and its necessarily moral foundations
- unity across divisions of class, geographic dislocation and cultural assimilation
- fierce criticism of and grievance against its enemies, internal as well as external
- acceptance of guilt for national failings and defeats and grief-ridden penitence leading to moral reform
- hopes for freedom, regeneration and the ingathering of exiles
- longing for a messianic age of peace among nations
- vengeful hatred of oppressors, and readiness to fight and die for the nation
- interconnection of the personal life with that of the nation.[1]

The Hebrew Bible foreshadows conflict in national identity – between the individual and the group, chosenness and egalitarianism, narrowly national and the universal – and dangers of nationalism – the abuse of power, interminable conflict, undermining of faith. But it also has a Manichean conception of the nation, with its potential for creativity and destruction, good and evil, rebirth and corruption, the ideal and the reality. The Hebrew Bible has the first recorded instances in history of poets speaking truth to power and risking their lives for an ideal. Amos was expelled from Samaria, Jeremiah was imprisoned, and Isaiah ben Amotz, according to legend, was executed, as were many other prophets whose moral teachings challenged the existing order.

The Hebrew Bible is the great model of the Nation pickled, as it were, in literature and preserved to survive defeat, failure and exile. Its vivid stories, characters, down-to-earth imagery, rhythmic excitement and extraordinary range of emotion became an artistic yardstick for Western literature, particularly in English and German translation. The fabulous tale of the slaves who rebelled, won freedom, accepted their own laws and sacred scripture and themselves as a new nation and established their own state has had decisive influence on modern nationalism. In translation, the Psalms and the fifteen prophetic books, with their extremes of universal ideals and militant chauvinism, of liberty and violence, of justice and vengeance, are the most influential poetry in cultural history.[2]

DEFEAT AND BIBLICAL NATIONALISM

The power of the Hebrew Bible was in inverse proportion to the political and military weakness of the people who created it. People whose history was one of inner discord, conflict with imperial powers, defeat and exile. Spanning a period of at least 600 years (8th–2nd centuries BCE), the Hebrew Bible evolved with the crushing defeat and exile of the two monotheist kingdoms, Israel in 721 BCE and Judah in 587 BCE. Much modern cultural nationalism, too, comes from the experience of defeat and humiliation.[3] Jewish survival after defeat was an inspiration to later national movements as was the implied lesson that a national religious culture could be stronger than political and military force. Consequently, many modern nations have learned to preserve memories of heroic cultural struggle after military conquest, strengthening national unity, resolve and distinctiveness. The Hebrew prophets were, perhaps, the first to recognize that a weak nation can survive by remembering its defeats. The memory of defeat can be a more powerful stimulant of nationalism than victory. The experience of defeat, persecution, weakness and chaos can teach a nation to treasure their opposites as ideals, to be achieved, if not through politics then through apocalypse.

Defeat can steel national identity in countries which treat the Hebrew Bible as their true heritage, their licence of chosenness as the 'new Israel': the Armenians, Hungarians, Irish, Poles, Romanians, Scots, Ukrainians, as well as many Black Africans and Latin Americans, Their national identity was forged by conquest, slavery, colonization and/or exile. As a forerunner of dissident national literature with great sympathy for the defeated and downtrodden and faith in an ethical power beyond the temporal, the Hebrew Bible offered consolation and hope in a world dominated by often-cruel, rapacious empires.

In the biblical world, however, defeat as a lasting spur to national identity was rare. Defeated peoples – even great empires such as Assyria and Babylonia – were mostly decimated or destroyed, or they assimilated and died and their culture was lost or incorporated into other cultures. In ancient near-eastern literature, victory is trumpeted; defeat is usually passed over in silence. It seems that no ancient people reacted to defeat as the Jews did.

The nature of this defeat in the biblical age was little different from that inflicted on many other small nations who got in the way of the great powers of the time. What was unusual, perhaps, was the perspective in exile of a defeated kingdom, Judah, whose people had witnessed the fatal defeats of the two greatest empires the world had yet seen – Assyria and Babylonia. This does not mean that the Jews would not have preferred victory. The first six books of the Hebrew Bible have as their main theme the emergence of the Israelites from slavery in Egypt and their conquest of Canaan. The study and recital of Scripture in synagogue was a constant reminder of the possibility of a victorious struggle against the odds. Yet Judaism in practice evolved as an anti-triumphalist religion in which defeat was given unique emphasis as the communication of God's judgement and will and as a challenge to moral renewal. The Judeans in 6th century Babylonia are the first known example in history of an exiled diaspora community that in the long run did not totally assimilate but kept its identity and the hope of return to its homeland. They turned to their religious culture as an exclusive means of preserving in sacred texts and memory their religious-national identity. As a defeated people, the Jews underwent a variety of metamorphoses but kept their identity until modern times.

Meanwhile, missionary Christianity brought the Bible to Africa and South America, grafting it on to local cultures in the process of establishing colonial rule. The cultural imperialism represented by the Bible called up deep ambivalence in Third World countries struggling for independence. The Christianity of the empires was often felt as an imposition: 'The Church in the colonies is the white people's Church, the foreigner's Church' (Fanon 1983: 32). In a famous witticism, 'When the white man came to our country he had the Bible and we had the land. Then the white man said "let us pray". After the prayer, the white man had the land and we had the Bible'. Yet, the bargain was not quite as unfair as that by which native Indians traded Manhattan for a few worthless baubles. The Bible was not just a tool of colonization but also empowered the colonized. The story of the escape of African slaves from bondage and their struggle for independence in the Promised Land was a clarion for liberation, inspiring colonized peoples to do likewise. Many defeated and suppressed peoples embraced this culture not out of identification with the empires that ruled them but, as in the case of European peoples struggling for freedom, with ancient Israel breaking out of slavery. The language of African poetry is filled with biblical imagery. The Ugandan poet Okot p'Bitek describes the Luo tribe retreating before the colonists in *Song of Ocol*: 'Had you given chase/ they might have perished in the water/ like the Egyptians in the Red Sea'. Similarly, the Malawian poet Felix Mnthali alludes to the Book of Jeremiah (ch. 31) in 'The Dance' in its portrayal of murderous kings who die in bed, 'unaware of the cry heard in Rama/ of Rachel mourning her sons/ because they are not'.[4] The adoption of biblical faith was a political act: it meant acceptance of a system in which divine rule and messianic hopes are above temporal rule, and every human being, created in God's image, is equal in the eyes of God.[5] In the struggle for independence, imperial colonies and ex-colonies could draw on biblical authority in asserting cultural distinctiveness and universality, national self-awareness and self-criticism, and resistance to the oppressor, transforming the legacy of slavery, suffering and hate, as Israel did, into a source of proud collective identity, divine discontent and hope for a better future.

The hope, ultimately fulfilled to the astonishment of the ancient Israelites, for the fall of tyrannical empires has evidently left its mark on modern nationalism. Apart from ancient Egypt, the hated, persecutory 'Other' in the Hebrew Bible is Mesopotamia, home of the great idolatrous empires of Assyria and Babylonia. Vengeful rage similar to that of the prophet Nahum against Assyria, or Jeremiah against Babylonia, appears in the national culture of defeated peoples such as the Irish, the Scots, the Greeks, the Poles and the Ukrainians, under the heel of powerful, often ruthless, empires. As biblical prophets found, so do modern cultural nationalists, cultural victory can be snatched from political defeat. Modern nationalist works such as Mickiewicz's *Pan Tadeusz* follow the Hebrew Bible as cultural 'victories' over a hated oppressor, ensuring the literary survival of a destroyed world and the hope of its restoration. In the struggle for independence, national poets, often inspired by the prophets, rage not only against external oppressors, but also against the nation itself and its traitors.[6] Mickiewicz (*ibid.*, ix 133–6) echoes the prophets in his attacks on Poles who assimilated into foreign cultures, neglecting their own. Shevchenko, steeped in the Bible, castigates the cruel, indifferent Ukrainian landlords and the elite (1964: 255). The religious establishment is a common target for national poets from the Hebrew Bible onwards, for it allegedly betrays the moral integrity of the Nation. The prophetic attacks on the Temple priesthood and the religion of mere ritual anticipate modern national poetry – of Botev, Gibran or J.L. Gordon, for example – which condemns the clergy who allegedly fail the people.[7] Instead of leading them in revolt, the clergy defend the corrupt status quo. The ideology of self-sacrifice adopted by some modern nationalists can be traced to the Hebrew Bible. Modern national poets – Petöfi, Botev, Marti, Plunkett and Pearse, among others – find biblical inspiration for martyrdom in the name of the moral integrity of the Nation.

THE PARADOX OF NATIONALISM AND UNIVERSALISM

The Hebrew Bible exemplifies the tension, familiar in modern nationalism, between national identity and universal humanity, the sense of being chosen and special on the one hand and being like everyone else and aiming for similar worldwide goals on the other. Biblical poetry is the poetry of one nation but also the poetry of many nations. In particular, several dozen sections of biblical prophecy are addressed to 'the nations'.[8] By implication, the message of ethical monotheism applies even to those who do not believe in God. Weber (1961) underlines the universal significance of the Hebrew prophets in suggesting that in some ways they prepared the ground not just for modern Jewish national identity but in general for the modern world. The universality of prophetic poetry is apparent in its emphasis on internal, abstract reality in metaphors and religious concepts, the prophets' intense social conscience, its violent opposition to magic and superstition, and its criticism of the status quo, which have no parallel in other surviving ancient near-eastern texts (Pritchard 1969). The Hebrew Bible has an elective affinity for radical change, social reform and transformation of an imperfect world through moral ideals and the *imitatio dei*. Political and religious movements which stress the value of social justice and compassion oppose materialism and the unjust distribution of wealth, object to ritual at the expense of spirituality and to the emphasis on the letter of the law rather than its spirit and belong to a tradition pioneered by the biblical prophets. The prophets were hostile to national distinction as expressed in existing power structures, in monarchy and cultic ritual. In their view, national aspirations are meaningless unless directed by moral ideals based on monotheist faith. Though this faith derives from the land of Israel and the Temple on Mount Zion, it draws the believer away from the confines of the national to look at the world in terms of humanity as a whole.[9] A person's value rests not on his or her being a member of a nation or tribe but on being human. The messianic ideal of the prophet Isaiah (2:4), of weapons transformed by all nations into instruments of peaceful cooperation and productivity, is not the assertion but the dissolution of national separation. It is the harmonizing of the babel of conflicting nations and their unity in common humanity and faith.[10]

THE HEBREW BIBLE, MORALITY AND THE NATION

In the next few pages, I will look at some biblical poetry which has influenced modern cultural nationalism through Bible translation in the vernacular. This poetry is dominated by the inseparability of national identity from morality, an idea prevalent in modern cultural nationalism.[11] The prophetic view of the nation, based on a conception of human beings as 'a little lower than the angels' (Psalms 8: 5), is incompatible with modern forms of exclusive racial nationalism. Israel's survival is predicated on conduct. Its identity as a chosen people depends on a conviction of moral inferiority, certainly to the divine ideal and at times to other nations. The blunt humble acceptance of shameful imperfection and incompleteness (which can lead to defeat and exile) can give a nation a moral aim, a basis for community and a reason for survival impossible if it believed arrogantly in its perfection and power.[12]

The book of Amos contains some of the earliest written literature to define a concept of national identity – not just of Israel but of all 'chosen' peoples – in purely moral terms. Amos lived in the last days of the Israelite monarchy, shortly before the Assyrian exile in 721 BCE. To Amos, Israel's chosenness depends on moral stature. Otherwise it is no different from other nations:

> ... Are you different from the Ethiopians,
> children of Israel?
> For though I took Israel from Egypt
> I did the same for the Philistines from Cyprus
> and Aram from Kir!
>
> (9: 7–8)[13]

To keep its side of the divine covenant and survive as a nation, Israel must paradoxically transcend nationalism and reach for universal values to fulfil its responsibilities to the poor and the helpless. Israel's chosenness is defined by the privilege of being aware of its failings:

> You alone have I known
> among the families of men:
> Therefore I will punish you for your sins!
>
> (Amos 3: 2)

The prophets regard the individual and the Nation as equally responsible before God. The value of a person and of a nation, and the justification for their continued existence, are measured not by military and political power but by Godly conduct.[14]

> What does the Lord want of you?
> Only to do justice,
> to love kindness,
> to go humbly with your God ...
>
> (Micah 6:8)

The prophets condemn their own people for moral backsliding, materialism, arrogance and insufficient regard for the sacred values of justice and truth, and for bringing disaster upon the nation. The principle associated with the Magna Carta, of the limitation of the power of rulers, has authority in Scripture: the king was required to write his own copy of Scripture, to ensure that he knew the law and obeyed it all the days of his life (Deuteronomy 17: 18–19). It is not unusual for prophets to attack kings: Nathan condemns David; Elijah denounces Ahab; and Jeremiah fearlessly attacks Jehoiachin for betraying the faith (the king's punishment is to be deported by Nebuchadrezzar to Babylonia).[15] These examples encouraged national identity based on the idea that, unlike human power, truth and justice are absolute, however humble their origins. Though idolatry could also inspire virtue, its gods tended to reflect the weaknesses of those who believed in them. Monotheism, with its impossible divine standard, could drive human beings to imagine and try to create a better world.

WAR POETRY IN THE HEBREW BIBLE

At the same time, the Hebrew Bible accepts violence, conflict and war as part of the human condition. Violence is at the climax of the archetypal image of the nation emerging to freedom – the exodus from Egypt. The victory of the escaping slaves glorifies not war but faith:

> Your right hand, God, glorious in power,
> your right hand, Lord, shatters the enemy,
> your fury loosed to eat them like straw.
>
> You blew – up the water piled in a dripping heap
> frozen in the sea's heart.
>
> The enemy said: I'll overtake, split the spoil,
> do what I want, draw sword and destroy.
>
> You blew – down the water came.
> They sank like lead in the foam.
>
> (Exodus 15: 6–10)

The return to the ancestral homeland in the Hebrew Bible (as in *The Odyssey*) is accompanied by violence. The entire history of the monotheist kingdoms is stained with internecine war and war with neighboring kingdoms, ending in defeat and exile. War transforms a tribal society to a militant nation kingdom, with its tribal/national god:

> I will sharpen my lightning sword
> for justice on my foes!
> I will make my arrows drunk
> with blood of captive and slain!
> My flesh-devouring sword
> on the heads of the wild-haired foe!
>
> (Deuteronomy 32: 41–2)

War unites the nation in the age of the Judges:

> The kings came and fought,
> the kings of Canaan fought at Ta'anach
> by the waters of Megiddo –
> no silver spoil for them!
>
> The heavens fought,
> the stars fought Sisera in their orbits,
> the river Kishon swept them away,
> ancient river, river Kishon.

> Tread valiantly, my soul!
>
> The pounding of horses' heels
> went galloping galloping on.
>
> (Judges 5: 19–22)

Even Isaiah, who paints a roseate picture of a world of peace and harmony, of a messianic future when the wolf will live with the lamb, also imagines the annihilation of Israel's enemies (11:11–16; also Micah chs. 5–6).

To the great Mesopotamian empires, war was a way of life. Much biblical poetry is a record of imperial conquest. The Babylonian final destruction of the Assyrian empire at Nineveh (612 BCE) is depicted vividly by the prophet Nahum:

> Red the attacker's shield,
> warriors decked in scarlet.
> Torch-like the chariots flash,
> javelins tremble poisonously:
> Lightning torches streak.
> Chariots frenzied roar in the squares,
> the clang of steel in the streets.
>
> (2: 4–5)

The crucial Babylonian victory over Egypt, Assyria's allies, at Carchemish (605 BCE) is hailed by Jeremiah as the will of God:

> Why do I see them tremble
> in retreat,
> warriors cut down,
> they don't look back when they run,
> the terrors round them –
> the Lord declares!
>
> The swift will not escape,
> nor the mighty,
> but they stumble, fall
> up north, by the Euphrates.
>
> (46: 5–6)

Yet, the prophet's hope for Judean independence is shattered as Babylonia turns on Judah, conquers Jerusalem and exiles many of its inhabitants (597 BCE).

> The city empties.
> All race for the caves,
> crouch in thickets,
> scramble up cliffs.
> The city is left, deserted.

Plundered one!
Why do you dress in scarlet
and put on ornaments of gold?

(4: 29–30)

DEFEAT, GRIEVANCE AND REVENGE

Unlike other extant ancient literature, the Hebrew Bible does not censor defeat. Rather, it treats defeat as a divine message delivered by the enemy – mainly Assyria and Babylonia – as the 'rod' of God's wrath. Uniquely in ancient literature, defeat in the Hebrew Bible galvanizes national consciousness. The destruction of the kingdom of Judah (early 6th century BCE) is traditionally believed to be the background to the Hebrew book of Lamentations, unflinching in its picture of national humiliation and self-blame, of guilt at having 'abandoned' God and of desolation at being 'abandoned' by God:

Remember, Lord, what befell us,
see our shame!
Our land and homes in strangers' hands ...

Orphans we became, our mothers – widows.
Silver we paid for water.

... On the waste of mount Zion
jackals prowl.

But you, Lord, reign forever!
Why do you forever forget us?
Why do you abandon us?
Return us, O God, to you.
Let us be restored,
as we were ...

(5:1–3, 18–21)

Yet defeat cannot always be faced calmly, as the will of God. Memories of defeat and humiliation in biblical poetry are sometimes filled with lust for revenge. The prophets took comfort in an apocalyptic day of judgment and punishment, not only of Israel but also of its hated enemies.[16] Psalm 137, dating from the late 6th century BCE, illustrates the close link between humiliation and nationalism in its picture of the captivity in Babylonia and the yearning for Zion and Jerusalem. It ends with a brutal curse at fallen Babylon, which had destroyed Judah and burnt down the Temple in Jerusalem:[17]

By the waters of Babylon we sat and wept
when we remembered Zion.

> On the branches of the willow trees
> we hung our harps
> when our tormentors mocked us,
> 'Sing us a song of Zion'.
>
> How can we sing a song of the Lord
> on foreign soil?
> If I forget you, Jerusalem,
> let my right arm be paralyzed.
> Let my tongue stick to my mouth
> if I do not remember you.
>
> O daughter of Babylon, you destroyer:
> Happy is he who pays you
> what you've done to us!
> Happy is he who takes your little ones
> and smashes them on the rock!

HOPE OF RESTORATION

The biblical hope for renewal of national political identity and the return of the 'saving remnant' to their land has had incalculable influence on modern nationalism. In the Book of Hosea, the negation of nationhood ['Not-my-nation' (*Lo-Ammi*, Hosea 2: 23)] will be put right when Israel abandons her idolatrous promiscuity to become again 'My-nation' (*Ammi*). Only then will God abolish war and make a new covenant with all living things. Here again, national realization is possible only in the sphere of universal moral action:

> I will betroth you to me forever.
> I will betroth you to me in righteousness,
> in justice, mercy and love.
> And I will betroth you to me in faith –
> and you will know God.
>
> (Hosea 2:21–22)[18]

But these were dreams of a future time. For the time being, the prophets of the surviving monarchy of Judah were sharply aware that political power does not last. They had the example not just of the fall of the kingdom of Israel and many other small nations but also the destruction of the Assyrian empire (the most powerful up to that time) in the late 7th century BCE. The total eradication of Assyria from history taught the prophets the need to strengthen national identity to outlast defeat and exile. A small defeated nation could be resurrected – its 'dry bones' could live – if it based its survival on moral ideals. After the fall of Judah and the exile of most of its inhabitants to Babylonia in the early 6th century BCE, Ezekiel predicted national rebirth:

> Son of Man!
> These bones are the people of Israel.
> Some say our bones are dry,
> our hope is lost
> we're clean cut off.
>
> Prophesy! Tell them:
> I will open your graves and bring you to life.
> I will bring you back to the land of Israel!
>
> (37:11–12)

After the Persian conquest of Babylonia in 539 BCE, the Judean exiles were allowed to return to their land. This is the first known case when a defeated, exiled nation went back to its homeland and rebuilt it. At the time, national revival could be linked to ancient messianic hopes and to apocalyptic visions of Jerusalem not just as a national capital but as a universal one (see Ezekiel 5:5; Zachariah 9:9–10).[19]

THE SOCIOLOGY OF BIBLICAL NATIONALISM

What is the sociological basis of biblical literature as 'national'? The Bible is evidently the first literature aimed not at an elite, nor even just at the nation, including its illiterates and those as yet unborn (cf. Deuteronomy 29:13–14), but also at all nations. No extant literature from the ancient world placed more importance upon social welfare and the responsibility of the better-off toward the poor. The concept of *tzedakah* (meaning both righteousness and charity), which originates in the Hebrew Bible, encouraged national consciousness, though it also pointed Judaism in a universalist direction. Israel's centrality in the ancient trade routes and exile among non-Jews inclined Judaism to cosmopolitanism and the application of abstract ideals such as liberty, love, justice and faith to all nations. The idea of mission, of reaching out to non-believers and their conversion, evidently begins in the Hebrew Bible (see Isaiah 56: 3). Much biblical literature was sung or spoken, and biblical poets included Jeremiah, a priest, and Amos, who describes himself as 'a shepherd and a dresser of sycamore trees' (7:14). As the biblical works were regarded as sacred long before the canon was fixed, by the beginning of the 2nd century CE, ordinary people (including, presumably, some women) were familiar with them, either in public recitals or speeches or as part of Temple and, later, synagogue service.[20] Much of the Hebrew Bible can be understood by children and recited aloud by illiterates. Even when it was still a Jewish sect, ancient Christianity had little room for narrow nationalism. While the core of the Hebrew Bible is the birth of a nation, the core of the Greek Bible is the expectation of universal messianic redemption. The authors of the Greek Bible, written mostly by the start of the 2nd century CE, believed in the imminent Second Coming. The prophecies in the Hebrew Bible would be fulfilled. The messianic age was at hand. Nations would soon be one family of mankind united in faith, as in Isaiah's prophecy. When this did not happen, messianic hopes faded and Christian dogma forced a split with Judaism. The Hebrew Bible, in contrast, does not assume that the world is about to end. Rather, we must make do with this world, the world of peoples or nations (*amim*). As new nations grew and converted to Christianity, the Hebrew Bible (the 'Old Testament') rose in importance. It satisfied the instinct for this-worldly national assertion. It expressed the conflict many nations experience between national particularity and a universal ideology of moral values. Above all, it gave the masses a ready-made portable culture whose beauty, as much as its moral and national content, had ensured its preservation by the Jews and led to its eventual adoption as sacred, even in translation, by a large part of the world's population.

The Church already in the early Christian era took on the identity of the 'true Israel'. Ancient Israel became the model for the evolving nation-state in European culture. The survival of ancient nations that translated the Bible into the vernacular (notably Armenia and Ethiopia around the 5th century) underscored the power of biblical nationalism among non-Jews. The return to the Hebrew Bible in the Renaissance might be seen as the start of modern nationalism.[21] Bible translation into the vernacular throughout Europe in the century after the invention of printing by Gutenberg in the 1450s (translation into German, English, French, Spanish, Italian, Dutch, Swedish, Danish, Finnish, Czech, Hungarian and Polish, among others) became the chief tool of nation building. 'Of all the works published, translations of the Bible were the most important, not only in the history of the Reformation but also in the history of languages' (Elton 1971: 289). When the Bible was published in the language of the people, a crucial step was taken in the creation of the modern world of nations. It encouraged literacy in a broad cross-section of society, reaching, as Erasmus enthused, 'the farmer, the tailor, the stonemason, prostitutes, pimps, and Turks' (Wright 2001: 199). The ancient Jewish intoxication with vernacular Scripture could now be shared by the European masses. The German translation of Luther, a lecturer in Hebrew at the University of Wittenberg, ran into 377 editions by the time of his death in 1546! (Elton 1971: 289)[22]

Yet the translation and publication of the Bible in the vernacular was at first an act of heresy, a crime like witchcraft punishable by death. Why? One answer is that translation, by making the content of the Bible clear to the common people, could undermine Church authority. The Church had treated Scripture as being in its control. It blinded the mostly-ignorant common people with Latin and Greek. The Latin Vulgate had supreme authority, but most people could not read or understand it. In 1530 Henry VIII prohibited the possession of the Bible in English translation as it could 'stir

National Poetry and the Hebrew Bible 47

and incense [the people] to sedition and disobedience against their princes, sovereigns, and heads' (Seldman 2006: 119).

Vernacular translations of the Hebrew Bible were not just seditious in their time but also had subversive consequences far beyond what was imagined. The Reformation idea of 'Scripture alone' without a clerical intermediary implied not just that people should read the Bible on their own and make up their own minds about it, but also that, in principle, they could and should think for themselves (Hill 1994: 414). As a vital part of a humanist education, the Bible was now subject to critical study. Resultant theological debate leading to comparative critical Bible editions helped create a climate for secular scientific investigation, including social studies and theories of nation-building. In this way, the growth of scientific method in the study of ancient Israel encouraged the historical consciousness of nations.

Especially in the age of nationalism during and after the American and French revolutions, nations struggling for independence were often compared with the Jews (even, ironically, when these nations were known for hatred of Jews). Their political system, directly or indirectly, could not help but be influenced by the Bible. The idea of the covenant between God and Israel (e.g., Exodus 19:3–8) might be seen as a theological precursor of constitutional monarchy, the 'consent of the governed', and the free society (Sacks 2002: 134). The Puritans and, later, revolutionaries in America, France, Italy and elsewhere, including Washington, Robespierre and Garibaldi, carried the torch of the prophets. Political revolutionaries brought increasingly secularized ideals of liberty, human rights and equality into the forefront of what was to become Western democracy (Kohn 1946). Even as the 'sea of faith' retreated in the face of secular enlightenment, the ideological influence of the Hebrew Bible persisted in secular forms.

In short, the influence of the Bible on modern nationalism has been overwhelming. Biblical influence was central in the German poetry of Klopstock (notably *The Messiah*, 1748–73), whose conception of the poet was that of prophet, teacher and patriot. Goethe saw the Hebrew Bible not just as the book of one nation but also as the archetype for all nations. In Hungary, translations of the Psalms and Karolyi's Bible translation 'influenced the development of Hungarian literary language for centuries' (Szakaly 1990: 94). Biblical language of the emergence from slavery, prophetic denunciations of the wicked and hopes for freedom not only for Hungary but for the world are frequent in Petőfi's poetry. In 1848, the year of revolution, he called on Hungarians to set out en masse from Egyptian bondage to the Promised Land, with poets such as himself as the pillars of fire guiding the way through the wilderness.[23] The Ukrainian poet Shevchenko was deeply influenced by the Hebrew Bible and the alleged similarities between Jews and Ukrainians (Shevchenko 1964: *l*). He translated biblical passages which he felt applied to the modern Ukraine under Russian rule. Biblical influences are plentiful, too, in the poetry of Mickiewicz, whose Polish nationalism

48   *National Poetry and the Hebrew Bible*

has likewise been described as 'Judaic': 'that of a conquered, humiliated and oppressed nation dreaming of resurrection' (Talmon 1967: 96).

In a world of evolving nation-states in which secular culture had not yet taken full hold and *the* Book was still the Bible (and Church attendance was usually mandatory), such influences were perhaps inevitable and were found among poets as diverse as Byron, Ibsen and Bialik. Lönnrot's *Kalevala* (1834), based on oral Finnish tradition, has many biblical echoes from the book of Job and Judges.[24] Verdi's 'Chorus of Hebrew Slaves' (*Va pensiero*) in the opera *Nabucco* (1842), written two decades before Italy's independence, is a patchwork of biblical texts.[25] In its longing for freedom, sung by the Israelite slaves in Egypt, *Va pensiero* became Italy's unofficial national anthem:

> Sing again songs of our homeland,
> of the past.
>
> We have drunk the cup of sorrow,
> and repented in bitter tears.
>
> Inspire us, God, with courage
> to endure to the end.

THE BIBLE AND BRITISH NATIONAL IDENTITY

The chief influence of the Hebrew Bible on national identity has been through the English language and literature. The scholars who translated the King James Bible (1611) 'forged an enduring link, literary and religious, between the English-speaking peoples of the world' (Churchill 2002: 124). The Bible spread with the British empire, and it should not be forgotten that 'the British ruled over much the largest and most diverse empire the world had ever known. It extended over every one of the world's climatic zones, over every inhabited continent and across all the world's major religions and civilizations' (Lieven 2000: 89). Perhaps no people, apart from the Jews themselves, have so totally absorbed the Bible as the British.[26] British history is, in a sense, biblical history. Long before the Norman conquest of 1066, the Bible was the main unifying force of the different, often warring, groups in the British isles. In the distinctiveness and cohesion of its national identity, England was centuries ahead of other west European societies (Hastings 1997). The Anglo-Saxon poem describing the battle of Maldon of 991, for example, is an appeal to the nation to stand firm, as Israel did, against invasion (*ibid.*, 42; also see Gillingham 1992). From the 11th–14th centuries, England was dominated by French-speaking Normans. After that, the Bible played a primary role in forging English nationalism, using the newfound power of the English language in a vernacular largely created by translation from the Hebrew. Henry VIII's break with the Church of Rome helped free the Bible from clerical control and gave English Bible translation the royal imprimatur. The English translations of the Hebrew Bible in the 16th and 17th centuries, above all, the King James Bible – 'the most influential version of the most influential book in the world, in what is now its most influential language' (MacGregor 1968: 170) – were revolutionary in British (and European) history and in English literature. The Bible was no longer prohibitively expensive and read exclusively by Church-dominated Latin readers. It could now be read by the much larger numbers who knew English and could afford cheap printed editions (Dickens 1970). For these reasons, the English Bible, more than other translations of the Hebrew Bible, had massive influence on the growth of the vernacular among the general population and on English national identity. Between 1560 and 1611, there were over 100 editions of the Bible in English (including, by 1557, a cheap pocketbook edition), and between 1611 and 1640 there were about 140 editions of the King James Version (Hastings 1997: 58).

The translations of William Tyndale were milestones in the growth of English vernacular and literary language and English national identity. Before Tyndale the English language 'was a poor thing, spoken only by a few in an island off the shelf of Europe, a language unknown in Europe' (Daniell 2003: 249). Latin was the main language of educated men. England lagged behind the Continent as translation into English was prohibited by the Constitutions of Oxford of 1407–09. Tyndale, a heretic in exile from a still-Catholic England, pioneered Bible translation into English, in Cologne and Worms in the 1520s. Tyndale took the revolutionary view (in fact, the norm in Judaism) that a ploughman could understand the Bible as well as, if not better than, a bishop. George Steiner sums up Tyndale's importance:

> 'Beyond Shakespeare, it is William Tyndale who is begettor of the English language as we know it ... It is Tyndale's cadences, sonorities, amplitudes and concisions (he is a master of both) which, via his commanding effect on the Authorized Version, characterize global English as it is spoken and written today. No translation-act, save Luther's has been as generative of a whole language' (1996: 49).

Tyndale's assistant, Miles Coverdale, printed the first complete Bible in English (1535), probably in Zurich, dedicated to King Henry VIII. In 1539, a revised version of Coverdale's Bible was printed and put in every parish church in England. (Later, Bibles had to be chained to the pews because of their popularity.) For the first time, large numbers of English readers could respond, as the Jews had done for 2000 years, to the full literary splendor of biblical stories and poetry. Coverdale's translation of the Psalms is the best-known and, to many, best-loved poetry in English. It was incorporated into the *Book of Common Prayer* (1662), which was used each day:[27] 'Even in their obscure moments they have the mellow beauty of some ancient, familiar window with slightly jumbled glass' (Dickens 1970: 185). Most notable English poets between Wyatt and Milton tried their hand at translation from the Psalms. In this way, the Hebrew Bible largely determined British national identity, not just through its content but also through its language. It gave Shakespeare and all later English writers their chief model of literary excellence.

Many biblical phrases became so assimilated into the English national heritage that their origin was often forgotten. If, for example, you stand at the parting of the ways, are in jeopardy of your life, play the fool, set your house in order, harden your heart, love your neighbour as yourself or turn the other cheek, you are quoting from the Hebrew Bible translated into English. If you believe the race is not to the swift; or that love is strong as death; feel like a voice crying in the wilderness, a still small voice; are slow of speech or slow to anger at those who multiply words without knowledge. If you are full of sour grapes, do not see eye to eye with your friends or put your trust in princes, you are using Hebrew expressions. If you believe that the leopard cannot change his spots, that you must cast your bread upon the waters, that for everything there is a season or that if you sow the wind you reap the whirlwind, you are using Hebrew imagery. If you escape by the skin of your teeth, you believe that if you spare the rod you spoil the child or that you have punished a scapegoat, you are quoting from the Hebrew. Examples can by multiplied a hundredfold, not just in English but in all the languages into which the Bible was translated.

In a society in which Church and State were one, Protestant Britain learned its history in the light of biblical history and saw itself as virtually the fulfilment of the Bible. Major events in British history (coronations, marriages, wars, deaths, the Gunpowder Plot of 1605, the English Revolution) were commonly identified with biblical texts, especially the 150 psalms, which were recited once a month. To Tyndale, England and ancient Israel were one: 'As it went with their kings and rulers, so shall it be with ours. As it was with their common people, so shall it be with ours' (Daniell 2003: 237–38). Many English kings were commonly identified with biblical kings, Henry VIII as David, for example, or Edward VI as Josiah (*ibid.*, 208). In particular, the Geneva Bible of 1560 'was the source book for public and personal lives in Britain, and a motor that drove revolution' (*ibid.*, 221). Oliver Cromwell treated the Geneva Bible as a guide in war, revolution and statecraft.[28]

English literature – Chaucer, Shakespeare, Spenser, Milton – is packed with biblical themes and allusions. Particularly in the Elizabethan period, and in the time of the English revolution in the 17th century (in some ways a model for later revolutions), the Bible was the chief inspiration of nationalism. In the age of Elizabeth, an English population of under six million bought half a million copies of the Bible (Daniell 2003: xiv). The imperialism of the Elizabethans – the 'ancestor of modern nationalism'

(Kermode 1965: 12) – is reflected in their literature, notably Spenser's *The Fairie Queene* (1590, 1596) in which corrupt Catholic Spain and Ireland are set allegorically against the 'true Israel' of the Protestant Church. Spenser is described by Hastings as 'an out-and-out English Protestant nationalist' (1997: 84) and *The Fairy Queene* is described as 'the quintessence of Elizabethan nationalism'. Celebrating the union of England and true religion under the sovereignty of Elizabeth, it is 'a work of reconciliation between old Englishness and new Englishness, a closing of ranks between the "Merrie England" which Catholics claimed had been lost with the Reformation and the Protestant gospel' (82–3). Spenser transforms the war between Protestant England and Catholic Spain into myth, the divine Una, the true universal English Church and its virgin empress Elizabeth I, opposed to Duessa, the satanic Roman Church. In Book I, after his struggle with moral impurity, the saintly Red Cross Knight – St. George the dragon killer, symbol of England, defender and future husband of Una – arrives Moses-like at the top of a holy mountain where he glimpses the heavenly Jerusalem and the likeness of its earthly counterpart, Cleopolis (London):

> The new *Hierusalem*, that God has built
> For those to dwell in, that are chosen his ...
>
> (X 57)

England's identification with Israel reached its height during the mid-17th century Puritan revolution, whose outstanding poet was Milton. The revolution was driven by the religious-nationalist ideology and fervor of the prophets, by self-identification as a chosen people with a divine covenant and messianic hopes, a love of liberty and opposition to overweening monarchic rule. Milton read the Bible in Hebrew. Among Milton's earliest writings were translations of Psalms 114 and 136, which relate Israel's escape from slavery to freedom. The motif of freedom would later become central in Milton's poetry, including *Paradise Lost*, and in his political works supporting Cromwell and the revolution. Milton's English nationalism derives mainly from the Hebrew Bible and the idea of a 'national community bound by Covenant-bonds to its divine king' (Fisch 1964: 123–24). The last book of *Paradise Lost* includes a prophecy of the birth of the nation of Israel, to which England would be heir.

Though strongest in the 17th century, the influence of the Bible on the English language and on British nationalism predominated until the 20th century.[29] In his translation of the Psalms in 1719, Isaac Watts was moved to replace 'Israel' with 'Great Britain' (Hastings 1997: 62). Burns was taught to read mainly from the Bible. Coleridge, in the *Biographia Literaria* (1817), points out that fine English is less likely to come from scholars, whose style is artificial and burdened with linguistic knowledge, than from those who regularly read the Bible (1975: 190–1) Byron's *Hebrew Melodies* reflect similar identification with the world of the Bible.[30] To Blake, immersed in biblical prophetic imagery, the visionary ideal of England is a 'new Jerusalem':

> I will not cease from mental fight,
> Nor shall my sword sleep in my hand
> Till we have built Jerusalem
> In England's green and pleasant land.
>
> ('Jerusalem' 1804)

Biblical influences saturate Victorian literature and the poetry of Kipling, 'poet of empire',[31] and even modernists such as D.H. Lawrence and T.S. Eliot (Aberbach 2003b: 145–46).

MODERN JEWISH NATIONALISM AND NEO-PROPHECY

If the Bible in translation could give the English, Americans, Germans, Spanish, Dutch, Scandinavians, Poles, Hungarians, Africans, Latin Americans, etc., a sense of chosenness in their 'new Jerusalem', how much more could the Bible in the original Hebrew stimulate national identity among the Jews. As we shall see in the next chapters, rabbinic Judaism for the most part facilitated the nationalism of longing and lost the name of action. Among medieval Hebrew poets, Judah Halevi (c. 1075–1140) stands out as an outspoken poet of Jewish national identity, illustrating the continuing potential power of biblical nationalism among the Jews: 'I'd lightly leave the good of Spain/ to see the Temple's dust again' (Carmi 1981: 347).[32] The dream of the lost homeland and hope for national regeneration are consistent motifs in Hebrew poetry from the Bible to modern times. The continuing influence of this poetry was ensured by the inclusion of much of it in the Jewish liturgy.

Yet, the Christian nations of Europe, deriving their national identity as chosen peoples largely from the Bible, adopted the doctrine that they were the elect heir to Judaism. Judaism was now an obsolete fossil. The Jews could live on purely as a token of the supremacy of the Church, damned in the eyes of God as murderers of the savior, identified with contemptible material existence devoid of spirituality, having no original cultural development of their own, subject to ceaseless hatred and persecution. As guardians of a crushed religion, the Jews were the most reluctant of European nationalists, among the last to emerge from the world of the Middle Ages and to discover their national identity. Initially, the growth of universalist secular Enlightenment encouraged not Jewish nationalism but political loyalty of Jews to the countries in which they lived. The granting of emancipation to most European Jews in the eighty or so years after the French Revolution and the spread of secular enlightenment, led to their assimilation and upward social mobility.[33] Assimilated European

Jews were perfectly willing to concede to their countries of citizenship their albatross identity as a chosen people in exchange for equality and human rights. The French Jews, for example, introduced a 'Prayer for France' into their prayerbook, identifying France as God's chosen nation: 'France is of all countries the one which You seem to prefer, because it is the most worthy of You' (Marrus 1971: 118). Nineteenth-century European nationalism, however, precipitated anti-Semitism and brought about widespread acceptance of a new doctrine; even conversion to Christianity could not eradicate the wickedness of the Jew, which was in the blood (Wistrich 2010). Even France, with its enlightened revolutionary ideals, was infected by Jew-hatred. In these circumstances, political Zionism was forced upon the Jews, who then discovered its overwhelming power of regeneration: 'The force we need,' wrote Theodor Herzl, founder of the World Zionist Organization in 1897, 'is created in us by anti-Semitism' (Mendes-Flohr and Reinharz 1995: 536).

Jewish nationalism, with its inevitable biblical undertones, led to the revival of Hebrew prophetic poetry in free verse. Chaim Nachman Bialik (1873–1934) and Uri Zvi Greenberg (1896–1981) are the two outstanding neo-biblical poets, politically as well as culturally.[34] Both responded forcefully to anti-Semitism. Yet their poetry raises a fundamental question: is modern Jewish nationalism a continuation of or a rebellion against Judaism? In some ways they are unlike the biblical prophets who offer hope and tend to be pacifists, teaching a morality which transcends the nation. The nation's enemies carry out God's will, which must be accepted. In contrast with their biblical sources, Bialik is uncompromising in his despair, and Greenberg in his violent militancy. Both are concerned less with prophetic ideals than with Jewish survival. Yet like the prophets, Bialik established his credentials not through praise but condemnation. In a poem quoting the Book of Amos, 'Prophet, run away' (*Hoze, lekh brakh*, 1908), the poet declares:

> My axe-like word strikes to damn,
> I never was a yes man.
>
> (Bialik 2004: 132)

Bialik's most notable neo-prophetic poems, or 'poems of wrath,' date from 1903–6, responding to widespread pogroms in Russia and expressing the despair that drove the national movement.

In particular, Bialik's in *The City of Slaughter* (*Be-Ir ha-Haregah*), written in 1903 after the pogrom in Kishinev in southern Russia, had a volcanic effect on Jewish nationalism. The poet visited the town shortly after the pogrom and describes it in gory detail. But instead of condemning the perpetrators, he attacks the Jews. The descendants of the heroic Maccabees were cowards, he claims: they hid like mice. (In fact, some of them did fight back, but Bialik does not mention this.) The poem is revolutionary in treating the

Jews not as an ethnic group living in Russia but as a nation in its own right. Bialik's majestic prophetic diatribe catches the spirit of a nation which no longer aims at assimilation but accepts in despair that it is different, and is hated. Later in 1903 this poem helped inspire one of the first instances of organized Jewish military resistance since the Bar Kokhba revolt, in the Gomel pogrom.

Smith's description of Bialik as writing of a 'Davidic cultural and political renaissance' (1999: 82) is perhaps even more true of Greenberg. Bialik ideologically was a disciple of the philosopher Ahad Ha'am, who believed in a secular cultural form of Jewish nationalism, built on traditional Judaism. It is Greenberg who writes of the realization of messianic longing through restoration of the so-called Jewish 'kingdom'. For this reason, Greenberg was condemned, and his poetry was neglected by the Israeli literary establishment, which is predominantly secular, liberal and generally unsympathetic to exclusivist nationalism. No modern Hebrew poet – perhaps no poet in any literature – has so passionately identified himself as a reincarnation of a biblical prophet as Greenberg. For Greenberg even more than Blake, the biblical celestial Jerusalem can be created on earth. Like a modern Jeremiah, Greenberg uses poetry to inspire national rebirth, holding up his personal biography as a symbol of the life of the people. The poet was totally identified with the divine calling of the prophet:

> Like prophetic chapters my life burns
> in total revelation,
> my body a metal mass for smelting.
> My God the blacksmith hammers me:
> every past wound opens in me,
> spits fire shut in my bones.[35]

The first half of Greenberg's life was a unique personal journey, which he came to regard as symbolic of the collective transformation of the Jewish people: from orthodox Hasid to Yiddish expressionist to poet of World War I to Palestinian Hebrew poet. He was the fiercest, most ardent and original poetic spokesman for Jewish religious-nationalist chosenness. The two great emotional poles of Greenberg's work were Jew-hatred and the re-establishment of a Jewish state. Greenberg saw his poetry not as art but as God-given prophecy meant to influence events and ultimately bring about messianic salvation. Greenberg was no aesthete. He rejected aestheticism, which he associated with hated Hellenism (Aberbach and Leoussi 2002). He believed in action. He has much in common with 19th century militant national poets, such as Mickiewicz, Petőfi and Botev (see Aberbach 2003). His poetry, born in violence, is full of violent images and gestures: perhaps no word echoes more angrily and insistently in his writings than 'blood'. Hebrew, he declared, was not his mother-tongue, but 'the language of my blood'.

National Poetry and the Hebrew Bible 55

Uprooted from his Hasidic home in Polish Galicia and conscripted into the Austro-Hungarian army in 1915, Greenberg, then eighteen, was thrust into the Serbian front on the Sava river. There he witnessed grotesque horrors which never left him – the lifeless bodies of comrades dangling upside down on the barbed wire fences. Toward the war's end, Greenberg deserted. In Lemberg during the pogrom of November 1918, he and his family were captured by Polish anti-Semites and lined up against a wall in a mock execution. Greenberg never forgot this nor the ordeals which he suffered during the war. In the poem 'Radiance' (*Hizdaharut*, 1926), he alludes to the fate that was almost his:

> Miraculously I survived the grasp of *goyim*.
> May father's God be blessed!
> I'm not lying in Slav earth, a Jew cut to pieces,
> eaten by worms.[36]

His grim view of Jewish history was largely formed by the time he arrived in Palestine in December 1923. Long before the Holocaust, he wrote powerful valedictions to centuries of Jewish life in Europe. In *Earthly Jerusalem* (*Yerushalayim shel Matah*, 1924), he describes his generation in the biblical language of trial by ordeal (Numbers 5:11f) and crucifixion, driven to nationalism by anti-Semitism:

> Forced to leave all valuables, we dressed for exile,
> slung satchel on shoulder.
> We sang like new recruits in an army barefoot
> on Mediterranean sands.
> We were forced to go.
> The earth screamed under our feet, rattling our beds.
> Mouldy bread sickened us to death.
> Adulteress water turned us green with terror.
> Everywhere we looked we were nailed to the cross,
> agony filled our lives ...[37]

To Greenberg, only national regeneration could save Europe's Jews. In the 1920s and 1930s, he celebrated the growth of the Jewish settlement in British Palestine. In common with other Palestinian Hebrew poets of the period (many of whom, including Bialik, Shlonsky and Shin Shalom, former Hasidim), he adhered to the 'religion of labor' taught by the labor socialist philosopher, A.D. Gordon. In 'Radiance', the poet is an incandescent vessel of messianic song, and the land of Israel is depicted in prayer, its geography the phylacteries, and the thirty-six righteous men of Jewish legend in the kibbutzim:

> Jerusalem – *tefillin shel rosh*, the Emek – *shel yad*!
> *Lamed vavin* in all kibbutzim,

> divine grandeur of all who suffer for the Kingdom!
> Sinai smoking over father's shoulder in Poland,
>
> face twilight-red ... at times wax-like!
> Candles in the seven-branched candelabrum mother lights
> such Jerusalemite radiance: our Jerusalem!
> Is this my light's source? – –
> Answer me, God of my father in Zion![38]

Greenberg wrote for Jews alone, not for those whom he regarded as murderous despicable *goyim*. Their culture, though magnificent in some respects, hid deep-rooted barbarity. Greenberg refused to be judged by gentile aesthetic criteria – though there was inconsistency here as his chief influences included Whitman as well as contemporary Expressionists such as Peretz Markish and Else Lasker-Schüler. His ultra-nationalism hardened with Arab opposition to Jewish nationalism. The anti-Jewish Arab pogroms of 1929 drove Greenberg to join the right-wing Revisionists, led by Jabotinsky, where he became a leading figure. He was convinced of an eternal hostility between Jews and non-Jews and indeed of Jewish racial superiority. He advocated the creation through force of a powerful Jewish state extending from the Nile to the Euphrates as the only way to overcome Jewish powerlessness and to defeat the rapacious anti-Semitic beast.

In despair, Greenberg watched in the late 1930s as the nations whose languages and religious cultures owed most to the Hebrew Bible brought the European Jews to the brink of extermination: Germany, by making Europe a lethal trap; and the United States and Britain, master of the largest empire in history (including the Jewish National Home in the Land of Israel), by keeping the gates of immigration closed.

For several years, Greenberg was stunned into silence by the Holocaust, which included the murder of his parents. He joined the Jewish underground, the Irgun, with the aim of forcing the British out of Palestine and saving some of the European Jews. Between the end of the war in 1945 and the establishment of the State of Israel in 1948 (when he became a member of Knesset in Begin's Herut party), he wrote a series of dirges collected in *Streets of the River* (*Rechovot Ha-Nahar*, 1951), including savage invectives against the Christian world:

> The snow has melted there again ...
> murderers turn back to farmers.
> Out they go to plough, in the fields of my dead!
> If the ploughtooth rolls out from under the furrow
> a skeleton, mine,
> the ploughman will have no fear or sorrow.
> He'll smile ... He knows it ... for the blow of his tool
> he'll see again.[39]

Greenberg also lashed out at those Jews who failed to return earlier to their homeland:

> Now – our bodies made holy in their blood
> rot there, the inheritance of worms,
> house and vessels bathed in holiness
> of Sabbath and festivals,
> song of deep longing, the flap of the Shekhinah's wings –
> the inheritance of *goyim*: for in their land
> we built houses and synagogues and dug graves
> not in Jerusalem
> Jerusalem of rock of gold
> *Allelai Amen.*[40]

In Greenberg's eyes, the Holocaust proved that the gentile world, in Europe at any rate, consisted mostly of murderers, collaborators and indifferent onlookers. The surviving Jews had no choice but to arm themselves to fight. His dirges (*kinot*) for the Holocaust victims, collected in *Streets of the River*, perhaps more than any other single literary work, convey the force of Jewish national grief and rage in response to genocide. In these poems, Greenberg transcended his role as a poet of the far-right and emerged as a prophetic spokesman for the Jewish people as a whole. Ironically reversing the traditional call by Christian intellectuals such as von Dohm and Kant for the baptism of emancipated European Jewry, Greenberg declared in his poetry that, after the Holocaust, there was only one atonement for the Christian world: to adopt Judaism.

In Greenberg, there is no split, as in much modern poetry, between the 'man who suffers and the mind which creates'. He gives the impression of being an almost wholly public poet, with no private life, or none that really matters, and no ambivalence or regret toward his role. In this respect, too, he has much in common with 19th century national poets, especially Whitman, who looked to the prophets for inspiration. Greenberg shares with other Bible-based national poets an explosive mix of creative passion and militant nationalism. But there is also a sense in which Hebrew nationalism comes full circle with Greenberg. Greenberg revives a dormant biblical national militancy in the original Hebrew that for hundreds of years had been largely the province of rising European nations in vernacular languages that had been decisively influenced by translations from the Bible. The European Jews had tried futilely to become assimilated into these nations, but had encountered hatred, persecution and ultimately genocide. Greenberg's prophetic poetry consequently despairs of Europe, asserting instead a revived Jewish nationalism, based ironically on the same literary heritage that inspired European nationalism, but in the original Hebrew. It demonstrates the power of the Bible as a living, if mostly unacknowledged, force in modern political, social and cultural life.

NOTES

1. Smith (1991: 50) sums up the importance of the Hebrew Bible in the growth of nationalism: "The profound consequences of the concept of a chosen people, and the passionate attachment to sacred languages and scriptures proved to be an enduring legacy for many peoples from late antiquity to modern times, sustaining their sense of uniqueness and nurturing their hopes of regeneration." See also Novak (1995) and Smith (1998, 2003) as well as the Introduction, pp. 11–12. On England and America as 'chosen peoples', see Longley (2002). For fuller accounts of national aspects of biblical literature, with bibliography, see Walzer (1985), Aberbach (1993), Kidd (1999) and Grosby (1999).
2. Though much modern cultural nationalism is true to the idealistic international spirit of the Hebrew prophets, there is also significant divergence from the biblical source in setting the Nation above moral principles. The adoption and perversion in the name of Christianity of the concept of chosenness, dependent in the Hebrew Bible on moral behavior, has brought national conflict, racist ideology, and the Holocaust: '… the more powerfully one identified one's own nation as chosen, the more one might want to eliminate the first chosen nation, the Jews, from the face of the earth' (Hastings 1997: 198). Hastings' view (which, if correct, does not bode well for future relationships between secularized Judaeo-Christianity and fundamentalist Islam) might be compared with that of Freud (1939: 88) who (naturally) saw the conflict between Judaism and Christianity in Oedipal terms, the 'Son-religion' (Christianity) aiming to murder the 'Father-religion' (Judaism). Biblical influence on Islam is illustrated in the Indian national poetry of Mohammed Iqbal, for example in 'National Song for Indian Children:'

> Its denizens, wise like Moses,
> its mountains, grand like Sinai,
> its oceans, the anchor for Noah,
> its earth a stairway to the skies;
> a breathing paradise on earth.
> This is mine, my native land.
>   (Burney 1987: 6)

The Palestinian Arabic poet Mahmoud Darwish, too, alludes often to biblical sources: 'I gaze upon the procession of ancient prophets/ climbing barefoot to Jerusalem' (Darwish 2003: 56). The poet seeks his identity in the Hebrew Bible: 'Who am I? The singer of the *Song of Songs*?/ The wise one of *Ecclesiastes*? Or both?' *(ibid.,* 154).

3. According to Kedourie (1960), modern nationalism starts with Germany's defeat by Napoleon at Jena in 1806. Kedourie, however, does not recognize that defeat characterizes certain forms of pre-modern nationalism, notably that in the Hebrew Bible.
4. See p'Bitek (1984: 135) and Zimunya (1989: 107). On the biblical Song of the Sea, see p. 41.
5. Biblical messianism has had far-reaching influence on modern nationalism: '… the mainspring of nationalism in Asia and Africa is the same secular millennialism which had its rise and development in Europe and in which society is subjected to the will of a handful of visionaries who, to achieve

National Poetry and the Hebrew Bible 59

their vision, must destroy all barriers between private and public' (Kedourie 1971: 106).

6. On attacks against 'traitors' in national poetry, see pp. 253–9.
7. On attacks on the allegedly corrupt clergy in national poetry, see pp. 38, 173, 256, 265 note 29.
8. For translations of some biblical 'prophecies to the nations', see Aberbach (1993).
9. The Hebrew Bible is extraordinarily welcoming to the stranger: 'you shall love him as yourself; for you were strangers in the land of Egypt' (Exodus 19: 34). Even if he belongs to an enemy nation, the stranger must be treated according to the same law as native Israelites (Exodus 12: 49). A non-Israelite such as Ruth the Moabite who exemplifies moral behavior is regarded more highly than an Israelite such as Miriam, Moses' sister who takes him to task for marrying a Cushite (evidently Black) woman (Numbers 12).
10. Whitman's poetry is particularly striking in its allusions to universalist prophetic ideals:

    Each of us inevitable,
    Each of us limitless – each of us with his or her right upon the earth,
    Each of us allow'd the eternal purports of the earth,
    Each of us here as divinely as any is here.

    Whitman, imitating biblical free verse and parallelism, created in his poetry what he called a 'New Bible' in an age in which the Bible was still overwhelmingly the determining book of American identity (Perry 1969, p. 96). The Bible, Whitman wrote, was the 'principal factor in cohering the nations, eras, and paradoxes of the globe, by giving them a common platform of two or three great ideas, a commonality of origin, and projecting cosmic brotherhood, the dream of all hope, all time' (Whitman 1964, ii 548). The American self-image as 'a light unto the nations', which Whitman brilliantly reflects, has had not-inconsiderable political repercussions. What is sometimes denounced as naked American imperialism is, to an extent, a genuine attempt to bring the secular gospel of freedom and democracy to oppressed people. Biblical influence on this sense of responsibility as the 'true Israel' should not be underestimated.

11. On cultural nationalism and moral values, see Hutchinson (1987) and Hutchinson and Aberbach (1999).
12. Monotheist faith is undermined even at the moment of the giving of the Torah to Moses on Mount Sinai. As the Israelites below worship the Golden Calf, monotheism and national identity are joined momentously in the opening of the Ten Commandments, which does not read simply, 'I am the Lord your God', but 'I am the Lord your God who has brought you out of the land of Egypt, from the house of bondage' (Exodus 20:2; Deuteronomy 5:6). This is not only a call to difference but to common humanity. It applies to all who accept the Law and enter the covenant of faith as chosen peoples yearning for exodus from oppression, and freedom. In Western and much Eastern civilization, nations have emerged from the 'house of bondage'. Even the most secular modern societies often contain more than a residual trace of religion, and this is certainly true of nationalism:

    'The secularization of society does not so much mean the disappearance of religion as it does the weakening of the hold of religion in its traditional forms, along with the disappearance of religious emotion into other areas, particularly the political' (Tucker 1968: 733; also see Aberbach 1996: ch. 4).

60 *National Poetry and the Hebrew Bible*

13. Translations from the Bible in this chapter are by David Aberbach.
14. The moral purpose of the nation and of humanity as a whole is summed up in a section of the Book of Isaiah which apparently dates from the late 6th century BCE, at the time of the return of the Judeans to their homeland:

    It is not enough you are my servant,
    not enough to restore the tribes of Israel,
    or to bring the survivors back –
    I have made you a light of salvation
    to all peoples!
    (Isaiah 49:6)

15. 2 Samuel (11: 1–13), 1 Kings (21:17f), 2 Kings (24:9).
16. The prophet Joel, for example, warns of the day when the nations would gather to be judged in the valley of Jehoshafat in Jerusalem:

    The harvest is ripe for the sickle –
    Wield it!
    The vats overflow with grapes –
    Tread them!
    For there is much wickedness!
    Multitudes, multitudes, in the valley
    of decision ...
    (4:13–14)

17. Later poets, including Byron, Shevchenko, Ibsen and Bialik, have been particularly drawn to Psalm 137 and its combination of longing, humiliation, idealization of the homeland in exile and lust for revenge. The genocidal lashing out in this poem can be seen as a foreshadowing of modern poets such as Njegoš of Serbia and Gökalp of Turkey. On revenge in national poetry, see pp. 24–5, 43–4.
18. Hosea's imagery of a renewed betrothal of God and Israel is adapted by Jeremiah: an aggrieved God remembers from long past his gracious bride 'when you went after me in an unsowed land' and promises a future when again the sound of joy, of bride and groom, will be heard in Jerusalem (Jeremiah 2:2; 33:11).
19. Kedourie, dividing the noumenal from the political, argues against the political significance of the passage from Isaiah (2:3), 'from Zion the Torah shall go forth, and the word of the Lord from Jerusalem', as 'simply the word of the Lord' (1971: 61). However, in the prophets (as among modern fundamentalists) no distinction is made between politics and religion. National feeling for Jerusalem as capital of the ancient Jewish state, 'its vistas the earth's delight' (Psalm 48), determined modern national feeling for Jerusalem as capital of Israel, much as the ancient Greek view of Athens made its choice as capital inevitable – despite the initial unsuitability of both places, backwaters of the Ottoman empire. As Jerusalem, however degraded, is eternally crowned by the Psalms, so also Athens shines in eternal glory in Pindar's ode: 'bulwark of Greece, city of the gods' (Trypanis 1984: 196).
20. The Hebrew synagogue service, whose origins date from the biblical period, includes many selected readings from biblical poetry, which have helped keep Jewish national identity alive in literary-religious form. See Aberbach (2008: ch. 3).

21. On the Bible and modern nationalism, see Greenfeld (1992).
22. 'Protestantism ably exploited the vernacular market in order to reach the masses in its war against the Papacy and the monarchy; if print-capitalism aided the spread of Protestant ideas, the latter increasingly required familiarity with the Bible on the part of every believer, and hence put a premium on literacy and understanding in the local vernacular' (Smith 1998: 135).
23. See Petőfi (1973: 340; and 1974: 203). From the time of the Turkish conquest of Hungary in the 16th century, the Hungarians had taken comfort from the divine salvation of ancient Israel: 'Just as He had liberated the Jews from their Hungarian and Egyptian captivities, He would certainly free the Hungarians from the Turkish yoke' (Szakaly 1990: 94). In general, ancient religious cultures, however they survived into the modern age, have left their mark on modern national identity. On nationalism in Asia, see Gungwu (in Kamenka 1976: 83).
24. Echoes of the Book of Job are particularly strong in *The Kalevala*, despite its predominantly pre-Christian character. In Canto 3 ('The Singing Match'), old Vainamoinen taunts his young rival, Joukahainen, in language reminiscent of the voice of God admonishing Job from the whirlwind (ch. 38). In Canto 4 ('The Drowned Maid'), Aino, refusing to be wed to Vainamoinen, declares, as Job does (ch. 3), that it would have been better had she never been born. Ibsen's *Peer Gynt*, set mostly in Christian Europe in the early 19th century, is greatly enriched by its mostly ironic biblical allusions. The moral purity of Peer's beloved Solveig is stressed as she is associated with the book of Psalms.
25. Biblical references in *Va Pensiero* include: Psalms 48:5, 137:2–3; Isaiah 22:4, 51:17 and Song of Songs 8:14. The British national anthem is similarly indebted to the Bible. For example, 'God save the King' is found for the first time as a salute to Saul, first king of Israel (I Samuel 10: 24) and 'O Lord our God arise/ Scatter his/her enemies' comes from Numbers (10:35).
26. The Welsh in particular came to identify themselves with ancient Israel: 'The Welsh myth of election pictured the community as the lost tribes of Israel, a latterday chosen people' (Smith 1999: 136–7). In the poetry of Saunders Lewis, widely regarded as the main 20th century Welsh language poet, Wales is depicted in the prophetic language of the Bible as the 'new Israel', a disappointment to the poet as to the prophet Isaiah (ch. 5):

A vineyard placed in my care is Wales, my country,
To deliver unto my children
And my children's children
Intact, an eternal heritage:
And behold, the swine rush on her to rend her.

(Elfin and Rowlands 2003: 77)

The translation of the Bible into Welsh in 1563 rejuvenated Welsh national consciousness. (The decision of John Knox and the Scottish reformers to adopt the English Geneva Bible of 1560 and the King James Version of 1611 and not translate the Bible into Scots was an important factor in weakening the Scots language and Scottish national identity, leading to increasing cultural and political union with England.) In the half-millennium after the translation of the King James Bible, there were hundreds of English Bible translations. On the influence of the Bible on English, see Hill (1994), Daniell (2003) and Crystal (2010). Also see Colley (1992). For a comprehensive dictionary of biblical motifs in English literature, see Jeffrey (1992). Broad selections of English literature influenced by the Bible are given by Jasper and Prickett (1999) and Atwan and Wieder (2000). On national poetry in the British isles and the empire, see chapters 5 and 12 (this volume), respectively. The British 'temptation/ To belong to other nations', as W.S. Gilbert put it in *HMS Pinafore*, or at any rate to identify with other nations, can also be attributed partly to the universalist spirit in the Hebrew Bible: this is apparent, above all, in Byron, but also in Swinburne, Clough, the Brownings, Kipling and T.E. Lawrence, among others.

27. The Psalms are so well-known that in the *Oxford Dictionary of Quotations* they appear not in the section on the Hebrew Bible but under *The Book of Common Prayer*, and there are more quotations there from the Psalms than from any other book, including *Hamlet*.
28. Cromwell would lead his men to battle with the opening of Psalm 68: 'Let God arise and let his enemies be scattered'. After the battle of Dunbar in 1650, Cromwell interrupted his pursuit of the Scots to sing Psalm 117: 'Fortunately,' Hill observes, 'it is the shortest in the book' (1994: 356). The Scots, for their part, had the consoling memory of the battle of Bannockburn (1314), in which the Scots, led by Robert the Bruce, annihilated the English army of Edward II. In Barbour's epic, *The Bruce* (c. 1370), English bodies filled the River Forth until the Scots could cross dryshod; so the Israelites had crossed the Reed Sea while their Egyptian pursuers, horse and rider, drowned: 'That apon drownyt hors and men,/ Men mycht pas dry out-our it then'.
29. During the Napoleonic wars, a profusion of biblical epics affirmed British national identity. After 1815, these epics lost their purpose. See Tucker (2008: ch. 4).
30. On Byron's use of biblical sources, see Slater (1952).
31. Kipling, in 'The White Man's Burden' (1899), draws on the Bible (specifically Numbers 11:5) in accusing colonized peoples in the British empire of ingratitude. If only to a limited extent, he posited, the empire had liberated them like ancient Israel from the 'Egypt' of ignorance and backwardness: 'Why brought ye us from bondage,/ Our loved Egyptian night?' Some poets who lived under British colonial rule, such as Mqhayi and Walcott, have attacked the use of the Bible as a tool of imperial conquest. Yet, the Bible itself is strongly anti-imperialist, and many colonized peoples did in fact identify themselves with ancient Israel in their struggle for independence. They often came to regard the Bible as a charter of independence, and their literature reflects deep immersion in the Bible. See chapter 12 (this volume).
32. On Judah Halevi and other medieval Hebrew poets, see chapter 4 (this volume).
33. On secular Enlightenment and emancipation as factors in the diminution of Jewish nationalism, see Aberbach (2013).
34. On Bialik, see Aberbach (1988) and Bialik (2004); on Greenberg, see Aberbach (2003a). Standard Hebrew editions are Bialik (1983–2000) and Greenberg (1990–1998).
35. Translation by David Aberbach (2003a: 17).
36. *Ibid.*, p. 23
37. *Ibid.*, pp. 20–1.
38. *Ibid.*, p. 23.
39. *Ibid.*, p. 30.
40. *Ibid.*, p. 29.

2 Mythical History in National Poetry

Die Weltgeschichte ist das Weltgericht.
The world's history is the world's judgement.

(Schiller, 1789)

*Aggadah [Hebrew: myth, legend, folklore]: the beautiful
little stones lapped by the sea for centuries and generations
until they are cast up on the shore, polished and smooth.*

(Bialik, 1910)

A self-appointed task of many national poets – including Burns, Goethe, Lönnrot, Kollar, Shevchenko, Njegoš, de Rada, Wergeland, Tagore, Yeats and Bialik – is to spend years studying, editing and writing poetry about national myths. These poets use myth in their poetry as the royal road to a nation's identity. National poets are often ideological brothers to national historians. After the French Revolution, Hobsbawm (2001: 345) wrote, Europe was overwhelmed by a veritable 'epidemic of history-writing' – in France, Germany, Britain, Denmark, Bohemia, Russia, Sweden and Switzerland, among others. Poets, too, recreate an ancient world, largely forgotten, whether of historical fact or myth, which allegedly anticipates and justifies longed-for aims of nationalists in the here and now. If the nation is to have a future, as poets, historians and folklorists fervently believe, – it must know its past. A nation with no past must invent one. Myth is most potent among peoples who lose sovereignty or land, such as the Armenians, the Jews, the peoples of the Balkans or the Gikuyu nation in Kenya. Scholars of nationalism are sometimes inclined to relegate myth to a minor part of historical, anthropological, or sociological studies.[1] In fact, myth is the heart and soul of nationalism.

This and subsequent chapters explore mythical history, historical myth and some flagrant mythical distortions of history, among Scandinavian, Hebrew, African and Arabic poets, as well as poets of the British isles. From Homer on, myth is preserved in national epics, with exceptional meaning among exiled peoples or those with no land, for whom poetry can become a spiritual homeland. The next few pages highlight the heroic world-outlook in European mythology, inspiring national movements, especially among peoples with a history of defeat.[2] Poets portray the nation's (imagined) history, its real and fictional heroes and its victories and glory to stir up national pride, defiance and action.

Klopstock and Kleist elevated the 1st century CE Germanic hero Arminius (Hermann) whose army annihilated several Roman legions in the Teutoburg Forest. Burns acclaimed the Scots warriors such as Wallace and Bruce ('Scots wha hae wi' Wallace bled'). Grundtvig, the Danish heroes such as Neils Ebbesen (14th century). Lönnrot and Runeberg, the heroes of Finnish or Swedish myth such as Vainamoinen and Fjalar. Njegoš, Milos Obilic, hero of the battle of Kosovo Fields (1389). Leopardi and Cavafi, the heroes of Thermopylae. Petöfi, Spartacus. Bjornson, medieval Norwegian heroes. Mickiewicz, Konrad Wallenrod. Fishta, Skanderbeg. Yeats, mythical figures such as Cuchulain as well as Irish nationalists such as Wolfe Tone and John Mitchel. Bialik, the Maccabees and Bar-Kokhba. Blok, Russian heroes such as Dmitri Donskoy.[3]

The Hebrew Bible joins history and myth to shore up or recreate national identity.[4] Perhaps the archetypal nation-building poet is the biblical King David, conqueror of Jerusalem (c. 10th century BCE) and putative author of the Psalms. It does not matter that some Psalms date from long after David's death. Psalm 74, possibly alluding to the destruction of the Temple and Jerusalem in 586 BCE, is a collage of historical myths:

> You shattered the sea with your strength,
> broke the heads of sea-monsters,
> you crushed Leviathan's heads,
> fed him to the desert people,
> you split water from rock,
> and dried powerful rivers
>
> (13–15)

This Psalm records the exodus from Egypt (mythically allegorized as a seven-headed Leviathan), the journey across the split sea through the wilderness to the Promised Land, the miraculous feeding of the people in the wilderness and the splitting of the rock to obtain water. All are part of the story of the birth of the nation.

HOMER, THE EPIC AND THE ORAL TRADITION

Apart from the Bible, the great pre-modern epic poems from Homer to Milton defined aspects of national identity through a mix of language, stories, territory, customs, folklore, history, legend and fantasy.[5] As epics survived from generation to generation, they created to some extent a standard language, both literary and vernacular. The epic also brought out familiar conflict between artistic individuality and universal values on the one hand and national identity and aspirations on the other. Homer's poetry, perhaps originally written down and preserved for the pleasure it gave, was transformed into an inadvertent vehicle of cultural nationalism, of language and tradition. It asserted claims of nation and territory in wartime and expressed noble perseverance in defeat. Though for some, such as Nietzsche, Homer's poetry was a catalogue of barbarity. Homer was central in the classical education which predominated in Europe in the age of nationalism. His characters were models for nationalists and for national poets, most of whom had studied (and often translated) the Latin and Greek classics. In *The Odyssey* (*ix*), Odysseus, shipwrecked on the island of the Cyclops after years away from home, concluded that what a man loves most are his parents and homeland. In *The Iliad* (xii), Hector, before dying in battle, declared, 'One omen is left, to fight for one's country'.

Homer's legendary sources reflect a social-historical reality of inestimable importance in the history of nationalism; the Greeks were the first people with long-standing diaspora communities which kept up a cultural link to their native land. At the time *The Iliad* and *The Odyssey* were written (c. 8th century BCE, about three centuries after the events in the poems allegedly took place), there was a thriving Greek trade in the Mediterranean. Many Greek seamen left home for long periods. *The Odyssey*, like the Hebrew Bible, taught that a broken bond with one's homeland can be mended[6] – even among those born elsewhere. Greek poetry proved that defeat or exile, or a life at sea, does not necessarily sever ties to the homeland. Homer's vivid description (whether accurate or not) of the Ithaca coast to which Odysseus returns after many years fighting in the Trojan war reinforced, for all time, the link with Greece even (at times especially) among non-Greeks:

> Here two jagged cliffs jut out, slope in
> to the harbour, blocking wildwind waves,
> where strong-timbred boats rock untied by the road.
> A leafy olive tree stands at the harbor's head
> near a dark, pleasant cave sacred to Naiads
> where bees make honey among stone jars and bowls.[7]

Epic poetry often seems to take place outside national territory, at sea or on the road, encountering much that is new, strange, fascinating, mysterious and dangerous, seeking new trade or conquest of a holy land whose reality exists chiefly in the imagination. Much national poetry paradoxically explores worlds elsewhere, beyond the nation. If not wholly international, this poetry teaches some form of pluralism and tolerance, softening the harsh edge of nationalism. Homer has had particular value to Greeks, bridging the ancient world and the modern state of Greece. Yet, Homer's epics survived precisely because they were not just Greek national documents, read by Greeks. Most of Homer's readers were (and are) non-Greeks, drawn to his poetry for their tales of wonder.

Homer's influence is seen in later national epics, notably Virgil's *Aeneid*, written in honor of the Roman emperor Augustus (27 BCE–14 CE). *The Aeneid* asserts cultural nationalism and imperialism and defines Roman identity in relation to other national identities, especially Trojan, Carthaginian, Italian, and Greek.[8] Book 8 of *The Aeneid* ends with the shield of Aeneas, on which the whole history of Rome is engraved down to the time of Augustus. Yet even the living memory of the battle of Actium and the fall of Anthony and Cleopatra in 31 BCE, enhancing Augustus' glory and that of Rome, is colored with newly created myth, as the grieving Nile embraces Cleopatra after her suicide:

... the Nile, sorrowing end to end,
opened wide his robe, welcomed the beaten queen
to the breast of his blue waters ...[9]

Later epic poems had similar co-minglings of history and the imagination: through the pain of exile; the heightened awareness of oneself when travelling abroad for trade or war; through accident; the conquest of others or being conquered and the hatred of an enemy. Camões' *The Lusiads* (1572) is a particularly rich mix of history and myth, based on the voyages of Vasco da Gama in search of India. It includes the precise day of his departure from Lisbon, 8 July 1497, and giving details of his route and events on the way, including storms and plagues and the historic conflict with Islam.[10] It also includes imaginary creatures and Greek gods such as jealous Bacchus, angry Neptune and loving Venus. Modelled partly on Homer and *The Aeneid*, *The Lusiads* is the great epic of Portugal in its period of imperial might and wealth (late 15th century), but written nearly a century later in an age of catastrophic decline. *The Lusiads* encourages Portuguese national feeling by recalling the wars and voyages of discovery that made Portugal a world power.[11] As the *Aeneid* depicts Rome's history on the shield of Aeneas, *The Lusiads* portrays the history of Portugal on the banners of Da Gama's ship.[12] Into this epic, Camões poured his travels to India, Arabia and East Africa and periods of residence abroad in Goa, Macau and Mozambique in the 16th century. His knowledge of other countries cemented his Portuguese identity:[13] 'He learned what it was to be Portuguese, to come from a landscape whose towns and rivers he loved, whose plains and castles were haunted by ghosts of warriors who had fought for this territory, whose provinces were part of Christendom and the Holy Roman empire but were emerging as a "state", and whose people were learning loyalty to a concept of a nation which transcended loyalty to kings' (White in Camões 1997: *xx*).

BALKAN ORAL POETRY

From the Bible onward, much national poetry comes from oral tradition, often sung with instrumental backing. Particular instruments were associated with national identity: in ancient Israel and medieval Ireland it was the harp; in Poland it was the dulcimer; in Finland, the *kantele*; in Ukraine, the *kobza* and in Serbia, the *gusle*. Something of the ancient power of oral poetry survived into modern times in Scandinavia and the Balkans and was preserved by ethnographers.[14] The Bosnian novelist Ivo Andrić (1892–1975) in *The Bridge on the Drina* (1945) described the hallowed atmosphere in which the *guslar* sang, in a scene set in the 16th century but which Andrić experienced as a child growing up in Visegrad (where the novel is set), near Sarajevo. The *guslar*, from Montenegro, starts a song, 'The Serbian tsar Stefan/ drank wine in fertile Prizen': 'The peasants pressed closer and closer around the singer but without making the slightest noise; their very breathing could be heard. They half closed their eyes, carried away with wonder. Thrills ran up and down their spines, their backs straightened up, their breasts expanded, their eyes shone, their fingers opened and shut and their jaw muscles tightened. The Montenegrin developed his melody more and more rapidly, even more beautiful and bolder, while the wet and sleepless workmen, carried away and insensible to all else, followed the tale as if it were their own more beautiful and glorious destiny' (Andrić 1977: 34). In this scene, set in a stable among peasants forced to labor without pay in building the bridge over the Drina, exhausted, filthy, frustrated, frightened and powerless, the value of the oral tradition – regardless of its origin, Muslim or Christian – is clear. 'Forgetfulness heals everything and song is the most beautiful manner of forgetting, for in song man feels only what he loves' *(ibid.,* 81). Three hundred years later, Andrić wrote, the *guslars* had not lost their power to stir the imagination nor the conflicting feelings of a proud but oppressed people. In a song beginning 'The sprig of basil began to weep', the rapt audience, now under Austro-Hungarian rule, 'seemed to see the victories so desired, the fights, the heroes, the glory and the glitter, such as existed nowhere in the world' *(ibid.,* 188). Muslims and Christians share this vision through centuries-long existence side by side, and the tensions between them cannot obliterate their siamese cultural bonds: 'In that great and strange struggle, which had been waged in Bosnia for centuries between two faiths, for land and power and their own conception of life and order, the adversaries had taken from each other not only women, horses and arms but also songs' *(ibid.,* 87).[15] As the Balkans fragmented into national groups, this shared oral tradition was ransacked to create separate national identities.

HERDER, NATIONALISM AND MYTH

The idea that myth helps build and defend a nation's identity is associated with the German thinker and Lutheran pastor Johann Herder (1744–1803).

He was among the first educated Europeans to see myth, legend and folk literature not as a mass of foolish beliefs, an evanescent popular culture, a false comfort to the illiterate, best forgotten and replaced by 'rational' education, but as the fingerprints of the nation, a sign of its age and distinctiveness, and its potential for renewal. Living in Riga (1764–69), Herder saw that German landowners sponsored the study of Latvian languages and folklore. Sympathetic himself to the national aspirations of Latvians, Lithuanians and Estonians under Russian domination, Herder studied and collected Latvian folksongs. Long before German unification, Herder saw the German language and folk culture as forces of national cohesion. The same was true of any people, however weak and downtrodden, which clung to its own culture (even orally in a largely illiterate society) especially those who, like the Jews, were a minority amid a hostile majority. A people under foreign rule, Herder believed, could gain freedom, spiritual and political, through immersion in their own original culture. The great mythologies of the past, including those in German lands and in England, were unjustly neglected.[16] They represented not blind worthless superstition but a 'gold mine' of culture (Herder 1993: 80). Herder scorned imitation and assimilation. He loved cultural pluralism. John Plamenatz sums up Herder's view that just as human beings are unique, so also are nations:

> 'A human being becomes an individual, a rational and a moral person capable of thinking and acting for himself, in the process of acquiring the language and the culture of his people. He becomes a person distinct from others, in his own eyes and in theirs, by developing potentialities which can only be developed in assimilating a culture and learning to belong to a community. Diversity is desirable as much within the nation as between nations if the life of the individual is to be enriched. Herder respected the culture of the illiterate, of peoples and classes held to be uneducated because they lack the skills that bring power and wealth to their possessors. He also sympathized with the Jews in their desire to pursue their communal identity among hostile populations, and with the Slav peoples dominated culturally by the Germans. Peoples ought neither to cut themselves off from one another nor allow themselves to be submerged or absorbed. They should preserve and develop their particular inheritance, borrowing from others but not becoming mere imitators of them and so spiritually impoverished. For what impoverishes any people impoverishes mankind'
> (in Kamenka 1976: 27–8).

Herder's view of national culture was not unlike that of Rousseau toward the individuality of the child in *Émile* (1762): each culture must be free to grow and be valued on its own terms. In particular, the German sense of inferiority toward the French was misguided. In 'To the Germans' (1768), Herder urged his countrymen to stop speaking French and speak German instead: 'Spew out the ugly slime of the Seine./ Speak German, O you Germans!' (Blanning 2010: 115).[17] Several generations before Darwin, Herder encouraged variety as a sign of health and cultural richness. Herder, ironically, prophesied both militant German nationalism and political Zionism. The Hebrew Bible, in Herder's view, was a model of national distinctiveness: '... the superiority of the Hebrew scriptures over all the other ancient religious writings is unmistakable' (Herder 1997: 261).[18] Germans and Jews had a distinguished ancient military history, having inflicted major defeats against Roman armies. Herder believed that in modern times, Jews and Germans, though facing formidable challenges, should aim to recover ancient glory and be proud independent nations. Herder's faith was borne out in ways scarcely imaginable in his lifetime.

MYTH AND HISTORY FROM THE FRENCH REVOLUTION TO WORLD WAR I

The French Revolution and the Napoleonic wars, by triggering national awareness, mainly in Europe but also elsewhere, raised the status of myth and legend. To some national poets, such as Shevchenko, the nation's degradations must be overcome by glorifying its history and mythology. Shevchenko articulated belief in Ukrainian national mythmaking:

> '... never before in the history of the Ukrainian people had any poet described the vicissitudes of the Ukrainian historical, particularly its Cossack, past in such glowing and exalted terms, or written about it with such patriotic fervor'
> (Andrusyshen, in Shevchenko 1964: xv).[19]

Though myth predates recorded history, it expresses collective social identity, a form of poetic ur-nationalism. Even when neglected or forgotten, myth can be revived and adopted by national movements. To Yeats, editor of several volumes of Irish myth in the 1890s, what was best in Irish literature came from Irish legend, through a slow anonymous process (Pritchard 1972: 36). Similarly, in 1910, while co-editing the legends and folklore (*aggadah*) in the Talmud and Midrash, Bialik defined *aggadah*:

> '*Aggadah*: the beautiful little stones lapped by the sea for centuries and generations until they are cast up on the shore, polished and smooth. Legends pass from generation to generation. Everything superfluous passes away. What remains is the best, the most beautiful, and most worthy of keeping and remembering' (1937, i 274).

Yet myth on its own can be sterile. To have meaning it must live in the culture and politics of the present. Yeats saw himself not just as a teller of legends but as a legendary figure himself, identified with Ireland and resurrecting its dead mythology for the modern world (Ellmann 1968: 18). In an early poem 'To Ireland in the Coming Times' (1892), Yeats found his poetic lineage among Irish national poets of the past. Mythical history or historical myth opens up a nation's intimate unique identity, its collective unconscious: *'Of things discovered in the deep,/ Where only body's laid asleep'*. Yeats' younger contemporary Patrick Pearse identified himself even more directly with Irish myth:

I am Ireland:
I am older than the Old Woman of Beare.

Great my glory:
I that bore Cuchuloainn the valiant.

Great my shame:
My own children that sold their mother.

I am Ireland:
I am lonelier than the Old Woman of Beare.

(Pearse 1917: 323)

Some national poets, such as Whitman, embrace the role of mythmaker, while a minority of others, notably Tagore, are hostile.[20] Tagore is rare among poets in using myth not to justify but to subvert nationalism. In his view, nationalism is evil: 'the spirit of conflict and conquest is at the origin and centre of Western nationalism;' the Nation 'will never heed the voice of truth and goodness' (Tagore 1917: 12, 24). Ancient Indian myth helps to comprehend and combat the moral degeneracy brought by modern nationalism. Tagore retells the legend of the man who, seeking immortality, is lured to disaster by Indra, Lord of the Immortals:

'The West has been striving for centuries after its goal of immortality. Indra has sent her the temptation to try her. It is the gorgeous temptation of wealth. She has accepted it, and her civilization of humanity has lost its path in the wilderness of machinery'

(*ibid.*, 78).

Tagore alludes to these ideas in the poem 'The Sunset of the Century', written at the end of the 19th century. The West was India's doom, he prophesied, a 'funeral pyre' upon which the nation would immolate itself through self-love and materialistic excess (*ibid.*, p. 81). In contrast, the radical Indian nationalist B.G. Tilak (1856–1920), who campaigned against the British authorities in 1905 after the partition of Bengal, found in Indian myth harbingers of Indian independence. In the Hindu epic the *Bhadavad-Gita*, he found opposition to passive suffering and support for decisive though impassive action. In one scene cited by Tilak, the Lord Krishna advises the hero Arjuna to rise on the field of battle and conquer his enemies, to fulfil his predestined role: 'These men were slaughtered long ago/ by me, you just carry it out' (xi 33) (Goodall 1996). Tilak and other Indian nationalists interpreted these lines as a call to modern India to accomplish its fate through revolt against British rule.

NATIONAL POETRY AND THE DISTORTION OF HISTORY

Much national poetry is based on myth-making and imaginative distortion, which Renan (1882) saw as basic in nation-building.[21] Poets have licence to use history creatively. They need not always be factually correct, as Goethe put it: 'There is no contradiction in poetry (*In der Poesie gibt es keine Widersprüche*)'. Some poets, such as Macpherson, Morganwg and Hanka, invent an ancient poetry – should this be called forgery? – to fit a modern national need.[22] Yet, poetic use of history can sometimes communicate feeling absent in purely factual accounts. Myth, conversely, can express historical realities. The emotional complexity of national poetry can have deeper truth than the truth of historians. 'Art is a lie', Picasso said, 'by which we learn the truth'. Ibsen starts *Peer Gynt* with Peer's mother calling him a liar. Plato did no less with Homer. Some historians, suspicious of nationalism, are skeptical toward its mythmaking.[23] Poets tend to see history in terms of recurrence rather than linear development. They are often closer than historians to the 'soul of the nation.' The Irish playwright J.M. Synge, illustrates the use of myth to define identity in *The Playboy of the Western World* (1907). A cowardly braggart is falsely believed to be heroic by people who do not know him. Through the 'myth' of his heroism, he finds in himself the confidence to overcome his timidity. This is a powerful message of modern nationalism: a fiction can become fact, a nation can be what it believes itself to be.

In some traditions, the poet is the key to national survival and regeneration, a kind of shaman preserving collective memory. In the Hebrew Bible, the poetry of the prophets is the burning core of Israel's national identity in history and myth.[24] Countries influenced by the Bible, particularly England and her colonies, were receptive to prophetic poets such as Blake who identified fervently with the nation as the 'new Israel' and, through its history and myth, aimed to build a 'new Jerusalem'. Similarly, Homer's mythology defined and empowered the Greek nation, though retaining an individual voice.[25] In *A Journey from Munich to Genoa* (1829), Heine gives the Romantic view of 'true' history as poetry:

> '[A people] demands its history from the hand of the poet rather than that of the historian. It does not ask for faithful reporting of naked facts; what it wants is to see these dissolved again into the original poetry from which they sprang'.[26]
>
> (Heine 1961 iii 209)

Poetry, older than recorded history, goes deeper than history into the popular psyche. Memory in poetry and song can heal.[27] In Germanic pre-Christian mythology, Odin the God of War is also God of Poetry and patron of poets.[28] A poet in Mickiewicz's *Konrad Wallenrod* (1828) teaches the hero to love his homeland and fight the oppressor. In Tennyson's *Idylls of the King* (1859–1885), Arthur's mentor, the magician Merlin, is also a bard. What makes myth vital in nation-building? If history judges the past, reflects the present, and predicts the future, so does myth. Vico claimed in *La Scienza Nuova* (1725) that myth is a form of poetry, itself a vehicle for myth – which in turn becomes part of the history of nations. The cycle is perpetual. National poets create or invent characters and symbols out of the myth, legend and folklore of a people, making them a representative experience of the nation, justifying national struggles for survival and independence. Though often historically untrue, poets give myth the vividness of reality. As in the case of childhood memories of individuals (Freud called these *Deckerinnerungen*, 'screen memories') transformed later in life (often in times of breakdown and chaos) into a source of cohesion, strength and insight, national memory and myth can also help the nation in crisis to endure (Aberbach 1983, 2003). Poets in countries with weak or incoherent national identities use myth as a kind of yeast to hold the ingredients together and – to follow the metaphor further – make the nation rise.

National unity is at times better served by myths of the distant past – for example, the biblical stories of Elijah and Elisha, the Mujo-Halil songs in Albania, the stories of Cuchulain in Ireland or the *Nibelungen* in Germany – than by often-divisive cultures of the present. In Albania, Father Gjergj Fishta is sometimes called a 'national poet', but he belonged to the Catholic North. As long as serious religious and ethnic divisions remained, no Albanian poet could truly represent the whole of this war-torn country (Preminger 1993: 27). For this reason, Albanian 'national' identity is best expressed in ancient songs and epics (e.g., the Mujo-Halil cycle), much of which opposes Ottoman Turkish rule (which lasted over four centuries, until 1912) above all in the exploits of the 15th century national hero George Castriota, or Skanderbeg.[29] The *Nibelungen* in Germany, the *Bhavagad-Gita* in India and the *Kalevala* in Finland have had parallel influence in the process of cultural unification. For Greeks, Homer was the great force of cultural unity in the creation of the modern Greek state.

In their use of myth, poets aim symbolically to defeat alienation and inner division by becoming one with the nation, becoming whole themselves and making the nation whole by revealing the coherence of the nation in its mythical past.[30]

Remaking the past, real or mythical, can open up a nation's intimate unique identity, inspiring poets in national (and universal) mythmaking. Myths voice the tragedy of a nation's defeat and exile and inspire resistance against foreign rule and hope of survival. This was the case among some nations of the ancient and medieval world, including the Jews and the

Armenians. The Jews created a vast literature of *aggadah* (legend, folklore, etc.), especially after the destruction of the Temple in Jerusalem in 70 CE (Bialik and Ravnitzky 1992).[31] The Armenian epic *Sassna Dzerek*, written down by Servantsediants in the 19th century but going back a thousand years, has inspired the Armenians with its tales of legendary heroes who killed tyrants and freed the people. Myths also furnish models for moral depravity, dehumanization, damnation and self-destruction, for example, in Kleist's play *Hermann's Battle* (1808), Goethe's *Faust* (1832) or Wagner's *The Ring of the Nibelungen* (1853–74) – the single greatest literary influence on Hitler.[32] Kleist's play, set in the 1st century CE, expresses German humiliation and rage after the defeat by Napoleon at Jena in 1806. Hermann, the Germanic leader, is ruthless in the war against the Romans. In a gory scene reminiscent of the biblical story of the Concubine in Gibea (Judges 19: 29), a father who has murdered his daughter after her rape by Romans is commanded by Hermann to cut her body up and send the pieces to the German tribes. This symbolic act will lead to national insurrection and freedom:

> From all Germany an army will come in revenge –
> a storm will roar in the forests: Revolt!
> the waves will roar against the shore: Freedom![33]

The power of myth is invoked by Wagner in *The Ring*: the man who fashions the magic gold into a ring will rule the world but must first renounce love. The cursed ring ruins all who have or seek it, gods and men alike. In the end, in a scene of mass destruction, the ring is returned to Nature. Reason, Wagner believed, leads to illusion and enslavement. The ring on one level represents (ironically, in view of Wagner's influence on Hitler) a warning against the arrogance, the seeking for power and absolute knowledge and the dehumanized dogma and violence of extreme nationalism, in which men seek to be gods.

Together with artistic motives, historical distortion or allegorization can also help a nationalist work pass the censor in a repressive regime. Mickiewicz's historical poem *Konrad Wallenrod* (1828), written under Tsarist rule, describes Lithuania's 14th century war against the Teutonic Knights; in fact, it is an allegory of Poland's struggle against Russia.[34] Shevchenko in 'The Neophytes' (1858), a bitter attack on despotism and persecution of minorities, evaded Russian censorship by setting the poem in the time of the Roman emperor Nero. One of Bialik's most militant nationalist Hebrew poems was passed by the Tsarist censor under the pretence that it referred to the final Jewish revolt against Rome, in the 2nd century CE.[35] *The City of Slaughter* (1903), transparently about the pogrom in Kishinev, was originally called *The Burden of Nemirov*, after a Polish village whose Jewish inhabitants were massacred by the Cossacks in the 1648–49 pogroms.

74 *Mythical History in National Poetry*

In countries with a free press, too, myth creates images of what the nation might become, against the odds. Distortion in nation-building can reflect, or create, a deeper truth. National poetry describes many things which never took place but which take on the power of reality. Biblical Israel, for example, was politically little more than a pawn in power struggles among the great empires of Assyria, Babylonia and Persia.[36] Yet, inspired by the Hebrew prophets, Israel came to see itself as conditionally chosen, potentially powerful. This self-image, ensuring Jewish religious survival, was adopted by other 'chosen peoples' (Smith 2003). Similarly, the heroic exploits in Macpherson's poems of Scotland – *Fingal* (1761), for instance – are mostly either conjured from the poet's imagination or derive from Irish, not Scottish, history.[37] The Polish 'victory' over the Russians in 1812 as Mickiewicz describes it in *Pan Tadeusz* (1834) never happened. The idea that the Russians could be annihilated by a cheese house collapsing on them, as happens at the climax of *Pan Tadeusz*, is a joke assuaging the pain and humiliation of the Polish defeat:

> ... where ranks had stood
> lay beams and corpses, cheeses stained with blood
> and brains.[38]

Shevchenko, too, distorts history by elevating the Cossacks as models of heroism and lovers of freedom, inspiring 19th and 20th century Ukraine to independence. In 'The Haydamaks' (1841), for example, Shevchenko idealizes the Cossacks of the 18th century, magnificently arrayed with banners and swords, decked in gold, boasting of their exploits:

> ... how long ago
> they built their fortress on the isle of Sich,
> ran the rapids in their canoes
> into the open sea, and burned Skutari down;
> how they lit their pipes from Polish towns they set ablaze;
> returning to Ukraine to celebrate and feast,
> they shouted: 'Kobzar, play! Innkeeper, pour!'[39]

It is clear from the atrocities described – 'the ill, the cripples, children too,/ All die'[40] – that the Cossacks were cold-blooded murderers, of Poles and Jews, and left a trail of destruction. Yet, the poet insists in the Epilogue that this was a glorious chapter in Ukraine's history. Whitman, likewise, gives a misleading picture of American history as part of national mythmaking. 'Starting from Paumanok' (1860) romanticizes the Indians as part of American history. He suggests that the Indians simply melted away leaving lovely names to the White Americans. In fact, they were massacred and the survivors herded into reservations. Whitman, like Longfellow, the most popular poet of the mid-19th century, whitewashes American racism and discrimination:

> The red aborigines,
> leaving natural breaths, sounds of rain and winds, calls as of birds
>   and animals in the woods, syllabled to us for names,
> Okonee, Koosa, Ottawa, Monongahela, Sauk, Natchez,
>   Chattahoochee, Kaqueta, Oronoco,
> Wabash, Miami, Saginaw, Chippewa, Oshkosh, Walla-Walla,
>   leaving such to the States they melt, they depart, charging the water
> and the land with names. (16)[41]

No less inaccurate is Bialik's account in *The City of Slaughter* of the cowardice of Russian Jews during the 1903 pogrom in the town of Kishinev.[42] The pogrom was as bad as it was precisely because some Jews did take up arms against their attackers. Yeats is similarly unfair when in 'September 1913' he contrasts what he then regarded as the failure of Irish nationalism, its descent into pettiness, with heroes of Irish history such as Edward Fitzgerald (1763–98), Robert Emmet (1778–1803) and Wolfe Tone (1763–98), all martyrs for Irish independence. The 'wild geese' are Irish traitors who served in foreign armies:[43]

> Was it for this the wild geese spread
> The grey wing upon every tide;
> For this that all that blood was shed,
> For this Edward Fitzgerald died,
> And Robert Emmet and Wolfe Tone,
> All that delirium of the brave?

After the 1916 revolt, Yeats implicitly admitted in 'Easter 1916' that he was wrong about the Irish lack of spirit.[44] Deceptive, too, is Robert Frost's American 'history' in the poem 'The Gift Outright' (1942). Read by the poet at Kennedy's presidential inauguration in 1961, it creates a sense of national unity while omitting, even more blatantly than Whitman does, disruptive collective memories – of Black slavery, civil war, genocide of Indians, and the heterogeneous nature of American society as a nation of mostly-recent immigrants. The American people gave themselves to the land cleanly, their deed the wars they fought for the land, 'still unstoried, artless, unenhanced'.

MYTH IN SCANDINAVIAN EPIC POETRY

Among the Scandinavians, myth and folklore preserved in epic poetry, notably *The Kalevala* and *Peer Gynt*, helped guard national distinctiveness and the idea of nationhood. Probably in no other country has the marriage of folklore and nationalism had such dramatic results as in Finland after the publication of the *Kalevala* by Elias Lönnrot in 1835:

> 'The *Kalevala* and the cultural works based on it gave the Finns a newfound pride in their past, a courage to face an uncertain future, and, above all, a feeling of self-esteem they had never known before. That this small and seemingly insignificant nation had produced an epic comparable to the world's greatest was to be a never-ending source of pride to the Finns. The *Kalevala* thus became their book of independence, their passport into the family of civilized nations'.[45]
>
> (Wilson 1976: x)

The *Kalevala* (roughly translated as 'The Land of the Heroes') is an anthology of ancient oral folk poems collected by Lönnrot and, together with some material original to Lönnrot (e.g., the tales of Aino and Kullervo), skillfully edited into a unified epic. Finns were elevated through their links with gods such as Vainamoinen, 'the eternal bard', and Joukahainen, who fight a Finnish duel of poetry in song. The *Kalevala* had enormous political importance. Elements of national distinctiveness – the Finnish myths and legends, the Finnish language and culture – combined to assert Finland's cultural independence both from Russia, which ruled Finland until 1917, and from Sweden, which had ruled Finland from the 12th century until 1809 and whose culture still dominated Finland. Under Russian rule, Finland was subjected to Russification, with Russian the official language. The *Kalevala* was written in the national language, Finnish, at a time when that language was often denigrated and abandoned in favour of Swedish or Russian.[46] In these circumstances, the study of Finnish myth, folklore and language was a political act. As A.I. Arwidsson put it: 'We are not Swedes, we will not become Russians and so we must be Finns' (Preminger 1975: 277). When Tsarist Russia collapsed in 1917, Finland declared political independence, but the *Kalevala* was, in a deeper sense, its true declaration of independence.

Lönnrot saw Finnish legend as the fingerprints of the nation. In the *Kalevala*, he aimed to give a mythic history of Finland from prehistory to Christianity. What makes the *Kalevala* Finnish? The stories begin with the creation of the world and describe the exploits of Finnish heroes, Vainamoinen, Ilmarinen, Lemminkainen and others in a mythological world of magic, witches, song, stirring conflict and adventure. The poem breathes an ideal Finnish view of life – stoical, good-humored, and heroic. In the opening story, Vainamoinen, the old God-like singer-hero, wins his singing contest against Joukahainen, young and arrogant. As his prize, he forces Joukahainen to give his sister Aino to be his bride. Then sorrow comes. Aino, distraught at having to marry an old man, drowns herself. Joukahainen is mad for revenge, but his mother begs him not to shoot Vainamoinen, for then the world would be without song or joy: 'Joy is better in the world, song more fitting on the earth/ than in the Dead Lands, those cabins of Tuonela' (6: 125f). Seeking a bride elsewhere, Vainamoinen asks one of the daughters of Louhi, king of the North Country, to marry him. She demands that he seek out Ilmarinen, the mighty smith who has forged the sky, to make the Sampo, the mill of plenty. Vainamoinen raises a great wind to carry Ilmarinen to the North Country where he agrees to forge the Sampo (though after the Sampo is made and presented to the king, his daughter refuses still to marry Vainamoinen):

> '... I can forge a Sampo
> with many-colored lid
> from one swan's feather, one fleece,
> one barley grain, bits of one distaff,
> for with no blueprint I have forged heaven
> with nothing to start with,
> not even a string'.[47]

The stories of the *Kalevala* are national in being uniquely Finnish, though in ways characteristic of myths. Set in the landscape and culture of Finland, they express a Finnish national spirit in their use of myths particular to Finland and its heroic tales, describing – some would say creating – a sense of Finnish cultural distinctiveness and independence. Their artistic quality, which gives them universal value and appeal, enhanced the national spirit which gave them life.

The mythology of Norway fills Ibsen's early writings, particularly *Peer Gynt* (1867). The background to Ibsen's work was Norway's struggle after hundreds of years of Danish domination to re-emerge as a nation.[48] Norway had been in the shadow of Denmark from the 15th century until 1814 when it became united with Sweden, a union dissolved in 1905.[49] Ibsen appeared at a time when 19th century Norway was ripe for a new literature proclaiming independence:

> 'The poet was expected to tell of the strong and simple pieties of the people, its pagan courage, the poetic vigour of its language, the virility of its native Northern culture in contrast to the effete sophistication of Southern lands. Popular delight in folk superstition and the inhabitants of the Nordic supernatural world – trolls and nisses and hulders and hill-people and goblins – was clearly something that called for literary exploitation. Inevitably, the ancient saga and the medieval ballad, the folk song and folk tale, history and legend were all energetically explored in the search for inspirational material. The result was a literature nationalistic in sentiment, romantic in its preoccupation with the past, folksy in its outlook, pastoral in its values, and yet for all that heroic in its aspirations'.
>
> (McFarlane and Orton 1970: 4–5)

Ibsen began his career as a writer in 1848, inspired by the revolutions in Europe. He was hired in 1851 by the new Norwegian Theatre in Bergen to write Norwegian nationalist plays. Most of his early plays were romantic nationalist verse dramas. Ibsen used the traditional skaldic or bardic figure to express a mythic conception of the Norwegian landscape as a protection against social corruption: 'that Norway's mountains constituted some safe-deposit of cultural values, that their isolation and remoteness provided a simple but effective protection against the contagion of social evil, and that simple goodness endured ... though it was sorely vulnerable if abused or insensitively treated' (*ibid.*, 27). Yet Ibsen felt himself to be held back artistically by his sense of obligation to serve the Norwegian Myth and conform to the skaldic image. His self-exile from Norway in 1864 marked his freedom from the 'bondage' of Norwegian nationalism. This was the start of his career as a great independent playwrite, starting with *Peer Gynt* (1867), whose overriding theme is the achievement of innate potential, for good or bad, and personal fulfilment. *Peer Gynt*, Ibsen's satiric fantasy in verse, bridges the romantic nationalism of his early work with the anarchic individualism of his later drama. In an irony familiar in national poetry, Ibsen's later work, written in a distinctive Norwegian, though un-nationalistic in voice, is recognized far more than the early work as the expression of Norwegian national identity.[50] While ostensibly asserting Ibsen's new-found independence from Norway and Norwegian nationalism, *Peer Gynt* is saturated with Norwegian myth: elves, trolls and monsters (the Great Boyg), picaresque wanderings of the hero, conflict and adventure in exotic settings. The play culminates in Peer's meeting on a Norwegian heath with the Button Moulder who tells him that he must be melted down in his ladle unless he can prove himself a sinner worthy of hell. Peer's life is a series of failures, betrayals and disappointments. It is not enough that Peer stole a bride and abandoned her, is unfaithful to Solveig, the one woman who loves him, and behaves like a self-centred cheat for much of his life. He also has megalomaniac fantasies of ruling the world and is ruled by the lust for profit. With brazen perfidy, working as a slave trader, he lends money to the Turks during the Greek War of Independence. Shipwrecked, he ruthlessly saves his own life, making another man drown. Exhorted by the Button Moulder to 'Set thy house in order', he sees Solveig again and, demanding judgement from her, is cleared: 'You have made my life into a song./ Bless you for coming back to me at last' (Ibsen 1963: 157). In a sense, this was Norway's judgement of Ibsen. Ibsen broke Norway out of its cultural provinciality and social inertia and brought it into the avant garde. The artist true to himself – even to the point of betraying his loved ones and exiling himself – is true to his nation.[51]

MYTH IN MODERN HEBREW POETRY

Exile and persecution haunt modern Hebrew poetry, drawing on biblical memories as well as an ancient homiletic tradition. Hebrew enlists the past, including legend and folklore, in national struggles. Hebrew poetry preserved in exile helped the Jewish people survive. The Bible and rabbinic literature acted as massive quarries for wisdom, heroism and warnings of moral dangers bringing catastrophe. Much of 19th and early 20th century Hebrew literature might be described as modern Midrash, of which the outstanding practitioner is Bialik.[52] Bialik's characteristic blending of the modern and the traditional is seen in a poem dating from 1902 in which the torment of an isolated couple is fused with national exile:

> Distant islands, lofty worlds
> of our dreams
> they made us into strangers
> wherever we went
> they made our lives hell.
>
> Golden islands we thirsted for
> as for a homeland
> all the stars hinted
> at them
> with trembling light.
>
> And on these islands we remain,
> friendless, like two flowers
> in a desert, two lost souls searching
> for an eternal loss
> in a foreign land.[53]

In a later poem, Bialik sets Jewish legend against the background of rising assimilation among the young generation of Russian Jews and their rejection of both traditional Judaism and Jewish nationalism:

> You'll raise Pithom and Rameses for your oppressors,
> using your children as bricks;
> when their cry lifts from the wood and the stone –
> it will die before reaching your ears.[54]

Bialik refers here to ancient legends of Israel enslaved in Egypt, Pithom and Rameses (Exodus 1:11) being cities built by the slaves.[55] Bialik recasts these legends (which he included in his collection of aggadah) to convey his bitter anger at the younger generation of Jews who ignored their own heritage and wasted themselves (as he saw it) on the cultures of other nations (Germany, for example, or Russia) who hated them.[56] In another poem, Bialik recasts a talmudic legend in which an Arabian merchant offers to show Rabba bar Bar Hanna the Israelites who died trying to force their way into the Promised Land (Numbers 14). The dead warriors lie in gigantic shapes where they fell in the desert:[57]

> '"Come and I will show you the Dead of the Wilderness." I went with him and saw the dead men looking as though they were ecstatic. They lay supine and the knee of one was lifted. The Arabian merchant passed under the knee riding on a camel and holding a spear erect – and he did not touch it'
>
> (*Bava Batra* 73b–74a).

Bialik turns this aggadah into a magisterial allegory of the somnolent condition of the Jews of his time and of their immense latent power. The climax of the poem inspired Bialik's generation and later ones as virtually a declaration that the Jewish exile was over:

And then –

gripped with wild power the awesome warriors wake,
a mighty generation, ready for war,
lightning-eyed, blade-faced, hands on sword!
Thundering in unison, the sixty myriads,
their voice rips through the gale,
clashing with the desert roar, ringed
with storm and rage they cry:
We are heroes!
The last generation of slaves,
the first to be free![58]

Yet the warriors remain where they lie in the desert, and the poem ends in despair. Tchernichowsky uses the same source more hopefully in fiercely nationalistic poetry written during World War I, when the poet served as a Russian army doctor on the eastern front. The poet identifies with 'the dead of the desert' not as failures but as conquerors who will conquer again. He rejects traditional images of Jewish martyrdom, of being led 'like the lamb to the slaughter', reciting the *Shema* ('Hear O Israel, the Lord is God, God is One') as they die.[59] Again there is marked contrast with Bialik, who extols Jewish martyrs as authors of Jewish survival. Tchernichowsky recoils from the lesson of the talmudic aggadah of the martyrdom of Hanina ben Teradion during the Hadrianic persecution (135–38 CE) – that martyrdom is the highest form of the sanctification of the Name of God. Hanina was burned to death by the Romans for teaching the Torah in public. To ensure a slow death, the Romans placed wet wool sponges on his heart. The poet, in contrast, would rather die fighting: 'On heart empty of God, wool sponges/ have no use to the man/ ready with shield and sword'.[60] Whereas Bialik mourns the destruction of the Temple in Jerusalem as symbol of national ruin, Tchernichowsky is drawn to Greek revenge. Turning from the tragic-heroic images of Jewish history – the martyrs of Spain and of the Cossacks in 1648–49 or the Maccabees – he seeks the youthful power of pre-historic Cannaanite culture, 'fresh, strong, wrestling with its God, despising its enemies' swords':

> Who are you, burning blood in me?
> Blood of martyrs of 1648–49?
> I'll not let my throat be cut
> nor turn Christian, but die fighting!
> No, no! I hold a sword, my fist is hard –
> when hit, I hit back blood for blood.
>
> Who are you, burning blood in me?
> Blood of martyrs in Spain?
> I'm no lamb for slaughter –
> I'd kill myself first![61]

Tchernichowsky shared with Byron an admiration for Saul, Israel's first king, who won independence for his nation, was defeated by the Philistines and died nobly in battle on Mount Gilboa near the Sea of Galilee.[62] His poems on Saul, extending over four decades, reflect his changing national views. In 1898, the star-struck idealistic young poet envisaged the messianic age in which Saul, about to take revenge on the gentiles, is commanded by God to love them instead. At this time, Tchernichowsky had a belatedly liberal universalist view of national identity (not unlike that of Byron in the early 19th century). The cruelty of early 20th century history brought the poet to a more narrow spirit of national struggle, especially after the Arab massacre of the Jews in Hebron in 1929. His last poem about Saul, in 1936, is an imagined reconstruction of King Saul's burial calling for a revived 'covenant with the sword'.[63]

Overhanging the mythmaking of modern Israel is the Roman siege of Masada.[64] Josephus' history of the Roman-Jewish war of 66–73 CE is the sole literary source. Masada was the last independent Jewish outpost, perched dramatically on a large rock in the Judean desert by the Dead Sea. The Jewish fighters held out for three years after the fall of Jerusalem, preferring in the end to die by their own hand rather than fall to the Romans. To modern Jewish nationalists, Masada became a symbol for a defiant, perhaps futile, stand against a hostile world. The Hebrew poet Isaac Lamdan in *Masada* (1927) describes the fortress as a symbol of last hope, 'outcast between desert and sea':

> Under an orphan bush in the desert flung
> not Hagar's son but Isaac faints with thirst ...[65]

To Lamdan, Masada recalls Hagar, the rejected concubine driven from home in Genesis (21:15), placing her child, Ishmael, beneath a bush in the blistering heat to delay his death. Yet, in the poet's own time, shadowed by anti-Semitism and culminating in the Holocaust, the endangered child is Isaac, ancestor of the Jewish people in the land of Israel.

NATIONAL POETRY AND AFRICAN MYTH

In Africa, imitation of Western poetry, including its rediscovery or invention of myth, strengthened awareness of African tradition and facilitated the emergence of national identities.[66] African poets such as Senghor, Kunene and p'Bitek recall the great African empires and mythical characters and events of pre-colonial times (e, g., Mali, Ghana, Zimbabwe). At times they create in poetry the impression of a proud, independent past where little or none existed.[67] African poetry and songs, too, illustrate the potency of myth in bringing to life a sense of national identity. The Kenyans, for example, tell of the supreme god Ngai or Mogai on Mount Kenya, who gave the land to Gikuyu and Mumbi, ancestors of all Kenyans. This myth was easily adapted to the Kenyan national aim of recovering land lost in the 19th century imperial 'scramble for Africa'.[68] Such myths became part of the struggle against the British, notably in the Mau Mau revolt (1952–1956), and inspired political songs of revolt declaring that the British robbed the Kenyans of their land: 'God blessed this land of ours, we Kikuyu/ And said we should never abandon it' (Barnett and Njama 1966: 75–6). Myth in Kenya took on a national-religious colouring not unlike that in European nationalism:

> 'Since in traditional terms nationalism meant the recovery of the God-given land, the Kikuyu believed their cause had the highest moral and religious sanction. The concepts of land, God, and Kikuyu political identity were thus symbolically fused together in the prophetic ideology of the nationalist movement'.
>
> (Ray 1976: 168)

In South Africa, similarly, poetic myth contributes to national identity in the stories of the Zulu Emperor Shaka (c. 1795–1828), who forcibly unified many of the tribes on the Cape. In Shaka's time, 'the poet and the singer became central figures in Zulu society. They defined social values, celebrating what was historically significant and acting as democratic agents to reaffirm the approval or disapproval of the whole nation' (Kunene 1979: xxv–xxvi).[69]

HISTORY AND MYTH IN ARABIC POETRY

Modern Arabic poets have rich, dynamic stores of mythical history, with ever-present memories of glory and defeat. National awakening among Arabs after the French Revolution stimulated a revolution in poetry. Poets reacted to the encroachments and allurements of the West. Nationalism became central in Arabic poetry, though, to Islam as to traditional rabbinic Judaism, nationalism is 'essentially a western, Christian-rooted concept' (Hastings 1997: 202).[70] Modern Arabic poetry depicts and is itself part of the split in Islamic identity between the claims of tradition and the call of social revolution. Born of conflict between East and West, modern Arabic poetry returns to the Arab literary past: 'the modern Arabs asserted their own cultural identity in a world threatened by alien forces' (Badawi 1976: 15). Ahmad Shawqi, formerly poet of the Egyptian court, became in the 1920s a poet of Egyptian nationalism, singing the glorious treasure and endless variety of Egyptian cultural history:[71]

> ... papyrus and Psalms, Torah, Gospel and Koran, Mena and Cambyses, Alexander and the two Caesars, and Saladin the Great ...[72]

In another poem, Shawqi has the God-like Sphinx survey the panorama of Egyptian history, including 'mighty Pharaoh/ who claimed descent from sun and moon' and 'tyrannous Caesar,/ enslaving us like donkeys' (Hourani 1991: 342–43). The Iraqi poet Maruf al-Rusafi recalls with nostalgia the glory of early medieval Islam, which conquered much of the civilized world: 'East and West surrendered'.[73] He exhorts modern Muslims to renew that glory through struggle, brotherhood and faith in the All-Merciful, to wake and be united again. The Syrian-Lebanese poet Khalil Mitran likewise recalls early Arab history, notably the conquests of Mohammed (the 'Qurashite orphan') in the 7th century:

> ... from when Qahtan found a hero's grave to Shaiban's Qais and brave Antar,
> to that Quraishite orphan, lord of wisdom, mighty in sword,
> speaking the word of God, defeating Kisra, taking Caesar's crown.[74]

The memory of the past inspires Arab nationalist poets to call for sacrifice. The Egyptian poet Al-Khamisi echoes Solomos, Petőfi and other 19th century national poets in his 'Hymn to Liberty':

> O beautiful Liberty! To shed blood for you is nothing:
> Life meets Death before your throne, time sings your praise alone.[75]

* * * *

What do poets teach us about the use of myth and history in nation-building? Poets diverse as Yeats, Lönnrot, Ibsen, Shawqi, Bialik, Fishta, Tagore and Whitman use myth and mythical history as a shifting tapestry of national identity. They explore or invent the unique character of the nation, emphasizing what seems most original and distinctive and most likely to enable the nation to hold together and resist oppression, to endure and to prosper. They recreate national heroes, give hope in victory, display wisdom in failure and reveal unity in defeat. They instil pride in national accomplishments even when the nation is defeated and powerless. They emphasize core ideals to give legitimacy and power to a nation, to 'the great Idea', as Whitman put it, 'that is the mission of poets' ('By Blue Ontario's Shore' 11).

NOTES

1. In many important studies of nationalism [e.g., Gellner (1964), Seton-Watson (1977), Armstrong (1982), Hroch (1985), Hobsbawm (1990), Breuilly (1993)], 'myth' does not appear in the index, and poets are rarely mentioned. Influential literary critical studies of symbol formation [e.g., Ellmann (1968), Bloom (1969), Frye (2000)] tend to emphasize individual rather than national significance.
2. On defeat as a spur of nationalism and national poetry, see pp. 22–4, 42–4.
3. On heroes in British myth, see chapter 5 (this volume).
4. For examples of the union of history and myth in biblical poetry, see Psalms 78, 106 and 114. On the Hebrew Bible, see chapter 1 (this volume).
5. On Homer's importance in the survival of Greek identity and in the emergence of Greece as a modern state, see chapter 6 (this volume). On oral literature in Scandinavia and the Balkans, see pp. 67, 75ff.
6. The salient method used by Assyria, the leading empire of the early 1st millennium BCE, to break national resistance was exile. Consequently, portable cultures such as those of the Greeks and the Jews, which taught that assimilation in exile and the loss of national identity were not inevitable (that culture could have more lasting power than military might), had far-reaching importance in the history of civilization by encouraging cultural survival. On exile and national identity in the Bible, see chapter 1 (this volume).
7. From *The Odyssey* (xiii), translated by David Aberbach.
8. On nationalism in *The Aeneid*, see Reed (2007).
9. Translated by David Aberbach. The Latin reads:

    … corpore Nilum
    pandentemque sinus et tota veste vocantem
    caeruleum in gremium latebrosaque flumina victos. (viii 711–13)

10. On the conflict with Islam in *The Lusiads*, see p. 99.
11. On *The Lusiasds*, see p. 66.
12. See Cantos 3 and 8 of *The Lusiads* for highlights of Portugal's history.
13. Compare the 'Lucy Poems', in which Wordsworth alludes to his travels in Germany in 1799:

    I travelled among unknown men,
    In lands beyond the sea;
    Nor, England! Did I know till then
    What love I bore to thee.

14. On myth in the *Kalevala*, see p. 75ff.
15. Yet, Ismail Kadare observes in *Three Elegies for Kosovo*, from 1389 on, rival Muslim and Christian minstrels were locked into conflict and could not escape singing of it, even when faced by a common foe. See p. 28, note 16. I am grateful to Professor David Elmer, director of the Milman Parry collection of Balkan folksongs, Harvard University, who drew my attention to the decorations on a *gusle*, including carvings of events considered glorious in Serbian history, from the battle of Kosovo fields in 1389 to Princep's assassination of the Archduke Franz Ferdinand in 1914, leading to World War I.
16. On the neglect of the Arthur legends in England, see p. 140.

17. Others, too, followed Herder in praising the use of the national language, however neglected and derided. See p. 255. Herder has antecedents in the ancient world among the rabbis who encouraged the use of the Holy Tongue to preserve Judaism and Jewish national identity and attacked the use of other languages, especially Greek (Aberbach 1998: 69–72).
18. Herder regarded the interweaving of history and myth in the Hebrew Bible as integral to Jewish national identity. On myth in the Bible, see p. 64.
19. Herder preceded Shevchenko in seeing the potential for Ukrainian nationalism through its rich folklore, predicting that 'Ukraine will become another Greece' (Subtelny 1988: 228).
20. On Whitman, see chapter 9 (this volume). On Tagore's critical view of nationalism, see pp. 277–8.
21. According to Renan, 'Forgetting and, I would even say, historical error are an essential factor in the creation of a nation' (Woolf 1996: 50).
22. On forgeries in national poetry, see p. 86 note 37, 137, 144 note 9.
23. On a variety of historians' views on nationalism, see Smith (1996a).
24. On the Hebrew prophets, see ch. 2 (this volume).
25. It may be that the Greek poet Hesiod was the first to express the idea that 'all Greeks had a common progenitor, Hellen, grandson of Prometheus and great-great-grandson of Heaven and of Ocean' (Finley 1975: 125). In *Theogany*, Hesiod depicts the Muses on Mount Olympus choosing him as a poet, telling him that they knew to tell lies that seemed true as well as the truth, when they wished.
26. A view similar to Heine's was held by Novalis (Friedrich von Hardenberg), who had much influence on Wagner: one day, he believed, poetry and myth would be recognized as true eternal world history. Wordsworth, too, writing of the Prometheus myths, described them as 'Fictions in form, but in their substance truths' (*The Excursion*) (Blanning 2010: 157, 158).
27. The return to the past is a frequent motive among cultural nationalists – including the Germans, the Finns, the Romanians, the Albanians, and the Jews – who seek an identity in the distant past which transcends the crises and limitations of the present.
28. 'Men knew that the gods whom they served could not give them freedom from danger and calamity, and they did not demand that they should. We find in the myths no sense of bitterness at the harshness and unfairness of life, but rather a spirit of heroic resignation: humanity is born to trouble, but courage, adventure and the wonders of life are matters for thankfulness, to be enjoyed while life is still granted to us. The great gifts of the gods were readiness to face the world as it was, the luck that sustains men in tight places and the opportunity to win that glory which alone can outlive death' (Ellis-Davidson 1974: 218).
29. On Albanian national poetry in the context of the history of Islamic conflict with Christianity, see pp. 153–4.
30. See Aberbach (1996) and Hutchinson and Aberbach (1999). On the interconnection of personal and collective motives in national poetry, see the Conclusion.
31. On uses of aggadah by modern Hebrew writers, see Jacobson (1987) and Aberbach (1994).
32. Wagner's influence on Hitler evidently only went so far. In conversation, Hitler is reported to have said: 'It seems to me that nothing would be more foolish than

to re-establish the worship of Wotan. Our old mythology ceased to be viable when Christianity implanted itself' (Cameron & Steven 1953: 51).
33. Translated by David Aberbach. The German reads:

> Der wird in Deutschland, dir zur Rache,
> Bis auf die toten Elemente werben:
> Der Sturmwind wird, die Waldungen durchsausend,
> Empörung! rufen, und die See,
> Des Landes Ribben schlagend, Freiheit! (IV vi 1616–20)

34. In Baranauskas' 'The Pine Grove of Anyksciai' (1858–9), the tragedies of Lithuanian history are allegorized in the story of a once-verdant forest cut down by invaders (Tsarist Russia): '... nightly they hacked, they stealthily bartered,/ selling our trees, they swindled their masters,/ they silenced the grieving folk of Anyksciai with a fist in the mouth' (Landsbergis & Mills 1962: 64–5).
35. On Bialik's 'Bar Kokhba' (1899), see p. 237.
36. For an account, with bibliography, of ancient Israel and its prophetic culture in relation to the great empires of Mesopotamia and Egypt, see Aberbach (1993).
37. On the 'invention' of the Scottish Highland tradition, see Trevor-Roper in Hobsbawm and Ranger (1983). Trevor-Roper points out that the Highlanders prior to the late 17th century 'were simply the overflow of Ireland', and the literature of Celtic Scotland was 'stolen from the Irish' (15, 17). Also, some of the best Scottish and Welsh poems were forgeries. Macpherson's forgeries of Ossian were matched by Morganwg's forgeries of Dafydd ap Gwilym. Biblical poetry, too, derived partly from Mesopotamian and Egyptian sources which are mostly lost.
38. '... gdzie stały szeregi/ Leżą drwa, trupy, sery białe jako śniegi,/ Krwią i mózgiem slamione' (Mickiewicz 2013: 419). On *Pan Tadeusz*, see pp. 177–8.
39. 'Г'рай, коσзарю, дий, шинкарю!' (Kobzar, play! Innkeeper pour!) is revised from Shevchenko (1977: 60, 62). Skutari is a suburb of Constantinople; Kobzar is a bard. *The Kobzar* was the title of Shevchenko's first book of poems (1840). 'The Haydamaks' tells the story (related to Shevchenko as a child by his grandfather, a witness) of the 1768 Cossack uprising against the Poles.
40. *Ibid.*, 102.
41. On Longfellow's idealization of the American Indians in *The Song of Hiawatha*, see p. 222 note 23. The Chilean poet Pablo Neruda influenced by the 16th century Latin American poet Alonso de Ercilla treats the conquered natives as part of the national history of the conquerors, for example, in *The Heights of Macchu Picchu* (1948). (See p. 296.) However, the conquistadors were four centuries past, whereas the dispossession of the North American Indians was ongoing in Whitman's lifetime.
42. On Bialik's allegation of cowardice against the Jews in the Kishinev pogrom, see pp. 238, 256.
43. Earlier poets had sometimes extolled mercenaries for their devotion to ideals of justice and liberty. See Macpherson 'On the Death of Marshal Keith' and Mickiewicz on Kosciuszko in *Pan Tadeusz*.
44. On Yeats' 'Easter 1916', see p. 243.
45. For an academic English translation of *The Kalevala*, see Lönnrot (1969). For a literary translation see Lönnrot (1989).
46. The Finnish national poet, Johan Ludvig Runeberg (1804–77), wrote in Swedish, including the romance *The Tales of Ensign Stal* (1848) from which the Finnish

national anthem is taken. On nationalism in Finland in the Grand Duchy period (1809–1917), see Alapuro (1988: ch. 5) and Stenius in Árnason and Wittrock (2012: ch. 9).

47. 'Jo taisin takoa sammon,
    Kirjokannen kirjaella,
    Yhen joukkosen sulasta,
    Yhen villan kylkyestä,
    Yhen ostrasen jyvästä,
    Yhen värttinän murvista;
    Kun olin taivoista takova,
    Ilman kantta kalkuttava,
    Ilamn alkosen alutta,
    Riporihman tehtysättä'.

    (*The Kalevala*, 1835 edn., V 214–223)

48. While 'landsmal' was the spoken language of Norwegian dialects, 'riksmal', a form of written Danish with Norwegian vocabulary, was the language of the Norwegian educated classes, including Ibsen. On the language conflict as reflected in Ibsen's *Peer Gynt* (1867), see p. 264 note 26.
49. On Denmark as 'Freya's palace' in Oehlenschlager's anthem, see pp. 77–8. Iceland, too, being under Danish rule for centuries (full independence came in 1944) developed an impressive poetic tradition containing a vast repository of history and legend. The only known author of Icelandic sagas is Snorri Sturluson (13th century), to whom *Egil's Saga*, *Heimskringla*, *King Harald's Saga*, *Prose Edda* and *Poetic Edda* are attributed.
50. Ibsen's compatriot, the poet Bjornson, was more conventional, evoking Norway's mythic history in his 'Fatherland Song' as the land of heroes, of Harold, Haakon, Olaf, Swerre, and Oevin the bard: 'Olaf with his blood has printed cross upon her loam;/ From her highlands Swerre stinted not tomtalk to Rome' (Van Doren 1936: 986).
51. Feminism, which often accompanies modern nationalism, can be seen as an extension of Ibsen's nationalism in *A Doll's House* (1879). The Danish and Swedish hold on Norway is duplicated in Helmer's hold on his wife, Nora. The subjugated nation, like the subjugated wife, lives in a 'doll's house'. The husband's possessiveness (Nora's beauty is 'mine, mine alone, all mine') echoes the idea that Norway is merely a 'possession' of Sweden, or culturally of Denmark. Nora, like Norway, has a duty to herself and must educate herself to make her own decisions. As Norway must break away to be free, so also Nora must leave her husband (as Ibsen left Norway) to be fully independent. However, being oneself, Ibsen points out in *Peer Gynt*, is not necessarily a good thing; at times it can be suicidal.
52. On Bialik, see chapter 10 (this volume); also see Jacobson (1987).
53. Translated by David Aberbach (Bialik 2004: 54).
54. *Ibid.*, 102.
55. According to the Midrash, for example, the one on Exodus 2:24 – 'and God heard their groaning' – children were used as bricks: 'Rabbi Akiba said: "Pharaoh's butchers would use the Israelites as mortar in the walls – and the Holy One, blessed be He, would hear their cries."' In another aggadah from the Book of Exodus, the angels in heaven try to persuade God not to drown the Egyptians

88 *Mythical History in National Poetry*

in the sea. The angel Gabriel fetches a brick with a baby sunken into it and declares to God that this was the way the Egyptians treated the Israelites. God then decides against the Egyptians.

56. Other poets, too (e.g., Shevchenko and Diop), express anger at their people for neglecting their own national culture. See pp. 255, 313. Yeats, in 'September 1913', attacks Irishmen who served in the armies of foreign countries. See p. 75. Bialik's attacks on his own people are discussed on p. 238.
57. This image of the dead warriors of myth recalls Petőfi's 'Homer and Ossian'. See p. 144 note 9.
58. Translated by David Aberbach (Bialik 2004: 62).
59. *Mangina Li* (My Song, 1916) in Tchernichowsky (1954: 217). On martyrdom in Hebrew and other poetry, see pp. 190–2. Tchernichowsky's "My Song" is quoted further on p. 81.
60. Babylonian Talmud, *Avodah Zarah* 18a.
61. Translated by David Aberbach from Tchernichowsky (1954: 217). The contrast with Bialik needs qualification as Bialik, too, occasionally expressed a spirit of revenge in his poetry. See p. 237.
62. On Tchernichowsky's depiction of King Saul, see p. 281. See Byron's poem 'Song of Saul Before His Last Battle'. On death in battle as an ideal in ancient Greek and Hebrew poetry and on martyrdom in national poetry, see pp. 65, 190–2.
63. See p. 281.
64. On the use of Masada in Israeli nationalism, see Ben Yehuda (1995).
65. Translated by David Aberbach from Lamdan (1962: 54).
66. On African poetry under colonial rule and after, see chapter 12 and Appendix (e) (this volume). While imitation of Western poetic myth enhanced modern African national identities, other forms of imitation broke down native traditions: 'To retain their sense of nationality, their separate cultural identity, they had in many ways to imitate the foreigners with whom they refused to identify themselves. And in so doing they could not help but loosen the hold over themselves of ancestral ways' (Plamenatz 1975: 31). See p. 283.
67. On history in African poetry, see Okpewho (1983: ch. 4). In former slave societies, the lack of a surviving native culture, or its perceived inferiority to colonial culture, often results in profound ambivalence of natives toward both cultures. See p. 311ff.
68. Jomo Kenyatta (c. 1897–1978), first president of Kenya (1964–1978), describes the myth of Mount Kenya as follows:
'According to the tribal legend, we are told that in the beginning of things, when mankind started to populate the earth, the man Gikuyu, the founder of the tribe, was called by the Mogai (the Divider of the Universe), and was given as his share the land with ravines, the rivers, the forests, the game and all the gifts that the Lord of Nature (Mogai) bestowed on mankind. At the same time Mogai made a big mountain which he called Kere-Nyaga (Mount Kenya), as his resting-place when on inspection tour, and as a sign of his wonders. He then took the man Gikuyu to the top of the mountain of mystery, and showed him the beauty of the country that Mogai had given him. While still on the mountain, the Mogai pointed out to the Gikuyu a spot full of fig trees (*Mikoyo*), right in the centre of the country. After the Mogai had shown the Gikuyu the panorama of the wonderful land he had been given, he commanded him to descend and establish

his homestead on the selected place which he named Mokorwe wa Gathanga. Before they parted, Mogai told Gikuyu that, whenever he was in need, he should make a sacrifice and raise his hands towards Kere-Nyaga (the mountain of mystery), and the Lord of Nature will come to his assistance' (1938: 3).
69. On the legendary Emperor Shaka, see pp. 283–4. The centrality of myth and song among West African tribes prior to the colonial era is attested in Achebe's novel *Things Fall Apart* (1958).
70. Jewish nationalism was fiercely opposed by rabbis, both Orthodox and Reform, until the Holocaust, when the need for a Jewish homeland overrode the opposition, except among a minority of ultra-Orthodox Jews.
71. Shawqi's assertion of national identity through cosmopolitanism recalls Whitman and Tagore. See pp. 201 note 16, 205. Egyptian nationalism was unique in the Arab world in being territorial and non-confessional. See Avineiri (in Kamenka 1976: 50). Though Arabic poetry had especial functional value in the colonial period, it did not cease to have relevance later. Of post–World War II Arabic poetry, Hourani (1991) wrote: 'A new Arab nation, a new Arab individual, needed to be brought into being, and the poet should be the "creator of a new world"' (396).
72. Revised from Arberry (1965: 160–1). The Arabic reads:

تـوراة والـفـرقـان والإصـحـاح   فيها مـن الـبُـرْدِيَّ والـمـزمـور والـ

فالقيصرَيْن فـذى الـجـلال صلاح   وبِـنَـا وقـمـبـيـزٍ الـى إسـكـنـدرٍ

73. *Ibid.*, 167. On the conflict between Islam and the West as reflected in national poetry, see chapter 3 (this volume).
74. Revised from Arberry (1967: 15–16).
75. *Ibid.*, 33. For similar calls among national poets for sacrifice and even martyrdom, see p. 191.

3 European National Poetry, Islam and the Defeat of the Medieval Church

> ... *we have lived to see the holy place lost*
> *where for our sake God suffered torment and death.*
> (Conon de Bethune, France, 12th century)
>
> *The day Muslim armies rode out,*
> *their banners waving tall,*
> *glory escorted their ranks,*
> *armed with the ridged Indian sword –*
> *East and West surrendered.*
> (Maruf al-Rusafi, Iraq, early 20th century)

Medieval Muslim conquests of Christian territories, in the Middle East and Europe, and the centuries of rivalry that followed are mapped out panoramically in European vernacular national poetry, or poetry which came to be seen as national.[1] The long violent history of Islam in Europe roused national identity in European territories that came under Muslim rule or were threatened as the 'House of War' by Islamic armies which fought for victory over Christianity as a religious duty.[2] For example, there was the poetry of the French troubadour Marcabru (c. 1150), who sang of crusaders 'cleansing' the lands of the enemies of Christ (Rosenberg *et al.*, 1998: 51–3); the early medieval French *Chansons de Geste* ('Songs of Action'); the 12th century Arthurian romances of Chrétien de Troyes; the anonymous Spanish epic *The Cid* (early 12th century); as well as the poetry of Judah Halevi (c. 1075–1141) and other Spanish Hebrew poets in the 11th–12th century.[3] There was also Wolfram von Eschenbach's early 13th century German adaptation of Arthurian legend *Parzival*, Geoffrey Chaucer (c. 1340–1400) in England, Luis de Camões (1524?–1580) in Portugal, Pierre de Ronsard (1524?–1585) in France and Torquato Tasso (1544–1595) in Italy. In Eastern Europe, Ivan Gundulic (1588–1638) in Croatia, Nicholas Zrinyi (1616–1664) in Hungary, and Mikhail Lomonosov (1711–1765) in Russia wrote epic poems, famous in their day, on Muslim invasions of Eastern Europe (16th–18th century).

After 1789, religious rivalry in the Balkans, the last outpost of Muslim rule in Europe, fueled nationalist conflict. Balkan national poetry sprang from ancient oral literature telling of local or border clashes or wars in time of Ottoman expansion or decline. Poets in southeastern Europe rediscovered, reinterpreted, or reconstructed their country's history in conflict with Ottoman rule.[4] For example, we can include Rigas Velestinlis (or Feraios) (1757–1798) and Dionysios Solomos (1798–1857) in Greece, Petar II Petrovic-Njegoš (1813–1851) in Serbia/Montenegro, Hristo Botev (1849–1876) in Bulgaria, Mihail Eminescu (1850–1889) in Romania and Gjergj Fishta (1871–1940) in Albania. Much of this poetry expressed a growing desire of a largely Christian population to be free of Muslim rule and overcome the defeat and humiliation of medieval Christendom by Islam. Balkan churches supported liberation from Islamic rule despite the danger of secularization. Two major Balkan national poets, Njegoš and Fishta, were priests. An overall picture emerges in European poetry from *The Song of Roland* (c. 1100) to Njegoš's epic *The Mountain Wreath* (1847). Though the medieval defeat of Christianity by Islam was only part of a complex shifting relationship extending from the birth of Islam to the modern period, this defeat stirred up European nationalism. Poetry helped unite Christian Europe defensively against Islam through the idea of a Europe of nations.

ISLAM AND EUROPEAN NATIONAL POETRY

Muslim conquests in the Middle East and southwestern Europe in the 7th and 8th centuries challenged and motivated the Christianization of Europe and stimulated nationalistic schisms and cultures.[5] Europe then was still mostly heathen and in the process of Christianization after the Roman empire collapsed and fell. Muslim conquests from the 7th century chart European poetry as national identities grew in reaction to defeat over a millennium and more. By conquering the three Middle Eastern Christian patriarchies (Jerusalem, Antioch, and Alexandria), Islam turned Europe into Christianity's main base. Islam militarily cut Latin Christendom off from the truncated Christian Byzantine empire and from other religions and civilizations, reducing it to 'a narrow corridor running from the British isles to central Italy' (Davies 1996: 257, 287).

Medieval poetry suggests that Islam forced Christian Europe into far greater political and economic autonomy, and cultural creativity, than would have been likely otherwise. Islam became the Other by which, to some extent, emerging European nations defined themselves. The conquest of Jerusalem in 638 was a grief throughout Christian lands for centuries,[6] as was conversion to Islam of the predominantly Christian Middle East – including Syria, Palestine, Egypt and North Africa. Muslim military expansionism in the Iberian peninsula, France, Sicily, Sardinia, Malta, and parts of Eastern Europe conquered or threatened by Islam. Major poetic cultures emerged consistently from this European history and fortress mentality. First, in early medieval oral traditions, poetry developed in regional languages and was later written down, notably in *Chansons de Geste*. It appeared as part of the

Christian crusading holy wars of the 11th–14th centuries which aimed to regain and defend the Holy Land, particularly Jerusalem, from the Muslim 'infidel'.[7] Poetic cultures continued to emerge after the Islamic reconquest of the Holy Land by 1291 with the immense spread of Muslim Ottoman territory, climaxing in the conquest (1453) of the Byzantine capital, Constantinople, to become the most powerful empire in Europe. This conquest took the islands of Rhodes (1522), Cyprus (1570), Crete (1669) and ruling lands that later became or formed parts of the modern states of Greece, Albania, Serbia, Montenegro, Romania, Bulgaria, Hungary, Poland, Russia and Ukraine. These tumultuous events and setbacks to Christian Europe, framed in the end a huge, diverse body of poetry in the many languages of the emerging European nations over a period of centuries. From the time of *The Song of Roland* until the early 20th century, poets of European countries under Islamic rule, including Greece, Bulgaria, Romania, Albania and Serbia, saw Islam as the hated 'Other' that had defeated and enslaved them. Even after the failure of the Ottoman siege of Vienna in 1683 – the turning point after which Islamic power in Europe faded – the memory of earlier defeats lingered, especially in the Balkans.

In their poetry, European nations emerged with separate languages and cultures, a bulwark of Christianity (*propugnaculumChristianitatis*) against Islam, while the authority of the Papal Monarchy was weakened as it sent tens of thousands of Crusaders to defeat. One after the other, the Popes proclaimed the Crusades as 'just wars' to reconquer the Holy Land for Christendom. How then had they failed? How could Islam have triumphed, for it was allegedly a form of idolatry, the creation of Satan, an insult and threat to Christianity which had to be destroyed? Where was justice now that Islam ruled the holy sites of Christendom, including the Holy Sepulchre in Jerusalem, profiting from Christian pilgrims, from tolls and tributes, and from the sale of souvenirs? For centuries, poets as diverse as Alcuin, Conon de Bethune, Ariosto and Njegoš asked such questions. The 'universal Christian Church' was hemmed in by land and sea. The challenge to Church authority contributed to growing awareness of national particularity and the political and cultural aspirations of emerging individual nations.

The Spanish crusades, in particular, developed into 'wars of national liberation', and Crusade leagues were adapted to the needs of emerging states (Riley-Smith 2002: 17, 23). The universal Christian Latin language (the vernacular in the age of Charlemagne) evolved into secular vernacular languages, with their heretical national implications, in France, northern Spain and Lombard Italy.[8] Poems sung and recited by generations of crusaders rejected the Christian belief that war was futile: 'all they that take the sword shall perish with the sword' (Matthew 26: 54). Rather, holy war was essential to Christianity.[9] Yet, by the late 13th century, the Crusaders had lost: many had indeed perished by the sword, and the Holy Land was again in Muslim hands. It may be partly for this reason that *The Song of Roland*, a poem whose historical basis is the defeat of the Franks (ironically, by Christian Basques) at Roncesvalles in 778, became the single most widely read, recited and translated medieval poem. It was an inspiration in defeat. Although there was some European national poetry that trumpeted historic victories against Islam: notably, in 732 when Charles Martel halted the Muslim invasion of France and in 1099 when the First Crusade temporarily regained Jerusalem for Christendom.[10]

THE SONG OF ROLAND

The Song of Roland portrays a 'nascent national consciousness' (Auerbach 1974: 121) of France united under Charlemagne (742–814), Martel's grandson, against the Muslim invasion of Spain and France in the 8th century. The poem indicates that early medieval European Christians shared with Middle Eastern and North African Muslims the militant fervor of recent converts to monotheism, with enthusiasm for holy war against 'infidels'. Aiming to consolidate Christian rule and identifying himself with the biblical King David, both ruler and poet, Charlemagne had attracted to his court an international elite of Latin poets (Godman 1985). Among these was Alcuin of York, who mourned the loss of Jerusalem:

> How shall any man restrain his tears
> when he looks upon [Jerusalem's] end,
> For a people hostile to God [*gens inimica deo*]
> now holds sway over its dwellings?
>
> (*ibid.*, 129)

For centuries, poets portrayed Charlemagne as the greatest Christian warrior of his age, chief opponent of Islamic expansion and originator of the Holy Roman Empire, aiming to restore the idealized order, unity and power of the Roman empire; to defend Christendom and to regain the Holy Land. Charlemagne and other characters in poetry set in the initial 8th century conflict (notably Roland) appear prominently in vernacular European literature until the Renaissance, most famously in Ariosto's Italian epic *Orlando Furioso* (1516, 1532), and later. *Chansons de Geste* such as *The Song of Roland* exalt Charlemagne and denigrate Muslims as pagan, exotic, cowardly, 'evil others' whose worship of Mohammed is idolatry.[11] The Bible-based French king-state-nation matrix of *The Song of Roland* became a model for later European states.[12] Written possibly at the time of the First Crusade (1096–99), the poem describes an 8th century Muslim attack in the Pyrenees in which the heroic knight Roland Charlemagne's nephew, dies defending the Cross against the Crescent. *The Song of Roland* was second only to the Bible as an influence on militant Christianity in medieval Western Europe, with extant translations into Middle High German, Old Norse, Welsh, Dutch and Middle English.[13] Yet it is also a French national poem with enduring popular appeal (particularly on pilgrim routes and trade routes) and a gripping story, with precise, vivid vernacular language, striking characters and exciting battle scenes. Roland affirms Christian faith against the Muslim 'pagans'; Charlemagne is sacred Emperor, Champion of Christendom: 'The pagans are wrong and the Christians are right' (*Paien unt tort e chrestïens unt dreit*) (st. 79; 1990: 61, 191). By the time *The Song of Roland* was written, most Spanish Christians had converted to Islam, as had happened in most other lands of Muslim conquest.[14] The ultimate aim of the Muslim leader Baligant, the emir of Babylon, is to convert Charlemagne to Islam (st. 193). Awareness of an unprecedented international religious war is strong in the poem: the Christian army is drawn from most Christian lands (st. 217–225); Muslim warriors come from throughout the Muslim world (st. 232–34). *The Song of Roland* transforms a local 8th century skirmish in the Pyrenees into virtually a world war. The poem can even be read as a preparation for the trials of crusade against Islam. It promises Christian soldiers a place in paradise among the angels but does not dodge the brutality and sorrow of war. Charlemagne faces the invaders with Christian virtues: religious devotion, wisdom, justice, kindness, valor, mercy and prudence. Much of the poem remained current in future centuries, for example, in the Archbishop's exhortation to the troops to preserve Christianity and defend the king (st. 89) or in Charlemagne's determination to fight for the justice of his cause: 'I must render to a pagan neither peace nor love' (*Pais ne amor ne dei a paien renore*) (st. 260). The Muslim threat encourages Christian solidarity in the name of the true faith and French national unity: 'The Franks will die, if they risk battle with us.../ The Franks will die and France will be bereft' (*Franceis murrunt, si a nus s'abandunent.../ Franceis murrunt e France en ert deserte*) (st. 74, 75). All France is in danger. Christians from every part and class of France join Charlemagne's army and share in the hope of ultimate victory.

THE CRUSADES AND VERNACULAR NATIONAL POETRY

Vernacular national poetry in various European countries, particularly France and Spain, responded to continual defeats (despite the Pope's blessing) of the Crusades and universal Christianity. French and Spanish troubadour Crusade poetry transformed 12th century European culture. The best known early *chanson de croisade*, in medieval French, by Marcabru exhorts the French to join the Second Crusade (c. 1149), to regain territories lost in the First Crusade. Not to fight would be an unnatural rejection of a divine task: '*Desnaturat son li Frances/ Si de l'afar Dieu dizon no*' (Rosenberg et al., 1998: 53). The crusader *trouvère* Conon de Bethune responded with shame and vengeful rage – '*S'irom vengier la honte dolereuse*' – to the Muslim reconquest of Jerusalem in 1187, in one of the most popular crusade songs:

... we will go avenge the painful offense
that must leave everyone angry and ashamed,
for we have lived to see the holy place lost
where for our sake God suffered torment and death.

(*ibid.*, 243; see also 290)

Chivalric virtues of holy war against Islam are sung by the French poet Rutebeuf in *La complainte de Monseigneur Geoffrei de Sergines* (1255–56), a portrait of the ideal Crusader who loved Louis IX of France, his liege-lord, so much that he went with him to the Holy Land ('Outremer') to avenge the 'shame of God':

Son seigneur lige tint tant chier
Qu'il ala avec li vengier
La honte Dieu outre la meir ...

(Rutebeuf 1989: 120)

HOLY WAR AND NATIONAL POETRY: FROM CHARLEMAGNE TO TAMBURLAINE

Chansons de Geste (c. 1100–1300) had a vast audience both for oral recital and in written form.[15] Translations of these epics (of which about a hundred survive) appear throughout Western Europe, Germany, Norway, Denmark, Italy, England and Wales (Newth 2005). In the anonymous French epic *The Pilgrimage of Charlemagne* (12th century), Charlemagne makes a pilgrimage to Jerusalem where he is given relics of the crucifixion, and he vows to rid the Holy Land of Muslim rule. The Spanish epic, *The Cid* (12th century), romanticizes the lengthy Christian recapture of Spain, not completed until 1492, when the Muslim kingdom of Granada was defeated by the forces of Ferdinand and Isabella. Based on an historical figure, Rodrigo de Vivar, the Cid embodies the virtues both of a Spanish Christian and a Spanish national hero at a time when Christian Spain was threatened by the Almoravid invasion in the late 11th century. The Cid, a soldier of fortune, is unjustly exiled by the Christian king Alfonso VI of Castile. He then fights a series of successful battles against the Muslim invaders in eastern and southern Spain – he slaughters them and exiles the survivors and makes Valencia a Christian city. In doing all this, he regains the king's favour,[16] and in the end, he marries his daughters to the kings of Navarre and Aragon: 'Now the kings of Spain are his kinsmen' (*Oy los reyes d'España sos parientes son*) (Merwin 1959: 240). With this crystallization of Spanish national identity, the poem ends.

Also in Castile in the late 11th and early 12th century, the Spanish Hebrew poet Judah Halevi wrote his poems of Zion in response to the First Crusade.[17] The conquest of the Holy Land, though a disaster for the Jewish community there, aroused messianic hope in Spain that Jewish national redemption was imminent, for the poet's heart remained in the East (לבי במזרח), and Hebrew could be restored as a vernacular language:[18]

> My heart is in the east and I –
> on the end of the west: how can I enjoy,
> how taste my food, how keep my vows
> while Zion is in Christian hands
> and I in Arab chains.
>
> (Aberbach 2008a: 37)

Other medieval poems display further effects of Islamic conquests and the Crusades. In the early 14th century, the challenge of Islam influenced Dante's *Commedia* (Menocal 1987: ch. 5). Dante writes in vernacular Italian, which had much influence on Italian nationalism. Although Dante expresses veneration for Averroes and Avicenna as well as Saladin, who reconquered Jerusalem for Islam in 1187, he gives no Muslim a place in Paradise. He rudely puts Mohammed in the Circle of Fraud among Sowers of Discord, 'from the chin/ Down to the fart-hole split as by a cleaver' *(rotto dal mento infin dove si trull)* (XXVIII 23–4; 1973: 246).[19] Dante's contemporary, Petrarch, in the *Canzoniere*, follows Dante in combining the assertion of Christian unity with the growth of a national culture in the vernacular. When Philip VI of France proclaimed a crusade in 1334, Petrarch saluted him as the 'seed of Charlemagne', through which the crucified Jesus sought unchristian revenge against the Muslim foe, 'breathing into our new Charlemagne/ the vengeance it were sinful to delay/ and Europe long has longed to venture on' *(onde nel petto al nove Carlo spira/ la vendetta ch'a noi tardata noce/ sì che molt'anni Europa ne sospira)* (Petrarch 2002: 24, 26). In Chaucer's *The Canterbury Tales* (later in the 14th century, after the Black Death), the effects of Islam are also felt, for by this time the Ottoman Turks had captured much of eastern Europe. In Chaucer's Prologue, the Knight, first and most esteemed of the pilgrims, is a protector of Christian Europe against Islam and has fought nobly for his king: 'Ful worthy was he in his lords werre,/ And therto hadde he riden, no man ferre' (Chaucer 1957: 17, lines 47–8). For over twenty years, the Knight served in the Iberian peninsula, the Baltic region and the eastern Mediterranean, fighting Muslims in Morocco (1342–4), and in the army of King Peter of Cyprus which took Antalya (Satalye) in southern Asia Minor (1361) and occupied Alexandria (1365). Later he returned to Asia Minor to take part in a raid on Ayas (Lyeys) in Cilicia (1367):

> In Gernade at the seege eek hadde he be
> Of Algezir, and riden in Belmarye.
> At Lyeys was he and at Satalye,
> When they were wonne; and in the Grete See
> At many a noble armee hadde he be.
>
> (*ibid.*, lines 56–60)[20]

Yet the Knight's crusading days appear to be past. He is a pilgrim not to the Holy Land (now back in Muslim hands) but locally, to Canterbury, to commemorate an English martyr, and in an English poem, not Latin; and gently, with the subtlety of Chaucer's experience as a court diplomat, hinting at new national concerns during the Hundred Years War.[21]

After Chaucer, Islam spread further as the Ottoman empire expanded: its crowning military achievement – the capture of Constantinople in 1453 – coincided with the invention of printing, which gave this catastrophe the widest possible publicity.[22] By this time, the Roman Church, despite its power, could no longer claim to unite Christian Europe under its authority. When in 1460, Pope Pius II wrote to Mehmet II, conqueror of Constantinople, to persuade him (futilely) to convert to the allegedly superior Christian faith, he emphasized not the power of the 'universal Christian Church' but individual qualities of European nations: 'Spain so steadfast, Gaul so warlike, Germany so populous, Britain so strong, Poland so daring, Hungary so active and Italy so rich, high-spirited, and experienced in the art of war' (Southern 1962: 100).

In Italy, three vernacular epics, infused with the new world of exploration and humanistic learning, science and art (much of which derived from contacts with Muslims), were among the most widespread and influential newly printed books, after Bible translations: Boiardo's *Orlando Innamorato* (c. 1483), Ariosto's *Orlando Furioso* (1516, 1532) and Tasso's *Gerusalemme Liberata* (1580–81).[23] These poems, though set in times of Christian/Islamic wars in the 8th and 11th centuries, express alarm at contemporary Ottoman conquests and seek salvation in a united Christian Europe. At the same time, they assert Italian distinctiveness and cultural unity. Boiardo, writing after the fall of Constantinople in 1453, adapts *The Song of Roland* for Renaissance readers, adding romance to the tale of Roland (Orlando) and combining elements of Arthurian chivalry with the story of Charlemagne. He bridges the seven centuries between Charlemagne and 15th century Europe with a menacing picture of a dynamic, rapidly spreading Islam: by this time the Muslim Turks ruled the lands of the Greeks, Romanians, Albanians and Slavs and threatened Venice and other Italian ports. The army of Sultan Suleiman the Magnificent (1520–66) penetrated the heartland of Latin Christendom (1521–6), conquering the kingdom of Hungary, Europe's '*Antemurale*' (bulwark) against Islam.[24] By this time, it seemed to some that 'the centralized, disciplined power of the Ottomans must surely prevail over a weak, divided, and irresolute Christian Europe' (Lewis 1993: 84).

Orlando Furioso, written as Suleiman overran Hungary, laid siege to Vienna (1529) and invaded Germany as far as Regensburg, is a swashbuckling story of a Muslim siege of Paris in the time of Charlemagne. This poem, the most famous and widely read in the Renaissance, spoke to Ariosto's 16th century readers. Following *The Song of Roland*, *Orlando Furioso* as a vernacular poem expressed both the idea of a culturally united nation, an Italy linguistically distinct from other European countries (and with potential for national unity) as well as the idea of a Christian Europe united against Islam. Charlemagne could be seen as an antecedent of Ariosto's contemporary, the Emperor Charles V, 'the last of the Holy Roman Emperors to pursue the medieval ideal of universal empire. He saw clearly the need for Europe to present a united front against the Turkish menace; and as heir to the Spanish throne he had inherited the traditional struggle of the Spanish kings against Islam' (Reynolds in Ariosto 1975: 14). At one point, Ariosto steps out of his 8th century narrative to excoriate the contemporary 16th century European powers, to their eternal shame (*'con eterno obbrobrio e vituperio'*), for weakening themselves with internal wars and religious schisms, far from the Holy Land, where their military intervention is most needed:[25]

> ... the Turks of late
> To our eternal shame and contumely,
> With their usurping presence desecrate,
> While Europe blazes, everywhere at war,
> Except where Christian arms most needed are.
>   (xv 99; 1975: 471)

Ariosto implores European Christians to stop fighting among themselves: '*perché Constantinopoli e del mondo/ la miglor parte occùpa il Turco immondo?*' –

> Why do you leave in dire captivity
> Jerusalem, by infidels polluted?
> Why do you let the unclean Turk command
> Constantinople and the Holy Land?
>   (xvii 75; 1975: 519)

Ariosto begs Pope Leo X, elected in 1513, to deliver a Christian roar worthy of his leonine name and divinely appointed office, for Italy's sake: '*e scelto il fiero nome,/ perché tu ruggi*' (*ibid.*, xvii 79). Ariosto's appeal is not in Latin, the language of the united European church, but Italian; and *Orlando Furioso*, translated into many languages, contributed to a Europe of nations.

Sixteenth century Christian Europe, divided by doctrine, was united by shared peril: fear of Muslim aggression was 'an essential background to the Reformation' (MacCulloch 2004: 57). The Council of Trent (1545–1563) coincided with the peak of Ottoman power. As papal authority was challenged by the Reformation, by the resurgence of Islam and by the rise of secular humanism and science, vernacular languages and literature spread. The generation of Erasmus, which lived through this cultural revolution, was the last to use Latin widely as a vernacular language. The first printed English Bible appeared as the Muslims triumphed over Hungary at Mohács (1526). In Islamic slave raids from 1530–1640, a million Western European Christians are estimated to have been enslaved (*ibid.*, 57). Tasso's late

16th century epic poem, *Gerusalemme Liberata*, set during the First Crusade in the late 11th century, speaks for widespread contemporary anti-Islamic feeling as the Ottoman empire expanded. The poet encourages his patron, Alfonso d'Este, duke of Ferrara, to renew the crusade against the Turks:[26] 'Be you as Godfrey [of Bouillon] was of yore./ Attend my song and gird yourself for war' (*Emulo di Goffredo, i nostril carmi/ intanto ascolta, e t'apparecchia a l'armi*) (i 5; 2009: 4).[27] The destruction of the Turkish fleet at Lepanto in 1571 as Tasso wrote *Gerusalemme Liberata* roused hope that Muslim domination of the Mediterranean would soon end.[28] At the same time, Camões wrote *The Lusiads* (1572), the major Portuguese national epic of the 16th century, celebrating Da Gama's voyages of discovery and kings and heroes such as Afonso Henriques who led Portugal's wars of national liberation from Muslim rule in the 12th and 13th centuries. (Camões had himself fought in the Portuguese army, losing an eye in battle with Muslims at Ceuta [c. 1547].) Camões warns of the brutal dragooning of Christian children into the teachings of the Koran and exhorts the European Christian powers to drive the Turks back to the caves of the Caspian mountains and to Scythia in the Far East: '*Fazei que torne lá às silvestres covas/ Dos cáspios montes e da Scítia fria/ A turca geraçao*' (vii 12). Like Ariosto, he attacks 16th century Christian rulers – the 'rough' Henry VIII ('*duro Ingrês*') and the 'unworthy' Francis I of France ('*Gallo indigno*') – for their divisive, sybaritic behavior and their neglect of their duty to reconquer Jerusalem from Islam: 'While an infidel monarch occupies/ The earthly city of Jerusalem…/ the Holy Sepulchre/ Occupied by dogs [*possuída de cães*] who now encroach/ With one accord against your own terrain' (vii 9). He describes as miraculous Afonso's minor victory at Ourique in 1139 for Jesus 'appeared' at the battle prophesying that Portugal would be liberated from Islamic rule. The Muslims fled, crying futilely for help from the Koran ('*A ajuda convocando do Alcorão*'):

> So the startled Moors snatched up
> Their weapons hastily and at random;
> They did not turn, but stood their ground
> Launching their terrible cavalry.
> Without flinching, the Portuguese met them,
>
> Impaling them through their hearts;
> Some fell half dead, while the survivors ran
> Calling aloud for help from the *Koran*.
>
> (iii 50)

Elizabethan poetry, too, asserts rising nationalism amid fear of Islamic power: Marlowe in *The Jew of Malta* (I i 179f) and Shakespeare in *Henry IV pt. 2* (III ii 297; V ii 47–8) mention large tribute paid to Turks.[29] *Othello*, set against the 16th century Ottoman invasion of Crete, stereotypes Turks as liars prone to sudden violence (II i 116; II iii 163–5). In this world where East and West meet, Othello, a Muslim convert to Christianity, is both familiar and an outsider, and his suicide – 'in Aleppo once,/ Where a malignant and a turbaned Turk/ Beat a Venetian and traduced the state/ I took by th' throat the circumcised dog/ And smote him – thus' (V ii 848–52) – is self-punishment as an 'infidel' to Desdemona, a fate deserved by Muslim 'infidels'. In *Richard II*, the Bishop of Carlisle defends the banished crusader, the Duke of Norfolk, who fought 'For Jesu Christ in glorious Christian field,/ Streaming the ensign of the Christian cross/ Against black pagans, Turks, and Saracens' (IV i 83–6). Henry V, forgetful of his father's usurpation of the throne – 'This is the English not the Turkish court' (*Henry IV, pt. 2*, V ii 47) – hopes his son will 'go to Constantinople and take the Turk by the beard' (207). Spenser, in *The Fairy Queen* (1 ii), allegorizes Islam as Sansfoy (faithless), an antichrist in unholy alliance with Duessa (Rome), killed cursing the bloody Cross by Red Cross, knight of Una, representing the universal Church and England. While Tamerlane, the Mongol warrior who temporarily checked the Ottomans at Angora in 1402 and captured Sultan Bajazeth I, is the hero of Marlowe's play, *Tamburlaine* (1588). In one particularly lurid scene, he mocks Mohammed and burns the Koran declaring himself a divinely appointed avenger:

> Come, Mohamet, if thou have any power,
> Come down thyself and work a miracle:
> Thou art not worthy to be worshippèd,
> That suffers flame of fire to burn the writ
> Where in the sum of thy religion rests.
> Part 2 (V i)

EAST EUROPEAN EPIC POETRY

Muslim invasions are depicted in major 16th and 17th century Eastern European national epic poems, instrumental in fostering separate national identities and their vernacular languages: for example, the Croatian allegorical epic poems *Judith* (written 1501, published 1524) by Marko Marulik (1450–1524) and Gundulic's *Osman* (1626) – a glorification of the battle of Khotin (1621) when the Polish-Lithuanian army drove back the invading Turks. Tasso was a major influence on Gundulic and Zrinyi, whose Hungarian epic *The Peril of Sziget* (1651) depicts the Turkish invasion in 1566 under Suleiman the Magnificent and the heroism of the outnumbered Hungarians and Croatians. These militant poems betray fear of Islamic expansionism at least until 1683, when the Ottoman siege of Vienna was broken by Jan Sobieski, king of Poland, and Charles of Lorraine. This turning point is recalled by the Ukrainian poet Taras Shevchenko (1814–1861) in the poem 'The Haydamaks' (1841) and by Njegoš in the Serbian epic *The Mountain Wreath* (1847):

> The saddle-girth snapped on the Prophet's mare.
> Charles, Leopold's courageous voivode,

John Sobieski, too, the Duke of Savoy,
All together they broke the demon's horns.
... Burak [Mohammed's horse] stumbled just before Vienna.
The wagon was overturned down the hill.[30]

Shevchenko, in 'Ivan Pidkova' (1839), describes 16th century Cossacks attacking Istanbul (Shevchenko 1964: 40–2) and, in 'Hamaliya' (1842) describes 17th century Cossack raids on Muslim coastal towns in Ottoman Turkey (*ibid.*, 143–9). In the early 18th century, Ibsen's *Peer Gynt* recalls that Sweden under Charles XII fought the Turks. From the 18th century, Russia fought the declining Ottoman empire (see Lieven 2002), and Russian poetry expresses nationalist anti-Islamic feeling: Lomonosov's ode on the battle of Khotin in 1739 (published in 1751) exults in the Russian victory over 'the soulless ones' (Wachtel 2004: 68), one of many stereotypes of Islam going back to the early medieval period.

THE FRENCH REVOLUTION AND BALKAN NATIONAL POETRY

Centuries of Islamic rule meant that Balkan national liberation movements during and after the French Revolution and the Napoleonic wars had a strongly religious coloring and aimed to avenge medieval religious defeats: first in Greece, Serbia and Montenegro, then in Bulgaria and Romania, and finally in Albania (Stavrianos 2000). Balkan poetry of 1789–1914 generally opposes Ottoman rule both on religious and political grounds while mirroring the complications of Great Power intervention in Muslim affairs. Though the Balkans were widely seen as primitive and savage, their poets, mostly unknown elsewhere, were highly influential as a revolutionary force of education and modernization until by World War I Ottoman rule was overturned and replaced with independent states.

The French Revolution stirred Greek national consciousness not just in Greece but also among philhellenes throughout Europe and in America who had little difficulty in constructing a modern Greek identity and culture. The revolution inspired Greek nationalists such as the poet Velestinlis in Vienna, with its large Greek population. In the Greek newspaper which he edited there, Velestinlis called for a pan-Balkan uprising against the Turks and demanded that Greek be taught in schools. The poet's murder by the Turks in 1798 ensured that he would be remembered as the first modern Greek prophet of armed revolt and martyr of independence. His poem *Thourios* (War Song), recast into English by the admiring Byron, provided a famous slogan for revolt: better an hour of freedom than forty years of slavery.[31] Greek poets helped to rouse a successful modern national revolt, giving legitimacy to the national movement and helping to unite its disparate, conflicting groups of local chiefs and religious leaders, merchants and seamen, and the wealthy and influential Phanariot French-educated Greek elite in Constantinople.[32]

Greek poetry grew in two schools, on the mainland (the Romantic School of Athens) and on Greek islands (the School of the Ionian Islands). Both schools expressed a new Greek national consciousness and revitalized the Greek language. Like much national poetry, these schools emphasized love for the homeland, pride in the past, yearning for freedom and the humiliation of a proud people long under foreign domination. Greek nationalism, driven forward by the Romantic movement, inspired Solomos, the opening of whose *Ode to Liberty* (1824) became the Greek national anthem,[33] and Byron whose death at Missolonghi in 1824 contributed to Greece's ultimate victory in its war of independence (Aberbach 2008).

History fueled the Greek war of independence (1821–29) in which many fought for the restoration of the Orthodox Byzantine empire and the return of Constantinople to Christendom after three and a half centuries under Islam. Ancient religious stereotypes were revived: a war of Hellene against Turk was a war of civilization versus barbarism and noble Greece needed help against the Muslim infidel. In the Greek war, 'Religion was the only fixed line of demarcation, in full conformity with the pre-existing Ottoman system of religiously defined *millets*. It was a war of Christians against Muslims' (Gazi 2009: 103). Folk poetry, which had long lamented Greek defeats by the Turks (Alexiou 2002) and proclaimed Greek pride and determination to win freedom from the Turks, now took on new meaning. In one song, Mount Olympus, home of the gods, declares that each of its peaks conceals a Greek 'brigand' (κλέφτης) ready to defend the country from the invading Turks.[34] Greece unexpectedly won the war against Ottoman Turkey when Britain, France and Russia stopped the Turks from crushing the revolt. The support of Byron and other public figures of his time was decisive (Woodhouse 1991: 136).[35] The Greek success anticipated both the eradication of Ottoman rule from the Balkans and also revolutionary independence movements throughout Europe and elsewhere.

The memory of medieval defeat and humiliation of Christian powers by Islam drove Balkan nationalism and its poetry until World War I and after. Balkan poets often sought revenge. Valaorites' bitter allegory 'The Rock and the Wave' recalls the long humiliating occupation of Greece by Ottoman Turkey (Trypanis 1984: 530–32).[36] Serbian poets record a history starting with the 1389 Muslim defeat of the Serbs at the Battle of Kosovo Fields and leading to five centuries of Ottoman rule. This defeat is glorified as a necessary sacrifice, making the Serbs a chosen people who have gained 'the empire of heaven':[37] 'The national bard helped transform the tragedy of Kosovo into a metaphor for survival', and the epic poetry based on this defeat 'became an important educational tool responsible for the preservation of the national culture' (Gorup in Vucinich and Emmert 1991:117).[38] The 1804 uprising which led ultimately to Serbian independence was an epochal event in Serbian epic oral poetry (Foley 2002: 203).[39] Njegoš' *The Mountain Wreath* (1847) climaxes in a Serbian massacre of hated Serbian Christian converts to Islam: 'Our struggle won't come to an end until/ we or the Turks are exterminated'.⁴⁰ The poet hails Charles Martel's victory over the Muslim invaders 1,100 years previously, in the battle of Tours/Poitiers (732), as though it had just happened: 'If the French dike had not stood in the way,/ the Arab sea would have flooded it all' (Njegoš 1989: 5).⁴¹ Similarly, the Romanian poet Eminescu declares revenge as his dearest wish: 'Dreamed-for revenge, dark as a tomb,/ The enemy's blood sizzling on your sword,/ above their lopped-off hydra heads dreamed-of triumph streaming in the wind ...' (Carduner *et al.* 1986: 50). In his *Third Satire* (c. 1881), Eminescu recalls the heroic age of Vlad Tepes (the Impaler) and his grandfather Mircea the Old, medieval Wallachian leaders of a once-great nation, 'Heirs to the Romans' who defeated the invading Turks in battle: 'In vain the flag of the Prophet was raised high.../ row upon row of Arabs wavered and were cut down' (Eminescu 1980: 144–5).⁴² European support for revolt against the Turks was so widespread that to help the Turks, as the opportunistic Peer Gynt does in Ibsen's poetic drama (1867), was heretical. When the poet Botev led the failed Bulgarian revolt against the Turks in 1876, the entire European press supported the Bulgarians: over 2,000 articles appeared in 200 newspapers (Topencharov 1982: 80). This response encouraged Russian intervention, which led to Bulgarian independence two years later. In Botev's poem 'On Parting', a young man leaves home to fight the Turks – and this is what Botev actually did. On a boat commandeered by the rebels, Botev handed the captain a letter explaining the motives of the revolutionaries and concluding, 'Long live Christian Europe!' (*ibid.*, 76). Botev's martyrdom fighting the Turks ensured his elevation as Bulgaria's national poet. In *The Highland Lute*, the last of the great Balkan national epics prior to the fall of the Ottoman empire, Fishta extols the 15th century national hero George Castriota, or Skanderbeg, who fought for Albanian independence from the Turks (though at one time he was also allied with the Turks):⁴³ Albanians ponder how to free the country from the Turks 'and make it/ As when ruled by Castriota,/ When Albanians lived in freedom' (Fishta 2005: 4; Canto i 39–41).⁴⁴ In much of this poetry, the good that Islam had brought for centuries, particularly its relative tolerance for minorities and effective government, was forgotten, and the image of cruelty, corruption and extortion lived on.

CONCLUSION

Poetry from *The Song of Roland* (late 11th century?) to Fishta's *The Highland Lute* (mostly 1902–1909) is imprinted with the history of European nationalism coming from the clash of Islam with Christianity. In centuries of ascendancy, Islam was a factor in undermining the authority of the Pope, the universal Church, the Gospel and Latin, opening the way to narrower, more national and cultural concerns expressed in poetry and song. Much medieval European poetry was a call to arms against Islam, not just in the name of the Church but also, increasingly, in the name of emerging nations, each with its own vernacular language. The centrality of *The Song of Roland* in medieval Europe reflects the Islamic challenge to Christianity after the 7th century Muslim conquest of the Holy Land and the invasion of Europe in the 8th century. The poem heralds further religious warfare, in the Crusades and until the Ottoman siege of Vienna (1683) and after, when the *jihadic* threat to Europe weakened. The clash of Islam with Christianity in Europe provoked remarkable poetic cultures, often with strongly nationalist elements: a proliferation of the vernacular, with secular themes; an attachment to a particular territory; a sense of threat from a hated enemy on the frontier; the elevation of often-legendary heroism in the past and of creative individualism; the unification of diverse peoples; a sharp self-questioning and self-criticism and a powerful Bible-driven conviction of national chosenness which became increasingly prominent after the invention of printing in the mid-15th century and the consequent spread throughout Europe of vernacular Bibles.

The 8th century Islamic conquests brought to Christian Europe both the threat of annihilation and the most advanced civilization of the early medieval era, with an unusually high regard for the art of poetry. Muslim culture, including poetry, was transmitted, translated and often transformed through the variegated, porous frontier societies of Spain. Long before they were written down, vernacular poems about Charlemagne, Roland and other heroes in the wars with Islam were a staple of popular culture, reaching every level of society, in song and theater, even puppetry, throughout the Christian world in many translations and versions. Poetry helped strengthen emerging nations of European Christendom against the Muslim military and missionary threat, and it deepened consciousness of national differences based on language, culture, territory, history and religion. Focusing chiefly on the ages of Charlemagne and the Crusades, poetry assuaged longstanding frustration over defeat by the Muslim 'infidel'; re-established pride in the past; pointed to religious, social and political reform; supported a feeling of community weakened by religious conflict and provided rudimentary forms of education as well as entertainment. As Latin lost influence, vernacular languages flourished and found some of their most creative and popular expression in poetry. Poetry asserted both international Christian unity (even among warring Christian countries) and also the emerging national individuality of separate Christian states, each with its own language and vernacular Bible translations and its conviction of being a 'chosen people', a 'new Israel'. While Renaissance Italian epics recalled the age of Charlemagne, Islamic invasions of Eastern Europe from the 14th to the 18th century permeated national poetry in many languages, including Croatian, Polish, Hungarian, Ukrainian and Russian. After 1789, ancient religious conflict in the Balkans set off overtly national poetry as part of independence struggles against the Ottoman Turks. This poetry reveals great bitterness at Muslim rule and influence, but also at times (in Albania especially) a remarkable synthesis of cultures. In the clash of Islam with Christianity, poets explored imaginatively real fears and hopes, frustrations and longings. The freshness and authenticity of their poetry ensured for centuries their appeal and relevance – which today are not totally lost.

NOTES

1. On defeat as a precipitant of nationalism and national poetry, see pp. 22–4, 42–4. On Muslim/Christian rivalry as a spur of nationalism, see Armstrong (1982).
2. See Smith (2004: ch. 6) for a discussion of war as a stimulant of nationalism.
3. On Judah Halevi and other Spanish Hebrew poets, see chapter 4 (this volume).
4. Njegoš, for example, writes in the context of a rich Serbo-Croatian tradition of folk song (see Bartok and Lord 1951); while Fishta, likewise, in *The Highland Lute* draws heavily on oral tradition (see Elsie and Mathie-Heck 2004) – necessarily so as the vast majority of Albanians were illiterate, and the Albanian language and education had been suppressed by the Turks. On the importance of vernacular languages to nationalism, see Anderson (1991).
5. Islamic conquests in the 7th and 8th centuries, including Spain (by 713) and the invasion of France (732), spread fear of the invaders as far as the British isles. On Anglo-Saxon reactions to Islam, see Beckett (2003). Bede's association of Muslims with a biblical model of the Ishmaelite 'other' (1968: 347) – in common with other familiar pre-Islamic groupings (Arabs, Hagarenes, Saracens), tainted with barbarous anti-Christian aggression, immorality, idolatry and exile from God – seems to have been general in Christian responses to the Muslim invasion, retarding an accurate picture of Islam as a new religion.
6. On the hope to reconquer Jerusalem for Christendom, see, for example, the poetry of Alcuin (Godman 1985: 129), the medieval French epic *The Pilgrimage of Charlemagne*, Crusader poems (e.g., Rosenberg *et al.*, 1998: 243), Ariosto's *Orlando Furioso* (xvii 75), Camões' *The Lusiads* (vii 9), and Ronsard (2002: 178). Outrage at the Muslim conquest of the Holy Land persists in European poetry until the 19th century: 'How long by tyrants shall thy land be trod?/ How long thy temple worshipless, Oh God?' (Byron, 'On Jordan's Banks', 1815).
7. Criticism of the Church intensified in the 13th century as Islam reconquered the Holy Land. For example, the poet Guillam Figueira accused the Church of selling indulgences: 'For pardon, you demand/ That money changes hands' (*Car vos perdonatz/ Per deniers pechatz*) (Kehew 2005: 288–9).
8. On the evolution of European languages in the Middle Ages, see Wright (1991).
9. Islamic poetry of victory over Christian armies in the Crusades – for example, Saladin's triumph at Hattin (1187) and the conquest of Acre (1291) – has no comparable nationalist character but instead is jihadic poetry in Arabic of the victory of Islam over Christianity (Hillenbrand 1999: 179, 240).
10. See, for example, Njegoš' *The Mountain Wreath* (1989: 5) and Tasso's *Gerusalemme Liberata* (i 5).
11. On anti-Muslim prejudice in *Chansons de Geste*, see Newth (2005: ix). Belief in Islamic polytheism persisted for centuries: Petrarch, writing in the 14th century, attributes to Islam a 'great variety of gods' (2002: 26). In Muslim poetry, similarly, Christians are described as 'polytheists' (Hillenbrand 1999: 70). The Christian view of Islam became more hostile after the conversion of the Mongols in

the 13th century [and later, after the Ottoman conquests (Bisaha 2004)] when Islam was seen increasingly as 'the single most significant obstacle to Christianity' (Cruz 1999: 66). On portrayals of Muslims in *Chansons de Geste*, see Bancourt (1982). On Crusader poetry, see Dijkstra (1995). For bibliography on Crusader literature, see Riley-Smith (2002: 103–4).

12. '... a Europe of nations would have been inconceivable without the peculiar combination of circumstances that first produced a France' (Armstrong 1982: 158–9). The translation of *The Song of Roland* cited here is by Burgess (1990). The French edition of *Le Chanson de Roland* is by Moignet (1989).
13. European nations adopted the Hebrew Bible as the source of their identification as 'chosen peoples' (Aberbach 2005), while Muslims preserved belief in the chosenness of Islam as a whole (Fletcher 2004: 159).
14. On conversion to Islam in Christian Spain, see Glick (1979).
15. A longstanding oral tradition may be assumed before the *Chansons de Geste* were written down, mostly, it seems, from the 11th century when Christian Europe gained ground against Islam and economic conditions improved. Stone castles, churches and schools (especially French cathedral schools) were built where poetry was preserved, written, recited and studied. Prior to 1050, the word 'poet' was hardly used: 'God was the sole creator' (Preminger *et al.*, 1993: 748). Hebrew was among cultures transformed by the rise of Christian Europe.
16. This story, current for centuries, was notably adapted by Corneille (1636) in the first masterpiece of French classical tragedy.
17. On Judah Halevi and other medieval Spanish Hebrew poets, see chapter 4 (this volume).
18. In Spain, however, there were long periods of fruitful Muslim, Christian and Jewish coexistence, reflected in their poetic cultures (Dodds *et al.*, 2008).
19. In Dante's *Paradiso* (xviii 39), Charlemagne and Roland are given a place in paradise, in the Heaven of Mars. On Western attacks on Mohammed, see Daniel (1993).
20. In Coghill's translation:

    When, in Granada, Algeciras sank,
    Under assault, he had been there, and in
    North Africa, raiding Benamarin,
    In Anatolia he had been as well
    And fought when Ayas and Attalia fell,
    For all along the Mediterranean coast
    He had embarked with many a noble host.

    (Chaucer 1972: 20–1)

21. Chaucer's Knight contributed to 'a dramatic reversal of the pattern of victimization' of Christian Europe by Islam in the 14th century, accompanied by impressive growth of Romance and Germanic languages (and the decline of Arabic in Spain) which were particularly important in defining nationality (Bartlett 1993: 292–3, 198ff). On the complex interconnection of medieval English and French nationalism as reflected in poetry, see Butterfield (2009).
22. The fall of Constantinople in 1453 was for centuries a subject of poetry. In one Greek folk poem, a heavenly voice calls for three ships, one to carry the cross, a second for the Bible, and a third for the altar, 'before the Turkish dogs desecrate it' (Trypanis 1984: 470). See p. 147. Compare Njegoš in *The Mountain Wreath*

[1989 (1847): 6, 83]: 'a mosque arises where the broken cross lies/... Omar's church has reared unto the sky/ on Solomon's sacred foundations;/ St. Sophia is but a stable now'. Arabic poetry lamented similarly after the First Crusade: 'How many a mosque have they made into a church!' (Hillenbrand 1999: 298).

23. Boiardo, Ariosto and Tasso all had patronage at the court at Ferrara, one of the most modern cities in the Renaissance world. The fame of Ariosto and Tasso increased through the adaptation of their epics in innumerable operas.

24. In 1848, Petőfi (1973: 251) recalled that Hungary 'once defended all the world/ against the Tatars and Turks.'

25. So bitter was infighting among Christian countries that they sold weapons to Muslims in their wars against other Christian countries (Lewis 1993: 74–5). In fact, Kidd (1999) points out that Islam 'fared little worse than Roman Catholicism in a Protestant demonology which associated the latter's rites with pagan superstition and its hagiolatry with polytheism' (290).

26. The Turks challenged Venetian naval power in the eastern Mediterranean and raided Sorrento, Tasso's birthplace, in 1558. Tasso, then fourteen, was falsely informed that his sister had been killed in the raid. Within the next two years, Tasso began his narrative poem about the First Crusade, which grew into *Gerusalemme Liberata*.

27. In a poem commemorating the successful defence of Metz against Charles V of Spain (1552–3) by François, duke of Guise – who traced his ancestry to Godfrey of Bouillon – Tasso's contemporary, Pierre de Ronsard (1524–1585), describes François's armour on which was carved a white-bearded Pope Urban 'gravely admonishing/ Christian Kings to fight the Saracens/ and conquer the Holy Kingdom of Jerusalem' (Ronsard 2002: 178).

28. For a stirring poem on this battle, see Chesterton's 'Lepanto': '*Vivat Hispania*!/ *Domino Gloria*!/ Don John of Austria/ Has set his people free!' Cervantes' parody in *Don Quixote* (1604) of chivalric romance which had dominated European poetry for centuries might be linked to the aftereffects of the battle of Lepanto in 1571 (in which Cervantes took part), 'when the insolent pride of the Ottomans was broken forever' (Cervantes 1975: 348) and traditional knightly behaviour became increasingly anachronistic – and quixotic – thereafter. The Cretan Renaissance (1580–1669), whose outstanding poem was Kornaros' *Erotokritos* (early 17th century, when Crete was under Venetian rule), is linked by scholars to the effects of the battle of Lepanto, particularly Book 2 in which Rotokritos, the Cretan commoner hero, fights a duel with the Karamanite Turk (Holton 1991: 52). Though set in Greece of pagan antiquity, and with little overt national content, the poem, written mostly in Cretan dialect, became a focus for national hopes after the Turks conquered Crete, in the Turco-Venetian war of 1645–69.

29. The Turkish siege of Malta in 1565 is the subject of the Cretan poet Antonios Achelis' poem *Maltas Poliorkia*. Malta had no written language of its own until the 19th century. Malta's national poet, Dun Karm Psaila (1871–1961), recalls highlights of Malta's history: the medieval warrior Roger the Norman, who freed Malta from Muslim domination: the Knights of Malta, 'sworn enemies/ Of the Muslim wolves'; and resistance to the medieval Muslim threat, together with the Maltese revolt against the French in 1799, as integral to Maltese national identity (Arberry and Grech 1961: 83, 91, 143). Psaila frequently alludes to the period of the Muslim conquest and the Great Siege of 1565, e.g., in 'The Lamp in the

Museum' (1920), 'To Malta' (1925), 'Non Omnis Moriar' (1927) and 'Wied Qirda' (1933). In his sonnet 'St. John's Day' (1939), the victorious Knights of Malta march in the annual procession through Valletta's streets strewn with laurel leaves as church bells toll (*ibid.*, 123). The siege of Malta is the subject of a 16th century Cypriot ballad in which the Turks acknowledge their defeat: 'Malta of gold, Malta of silver, Malta of precious metal,/ We shall never take you' (Bradford 1979: 219).

30. Пуче колан свечевој коôнлн.
    Леололдов храôрн војевода,
    Соôњевскн војвода савојскн
    саломнше демону рогове...
    Пред Бечом је Бурак посриуо,
    оôриуше кола ииза сграиу.

    (Njegoš 1989: 41; lines 1143–6, 1149–50)

31. On *Thourios* in the context of Greek poetry of independence, see pp. 150–1.
32. For a fuller account of Greek national poetry in response to the war of independence, see chapter 6 (this volume).
33. For a selection in English translation, see Solomos (2000).
34. See pp. 147–8.
35. An indication of the importance of Great Power support for national movements in the Balkans is that during the continent-wide revolutions of 1848–49 no comparable support was offered to any of the uprisings, and all failed.
36. On Valaorites' poem, see p. 156.
37. See Pennington and Levi (1984: 17–18), Vucinich and Emmert (1991: chs. 8, 11, 14) and Kaufman (2001: 171). For texts in English translation, see Karadžić (1997: 42–158). Njegoš' *The Mountain Wreath* (1847), though set c. 1700, alludes to a tendency among Serbs to relive Kosovo in the memory of it, fighting alongside Prince Lazar against the Muslim 'sons of death'. A Serb declares to his Turkish enemy, 'Weren't we both on the field of Kosovo?/ I fought then and I am still fighting now,/ you were traitor then and you are one now' (1989: 16). On the memory of Kosovo among later Serb poets, see Mihailovich in Vucinich and Emmert (1991: 152–3).
38. On Ismail Kadare fictional reconstruction of the battle of Kosovo in 1389 and its effect on poetry, see p. 28 note 16.
39. On Bosnian and Albanian oral poetry with a Muslim view of the conflict with Christianity, see Parry (1974), Foley (2002) and Elsie and Mathie-Heck (2004). This is poetry of loyalty to the Ottoman empire and nostalgia for the early 16th century, when the empire reached the height of its power. As Serbian Christians and Muslims lived in close proximity, it is not surprising that their folk poetry overlaps at times. Ivo Andrić, in *The Bridge on the Drina* (1945), tells of a Muslim song: 'When Alibeg was a young beg/ A maiden bore his standard', which was converted during Karageorge's revolt (1804–13) into a Christian song – 'the most precious of booty' – of the revolt: 'When Karageorge was a young beg/ A maiden bore his standard'. It was a capital offence to sing this version (1977: 87, 88). Much Albanian folk poetry, too, is notable for its opposition to Turkish rule, which lasted over four centuries, until 1912 (Pipa 1978). This poetry finds roots of Albanian national identity in ancient Greece (Ilyria). For Albanian folk songs on the Greek War of Independence, see Ruches (1967: 41–60).

40. ђорђи иашој краја ђити иеће
    до истраге турске али иаше...

    (Njegoš 1989: 8, lines 131–2).

    The virulence of anti-Muslim feeling expressed in Serbian national poetry 'may, sadly, be a reaction to the reality of history in which Orthodox Serbs were for centuries the principal Balkan Christian co-operators with the Turkish empire' (Hastings 1997: 133). In Serbian painting, too, the image of Judas came to symbolize the Serbs who defected to Islam (*ibid.*, 132). The genocidal impulse in *The Mountain Wreath* might be linked to the Serbian massacre of Bosnian Muslims in 1992 (Sells 1996, Kaufman 2001). Similar Muslim atrocities are described by Armenian Christian poets, including Daniel Varoujan (1884–1915) and Siamanto (1878–1915), both killed by the Turks (Hovanessian & Margossian 1978).
41. Француского да не ђн ђрњега,
    аравнјско море све потопн!
42. '*In zadar flamura verde o ridică înspre oaste* .../ *Cad asabii ca şi pîlcuri risipite pe cîmpie*'. For Eminescu in the context of Russian-Ottoman imperial rivalry, see pp. 172–3.
43. Similarly, in the 12th century Spanish poem, *The Cid*, the fact that the Cid was historically a mercenary in Muslim service is glossed over, making him an 'exclusively Christian, crusading, Castilian patriot' (Fletcher 2004: 86).
44. Hostility to Turkish rule dominated Albanian poetry after the Congress of Berlin (1878), though Albania had been the main support of Turkish rule in the Balkans, vital to the defence of Constantinople and with a Muslim majority.

4 Medieval Spanish Hebrew National Poetry

לבי במזרח ואנכי בסוף מערב

My heart is in the east and I –
on the end of the west ...

(Judah Halevi)

Hebrew poetry in medieval Spain expresses Jewish nationalism as the Bible does, by being in Hebrew, its Golden Age in the 11th and 12th centuries, when most Jews still lived in the Middle East after centuries under Islamic rule. As the Iberian Peninsula was part of the Islamic empire, and had been since the 8th century, the Jews generally felt more at home there than in Christian Europe, where the Crusades brought havoc to many Jewish communities. All Spanish Hebrew poets were native Arabic speakers and writers. Their use of Hebrew was a matter of choice, signifying that however assimilated they were in Arabic society they were Jews in exile from the land of Israel. This lachrymose self-image, universal among Jews until 1789, was in line both with Judaism and with Christian and Islamic perceptions of Jews as tolerated infidels. The high point of Hebrew poetry in medieval Spain came in the late-11th century, when the Crusaders conquered the Holy Land from Islam (1099), briefly raising messianic hopes of a return from exile.[1] These hopes were expressed most notably in the poetry of Judah Halevi (c. 1075–1141), which entered the Jewish liturgy and remains so to this day. Halevi's poems of Zion, written in Spain – 'the end of the west' – express yearning not only for the land of Israel as it was in the time of Jewish sovereignty but also as it might become in future.[2]

My heart is in the east and I –
on the end of the west: how can I enjoy,
how taste my food, how keep my vows
while Zion is in Christian hands
and I in Arab chains.
I'd lightly leave the good of Spain
to see the Temple's dust again.[3]

Medieval Spanish Hebrew National Poetry   111

Halevi's poem beginning 'Zion, will you not ask' is the best-known Hebrew poem between the biblical and modern periods, recited by observant Jews on the eve of Tisha B'Av, the ninth of Av, the anniversary of the destruction of both Temples in Jerusalem. This poetry reflects Halevi's anxiety at being caught between two religions at war and his hope for the messianic redemption of the Jews and their return to their homeland.

> Zion, will you not ask about your captives?
> They ask for you, the last of your flock.
> Accept their greeting, west and east, north and south,
> far and near on every side; my greeting too,
> lust-locked to weep Hermon's dew across your hills:
> A jackal I am, wailing out your grief,
> a harp for the dream-song of your exiles' homecoming.[4]

Yet, while Hebrew poetry in Muslim Spain in the 11th and 12th centuries is linguistically nationalistic, it is mostly assimilative in content. Hardly any of it is about Zion. Conspicuous in Hebrew for non-theological elements, this poetry has for its most immediate influence contemporary Arabic poetry with its various genres: love poetry, including homosexual poetry, poetry of friendship, wine songs, war poetry and so on. This was the outstanding Hebrew poetry between the end of the biblical age and modern times. Most of it belongs to the years 1031–1140 when the Umayyad empire fell apart while Christian Europe in some ways overtook Islam, militarily, economically and culturally. Hebrew poets adopted Arabic versification and themes from Arabic poetry and the secular court lifestyle while evidently keeping strictly to Jewish tradition and writing poems for the synagogue liturgy. How did Jewish literature move from its relatively assimilationist stance in the early 11th century to nationalist longing a few decades later?

In the 11th century there was a decisive historical shift in the global balance of power. Islam weakened as Christian Europe became stronger.[5] The Islamic empire, including most of the Mediterranean area, had split into three caliphates: the Abbasid, Fatimid and Umayyad, whose cultural unity was based mainly on the use of Arabic. The 11th century began with the collapse of the Umayyad caliphate. It ended with the conquest of Muslim-held Sicily and the east Mediterranean, including Palestine, by the Crusaders. By 1099, Jerusalem after four and a half centuries under Muslim rule was in Christian hands. The fragmentation of the seemingly stable and powerful Muslim empire in the west Mediterranean into over two dozen city-states (*taifas* = 'parts') provoked civil war in Spain. Fanatical Berber Muslims invaded from North Africa. Gradually, the Christians reconquered Spain from the north. The First Crusade and internecine war in Spain were disastrous for the Jews and, as is often the case in Jewish history, stimulated renewed longing for the land of Israel, notably in Halevi's poems of Zion.

This age of imperial collapse and failed recovery in Muslim Spain was marked by two distinct periods: (1) civil war among the splinter-kingdoms and (2) Berber invasions from North Africa. The two Hebrew poets who dominated the first period were Samuel Hanagid (993–1056) and Solomon ibn Gabirol (1021/2–1056?), of whom Gabirol is acknowledged as the greater. In the second period there were also two outstanding Hebrew poets: Moses ibn Ezra (c. 1055–after 1135) and Judah Halevi (c. 1075–c. 1141). With Halevi, post-biblical Hebrew poetry reached its artistic peak prior to modern times. The poetry of Hanagid and ibn Gabirol is set against the fall of the Cordoba caliphate, while the poetry of Ibn Ezra and Halevi has for its background the Berber invasions of 1090 and 1140. This explosion of creativity came from a society torn apart by war and the spasmodic drive south by the armies of Christian Spain, yet culturally among the most advanced in the Middle Ages. Its relatively secular, pluralistic outlook might be seen as a harbinger of the modern age.

Spanish Hebrew poets themselves might have wondered to learn that later generations saw theirs as a golden age. Their own experience was war, chaos, instability and exile, conditions ripe with messianic hope, as shown in the following list of events:

1009–1031	Collapse of the Umayyad caliphate.
1013	Fall of Cordoba. Exile of Samuel Hanagid from Cordoba, his birthplace, to Malaga.
1031–1091	Over two dozen splinter-kingdoms rule Andalusia, often at war with one another.
1066	Massacre of Jewish community of Granada.
1085	Conquest of Toledo by Christian army of Alfonso VI.
1086	Almoravid invasion and defeat of Christian army at al-Zallaqah, near Badajoz.
1090	Destruction of Jewish community of Granada by Almoravids, witnessed by ibn Ezra and Halevi.
1091–1145	Almoravid rule of Muslim Spain.
1096–99	First Crusade, culminating in Christian conquest of the land of Israel from the Muslims.
1135	Capture of Seville by Christian army of Alfonso VII.
1140–50	Almohad invasion and conquest of Muslim Spain.
1147	Capture of Seville by Almohads. Maimonides and his family, resident in Cordoba, are forced into exile.
1147–49	Second Crusade.

Jewish nationalism fructified in this volcanic soil. From the time of the Arab conquests of the 7th and early 8th centuries until the 13th century, the world Jewish population was still largely concentrated in the

Middle East, chiefly in Babylonia under Abbasid rule. Economic decline and political instability, and the shift of the power centre of the Arab world from Baghdad to Cairo in the Fatimid empire, led many Jews to emigrate from Babylonia to North Africa or to Spain. Spain, conquered by Muslims in 711, was the frontier not just of Islam but also of the known world. Its large empty spaces and fertile land and its geographical position offered much opportunity within an Arabic culture familiar and congenial to most Jews.

The hardships of the Babylonian Jews, driving them to emigrate, appear in an undated liturgical poem by the last great religious leader of Babylonian Jewry, Hai Gaon, who died in 1038 having lived for a century. Hai Gaon writes bitterly of the Jews in exile:

> This the people that never were,
> eaten away, scattered, despoiled.
> Babylonia trounced them, Media knocked them out,
> Greece swallowed them, Islam did not vomit them.
> Why make their yoke heavier?
> Why double their misery?
> Powerless, what can they endure?[6]

At the start of the golden age, when these lines were written, most Jews spoke Arabic, which had replaced Aramaic as their *lingua franca*. Conditions in Spain encouraged assimilation, not longing to return to Zion. Spain's manifest superiority as a rich, elegant, culturally sophisticated society on Islam's toehold on continental Europe drew settlers from the east. The relative tolerance characteristic of Islam in Spain attracted Jews from the Middle East and North Africa. Throughout the Arab world, the Jews, like the Christians, had the status of a protected religious group (*dhimma*) and were respected as a 'people of the book' (*ahl-al-kitab*), a people who possessed holy scriptures recognized by Islam. Jewish immigrants to Spain easily fitted in, especially as the country was a frontier with many new immigrants. The similarities between Islam and Judaism also helped in the acculturation of Jews in exile. Both religions are monotheisms which teach salvation through obedience to divine commandments as revealed to a supreme prophet; both are based on religious jurisprudence interpreted by scholars and judges; both emphasize the importance of dietary laws and communal worship.

With their ancient, sharply-defined religious culture, the Spanish Jews had much indirect influence at a time when Spain, with its highly diverse population, struggled for national self-definition. The Jews' stress on their biblical lineage and chosenness, as bearers of a divine message in a pure and holy literature, was adopted by Christians and Muslims in shaping Spanish culture. Through its impact upon Europe and its empires overseas, this culture later became a seminal force in the making of modern civilization. Judaism, which was nowhere a state religion (except in the land of the Khazars in the 9th–10th centuries), was the more adaptable under Islamic (and, later, Christian) rule. Psychologically, the Jews' long experience of exile and minority status eased their adaptation within Spanish Muslim society, while Christians, unused to foreign rule, mostly converted to Islam or fled to Christian Spain. Hebrew poetry expressed the cultural synthesis for which Jews aspired in the Muslim world. But as for daily usage in Jewish life, Arabic went much the same way as Greek in the Roman empire and German in Christian Europe: all were instruments of failed assimilation. Jewish attempts to identify with the culture, however superior, of a hostile people have invariably led to disillusionment. In the long term, the Jews preserved only Hebrew as the language of national memory and hope.

Hebrew poetry in Muslim Spain came out of the struggle for acculturation against Jewish inferiority in Muslim society. Until modern times, Bernard Lewis has written (1984: 102), the Jews under Islamic rule were harassed and humiliated, mocked and insulted. They paid higher taxes than Muslims; they suffered restrictive laws of inheritance; they could not carry arms. There were limitations on the animals they could ride, the buildings they could build and the places of worship they could use. They were even limited in the clothes they could wear and were obliged to wear a special emblem, the origin of the notorious yellow star. In the 10th and 11th centuries, until the Berber invasions, these disabilities were not felt as acutely in Muslim Spain as elsewhere. In fact, there were advantages in being Jewish in Andalusia at this time. Under 'Abd ar-Rahman III (912–61), Muslim Spain broke away from the Abbasid empire. It became the most powerful, richest and most culturally advanced country in 10th century Europe. Its capital, Cordoba, was one of the largest cites of the time with an estimated quarter million inhabitants. Cordoba's central library had some 400,000 volumes (Baron 1957, iv 28). The Spanish Jews at this time may have numbered no more than 60,000 (Ashtor 1979, ii 34). Yet they were concentrated in the cities, at the hub of the social, economic and political life of Muslim Spain. The creation of an independent caliphate in Spain led to the independence of its Jewish population from the declining Babylonian religious authority. Consequently, the Spanish Jews were readier than in the past to take part in the life of the wider society, to experiment culturally. A sign of this new freedom was their use, for the first time, of secular forms and genres in Hebrew verse. The literature created by Jews in this period, in some respects, brings to mind the assimilationist Haskalah literature in the early and mid-19th century. While this literature rarely suggests a burning desire to return to the land of Israel before the advent of the Messiah, it is a continual reminder of the latent nationalist power of Hebrew.

Spain at the start of the golden age had unusually propitious conditions for minorities. Most Spanish Christians were recent converts to Islam.[7] The Muslim rulers, needing minority support, including Christians, Jews, neo-Muslims and others, were sharply alive to the need to ensure a sense of

Medieval Spanish Hebrew National Poetry 115

belonging, fairness and loyalty, through a tolerant universalist Arab culture, rather than narrow exclusive Islamic rule. The court, not the mosque, was the center of this culture. The splendid court of Cordoba and, later, the courts of the splinter-kingdoms, gave scope for Jewish courtiers. Imitating their Arab colleagues, they became patrons of Hebrew poets. When the courts vanished and patronage ceased, both literatures continued to grow, even more creatively.[8] The Jews' alliance with Islamic sovereignty discouraged Jewish nationalist feeling. The golden age of Hebrew poetry thus reflected short-lived hopes of ethnic and religious diversity and long lasting political conflicts and socio-religious problems of Hispano-Arab society (Wasserstein 1985; Brann 1991).[9]

The Spanish Jews comprised an essential part of the middle class, with hardly a profession in which they were not active. Their extensive trading links, cosmopolitanism and knowledge of languages, made them invaluable as translators, courtiers and diplomats. Their talents were a rich source of revenue. The shift of power in Andalusia in the 10th century from the aristocratic elite to the middle class worked to the Jews' advantage, especially in cities such as Granada, where they formed a large minority. Hebrew poetry expressed Jewish pride and self-confidence stemming from social and economic success and political power. A point alluded to earlier should be stressed: Spain's geographic position on the frontier of Christian Europe and the great unexplored Atlantic helped break down social barriers which blocked Jewish assimilation elsewhere. The high level of cooperation and social harmony between Spanish Jews and Muslims was virtually unique in the Middle Ages and unrepeated in modern times. These conditions were not conducive to Jewish nationalism. They encouraged Jews to think of the diaspora as home rather than return to the land of Israel.

THE CULTURAL BACKGROUND OF THE GOLDEN AGE

How then did Jewish nationalism emerge among the Spanish Jews and in their poetry? As usual in Jewish cultural history, the forces of change were gradual. Medieval Hebrew poetry had a long, complex socio-linguistic germination. A number of factors in addition to those given above were of special importance in promoting a national literature, stimulating cultural imitation and competition, and in heightening sensitivity to the Hebrew language and sharpening its usage:

1 Christian biblical exegetes often undermined Jewish interpretation. They forced Jewish exegetes, many of whom wrote Hebrew poetry, to study closely the vocabulary and grammar of the Bible in order to refute the Christians and achieve a clear interpretation of the Hebrew text.

2 The Karaites, a fundamentalist Jewish sect, denied the sacred character of the Oral Law and of post-biblical Hebrew, insisting instead that authentic Judaism was confined to the literal truth of the Five Books of Moses. The dispute with the Karaites, who had much influence in the 9th and 10th centuries and after, forced their 'Rabbanite' opponents to stop their neglect of the Bible and study closely the nuances of the Hebrew text.

3 The proliferation since the late-Roman period of synagogues led to an increasing demand for original Hebrew liturgical poetry which entered the Jewish prayer book (*siddur*), the earliest editions of which were edited in the 8th or 9th centuries.[10] All the great medieval Hebrew poets wrote for the synagogue as well as for secular reading.

4 The golden age was part of a flourishing of Jewish literature – legal, homiletical, polemical, exegetical, philological as well as liturgical – in the years 900–1200 (Baron 1958, vii 136). This literature was facilitated by the reunification of the majority of the world's Jewish population under Islamic rule and by the intellectual stimulus of the rise of Islam. It was also part of a great surge in European literary activity resulting from a revolution in book manufacturing. Paper reached the Islamic empire by the end of the 8th century. Within two centuries, Spain became a world center of paper and book production.

5 The increasing split between Jews living under Muslim and Christian rule made vital the use of Hebrew in contacts between the two groups as this was often their only shared language.

6 The explosion in the use of Arabic and the growth of Islamic court culture, in which Arabic was used in the 8th and 9th centuries, led to the enrichment of the Arabic language and high valuation of correct grammar, stylistic excellence and beautiful calligraphy:

> 'Perhaps in no period in human history did preoccupation with the correctness and purity of the spoken and written language become such a deep concern of the educated classes as during the Islamic Renaissance'.
>
> (Baron 1958, vii 4)

Muslims believed that the stylistic excellence of the Koran proved its divine inspiration and truth. Jews had a similar belief about the Hebrew Bible. As the first fully bilingual group of Jewish writers, Hebrew poets of Muslim Spain knew Arabic and the Koran, though as infidels were discouraged from writing Arabic. They preserved the rabbinic belief that Hebrew is superior to all languages, being more ancient and beautiful but, above all, the language in which God revealed himself in the Bible. These poets revolted against the eastern style of Hebrew poetry associated with Saadia Gaon, with its flood of enigmatic talmudic and midrashic allusions. Instead, they favoured clear biblical language. The rediscovery of ancient Greek learning, philosophy and rhetoric (in which Jewish writers, often translators from Arabic to Latin, were intermediaries) further influenced Spanish Hebrew poetry, often via Arabic and its poetry.

POETRY, THE COURT AND ISLAM

The pre-eminent importance attached to poetry in the Islamic empire was the single main catalyst for Hebrew poetry, which was enriched immeasurably in imitation of and competition with Arabic poetry. This influence was not mutual, however: non-Jewish Arabic readers did not usually read Hebrew, and contemporary Hebrew poetry was apparently not widely translated into Arabic. Still, the high status of the art of Hebrew poetry among the Spanish Jews at this time was probably unique in Jewish history. Whole cities, such as Lucena and Seville, were known as 'cities of poetry'. Court life brought into being the professional Hebrew poet, employed by Jewish courtiers such as the physician and statesman Hasdai ibn Shaprut (c. 905–c. 970), whose influence in the court of the above-mentioned 'Abd ar-Rahman III made him the natural leader of the Jews in Muslim Spain. Imitating Arab courtiers, ibn Shaprut became the patron of scholars and poets. These included the two Hebrew poets who created the artistic basis for the golden age: Menahem ibn Saruq (c. 910–c. 970) and Dunash ben Labrat (?–c. 970). Neither had outstanding poetic gifts. Yet, ben Labrat revolutionized Hebrew poetry by imitating the quantitative metres and secular themes of Arabic poetry. He was also the first to criticize the artificiality of forcing Hebrew verse into Arabic prosody and the blasphemy of using the Holy Tongue for secular purposes. This criticism reached its bitterest expression in the writings of Judah Halevi. The golden age ironically began and ended with blasts against new-fangled Hebrew imitations of Arabic, with the further irony that this criticism was also imitative. The Arabs frequently complained of Arabic poetry of the Cordoba caliphate: as a reflection of the artificiality and corruption of court life, the abuse of artists as mere functionaries flattering their patrons, sycophantically toeing the party line. Hebrew imitation of Islamic aesthetic norms represents on one level increasing assimilation of Iberian Jews and an evident lack of interest in active Jewish nationalism. Yet, the very fact that Spanish Jewish poets wrote in Hebrew – even with the aim of acculturation under Islam – inadvertently had a national significance. Thematically, Hebrew poets were drawn to Zion, even as they learned to mime Arabic literary conventions. The first known medieval Hebrew wine song, by Dunash, echoes both the *Song of Songs* and the typical temptations of sensuous Arabic verse:

> Drink vintage wine
> in an orchard of myrrh, lilies, henna, aloes,
> pomegranates, palms, tamarisks and vines,
> as fountains gush singers sing,
> lutes and flutes, lyre-strings –

118 *Medieval Spanish Hebrew National Poetry*

The poet cannot live this sybaritic life:

> You left off study of God's Torah
> to have fun – while jackals prowl Zion's ruins!
> How can we, despised, drink wine –
> for we are nothing ...[11]

Though overlaid with religious guilt, this poetry also anticipates the largely secular character of modern Hebrew poetry and its Greek influences, especially in the work of Tchernichowsky.[12]

The attractiveness of Jewish nationalism increased when the Umayyad empire fell and splinter-kingdoms replaced it in the first half of the 11th century. This upheaval galvanized both Hebrew and Arabic literature. The technical and thematic revolution of the 10th century was now harnessed to a radical change in psychological outlook and sensibility. For a brief period, both literatures created poetry of exceptional artistic quality, if not genius. In Hebrew, this change led ultimately back to Zion.

The Jews had mastered the dominant high culture of the early Middle Ages and gained entrée into the highest social and political circles at the zenith of the Umayyad caliphate. Now they realized that their position under Muslim rule in Spain was untenable. Precisely at this moment – in the first half of the 11th century – the Jews reached the high point of their political power and cultural achievement between the destruction of the Second Temple and modern times. Why was this so? One explanation is that the Jews, as part of a society in chaos, were liberated for a while from the normal social shackles of being Jewish in the medieval world. The Hebrew poet was, to an extent, temporarily free of social constraint and able to use advances in Hebrew poetry to find an original poetic voice. Like Van Gogh's sunflowers, this golden Hebrew culture was dying, and dying in the very poetry which was its brightest sign of life.

The destruction of court society centralized in Cordoba meant the end of 'official' court poetry. It freed the individual poet, Muslim and Jew, to explore personal emotion as a subject worthy of poetry (Monroe 1975: 21). This liberation prepared the way for the deeply personal poetry of Halevi, including his laments for Zion. The social anarchy described in the poetry of Hanagid and Gabirol belongs specifically to the 11th century. The following lines by Gabirol, though typically they echo a biblical passage (Micah 7:6), could not describe 10th century Andalusia, when the caliphate was strong. They are a grim picture of the chaos, civil strife and despair in Andalusia after the caliphate fell apart:

> Man has no joy on earth:
> Slave murders master.
> Servant girls attack their queen.
> Son strikes parents.
> Daughter does the same.
> Friend, the best remedy I know – madness.[13]

The social stratification in Muslim Spain, already greatly weakened in the 10th century, was largely swept aside. The splinter-kingdoms, battling among themselves, sought allies – Jews and Christians alike – where they could find them. As a result, Jews could take part in Islamic society to a degree unknown in Islamic history and unrepeated since. The collapse of the caliphate meant that Arabic poets such as ibn Hazm (994–1064) and ibn Zaidun (1003–1071) and their contemporary Hebrew poets Hanagid and Gabirol could give new emphasis in their poetry on the individual sensibility as well as its technical mastery. The following lines by ibn Hazm, for example, strike a new note in Arabic poetry:

> I am seen as a youth desperate with love,
> my heart broken, my spirit troubled. By whom?
> Men glance at me and know,
> but on closer look are left in doubt.
> I am like clear handwriting, meaning obscure,
> like a dove cooing every which way
> in its little forest, delighting the ear
> with its melody, its meaning untapped...
> A girl once loved me, I surprised her with a kiss:
> That kiss was my only life, however long my life is.[14]

In the poetry of ibn Zaidun, too, true feeling counts more than the artifice of court life. Most of ibn Zaidun's poems were inspired by his love for an Umayyad princess in the last days of the caliphate and for some time after. His poems of lost love recreate a vanished world in deeply personal tones:

> Yes, I remembered you, longed for you, as you were
> in az-Zahara', the sky blue, earth alight,
> the evening breeze languid with pity for me.
> And the garden smiled. A day like the lost pleasure time
> we thieved our nights away as fortune slept.
> Flowers caught our eye, bent with dew as if in tears
> for my sleeplessness.[15]

In the poetry of ibn Zaidun, Arabic poetry reached a peak of artistic perfection, 'the last flowering of an original and personal lyrical [Arabic] poetry before modern times' (Hourani 1991: 194).[16] The same was true of ibn Zaidun's Jewish contemporaries, whose best work is unequalled until modern times.

HANAGID AND GABIROL

The new individual voice of Arabic poetry reached Hebrew with lasting impact in the poetry of Hanagid. Hanagid had a varied and interesting life and career, though what is known of him can be summed up in a few lines.

As well as being the first major Hebrew poet of the golden age, he was also an important rabbi, the leader of the Granada Jewish community, ultimately first citizen of Granada as vizier (from 1027) and minister of war (from 1038) and commander of the Berber Muslim army for nearly two decades of almost constant war. He reportedly never lost a battle.

The complexity of Hanagid's career and the extent of his power are themselves the clearest indication of the new life chances which opened to Jews in Muslim Spain after the fall of the caliphate. The formative trauma of Hanagid's early manhood was, in fact, the end of the caliphate – the horrific siege of Cordoba, his hometown, by the Berbers. This siege lasted for several years until the Umayyad capital fell in 1013. Exiled from his native city, Hanagid was an eyewitness of the appalling effects of the fall of the caliphate and the civil wars which followed. His rise to power in Granada was, paradoxically, made possible by the very fact of his being Jewish. Jewish nationalism in any political sense evidently meant little to him. His immediate wholehearted loyalty was to the kingdom of Granada, and this was also in the interests of the Jewish community. The Spanish Jews, representing the economic strength of the middle class, helped create a precarious stability in the balance of power between the Berber rulers and the Arab aristocratic elite. Yet again, the fact that Hanagid's verse was in Hebrew, not Arabic, suggests deeper religious feelings and cultural loyalty. When Hanagid saw how the neighboring Christian powers began what amounted to a protection racket by which the fragile Muslim kingdoms obtained military aid against their Muslim rivals, the poet called for the renewal of his people as he cursed the Christians in impeccable metre and rhyme:

> Evil queen, cease your reign!
> Reign instead, hated Jews,
> long asleep on bed of pain.
> Wake! There's medicine for you,
> and recompense for being true.[17]

The fascination of Hanagid lies in the contradictions of general and poet, leader of an Arab army and head of the Granada Jewish community, public man and tough individualist, religious Jew and secular poet. Hebrew war poetry was a rarity for over a thousand years prior to Hanagid. The harsh directness of his war poems had not appeared in Hebrew since the Bible and was not to appear again until the 20th century, when most Hebrew poets have also been soldiers:

> I stationed a regiment in a fortress
> destroyed long ago in war.
> There we slept, below us the dead ...
> If they woke to life, they'd kill us
> and take everything we have.
> It's God's own truth, by tomorrow
> we'd all be stone-cold as they.[18]

The kingdom of Seville was Granada's main rival. Many of Hanagid's poems describe wars which he fought against Seville. Although Hanagid commanded a Muslim army, he writes as though Jews are at war with the infidel, not Muslims fighting against Muslims. (He never mentions, incidentally, that there were Jews in the armies against which he fought.) Instead, his victories are the victories of God in the Bible.

> In Seville they did evil to the Jews – conspiracy, weapons, chains –
> to murder Jewish mothers and babies,
> rich and poor alike.
>
> We laughed at their king for his arrogant speech.
> We crossed the border to avenge our people,
> swarming locust-like, our warriors savage as lions ...
>
> God tied their hands with rope, their hearts too.
> They stumbled over their chariots,
> their horses' chains on their feet.
>
> In a word, he broke them as a weaver snaps thread.
> Famous warriors in chains, dragged before the king –
> at his will they lived or died.
>
> I was faint at the bloody torture,
> the pampered foot stabbed with thorns,
> warriors' corpses tossed on a pile.[19]

The Arabs led by Hanagid were not so secular as to overcome their prejudice against him as an infidel Jew, damned to perdition. Neither were they so devout as to shirk from the leadership of an inordinately gifted Jew. As a prominent figure in the Granada court, Hanagid had his Jewish retinue, including the young Gabirol who seems to have admired Hanagid's poetry as well as his statesmanship. In a panegyric for Hanagid, Gabirol compares him with his namesake, the prophet Samuel:

> Wisdom-seeker, delver into her mysteries
> to gather her from exile,
> making her treasures his,
> her silver and gold.[20]

To Gabirol, Hanagid was a model of the synthesis to which he aspired between Arab culture and the Jewish tradition. As a poet, however, Gabirol went much further than Hanagid in using the new-found freedom of Andalusian poetry. Whereas much of Hanagid's poetry is outgoing and public, Gabirol's is deeply personal. The sadness and loneliness in Gabirol's poetry is unparalleled in any other medieval Hebrew poet. His works reflect not only his physical illnesses and mental tortures but also – a stage toward the renewal of Jewish national feeling – his awareness that the hoped-for cultural synthesis between Jews and Muslims in Spain was a pipe dream:

> I am buried – not in a desert but in my house,
> my coffin. I agonize, orphaned of mother and father,
> brotherless. Young, alone, poor. Thought
> is my only friend. My tears are stirred in blood and wine,
> thirsting for a friend –
> I will die before that thirst is quenched.
> The heavens block my yearning.
> Alien am I to all.[21]

> If you want to join the man forever young,
> as your soul gutters by the underworld's flame –
> mock worldly things, be not the fool
> of wealth and honour, a son to have your name.
>
> Value poverty and humility, then die
> as Seled did, with no son.
> Try to know your soul well. It alone
> will live when skin and flesh are gone.[22]

Gabirol's fears were borne out by the execution of his patron, Yekutiel ben Isaac ibn Hassan, in 1039. It is recorded in the following lyric:

> See the sun red-cloaked at dusk,
> stripping itself of north and south,
> dressing itself crimson,
> leaving the land naked, to sleep
> in night's dark shelter.
>
> Then the sky went black as a sack
> for the death of Yekutiel.[23]

In the face of outrage to his body, his soul and his social world, Gabirol retreats to his infinitely gentle, suffering spirit, to a dialogue with soul or Creator. The poet is trapped in a shifting no-man's land in the long religious war between Muslims and Christians, in which the Jews are losers. Terrified, he calls to God, the beloved in rabbinic interpretations of the Song of Songs:

> Open the gate, my love!
> Get up, open the gate!
> I tremble in terror. Mother's slave,
> Hagar, mocked me in her arrogance,
> for God heard her son Ishmael's cry.
> In the dead of night

Medieval Spanish Hebrew National Poetry   123

the wild-ass Muslims chased me,
the wild-boar Christians trampled me.
When my exile's end was fixed
my heartache grew worse.
No one can explain – and I am dumb.[24]

SOCIAL BREAKDOWN IN ANDALUSIA AND HEBREW CREATIVITY

The pessimism of Gabirol's poetry foreshadowed the end of Andalusian Jewry under Muslim rule and Halevi's laments for Zion. In 1066, Hanagid's son Joseph, who had succeeded him as vizier of Granada, was murdered. In one of the earliest pogroms in European history, several thousand Jews in Granada were murdered. An Arabic poem by Abu Ishaq helped to trigger the pogrom. It incited Badis ibn Habbus, king of Granada, to wipe out Jewish influence in the Granada government:

This was Badis' fatal mistake, making our enemy rejoice:
Not Muslim but Jew he made his minister.
Now the Jews are not just low-down:
They're arrogant, insolent too.
They got more than they ever dreamed of,
ignoring Muslims dying in misery.
How many noble Muslims are brought low
before this wretched monkey-Jew![25]

It is possible to see this poem and the pogrom which followed as a turning point in the history of the Andalusian Jews, a warning that they lived on an live volcano:

'The slaughter in Granada showed them the tenuousness of their position in alien lands. Over the generations they had come to believe [sic] that they were as much citizens of Spain as were the Muslims and Christians, the Andalusians and Arabs, the Berbers and Slavs – now it was clear: Spain was a land of exile as were all the other diasporas'.
(Ashtor 1979, ii 191)

As in Russia 700 years later, anti-Jewish violence in Muslim Spain was a gauge of general political and social instability, not only in the splinter-kingdoms that sprang from the ruins of the Umayyad empire but in the Islamic world as a whole as the balance of power between Muslims and Christians shifted to the clear advantage of the Christians. The lack of strong central authority in the Arab empire led to political breakdown and to Christian military success, in Spain and the Holy Land. The Christians won control of trade in the Mediterranean. The Muslims lost economic power in lands controlled by Islam. The defeats in Spain and the Holy Land at the end of the 11th century were not just military blows. They were also unprecedented religious and psychological setbacks to Islam. They led to growing fanaticism among the Muslims, which increasingly soured relations between Muslims and Jews and stirred up Jewish national longing. To devout Muslims, the integration of Jews within Spanish Muslim society was a sign of defeat, even of moral decline and corruption. After the fall of Toledo in 1085, the splinter-kingdoms invited the Almoravid Berbers to cross the strait of Gibraltar to save them from the Christian infidel. In 1086 the Berbers defeated the Christian army of Alfonso VI of Castile at Sagrajas. Between 1090–1102 they ended the disunity which had prevailed since 1031. They seized Andalusia and made it a province of their North African empire. This military feat led to the migration of most Andalusian Jews to Christian Spain. Unexpectedly, it heralded an Indian summer of Hebrew poetry, and a turn to Zion.

MOSES IBN EZRA AND JUDAH HALEVI

Hanagid and Gabirol were wholly Andalusian poets in the time of the splinter-kingdoms and civil wars, but after the Almoravid invasion they were exiled to Christian Spain.[26] Unlike Halevi, and despite maltreatment by the Andalusian Muslims, ibn Ezra remained nostalgic for the Andalusia of his youth. No other Hebrew poet applied so expertly Arabic metrics, themes and images to Hebrew.[27] The following poem, for example, bears an Arabic imprint in its meter (in the Hebrew ABCBDB), its imagery and feeling:

> Let man always know
> unto death he moves.
> As day to night creeps past
> he may think he is at rest –
> at rest on a boat
> flying in the wind.[28]

Ibn Ezra's affection for Andalusia evidently grew as he discovered the pains of being a stranger and a Jew in Christian Spain. In one of his poems, the world is a mother with a stillborn child in her belly and a dying child on her back. He might have been thinking of his own life.[29] To ibn Ezra as to Gabirol, poetry consoles the poet and his readers. He invites the heartsick to seek medicine for their grief in the garden of his poems:

> Compared to my songs honey is bitter
> incense stinks: these poems make the deaf hear

the stammerer speak, the blind see,
the lame run. The grieving, the heartsick,
those who cry bitterly find joy in them.³⁰

To Halevi, his protegé, ibn Ezra poured out his heart, revealing his feelings of betrayal and depression:

I dwell among wolves for whom
the word human means nothing.³¹

Ibn Ezra's destination as a wanderer in his poetry remained uncertain, but Halevi's unhappiness in Spain drove him to think with longing of Zion. Yet, as among many modern Zionists, even his Zionism was filled with love for his native land. He vainly entreated ibn Ezra in verse to return to Muslim Spain:

How can I find peace with you gone?
My heart beats after you.
If I left off waiting for your return
I'd die. Look, the mountains of our separation
testify: clouds are cheap with rain. I cry buckets.
Come back to Muslim Spain, lamp of Muslim Spain.
Make your mark on every heart and hand.
Pure of speech among the stammerers:
Why spread Hermon's dew on cursed Gilead?³²

Halevi was born in Tudela, then under Muslim rule, near the Christian border. As a young man, he came south to Granada where he met Ibn Ezra. The Almoravid invasion drove him to Toledo, recently (1085) captured by the Christians, where he worked as a doctor. After the Toledo Jews were set on by a bloodthirsty mob in 1109 and his patron was murdered, Halevi came back to Andalusia. He lived in Cordoba for some thirty years. When the Almohads invaded southern Spain, he set out for the Holy Land. It is not known if he reached his destination.

The two decisive events in Halevi's life were the Almoravid invasion of Andalusia in 1090 and the Christian conquest of the Holy Land in 1099. The first aroused his disillusionment with Muslim Spain – indeed, with any form of gentile rule – and the second aroused his yearning for messianic redemption and the return to the land of Israel. To the North African scholar, Rabbi Habib, Halevi confessed in a letter that 'Greece and its wisdom have drowned me in thick black grease; Islam and Arabic have blackened me; Christianity has torn me apart, destroyed me' (Brann 1991: 90). In poetic dialogues between the Congregation of Israel and God (the Lover), again based on the Midrash on the Song of Songs, Halevi confesses the torment of entrapment between two rival religions and frustration that Jerusalem, 'my palace', was now ruled by the Crusaders:

> Friend – suffering forces me to live
> with viper and scorpion, captive.
> Pity me!
>
> I despair of sunrise.
> Day by day I cannot hope.
>
> What can I say, lover?
>
> Crusaders, freeborn, in Jerusalem, my palace,
> while I slave for Arab and Christian –
> a dog in their tormenting hands.[33]
>
> Lover, have you forgot how you lay between my breasts?
> Why have you sold me for all time?
> Did I not follow you in the wilderness?
> Let the mountains be my witnesses –
> Seir and Paran, Sinai and Sin!
> My love was yours, you wanted just me –
> how can you share yourself with others?
> I am crushed by the Persians,
> scorched by the Greeks,
> thrust among Christians, driven among Muslims:
> Is there a savior but you?
> A prisoner of hope but me?
> Give me your power, I'll give you my love![34]

The suffering of the people of Israel is seen by the poet as an expiation for sin. Israel takes almost masochistic pleasure in its persecution – this is God's will, but it is also God's will to free his people as he did in the past:

> Since you became love's home,
> my loves are pitched by you.
> My enemies' curse makes me glad.
> Let them curse me – as you did.
> They learned to hate from you
> and I love them – they hound the one you hurt.
> The day you scorned me I felt the same.
> How can I love the one you hate?
> Till your fury goes and you free again
> your people whom you freed from Egypt.[35]

The conquest of the Holy Land by the Crusaders after four and a half centuries of Muslim rule was a disaster to the Jewish communities there (as of those in Europe). Yet it also awakened in the diaspora the Jewish hope of return to the land of Israel at a time when most Jews still lived in the Middle East. The memory of Hanagid's military genius was still green: was Jerusalem's conquest by Christians not a sign of imminent redemption? Halevi's messianic hope was roused, too, by the rise of the Almohads in the second and third decades of the 12th century. Halevi's decision to go to the Holy Land, to which his poetry points as inevitable, was part of a general religious upsurge in the early 12th century. Like earlier invaders, the Almohads were a fanatical North African Berber tribe. However, they were a messianic movement, their founder revered as the savior, destined to restore Islam to the true path and create a kingdom of heaven on earth. The Almohads were, in fact, the last gasp of the Islamic empire which had ruled Andalusia since 711. They ended Andalusian Jewish life under Islam when they invaded in 1140. Halevi's contemporary, Abraham ibn Ezra, escaped to Egypt where he heard of the massacres in Spain and responded with a lament:

> How has Cordoba been abandoned, a sea of ruin –
> its wise, powerful men dead of hunger and thirst!
> Not a single Jew left in Jaén and Almeria ...[36]

Halevi's poems of longing for Zion are among the best-known Hebrew poems outside the Bible. Yet they belong to no genre or tradition. Rather they are the response of one unusually gifted poet to a decisive crisis in medieval Jewish life. They express nostalgia not just for a Zion that Halevi had never seen – and which had never existed except in the world of Jewish legend – but also, implicitly, for a lost, once powerful and splendid Andalusia in which great hopes and illusions had died.[37] In these poems, a western voice speaks at a time when the demographic process that was to bring most Jews westward was not yet completed. For brief moments, Hebrew, engaging the obsession closest to its heart, breaks out of the shackles of Arabic ornamentation and speaks with real individuality and passion.

In contrast with most medieval Hebrew poetry, the longing and searching of the Zion poems were not literary conventions. They expressed feelings of an ageing poet, driving him to leave Spain for the land of Israel. The plangent, questing mood of the Zion poems seems to pervade Halevi's work, the secular love poems as well as the liturgical ones.

> Ophrah washes her clothes in my tears.
> She spreads them in the sunshine of her life.
> She has no need of fountains,
> nor sun to beautify her light.[38]

> Time's slaves – slaves of slaves,
> but God's servant is free.

For his part in life man prays:
My part in you I see.³⁹

God, where can I find you,
hidden in heaven on high?
And where can I not find you –
you fill the universe with glory!⁴⁰

CONCLUSION

Halevi left Spain in 1140 (he died a year or two later), the Almohads conquered Andalusia, and the Spanish Jews and Hebrew poetry were exiled. Then, by the start of the 13th century, the Almohads were themselves defeated by Christian armies, and the empire of Islam was driven from western Europe. And so, we see now, the flowering of Hebrew poetry in the years 1031–1140 was the final creation of a dying empire that had made Spain the cultural center of the Western world. It was a long goodbye of a minority once integrally a part of this empire, whose alienation and decline – and its turn from assimilation to Jewish nationalism in despair – marked the empire's fall. Halevi to some extent broke with the artificiality of Arabic rhetoric and thematic conventions, 'the emphasis on the manner of saying a thing rather than on the meaningful content' (Watt 1984: 48). Halevi's Zion poems, though a step down from a more glorious literary past, mark a turning point in Jewish socio-cultural history. However much influenced by secular Arabic poetry and lifestyle, Hebrew poets wanted to assert firm loyalty to the Jewish faith. They wrote Hebrew poetry because, despite the inherent artificiality of its adopted poetics, it was best capable of expressing their strongest feelings. In Hebrew, this poetry could be widely read only by Jews. At the same time, it was an act of cultural synthesis, of alliance and mimicry, of assimilation and competition. Enthusiasm for this assimilationist ideal might have led some Hebrew poets to adopt, at times, a secular voice alien to them.

Symptomatic of the twisted state of Jewish–Muslim relations of the latter part of the 'golden age' is the fact that the most famous Jewish philosophical work of this period, Halevi's *Kuzari*, written in Arabic in the early 12th century, was a defense of the allegedly inferior religion Judaism. More than this, 'The *Kuzari* was a glorification of rabbinic Judaism and an unabashed statement of nationalism, very much in the modern sense of the word' (Stillman 1979: 60). In one passage, the Rabbi extols the land of Israel to the King of the Khazars:

> 'Moses prayed to see [the land of Israel]; he considered it a misfortune when this was denied him, and as an act of grace, when the land was shown to him from the summit of Pisgah, Persians, Indians, Greeks,

and other nations begged to have sacrifices offered and prayers to be said for them in that Holy House, and they spent their wealth on it, though they believed in other religions, since the true religion did not admit them. Today, also, the country is honoured, although the Shekinah no longer appears in it; all nations make pilgrimages to it, long for it – excepting we ourselves, being oppressed and homeless'.

The King of the Khazars asks in reply why Jews do not return to the Holy Land:

'If this be so, thou fallest short of thy religious duty, by not endeavouring to reach that place, and making it thy abode in life and death, although thou sayest: [in the synagogue blessings concluding the Torah readings] 'Have mercy on Zion, for it is the house of our life', and thou believest that the Shekinah will return thither'.

(Halevi 1947: 68–9)

The defense of Judaism in the *Kuzari* and its declaration that the Jews had a duty to return to Zion might have been unnecessary if the Jews had been accepted as equals in Arab society. Especially after the pogrom in Granada in 1066, it was clear that the Jews were not tolerated in positions of power under Muslim rule.

The artificiality of Hebrew poetry might be seen in this light as an inadvertent enactment of the artificiality and awkwardness of Jewish life under Muslim rule in medieval Spain. Hebrew poets were most completely freed from this artifice when, caught among the warring fragments of the Umayyad empire and in a 'holy war' of Christians and Muslims, they could no longer see Spain as a 'new Zion'. In much Hebrew poetry emerging from this crisis, bitter despondency toward Arab society was implicitly far greater than that toward any aspect of Judaism. Jewish acculturation in Muslim Spain was based on the assumption of a realizable parity within a tolerant, essentially secular Arabic civilization. The fall of the Umayyad empire led, instead, to a failure of Arab universalism and a resurgence of Islamic religious militancy in which the Jews were seen as part of the problem of the empire's decline. The nationalist undercurrent in Hebrew poetry may be seen as a reaction to this exclusivist zealotry.

In the *Kuzari*, Halevi argues that the Jews are distinguished above all other peoples through their capacity to receive divine prophecy. Only in the land of Israel could they fulfil their prophetic destiny. Such open religious nationalism is not found among the great earlier poets of the golden age Hanagid and Gabirol, who lived prior to the Almoravids and the First Crusade. The fervor of Halevi's Zionism betrays the poet's disillusionment with Muslim Spain and evident hope that the Crusader conquest of the Holy Land from the Muslims by 1099 was a prelude to messianic redemption and the return to Zion. Hebrew poetry in the half-century between the First

Crusade and the Almohad invasion expresses nagging unease and, at times, despair of Spain. Hebrew poets of this period created an ideal alternative world in their poetry. In so doing, they were part of a Continent-wide phenomenon by which the conflict between Islam and Christian Europe stimulated the growth of languages and national cultures.[41] They also anticipate an independent secular modern Hebrew literature, part of the resurgence of Jewish nationalism in the late 19th century.[42]

NOTES

1. The commentary of Rashi (c. 1040–1105), the most important Jewish commentator on the Bible and Talmud, who lived in France, dates from the same period as Halevi's poems of Zion. His gloss on the opening of Genesis suggests a Jewish nationalistic aim similar to that of Judah Halevi. The two evidently never heard of one another but were deeply affected by the First Crusade.
2. Bilingual selections of medieval Hebrew poetry include Carmi (1981) and Scheindlin (1986, 1991). For a general history of the Jews in Muslim countries, see Gilbert (2010). For a brief but comprehensive introduction to medieval Hebrew poetry by an important modern Hebrew poet, see Pagis (1970). Also, see Goldstein (1965) and Stillman (1979). Texts are taken mostly from Schirmann (1959).
3. Translated from the Hebrew (*Libi be-mizrach*) by David Aberbach, as are all translations in this chapter, unless indicated otherwise. For the Hebrew original, see Schirmann (i 489).
4. From the poem beginning '*Zion, ha-lo tishali ...*' (ibid., 485–6).
5. On changes in the balance of power in the conflict between Islam and Christian Europe, see chapter 3 (this volume).
6. '*Akhen sar mar ha-mavet ...*' in Carmi (1981: 303).
7. On conversion to Islam in medieval Spain, see Glick (1979). From a sociological viewpoint, Spain was unique in a number of other ways: in having been a Roman province, then later becoming an undifferentiated province of Western Christianity, and in having undergone Germanic conquest, with the result that 'Even the Christians displayed a degree of assimilation that is scarcely paralleled in the east' (Crone and Cook 1977: 115).
8. On the creativity of Arabic and Hebrew poetry after the collapse of the Umayyad caliphate in the 11th century, see p. 119ff.
9. The complexity of early medieval Spanish society and the potential advantage of being Jewish in Spain is summed up by Brann: 'Abd ar-Rahman III's Umayyad predecessors repeatedly sought to exert Cordoba's centralizing authority over a territory and population torn by numerous tribal, ethnic, and social cleavages, socio-economic and religious struggles, and factional rivalries: Arabs battled with Berbers, Syrian Arabs quarreled with Yemenis, and Arab Muslims competed with native Iberian neo-Muslims and their descendants (Ar. *muwalladun*). The *saqaliaba* or 'Slavs', praetorian guards of diverse European origin, brought to Spain as slaves at a young age, were involved in revolts against Umayyad authority as well as Mozarabic Christians, not without considerable ambivalence, occasionally resisted the idea of living with an Islamic polity. Under such complex and unpredictably shifting political circumstances, it is easy to

appreciate why the Jewish community, which had no stake in the various internecine disputes among Muslims and which could be neither accused of harboring a subversive allegiance to any sovereign power nor suspected of entertaining an obligation to any anti-Umayyad cause, might have warranted the trust of the Umayyads' (1991: 4). The diversity in Muslim Spain was, at the same time, part of the wider unified Islamic empire: 'It is precisely this pattern of regional disjunction within a broader context of fundamental social unity, as part of the universal society of Islam, which marks Iberian Islam from start to finish' (Wasserstein 1985: 294).

10. On the history of the Hebrew prayerbook, see Reif (1993). On national elements in the prayerbook, see Aberbach (2006).
11. '*ve-Omer al tishan ...?*' Schirmann (i 34, 35). On the echo from the book of Lamentations, see p. 43.
12. On the ambivalence to Hellenism in Jewish culture, see Leoussi and Aberbach (2002).
13. '*Ve-lev navuv ...*' in Schirmann (i 230–1).
14. From Monroe (1975: 174–5). The translation of this and the other Arabic verse quoted below has been revised by David Aberbach.
15. From Arberry (1965: 114–5).
16. For a more detailed argument that the most original Arabic poetry was written in its earliest phase, in the 9th–11th centuries, see Giffen (1971).
17. The opening words of the poem, *Malkah resha'ah* (Evil queen, i.e., Christian Spain), are apparently a play on *malkhut resha'ah* (evil kingdom) which in the Talmud (e.g., *Berakhot* 61b) describes Rome. See Schirmann (i 146). The collected poems of Hanagid are edited by Jarden (1966). For a bilingual edition of Hanagid's poetry by Hillel Halkin, see Hanagid (2000).
18. '*Halinoti gedud ...*' in Schirmann (i 132).
19. The imagery and language in this poem ('*Ha-li ta'as bekhol shanah ...*' in Schirmann i 95, 96) owe much to the book of Nahum.
20. '*Mi zot kemo shachar ...*' in Schirmann (i 206).
21. '*Nihar be-kori groni ...*' (*ibid.*, 207).
22. For the text of '*Im te'ehav lihyot be-anshe Kheled ...*', see Jarden (1975: 33). Schirmann (i 231) has *lihyot* (to be) rather than *likhyot* (to live).
23. Schirmann (i 202) dates this poem ('*Re'eh shemesh ...*') 1039–40. Halevi also experienced the violent loss of his patron. See p. 125.
24. Schirmann (i 243) notes the biblical references in this poem ('*Sha'ar petah ...*'): Genesis 16:12, 21:17, Psalms 80:14 with its gloss in *Lev. Rab.* 13, 'The pig is Edom' [i.e., Rome].
25. From Monroe (1975: 206–7).
26. For a poem on ibn Ezra's flight from Granada, see Schirmann (i 379).
27. For a literary study of Ibn Ezra's poetry, see Pagis (1970).
28. '*Yizkor gever ...*' in Schirmann (i 401).
29. '*Pnei ha-El levad ...*' (*ibid.*, 402).
30. '*Kol ish deveh levav ...*' (Aberbach 2008a: 51).
31. Translated by Gabriel Levin (1992:36).
32. '*Ech aharecha emtza margo'a ...*' in Schirmann (i 461–2).
33. '*Yodi, hefitzuni yeme oni ...*' (*ibid.*, i 482).
34. '*Yedidi, hashakhahta ...*' (*ibid.*, i 466–7).
35. '*Me'az me'on ahavah ...*' (*ibid.*, i 467–8).

36. 'Aha yarad ...' (ibid., i 570)
37. See, for example, Schirmann (i 386, 460), where Halevi describes Andalusia in biblical language reminiscent of his poems of Zion. Halevi's hope that messianic redemption from what he describes as arrogant and oppressive Muslim rule would occur in 1130 is expressed in the poem beginning 'Namta ve-nirdamta ...' (ibid., 480).
38. 'Ophrah tekhabes ...' (ibid., i 439).
39. 'Avdei zeman ...' (ibid., i 521).
40. 'Yah, ana emtza'akha ...' (ibid., i 524).
41. On the Crusades and their stimulus of local nationalism and vernacular languages, see p. 94ff., 104.
42. On modern Hebrew national poetry, which accompanied the rise of political Zionism, see pp. 175–6, 181–2, ch. 10.

5 Poetry of the British Isles
History, Myth and Nationalism*

RISE, Britons, rise, if manhood be not dead …
(Tennyson)

English poetry, rooted in myth and history transformed to myth, helped define the modern concept of national identity. Conversion to Christianity by the 7th century and the growth of Old English, which has the oldest Western European literature in the vernacular, ensured Britain's cultural distinctiveness. The high status of early medieval English vernacular, unprecedented elsewhere in Europe, is evident already in Bede's *Ecclesiastical History* (732), in the reverent story of how the illiterate farm labourer Caedmon became a poet: he dreamt of being called to sing of the Creation of all things and did so not in Latin, which he did not know, but in English. History set the course of British national poetry. Medieval England absorbed much foreign influence through invasion and conquest: by Germanic tribes (5th century), the Danes (9th century) and the Normans (1066), the Reformation and the wars with France and Spain, the English Civil War and the Restoration, the French Revolution and Napoleonic wars and the two world wars in the 20th century.

The poetry of the British isles seems to reach artistic peaks in moments of heightened national self-awareness, when independence is threatened or lost, whether because of foreign invasion or internal wars or disasters. The battle of Maldon fought against the Viking invaders in 991 is commemorated in a magnificent Old English poetic fragment culminating in the death of the old warrior Byrhtwold. Raising shield and shaking spear, he emboldens his men with dying breath:[1]

> Hige sceal þē heardra,   heorte þē cēnre,
> mōd sceal þē māre,   þē ūre mægen lȳtlað.
>
> (Strength fails, spirit must be firmer,
> heart bolder, courage greater.)

Britain's greatest crisis after the Norman invasion, the Black Plague in the mid-14th century in which an estimated one-third of Europe's population died, was followed by literary flourishing, including works of Chaucer, Langland's *Piers Ploughman* and *Sir Gawain and the Green Knight*. The Reformation and the conflict with Spain are the background to much Elizabethan poetry, notably Spenser and Shakespeare.[2] The deposition and execution of Charles I, the English civil war in the 1640s and Cromwell's rule and the restoration of the monarchy in 1660 were crucial influences on Milton's poetry, especially *Paradise Lost*. In the 18th century, war with France stimulated British patriotism, and a number of poets – Collins, Gray, Goldsmith, Cowper and Smart – wrote of national issues and aspired to the role of 'my country's poet' (Griffin 2002: 292). The French Revolution and Napoleonic wars marked English poetry in the Romantic period as did the two world wars in the 20th century.

These crises and others appear in the poetry of England, Ireland, Wales and Scotland both as separate and shared histories. Each country, distinct in time of conflict with one another but in peacetime and at war with a common foe (notably France, Spain or Germany), united as parts of Great Britain. There is a significant literature in Welsh, Scottish Gaelic and Irish Gaelic, in which relations with England are a common thread. In 'The True-Born Englishman' (1701), Defoe savagely mocks what he sees as the violent indecent yokings together that created 'the mongrel half-bred race' of English identity:

> In eager rapes, and furious lust begot,
> Betwixt a painted *Briton* and a *Scot*:
> Whose gend'ring offspring quickly learnt to bow,
> And yoke their heifers to the *Roman* plough:
> From whence a mongrel half-bred race there came,
> With neither name nor nation, speech or fame
> In whose hot veins new mixtures quickly ran,
> Infus'd betwixt a *Saxon* and a *Dane*.
> While their rank daughters, to their parents just,
> Receiv'd all nations with promiscuous lust.
> This nauseous brood directly did contain
> The well-extracted blood of Englishmen ...
>
> (336–47)

This jaundiced swipe at English national identity, which recalls the prophetic denunciations of Israel as harlot (e.g., Hosea 1–2, Ezekiel 23), can paradoxically signify the nation's strength. Colley (1992) describes these lines as a 'powerful demonstration of English confidence. Far more than the Welsh and Scots felt able to do, the English could – occasionally – ridicule themselves because they had a strong sense of who they were and of their own importance' (15–16).

The British isles might have lain down a slut, as Defoe suggests, but rose a woman of valor. After centuries of turmoil and mixing, some of the greatest poets writing in English were Scottish (Byron), Irish (Yeats) and Welsh (Dylan Thomas). Monogamous nationalism exacted a price, though. By the 19th century, poetry in Welsh and Gaelic was greatly diminished by English intrusion and emigration. Nevertheless this poetry retains its power to inspire a strong, even militant, national identity.

MEDIEVAL WALES AND SCOTLAND

Memories of Welsh and Scottish independence survive in medieval poetry. Scottish poems, such as John Barbour's *The Bruce* (c. 1370) and Blind Harry's epic *Wallace* (c. 1460), record Scottish courage and defiance. Though Scotland and England have shared a monarch (since 1603) and a Parliament (1707–1999), Scotland preserves in poetry the memory of its revolt against England under Robert the Bruce and its triumph over England in 1314 in the battle of Bannockburn, after which (in 1328) England recognized Scottish independence.

Long before the loss of Welsh independence in 1282, there was a remarkable tradition of Welsh poetry, notably the *Hengerdd* (old song). Welsh history, particularly the medieval struggle against the Normans, stimulated some of its greatest poetry. Affirming Welsh national identity in Welsh was Cynddelw Brydydd Mawr's elegy for Madog ap Maredudd, prince of Powys, who died in 1160, the heroic 'hope of minstrels':

> Portcullis he was, buckler and shield,
> hero on battlefield,
> through greensward foe he flamed,
> sung by a myriad ...[3]

In the 12th and 13th centuries, Wales went from being an autonomous state under Welsh rule into a feudal vassal of England. Gruffudd ab yr Ynad Coch wrote a haunting lament for Llywelyn ap Gruffudd, last prince of independent Wales, killed by the English in 1282:

> Mine now to rage against Saxons who've wronged me,
> Mine for this death bitterly to mourn.
> Mine, with good cause, to cry protest to God
> Who has left me without him.[4]

In Wales, the annual Eisteddfod (bardic festival), which dates from 1176 when Wales was still free, has a strong nationalist character. Restarted in 1789, it keeps alive the memory of the past, and the hope of the future, Welsh independence.

ENGLISH HISTORY AND MYTH: FROM SHAKESPEARE TO TENNYSON

Mythical history and myth dominate much English poetry. English nationalism and its poetry commonly flare up in crisis. Shakespeare's history plays, for example, date mostly from the 1590s, after the defeat of the Spanish Armada in 1588, 'the years of the Spanish war at its fiercest' (Hastings 1997: 207).[5] In *Richard II* (c. 1595), John of Gaunt's dying speech (II i 40f) reminds a nation threatened with invasion of its God-given blessings and worth and its protection as an island fortress 'bound in with the triumphant sea'. In the late 16th century, as in the time of Richard II two centuries earlier, internal discord could be more dangerous to England than foreign threat, leading to 'shameful conquest of itself'. *Henry V* (c. 1599), too, reflects the national spirit of the age, stirring up the nation's fighting spirit. The king's speech at the battle of Harfleur is a classic of nationalist propaganda:

> And you, good yeomen,
> Whose limbs were made in England, show us here
> The mettle of your pasture; let us swear
> That you are worth your breeding; which I doubt not;
> For there is none of you so mean and base
> That hath not noble lustre in your eyes.
> I see you stand like greyhounds in the slips,
> Straining upon the start. The game's afoot:
> Follow your spirit; and, upon this charge
> Cry 'God for Harry! England and Saint George!'
>
> (III i 25–34)

Again, on the night before the battle of Agincourt (1415) Henry V inspires his men with a fighting national spirit:

> We few, we happy few, we band of brothers;
> For he to-day that sheds his blood with me
> Shall be my brother; be he ne'er so vile
> This day shall gentle his condition:
> And gentlemen in England, now a-bed
> Shall think themselves accurs'd they were not here,
> And hold their manhoods cheap whiles any speaks
> That fought with us upon Saint Crispin's day.
>
> (IV iii 60–67)

There is little proof that Henry V actually said anything like this, but this is what he *should* have said.

In a later age of crisis, when France threatened to invade, Coleridge in 'Fears in Solitude' (1798) declared love for Britain as a divine being, a temple of worship and love. The madonna-like national image in this poem is as far removed from reality as Defoe's slut, yet such national feelings in crisis are common.[6] In quieter, more stable periods, English poets often seem more vulnerable to doubts. As the British empire reached the height of its power in the 19th century, some English poets, such as Tennyson and Kipling, became uneasy.[7] They feared the corruption of power and imperial decline. In some cases, their poetry was a form of spiritual revitalization, providing moral guidance through British historical figures and events. Tennyson, Poet Laureate from 1850–1892, wrote a series of historical dramas, 'Queen Mary' (1875), 'Harold' (1876) and 'Becket' (1884), to illustrate the strengthening force of crisis. In poems such as 'Puck's Song' (1906), Kipling called up defining historic moments associated with spots in the English landscape:

> See you our stilly woods of oak,
> And the dread ditch beside?
> O that was where the Saxons broke
> On the day that Harold died.
>
> See you the windy levels spread
> About the gates of Rye?
> O that was where the Northmen fled,
> When Alfred's ships came by.[8]

POETRY AND HISTORICAL MYTH IN SCOTTISH NATIONALISM

The Scottish poets Macpherson, Burns and Scott have had especially strong influence on Scottish nationalism, drawing on Scotland's rich store of history and myth either to support independence from or union with England. Burns' use of myth is less apparent than that of Macpherson and Scott. The poetic fragments of the legendary 3rd century CE bard Ossian, however fraudulently presented by Macpherson in the late 18th century (Samuel Johnson derided them as 'impudent forgeries'), roused Scottish nationalism.[9] Macpherson's poetry, like that of Burns, is poetry of Scottish defiance after its defeat by England at Culloden in 1746.[10] The controversy over Ossian was not just over scholarly authenticity but over national authenticity: did Scotland have a national identity distinct from that of England? The fame of Ossian, amounting to a craze in 18th and 19th century continental Europe, brought the past alive in the nation's hopes.

Scott is unusual as at different times he hoped for Scottish independence from England and supported union with England. His deep-bred Scottish nationalism was at times neutered by his commitment to Britain and Tory politics. Scott was raised in late 18th century Edinburgh in an atmosphere of resentment for: the Treaty of Union of 1707; the Scottish defeat and humiliation in the uprising of 1745–46; bitter memories of the atrocities committed by the English army; the consequent English military presence; the proscription of Highland customs and the Highland clearances. As a child, Scott absorbed Scottish culture – the language, stories, songs, the great medieval poems and ballads, and the folk culture – from people who, in some cases, had seen or taken part in the Scottish revolt. In the introduction to Canto III of *Marmion* (1808), Scott called up childhood memories of Scottish lore and heroism:

> ... ever, by the winter hearth,
> Old tales I heard of woe or mirth,
> Of lovers' slights, of ladies' charms,
> Of witches' spells, of warriors' arms;
> Of patriot battles, won of old
> By Wallace wight and Bruce the bold;
> Of later fields of feud and fight,
> When, pouring from their Highland height,
> The Scottish clans, in headlong sway,
> Had swept the scarlet ranks away.

Scott could easily have become a revolutionary but was born too late. In 1813, after he stopped writing poetry, he confessed:

> 'I am very glad I did not live in 1745 for though as a lawyer I could not have pleaded Charles's right and as a clergyman I could not have prayed for him yet as a soldier I would I am sure against the convictions of my better reason have fought for him even to the bottom of the gallows'.
> (Scott 1932, iii 302)

In time, the bitterness of the Scottish defeat shrank. Scotland kept its own Church and legal system, which came to symbolize Scottish independence. Scott trained in law, as did many Scottish historians, philosophers, literary artists and essayists. The Scottish Enlightenment was an outburst of new-found confidence of a rational, modern people. An entire generation was transformed by the Napoleonic wars as English and Scots had an enemy in common – the French – and fought bravely and successfully side by side. The Union on paper was sealed in blood. Scott's career as a poet was almost entirely confined to the Napoleonic period, when French invasion of Britain was a constant threat. Scott's choice in *Marmion* of the Scottish defeat by England at Flodden in 1513 – 'the greatest catastrophe in Scottish history' – 'seems to have been in the service of a higher patriotism towards Britain' (Sutherland 1995: 125).[11] There is an 'extinction of Scotland' in *Marmion*. In the first Epistle, for example, instead of 'Scotland' and 'Scottish', 'Britain' and 'British' appear twelve times (and 'English' once), and the poem is pure English, with no trace of Scottish dialect (*ibid.*, 126). Had *Marmion* been published in 1758 rather than 1808, the stress would probably have been on Scottish nationalism and English villainy. The omission of Scotland seems to reflect the unification of the British isles by war with France.

Yet, Scott regretted Scotland's loss of independence. His wavering to and from Scottish nationalism continued after he turned from poetry, poleaxed by Byron's success in *Childe Harold's Pilgrimage* (1812), to the novel: the hero of *Waverley* (1814) is both Jacobite and Hanoverian and fights on both sides.

Scott's romantic Scots nationalism was watered down both by Enlightenment internationalism and by self-interested (but not bogus) loyalty to Great Britain. The strands of Scottish nationalism and commitment to Great Britain are intertwined in Scott's life and works, which themselves became an act of union. From childhood, Scott was drawn more to coarse and primitive but alive Scottish language than to the genteel, elegant English of the Enlightenment. He admired the work of Fergusson and Burns to revive Scottish poetic language. One of Scott's earliest publications, before he became a poet and novelist, was his collection of Scottish ballads *The Minstrelsy of the Scottish Border* (1802), influenced by Bishop Percy's ballad collection *Reliques of Ancient English Poetry* (1765) and by the German Romantics, by Herder and Goethe. Poetry as tool of national survival and regeneration is implicit in Scott's *The Lay of the Last Minstrel* (1805). Whoever is cold to the joy of national feeling in the minstrel's song will die 'Unwept, unhonour'd, and unsung'. Song brings health and freedom and breaks the staff of evil. When the minstrels sing their songs of the past, the evil dwarf magician is driven away. Though the poem is set in 16th century Scotland, it is alive with Scottish national feeling of the late 18th century and early 19th century when the minstrel was needed as 'an apostolic link with that period [the 16th century]' when, as Scott (anticipating Heine) put it in his 1824 essay on 'Romance', 'poets were the historians and often the priests of their society' (Sutherland 1995: 100). Scott's narrative poems helped define Scottish national identity within Great Britain as Scottish customs, speech, dress and landscape first became widely known through Scott. *The Lady of the Lake* (1810) set off a wave of Scottish tourism at a time when the Grand Tour of continental Europe was impossible because of the Napoleonic wars.

At the same time, as a successful writer, Scott became a leader of the British Establishment. His politics were High Tory, and he eventually became a baronet and – his financial coffin – laird of Abbotsford. During the war with France, he joined the Edinburgh Volunteers Light Dragoons (Burns, similarly, after early sympathy with the French Revolution, joined the Dumfries Volunteers). His military zeal was at odds with his writings, in which war is cruel and senseless. He supported Henry Dundas, Scotland's virtual ruler, despised by Scottish nationalists as a traitor. His conservatism was such that, panicked at the thought of popular revolt, he defended the Peterloo massacre in 1819. When George IV visited Scotland in 1822, Scott escorted and introduced him as the monarch of the Highland clansmen.

Scott's complex form of nationalism was not unlike that of the exiled Jews after the loss of territorial sovereignty who, while remaining scrupulously loyal to the countries where they lived, preserved a healing memory of past glory, noble battles and great men and women – but in culture, not aimed at political action. Daiches (1971) sums up the therapeutic ambivalence to Scottish nationalism in Scott's writings:

> 'Scott's aim in much of his writing was a healing one: to present the glamour of Scottish history and landscape, with the heroic violence that made part of the glamour modulated quietly into the past tense so that Scotland could be seen now as part of a peaceful and enlightened Britain' (p. 83).

THE BRITISH EMPIRE AND TENNYSON'S REVIVAL OF ARTHURIAN LEGEND

Tennyson's revival of the legends of the 5th century King Arthur, much of which came from oral tradition, coincided with the emergence of Britain as the most powerful empire in history. These legends are taken for granted as part of 'British national consciousness'. Yet, as in the case of many other mythologies, such as the *Kalevala* and the *Nibelungen*, this literature was largely forgotten until the Victorian era. The rediscovery of Arthur and the Round Table was mainly the work of Tennyson, in his epic poem and life work *Idylls of the King*. The poem was begun in the 1830s and not published in its complete twelve-part form until 1885.

Prior to the imperial age, Milton and Wordsworth had rejected Arthur as an inappropriate subject for an English national epic.[12] Sir Thomas Malory's 15th century epic *Morte d'Arthur*, Tennyson's chief source, was never widely popular. Consequently, the stories were unknown to the English-reading public. On publication of the first edition of the Tennyson's *Idylls* in 1859 (comprising 'Enid', 'Vivien', 'Elaine' and 'Guinevere'), the *Saturday Review* described the material as 'a forgotten cycle of fables which never attained the dignity or substance of a popular mythology' (Shaw 1973: 83). The stories of Arthur did not stay forgotten for long: the *Idylls* sold 10,000 copies in the first week (*ibid.*, 82).

Tennyson was influenced by 19th century research into ancient texts as part of the recovery and invention of tradition and by the suggestion of Albert, the Prince Consort (himself a German prince), that 'the Arthurian cycle was the equivalent of German's national epic the *Niebelungenslied*' (Jordan 1988: 157). Occasionally Tennyson could strike a militant, even chauvinist note, for example, in the poems he wrote after the French *coup d'état* of 1851 ('RISE, Britons, rise, if manhood be not dead'). Yet he was chiefly an introspective, spiritual poet ('the saddest of poets,' as T.S. Eliot described him). Tennyson used the stories of Arthur, Queen Guinevere,

Arthur's sword Excalibur, the Knights of the Round Table, Merlin the magician and the Holy Grail not to justify imperial conquest but, as in the poetry of the biblical prophets, to highlight spiritual ideals. There are unforgettable mythic images, such as Sir Bedivere's return of Excalibur to the Lady of the Lake as Arthur lies dying:

> Then quickly rose Sir Bedivere and ran,
> And, leaping down the ridges lightly, plunged
> Among the bulrush-beds, and clutch'd the sword,
> And strongly wheel'd and threw it. The great brand
> Made lightnings in the splendour of the moon,
> And flashing round and round, and whirl'd in an arch,
> Shot like a streamer of the northern morn,
> Seen wher the moving isles of winter shock
> By night, with noises of the northern sea.
> So flash'd and fell the brand Excalibur:
> But ere he dipt the surface, rose an arm
> Clothed in white samite, mystic, wonderful,
> And caught him by the hilt, and brandish'd him
> Three times, and drew him under in the mere.
> ('The Passing of Arthur' 301–14)

Tennyson defines heroism in biblical, not pagan, terms. As we have seen, Arthur's wise mentor Merlin is a prophet-like bard. Conquest of enemies counts less than conquest of the self, of the inner defiling monster of ethical frailty (particularly Guinevere's sexual betrayal of Arthur) which ruins the social order.[13] As in Tennyson's best-known long poem *In Memoriam*, loss and the prospect of loss fill the *Idylls* and question British power. The *Idylls*, like the *Nibelungen*, is concerned less with the pride and confidence of the nation than with its dark-edged dignity in decline. As national poems, both foreshadow the weakening of the monarchy and in the case of Germany, its fall.

YEATS AND IRISH LEGEND

An attraction of Irish legend to those who sought independence from England was that it preceded the English conquest. England had controlled parts of Ireland for centuries but gained absolute rule only in the 17th century. In the Act of Union of 1801, England and Ireland became the 'United Kingdom of Great Britain and Ireland'. The consequent decline of Ireland led to the rise of Irish nationalism, the revival of Irish language and an outstanding literature, dominated in poetry by Yeats.[14] Influenced by Irish cultural nationalists such as Standish O'Grady, John O'Leary and Douglas Hyde, Yeats became a connoisseur of Irish legend, much of which survived in oral Gaelic tradition among the western Irish peasantry. He edited several volumes, including *Fairy and Folk Tales of the Irish Peasantry* (1888), *Stories from Careleton* (1889), and *Representative Irish Tales* (1890), and he used this material in his own poetry. Yeats discovered in this ancient literature a pristine national spirit more powerful than British culture, which could be seen as corrupted by the power of empire. Yeats wrote of the Irish legends he edited:

> 'All that is greatest in our literature is based upon legend – upon those tales which are made by no one man, but by the nation itself through a slow process of modification and adaptation, to express its loves and its hates, its likes and its dislikes'
>
> (Pritchard 1972: 36).

Yeats saw himself not just as a teller of legends but as a legendary figure himself:

> '... the artist was to conceive of himself as a representative figure, to identify himself with all men, or with Ireland, or with some traditional personage. In this way the correspondences of old legends with modern life could be established, and so, as Yeats proposed, a dead mythology might be changed to a living one'
>
> (Ellmann 1968: 18).

In an early poem 'To Ireland in the Coming Times' (1892), Yeats declares his kinship with Irish national poets of the past. He uses Irish myth to unlock the national unconscious:[15]

> *Nor may I less be counted one*
> *With Davis, Mangan, Ferguson,*
> *Because, to him who ponders well,*
> *My rhymes more than their rhyming tell*
> *Of things discovered in the deep,*
> *Where only body's laid asleep.*

To Yeats, as to Shelley, poetry is meant to educate, to remind its listeners of their heroic past and to unite them in hope. Heroes such as Oisin and Cuchulain are archetypes of heroic resistance. In Yeats' 'The Wanderings of Oisin' (1888), the chained woman whom Oisin liberates resembles Ireland in English chains, and Oisin's 'battles never done' recall the never-ending Irish struggle for independence (Ellmann 1968: 18–19). Similarly nationalistic is Yeats' 'Cuchulain's Fight with the Sea' (1892), which draws on one of the most famous images in Irish legend:

> Cuchulain stirred,
> Stared on the horses of the sea, and heard

The cars of battle and his own name cried;
And fought with the invulnerable tide.

Like Tennyson's Arthur, Yeats' creation of Cuchulain was greatly influenced by the *Nibelungenlied* (both the medieval poetry and Wagner's music) as a pure expression of national spirit.

Yeats in 'September 1913' unfairly contrasted what he then regarded as the failure of Irish nationalism, its descent into pettiness, with heroes of Irish history such as Edward Fitzgerald (1763–98), Robert Emmet (1778–1803) and Wolfe Tone (1763–98), all martyrs for Irish independence. After the 1916 revolt, Yeats implicitly admitted in 'Easter 1916' that he was wrong about the Irish lack of spirit: 'a terrible beauty is born'. By the end of his life, in 'The Statues' (1938), Yeats was skilfully using Irish legend for contemporary needs. Echoing Blake's 'The Tyger', he writes in wonder of the Irish martyrs in the 1916 uprising who had a cult of Cuchulain – their fight being equally heroic and, in the short run, futile – remembered by the Irish government with a statue of Cuchulain in the Dublin Post Office where the rebels held out for a few days against far superior British firepower:

> When Pearse summoned Cuchulain to his side,
> What stalked through the Post Office? What intellect,
> What calculation, number, measurement, replied?
> We Irish, born into that ancient sect
> But thrown upon this filthy modern tide
> And by its formless spawning fury wrecked,
> Climb to our proper dark, that we may trace
> The lineaments of a plummet-measured face.

The contradictions in Yeats made it hard for the Irish to see him in his lifetime as a true national poet. Even as he extolled the virtues of Gaelic, rural Ireland and the peasantry, he wrote in English (indeed, in the English Romantic tradition) and lived in cities. Much of his poetry stands out less in its Irish nationalism than in its universalism. Yet, with the passage of time, it has been possible even for the Irish to accept Yeats as a master of Irish legend and representative of national identity and hopes.

NOTES

* * I am grateful to Athena Leoussi for editing an earlier version of this chapter for a *Festschrift* in honor of Anthony D. Smith.
* 1. The translation is by David Aberbach, admittedly one of Sir Randolph Quirk's less illustrious pupils of Anglo-Saxon at University College, London, but thankful nevertheless that some vague (perhaps mythical) memory of Sir Randolph's classes might remain. Corrections would be gratefully accepted.

2. On the 16th century as a turning point in the emergence of English nationalism (as well as European nationalism in general), see Baker (2001).
3. Translated by David Aberbach. For the passage in full, see Conran (1967: 118).
4. *Ibid.*, 128
5. A decade after *Henry V* (1598–99), in *Cymbeline* (1609–10), Shakespeare depicts Britain in the age of Augustus, when there was a similar threat of invasion. In lines which to a Jacobean audience must have immediately called up the failed Spanish Armada, the Queen argues against payment of tribute to Rome in view of Julius Caesar's failure in 55–54 BCE:

   … he was carried
   From off our coast, twice beaten; and his shipping,
   Poor ignorant baubles on our terrible seas,
   Like eggshells moved upon their surges, cracked
   As easily 'gainst our rocks.

   (III i 25–9)

   Britain was eventually invaded successfully by Claudius in 43 CE. Apart from *Cymbeline*, the invasion of England or Britain occurs several times in Shakespeare's plays: *3 Henry VI* (1590–91), *Richard III* (1592–93), *King John* (1596–97), and *King Lear* (1605–06).
6. Coleridge's emphatic patriotism in 'Fears in Solitude' may be linked to the fact that as a radical he was a suspected traitor (Crocco 2014: ch. 4).
7. On national poetry in the British empire, see chapter 12 (this volume).
8. Kipling's brief mention of King Alfred in 'Puck's Song' may be contrasted with John Fitchett's epic poem about Alfred remembered, unfortunately, only for its exceptional length (over 130,000 lines) and the time it took to write (nearly 40 years and incomplete at the time of the poet's death in 1838).
9. Ossian greatly inspired nationalism in the century after the French Revolution. On Ossian and the forgeries of the Slavonic poet Vaclav Hanka, see pp. 179–80. The Hungarian poet Sandor Petőfi in 'Homer and Ossian' (1847), recalls the glory of the dead, defeated warriors depicted by Ossian as an inspiration to those who, like the Hungarians against the Russians, rebelled against tyranny (Petőfi 1974: 93). Another improbably successful forgery was made from the 14th century Welsh poet Dafydd ap Gwilym by Iolo Morganwg.
10. See Tobias Smollett's elegy for defeated Scotland 'The Tears of Scotland. Written in the Year 1746': 'Mourn, hapless Caledonia, mourn/ Thy banished peace, thy laurels torn!/ Thy sons, for valour long renowned,/ Lie slaughtered on their native ground' (Lonsdale 2003: 407).
11. On 'the scar of a national history' in *Marmion* and other epics in English, many with biblical themes, see Tucker (2008).
12. Milton's Latin poem *Mansus* (1639) has a nationalist emphasis as 'a defence of English poetry in its entirety and the claim that John wants to bring King Arthur back to life in his poetry' (Beer 2008: 99). Dante, a poet whom Milton loved, had argued similarly in Latin for the Italian vernacular in *De Vulgari Eloquentia* (On Vernacular Expression).
13. On Tennyson's *Idylls* in the context of Victorian nationalism, see Graham (1998: ch. 3).
14. On Yeats, see chapter 10 (this volume).
15. Yeats' younger contemporary Patrick Pearse had a similar mystic identification with the nation, in 'I am Ireland'. See p. 170.

6 The Greek War of Independence and its Poetry

'Απ' τὰ κόκκαλα βγαλμένη
τῶν Ἑλλήνων τὰ ἱερά,
καὶ σὰν πρῶτα ἀνδρειωμένη
χαῖρε ὢ χαῖρε, Ἐλευθερια!

Hail Liberty! you I greet
who springs bold
from holy bones of Greeks,
brave as of old ...

(Solomos)

The Greek War of Independence against Ottoman Turkey (1821–29) was the first successful modern European national revolt against an imperial power. Revolutionary too was the simultaneous revival of Greek poetry in two schools, on the mainland and on the islands.[1] The war and its poetry, particularly its association with Byron, came to define European nationalism as a struggle for independence led not just by soldiers and politicians but also by poets, priests and other tradition-bearers. Greece thenceforth was 'the myth and inspiration of nationalists and liberals everywhere' (Hobsbawm 2001: 173). Inspired by Homer and later Greek literature, as well as by the ideals of the Enlightenment and the French Revolution spread by the Napoleonic wars, modern Greek poets starting from Rigas Velestinlis (or Feraios, 1757–1798) helped to create a modern national Greek culture. This chapter explores poetry of the revolt and its significance both in the history of nationalism and as part of a long European poetic tradition depicting conflict between Islam and Christianity. Highlights of this revival were works by Dionysios Solomos (1798–1857) and Alexander Soutsos (1803–63); folk poetry in Greece and Albania; and Byron, whose martyrdom (as it came to be seen) for Greece at Missolonghi in 1824 created a new, much imitated image of the poet ready to fight and, if necessary, die for a national cause.

In this remarkable history, the Greek island of Zakynthos (Zante), mentioned by Homer, gives a uniquely vivid education in the importance of poets in a nation's history. The island airport is named for Solomos, a native of Zante, whose flights of poetry include the Greek national anthem.[2] Through a landscape, described lovingly by its poets, of verdant fields and vineyards heavy with fruit where the scent of lemons drifts to sea, Zante Town comes into view at the base of a steep hill by the sea and with an unusually large square, again named for Solomos, with an impressive statue of the poet. A stone's throw from the square is the Solomos Museum, a memorial of the Greek struggle for independence and a national shrine where Solomos and his fellow Zante-born poet Andreas Kalvos (1792–1869) are buried. On the hill overlooking the town is the old fort. Its ruined ramparts are a memorial to once-powerful empires, including the Ottoman Turkish and the British, and yet another shrine to Solomos. The poet is said to have wept there during the Turkish siege of Missolonghi, across the bay on the distant Greek mainland.

Solomos and other Greek poets, venerated in Greece, have unusual importance in modern European history as inspirers of the revolt which brought Greek independence from Ottoman Turkey and marked the beginning of the end of Islamic rule in the Balkans. At the same time, the Greek poetic tradition is one of the oldest in the world, going back to Homer. An exploration of Greek poetry reveals much about the evolution of national poetry from the ancient world to modern times.

HOMER AND GREEK NATIONALISM

Historically, Homer's epic poems have had far more influence as universal documents, the lion's part of a living classical literature in Western civilization, than as a source of Greek nationalism. Still, in the Greek struggle for independence, Homer was an inspiration and binding force. Against those who doubted (with good reason) that modern Greeks had or could have a collective identity, Homer was a powerful answer.[3] As a genre, the epic poem has defined national identity from ancient to modern times while embodying the fundamental conflict between artistic genius and universal values on the one hand and national identity and aspirations on the other. To most educated Europeans at the start of the 19th century, Greek identity lived in Homer's epics: in war, heroism; in defeat, noble perseverance. Homer was essential in European classical education which, in an age of growing nationalism, helped construct modern Greek identity. Greece could not fight a war of independence without associations with Homer and the classical age. In Solomos' 'The Shade Homer', the poet of Greece reborn encounters Homer, no longer blind. Theodoros Kolonctronis (1782–1827), a Greek hero of the war, wore a helmet to recall ancient glory. As with other pre-modern mythical poetry, such as the *Niebelungen* or the *Kalevala*, Homer represented a world outlook, a way of life and a moral standard.[4] To poets of the War of Independence, most of whom studied and translated Latin and Greek classics, Homer's characters were models of 'national' virtues or failings. The classical revival in 18th century Europe and the United States made the emergence of modern

Greece seem natural, even inevitable. Modern Greek poetry of a renascent nation seemed umbilically joined to the classical age. Ancient Greece in any case had claim as progenitor of the ideology of independence struggles, of democracy and freedom. Revolutionary Greece was in a sense rediscovering its own heritage. If not for the memory of ancient Greek culture, Homer above all, the sense of Greece as a living presence might have been lost. As for the Greek masses in the early 19th century, few could read or write. They did not know Homer and were largely ignorant of the classical world which educated Europeans, a small minority at the time, associated with them. Solomos' *Ode to Liberty* and his poem in praise of Byron (1824) were above their heads (Trayiannoudi 2004: 426–7). Their sense of national unity was practically nonexistent. Even so, the memory of the past, though confined mainly to an educated minority, was crucial in the War of Independence, in the aim of creating a modern westernised national state inspired by the classical world, particularly Periclean Athens (450–400 BCE). Yet, religion was also a major element in the War, which revived the bitter medieval conflict of Christian Europe and expansionist Islam, and was fought in hope of restoring the Orthodox Byzantine empire and returning to Constantinople, conquered by the Turks in 1453.[5] For these reasons, Greek poets, though geographically on the margin of Europe, could be seen culturally at the centre, the living voice both of ancient and modern Greece.

GREEK FOLK POETRY

Greek national poetry had precedents in anonymous folk poetry surviving orally, often sung in the War of Independence. Though there is debate over the continuity of Greek literature from ancient to modern times, there are distinctive recurrent elements (Alexiou 2002a).[6] The long history of Greek defeats from the 15th century – above all, the fall of Constantinople to the Turks under Sultan Mehmet II (1453), but also the fall of Athens (1456), the siege of Malta (1456), the fall of Cyprus (1570) and Crete (1669), among others – has endless sources for the Greek lament (Alexiou 2002: ch. 5).[7] 'The Last Mass in Santa Sophia' describes the fall of Constantinople in 1453: a heavenly voice declares that it is God's will that the city will fall to the Turks (γιατὶ εἶναι θέλημα θεοῦ ἡ Πόλη νὰ τουρκέψη) and exhorts the priests to put out the candles and load the sacramental vessels, the Cross, the Bible and especially the Altar – 'to stop the Turkish dogs from defiling it' (μὴ μᾶς τὴν πάρουν τά σκυλιὰ καὶ μᾶς τῆ μαγαρίσουν) – on three ships sent from the Christian world to rescue them.[8] Other Greek folk poems, such as 'The Battle of the Mountains', convey Greek pride and determination to win freedom from the Turks. In this poem, Mount Olympus – the twenty-five mile range in northern Greece between Thessaly and Macedonia, whose summit nearly two miles high is the highest point in Greece, in Greek myth the home of the gods and in modern Greece symbol of the free Nation – addresses

Kisavos, a Thessalian mountain where the Turks had their headquarters during the War of Independence:

> I am ancient Olympus, world-famous,
> I have 42 peaks and 62 sweet springs.
> On every peak flies a flag, behind each branch
> a Greek rebel waits ...[9]

For centuries, a Greek legend of the *xanthon genos*, a fair-haired race of liberators from the north – evidently the Russians, the only Orthodox people not under Ottoman rule – persisted in folk memory. In the 17th century, Matthaios, Metropolitan of Myra wrote, 'We hope for the fair-headed races to deliver us,/ To come from Moscow, to save us' (Clogg 2002: 17). Russian victories over the Turks in the 18th century revived this hope among Balkan Christians, especially as Catherine the Great planned to divide the Balkans with Austria and re-establish a Byzantine empire. As Ottoman power waned and the empire became increasingly vulnerable to corruption, internal revolt and the manipulations of the Great Powers, local Muslim rulers also dreamed of freedom from the Porte.[10]

GREEK NATIONALISM AND ITS POETRY

As we have seen, Greek cultural nationalism could be traced to, or constructed from, the classical world, including Homer, with medieval antecedents and a living folk poetry, both within Greece and its islands and in the Greek diaspora. The French Revolution and Enlightenment ideals of liberty and progress stirred Greece to rebirth as a modern nation. The rise of Greek nationalism and the Greek War of Independence in the 1820s totally transformed Greece and its literature.[11] Greek poetry, infused with liberal Enlightenment ideals, helped create modern Greek culture, its language and its literature. The effect of the French Revolution and the Napoleonic wars throughout the Balkans was to make their peoples, subject to the Ottoman Turks, 'more restless, more independent, and more determined to win their freedom' (Stavrianos 2000: 211). The Greeks heartened peoples in Europe and elsewhere to struggle for independence and create their own national cultures. Greek poetry was transformed in the early 19th century as part of a surge of cultural nationalism – in the classical revival, folklore, history, linguistics, archaeology, philology, and philosophy. In Greece and in other emerging modern European states, an emerging middle class and new school systems created a market and an educational outlet for national poetry (Lambropoulos 1988: 9).[12] Greek poetry gave legitimacy to the Greek national movement and united its disparate, often-conflicting, groups of local chiefs and religious leaders, merchants and seamen, and the Greek diaspora, notably its communities in Vienna and Odessa, and among

The Greek War of Independence and its Poetry   149

the wealthy and influential Phanariot French-educated Greek elite in Constantinople.[13] The wealthy Greek merchant class supported liberal education of young Greeks abroad, mainly in France and Germany, as well as the publication of modern editions of Greek literature by scholars such as Adamantios Korais, whose Greek classics series began with an edition of Homer in 1805.

Prior to the French Revolution, Turkish rule had isolated the Greek world. With notable exceptions – for example, in Crete and the Greek diaspora – the great transformations in European history, the Renaissance, the Reformation, the 17th century scientific revolution and the Enlightenment had largely passed Greece by.[14] Previous Greek revolts against Ottoman rule on the mainland had failed. The slow, hard fight by which the Ottomans put down the first Serbian revolt (1804–13) – 'a small border war against poorly armed and disorganized Christian farmers and traders' (Mazower 2000: 80) – exposed the chronic weaknesses of the empire. Greek nationalism was driven forward by an array of pre-modern and modern cultural forces, in which poetry stood out. Apart from Homer, whose epics had kept alive the illusion, if not the reality, of Greek national identity, there was the 2nd century BCE Greek Bible (the 'Septuagint'), translated from the Hebrew by Alexandrian Jews; Byzantine culture and the medieval tradition as well as an oral folk tradition; the Romantic movement, particularly Byron, whose death in Greece in 1824 helped to inspire Greeks to fight and created invaluable propaganda for Greek independence; and the many Greek scholars and poets, notably Solomos in his *Ode to Liberty* (1824), who helped define modern Greek national identity, creating a momentum to independence. Greek poetry was also born from an unsavory fusion of racial, religious and cultural conflicts: Christian Greeks versus Muslim Turks, White versus non-White, Romanticism versus the established order, European versus foreign. European enthusiasm for the Greek revolt was widespread:

> 'The War was the tangible manifestation and at the same time the crowning achievement of the Romantic Movement, which had found its first great expression in the French Revolution. All the love and gratitude of every educated man for Ancient Greece, all the admiration felt by the world for the poetry, the nobility, the romance of Lord Byron, swept away like chaff the resistance of Czars, Emperors and Kings: What! was the Sparta of Leonidas to be inhabited by the Arab and the Negro? Was Athens to remain for ever under the government of a black eunuch? And so the money poured in, volunteers of high capacity, such as Hastings, Gordon and Cochrane, joined the cause; Canning assumed the reins of the Foreign Office, and the issue was set beyond doubt'.
> (Jenkins 1940: 45–6)

Modern Greek poetry responded to these events in two schools, one on the mainland, known as the Romantic School of Athens with enthusiastic support from the Phanar district of Constantinople; and, on Greek islands, the School of the Ionian Islands under British rule, mainly associated with the two islands where Solomos, its leading poet, lived: Zante and Corfu. Both schools aimed to express the new Greek national consciousness and revitalize the Greek language. Their poetry shared with similar poetic movements throughout Europe the love for the homeland, pride in the past, and yearning for freedom – and the humiliation of a proud people long under foreign rule. Both schools, though largely secular, tended to respect the Greek Orthodox Church, despite its natural rejection of the anti-clerical secular Enlightenment. The Church, having little choice, joined the war against Islam.[15] More anti-Ottoman than pro-Western, the Church supported the revolt in hope of the revival of the glory of Christian Byzantium – not the ancient pagan Hellenic spirit of Leonidas, king of Sparta, who in the Persian invasion in 480 BCE held the pass at Thermopylae until all the defenders were killed. Poets of the Ionian islands had conditions far different from those on the mainland. Except for Leucas, the islands were never under Turkish rule. The upper classes among the islanders as well as overseas Greeks were philhellenists in their Western European outlook, while mainland Greeks, despite periodic revolts, were mostly illiterate peasants resigned to the centuries-old Muslim empire. The War of Independence unified these different groups. Most of the 750,000 Greeks in the newly-formed Kingdom of Greece in 1833 were Greek speakers. In the evolving Greek educational system which followed independence, Greek poetry formed part of the curriculum.

MODERN GREEK POETRY: THE HISTORICAL BACKGROUND

Modern Greek poetry, rising on the post-1789 nationalist wave, was widely seen as a Romantic revolt against imperial Turkish despotism (*Turkokratia*),[16] going back to 1453. Under Ottoman rule, knowledge of Greek history and language declined, and churches were turned to mosques. Its rugged land closed Greece to most travellers. Pre-revolutionary French travel literature glorifies ancient Greek monuments and landscape while maligning contemporary Greeks alongside their putative ancestors (Augustinos 1994). The French Revolution put the question of Greek independence in the news. A small band of Greek intellectuals, most famously Velestinlis, began to call for revolution against the Turks and the reawakening of Greek culture.[17] In Vienna, with its large Greek population, Velestinlis called for a pan-Balkan uprising; he published a Greek constitution and a collection of war songs and was active in the emergence of a modern Greek press; he demanded the study of Greek in schools and stressed the value of Greek antiquity to modern Greeks. After the poet was executed by the Turks in 1798, he was revered as the first modern Greek prophet of armed revolt and martyr of independence. Lines in his poem *Thourios* (War Song), which Byron translated, became a slogan of revolt: 'Better one hour of free life/ Than forty years of slavery and prison' (Clogg 2002: 29). By the early 1800s, Greek parents began to name their children after ancient Greeks such as Socrates, Plato and Aristotle, and Greek municipal authorities named streets after Greek heroes rather than saints. In 1805 Christopoulos published a grammar of spoken Greek. Greece became more accessible to the outside world; Byron first visited in 1809.

The French Revolution and the Napoleonic wars stirred Greek national consciousness not just in Greece but also among philhellenes throughout Europe and in America who had little difficulty in constructing a modern Greek identity and culture. Greece roused the interest of politicians and literary figures such as Byron and Goethe. A vague humanistic, literary, philanthropic or antiquarian feeling for Greece was transformed into concrete political aims. In 1814 in Odessa, a secret society, the *Philiki Hetairia*, was created to free Greece and found a Greek empire. In his narrative poem *Laon and Cythna* (1817), Shelley anticipated a Greek struggle for liberty against Ottoman rule. In 1821, the president of the *Hetairia*, Count Alexandros Hypsilantis, a former general in the Russian army, assembled an army of about 4500 in a Greek revolt against the Turks in the Danubian principalities of Wallachia and Moldavia:

> 'Let us recollect, brave and generous Greeks, the liberty of the classic land of Greece; the battles of Marathon and Thermopylae, let us combat upon the tombs of our ancestors who, to leave us free, fought and died'
> (St. Clair 1972: 23).

This revolt, quickly crushed, was followed by a successful peasant revolt in the Peloponnese. Hypsilantis' declaration of Greek independence roused the imagination (as intended) of Europeans with a classical education. 'We are all Greeks', responded Shelley in the preface to his poem *Hellas* (1821), in which the Muslim tyrant Mahmud faces ultimate defeat and the fall of his empire while the poet predicts a new birth of liberty in Greece, a 'brighter Hellas' and a renascent Athens. The decline of Christianity spurred identification with Greece as secular Enlightenment and science spread: 'The retreat from Christianity made faith in Greece a necessity for Western intellectuals' (Zamoyski 1999: 236). Cultural landmarks included Korais' modern editions of Greek classics (with introductions in the vernacular), Pouqueville's *Voyage dans la Grece* (1820) and Fauriel's collection of Greek folk songs *Chants populaires de la Grece moderne* (1825–26).[18] Even Greek atrocities during the war were not allowed to dampen revolutionary ardor for Greece.[19] In contrast, Turkish atrocities, notably on the island of Chios, were widely publicized to stress the moral superiority of Greeks over Turks, and of Christianity over Islam. The Greeks and the Christian world were incensed and unified by the murder of Gregorios, Patriarch of Constantinople, and other clergymen by the Turks on Easter Sunday 1821. Though the Patriarch had warned against the revolt and excommunicated the rebels, the Turks accused him and his colleagues of fomenting revolt. Ancient stereotypes of religious war were revived: of noble Greeks fighting barbaric Turks, of European Christian civilization at war with the Muslim infidel (Gazi 2009: 103). Hundreds of volunteers came from across Europe and from America to fight with crusading zeal for Greek independence. Volunteers came even when the Greeks did not want them (as in Hydra, for example, where the population mostly spoke Albanian) and simply wanted to be left alone, or if they were cowardly or cruel, or fighting one another, or even if they threatened the lives of their 'saviors'; it made no difference. Hellenic aid committees sprang up throughout Europe. During this frenzied period, thieves and cut-throats suddenly became incarnations of Odysseus and Leonidas: 'It seemed impossible to represent any event in Modern Greece as an event in its own right without overwhelming it with misleading classical allusions' (St. Clair 1972: 24).[20] Key events of the War of Independence transformed national consciousness and created Greek unity: the convening of the first national assembly at Epidaurus (1822); the publication of Solomos' *Ode to Liberty* (1824); the destruction of the Ottoman fleet at the battle of Navarino (20 October 1827); and the Treaty of Constantinople (1832) in which Greece was recognized as a free country.

These events fill the poetry of the Romantic School of Athens, founded and led by Alexander Soutsos,[21] a veteran of the War of Independence. Soutsos' 'The Roumeliote Veteran' conveys the national spirit roused by the war but largely lost after independence, when the effects of the devastation – over 200,000 had died in the war – were felt: 'With the war concluded there were no more heroics to be sung. What was left was a ravaged country whose war-devastated people bore little or no resemblance to the celebrated ancients' (Augustinos 1994: 289). Soutsos' poem highlights stirring moments, particularly in the district of Roumeli in southern Greece, known for its revolutionary feeling against the Turks.

> Attacked by the Skorda mob at Karpenisi, how at once, unafraid,
> Botzaris scattered them, then hid his mortal wound
> from us, giving us courage with his last look,
> Remember our heroic years?
>
> How the Turks swarmed over the valleys of our brave Roumeli,
> our children and parents besieged by Arabs in Missolonghi?
> How it rose to the stars in the eyes of hard-hearted Europe?
> Remember our heroic years?
>
> When Karaiskakis came to Athens with his chosen three hundred,
> How Kioutahi Pasha lost his courage and wits?
> Within a month Roumeli joined the fight,
> the soil of Arachova stained with blood. Remember?[22]

Soutsos pictures the rugged landscape of Arta, Karpenisi and Arachova (near Delphi), which shielded Greek fighters as well as heroes of the war, including

Markos Botzaris, who died leading the Greek attack at Karpenisi and was buried at Missolonghi in 1823,[23] and Georgios Karaiskakis, who fought against the Turks led by Hoursit Pasha and Kioutahi Pasha and died in action at the time of the Turkish siege of the Acropolis in 1827. Modern and ancient Greece are linked in the setting: the vicinity of Mount Olympus, home of the gods in ancient Greek mythology and a battle site in the seven-year War of Independence. How are events in the war recounted in Albanian folk poetry?

ALBANIAN POETRY OF THE GREEK WAR OF INDEPENDENCE

Albanians were prominent in the multiethnic society preceding Greek independence. A large part of northern Greece was ruled by the Muslim Albanian Ali Pasha. Like the Greeks, the Albanians had a long poetic tradition of independence from Ottoman rule. Albanian epic poetry relates the exploits of Skanderbeg, who fought for Albanian independence from the Turks in the 15th century. Albanian folk poetry, too, opposes Turkish rule, which lasted from 1479–1912 (Ruches 1967). Though raised among the Turks and allied with them, Skanderbeg came to symbolize Albanian freedom. He rediscovered his Christianity, united the Albanian tribes and defeated the Turks (1444–1466). After his death, Albania became a Turkish province, though its mountainous terrain made full Turkish control impossible and revolt was frequent. Albania, 'the chief pillar of Turkish rule in the Balkans' (Stavrianos 2000: 508), was vital to the defense of Constantinople, and the Ottomans did much to persuade Albanians to convert to Islam: by the 19th century, about two-thirds of Albanians were Muslims.[24] At the same time, the Albanian Catholic diaspora grew, particularly in Italy where Albanian literature was published, in contrast with Albania itself where the Turks banned Albanian publications. Albanian poetry of the Greek War of Independence gives a remarkable dual picture of the war, mostly the Christian viewpoint but also the Muslim side.[25] A failed Greek cavalry charge against the Turks led by Hypsilantis on 7 June 1821 is commemorated in this Albanian song:

> Strike the Turkish traitor down
> for the Greeks he drowned in the Danube!
> for the troops of Hypsilantis slain
> on the ridge of Dragatsani.[26]

Other Albanian songs recall Markos Botzaris who united various Greek factions against the Turks. One song addresses Ali Pasha, the Porte's powerful and rebellious provincial governor, whose revolt against Constantinople in 1821 triggered the War of Independence[27] and whose Greek-speaking capital Jannina was Botzaris's childhood home:

> Do you recall, Old Man Ali, that little boy at court?
> That little devil, that black dog, that odious serpent –

Markos Botzaris – now he's more famous than you –
Pouncing like a lion, he cut down forty officers, damn him!²⁸

In the siege of Missolonghi in 1822, (where the defenders were mainly Albanian and Greek–speaking Christians), the Albanian-speaking Muslims attacked on Christmas eve, but the defenders were not in church but waiting for them: 'The garrison stayed at the battlements,/ Like doves they fought, their feet off the ground'.²⁹ The siege continued in 1823:

> Wait, wait, Roumelia, for an army of all colors:
> Anatolian, Gheg, Tosk;
> come see Shkodra's pasha attack
> with twenty thousand lions ...³⁰

Like Gideon in the Book of Judges, Botzaris chooses three hundred men and in a night raid vengefully destroys the Albanian camp (which, significantly in the evolution of Albanian national identity, could not distinguish Christian from Muslim, or the language of the Christians from the language of Muslims): 'they have roasted us, set us ablaze/ By Mohammed and the Koran' (*se ne poqi, na vu zjarrë/ Muhameti me Kuranë*).³¹ Botzaris died in the melee. Byron, arriving at Missolonghi in January 1824, visited Botzaris' grave, and when he died a few months later was at first buried next to Botzaris. The siege continued until the Greek capitulation in 1826. In the Aegean, meanwhile, the Muslim fleet went from island to island – most notoriously to Chios, on 10 March 1822 – butchering the inhabitants and selling survivors as slaves. The admiral of the fleet is denounced in one Albanian poem: 'Damn you, Ottoman dog of dogs/ Courageous in cutting children down!' (*Qën i qënit Osmanlli!/ Nem paç! Me çilimi/ gjete të bëc trimëri?*').³² The Muslim siege of Athens in 1826 is recalled in both Christian and Muslim Albanian poetry. The Greek defender, John Gouras, sends for aid from Karaiskakis, commanding general at Thessaly: 'While a single drop of blood remains in me/ I shall not give up the fort' (*se unë kalanë s'jap/ sa të kem një pike gjar*).³³ Greek defiance is matched by the bitterness of the Muslim besiegers:

> Hey Greece, black Greece, how many brave men
> did you take from us?
> mothers blinded, fathers executed,
> brothers bereaved, sisters cuckolded, women widowed?³⁴

Another Albanian ballad grieves the fall of Athens and the death of the Muslim commander Mustafa Bey:

> What is this, o Mustafa Bey,
> Nine days under siege with no bread or supplies.
> They have slain us and cast us to earth.³⁵

While the idea of a distinct Albanian national identity comprising both Christians and Muslims had not yet emerged at the time of the Greek revolt in the 1820s, the Albanian poetry of the revolt might be regarded as a harbinger of this development a half century later, in the poetry of Vasa, Frasheri and Fishta, among others.[36] By the end of the Greek War of Independence, Christian Albanians in Albania were ready to revolt (Dakin 1973: 221).

THE SCHOOL OF THE IONIAN ISLANDS

Solomos created and dominated the School of the Ionian Islands,[37] whose other leading poets were Kalvos and Aristotle Valaoritis (1824–79). Like other national poets, Solomos set out to create a vernacular language linking his people with a heroic past. Yet, Solomos' background indicates the confused nature of Greek national identity and culture, especially prior to the War of Independence. Solomos was born a French subject; from 1815 until his death, he lived under British rule in the Ionian islands,[38] never visiting the mainland; and his native language was mostly Italian. The notes and drafts for his Greek poems are mainly in Italian, and the only book of poems he published in his lifetime was in Italian.[39] During his early life, he read little in Greek, and his knowledge of Greek was mostly in the spoken language. When in 1822 the Greek historian Spiridion Tricupis suggested to him, after reading some of his Italian poetry, that he should write in Greek, Solomos is reported to have replied: 'I don't know Greek, how could I write well in Greek?' (in Jenkins 1940: 54). His *Ode to Liberty* was practically the first poetry he wrote in Greek, and the first important poetry in Greek since the fall of Crete to the Ottomans in 1669. It describes various battles of the Greek revolt, including those at Tripolytza, Valtetzi, Corinth, Missolonghi (where the ode was published) and Achelous.[40] In some ways weak and derivative, the poem became an instant sensation and was admired by leading European writers, including Goethe, Hugo, Lamartine and Chateaubriand. Solomos, though committed to the idea of liberty rather than the creation of a modern national state, found himself a major figure in Greece's struggle for independence. Ironically at first, as Tricupis observed in 1825, his poem was read in Greek throughout the civilized world – except in Greece (*ibid.*, 1). Yet its opening became in 1865 – the year after the Ionian islands gained independence from Britain – the Greek national anthem:

> I know you by the sword,
> its sharp edge,
> I know you by the look
> that sizes up the earth.
>
> Hail Liberty! you I greet
> who springs bold
> from holy bones of Greeks,
> brave as of old ...[41]

Though Solomos is mainly associated with his Ode, the love of liberty recurs in his poem *The Cretan* (1833–34), in which a Cretan youth escapes after his family is slaughtered by the Turks.

In Kalvos' poetry, myth is a key to Greek national identity. Zakynthos – his birthplace (and Solomos') – is an enchanted isle populated with figures of Greek myth.[42] For many years Kalvos lived abroad. European influences from Ausonia (France) and Albion (England) enhanced the poet's sense of Greek identity, and his love of Zante, site of Greek myths of Artemis, the virgin goddess of the moon and the hunt:

> Albion, farewell, Ausonia too; farewell glorious Paris;
> Zante my only mistress, whose forests and shady hills heard
> the message of Artemis' silver bow.[43]

Valaorites, born during the revolt in 1824, hoped that all Greek lands and their Greek populations (most of whom at the time of independence still lived under Ottoman rule) would join the Greek state. Valaoritis was a politician as well as a poet. He represented the island of Leucas in the Ionian parliament and, after union with Greece, in the Greek parliament; and his poetry reflects his political views. His historic poem *Photeinos* is set on the island of Leucas during a revolt against the Franks. Another poem, *Astrapogiannos*, is the heroic tale of a *klepht* (bandit) who obeys his wounded leader's command to kill him and behead the corpse to prevent it falling into the hands of the Turks. 'The Rock and the Wave' is a bitter allegory of Greek revenge for the long humiliating Ottoman occupation and the ongoing conflict with the Turks. The vengefulness of the sea against the rock recalls the poetry of other defeated peoples, such as the Irish, the Scots, the Poles and the Ukrainians, dominated by powerful, ruthless empires.[44] Valaoritis' poem is a Promethean roar of fury at enslavement, calling up the revenge motif deep-rooted in classical Greek culture, including Homer and Sophocles. The poem culminates with a cry for revenge, an echo of ancient Greek drama in which catharsis comes with bitter accusations –

> you made me a bed of death...
> you piled me with corpses, exiled me, poisoned me
> with alms, laughed at my death rattle[45] –

and concludes with a sentence of extinction as the sea crushes the rock and drowns it.

BYRON AND THE GREEK WAR OF INDEPENDENCE

The Greek revolt was supported by the European powers and leading writers and thinkers, including Shelley and Byron, whose 'shadowy presence

[was] a major factor in the propaganda war' (MacCarthy 2003: 545). At the time when Byron, the most famous Briton of his age, joined them, the Greeks were fighting a civil war. The rise of Greek nationalism and the War of Independence briefly and crucially overcame European prejudice and indifference toward modern Greeks and gave them a halo of ancient heroism. Alone among the great early 19th century Romantics, Byron gave his life for a national cause. In a letter of 30 January 1824, written shortly before his death, Byron summed up to Andreas Londos, a leader of the Greek war, what Greece meant to him: 'Greece has ever been for me, as it must be for all men of any feeling or education, the promised land of valour, of the arts, and of liberty throughout all the ages' (Moore 1932: 620). As a martyr to the Greek cause, Byron transformed the climate of opinion toward independence struggles and defined the meaning and role of the poet in the age of nationalism:

> 'The self-sacrificing death of the poet was to have a profound effect on the European imagination, focusing attention on the cause that he had died for. Byron's death, above all, helped define Greece as a country with its own recognisable character and political validity'.
> (MacCarthy 2003: 530)

Byron used his poetry – the height of fashion in the early 19th century and with a huge market – to create empathy for the Greeks, though 'Greece appealed to him mainly as a fight for Liberty, not as a fight for Greeks as such' (St. Clair 1972: 151).[46] Byron's call (in *Childe Harold's Pilgrimage* II 73) to

> Fair Greece! sad relic of departed worth!
> Immortal, though no more; though fallen, great!
> Who now shall lead thy scatter'd children forth,
> And long accustom'd bondage uncreate?

echoed through European countries, in many cases galvanizing their cultures to help produce poets ready to fight and, if necessary, die for the national cause. After Byron's visit to Greece in 1809, his poetry – *Childe Harold's Pilgrimage* (Canto II, 1812), *The Giaour* (1813), *The Bride of Abydos* (1813) and *The Siege of Corinth* (1816) – gave the definitive literary portrait of the Greeks in his age: as a once-great nation under the heel of the barbaric Turks, yet capable of renewal and liberation. Some sympathizers such as Pushkin, who wrote an ode to Eleutheria (freedom), regarded modern Greeks as the heirs of Homer and Themistocles, until they actually met some Greeks – who made a poor impression, of confusion, disunity, subservience, indiscipline, corruption – and changed their minds.[47] Byron, in contrast, saw the marks of a long history of subjugation, which independence would ameliorate and restore the true underlying greatness of Greek cultural lineage. In *Don Juan*, Canto III (1810), Byron famously expressed the Romantic hope for Greek freedom:

> The mountains look on Marathon –
> And Màrathon looks on the sea;
> And musing there an hour alone,
> I dream'd that Greece might still be free;
> For standing on the Persian's grave,
> I could not deem myself a slave.
>
> (86, 1)

He imagined a resurrection of ancient Greek heroism:

> Earth! render back from out thy breast
> A remnant of our Spartan dead!
> Of the three hundred grant but three,
> To make a new Thermypolae!
>
> (ibid., 7)

In *The Giaour*, Byron put starkly the choices for the Greeks: 'Freedom's home or Glory's grave' (105). In the manuscript of *Childe Harold's Pilgrimage* (ii 73), the poet addresses Greece five times with the question, 'Who now shall call thy scatter'd children forth?' and five times scrawls 'Byron' between the lines (Eisler 1999: 228).

In 1821, when the war broke out, Byron was invited by the London Greek Committee to visit Greece to help raise funds. He saw this as an invitation to emerge from between the lines and lead the revolt. Now Byron's romantic longings could become practical deeds. His arrival in Greece in December 1823 'transformed the philhellenic movement into the great romantic crusade of the early 19th century' (Woodhouse 1991: 140–1). For some, the fight for Greek independence was a secular substitute for the Judaeo-Christian tradition, which Enlightenment and Reason called into question. Those who, like Byron, had their imagination stirred by a classical education, could believe that Greece was a nation, Athens was 'holy ground' (*Childe Harold's Pilgrimage* II 88) and the Greeks were lineal descendants of the heroes of Marathon and Thermopylae – though to more sober minds all this was doubtful.[48]

In his loyalty to Greece unto death, Byron set an example to European nationalists. Byron's death was a factor in shaming European rulers to admit that 'the war in Greece was a disgrace to civilization' (Woodhouse 1991: 143) and ultimately to take action to ensure Greece's independence.[49] The support of Byron and other poets of his time was a decisive weapon:

> 'The names of Byron and Shelley, Goethe, Schiller and Victor Hugo meant nothing to the Sultan, but these were his real enemies. He was left to depend on Metternich and Castlereagh – an unequal match, as history was to show'.[50]
>
> (ibid., 136)

Byron's total identification with the ancient Greeks by the time of his death is clear in his poem 'On this day I complete my thirty sixth year', written at Missolonghi on his thirty-sixth birthday (1.22.1824):

> The sword – the banner – and the Field
> Glory and Greece around us see!
> The Spartan borne upon his shield
> Was not more free!

After Byron's death, British and French demands for recognition of Greek autonomy, and the Ottoman refusal, led to the destruction of the Turkish/Egyptian fleet at Navarino (1827). This was followed by a brief war between the Russians and the Turks (1828) and a resultant treaty affirming Greek independence. Athens, an insignificant town prior to the war, was chosen for its classical associations as capital of the new Greek state.

CONCLUSION

The Greek War of Independence greatly stimulated Greek national culture, including poetry in two schools, on the mainland and the islands. It also helped create a nascent Albanian identity, expressed in folk poetry during the war, with dual Christian and Muslim points of view. Greece was the first Balkan country to win at least nominal independence, having the advantage of an internationally recognized classical culture to justify the idea of a continuous historical culture and a modern Greek nation. As elsewhere in Europe, poetry in Greece was part of wider cultural developments, giving evolving nations an identity through the study of history, myth, folk literature, archaeology and linguistics. In the Balkans, last European outpost of Muslim rule, religious rivalry stimulated nationalism after 1789. Greek poetry of the War of Independence was part of Balkan poetry of independence struggles against the Turks but also of a centuries-old tradition of European poetry responding to clashes of Islam and Christianity.[51] It also foreshadowing more Balkan conflict as newly-emerging nations struggled for independence from Ottoman rule.

With its complex, tumultuous background, the Greek struggle for independence could not help but renew the clash of Islam and Christianity. This lead to unusually widespread and effective European support for the Greeks, without which their revolt would have failed. Byron and other European liberals hoped that the Greek War of Independence would fulfil the secular ideals of the Enlightenment and the French Revolution. Indeed, Greek independence brought wholesale abandonment of Balkan Orthodoxy, the breaking of clerical control and the establishment of secular schools. Yet, revolt against Ottoman rule inevitably had a religious dimension: Russia was inclined to help its Orthodox co-religionists in the Balkans in fighting their common Islamic enemy; the Church was a bulwark against Islam as 'it was the peasants whose uprisings actually created the new nation-states, and they remained firmly attached to their Church'; and the Great Powers, while propping up the tottering Ottoman empire as a buffer against Russian expansion, supported 'Christians oppressed by Muslim despotism' (Mazower 2000: 75, 79). As many as 7,000 priests as well as many bishops were killed in the Greek War of Independence (Frazee 1969: 101). Athanasios Diakos, a priest who took up arms and fought heroically against overwhelming numbers, was taken captive. Pressed to convert, his reply became famous: 'Go you and your faith, you filth, to hell with you!/ I was born a Greek, a Greek will I die' (Stavrianos 2000: 281). This martyrdom is glorified in a poem by Valaorites.[52] A venerable, largely oral literature telling of local or border clashes or wars in time of Ottoman expansion or decline – often involving conflict between Muslims and Christians – was transformed into national poetry as poets rediscovered, reinterpreted or reconstructed their country's history in opposition to Ottoman rule.[53] During the war, the poet Panagiotis Soutsos (1828) expressed the intense chauvinism and anti-Islamicism of the time. Lines such as 'Islam mourns, retreats at speed at the sight of the cross' (22) mark a violent break from the multiethnic society, in which most Greeks were resigned to Ottoman rule, and a revival of ancient religious conflict within an ideological framework of secular nationalism.

Greek poetry reflects a new sense of national pride and confidence, and the international image of the Greeks and the Turks was transformed. Prior to the war, Greeks were often seen in a negative light, while images of the Turks were positive (Todorova 2009: 92–3). Byron's intervention in the war in 1824 was a turning point in the national fortunes and image of Greece, as a focus of liberal hopes whose independence struggle the Great Powers could not allow to fail. The same proved to be the case throughout the Balkans as Muslim rule was brought to an end before World War I. In contrast, the continent-wide nationalist revolutions of 1848–49 had similarly inspirational poets – Mickiewicz, Lamartine, Petőfi and Mameli, among them – but with no comparable history of religious conflict provoking effective international intervention. All failed.

NOTES

1. On the Greek War of Independence, see St. Clair (1972), Dakin (1955, 1973), Diamandoupos (1976), Gerolymatos (2001) and Beaton and Ricks (2009). On Greek nationalism in the general context of Ottoman rule of the Balkans, see Stavrianos (2000) and Mazower (2000). The Ionian islands passed from Venice to France (1797), to the Russians and Turks (1798), to France again (1807) and then with Napoleon's fall in 1815 to Britain until independence in 1864. On the nationalism of the *Rizopastai* (Radicals) in the Ionian Islands prior to independence, see Calligas (2009).
2. See Mackridge's biography of Solomos (1989). For a selection of Solomos' poetry, see Solomos (2000).

3. On Homer and the epic, see Bowra (1965) and Ricks (1989). A lesser-known though important Greek poem, the *Epic of Digenes Akrites*, thought to originate in the Byzantine era, survived in manuscript and fragmented oral form until it was published in the late 19th and early 20th centuries (Ricks 1990). Yet it had nothing like Homer's inspirational influence. On the question of the ancient origins of nationalism, see Armstrong (1982) and Smith (2000). On the disputed unity and continuity of Greek national identity, see for example Kitromilides (1998) and Mackridge (1998).
4. In *The Odyssey*, for example, after Odysseus' companions swear not to kill the Oxen of the Sun and break their vow, they pay with their lives. Penelope's suitors, too, perish because of their wickedness, their greed and their lack of self-control. Odysseus stands for justice; his bloody revenge restores the moral order in the end.
5. On the view that modern Greece's chief source of national identity is not the ancient heritage but Byzantium, see Ricks and Magdalino (1998).
6. Among elements of continuity between the medieval and modern periods, since the 12th century there has been a single basic metre in both folk and written Greek poetry (Ricks 1990: 1). Yet, the Greek word for 'folklore' was coined as late as 1884 (Peckham 1998: 96).
7. For some, Greek defeats went back far earlier than 1453. There is a view that Greek independence ended in 338 BCE with the battle of Chaeronea. Greek folk poetry is discussed in the context of the long history of conflict with Islam in chapter 3.
8. For the text of this poem, see Trypanis (1984: 469–70).
9. Translated by David Aberbach. The Greek reads:

'Ἐγώ εἶμ' ὁ γέρος Ὄλυμπος στὸν κόσμο ξακουσμένος,
ἔχω σαράντα δυὸ κορφὲς κι ἐξήντα δυὸ βρυσοῦλες,
κάθε κορφὴ καὶ φλάμπουρο, κάθε κλαδὶ καὶ κλέφτης.

(ibid., 480)

The word κλέφτης (klephtis) may be translated as 'brigand', but in the Greek folk imagination (as elsewhere in Europe), brigands were the rebels who fought institutionalized injustice. See Koliopoulos (1990). On a heroic brigand in Valaorites' poem *Astrapogiannos*, see p. 156. Also see p. 173 on Botev's ballad of the Bulgarian brigand Hadzhi Dimit'r.
10. While the latent power of Greek nationalism is evident in hindsight, most of the Balkan population prior to the French Revolution were interested less in national independence than in autonomous territory free of Ottoman interference. This was the case in Epirus, ruled by the Albanian Muslim Ali Pasha (1741–1822), 'the Lion of Jannina', whose revolt against Constantinople in 1821 lit the fuse for the Greek revolt. On Ali Pasha in Albanian poetry of the war, see pp. 153–4 Both Byron, who gave the Greek revolt Romantic liberal credentials, and Solomos, the leading Greek 'national poet' of the early 19th century, wrote for the cause of liberty, not a Greek national state.
11. For histories of Greek literature, see Politis (1973) and Trypanis (1981).
12. The neoclassical revival in late 18th century Europe owed much to German poets and intellectuals such as Goethe, Schiller, Hölderlin, Winckelmann, Schelling and Hegel. (Hölderlin's *Hyperion* [1797] tells of a Greek patriot fighting for his country's freedom.) To German thinkers, ancient Greece with its sublime ideals of youthful beauty, grace, harmony and moral virtue was often seen as the antithesis of Germany. Ancient Greek culture might shore up weak German

162 *The Greek War of Independence and its Poetry*

national identity; and in Germany and elsewhere in Europe, the Greek heritage might replace the allegedly failing Judaeo-Christian tradition.

13. See Breuilly (1993), Clogg (2002) and Koliopoulos and Veremis (2002). Geanakoplos (1976) observes that Greek diaspora communities made the educational preparations for Greek nationalism: '… for almost four centuries the Greek diaspora communities *were* the Greek nation-in-exile' (77).
14. The 'Cretan Renaissance' (c. 1570–1669) produced the last surviving Greek poetry of importance before Solomos; see Holton (1996). On discriminatory practices of Ottoman rule against Greek Christians, see Vryonis (1976): for example, the Greeks were about 90 percent of the population of Greece but owned only about one-third of the land; and the testimony of a Christian was invalid in a Muslim court.
15. On the role of the Orthodox Church in the Greek War of Independence, see Frazee (1969). On the interconnection of resurrectionary religious and insurrectionary modernist forces in the war, see Hatzopoulos (2009). In considering the support of the Greek Orthodox Church for the Greek revolt, it is notable that national poets elsewhere were often at odd with established religion. The Bulgarian poet Hristo Botev, for example, borrowing imagery from Pushkin, attacks corrupt, drunken traitorous priests leading the Bulgarians like sheep to the slaughter: 'Priest and Church with faith attend/ The man who tortures all the land' (Botev 1974: 51). See p. 173.
16. For a concise summary of the historical background, see Clogg (2002: ch. 2).
17. On Velestinlis in the context of the long history of conflict with Islam, see chapter 3 (this volume).
18. The dubious notion that Greek national identity was continuous from the ancient world was encouraged by the work of Korais, Pouqueville and Fauriel and given an official stamp in Paparrigopoulos' *History of the Greek Nation* (1st ed., 1860–74). Paparrigopoulos' work influenced historians in other parts of the Balkans – Iorga in Romania and Zlatarski in Bulgaria, for example – to argue a similar national continuity with the past. In the same period, Graetz wrote his massive *History of the Jews*, which, likewise, shows an unbroken national link of the Jews with their ancient biblical history.
19. The philhellene Scot, Thomas Gordon of Cairness, brought arms from Scotland for the rebels, but was disgusted to witness their massacre of 8,000 Turks at the siege of Tripolitsa in 1821 (Dakin 1955: 28ff.).
20. Panagiotis Soutsos (1828: 96, 130, 160) refers repeatedly to Leonidas in his poetry of the War of Independence. At moments in the war, however, ancient associations seemed justified. When in April 1821 Athanasios Diakos died defending the bridge at Alamana against a Turkish assault, it was impossible not to think of Leonides and his three hundred Spartans defending the pass of Thermopylae (a few hundred yards away) against the Persians in 480 BCE. This modern act of valor is commemorated by Valaorites in the poem 'Athanasios Diakos' (1864–6).
21. Other noted poets in the Romantic School of Athens were: John Karasoursas (1824–73), Theodore Orphanides (1818–86), Alexander Rizos Rangavis (1809–92), Panagiotis Soutsos (1805–68), Elias Tantalides (1818–76) and George Zalokostas (1805–58). Later figures included Demetrios Paparrhegopoulos (1843–73), George Paraschos (1822–86), Alexander Vizantios (1841–98), George Vizyenos (1848–94), Angelos Vlachos (1838–1919), and, most notably, Achilles Paraschos (1838–95). See Trypanis (1984).

The Greek War of Independence and its Poetry   163

22. Translated by David Aberbach from Trypanis (1984: 511–13).
23. The second siege of Missolonghi (1825–26) is the subject of Solomos' poem 'The Free Besieged', in which Turks and Arabs, symbolizing brute force, try unsuccessfully to demoralize the besieged Greeks and lure them to surrender by promising to spare them if they convert to Islam.
24. On Albanian poetry in the context of Ottoman/Tsarist imperial rivalry, see pp. 169, 173–5.
25. Serbian poetry has a similarly dual perspective. For example, Muslim poems on the Battle of Kosovo Fields coexist with Christian ones, but the Muslim side (which survived in oral literature) was mostly suppressed by Serbian nationalists. I am grateful to Professor David Elmer who, on my visits to the Milman Parry collection at Harvard University, drew my attention to this literary history.
26. As i biri Turk jezitit!
    Në Dunë të gjithë i mbiti.
    Në qafë të Dragocanit
    u vra llohu i Ipsillantit.

    (Ruches 1967: 42)

27. An Albanian song recalling the revolt, defeat and execution of Ali Pasha, 'Lion of Jannina', was composed and preserved by the Muslims of Epirus: 'In your seventy years you shone/ in conquest like the sun./ Jannina did not betray you –/ the empire tore you down' (Ruches 1967: 37). The high level of cultural interchange in the territory controlled by Ali Pasha is indicated in the fact that he had a personal poet, Haxhi Shereti, who wrote an epic, the *Alipashiad*, in his honor – in demotic Greek.
28. *Ibid.*, 43.
29. *Ibid.*, 45.
30. *Ibid.*, 46.
31. *Ibid.*, 49.
32. *Ibid.*, 54.
33. *Ibid.*, 56.
34. *Ibid.*
35. *Ibid.*, 59.
36. On Albanian national poetry, see pp. 169, 173–5.
37. On Solomos, see Politis (1973: ch. VII) and Mackridge (1989). Other noted figures in the School of the Ionian Islands included Gerasimos Markoras (1826–1911), Lorentzos Mavilis (1860–1912), George Tertsetis (1800–74) and Julius Typaldos (1814–83).
38. Solomos' house in Corfu, where he lived from 1828 until his death in 1857, during the period of British rule, is today a Solomos museum. As elsewhere in the British empire (see chapter 12 [this volume]), the British presence in the Ionians encouraged independence, which was achieved in 1865 with the full cooperation and help of the empire.
39. Like Solomos, the Albanian Gjergi Fishta and the Maltese Dun Karm Psaila were native Italian speakers and fought to establish Albanian and Maltese, respectively, not just as languages of poetry but also in daily life.
40. Solomos' poem 'On Psara' is a famous vignette of the Aegean island, site of a gruesome massacre by the Turks during the war:

164 *The Greek War of Independence and its Poetry*

> On Psara's coal-black ridge
> Glory walks alone
> thinking of these heroes,
> on her head a crown
> of thin grass
> of that desolate ground.
>
> Translated by David Aberbach (Trypanis 1984: 502)

41. Translated by David Aberbach. The Greek reads:

> Σὲ γνωρίζω ἀπὸ τὴν κόψη
> τοῦ σπαθιοῦ τὴν τρομερή,
> σὲ γνωρίζω ἀπὸ τὴν ὄψη
> ποὺ μὲ βία μετράει τὴ γῆ.
>
> 'Απ' τὰ κόκκαλα βγαλμένη
> τῶν Ἑλλήνων τὰ ἱερά,
> καὶ σὰν πρῶτα ἀνδρειωμένη
> χαῖρε ὦ χαῖρε, Ἐλευθερια!
>
> (Trypanis 1984: 501)

As the Greek national anthem, these are probably the best-known lines in modern Greek poetry.

42. On Kalvos, see Politis (1973: ch. VIII). On the love of Zante, see also Foscolo's Italian poem '*A Zacinto*'.

43. Χαῖρε Αὐσονία, χαῖρε/ καὶ σὺ Ἀλβιών, χαιρέτωσαν/ τα ἔνδοξα Παρίσια/ ὡραία καὶ μόνη ἡ Ζάκυνθος/ μὲ κυριεύει.
Τῆς Ζάκυνθου τα δάση/ καὶ τα βουνα σκιώδη/ ἠκουόν ποτε σημαίνοντα/ τα θεια τῆς Ἀρτέμιδος/ αργυρα τόξα.

> Translated by David Aberbach (from Trypanis 1984: 508)

44. On revenge in national poetry, see pp. 23–5, 43–4.
45. Translated by David Aberbach. The Greek reads:

> Μ' ἔκαμες Ευλοκρέβατο ... Μὲ φόρτωσες κουφάρια ...
> Σὲ ξένους μ' ἔριξες γιαλούς ... Τὸ ψυχομάχημά μου
> τὸ περιγέλασαν πολλοί, καὶ τὰ παθήματά μου
> τὰ φαρμακέψανε κρυφὰ μὲ τὴν ἐλεημοσύνη.
>
> (Trypanis 1984: 532)

46. Of the Italian revolutionaries whom he joined in Ravenna before he came to Greece, Byron wrote:

> 'They mean to *insurrect* here, and are to honour me with a call thereupon. I shall not fall back; though I don't think them in force or heart sufficient to make much of it. But, *onward!* – it is now the time to act, and what signifies *self*, if a single spark of that which would be worthy of the past can be bequeathed unquenchably to the future? It is not one man, nor a million, but the spirit of liberty which must be spread' (Moore 1932: 476).

47. The German scholar Fallmerayer opened a Pandora's box with his (now discredited) theory that modern Greeks are mostly of Slavic origins. In the poem *Modern Greece* (1817), Felicia Hemans expressed popular anti-Greece prejudices,

more common before the War of Independence than after, in suggesting that Greece fell as a result of a lack of patriotism on the part of its women, and that the nation was further debased by breeding with the Muslim population (Crocco 2014: ch. 5).

48. Chateaubriand wrote in 1806: 'I visited Sparta, Argos, Mycenae, Corinth, Athens; beautiful names, alas! nothing more... Never see Greece, Monsieur, except in Homer. It is the best way' (Augustinos 1994: 178).
49. On the influence of Byron's martyrdom on 19th century national poets, see Aberbach (2008).
50. In general, as seen in chapter 7 (this volume), Balkan revolts against Muslim rule tended to have the support of European Christian powers. The international character of Greek independence, which cut across national rivalries, is indicated in the facts. Otto I (1815–67), son of Louis I of Bavaria, became the first king of Greece (1832–62), installed by the Great Powers, and was succeeded by George I (1845–1913), son of Christian IX of Denmark.
51. See chapters 3 and 7 (this volume).
52. See p. 162, note 20.
53. Njegoš, for example, wrote in the context of a rich Serbo-Croatian tradition of folk song (see Bartok and Lord 1951). Fishta, likewise, in *The Highland Lute* (mostly written in 1902–09, shortly before Albania gained independence from the Ottoman empire), draws heavily on oral tradition (see Elsie and Mathie-Heck 2004) – necessarily so as the vast majority of Albanians were illiterate, and the Albanian language and education had been suppressed by the Turks. On the importance of vernacular languages to nationalism, see Anderson (1991).

7 National Poetry and Russian-Ottoman Imperial Conflict

> *O architect, with your marvellous creation ... beware of me!*
> (Pushkin, 'The Bronze Horseman')
>
> *The meal is served, eat, gentlemen, eat, till you gag ...*
> (Fikret, 'Free Meal')

National poetry bloomed in the rival Ottoman Turkish and Tsarist Russian empires after the French Revolution and the Napoleonic wars which spurred national cultures and vernacular languages throughout Europe, and frequent revolts.[1] Poets did their part in the fall of both empires, which collapsed in World War I. Inspired by the egalitarian ideology of the Revolution, they proclaimed in all their different languages that their nations, tired of imperial rule, were set on freedom. Poets rediscovered (or invented) and taught their national history, language and education. Asserting cultural independence, their poetry was political, its originality a mark of national distinction. They sought freedom in history and myth, in revivals of long-disparaged or neglected languages. They asserted as elsewhere the cultural and psychological independence of separate national groups, anticipating political independence.

In both empires, the dissident poet was often a leader and figurehead in national independence struggles and, not infrequently (for example, in Serbia and Albania, and in Poland and Bulgaria), deeply involved in the political, religious and educational life of the country. Both empires had national poets of their own, Turkish and Russian, expressing yearnings of subjugated peasant peoples with cultures alien to the ruling elite. To be a poet in a reactionary empire often meant to be a progressive and a rebel: Kondrati Ryleyev was hanged in 1826 for his part in the abortive Decembrist uprising against Tsar Nicholas I, Pushkin was exiled, Namik Kemal wrote in Turkish of the 'dogs of despotism' and of being imprisoned by the love of liberty and Tevfik Fikret laid bare the decay of the Ottoman empire in the last generation before its dissolution in World War I (Menemencioğlu and Iz 1978: 167, 169). Some poems, such as Solomos' Greek *Ode to Liberty* (1824) or Lönnrot's Finnish epic *The Kalevala* (1835), are practically declarations of independence, from the Ottoman and Tsarist empires, respectively.

From the French revolutionary era onward, poets in the Ottoman empire had high hopes that the French army would be their avant garde for independence.

National Poetry and Russian-Ottoman Imperial Conflict 167

Balkan poets had similar (more justified) hopes of Russian military intervention. The Tsarist empire championed Orthodoxy; the Ottoman empire was historically the most powerful and influential Muslim empire. Whereas poets in the Russian empire were angered by imposed Russification, Balkan poets, mostly Christian, played with fire in stoking up centuries-long conflict between Christianity and Islam. Hopes of independence grew in the Balkans as the Ottoman empire weakened after its defeats by Tsarist Russia in the 18th century. By the time of Byron, the Ottoman empire was little more than a prop of the Great Powers, a buffer against Russian expansion, consumed, as Ivo Andrić puts it in *The Bridge on the Drina* (1945), by a slow fever.

Though the two empires were bitter enemies and often at war, the Ottoman empire might be described as 'Russia's alter ego' (Hosking 2001: 193). Both were multiethnic religious autocracies, with traditions of tolerance toward minorities. Though the peoples in both empires were mostly illiterate, they had powerful religious cultures. Even in the remotest parts of the Tsarist empire the Bible was venerated; the Ottoman empire followed Islam in its high valuation of poetry, with a distinguished poetic tradition going back to the medieval Islamic conquests. Most of the Sultans who ruled the empire wrote poetry. Even in reaction against the empire and its religion, modern Turkish poets drew on Ottoman religious-cultural norms.

A bird's eye view of national poetry in the Ottoman and Russian empires reveals its exceptional variety, articulating the yearning for freedom of subjugated peoples. Both empires spawned a rich assortment of national poets, major figures in their respective countries, widely taught in school curricula, studied and sung, remembered and honored in buildings and streets, statues and money, and in many other ways. Celebrities at home, in foreign lands they are largely unknown, neglected even in the scholarship on nationalism. For their pearl of poetry, grit abounded, in the repressive Tsarist empire and in the Balkan 'front-line' in the conflict between Islam and Christianity (Lieven 2000: 148). What follows are vignettes of poets involved in these national struggles, some of whom appear elsewhere in this book in different contexts. In the Ottoman-ruled Balkans:

- Rigas Velestinlis (or Feraios) (1757–1798), Greece
- Petar II Petrovic-Njegoš (1813–1851), Serbia/Montenegro
- Hristo Botev (1849–1876), Bulgaria
- Mihail Eminescu (1850–1889), Romania
- Gjergj Fishta (1871–1940), Albania

In the Tsarist empire:

- Adam Mickiewicz (1798–1855), Poland
- Elias Lönnrot (1802–1884), Finland
- Taras Shevchenko (1814–1861), Ukraine

There were also poets of two scattered peoples caught in the conflict between the Ottoman and Tsarist empires: pan-Slavic, especially the poet Jan Kollar

(1793–1852); and Jewish, led by the Hebrew poet Chaim Nachman Bialik (1873–1934) in a unique revival of Jewish cultural nationalism originating mainly in the Tsarist empire in the 1881–1914 period, but focusing on the land of Israel, then under Ottoman rule.

Some Balkan poets spoke for nations whose existence was in doubt prior to the mid-19th century, such as Romania, Bulgaria and Albania, which won independence prior to World War I. While long-established countries under Tsarist rule, such as Poland and Ukraine, had to wait for independence at least until the 1917 revolution. Poets glorified national history: in Greece, the Greek War of Independence (1821–29), leading to independence in 1830;[2] in Serbia, independence struggles until 1878, when Serbia and Romania, too, won independence; Bulgaria gained autonomy; and even Albania, the only European country with a Muslim majority, began to resist rotten-ripe Ottoman rule, until independence came in 1912.

HOLY WAR IN THE BALKANS

The Balkans, last outpost of Muslim power in pre-1914 Europe, produced the only substantial body of 19th and early 20th century European national poetry reflecting the ancient clash of Islam and Christianity.[3] This subject, for centuries in the vanguard of European popular culture – in works such as *The Song of Roland* and *Orlando Furioso* – was mostly abandoned in European literature after the 17th century, when the Islamic expansionist threat to Central Europe receded. National poets in the Balkans often saw the Tsarist empire and its Orthodox Church as their allies against the Ottomans and Islam. To Balkan poets, unlike poets in Tsarist lands, national revolt was linked to religious conflict. Balkan revolutionary movements had the support of Christian powers (including Tsarist Russia) against Muslim rule. Christian insurrection in the Balkans invariably led to a declaration of Muslim holy war and threat of total annihilation. National Balkan poetry under the Ottomans is consequently more bloodthirsty and cruel than national poetry under the Tsars. Mickiewicz's Polish epic *Pan Tadeusz* (1834), for example, is shot through with occasionally violent longing for independence from Russia, but the poet's main aim is the depiction of Polish society in all its distinctive individuality. In contrast, Njegoš' Serbian epic *The Mountain Wreath* (1847) palpably lusts for the annihilation of the Muslim enemy – particularly Serbian converts to Islam – as a condition of Serbian survival. Conflict with Islam is the core of the poem.[4]

ANTECEDENTS: NATIONAL POETRY IN THE OTTOMAN BALKANS AND TSARIST RUSSIA

National poetry in the Ottoman and Tsarist empires after 1789 had pre-modern antecedents, both in oral literature – in Balkan folk poetry and song – and in eastern European epic poetry. Balkan poetry flowered from rich strata of centuries-old oral poetry in mountain regions whose rough remoteness helped survival, even of small peoples, and the growth of separate, though often intertwined, cultures.[5] Much of this oral poetry has medieval origins, in longstanding local border and religious disputes and 19th century Great Power conflicts – the Christian empires of Tsarist Russia and Austria-Hungary versus the declining Muslim Ottoman empire. Serbian poets mourn 14th century Ottoman conquests as though they just occurred. Romanian poets salute medieval heroes such as Mircea and Vlad Tepes, who fought the Turks. Albanian poets praise resistance to Turkish rule, lasting over four centuries until 1912. Central in Albanian poetry is the 15th century hero Skanderbeg,[6] ubiquitous in both oral and written Albanian, in works by de Rada, Frasheri and Fishta, among others. Though raised among the Turks, Skanderbeg returned to Christianity and led the Albanian tribes in a victorious war against the Turks (1444–1466). After his death, Albania was subdued by the Turks (1479), but its mountainous terrain made full control impossible. Skanderbeg's resistance made him a folk hero and for centuries an icon of Albanian hope for freedom; and there were frequent revolts in the mountains.

The leading Albanian poet of the 19th century, Jeronim de Rada (1814–1903) repeatedly stresses the 15th century as the turning point in Albanian history.[7] De Rada, son of a Catholic parish priest in Cosenza, Italy (a center of the Albanian disaspora), was fascinated by Albanian folklore. While studying law in Naples in the 1830s, he reworked this folk tradition into the first modern Albanian poetry. To de Rada, the gathering and reworking of fragments of folklore brought closer political unification of the Albanian people as a modern nation. In Greece, too, anonymous folk culture preserved nationalist longings. Among the early 19th century illiterate Greek masses, folk poetry, surviving orally and often sung, contributed to the building of the nation. Though scholars question the continuity of Greek literature from the ancient to the modern world, there are recurrent elements.[8] The long history of Greek defeats by the Turks from the 15th century on gave a flow of inspiration to the Greek lament, particularly on the fall of Constantinople in 1453 (Alexiou 2002a, ch. 5). Other poems declare Greek pride and determination to win freedom from the Turks.[9]

In Tsarist countries, too, national poetry had many pre-modern antecedents. From the 14th to the 17th century, Ottoman conquests threatened Christian Europe, triggering much vernacular poetry of emerging nationalism: for example, in epics by Ivan Gundulic (1588–1638) in Croatia, Nicholas Zrinyi (1616–1664) in Hungary, Waclaw Potocki (1625–1694) in Poland and Mikhail Lomonosov (1711–1765) in Russia. Gundulic's epic poem *Osman* (1626), set against the battle of Khotin (1621) in which the Polish-Lithuanian army drove back the invading Turks, glorifies the struggle of Christianity against Islam.[10] For centuries in the Balkans, folk memory preserved a Greek legend of the *xanthon genos*, a fair-haired race of liberators from the north – usually identified with the Russians, the only

Orthodox people not under Ottoman rule.[11] In the 18th century, this hope revived among Balkan Christians after the Russian victories over the Turks. Catherine the Great aimed to divide the Balkans with Austria and re-establish a Byzantine empire; and local Muslim rulers, too, lusted for freedom from Ottoman rule.

BALKAN NATIONAL POETRY UNDER OTTOMAN RULE, 1789–1914

Most major Balkan national poets – including Solomos, Njegoš, Botev, Eminescu and Fishta – were politically committed Christians opposed to Ottoman rule, and their poetry and cultural activities were directed to national independence. Insecure Turkish control of the Balkans was a creative stimulus: the Turks were protected by the Balkan population – about two-thirds Christian – but also feared them as a 'Trojan horse' (Lieven 2000: 149). Until the French Revolution, the Balkan population was defined mainly in religious terms. Under relatively tolerant Muslim rule for centuries, the Balkans guarded the Turkish capital, Constantinople, from attack by the European Christian powers, particularly the Habsburg and Tsarist empires from the north. The Balkans also controlled the Straits of the Dardanelles and the Bosporus, the gateways to the Black Sea and to the markets of Russia and Central Asia. Balkan poetry reacted to the Ottoman loss of control over the Straits. As the Ottoman empire weakened, old religious categories stiffened national identity and, at times, eclipsed it. No Balkan state could have won independence on its own from the Turks. Revolt was invariably crushed. Yet the Christian European powers periodically intervened and supported fellow Christians defeated by the Turks: Serbia (1810), Greece (1827) and Bulgaria (1876). Religion in the Balkans determined political alliances. For example, the Ottomans favored and protected Balkan Muslims; the Russians protected the Orthodox Serbs; and the Austrians protected the Catholic Albanians. National movements in the Tsarist empire (including those in the crushed continent-wide revolutions of 1848–49) did not have the historical 'front-line' advantage of the Balkan people. Yet, by encouraging independence struggles against the Ottoman empire and creating semi-autonomous puppet states in the Balkans with distinct cultures of their own, the Great Powers unleashed uncontrollable rival nationalisms and expansionist forces. National poetry in the Balkans as elsewhere signified a new, ultimately catastrophic militarism. The centuries-long conflict between Islam and the West can be seen as an indirect cause of World War I.

Serbia/Montenegro

For centuries in remote Balkan mountain areas, there was periodic resistance to Ottoman rule. The failed Serbian uprising of 1804–13 was followed by a successful war against the Turks and limited Serb autonomy by 1817, with full autonomy by 1830 and independence in 1878. The sense of history, both real and mythical, is strong in Serbian poetry. The poet and bishop-ruler Njegoš, one of the few literate Serbs of his time and author of the classic Serbian epic *The Mountain Wreath* (1847), takes comfort from Charles Martel's victory over the Muslim invaders in the battle of Tours/Poitiers eleven hundred years earlier: 'If the French dike had not stood in the way,/ the Arab sea would have flooded it all' (Францускога да не би брњега,/ аравнјско море све потопн!) (l. 7–8). Njegoš follows earlier Serbian poetry in glorifying the 1389 Muslim defeat of the Serbs at the Battle of Kosovo Fields which led to five centuries of Ottoman rule, as a necessary sacrifice, making the Serbs a chosen people who have gained 'the empire of heaven'.[12] Like many of his followers, devout Orthodox Serbs, the poet laments the aggressive efforts of Muslims to tempt them to Islam, through incentives such as bribery, freedom from taxation, trading advantages and the right to ride horses and carry weapons. Loyal Serbs came to see Orthodoxy as the core of their Serbian identity. Apostasy to Islam was a capital crime, the betrayal of the sacrifice and ideals of Kosovo. *The Mountain Wreath* treats Islam as a threat to 'true' Serbian identity. It celebrates as a 'victory' a Serbian massacre of converts and suggests that the conflict will not end until either the Serbs or the Turks are exterminated.[13] Njegoš goes against the Byronic internationalist liberal grain in early 19th century national poetry, foreshadowing instead later slaughters. Serbian nationalism is inseparable from Orthodoxy, yet the poem never considers that the genocide of converts to Islam is un-Christian.[14] At the same time, the case for Islam is put eloquently by the Muslim leader Mustaj Kadija. Even the Orthodox Bishop Danilo concedes that the infidel cannot wholly be blamed, for human nature is weak. Religious conversion and intermarriage are part of life; they become intolerable when they threaten Serbian religious-national survival.

Greek Nationalism and the Classical Revival

The French Revolution and Enlightenment ideals of liberty and progress helped give birth to the modern Greek state and its culture at a time of classical revival in Europe and the United States.[15] Prior to the French Revolution, Ottoman rule had isolated the Balkans: the Renaissance, the Reformation, the 17th century scientific revolution and the Enlightenment mostly passed it by. Of pre-1789 Balkan cultures, Greek had the most international prestige, as part of a well-rounded education in schools and universities. After the French Revolution, as European nationalism spread, Greeks increasingly began to search for their national identity in the classical world. A small number of Greek intellectuals, whose leading poet was Rigas Velestinlis, called for revolution against the Turks and the reawakening of Greek culture. Murdered by the Turks in 1798, Rigas was hailed as the first modern Greek prophet of armed revolt and martyr of independence. His

Thourios (War Song) widely sung, admired and translated by Byron, contemptuously rejects Greek 'slavery' in the prison of Islam and Ottoman rule: (Clogg 2002: 29).

The Greek War of Independence and its Poetry

Greece followed Serbia in its revolt against the Ottoman empire, with independence by 1830. As we saw in chapter 6, Greek poetry of this period and after reflects a new sense of national pride and confidence, transforming the international image of Greeks and Turks.[16] Key events of the war heightened Greek national consciousness and created Greek unity. Byron's arrival in Greece in 1824 to fight in the War of Independence made the war a 'great romantic crusade' (Woodhouse 1991: 140–1). When the Turks refused the British/French demand that Turkey recognize Greek autonomy, the Ottoman fleet was destroyed at Navarino (20 October 1827). A brief war between the Russians and the Turks (1828) was followed by a treaty affirming Greek independence, with Athens the capital. These events inspired the poets of the Romantic School of Athens, founded and led by Alexander Soutsos (1803–63).[17] Soutsos' poetry conveys the national spirit of the War of Independence. Himself a veteran of the war, Soutsos highlights stirring moments, particularly in southern Greece, renowned for its fighting spirit: 'How the Turks swarmed over the valleys of our brave Roumeli,/ our children and parents besieged by Arabs in Missolonghi?' (Trypanis 1984: 511). In response to the siege of Missolonghi, Dionysios Solomos (1798–1857) wrote *Ode to Liberty* (1824), the opening of which became, in 1865, the Greek national anthem: 'Hail Liberty! you I greet/ who springs bold/ from holy bones of Greeks,/ brave as of old …'.[18] Albanian poetry of the same period recounts events of the war from a Muslim viewpoint.[19]

Eminescu and Romanian Nationalism

Eminescu was the chief Romanian poet in the years before and after independence from the Ottoman empire (1878). Romanian nationalism was roused by the French Revolution via Greek influence, though belief in the antiquity and chosenness of the Romanian people as direct descendants of the Romans began among late 18th century Romanian students in Jesuit schools in Rome. These early cultural nationalists transformed the Romanian language, replacing Slovenian with Latin; purging the language of Slavic, Greek and non-Latin words; and establishing Romanian as the language taught in schools. Eminescu was part of this cultural upsurge, aiming to achieve the Herderian ideal of the nation defined by the vernacular. He did much to revive common idiomatic speech and traditional forms attuned to contemporary needs.

Yet, like Greece's Valaorites, Eminescu was also a poet of revenge against the Turks.[20] In 1867, a decade before independence, he rejoiced in their violent deaths: heads lopped off hydra-like, blood burning on slashing swords (Carduner and Natanson 1986: 50). The poet contrasts Romania's abject state now, in the late 19th century, with the heroic age of Vlad Tepes (the Impaler) and his grandfather, Mircea the Old, medieval Wallachian leaders of 'this once great nation,' who defeated the invading Turks in battle: 'row upon row of Arabs wavered and were cut down' (*Cad asabii ca și pîlcuri risipite pe cîmpie*) (Eminescu 1980: 144–5).

Botev and Bulgarian Nationalism

Many Bulgarian poets, including Chintulov, Rakovski, Botev and Karavelov, were influenced by Russian revolutionary literature in the struggle against the Turks. Still, prior to the second half of the 19th century the concept of Bulgaria as a self-governing state free of Ottoman rule hardly existed. Bulgarian nationalism kept hope for freedom alive after five centuries of Ottoman rule. Greek ecclesiastical domination was ended by replacing the Greek Bible with a Bulgarian translation, establishing an autonomous Bulgarian church in 1870 and creating a secular school system using vernacular Bulgarian.[21] Botev attacks corrupt, drunken traitorous priests who allegedly led the Bulgarians like sheep to the slaughter: 'Priest and Church with faith attend/ The man who tortures all the land (И на обществен тоя мъчител/ и поп, и черква с вяра слугуват)' (Botev 1974: 51). Yet, Botev also hated Ottoman rule. He saw Bulgarian nationalism as part of a religious war and compared the Turkish feudal state to an agonized body eaten alive by worms (Topencharov 1982: 68). The death of a rebel, Hadzhi Dimit'r, in 1871, inspired his ballad of that name whose opening was the cry of popular disbelief, 'He's alive, he's alive!' (жив е той, жив е!).[22] Botev evidently wanted such a death for himself, not for his country alone but with universal significance, for the poet aims to change the world (*ibid.*, 57, 60). He was killed on 2 June 1876 (a date commemorated annually in Bulgaria), leading the Bulgarians in revolt against the Turks. The entire European press supported the Bulgarians (*ibid.*, 80). Russian intervention brought Bulgaria to independence two years later.[23]

Albanian Nationalism and its Poetry

The Italian-born poet Jeronim de Rada was the leading 19th century Albanian nationalist. Apart from his poetry (including an epic on Skanderbeg), he gathered Albanian folklore and published the first Albanian newspaper in 1848. A tipping point in Albanian history was the Treaty of Berlin (1878), which granted independence to Romania, Serbia and Montenegro, and autonomy to Bulgaria, while ignoring Albanian concerns. This forced Albanian national awareness, leading to revolt and independence by 1912. Albanian poetry of this period is striking in its religious tolerance. It defines Albanian national identity through shared history and religious heritage. The Congress of Berlin in 1878 exposed the humiliating threat of piecemeal annexation of Albanian territory by Serbia, Montenegro and Greece, supported by the Great Powers. At this time, the Albanian poet Pashko Vasa (1825–92), a member of the League of Prizren (1878) which demanded Albanian autonomy, articulated the growing national frustration – shared by Christians and Muslims – at being part of a bitterly divided people vulnerable to the machinations of the Great Powers. Split into a hundred factions, Albanians were killing one another:

> Some say, 'I believe in God,' others 'I in Allah,'
> Some say 'I am Turk,' others 'I am Latin,'
> Some 'I am Greek,' others 'I am Slav,'
> But you are brothers, all of you, my hapless people!
>
> (Elsie 2005: 87)[24]

Vasa called for Albania to awake and unite as one nation:

> Let us all, as brothers, swear a common oath
> And not look to church or mosque,
> The faith of the Albanians is Albanianism!
>
> (*ibid.*, 88)

From the late 19th century, Albanian cultural nationalism spread with the proliferation of schools in the north, funded by Austria-Hungary, self-appointed protector of the Christian Balkan population. Nationalism grew with increased literacy in a society previously almost totally illiterate. Both Muslims and Christians looked to the past as a basis for national cohesion. The Muslim poet Naim Frasheri, 'apostle-poet of Albanian nationalism' (Stavrianos 2000: 505), drew on ancient folk tradition in yet another poem on Skanderbeg, the prototypical Albanian 15th century warrior.[25] Gjergj Fishta – a Franciscan monk, with close ties to Austrian Catholics – became administrator of schools in the district of Shkodra in 1902, when he began work on *The Highland Lute*, the last great European heroic epic before World War I. At this time, amid fear of Albanian partition between the Slavs and the Greeks,[26] Fishta helped change the language of instruction in northern Albanian schools from Italian to Albanian and so created the first generation of literate Albanians, able to read his poem.[27] *The Highland Lute*, completed after Albanian independence in 1912 (and Fishta became vice president of the Albanian government), depicts in fifty cantos the historical process from 1862–1913 by which Albania was transformed from a collection of tribes into a nation. Fishta's poem itself did much to shape a previously nonexistent Albanian national identity.[28] Like other epics, such as Mickiewicz's *Pan Tadeusz*, *The Highland Lute* is virtually a compendium of 'national' traditions, customs and beliefs in different social strata, such as the word of honor (*besa*), the blood bond, and the value of hospitality, the attachment to the Albanian landscape, as well as traditional grievance against the Turks and hope of independence inspired by Skanderbeg. Albania was no slice of fruit divided among strangers but 'the land of our fathers', birthplace of Skanderbeg, home of heroes who fought the Turks (Fishta 2005: 85–6).[29] *The Highland Lute* reads at times like an Albanian *Song of Roland*, with frequent cascades of severed heads and traditional glorification of conflict, bravery and honor that the Great War made absurd and anachronistic. Yet, in the poem Christian and Muslim cultures co-exist amid multiple viewpoints, as in Albanian poetry of the Greek War of Independence (Ruches 1967).[30] Fishta treats Albanian identity as inclusive, with Muslims and Christians united against common foes after the Congress of Berlin: Muslims swear on the Koran, Christians on the Gospels, to be loyal and defend Albania (Fishta 2005: 130, 131). In this poetry, nationalism supersedes religious conflict and points to an end of ancient divisions and rivalries:

> Will I ever see my people
> All united under oath and
> Out to fight and save their homeland?
>
> Will they ever join their forces,
> Ghegs and Tosks from Highlands, lowlands,
> Linked together our red-black banners,
> Here to spend blood for their birthplace?
> Yes, why not?

(*ibid.*, 52)

Yet, when independence came, in the Balkan war of 1912–13, many Balkan Muslims were shocked as the border with Turkey had withdrawn overnight by over 600 miles, and the power of the empire vanished like a great ocean tide, leaving them 'deceived and menaced, like seaweed on dry land, left to their own devices and their own evil fate' (Andrić 1977: 230).

NATIONAL POETRY IN TSARIST RUSSIA, 1789–1914

By 1914, for the first time since the 15th century, the Balkans were free from Ottoman rule. The Tsarist empire, with the largest army in Europe, kept all national groups under its rule until the 1917 revolution. Of the two empires, the Tsarist was the more repressive, in trying to impose a Russian-dominant culture. National poets in the Tsarist empire, in Poland, Finland, Ukraine and elsewhere, opposed Russification, asserting national distinctiveness in their own languages. The great exception was Hebrew which, from the 1820s until 1881, the Russian authorities allowed to develop among the Jews as a tool of secular education (Haskalah = the Hebrew Enlightenment) and ultimate Russification. Only after the pogroms of 1881 did Hebrew became an integral part of Jewish nationalism. Until 1881,

Hebrew poets were, in effect, agents of Russian patriotism, despite Russian anti-Semitism.[31] Typically obsequious, the poet Abraham Dov Lebensohn (1794?–1878) addressed the tyrannical Tsar Nicholas I:

> Peter the Great did wonderful things,
> Catherine the same.
> Alexander was best of kings,
> But Nicholas, yours is the greatest name.
>
> (Lebensohn 1895: 72)

The reforms of Alexander II after the Crimean War – the abolition of juvenile conscription and the admission of wealthy and professionally trained Jews into the Russian interior, as well as the optimistic spirit of the period – encouraged Jewish patriotism and hope that emancipation was imminent. The leading 19th century Hebrew poet, Judah Leib Gordon (1831–1892) responded to the freeing of the Russian serfs in 1861 with the classic expression of Haskalah delusions, in a Hebrew poem in which the Russian Jews are encouraged to speak, not Hebrew but Russian:

> Lift your head, straighten your back,
> with love set your sight.
> To wisdom open your heart:
> speak their tongue, seek the light.
>
> (Gordon 1973: 4)

Yet, Gordon also introduced in his poetry Jewish nationalist elements – such as alienation and violent revolt against authority and restraints – typical of national movements (Kedourie 1960: 100–1). During the Polish revolt against Russia in 1863, Gordon condemned the Jews and their rabbinic leadership for neglecting the martial arts:

> You're ruined, Israel:
> you did not learn the art of war,
> so you're burnt out, spiritless,
> stuffed with scribes' dust, pages of talk …
>
> (*ibid.*, 109)

Gordon believed the Russian Jews should assimilate in Tsarist Russia; yet his use of Hebrew and attacks on his people inadvertently gave his poetry a national character and contributed to the rise of Jewish nationalism.

Mickiewicz and Polish Nationalism

The exemplar of modern Polish nationalism was Mickiewicz, a Lithuanian Pole born under Russian occupation during the Napoleonic era.

Mickiewicz never forgot the stirring sight of Napoleon's army marching in 1812 on the road to Moscow, bringing freedom, so it seemed, to the Poles and other oppressed peoples. He set his epic *Pan Tadeusz* in 1811–12 to fix permanently in Polish culture this moment, when the invasion of Russia was joined by tens of thousands of Poles who saw Napoleon as their messiah: 'We shall be Poles once more!. .../ our Land will be restored!' (VI 246, 256; Mickiewicz 1962: 179). After the French defeat, the poet went on to study at the University of Vilnius and became a teacher in a school in Kovno, where he published his first book of poems. In 1824, he was banished to Russia for membership in a secret Polish nationalist group.[32] In 1829 Mickiewicz fled for France after the publication of *Konrad Wallenrod*, a thinly-disguised allegory of Poland's struggle with Russia, which made his reputation as Poland's national poet.[33] Set in the 14th century, the poem tells of Wallenrod, a gloomy Romantic kidnapped with Halban, a Lithuanian bard, by Teutonic Knights at war with Lithuania. Halban's song revives Wallenrod's national hopes. He becomes Grand Master of the Knights and leads them to defeat. Tormented by guilt at his own fox-like treachery, Wallenrod kills himself.[34] Halban preserves Wallenrod's heroic tale in song. In the Polish rising of November 1830, the political implications of the poem were clear: 'Every class, women and youths, the army and civilians drank in this great and patriotic poem with boundless enthusiasm' (Koropeckyj 2008: 95). Mickiewicz arrived from France to take part in the revolt to find that it had already been crushed. He then returned to the West and wrote *Pan Tadeusz* in Paris, with a hopelessly melodramatic prediction of Poland surfeited with slaughter, drenched in the blood of its dead foes.[35] *Pan Tadeusz* can be read as a literary 'victory' over Russia. Ending before Napoleon's defeat, it freezes the moment of hope together with all that makes Polish identity. The poem was written mainly for the thousands of expatriats who, like Mickiewicz, found refuge in Paris after the failed 1830 revolt, and for whom a national existence had been suspended. In the Epilogue of *Pan Tadeusz*, Poland is described as dead and buried: the poem will resurrect it. The time will come when knights in a free Poland will recall its former glory in song; in the meantime, there is the poem. Mickiewicz attacks Poles who degrade the nation by assimilating into foreign cultures, neglecting their own. In Book IX, he satirizes the Polish traitor Major Plut who, like other Poles, has changed his name and become both Russified and a Russian lackey, joining the Russian army only to be comically exposed in his cowardice by the fighting Poles.

Pan Tadeusz, published in Paris, out of reach of the Russian censor and set in a remote Polish estate – 'the center of our Polish ways' (VII 453) – is practically a handbook of Polish types and customs and instruction on how to be a Pole and a Polish Romantic: how to dress, eat, behave socially, to court, duel, hunt, fight, dance the polonaise – even how to gather mushrooms and make Polish coffee. The poem ends with a magnificent banquet which follows instructions in a book on medieval Polish customs, 'When Poland still knew happiness and power' (XII 270). This book, like the poem itself, will continue to guide Poles who value their traditions. *Pan Tadeusz* gives a marvellously detailed, psychologically rich and often comic portrait of a whole, harmonious Polish society about to be crushed by Russia. The poem has a strong anti-Russian undercurrent. Tadeusz, the young man of the title, is born at the time of the 1794 Polish revolt and named after Kosciuszko, leader of the revolt. The bear hunt in Book IV, in common with a similar scene in the *Kalevala*, is an implied attack on Russia, symbolized by the bear.[36] Feuding among Poles stops with the prospect of war with Russia: 'The Polish Commonwealth will bloom again' (VII 375). Even the assassination of the Tsar is imagined (*ibid.*, 250f). *Pan Tadeusz* reaches its absurd climax in Book IX when a garrison of Russian soldiers takes refuge in a collapsing cheese house and is chivalrously routed by Polish patriots.[37] This morale-boosting vision of military victory had no basis in political reality, and perhaps this is why Mickiewicz and his poem meant so much to Poland.

Lönnrot and Finnish Nationalism

In 1835, the year after *Pan Tadeusz* came out, the Finnish ethnographer Lönnrot published the *Kalevala*.[38] Finland, annexed by Russia in 1809, remained under Russian rule until 1917. The *Kalevala* more than anything else in Finnish culture gave national pride and self-esteem as Finland's 'book of independence' (Wilson 1976: x). The poem describes the exploits of Finnish heroes in a mythological world of magic, witches, song, stirring conflict and adventure. The *Kalevala* radiates a distinctive Finnish character and outlook and had enormous political importance. Elements of national distinctiveness – Finnish myths and legends, the Finnish language and culture – combined to assert Finland's cultural independence both from Russia and from Sweden, Finland's ruler from the 12th century until 1809, whose culture still dominated Finland. The *Kalevala* was written at a time when Finnish was generally regarded as inferior to Swedish or Russian.[39] When Tsarist Russia collapsed in 1917, Finland declared political independence, but the *Kalevala* was, in a deeper sense, its true declaration of independence. Finland celebrates Kalevala Day on 28 February, the date of Lönnrot's 1835 Preface to the first edition of *The Kalevala*.

Shevchenko and Ukrainian Nationalism

From the 1830s, Shevchenko's poetry roused Ukrainian national consciousness and promoted unity and moral regeneration in the struggle for independence from Russia. Ukraine, Shevchenko believed, must look inwardly for strength to break its chains: independence was not enough, it needed to create a just society (Shevchenko 1964: 249–50).[40] Somewhat incongruously, the poet elevates the Cossacks as models of Ukrainian heroism. He rages against traitors – particularly Ukrainian landlords – who 'crucify the mother' and suck her blood, as well as cultural 'traitors' who abandon the sacred Ukrainian mother tongue (*ibid.*, 255, 256).[41] Shevchenko's mockery of the Tsar and his wife and his championship of Ukrainian cultural independence led to his exile to Siberia and consequent elevation as Ukraine's national poet.

The history of Ukrainian subjugation by Russia meant that the role of Russians in promoting Ukrainian culture was sometimes overlooked. Shevchenko attacks Russians such as the critic Belinsky who mocked Ukrainians as uncultured and Ukrainian as a dead language.[42] In fact, many Russians were fascinated by the 'wild frontier' of Ukraine, by its history and folklore (Subtelny 1988). The leading promoter of early 19th century Ukrainian literature was a Russian, Izmail Sreznevsky. Russian journals published Ukrainian literature. Shevchenko himself had crucial support from Russians in his metamorphosis from serf to distinguished poet and artist.[43] Still, Russians were generally unwilling to accept the legitimacy of Ukrainian nationalism and the justice of Ukrainian independence, and their support for Ukrainian literature was seen as 'an enrichment of general Russian culture' (*ibid.*, 232). Shevchenko pointedly dedicated several of his poems to prominent Ukrainian writers, including Kotliarevsky, Hrebinka and Osnovianenko, with the aim of encouraging Ukrainian against encroaching Russification.

NATIONAL POETRY OF SCATTERED PEOPLES IN THE OTTOMAN AND TSARIST EMPIRES

Kollar and Pan-Slavic National Poetry

Shevchenko's dismissal of pan-Slavic nationalism[44] was not unjustified. This nationalism had no agreed-upon past or, it seems, future, though individual Slavic countries eventually gained independence. In the early-19th century, the Hungarian poet Ferenc Kölcsey blamed his own people, fellow Magyars, for 'our crimes' which brought the 'Turkish yoke' (Kirkconnell 1947: 26).[45] Kollar, pastor of the Slovak Lutheran community in early 19th century Budapest and chief poet of pan-Slavism, sang of a glorious future for the Slavs and hoped futilely for Slav independence from Russia.[46] Even so, pan-Slavic poetry helped undermine Russian imperial rule.

As a student at the University of Jena, Kollar was inspired by the French Revolution and German Romanticism, by Herder and Hegel. Kollar's work was part of a revival of Slavic cultural and national self-awareness in the 19th century, under the impact of the Revolution (Kirschbaum 1995: ch. 5). Slavophile nationalists were inclined to forge the nation, in every sense, using all means available. In 1817 – much as Macpherson did the 'poems of Ossian' – the poet Vaclav Hanka, archivist in the Museum of Bohemia, 'discovered' first an ancient manuscript of Slavonic poems (the 'Kralovedorsky

Manuscript'), and in the following year, 'discovered' a Czech epic of the 13th century, *The Judgment of Libusa* (the 'Zelenohorsky Manuscript', 1818). These forgeries of a heroic national identity and a bogus fight for freedom were a popular and scholarly success and made Hanka a national hero. The Czech historian and political leader Frantisek Palacky (1798–1876) wrote of his joy and national pride at reading the Zelenohorsky Manuscript after its 'discovery'. History became a branch of Slavic myth. In his historical writings, Palacky identified a continuous Slavic identity from the medieval to the modern period and traced modern progressive and liberal Western culture to Slavic influence. In 1823, the Borisov brothers founded a Society of United Slavs in the Ukraine. The term 'Panslavism' was coined by the Slovak scholar Jan Herkel in 1826. Around 1840, the Brotherhood of Cyril and Methodius, a society with a similar aim of Slav unity was set up by Vassily Bilozerski and Mikola Kostomarov in Kiev, capital of ancient Rus. Both Kollar and the poet and scholar Pavel Josef Safarik published collections of Slovak national songs: Safarik in 1823 and 1827, Kollar in 1834 and 1835. To Slav nationalists such as Kollar these nationalist stirrings presaged panslavic unity. Kollar regarded Judaic influence via the Bible as integral to Slav identity. The 'humanitarianism' of the Slavs was, in Kollar's view, 'a spiritual superiority which naturally dictated a messianic role to them' (Zamoyski 1999: 316).

Kollar, living in Austria and Hungary, roused some Slavic national awareness and a sense of cultural community. His sonnets, *Daughter of Slava* (1824), written mostly in Czech, are poems of hope for unification of all Slavs – Bulgarians, Croatians, Czechs, Hungarians, Poles, Russians, Slovenians and Ukrainians – and an end of oppressive German influence. Yet, this nationalism was wrecked by reality: the tearful poet sees Slavic lands as the graveyard of their national hopes. Kollar's Lutheran background meant that he belonged to a minority immersed in biblical Czech, a literary language in which the majority, Catholic Slovaks who spoke the vernacular, had no interest.[47] He knew national resurrection was unlikely. His hope that Slavic – the speech of slaves – would be a major language of science and the arts, spoken even by enemies of the Slavs, was a pipe dream. Few of Kollar's poems openly express national Slav identity. Toward the end of his life, as a professor at the University of Vienna, he supported the Austro-Hungarian monarchy.[48] Kollar believed, nevertheless, that the Slavic revival was possible – but only if he led it.

Jewish Nationalism in the Tsarist and Ottoman Empires

Jewish nationalism – the most ancient European nationalism and the last to find political direction in the 19th century – emerged in the no man's land between the Tsarist and Ottoman empires, with about 65,000 mostly Russian Jews emigrating to Ottoman Palestine in the period 1881–1914. Until the 1881 pogroms, the Russian Jews remained quiescent, seemingly oblivious to independence movements in the Tsarist empire. However, Balkan nationalism inspired some early Zionists, such as Rabbi Yehuda Alkalai of Semlin, Serbia, whose Zionist tract *Goral l'Adonai* (1857) anticipated Herzl's *Judenstaat* (1896) (Herzl's paternal grandfather Simon was a disciple of Alkalai's) and Ben-Yehudah, author of the first modern Hebrew dictionary, who came to Zionism during the period of nationalist fervor created by the Russian-Turkish war of 1877–78. Bialik's concept of *kinnus* (cultural ingathering) by which fragments of Jewish culture from many ages and lands of exile might be 'gathered in' and unified as a modern secular national culture recalls a similar program by the Albanian poet de Rada by which the restoration of folk fragments to unity would unite 'the dispersed nation' (Pipa 1978: 23). As a fighting people, the Greeks, both ancient and modern, encouraged some modern cultural Zionists, notably the Russian Hebrew poet Saul Tchernichowsky (1875–1943), translator of Homer into Hebrew (Leoussi and Aberbach 2002). Tchernichowsky, a doctor by profession, found in Greek mythology an antidote to the alleged sicknesses of Judaism. In a notorious poem of 1898, the poet paid homage to Apollo:

> I bow down to life, might and beauty,
> I bow to all beautiful things, robbed
> by rotten human carcasses,
> rebels against life, against *Tzuri Shaddai*,
> God of the gods of wondrous deserts,
> God of the gods of the conquerors of Canaan in storm –
> and tied him with *tefillin* straps ...
>
> (Aberbach 2003a: 174)

The strengths of early Zionism came partly from the weaknesses of the Tsarist and Ottoman empires: growing popular discontent in Russia after the serfs were freed in 1861; violent anti-Semitism and Jewish disillusionment with Russification and Haskalah ideals after the assassination of the Tsar in 1881; and the bankruptcy of the Ottoman empire, giving the Zionists, led by Theodor Herzl (1860–1904), political leverage (which they were unable at first to exploit because of the hostility or indifference of Western European Jews). In tandem with the Western political Zionist Organization, founded by Herzl in 1897, cultural Zionism thrived in Russia with a remarkable growth of nationalist Hebrew literature, whose outstanding poet was Bialik.[49] The instability of the Tsarist empire is memorably expressed by Bialik in a series of poems written during the pogroms of 1903–06, instigated in part by the government to divert widespread popular discontent against the Jews:

> Look how night envelops us, we are crushed
> by darkness, we grope like the blind.
> Something has gone wrong, no one knows what.

No one sees, no one tells,
if the sun has risen for us or set –
or set forever.
And chaos is all around, all around terrible chaos
and no escape.⁵⁰

Though the Zionist political organization was largely a creation of West European Jews – assimilated, highly educated, legally emancipated but exposed to social and racial prejudice – the Hebrew cultural revival after 1881 came mostly among the unemancipated Jews of the Russian Pale of Settlement – largely unassimilated, Yiddish-speaking, impoverished, deeply religious and subjected to increasingly violent state-tolerated anti-Semitism. The two waves of Tsarist Russian pogroms, in 1881–2 and 1903–06, led to the first two waves of modern Jewish *aliyah* (immigration) to Ottoman Palestine, where Hebrew culture was restored to its ancient roots.

CONCLUSION

Poets contributed to the demolition of the already-fragmenting Ottoman and Tsarist empires. Byron directly influenced poets in both empires, particularly Solomos and Mickiewicz. His death in Missolonghi in 1824 inspired a new militancy among poets, especially in Balkan national struggles against Ottoman rule. After Byron, it was not unusual for poets, notably Petőfi of Hungary and Botev of Bulgaria, to fight and die for the national cause. As Greek culture was renewed as part of a modern national movement aiming at political independence, so it was also among other peoples under imperial rule. In the Balkans, poets were the 'real enemies' of the Sultans (Woodhouse 1991: 136). The Tsars, too, were no match for the poets of their empire. By the time the Ottoman and Russian empires collapsed, these poets and their followers had shaped their national cultures into a new, distinctive force with political independence achieved or on the horizon.

NOTES

1. The Ottoman and Tsarist empires are compared by Lieven (2000). On nationalism in countries in the Ottoman and Tsarist empires, see Kedourie (1960), Hobsbawm (1990), Gellner (1983), Hourani (1991), Breuilly (1993), Hutchinson (1994), Cleveland (1994), Lewis (1995), Crampton (1997), Mazower (2000), Stavrianos (2000), Smith (2001), Clogg (2002) and Todorova (2009).
2. In contrast with the Greek revolt, the Polish revolt of 1830 brought no Great Power intervention, and was crushed.
3. On the clash of Islam with Christianity as reflected in national poetry, see chapter 3 (this volume).

4. To Armenians, too, poetry is part of the struggle against Islam for national survival. See pp. 190, 252.
5. The Milman Parry archive, Harvard University, has many recordings of Balkan oral poetry, mostly from the 1930s, giving unique insight into the process by which regional cultures can be transformed into cultural nationalism. On Balkan oral literature, see p. 67.
6. On Skanderbeg, see p. 153.
7. De Rada's first two, influential books of poetry (both published in Naples, which had a sizable Albanian population), look back to the 15th century, the age of Skanderbeg and Albania's resistance to the Ottoman invasion: *Poesi Albanesi del Secolo XV. Canti di Milosao, figlio del despota di Scutari* (15th Century Albanian Poetry: Songs of Milosao, son of the despot of Shkodra, 1836) and *Canti Storici Albanesi di Serafina Thopia, moglie del principe Nicola Ducagino* (Albanian Historical Songs of Serafina Thopia, wife of Prince Nicholas Ducagjini, 1839). Much of de Rada's poetry is set in the region of Shkodra, a center of resistance to Ottoman Muslim rule in the Catholic North. On Albanian national poetry in the context of other Balkan national poetry, see pp. 173–5.
8. See Alexiou (2002a: 455, note 21). For forerunners in Greek poetry, see Trypanis (1981: 627–28). Similarly, the Armenian epic *Sassna Dzerek*, written down by Karekin Servantsediants (1840–1892) but originating a thousand years earlier, resonates among Armenians with its tales of legendary heroes who kill tyrants and free the people. On Greek folk poetry in the context of the War of Independence (1821–29), see pp. 147–8.
9. For a Greek folk elegy over the fall of Constantinople, see 'The Last Mass in Santa Sophia'. Poems such as 'The Battle of the Mountains' assert Greek determination to win freedom from the Turks. See pp. 147–8.
10. Gundulic's main Croatian poetic predecessor Marko Marulik (1450–1524) is similarly concerned with the Islamic threat, notably in his allegorical epic poem *Judith* (written 1501, published 1524).
11. On the legend of the *xanthon genos* in the context of the Greek War of Independence, see pp. 169–70, and Clogg (2002: 17).
12. See Pennington and Levi (1984: 17–18) and Kaufman (2001: 171). For texts in English translation, see Karadžić (1997: 42–158). On the medieval history of Serbia, see Fine (1987: ch. 8).
13. On genocidal elements in *The Mountain Wreath*, see pp. 102–3, 255.
14. Though evidently based on a fictive genocide, this poem – 'the archetypal example of what to ban from the classroom' (Kaufman 2001: 216) – provided a grotesque model and inspiration for the Serbian massacre of Bosnian Muslims in 1992. On political implications of anti-Muslim Serbian poetry, also see Sells (1996: 37–45, 148–9).
15. On Greek poetry and the War of Independence, see chapter 6 (this volume).
16. Prior to the war, the Turks had a better European public image than the Greeks (Todorova 2009: 92–3), an indication that conflict with Islam was regarded as mostly a thing of the past.
17. For other noted poets in the Romantic School of Athens, see Trypanis (1984).
18. See p. 155.
19. See pp. 153–5.
20. On Eminescu in the context of other independence struggles, see p. 103.

21. The first lay school teaching in Bulgarian was established in 1834, increasing to about 2,000 by the liberation in 1878 (Crampton 1997: 61–2).
22. The cry, 'He's alive, he's alive!' was adopted by the Bulgarian resistance movement in World War II, in battle, at executions and burials (Topencharov 1982: 14–15).
23. On Botev and his poetry in the context of independence struggles, see p. 191.
24. Fishta, too, portrays the Congress of Berlin as a cruel exposure of Albanian weakness and a catalyst of nationalism. In *The Highland Lute*, he denounces the Albanians, as did Vasa. See pp. 257–8.
25. On Skanderbeg, see p. 169.
26. On the background of *The Highland Lute* and its structure, see Pipa (1978: 112–19).
27. Fishta's role as poet-priest-educator in Albania closely paralleled that of Njegoš in Serbia/Montenegro. See p. 63.
28. 'The modern Albanian nationalist myth [is] eagerly promoted to prove a national cohesion historically non-existent' (Ruches 1967: viii). Not until 1911 did Albania seek recognition as a separate state as opposed to the previous categories of Muslim and non-Muslim (Mazower 2000: 98). Still, the Greek War of Independence was evidently a watershed in the evolution of a distinctive Albanian identity, expressed in folk poetry. See pp. 153–5.
29. On Albania in Fishta's poetry as a land of heroes not to be broken up, see p. 253.
30. On Albanian poetry of the Greek war of Independence, see pp. 153–5.
31. On Jewish patriotism in Russia and elsewhere in Europe, see Aberbach (2013).
32. A poem by Mickiewicz after the river of St. Petersburg, the Neva, overflowed in 1824 – in which he described the statue of Peter the Great critically (as did Shevchenko later) as a symbol of autocracy – influenced Pushkin in the poem 'The Bronze Horseman' (1833): 'Tsars cannot master/ The divine elements' (С Бóжиеи стихиеи/ Царям не совладáть). The ambiguity of the poem – Pushkin was under house arrest at the time, and Tsar Nicholas I was his censor – is reflected in the central image of the equestrian statue of Peter the Great in St. Petersburg:

    Was it not so, fate-masterer,
    that with iron bit you held Russia up,
    rearing on the brink?

    (Не так ли ты над самой бездной,
    На высоте, уздой железной
    Россию вздернул на дыбы?)

33. Other well-known Polish poets in Mickiewicz's time were Julius Slowacki (1809–49) and Sigismund Krasinski (1812–59).
34. See p. 250. Bialik's poem *In the City of Slaughter* (1903), similarly a poem of suicidal despair set in the past – ostensibly during the Cossack massacres of Polish Jews in the seventeenth century but actually referring to the Kishinev pogrom in 1903 – was also interpreted (or misinterpreted) by its readers as a poem of national reawakening under Tsarist rule. Both poems, set in the past, evaded Tsarist censorship.
35. On Mickiewicz's portrait of a triumphant Poland, see p. 251.
36. Shevchenko, in 'A Dream' (1844) mocks Tsar Nicholas I as a dissipated bear. Pushkin might be alluding, similarly, to the Tsarist regime in Tatiana's nightmare of the frightening bear in *Eugene Onegin* (Book 5).

37. On the Polish 'victory' over the Russians, see p. 74.
38. On the *Kalevala* in the context of national mythmaking, see chapter 2 (this volume).
39. As A.I. Arwidsson put it: 'We are not Swedes, we will not become Russians, and so we must be Finns' (Preminger 1975: 277).
40. On Shevchenko's inspirational verses calling for an independent, just Ukraine, see p. 251.
41. On cultural 'traitors' to Ukrainian and other languages, see pp. 253–9.
42. On Shevchenko's mockery of Belinsky for his dismissal of Ukrainian, see p. 17.
43. V.A. Zhukhovsky (1783–1852), a Russian poet, painter and a tutor of future Tsar Alexander I, allowed a portrait made of him by Karl Briullov to be sold at the court and the proceeds used to free Shevchenko from serfdom, on 22 April 1838. Shevchenko dedicated his poem, *Katerina*, to Zhukhovsky later that year.
44. On Shevchenko's attack on pan-Slavic nationalism, see p. 255.
45. On the attacks by Kolcsey and his contemporary, Berzsenyi, on Ukrainian 'traitors', see p. 254.
46. On Kollar in the context of independence struggles, see p. 249ff.
47. Ireland, too, had a minority Protestant nationalism, whose greatest poet was Yeats, much to the chagrin of the Catholic majority (Hutchinson and Aberbach 1999).
48. In a similar irony, Macpherson, though a Scottish patriot, became an employee and supporter of the Hanoverian monarchy.
49. On Bialik, see Aberbach (1988, 1997) and Hutchinson and Aberbach (1999).
50. Translated by David Aberbach (Aberbach 2003a: 168). Bialik's searing account of the pogrom at Kishinev in 1903, in *The City of Slaughter*, with its graphic scenes of murder and rape, had a galvanising effect on Jewish nationalism (Aberbach 1988). Similar atrocities are described by Armenian poets such as Daniel Varoujan (1884–1915) and Siamanto (1878–1915), both killed by the Turks during the Armenian genocide in World War I. Siamanto's poem 'The Dance' (1909) recalls grotesque humiliations and massacres of Armenians by the Turks: 'O human justice/ I spit at your forehead' (Hovanessian & Margossian 1978: 144).

8 Byron to d'Annunzio
From Liberalism to Fascism in National Poetry, 1789–1933

I dream'd that Greece might still be free ...

(Byron 1810)

Vae Victis! La force barbare nous appele au combat sans merci.

(D'Annunzio 1914)

In a story scarcely believable if not corroborated by eyewitnesses,[1] in late 1920 the Italian poet Gabriele D'Annunzio invited the famous conductor, Arturo Toscanini, to give concerts in Fiume (now Rijeka, in Croatia, but allocated then by the League of Nations to Yugoslavia) – this was a year after the poet had captured the North Adriatic town, claimed it for Italy, and proclaimed himself dictator (*Duce*) – and like one of the more bloodthirsty Roman emperors, he used his troops, mostly demobilized Italian soldiers, to stage a battle for the entertainment of the orchestra – with live ammunition. There were many injuries and, as D'Annunzio related to the writer Osbert Sitwell, 'The members of the orchestra, which had been playing during the quieter intervals, fired by a sudden access of enthusiasm, dropped their instruments, and charged and captured the trenches. Five of them were badly hurt in the struggle' (Sitwell 1950: 140).

This cruel irresponsibility seems a light extravagance compared to the slaughter of World War I. Yet, in 1920 D'Annunzio was the most famous Italian – far better known than the struggling Mussolini whose failing fascist party was to try in desperation a few months later to replace Mussolini with D'Annunzio as leader (Ridley 1997: 116). The poet's every move attracted publicity. Universally hailed as Italy's greatest living poet, D'Annunzio was also a charismatic and much-decorated World War I hero. Italy alone had awarded him the maximum three silver medals for bravery; and he was honored by other countries, including Belgium and Serbia as well as France with the Croix de Guerre and England with the MC. Mussolini looked to D'Annunzio as a model of charismatic fascist leadership.[2]

D'Annunzio's dictatorship in the name of the nation, though colored by the poet's adulation of the ancient Roman emperors and his Nietzschean elevation of the *Übermensch*, owed much to Rousseau as interpreted by Robespierre. The xenophobia and ruthlessness of early 20th century fascism is evident in some early 19th century Romantic poetry, particularly in Germany. The destructive potential of nationalism may be glimpsed not just among violently nationalistic minor German poets such as Achim von Armin or Ernst Moritz Arndt,[3] whose militancy was stirred up by defeat and subjugation by the French, but also among more liberal poets such as Burns, Schiller, Mickiewicz, Shevchenko, Petőfi and even the young Whitman, who tended to glorify violence and revenge and sought national justification in history and myth. The early 20th century Futurist view of war as a sublime test of character can be traced to the Napoleonic wars (Bell 2007: 310–11). Talmon (1986) finds the origins of 'totalitarian democracy' and the 'necessary murder' in the French Revolution, and Gellner observes that even Nazi atrocities were in some ways 'a continuation of the Enlightenment, and [...] part of the Romantic reaction to it' (1996: 122).[4]

National poetry from Byron to D'Annunzio reflects a duality in nationalism: its moral idealism and emphasis on education and progress and its unleashing of demonic, destructive powers. In the age of Byron, nationalism was associated with self-determination and liberty. By the age of D'Annunzio, nationalism more often expressed hate for the Other. While there is no clear, inevitable, direct line from the Enlightenment to Nazism, there is, generally speaking, a transformation from liberalism to fascism, 'from humanity via nationality to bestiality', as the Austrian poet Grillparzer put it.[5] D'Annunzio's brutality would have been abhorrent to most early 19th century national poets, such as Solomos of Greece or Petőfi of Hungary, who often looked to Byron as a poetic paragon of moral leadership. Instead, D'Annunzio would seem to justify Plato's recommendation in *The Republic* that poets should be exiled. Yet, D'Annunzio reflected a profound, tragic and not wholly comprehensible change in the history of civilization and the character of nationalism between the French Revolution and World War I. National poetry changed too, from being an instrument for the idealistic transformation of the world for the better into a mirror of an altogether darker and more complex picture of violent intolerance and genocidal hatred (which D'Annunzio himself would have condemned). National poetry changed from Schiller's 'Ode to Joy': '*Alle Menschen werden Brüder/ Wo dein sanfter Flugel weilt*' (All men become brothers/ Under your tender wing) to Stefan George's prophecy of madness and slaughter in *The Star of the Covenant* (1913): '*Zehntausend muss der heilige wahnsinn schlagen*' (Ten thousand must the holy madness strike) (1968: 361) and culminating in the Great War. It changed from Byron's idealistic declaration in *Don Juan* (1810), 'I dream'd that Greece might still be free' (1810, III 86, 3),[6] to Wilfred Owen's nauseating images of the horror and pity of war, scrawled on the Western front in 1917, mocking the dangerously idealized justification of 'the old Lie: Dulce et decorum est/ pro patria mori'. Some war poets, such as Owen and Ungaretti, depicted the cheapening of life in the war. D'Annunzio exalted war as part of his culture of dictatorship, with the motto (adopted by Mussolini) *Me ne frego* (I don't give a damn).

World War I created widespread awareness that while nationalism can inspire survival, defiance, cultural creativity and the hope of freedom, it can also express the dark violent side, the fanatic heart of a nation, its abandonment of moral discipline, its secret wish for death in a blaze of violent glory rather than a life of humiliating, though peaceful, accommodation. The Great War made the militant enlightened idealism exemplified by poets in Byron's age and after seem naïve and foolish. After such slaughter, and the crises that followed, many felt the need not for Romantic liberation but salvation – forgetting the lesson of the French Revolution, that in crisis nations are vulnerable to charismatic saviors who, once in power, become cruel and greedy dictators. World War I was the culmination of a radical change in the meaning of nationalism – or, some might argue, the discovery of the 'true face' of nationalism – from the liberal, progressive universalism of the early 19th century to its opposite: intolerance, totalitarianism and genocidal 20th century fascism.[7]

The coarsening effect of the war was reflected in new, brutal uses of language; in the anti-Romantic poetry of Owen and Sassoon, whose experiences at the front made them hate war and in the writings of Marinetti and the Futurists, who embraced the war in all its horror and maintained to the end that, despite the differences in scale and technological advances in destructive means, war was as noble as it had been in the age of Garibaldi. 'There will always be corpses', exclaimed Marinetti in *War, the World's Only Hygiene* (1911–15). 'All the better! Then explosive materials will also increase, and this will be just what our so flaccid world needs' (Marinetti 1972: 83). Marinetti's aestheticization of violence is illustrated in the 'Manifesto of the Futurist Dance' dated 8 July 1917: 'I want to give the Italian carnality of the shout *Savoia!* that rips itself apart and dies heroically in shreds against the mechanical geometrical inexorable rolling-mill of the machine-gun fire' (ibid., 140).

By the end of the war, such hoped-for martyrdom for the nation seemed less noble and idealistic than sick and suicidal. It promised no new age of nations committed to universal ideals in peace and tolerance, as in Byron's time, but threatened ever more destructive wars among nations. By this point, Byron had lost much of his popularity,. He seemed to belong to a past age, a lost innocence. Yet, D'Annunzio kept up what in another age might have been described as the Byronic spirit – even toward the war's end, when he was attacked by Italian soldiers under his command, terrified and enraged that his love of war would get them killed. When thirty-eight of these men were executed, D'Annunzio wrote a cold, clinically precise account of their execution, including the flies swarming on their brains (Woodhouse 1998: 306–7). D'Annunzio was unusual in regretting the armistice. Hatred of the enemy, common at the start of the war (most famously in Lissauer's 'Hymn of Hate against England'), subsided among the victorious Allies in 1918. In contrast, D'Annunzio, paraphrasing the Lord's Prayer, declared to the fallen: 'Keep alive in us sacred hatred,/ As we shall never deny your love' (ibid., 312).

This hatred was the antithesis of the liberal spirit of Bryon's age, in which nationalism and even national rivalry were thought to be compatible with international brotherhood.

BYRON AS SERIAL NATIONALIST

Inspired by the ideals of the French and Scottish Enlightenment, Byron perhaps more than any poet of the early 19th century believed that nationalism could coexist with universalism. Byron, a serial nationalist, was motivated chiefly by sympathy for oppressed peoples and identification with their hopes for independence. These included the Armenians, Albanians, Irish, Italians, Jews, Poles, Spaniards and Latin Americans. He admired Simon Bolivar – as well as the Greeks. To the Scots-born Byron, the noblest prospect was the high road leading to the nationalism of weak and persecuted peoples.

Byron was active in Italy for the cause of Italian independence and in Greece for Greek independence. His death at Missolonghi in April 1824 was a major event in the history of nationalism. He became, and remains for many, the exemplar of 'hot' nationalism, which 'aims to instill the idea of the nation as a sacred and transcendent object of worship for which people must make sacrifices' (Hutchinson 2005: 129).[8]

Byron also inspired poets seeking national identity in the past through his fascination with cultural 'remains', folklore and archaeology. From the age of Byron onward, poets (e.g., Mickiewicz, Lönnrot, Kollar, Tennyson, Eminescu, Yeats, Bialik) frequently became students, collectors, editors or adaptors of legend and folk literature and became constructors and teachers of national identity.[9]

Byron's younger contemporaries, including Pushkin, Heine and Hugo, saw in Byron and his poetry the ideal of art wedded to politics. In addition, his self-perceived exile from England – he left in 1816, never to return – enhanced his sympathy for exiled and victimized peoples. 'His sympathy for victim nations was augmented by his sense of outcast self ... The experience of exile altered him. His resentment at what he saw as the injustices against him sharpened his moral outrage against cruelty in general' (MacCarthy 2003: 239, 374). Immersed since childhood in the Bible (Moore 1932: 536), the poet identified himself with the exiled Jews – 'I look'd for thy temple, I look'd for my home' ('On the Day of the Destruction of Jerusalem by Titus'). In the poem 'Magdalen', dated 18 April 1814 at the time Byron was writing his *Hebrew Melodies* and preserved in the Lovelace Papers, the poet expresses deep identification (perhaps as a child of the defeated Scots) with the defeated, exiled, degraded Jews pursued by an 'idiot hatred' (Ashton 1972: 20). Byron recognized, sooner than most Jews did, the power of Jewish culture to achieve a national renaissance. He was sensitive to the pathos of Jewish existence, 'the wail of a wandering and homeless people [and] the battle cry of Jewish nationalism', and he 'easily identified himself with an oppressed people reaching for freedom' (Marchand 1965: 134–5) – as did many English thinkers in his time (Slater 1952). Byron empathetically identified, too, with the cause of Spanish independence from French rule: 'Awake, ye sons of Spain! Awake! Advance!/ Lo! Chivalry, your ancient Goddess, cries ...' (*Childe Harold's Pilgrimage* i 37). Byron became a militant nationalist in Italy while living in Ravenna (1820–21), when he joined the Italian revolutionary group, the Carbonari, and had his own troop consisting evidently of several thousand men (Iamartino 2004: 109–10). At the same time, the poet was allied to the cause of Polish independence. In *The Age of Bronze* (1823), Byron alludes to the Russian annexation of Poland by Catherine the Great and her bloody suppression of the heroic Polish revolt led by Kosciuszko in 1794: 'On – on – on – the thirst of war/ Gasps for the gore of serfs and of their czar' (167–8). Byron's cosmopolitan sympathies were remembered long after his death. Mazzini read Byron for inspiration in the struggle for Italian unification, to 'awaken pride and push to action' (Smith 1994: 182). Similarly, at the time of the Turkish massacres of Armenians in the 1890s, the Armenian poet Toumanian found consolation in Byron's empathetic description of Armenia as 'an oppressed and noble nation ... though long a powerful kingdom, it was scarcely ever an independent one, and the satraps of Persia and the pachas of Turkey have alike desolated the region where God created man in his own image' (Moore 1932: 337).[10]

POET- MARTYRS

To Byron, a poet should be a political activist ready to fight and die for (what he felt to be) a noble national cause and to defend international ideals: above all, Freedom, a 'thunder-storm *against* the wind' (*Childe Harold's Pilgrimage* iv 98). A major underlying influence on this Romantic image of the poet as social reformer and revolutionary was the biblical prophet-poet, though Byron was also inspired by the Greek nationalist poet Rigas Velestinlis (or Feraios), who called for a revival of Greek and revolt against the Turks. Byron admired and translated his *Thourios* (War Song), with the famous lines: 'Better one hour of free life/ Than forty years of slavery and prison'. Velestinlis' murder by the Turks in 1798 ensured that he would be remembered as the first modern Greek prophet of armed revolt and martyr of independence. By going to Greece to lead the fight for Greek independence, Byron emulated Velestinlis. On 27 December 1823, the day before he left Cephalonia for Missolonghi, Byron wrote to Tom Moore anticipating the possibility of his death in battle, as happened to 'brother warblers' such as the German poet Theodor Körner, who died fighting the French in 1813 (Moore 1932: 607).[11]

Byron's death for the international ideal of national independence from oppressive powers inspired other poet-martyrs[12] – though the insurrections in which they took part mostly failed. In the year after Byron's death, the Russian poet Ryleyev was a leader of the abortive Decembrist uprising against Tsar Nicholas I. Sentenced to hang, he reportedly died clutching a book of Byron's poetry. The Polish poet Mickiewicz adopted Byron's style of dress, the way he wore his hair, his mannerisms, and aimed at similarly inspirational poetry and political impact. Above all, he took from Byron the idea that 'one should live the way one writes' (Modrzewska 2004: 308). The violence in Mickiewicz's poetry, as in other 19th century national poetry – especially that of defeated nations – is not gratuitous but seen as necessary in the cause of liberty. The poet died in Byronic fashion in 1855, organizing a regiment of Poles to fight Russia in the Crimean War. Similarly, the Hungarian poet Sander Petőfi died fighting for Hungarian independence against Russia in 1849. Petőfi saw no contradiction between the revolt for national independence and the struggle for World Liberty. Persistently in his poetry he seeks a violent heroic death battling tyrants: 'let me die fighting on the field' (Petőfi 1973: 168). The Italian poet Geoffredo Mameli died in the same year as Petőfi, in Rome fighting for Italian independence from Austria. He had previously fought in Lombardy and had entered Rome with Garibaldi's troops. His poem *Fratelli d'Italia* (1847) – from 1946 Italy's national anthem – recalls Byron's letter to Hobhouse of 2 January 1818 attached to Canto 4 of *Childe Harold's Pilgrimage*, alluding to Italy's longing for the 'immortality of independence'. Mameli invokes the Byronic spirit of sacrifice for the Nation: 'Stringiamci a coorte,/ Siam pronti alla morte:/ Italia chiamo!' (Let us gather in legions/ Ready to die:/ Italy calls) (Codignola 1927, ii 76–7). A quarter-century later, the Bulgarian poet Hristo Botev, following Mameli's example, fought and died in the war for Bulgarian independence from Turkey, in 1876. Botev, like Byron, anticipated, even welcomed, his death in battle for a universal cause: 'This poor man died/ for justice and freedom' (Botev 1974: 37). Botev's confidence that 'the civilized European people and governments will stretch out a brotherly hand' (Topencharov 1982: 77) to the Bulgarians, including himself, in the 1876 uprising against the Turks, had the precedent of Byron at Missolonghi, also fighting for the freedom of an oppressed people against the Turks. José Marti fought and died in 1895 for Cuba's independence from Spain. He wrote as *'el hijo de un pueblo esclavo'* (son of a land in chains) (1999: 263), a poet ready to give his life in the fight for his country's freedom. Other poet-martyrs were the Irish Joseph Plunkett and Patrick Pearse, who died in Dublin in the Easter 1916 revolt against British rule. In Plunkett's poem 'I see his blood upon the rose', Jesus, himself a rebel, is the exemplar of martyrdom: 'His cross is every tree' (Kennelly 1970: 301). Pearse's poetry treats national slavery as worse than death, and war as a purification (Martin, in Kamenka 1976: 74–5).

English poets, notably in the 1930s (e.g., John Cornford), followed Byron's internationalist idealism by fighting for causes further than at home.[13] Though national militancy was questioned in poetry even prior to World War I (e.g., in Whitman and Kipling) and, most powerfully, among World War I poets such as Wilfred Owen and Siegfried Sassoon, the Byronesque tradition of fighting poets continued despite the war: for example, D'Annunzio (Italy), Greenberg (pre-State Israel), and Rebelo (Martinique). Byron's life and poetry were especially meaningful to peoples struggling for independence from foreign dominant powers: Poland, Finland and Ukraine from Russian rule; Greece, Romania and Bulgaria from Turkish rule; Italy and Hungary from Austrian rule; Scotland, Ireland, India, Iraq and pre-State Israel from British rule; and the countries of Africa and Latin America from colonial rule.

Byron, in his time perhaps the most famous European after Napoleon – though untainted with the emperor's abuse of power, his betrayal of revolutionary ideals, and the ignominy of his defeat and exile in 1815 – was unusually well-suited to the role of national martyr. He was that rare creature, a poet who became rich from book sales: 10,000 copies of *The Corsair* were sold on 1 February 1814, the day of its publication. But Byron's fame exploded internationally with the unprecedented notoriety of his openly profligate sex life, the countless flirtations and affairs, the spicy hints of incest and sodomy. Byron's influence on nationalism spread as he was the outstanding 19th century antecedent of celebrity culture. His life was a subject of endless scandal and gossip; his death, like that of John Kennedy or Diana, Princess of Wales, was a trigger of international grief.

BYRON: THE CRIPPLED SELF AND NATION

From Byron on, the charismatic national poet exemplifies the damaged individual striving to heal or renew the self wedded to the nation. By becoming one with the Nation, the poet defeats alienation and inner division. 'Nationalism', wrote Isaiah Berlin, 'is the direct product of wounds inflicted on a sense of common nationhood, or common race or culture' (1996: 256). Hroch (1985) points out that language and culture often shore up weak nations. The wounded poet can, perhaps, best give expression to national wounds. Byron found consolation for his own physical and emotional infirmities through hopes for the revival of Italians, Greeks, Irish, Poles, Armenians and Jews, whose national condition in the early 19th century could be described in various ways as crippled.

Byron's self-image was largely determined by his father's disappearance and death (a possible suicide) when he was three. In 'Childish Recollections' (1806), he describes one of the emotional consequences of this loss as a need to 'seek abroad the love denied at home' (216). Poets who suffer severe trauma or disability, especially in childhood – there is a long list apart from Byron, including Burns, Solomos, Shevchenko, Leopardi, Pascoli, Shawqi, Bialik and Bharati – might identify strongly with a wounded, humiliated nation, long for it to be healed and revived, and work to rediscover (or invent) lost national unity.[14] Byron's Scots background might have inclined him to sympathy with nations which – like Scotland at Culloden in 1746 – had suffered humiliating defeat by a persecutory power.[15] For Byron, however, and most 19th century national poets, identification with the nation meant acceptance of moral responsibility – not, as in the case of D'Annunzio, a Dionysian letting go.

FROM BYRON TO D'ANNUNZIO

There is a historical gap between the age of Byron and D'Annunzio, between the idealism of post-1789 Europe and the despair of World War I, between the liberal and progressive forces which survived – were even stimulated by – Napoleon and the fascist totalitarianism which followed the Great War. The French Revolution, for all its shining ideals, had shown that the Nation could be a brutal amoral instrument (albeit with the veneer of 'politics of morality'), bringing a Reign of Terror and two decades of European war. Yet, Napoleon's defeat and the Congress of Vienna (1815) promised a new, more stable age in which nations could grow and prosper peacefully. Few major writers and thinkers of the age of revolution, 1789–1848, foresaw what seems obvious with hindsight: that the nationalism of weak nations or nations with corrosive feelings of inferiority, such as Russia or Germany, could be twisted into systematic policies of discrimination and murder. Until 1848, it still seemed possible to fulfil the biblical ideal by which national particularity coexisted with revolutionary universal values. This view of nationalism was associated above all with Byron:

> '... the deification of the nation necessitated the apotheosis of universal history and the oneness of mankind ... The risen nations, Italians or Poles, Frenchmen or Germans, would undergo a process of purification and rebirth. Freed from the yoke of foreign invaders or royal despots, the natural good impulses would assert themselves and stifle selfishness and class oppression, the evil breed of tyranny. The free peoples would realize the ideal of a nation as a family of brethren. Furthermore, this sense of solidarity within one nation would be extended to members of other nations'.
>
> (Talmon 1960: 29–30)

European history after the failed revolutions of 1848–49 has been recounted many times, but rarely in the context of changes in the character of national poetry. The overthrow of the French king Louis Philippe in February 1848, his replacement for several months by the liberal poet Lamartine as head of state and the dozens of revolutions which followed in 1848–49 resulted in failure and the frustration of liberal hopes throughout Europe. Post-1848 national poetry reflects a narrower, less liberal form of nationalism and a changed relationship of state and society. Increasingly secularized states with ever-growing populations sought justification less in universalist semi-religious ideals than in exclusivist national interests. Fear of revolution, which had gnawed at European states since the French Revolution and the Napoleonic wars, grew after 1848.

European monarchs, particularly Napoleon III and William I, became ever more militaristic. European monarchic dynasties struggled to shore up their positions; subordinate liberal reformism to political unity; eliminate dissent through increased state control and – helped immeasurably until 1873 by unprecedented uninterrupted economic growth – develop industry, education and the social services. Now more than previously, state bureaucrats wanted to know and control their populations, through more sophisticated administrative techniques, the use of the police, and a newly-compulsory educational system and conscription. The state appropriated the nation. It mobilized, influenced and indoctrinated its citizens. Ugly chauvinism and racist nationalism spread in the second half of the 19th century. The hoped-for biblical merging of nationalism and universalism of the Romantic age seemed more and more remote. Hegel took the place of Isaiah: that is, Isaiah's universalist vision of nations uniting in faith ('Nation shall not lift sword against nation') was replaced in the age of nationalism by Hegel's view that the policies and actions of each nation are determined by its own interests. The meaning of nationalism changed, from the enhancement and protection of individual freedom, progress and reform, to the increasingly paranoid defense of state interests, leading to World War I.

From 1873 Europe was plagued by a cycle of economic depression, reviving again the spectre of revolution. European states reacted with increasing hostility and rivalry toward one another – exacerbated by imperial conflicts of interests, especially in Africa – with intolerance towards and persecution of 'enemies of the state' and with growing suspicion and hatred of foreigners. The shift in the meaning of nationalism was strikingly reflected in changed attitudes of national poets towards Jews: from emancipation and the enthusiastic welcome of 'fellow brethren' in the age of Byron to genocidal racial hatred (which D'Annunzio did not share) by the end of the 19th century. From Byron's empathetic depiction of the Jews in 'Magdalen' (*Hebrew Melodies*, 1815) as 'Scourged – scorned – unloved – a name for every race/ To spit upon – the chosen of disgrace'(Ashton 1972: 20) to the biological racism in T.S. Eliot's 'Burbank with a Baedeker, Bleistein with a Cigar' (1919) as 'The rats are underneath the piles./ The Jew is underneath the lot', this shift in the meaning of nationalism was a practically unthinkable leap to the major pre-1848 national poets, many of whom – Mickiewicz, Petőfi, Shevchenko, Wergeland and the English Romantics – were philo-Semitic. Even those who, like Goethe, had conventional anti-Semitic views were generally immersed in the tolerant, liberal ideals of the French Enlightenment. In contrast, the perceived enervation, decadence and degeneration of *fin de siècle* Europe were accompanied by a Nietzschean hope for national regeneration and purging through ruthless heroic violence; and the xenophobia underlying biological racism was nurtured by nationalism. Poets such as Ibsen, Cavafi, Yeats and Bialik became more ambiguous and complex in their attitude to the nation and to their role. Some poets, notably Pound and Eliot, succumbed to racism. In his fascist tendencies both in his writings and his military-political career (1915–1920), D'Annunzio was a poet of his age. He saw his poetry as a 'war-cry' for the Latin peoples, to overcome the chaos and corruption of their modern existence and create a new Roman empire. Italian materialism – the lust to acquire (*acquerir*) rather than conquer (*conquerir*) – was odious. War would purify the nation and restore her to greatness.[16]

D'ANNUNZIO, WORLD WAR I AND FIUME

D'Annunzio, perhaps more than any other early 20th century poet, exemplifies how far nationalism had been transformed – some would say, distorted – from its liberal universalist origins in the age of Byron. In contrast with Byron, D'Annunzio saw nationalism in narrow, exclusivist terms, anticipatory of fascism. It is hard to imagine Byron approving of D'Annunzio's politics, his militant expansionist nationalism, irresponsible violence, self-aggrandizement as *Duce*, manipulation of crowds or use of his blackshirted followers to crush dissent. It can be claimed that 'without D'Annunzio the Fascist seizure of power would most likely not have taken place' (Ledeen 2002: xiii). Yet, the Byronic ideal of poet as warrior for the nation reached a climax of sorts in the life of D'Annunzio. D'Annunzio naturally identified with Byron – as a decadent, bohemian, unconventional Romantic rebel, a heroic type that had deeply influenced the young Nietzsche and determined his own *Weltangschauung* (Pointer and Geisenhansluke 2004: 266–8). For D'Annunzio, as for Byron, ancient Greece and Rome lived in the present. Byron was, furthermore, a fellow fighter-poet and leader committed to Italian independence.[17] If a foreign poet such as Byron could devote himself to a free Italy, to 'the very *poetry* of politics' as Byron put it in his Ravenna journal on 18 February 1821 (Moore 1932: 488), why should a native Italian poet not be prepared for self-sacrifice for his country? In August 1914, convinced that war, action and suffering would restore to Italy the grandeur of her classical past and expand her borders, D'Annunzio published the jingoistic '*Ode pour la rèsurrection latine*' predicting that Italy would enter the war. His enthusiasm at this time for conquest, and for military matters, was not untypical of its time or of national poetry in the past:

> *Vae Victis*! La force barbare nous appellee
> Au combat sans merci …
> O Victoire, moissonneuse farouche,
> je sens sur mon front, dans l'attente,
> la fraicheur du matin.[18]

As in the case of Byron after Napoleon's fall in 1815, D'Annunzio's poetry after Italy entered the Great War in 1915 was subordinated to politics. His view of war, somewhat like that of Futurists such as Marinetti, was deeply colored by a distorted (but, later, useful to fascism) popular notion of Nietzsche's *Übermensch* (Superman) and *Wille zu Macht* (Will to Power).[19] When Italy entered the War against Austria in 1915, D'Annunzio, though over fifty, did not hesitate: he volunteered for the cavalry and went on to serve with distinction in the army, navy and air force. He was usually in the thick of the fighting, exhorting the men to do their best for Italy, eulogizing the dead, or reciting his inspirational poetry to the combatants. Woodhouse (1998: 166) relates that on 21 July 1915, in an address to the survivors of the *Amalfi*, torpedoed by the Austrian navy off the mouth of the River Isonzo, D'Annunzio recited his poem, 'A torpedo-boat in the Adriatic' (*Una torpediniera nell'Adriatico*, 1892):

> Craft of steel, straight, swift, skimming,
> lovely as a naked weapon, alive, quivering,
> as though the metal enclosed a terrible heart;
> sharpened on man's cold courage alone,
> like a weapon on the whet-stone,
> you suffer no coward on the burning plates of the bridge,
> which throbs with the pulsations.

Among D'Annunzio's war aims was, ominously, the restoration of Austrian-held northeast Adriatic coast – *succiso adriatico fiore* (the 'cropped flower of the Adriatic'), he called it in *Alcyone* (1903) – to Italy, its rightful owner in his view (D'Annunzio 1988: 211).

Unlike many soldiers, whose early patriotic zeal turned to disillusionment, their war-fever dampened by the senseless carnage, D'Annunzio never lost his love of combat: 'He admitted that he hoped to be killed in action' (Rhodes, 1959: 161n). In contrast with war poets such as Owen and Sassoon, the horror of war which he observed at close quarters did not sicken him, dull his patriotism, or diminish his heroic posturing, even after the war ended.[20] In D'Annunzio's famous phrase, Italy, though on the winning side in the Great War, had been cursed with a *vittoria mutilata* (mutilated victory). In September 1919, he annexed and became dictator of Fiume, with about 50,000 inhabitants, many of whom spoke Italian. The Treaty of Versailles had given Fiume, originally in the fallen Austro-Hungarian empire, to Yugoslavia, but many Italian nationalists, resenting the Treaty as a humiliating wound to national pride, claimed Fiume for Italy. D'Annunzio's daring stroke was at first so popular that the Italian government could not risk sending the army into Fiume for fear of starting a civil war in which nationalists and socialists would join forces in a nation-wide revolution. The examples of Russia and other socialist revolutions and threatened revolutions, in

Germany, Hungary and elsewhere, were fresh. Instead, the navy was used to blockade Fiume for over a year. Only after the first Treaty of Rapallo, signed by Italy and Yugoslavia in November 1920, established an independent state of Fiume, were Italian forces used to bomb Fiume into surrender.

In itself a minor event, 'the consequences of Fiume were incalculable for the future development of European politics' (Woodhouse 1998: 351). Fiume exposed the weakness, later exploited by fascists in Italy and Germany, of a democratic government faced with paramilitary action led by a charismatic leader, with much popular support, in the name of the nation. D'Annunzio tried to some extent to govern according to liberal principles. He collaborated with syndicalist Alceste de Ambris in drafting the Carnaro Charter (*Carta del Carnaro*), ensuring universal suffrage, schools free of political and religious propaganda and influence, freedom of press, free trade union association and many other measures closer to liberal democracy than to fascist dictatorship. Yet, Fiume, like the Great War itself, also became for D'Annunzio 'a gigantic boy-scout jamboree, or of youth playing at war, but, tragically, using real ammunition' (*ibid.*, 339). Though D'Annunzio's actions had ideological and aesthetic underpinnings – particularly in Nietzsche's philosophy of the amoral *Übermensch* and among Italian Futurists who encouraged violence as an end in itself – they also expressed the poet's flawed, immature character. Foreboding the behavior of Italian fascist blackshirts and Nazi brownshirts, violence, drunkenness, racism and hooliganism were tolerated in Fiume as the expression of the highest ideals ('Arditism' or 'Fiumanism'). A British observer in Fiume summed up the irresponsibility of D'Annunzio and his followers: 'We are a handful of illuminated beings and mystic creatures, who will sow through the world the seed of our force – a force which is purely Italian and will germinate into the highest daring and violent irradiations' (Macdonald 1921: 171). When in December 1919 D'Annunzio held a referendum to decide the annexation of Fiume by Italy, he suspended the vote count, giving no explanation: '… he was fundamentally unwilling to let go of the absolute power which he now experienced for the first time in his life', and he evidently also wanted to keep up his supply of drugs and women and retain the power of a 'Renaissance despot' (Woodhouse 1998: 338).

As anarchy and immorality increased in Fiume, the poet's lust for power blocked peace negotiations and led to international hostility against him. The Treaty of Rapallo made D'Annunzio's position untenable. The Italian navy bombarded the town on Christmas 1920, when there were no newspapers to condemn the attack. After 56 deaths and 150 casualties, D'Annunzio surrendered and left Fiume.

D'Annunzio's dictatorship at Fiume had catastrophic implications. At a moment of unprecedented social and political collapse throughout Europe, when the great monarchies – in Germany, Russia, Austria-Hungary and Turkey – had been swept away by the Great War, D'Annunzio demonstrated the power of one 'Man of Action' operating with seeming disregard for conventional political structure or morality, and with no institutional backing or affiliation. If at this moment D'Annunzio had led a 'March on Rome', as Mussolini was to do in 1922, the poet – though tiny, semi hunch-backed, one-eyed, bald, with rotting teeth, and nearly sixty – could probably have become a national leader. As mentioned, he was by far the more famous and influential figure, and he had more followers than Mussolini, who alongside the poet seemed 'a boy from the back-blocks' (Bosworth 2002: 117) – intellectually, culturally, and socially his inferior. D'Annunzio's popularity in the immediate post-1918 years contrasted with the unpopularity of the fascists. At the inaugural meeting of Mussolini's *Fasci di Combattimento* (Combat Group) in Milan in March 1919, only about 100 people showed up. D'Annunzio was not among them. In the Italian election of November 1919, at the time of D'Annunzio's annexation of Fiume, no fascist deputies were elected. Mussolini, written off as a political 'corpse' – he declared to D'Annunzio, 'I am your soldier' (Woodhouse 1998: 336) – had reason to fear that he might be ousted by D'Annunzio (Ridley 1997: 123). In 1921, with Mussolini's career at low ebb, D'Annunzio was invited to replace the *Duce* as fascist leader. He declined, saying that he was not interested enough in Italian politics (*ibid.*, 116).[21]

Instead, D'Annunzio's capture of Fiume inspired Mussolini's March on Rome which, in turn, encouraged Hitler in his failed Munich Putsch in 1923.[22] Fiume was briefly a lightning rod of the anxiety and dissatisfaction of the post-war period, particularly among demobilized soldiers who were highly susceptible to 'salvation' by a lone charismatic who had served his country valiantly and had the scars to prove it. The poet became the dangerous example of that gifted and determined man, capable of establishing, with the aid of newly-developing scientific and technological advances, a strong personal bond with a group or groups, harnessing their fears and hopes to gain power. D'Annunzio was a model for fascistic one-man rule, with its capacity both for rapid beneficial social change and also for arbitrariness and moral irresponsibility, leading to catastrophe. D'Annunzio lit the fuse for the explosion made by Mussolini and Hitler. In this way, the Byronic spirit in national poetry – essentially liberal, progressive and universalist – went the way of nationalism generally as it took on a fascistic character in the early 20th century. In 1919, the year D'Annunzio captured Fiume, Yeats encapsulated this extraordinary transformation in lines no early 19th century poet, certainly not Byron, could have written:

> The best lack all conviction,
> While the worst are full of passionate intensity.
> 'The Second Coming'

NOTES

1. For details of this perverse 'entertainment', which reads like something out of Suetonius' portraits of sadism and decadence among the Roman emperors, see Sitwell (1950), Woodhouse (1998) and Santoli (1999).
2. In anticipation of Mussolini and the rise of fascism, the early 20th century Italian Futurists led by Marinetti (with whom D'Annunzio was sometimes associated) followed Nietzsche in their elevation of violence as a cleansing force. Yet, especially prior to the March on Rome in 1922, Mussolini may have regarded D'Annunzio less as an ideological influence than as a particularly attractive role model. The poet – unlike any of his contemporaries – had achieved the kind of international distinction in arms and culture of which the future dictator could only dream. On parallels between the two, see Farrell (2004), who concludes: 'They succeeded because they were able to create a myth which moved men to action' (87).
3. On the effect on German poets and poetry of defeat by Napoleon at Jena (1806) and its humiliating consequences, see Leerssen (2006). Hatred of the French transformed the poetry of Kleist, for example: 'Use their corpses to dam the Rhine' (*Dammt den Rhein mit ihren Leichen*) (ibid., 115, 274). Leerssen (117) describes the poet Theodor Körner, who wrote poetry of resistance against French tyranny, enlisted, fought and died in the liberation of Germany from the French in the Battle of Leipzig (1813), as the 'prototype' of the national poet, including Byron. Byron, however, was better known and had greater inspirational authority than practically any other 19th century poet, becoming 'one of those who did most to make nationalism the religion of the [19th] century' (Brinton 1966: 154). On Byron's immense and unparalleled international influence on nationalism and culture, see Cardwell (2004). The neglect of Byron by scholars of nationalism is striking: Hobsbawm (1990), Smith (1991), Anderson (1991), Greenfeld (1992), Breuilly (1993), Gellner (1997) and Herzfeld (2005) are among many who do not have a single entry on Byron in their indexes.
4. The French Revolution and the Napoleonic wars included blatant violations of freedom and human rights – in the name of freedom and human rights. The individual was subject to state terror – in the name of individualism. In particular, the massacres of the population of the Royalist Vendèe in Western France in 1793–4, which came close to genocide, 'evoke the cruelties of the SS' (Bell 2007: 181). Combatants and non-combatants were demonized and slaughtered indiscriminately. Extermination was carried out in the name of political ideals, of Liberty and Peace, as part of a cleansing war to the death against an inhuman, monstrous enemy, and it was justified even by men such as Robespierre who had previously opposed war. On Robespierre and the 'uneasy coincidence of democracy and fanaticism present at the birth of modern European politics', see Scurr (2006). Byron and many of his contemporaries, and later generations, exaggerated the high revolutionary ideals associated with Napoleon, though Napoleon did more than anyone to spread these ideals. Metternich alleged that in June 1813 Napoleon told him, 'I grew up on the battlefield. A man like me does not give a shit about the lives of a million men' (Bell 2007: 251). Though a line may be drawn from the barbarities of the French Revolution to 20th century fascism, the 'cunning passages' of history should not be forgotten. For example, remember that the leading German poets of the Napoleonic era were Goethe

and Schiller, both exemplars of liberal idealistic humanism and *Weltliteratur* (the word originates with Goethe), who recoiled from the excesses of the French Revolution. Schiller, in disgust, rejected the honorary citizenship offered to him by the French Republic in 1793 and from patriotic fervor in German lands. Remember also that the post–World War I era was, briefly, one of high idealism, expressed in the creation of the League of Nations, in Wilson's Fourteen Points and the Treaty of Versailles.
5. The German reads: '*Von der Humanität durch Nationalität zur Bestialität*'.
6. Scottish poets, in the shadow of the defeat at Culloden in 1746, rediscovered in the French Revolution the traditional hope for Scottish independence, a yearning going back to an earlier defeat at Bannockburn in 1314 which merged with the 18th century Scottish Enlightenment, with its liberal and progressive ideals. Robert Burns expressed in 1793 the classic enthusiastic for revolution: 'Tyrants fall in every foe!/ Liberty's in every blow' ('Scots Wha Hae'). Yet, just over a century later, as the Great War was breaking out, D'Annunzio sounded a totally different note – nationalism as barbaric bloodlust: '*Vae Victis*! The forces of barbarism/ summon us to ruthless combat ...' (*Vae Victis! La force barbare/ nous appele au combat sans merci*) ('*Ode pour la rèsurrection latine*', 1914). By 1939 W.H. Auden was attacking his age for its cowardice and 'intellectual disgrace', its paralysis in the face of chauvinistic nationalism, fascism and totalitarianism.
7. D'Annunzio, while appearing to exemplify a substantial shift from the international idealism and liberalism of early 19th century Romanticism as represented by Byron, could hardly be described as a wholly committed fascist. When Walter Benjamin in 1936 dissected 'the Fascist apotheosis of war' and its 'introduction of aesthetics into political life' (Benjamin 1999: 234), he cited not D'Annunzio but Marinetti, who wrote, 'My passion for Italy forbids me to savour any internationalism' (Berghaus 1995: 11). Yet, in considering the intellectual origins of Fascism, 'it is very difficult to cite Futuristic notions concerning violence and its employment as evidence of Fascism's unqualified commitment to its use – to the exclusion of thought and morality ... the thought of F.T. Marinetti had very little to do with the formal ideology of Fascism' (Gregor 2005: 255).
8. On Byron's importance in the Greek war of independence, and on Greek nationalism, see chapter 6 (this volume). Though Byron's militancy was stirred by the cause of national freedom, he hated post-1815 English triumphalism, expressed by other English poets such as Southey and Wordsworth after Napoleon's defeat. In *Childe Harold's Pilgrimage*, Canto III, written in 1816 shortly after he visited the battlefield at Waterloo, and in *Don Juan*, Canto IX, written in 1822, Byron expressed disgust at war: 'War's a brain-splattering, windpipe-splitting art' (*Don Juan* IX. iv). On the Napoleonic wars as seen by English poets, see Watson (2003).
9. In his encouragement of cultural nationalism, Byron was part of a general trend in the Romantic age in which Herder, the Grimm brothers, Brentano, Kleist and Arndt, Thomas Moore, and others were also influential. Hölderlin's *Hyperion* (1797) anticipates Byron as a story of a Greek patriot fighting for his country's freedom. Byron knew well Macpherson's scandal-ridden translations/forgeries from the legendary 3rd century bard Ossian, rousing Scottish nationalism and pointing the nationalist direction of 19th century poetry. However, the most immediate literary influence on Byron's nationalism may have been Walter Scott, whose poetry – commercially the most successful in early 19th century English before Byron – frequently invoked Scottish heroism and childhood memories of

Scottish lore. Unlike Scott, however, Byron broke with the English establishment and from 1816 until his death was an exile.
10. On Byron and Armenia, see Bekaryan (2004). Though the Turks were the enemy 'Other' against whom Byron fought, the poet, consistent in his Herderian estimation of varieties of national cultures, had high regard for Turkish and Islamic civilization. Many of his works are set in the Orient (Demata 2004).
11. Byron, nevertheless, would have appreciated Wilde's epigram: 'a thing is not necessarily true because a man dies for it'.
12. The Philippine poet José Rizal, executed by the Spanish in 1896, was unusual among 19th century national poets as he believed in change not through revolution but education, anticipating the nonviolent campaigns of Gandhi and Martin Luther King.
13. English poets from Byron's age until World War II – including Blake, Clough, Swinburne, the Brownings and Kipling – show a surprising degree of identification with foreign countries, and even a 'temptation to belong to other nations', as W.S. Gilbert put it in *H.M.S. Pinafore* – a phenomenon attributable to the combination of an essentially cosmopolitan culture taught by the Bible in translation (which also facilitated mission) and the tolerance of and interest in non-English cultures stimulated by the expansion of the British empire. See chapter 12 (this volume). T.E. Lawrence's sympathy both for Arab and Jewish national aspirations had a romantic affinity with Byron, who was similarly drawn to the Orient and its people.
14. On charismatic homogamy, see the Conclusion (this volume).
15. Byron's mother, though noble-born, sympathized not with her aristocratic class in the French Revolution but – as did her son – with the revolution (MacCarthy 2002: 6). Byron was 'thrilled by Napoleon's grand vision and his effrontery in implementing it, whilst being dismayed by the widespread savagery that the Napoleonic wars unleashed' (*ibid.*, 81). On Byron's liberalism, see Rosen (1992).
16. An attraction of Eastern poets such as Tagore and Iqbal in the West in the early 20th century is that they maintained the universalist ideals associated with early 19th century poets such as Schiller and Byron. In 'Pilgrimage to India' (1910), for example, Tagore welcomes 'India's ocean-shore of great humanity' – 'not one is alien' (Tagore 2004: 201). Iqbal, in 'Vision of a New World', expresses belief in 'A world without distinction of blood and colour' (Iqbal 2000: 126). On Tagore and Iqbal, see pp. 21–2.
17. D'Annunzio, already as a teenager, was immersed in the poetry of the English Romantics, and Carlyle's view, in *On Heroes*, that individuals determine history, deeply impressed him. Byron's personality and politics, rather than his poetry, influenced D'Annunzio most (Hallett-Hughes 2013: 101–02).
18. *Vae Victis*! The forces of barbarism
    summon us to ruthless combat ...
    O Victory, shy harvester,
    I feel already on my forehead as I wait,
    the freshness of dawn ...

    (Translated by David Aberbach)

19. The Turkish poet Ziya Gökalp, a contemporary of D'Annunzio, was also influenced by Nietzsche, through which he justified the idea of Turkish racial superiority over the Armenians and, ultimately, of genocide during World War I: 'let the waters of the Danube run red with blood' (Akçam 2006: 117).

20. Most poetry of the Great War was, nevertheless, chauvinistic (Marsland 1991). Particularly in the early months, when it was widely believed that the war would be short, poetry generally had a martial tone. Julian Grenfell's 'Into Battle' (1915), with its adoration for war and joy in battle, could almost be mistaken for a poem by D'Annunzio. D'Annunzio, however, at 52 was considerably older than most other combatants, and his heroic view of war more firmly entrenched. He was nearly twice Grenfell's age when the English poet was killed in France in 1915.
21. As a member of the Italian parliament, D'Annunzio found government boring and rarely attended. For him, 'the mass of humanity was as uninteresting as a railway siding'. At times he even found the Great War and his 'great adventure' in Fiume boring (Hughes-Hallett 2013: 556). Yet, D'Annunzio inspired many elements of fascism: Mussolini's oratory with its allusions to the glorious past of military triumph and cultural splendor; his use of blackshirted thugs; his adoption of the title *Duce* and his contempt for authority. The Roman salute, symbol of 20th century fascism adopted by Mussolini, Hitler and Franco, was revived by D'Annunzio, who each morning at his villa on Lake Garda held a flag ceremony to declare his love for Italy. Ironically, the poet had deeply ambivalent feelings about Mussolini's perversion of fascism, as he saw it. To D'Annunzio, fascism meant not the *Duce*'s dictatorship but heroic ideals of ancient Rome, the Risorgimento and Garibaldi. Yet, in D'Annunzio, the poet became the dangerous example of a Nietzschean *Übermensch*, above common morality, predatory and morally irresponsible.
22. Fiume inspired Mussolini prior to the 'March on Rome' in his marches into Bolshevized towns, 'capturing' them for fascism, which 'proved what could be achieved by nerve' (Toland 1977: 161). Hitler, hearing of Mussolini's successes, did the same at Coburg in Upper Bavaria in October 1922: 'Coburg proved to Hitler that he and his SA could emulate Mussolini' (*ibid.*, 163).

9 Walt Whitman, American Nationalism and the Revolutions of 1848–49

Európa csendes, ujra csendes,
Elzúgtak forradalmai ... Szégyen reá!
(Europe is quiet, quiet again,
    Its revolts have died down ... Shame on it!)

(Petőfi 1849)

'This is an age of the world when nations are trembling and convulsed. A mighty influence is abroad, surging and heaving the world, as with an earthquake. And is American safe? Every nation that carries in its bosom great and unredressed injustice has in it the elements of this last convulsion'.
(Harriet Beecher Stowe, *Uncle Tom's Cabin* 1852)

American national poetry in a distinctly American (as opposed to European) style begins mostly with Walt Whitman after the failed European revolutions of 1848–49. Whitman was the first poet to articulate an almost-Darwinian enthusiasm for American diversity – 'Here is not merely a nation but a teeming Nation of nations ...' (*By Blue Ontario's Shore* 5) – and perhaps the only 19th century national poet who, instead of wanting to shoot foreigners, made poetry out of welcoming them to New York. In the decade prior to the publication of *Leaves of Grass* in 1855, Whitman witnessed in New York the arrival of about three million immigrants, the largest proportionate increase at any time in American history. A large number were Irish Catholics fleeing the potato famine. These new arrivals were not welcome but were admitted in the absence of immigration restrictions.[1] America in the 1850s was in an economic crisis and gripped by one of its periodic bursts of religious enthusiasm. In the years leading to and including the Civil War, it was questionable if Americans could live with their fellow Americans, let alone millions of new immigrants. While the argument over slavery raged, a virtual civil war in New York was caused by the Protestant American party (the 'Know-Nothings'), who aimed to exclude Catholics and foreigners from public office and limit Irish and German Catholic immigration. The 'Know-Nothings' reached the height of their influence as *Leaves of Grass* came off the press in 1855. Whitman adopted some Know-Nothing attitudes 'to the extent that he would once say that America's digestion was strained by the "millions of ignorant foreigners" coming to its shores' (Reynolds 1996: 86). Yet in *Leaves of Grass*, Whitman's response to the new arrivals as Americans in the making, and the making of America, was a total rejection of immigration restrictions and nationalistic and ethnic hatred, which he associated with Europe after the failure of the 1848–49 revolutions: 'lend us the children of the poor', he writes in his notebooks, 'the ignorant, and the depraved'. America 'rejects none', Whitman declares in the 1855 Preface to *Leaves of Grass*; and Jesus-like he comforts the 'shunned men and women' of the world in 'Children of Adam': 'I will be your poet'.[2]

WHITMAN AND THE REVOLUTIONS OF 1848–49

What caused Whitman to abandon the xenophobia of his age and, instead, define American national identity as inclusive of many foreign immigrants with their diverse cultures? Whitman's Quaker background inculcated tolerance and belief in the 'inner light' which joins human beings to God. More immediate in the years before *Leaves of Grass* was Whitman's bitterness that the European revolutions of 1848–49 had all failed. The revolutions started in France, spread to Prussia and the German states, Italy, Austria, Hungary, Bohemia and Poland, with several dozen other conflagrations throughout Europe. Whitman was well-situated to follow the upheavals and judge their effect on America. There are striking parallels between the young Whitman and the young Karl Marx in the year of revolution, 1848: both about thirty, radical newspaper editors on the move[3] and maverick admirers of the French Revolution living temporarily in French-speaking cities – Whitman in New Orleans, Marx in Paris. Marx's *Communist Manifesto* and Whitman's *Leaves of Grass* express in different ways their hunger for radical change:[4] Marx was inflamed by revolution into a form of secular socialist messianism; Whitman was reacting to revolution with mystical American nationalism. Marx changed from being a promising poet – before 1848 his poetry was better than Whitman's was then, which is not saying much[5] – to a political and economic theorist. Whitman, in 1848 a hack journalist and failed story writer, turned into a national poet, visionary spokesman and embodiment of America.[6] Still, both were caught between the liberal optimism of the age of the French Revolution with its abortive new birth in the revolutions of 1848–49 and the disillusionment caused by the rise of militant exclusivist nationalism and totalitarianism in the second half of the 19th century, culminating in World War I.[7] Both belonged to the earlier, liberal stream of national poetry, sharing the biblical view of the Nation not as an end in itself but as a vehicle for the realization of universal values. Both were inspired by the biblical prophets who spoke for the Nation but, more importantly, with passionate concern for the future and spiritual well-being of all nations and all humanity. Whereas Marx saw nationalism and religion as chimeras disguising the universal reality of conflict between workers and capitalists, Whitman gloried in national difference as a child in a garden of butterflies.

> Each of us inevitable,
> Each of us limitless – each of us with his or her right upon the earth,
> Each of us allow'd the eternal purports of the earth,
> Each of us here as divinely as any is here.
>
> ('Salut Au Monde!')

The 1848–49 revolutions were widely covered in the American press, including the *Brooklyn Daily Eagle* and the *New Orleans Crescent*, which Whitman edited in early 1848. Whitman was in New Orleans when the French king Louis Philippe was deposed on 22–24 February 1848. The poet Alphonse de Lamartine, whom Whitman admired, became French head of state for several months. This was big news in the largest French-speaking city in America, but the poet for some time had kept a newspaperly eye on France. In the previous year (*Brooklyn Daily Eagle*, 11 February 1847), he prophesied that Louis Philippe, 'the false one, the deceiver', would soon be consumed by the flame of liberty (Whitman 2003: 194).[8] He hoped for a general European revolt: 'The mottled empire of Austria is filled with the seeds of rebellion – with thousands of free hearts, whose aspirations even tend to the downfall of despotism; and the numerous petty German states, too, have caught the sacred ardour' (*ibid.*). On 10 August 1847, in a review of Lamartine's *History of the Girondists*, Whitman again declared his sympathy for revolutionary causes, even for the Reign of Terror, in violent language that would have delighted Marx: 'In the overthrow of the despotism of that period [of the French Revolution] we hail a glorious work, for which whole hecatombs of royal carcasses were a cheap price indeed' (*ibid.*, 306). The pen, he had written feverishly in an article dated 22 September 1846, could 'make gaping wounds in mighty empires – to put the power of kings in jeopardy, or even chop off their heads – to sway the energy and will of congregated masses of men, as the huge winds roll the sea, lashing them to fury, and hurling destruction on every side!' (*ibid.*, 62). Here, in full revolutionary flow, was a fit companion to Robespierre, Byron, Marx and Engels, Bakunin and Garibaldi!

Whitman's youthful zeal for blood and gore in casting kings to the dung heap of history was frequent among nationalist 18th and 19th century poets, some of whom, including Macpherson and Burns, influenced him: 'our New World's chiefest debt is to old poems' ('Old Chants'). Whitman shared with Byron the idea of Liberty as a holy cause;[9] and, like Shelley, he believed that poets are lawgivers, with the power to change society, at times violently: in the 1855 Preface to *Leaves of Grass* he calls the poet 'the president of regulation' (Whitman 1964: ii 438). After the failure of the 1848–49 revolutions, his poem 'Europe' (or 'Resurgemus') – its original subtitle in the *New York Daily Tribune* (21 June 1850) was 'Poem of the Dead Young Men of Europe, the 72d and

73d Years of These States' – links in a Blakean flourish the hopes for European liberty with American freedom, though imperfect, achieved in 1776–1783.[10]

> Suddenly, out of its stale and drowsy lair, the lair of slaves,
> Like lightning Europe le'pt forth
> Sombre, superb and terrible
> As Ahimoth, brother of Death.
> God, 'twas delicious!
> That brief, tight glorious grip
> Upon the throat of kings.[11]
>
> (Whitman 1963: 38)

The defeat of European revolutionary liberalism was a trigger of *Leaves of Grass* between 1848 and 1855 and affected Whitman's perception of the Civil War in his later poems as he saw American internal discord as an international blow to democracy. Whitman, exhorting his readers in the 1855 Preface to *Leaves of Grass* to 'hate tyrants', meant European tyrants. Not unlike Jefferson after the erosion of French revolutionary ideals in the Reign of Terror and the Napoleonic dictatorship, Whitman felt that America stood alone, vulnerable. Whitman was rare among 19th century American poets in being un-European, even anti-European. Repeatedly, he calls on America's 'uncorrupted core of primal fresher soul' to overthrow Europe's 'moral rottenness' (Zweig 1984: 32). He condemns Europe in 'Song of the Redwood-Tree' for its 'old dynastic slaughter-house' and anachronistic monarchies, gripped by reaction after 1848. The axe, symbol of cruel arrogant European power, is in the hands of American frontiersmen a tool of progress, taming the wilderness. Europe is corrupt, maimed, a dying culture. The United States, he implies, was the only country left to guard democracy and liberty. America alone is the chance of a new start for humanity. This belief that democracy depends on America has powerful parallels in American political documents: for example, in Thomas Paine's *Common Sense* (1776), which defines America as uniquely tolerant of the many cultures of its citizens; in Jefferson's Inaugural Address (4 March 1801) in which America is 'the world's best hope'; and in the closing words of Lincoln's Gettysburg Address (19 November 1863): 'that government of the people, by the people, and for the people, shall not perish from the earth'. Whitman in the 1855 Preface to *Leaves of Grass* provocatively declares that the poetry of 'other nations' (i.e., in Europe) marked the end of the line. American poetry – namely Whitman's – is a new birth:

> 'Let the age and wars of other nations be chanted and their eras and characters be illustrated and that finish the verse. Not so the great psalm of the republic. Here the theme is creative and has vista'.[12]
>
> (Whitman 1964: ii 437)

Europeans disenchanted with the events of 1848–49 found refuge in America. Adolf Brandeis, father of the eminent American jurist Louis Brandeis, arrived from Prague in 1849, in advance of his future wife. He wrote to her: 'To your own surprise you will see how your hatred of your fellow-man, all your disgust at civilization, all your revulsion from the intellectual life, will drop away from you at once. You will appreciate that these feelings are solely the products of the rotten European conditions' (Sachar 1981: 167). Whitman came to share this aversion to Europe, as a 'lair of slaves', mostly overlooking the fact that Europe had emancipated its slaves, while America had not.[13] As the European monarchies hardened against democratic liberalism, American democracy, though imperfect, seemed all the more precious and vulnerable. The European retreat from liberalism put the burden on America to unify its divided house as civil war threatened, then came, in the most destructive conflict between the Napoleonic wars and World War I. Whitman's nationalism crystallized in his poetry, celebrating America, its liberty, democracy, tolerance and variety – and abhorring slavery and political corruption. Whitman's America was an ideal, not the reality.

Whitman loved to loiter by the New York docks, where he saw the country transformed by immigrants as they, in turn, were transformed into Americans. Whitman became their national poet. In his poetry, he does not write about American opposition to new immigrants, especially Irish Catholics. His America, unlike Europe, is tolerant and accepting of newcomers, 'curious toward foreign characters' (*By Blue Ontario's Shore* 5), too large to be swamped by them.[14] Europe, by comparison – especially after 1848 – was hostile to foreigners. As in the past, many immigrants had known persecution in Europe. European national poets of the post-Napoleonic period – Mickiewicz of Poland, Petőfi of Hungary, Shevchenko of Ukraine, Botev of Bulgaria and others – sing of the nation, not immigrants. As poet of a country independent many years before his birth, Whitman did not see American nationalism as a struggle to break free of tyranny, as in Europe. *Leaves of Grass* opens by celebrating not America but America's greatest achievement: the free self, a sensibility created by democratic government, untrammelled by kings and queens, in which individuals feel confident at their leisure to contemplate themselves and the universe.[15]

> I celebrate myself, and sing myself,
> And what I assume you shall assume,
> For every atom belonging to me as good belongs to you.
> I loafe and invite my soul,
> I lean and loafe at my ease, observing a spear of summer grass.

European national poets rarely 'loafe': most belong to defeated or subjugated nations – for example, Mickiewicz of Poland, Lönnrot of Finland or Petőfi of Hungary – yearning for freedom.[16] The poetry of Mickiewicz is tense with Polish defeats and humiliation and the desire for liberty and revenge.[17] At the core of Whitman's poetry is tolerance for the Other; European poets often define national identity through hate for the Other. Whitman's hatreds blew out in his journalism,[18] leaving his poetry an eye of calm. In *Leaves of Grass*, Whitman rejects the Europe of tyranny and servitude, blood and pain. In a suggestively Oedipal analogy, first stated in the 1855 Preface to *Leaves of Grass*[19] and repeated in *By Blue Ontario's Shore*, the son (America) inherits all from his dead father (Europe, the 'Old World'):

> [America] perceives the corpse slowly borne from the house,
> Perceives that it waits a little while in the door,
>   that it was fittest for its days,
> That its life has descended to the stalwart and well-shaped
>   heir who approaches ...
>   (*By Blue Ontario's Shore* 5)

Poetry is Europe's 'chief legacy', Whitman acknowledges in the end, in one of his last poems, 'Old Chants':

> Ever so far back, preluding thee, America,
> Old chants, Egyptian priests, and those of Ethiopia,
> The Hindu epics, the Grecian, Chinese, Persian,
> The Biblic books and prophets, and deep idylls of the Nazarene,
> The Illiad, Odyssey, plots, doings, wanderings of Eneas,
> Hesiod, Eschylus, Sophocles, Merlin, Arthur,
> The Cid, Roland at Roncesvalles, the Nibelungen,
> The troubadours, minstrels, minnesingers, skalds,
> Chaucer, Dante, flocks of singing birds,
> The Border Minstrelsy, the bye-gone ballads, feudal tales, essays, plays,
> Shakespere, Schiller, Walter Scott, Tennyson ...

This confession of being heir to a poetic legacy is remarkable as in the period when Whitman wrote the first poems of *Leaves of Grass*, he intentionally disacknowledged influences and predecessors: 'make no quotation and no reference to any other writers', he reminds himself in his notebooks.[20] Does this 'killing off' of influence parallel the supersession of the European paternal 'corpse' by the 'well-shaped heir'? The European poetic legacy, it is clear, filters and fibers Whitman's poetry; but he stresses the new – his vision of America as the mirror image of himself, not as he was but as he wanted himself to be: an heir come into his inheritance, open, loud and confident, resourceful and generous, comfortable with himself, speaking with quietly revolutionary egotism and egalitarianism the language of liberty and democracy:

> Walt Whitman, a kosmos, of Manhattan the son,
> Turbulent, fleshy, sensual, eating, drinking and breeding,
> No sentimentalist, no stander above men and women

> or apart from them,
> No more modest than immodest.
>
> Unscrew the locks from the doors!
> Unscrew the doors themselves from their jambs!
>
> Whoever degrades another degrades me,
> And whatever is done or said returns at last to me.
> Through me the afflatus surging and surging,
>   through me the current and index.
>
> I speak the pass-word primeval, I give the sign of democracy,
> By God! I will accept nothing which all cannot have
>   their counterpart of on the same terms.
>
> (Song of Myself 24)

WHITMAN: BIOGRAPHICAL SELF AND NATIONAL POET

Using his own self as model, Whitman adapts Jefferson's belief in individuals, not institutions, as the basis of democracy. Men are 'a law unto themselves'. Democracy could not be achieved through social organizations – political parties, trade unions, churches, etc. – only by individuals. The Self is above all things: '... nothing, not God, is greater to one than one's self is' (*Song of Myself* 48). Whitman is 'bard of personality' ('Starting from Paumanok'), not bard of the Nation. The Preface to *Leaves of Grass* does not declare: love the Nation, but: enjoy me on equal terms, I am no better than you. The Self expresses a universal soul, its thoughts are the thoughts of all men in all ages: 'If they are not yours as much as mine they are nothing, or next to nothing ...' (*Song of Myself* 17).

> What is commonest, cheapest, nearest, easiest, is Me,
> Me going in for my chances, spending for vast returns,
> Adorning myself to bestow myself on the first that will take me,
> Not asking the sky to come down to my good will,
> Scattering it freely forever.
>
> (ibid., 14)

The great poet knows the Soul alone, with its infinite variety: 'Encompass worlds, but never try to encompass me' (*Song of Myself* 25). Whitman's Me has multiple viewpoints: 'You shall listen to all sides and filter them from yourself' (*ibid.*, 2) and is morally complex: 'I am not the poet of goodness only, I do not decline to be the poet of wickedness also' (*ibid.*, 22), though in 'Starting from Paumanok' (7) the poet declares 'there is in fact no evil' – not even slavery.

Yet, the agonizing question for Whitman – as for America, with its rapidly changing identity – is: who is this Self of whom I sing? There is literal truth in Whitman's declaration that even by the end of *Song of Myself*, the reader 'will hardly know who I am or what I mean' (52). This autobiographical poem has almost no biographical facts: for example, that Whitman was born in Long Island in 1819 to a family with English and Dutch Quaker origins, one of eight children; that his father was a farmer and later a carpenter, sympathetic to radical thinkers such as Francis Wright and Thomas Paine; that in 1823, the family, struggling to make ends meet, moved to Brooklyn; that in 1831, aged twelve, Whitman left school and for many years worked as a printer, journalist, teacher and newspaper editor in New York; that some of his early writing appeared in the *Democratic Review*, a journal published by 'Young America', a group of nationalists convinced that a literary genius was about to forge an 'American' literature, to slough off prevailing, stifling European influence;[21] that Whitman tried in poems, stories and articles to be this literary redeemer but had little impact until 1848, when the European revolutions began and he moved briefly to New Orleans. Whitman was changed by his experience in 1848, but nothing in his writings shows clearly what happened. Later, after his father became sick in Brooklyn, Whitman nursed him while writing *Leaves of Grass* in the next room. The first edition came out in July 1855, a week after the father died. None of these biographical details figures in *Leaves of Grass*. Nor do we learn from the poetry of Whitman's retarded, possibly epileptic brother who shared a room with him; another brother who was syphilitic; a mentally ill sister; and a tubercular alcoholic third brother married to a once and future prostitute. These and other details about the poet's family history were pieced together by scholars and became publicly known only after his death.[22]

Whitman published *Leaves of Grass* at his own expense and to a mixed reception: praise from Emerson and a few others (including Whitman himself, in anonymous reviews) as an American genius; mostly denigration from the rest for the sprawl and apparent carelessness and egotism of his poetry and his open sexuality and hints of homosexuality. From 1861, the Civil War entered Whitman's poetry, when he volunteered as a hospital nurse in Washington, making hundreds of hospital visits and seeing tens of thousands of soldiers, and also worked as a government clerk and war correspondent. His hospital work ruined his health, and in 1873 he retired, semi-paralyzed, to Camden, New Jersey, where he was nursed by family and admirers until his death in 1891. Whitman revised and expanded nine editions of *Leaves of Grass*, but the early editions, in the 1850s, contain the bulk of his most radical, mysterious and enduring poetry.

Who, then, is the Me of *Leaves of Grass*, and how did this Me become a revolutionary national poet after 1848–9? An answer might be found in Whitman's inner transformation as poet-healer. Even before his father's death in 1855, Whitman was chief provider and head of his troubled household in Brooklyn. His voluntary responsibility as his father's nurse continued in his work as a nurse during and after the Civil War, expanding into his poetic role as lover and comforter of the sick, wounded Nation. In some ways, the poet was toughened into new confidence: 'It is I who am great' (*By Blue Ontario's Shore* 15):

> Behold, I do not give lectures or a little charity,
> When I give I give myself.
>
> You there, impotent, loose in the knees,
> Open your scarf'd chops till I blow grit within you,
> Spread your palms and lift the flaps of your pockets,
> I am not to be denied, I compel, I have stores plenty and to spare,
> And any thing I have I bestow.
>
> (*Song of Myself* 40)

Yet, Whitman often seems less a confident poet of national unity than a bundle of contradictions: easy-going yet remote, democratic yet vain, indolent yet practical, natural yet calculating, unliterary yet intellectual, calm yet hot-headed, 'rough' yet bookish, at ease with himself and the world yet humiliated by guilt. Loving ordinary men and women, he finds them at times ill-bred and repulsive; though he writes that marriage is sacred, he never married. Not unlike America itself, Whitman is 'torn between democracy and history, between what he appears to be and what he is'. He struggles with deep-rooted American problems: 'how to reconcile the desire for personal liberty with the demands of social union [...] the republican ideals of the past and the dislocations of a modern market economy' (Erkkila 1989: 165, 254, 256).[23] Whitman's Me is admittedly not always under control: 'You villain touch! what are you doing? my breath is tight in its throat,/ Unclench your floodgates, you are too much for me' (*Song of Myself* 28). At times, the poet, striving for American purity, seems plagued by European impurity. Prizing equability, the poet confesses evil and contrariety, for he 'lied, stole, grudg'd,/ Had guile, anger, lust, hot wishes I dared not speak' ('Crossing Brooklyn Ferry' 6): 'I am the poet of sin' he confesses in his notebooks (Whitman 1984: i 73). Even his trademark spiritual certainty is porous at times with doubt that 'may-be identity beyond the grave is a beautiful fable only ...' ('Of the Terrible Doubt of Appearances'). Without giving biographical details, Whitman probes deeply and often subtly his 'real Me', the dark underside of his buried life, his weaknesses and failings, and his knotty sexual identity. Whitman's real Self appears to be plagued with guilt and doubt, suffering, ignorant and unsure of himself and his poetry with its blab and arrogance. It is strange that so tormented and self-absorbed a poet as that of 'As I Ebb'd with the Ocean of Life' and 'Prayer of Columbus' could become a public spokesman for a new optimistic, forward-looking America, enemy of the Europe that had betrayed liberal hopes:

> O baffled, balk'd, bent to the very earth,
> Oppress'd with myself that I have dared to open my mouth,

> Aware now that amid all that blab whose echoes recoil upon me
> I have not once had the least idea who or what I am,
> But that before all my arrogant poems the real Me stands yet
>   untouch'd, untold, altogether unreach'd,
> Withdrawn far, mocking me with mock-congratulatory signs and bows
>   ('As I Ebb'd with the Ocean of Life')[24]

> Is it the prophet's thought I speak, or am I raving?
> What do I know of life? What of myself?
> I know not even my own work past or present,
> Dim ever-shifting guesses of it spread before me,
> Of newer better worlds, their mighty parturition,
> Mocking, perplexing me.
>   ('Prayer of Columbus')

Whitman's surviving notebooks and letters in some respects reveal more than the poetry about this private Me with its exclusion of women, from whom the poet evidently fled.[25] Among many unanswered questions about Whitman is why he never married – he had no known children, though he saw his work as progeny, his self-creation part of America's self-creation. In Whitman's inner world male bonding is an obsession, which his love poems in *Calamus* make clear. His notebooks contain lists of men, some of whom shared the poet's bed (though this was not in itself unusual at the time), and hint at a soul tormented by his sexuality, using a code to confess homosexual feelings in a puritanical age in which sex was taboo.[26] In manuscript, the haunting 'Once I Passed through a Populous City' refers not to a woman but a man:[27]

> Once I passed through a populous city imprinting on my brain
>   for future use, its shows, architecture, customs, and traditions,
> But now of all that city I remember only the man
>   who wandered with me there, for love of me,
> Day by day, and night by night, we were together.
> All else has long been forgotten by me – I remember, I say,
>   only onerude and ignorant man who, when I departed,
> Long and long held me by the hand, with silent lip, sad and tremulous.
>   (Whitman 1922, ii 102)[28]

The city might be New Orleans in 1848 but, if so, the poem is dominated not by revolutionary American and European politics which then filled Whitman's daily life as a newspaperman but the poet's far-reaching emotional revolution: 'All else has long been forgotten by me'. Politics, the failure of liberalism and the threat to American democracy receded in the face of a shining vision of a strong, tolerant America in which the private, secret, individual Self, greater than God, *was* America, free to assert itself. This was the birth of Whitman's conception of America as a 'Nation of nations'.

ANTI-POLITICS IN LEAVES OF GRASS

Composed in the revolutionary spirit of 1848–49 and with great love for and faith in America in its growing diversity, *Leaves of Grass* is at the same time the poetry of a man driven from American politics in despair at its corruption. In a vicious attack on American political ineptitude and self-seeking, 'The Eighteenth Presidency!', written in 1856 but not published in his lifetime, Whitman compared politicians to lice, maggots and venereal sores. American democracy seemed an experiment in danger of failing as the States were ripped apart by the controversy over slavery.[29] At the time of the first editions of *Leaves of Grass*, the 'United States' were headed for civil war. American leadership, including the three presidents prior to Lincoln, was dwarfed by the crisis it faced. Whitman's attack on 'the lair of slaves' in 'Europe' seemed to apply more to America than to Europe. Was America threatened by civil war better than Europe – a 'democratic slaughter-house'? Could Whitman state that slavery had no place in America, as Cowper could of England in the late 18th century: 'Slaves cannot breathe in England' ('The Task')? England ended the slave-trade in 1807 and banned slavery in its empire in 1833. America, whose southern states were largely dependent on agriculture and slavery, lagged behind, a hypocrite since 1776 to its democratic principles.[30] Jefferson tried to end slavery in the Declaration of Independence, but Congress would not agree, and Jefferson himself owned many slaves. The relaxed tone of *Leaves of Grass* belies the fact that American expansion made the controversy over slavery a dangerous and growing threat to the Union. American legislation to deal with slavery as the Union grew – notably the Missouri Compromise (1820–21), the Wilmot Proviso (1846), the Compromise of 1850, and the Kansas-Nebraska Bill (1854) followed by the Dred Scott case (1857) – exacerbated conflict.[31] None of this enters *Leaves of Grass*. The European failure in 1848–49 roused painful questions about the American ideals of liberty and justice for all, including Black slaves. Could these be realized without civil war? As a newspaper editor, Whitman was thoroughly familiar and disgusted with American politics.[32] In response to the Dred Scott decision, Whitman played the devil's advocate, contrasting Europe favorably with America, for Europe, unlike America, had killed slavery: 'Does the whelp [slavery] fall howling and dead under the blows of an English judge and have his full swing, with meat and drink to boot, from the caressing hand of an American judge?' (quoted by Erkkila 1989: 148). Whitman did not want to be a poet of the lost cause, like Heine who, as the first poems of *Leaves of Grass* were written, confessed himself a failure in the fight for freedom: *Verlorner Posten in dem Freiheitskrige* (a lost sentry in the war of liberation) ('Enfant Perdu').

Whitman opposed slavery but could not escape popular prejudice against American Blacks. Nor was he immune to White supremacist views. Whitman's journalism on Blacks lacks the idealism of his poetry. In the *Brooklyn Daily Times*, 6 May 1858, he writes: 'Who believes that Whites and Blacks can ever amalgamate in America? Or who wishes it to happen? Nature has set an impassable seal against it. Besides, is not America for the Whites? And is it not better so?' (Whitman 1932: 90). Whitman believed (as Lincoln did) in White superiority and in segregation,[33] even that slavery had its 'redeeming points' (*ibid.*, 88). Yet, in his poetry, Whitman accepted Black Americans on democratic principles – this is most evident in the 1855 edition of *Leaves of Grass*. Whitman's earliest surviving attempt at free verse, in a notebook of 1847–48, begins: 'I am the poet of slaves' (Whitman 1984: i 67).[34] Free verse is clearly associated in his mind with liberation. In the twelve-poem 1855 edition of *Leaves of Grass*, Whitman's portrayal of Blacks is unusual in contemporary American literature. He mentions Blacks in nine of these poems. Whitman embraces all peoples, includes slaves, for 'Whoever degrades another degrades me' (*Song of Myself* 24):

> The runaway slave came to my house and stopt outside ...
> He staid with me for a week before he was recuperated and pass'd north,
> I had him sit next to me at table, my fire-lock lean'd in the corner.
> (*ibid.*, 10)

Whitman goes beyond sympathy to a remarkable identification with slaves – 'I am the hounded slave, I wince at the bite of the dogs' (*ibid.*, 33) – and even with the vengeful rage felt by the oppressed: 'I hate him that oppresses me' ('The Sleepers'). The poet seeks 'a change of heart by *all* Americans to include Blacks and other marginalized peoples in a diverse and united democracy' (Klammer 1995: 157).

WHITMAN AND THE AMERICAN IDEAL

After 1848–49, as the crisis over slavery deepened, Whitman's poetry was increasingly absorbed by a vision of an ideal, transcendent, timeless, even mystical America. Unlike some national poets, such as Tagore of India who experienced nationalism in the trammels of colonial imperialism,[35] Whitman was in love with democratic national identity. America, as Wallace Stevens might have put it, was Whitman's 'interior Paramour', a love object. Whitman's ideal America is free and tolerant, open to new ideas and infinite possibilities, improvising, exuberant, optimistic, a force of unity and regeneration:

> Clearing the ground for broad humanity, the true America,
>   heir of the past so grand,
> To build a grander future.
>   'Song of the Redwood-Tree'

Whitman's confidence reflects the ideal American self-image since independence, based on the successful wars against Britain in 1776–83 and 1812, the great land acquisitions of 1803 and 1846 and growing wealth as the land was settled with immigrants from many countries. America fought to create itself, free, tolerant, open to new ideas and infinite possibilities, improvising, exuberant, optimistic. To be American, writes Whitman, is to be oneself, to be an individual, to know oneself, to be free:

> It is not the earth, it is not America who is so great,
> It is I who am great or to be great, it is You up there, or any one,
> It is to walk rapidly through civilizations, governments, theories,
> Through poems, pageants, shows, to form individuals.
> Underneath all, individuals,
> I swear nothing is good to me now that ignores individuals,
> The American compact is altogether with individuals,
> The only government is that which makes minute of individuals,
> The whole theory of the universe is directed unerringly to one single individual – namely to You.
>
> (*By Blue Ontario's Shore* 15)

America, dynamic, growing, prospering and increasingly diverse, impressed the idealistic Whitman as a source of good, identical with the divinely blessed individual self: 'These States, what are they except myself?' (*ibid.*, 18). A motive behind *Leaves of Grass* is nation-building in the belief that Democracy based on individualism is 'the destin'd conqueror' (*By Blue Ontario's Shore* 1), though the United States, Whitman (1964: ii 434) announces in the 1855 Preface to *Leaves of Grass*, 'are essentially the greatest poem'. In 'A Backward Glance O'er Travel'd Roads' (1888), Whitman (*ibid.*, 732) echoes other national poets, such as Leopardi and Yeats, in stating that great poetry comes from a national spirit. No longer the angry newspaperman raging at Europe and American politics, Whitman the poet speaks with the voices of a nation built out of virtually all other nations, in harmony and versatility. In his expansive free verse, the Nation is a revolutionary creative act, beautiful in its simplicity, original in its diversity and capacity for growth, mature in its achievement. Whitman the newspaperman in search of a broader circulation became the poet with a unique poetic style in *Leaves of Grass*, whose vocabulary and syntax are yet close to newspaper English, common and comprehensible as grass, 'the grass that grows wherever the land is and the water is' (*Song of Myself* 17).

Whitman's poetry is revolutionary in its eclecticism, grand and welcoming, uniting in its different sections high and low culture: the *Bhagavad Gita* with the *New York Tribune* (Emerson's description of *Leaves of Grass*); Homer, the Bible and Shakespeare with the dime novel; Thoreau and Emerson with popular books on history and science; Italian opera with treatises on phrenology, spiritualism and health. This jazzy freewheeling style, making use of whatever comes along, marks Whitman's poetry as revolutionary – and improvisationally American. Whitman's conception of America as a 'Nation of nations' – a conglomerate of peoples from all over the earth – recalls the prophetic self-image of biblical Israel: once the spiritual ideal is realized, all national and racial divisions will fall away as spiritual internationalism makes political nationalism obsolete (Aberbach 1993, 2005).

WHITMAN AND THE SECESSION OF THE SELF

Whitman was a self-declared embodiment of Union, sickened though he was by post-1848–49 politics, both European and American. He turned inward to poetry, a secessionist revolting against the confines of the Nation for the freedom of the Self.[36] He launches his persona across continents to distant lands. He reaches into outer space and the Universe, back in time or into the future. He enters the mystical realm. He burrows frantically into himself, his past, and into Sex or Death. In his voyages, he abandons trouble and limitation, not just of the oppressive Self but also of the Nation – the 'lair of slaves', the 'democratic slaughter-house' – shrinking the wounds of Self and Nation *sub specie aeternitatis*; retreating from the suffering world to return to it with new insight and new health; speaking the voice of 'Nature without check with original energy' (*Song of Myself* 1); aiming to 'add, fuse, complete, extend – and celebrate the immortal and the good' ('L. of G.'s Purport'). The reader opens *Leaves of Grass* to find 'this is no book,/ Who touches this touches a man' ('So Long!'). Even Whitman's assertion of the 'ever-united lands' in 'Our Old Feuillage' shatters into incoherence through comparison between the United States and the poet's body:

> ... my body no more inevitably united, part to part, and made out of a thousand diverse contributions one identity, any more than my lands are inevitably united and made ONE IDENTITY.

The ambiguity of Whitman's role as National Poet is implicit also in the 1855 Preface to *Leaves of Grass*, where the childless poet concludes – despite the attractions of Self, Nation and Universe – that nothing is greater than family life, having children and bringing them up well. Nor is the poet physically confined to the Nation (Whitman left the United States only when he visited Canada), but soars, as Ezekiel does in his prophetic visions, across the world:

> My ties and ballasts leave me, my elbows rest in sea-gaps,
> I skirt sierras, my palms cover continents,
> I am afoot with my vision.
>
> (*Song of Myself* 33)

The poet leaves America to sing the myths of other lands, notably in *Passage to India*, celebrating the completion of the Suez Canal in 1871 and the 'fables spurning the known, eluding the hold of the known,/ Mounting to heaven!' He even goes back in time, one of the first poets to suggest a concept of evolution, even as far back as dinosaurs:

> Before I was born out of my mother generations guided me,
> My embryo had never been torpid, nothing could overlay it.
>
> For it the nebula cohered to an orb
> The long slow strata piled to rest it on
> Vast vegetables gave it sustenance,
> Monstrous sauroids transported it in their mouths and deposited it with care.
>
> (*Song of Myself* 44)

The poet reaches out to the universe, like a noiseless patient spider in the poem with that title, exploring and spreading its web in a vast vacancy, casting his soul 'in measureless oceans of space,/ Ceaselessly musing, venturing, throwing, seeking the spheres to connect them'. Whitman's aims often seem closer to mysticism – his disciple, the psychiatrist Richard Maurice Bucke, called it 'cosmic consciousness' – than nationalism:[37]

> 'I will take each man and woman of you to the window and open the shutters and the sash, and my left arm shall hook you round the waist, and my right shall point you to the endless and beginningless road up along the sidewalks of eternity ... whose sides are crowded the rich cities of all living philosophy, and oval gates that pass you in to fields of clover and landscapes clumped with sassafras, and orchards of good apples, and every breath through your mouth shall be of a new perfumed and elastic air, which is love'.
>
> (Whitman 1984: i 63–4)[38]

Whitman's mystic spirituality, riven though it is with private doubts, infuses his conception of America, democracy and the Self:

> I say the whole earth and all the stars in the sky are for religion's sake.
> I say no man has ever yet been half devout enough,
> None has ever yet adored or worship'd half enough,
> None has begun to think how divine he himself is,
> and how certain the future is.
>
> I say that the real and permanent grandeur of the States must be their religion ...
>
> (*Starting from Paumanok* 7)

Yet, Whitman's language of cosmic harmony and love is not addressed to Americans alone, but to all, educated and uneducated alike:

> Each of us inevitable,
> Each of us limitless – each of us with his or her right upon the earth,
> Each of us allow'd the eternal purports of the earth,
> Each of us here as divinely as any is here.
>
> ('Salut Au Monde!')

Whitman's litany of ideals and aims in 'Gods' leaves the Nation out:

> Or Time and Space,
> Or shape of Earth divine and wondrous,
> Or some fair shape I viewing, worship,
> Or lustrous orb of sun or stars by night,
> Be ye my Gods.

The Nation is superseded, too, by the poet's immersion in death. In *Out of the Cradle Endlessly Rocking*, the poet as a child learns of death as he plays by the sea, savage mother of all life. Death, the poet confesses in the end, is the urge behind his poetry.[39]

> My own songs awaked from that hour,
> And with them the key, the word from the waves,
> The word of the sweetest song and all songs,
> That strong and delicious word which, creeping to my feet,
> (Or like some old crone rocking the cradle, swathed in sweet garments, bending aside,)
> The sea whisper'd me.

The poet, believing in the survival of the spirit in Nature, in 'leaves of grass' –[40]

> What do you think has become of the young and old men?
> And what do you think has become of the women and children?
> They are alive and well somewhere,
> The smallest sprout shows there is really no death,
> And if ever there was it led forward life ...
>
> (*Song of Myself* 6 –)

speaks spine-tinglingly from the grave: 'look for me under your bootsoles' (*Song of Myself* 52). As readers resurrect the poet, so the poet resurrects his readers. The 1855 Preface to *Leaves of Grass* recalls the dead-bones prophecy of Ezekiel: 'The greatest poet ... drags the dead out of their coffins and stands them again on their feet ... he says to the past, Rise and walk before me that I may realize you' (Whitman 1964: ii 443). This resurrection and Whitman's readers are not necessarily American. Where, then, is the poetry of nation-building?

WHITMAN AND THE CIVIL WAR

The 1850s, leading to the American Civil War (1861–65), was Whitman's most creative period, but the war was the pivotal event of his life. Had Whitman's idealistic picture of a tolerant, dynamic America in *Leaves of Grass* been a reality, the war would have been unlikely. In the war, Whitman returned to public involvement, committing himself to the Union not just as a poet but also as a participant, in hospitals. The war gave him a role and an identity, and a direction for his poetry. Whitman regarded himself as 'saved' by the war (Morris 2000: 3).[41] In the early months of the war, while still in New York, he expressed conventional war fever, reminiscent of 'Europe', in poems such as 'Beat! Beat! Drums!' and 'Song of the Banner at Daybreak':

> I hear the tramp of armies, I hear the challenging sentry,
> I hear the jubilant shouts of millions of men, I hear Liberty!

After Whitman volunteered as a nurse in war hospitals, such exhilaration vanished. When he nursed sick and dying soldiers, he made no distinction between men of the South and of the North, or Black and White. He made the tolerant inclusiveness of his poetry a living reality. Unlike most 19th century poetry, Whitman's war poems express the horror, not glory, of war.[42] They are, at times, brutally realistic, with nauseating imagery of bloody rags, piles of amputated limbs, stumps and terrified faces, foreshadowing World War I poets such as Owen and Sassoon: 'is there no hell more damned than this hell of war'? (Whitman 1984: ii 517). No longer does Whitman try to differentiate between America and the European 'slaughter-house'. Bloody though the revolutions of 1848–49 were, the Civil War was a far worse butchery:

> Arous'd and angry, I'd thought to beat the alarum,
>   and urge relentless war,
> But soon my fingers fail'd me, my face droop't and I resign'd myself,
> To sit by the wounded and soothe them, or silently watch the dead ...
> To the long rows of cots up and down each side I return,
> To each and all one after another I draw near, not one do I miss,
> An attendant follows holding a tray, he carries a refuse pail,
> Soon to be fill'd with clotted rags and blood, emptied and fill'd again.
>   ('The Wound-Dresser' 1, 2)[43]

These poems are nationalistic not in war-fever, as in his earlier poetry, but in grief and compassion:[44]

WHITMAN: NATIONAL POET AND POET OF THE SELF

In the years 1848 to 1865, when Whitman emerged as a national poet, his contradictions could mirror those of the Nation; his despair and hope merge with those of the Nation. In his poetry, as in life, Whitman saw himself as a father-healer. The interaction of his private life, particularly his father's death in 1855, with his role as national poet has many parallels in the history of cultural nationalism. Loss is often a motivating force in creativity.[45] Whitman's writings suggest that in much the same way that he took over his father's role, he saw America taking over from Europe the chief responsibility for the survival of liberal democracy. Rather than be the secretive, gloomy son of a decaying family, Whitman chose to identify himself with an ideal imagined America, healthy, forward-looking, dynamic. Whitman's new Self was that of America, the young 'truculent giant', powerful, confident, creative, heir to the European liberal tradition, a 'corpse' after the failed revolutions of 1848–49.

Through his inner conflicts, his raving questions and uncertainties about his true Self, Whitman spoke for the uncertainties of American national identity after 1848. Even in his imaginative escape from the Nation, Whitman's poetry revealed his power, and that of the Nation, to contain and resolve painful contradictions and grow through them. In this way, too, a stronger and more tolerant America could emerge. The Civil War made Whitman both spiritually and physically the Nation's healer, but the war also helped Whitman to heal himself. As the Nation could not be destroyed by Civil War, so also the poet could not be obliterated by inner conflict. As the Nation transformed the poet, so also the poet transformed the Nation, as the prophets did, into an ideal. Whitman's poetry prescribes health and Eros as an antidote to disease and Thanatos, and all life, and death too, is good: 'To die is different from what anyone supposed, and luckier' (*Song of Myself* 6). Whitman bridges the liberal optimism of the pre-1848 era and the ensuing disillusionment: at first a chauvinist like other 19th century national poets, Whitman in his Civil War poetry foreshadows the anti-war national poetry of World War I. Whitman, more than most national poets, came to embody the thorny paradoxes of nationalism and internationalism, public man and tormented artist, Self and Universe. His cosmic-confessional individuality signified the democratic Nation's strength in diversity. Later national poets, such as Ibsen, Yeats and Bialik, shared Whitman's view of poetry as a tool for national regeneration as well as self-creation and healing of the wounded Self.

NOTES

1. In the North, there was much hostility towards Irish immigrants because they were Catholic and tending to support slavery. See Reynolds (1996).
2. See Whitman (1984: i 149) and Bowers (1969: 62).
3. In 1848, Marx edited the *Neue Rheinische Zeitung*; Whitman edited the *New Orleans Crescent*. On Whitman and Marx, see Erkkila (2007).
4. Grunzweig (2006: 151) writes that many leftists regard *Leaves of Grass* as a 'lyrical correlative to Karl Marx's *Communist Manifesto*'. Whitman's socialist sympathy might be seen in the 1855 Preface to *Leaves of Grass*, where the poet tells the reader to 'devote your income and labor to others', though the rhetoric here as in the poetry has a strongly biblical resonance.
5. Compare, for example, Whitman's 'The Columbian's Song' (1840) – 'What a fair and happy place/ Is the one where Freedom lives,/ And the knowledge that our arm is strong,/ A haughty bearing gives!' (Whitman 1963: 12) – with Marx's verse tragedy *Oulalem*, written around the same time – '... we are chained, shattered, empty, frightened,/ Eternally chained to this marble block of being,/ We are the apes of a cold God' (Payne 1968: 71).
6. Zweig (1984: 4) perhaps exaggerates in describing Whitman prior to *Leaves of Grass* as an 'ordinary American man with no visible talents'. Still, Whitman's journalism and his poems and stories prior to *Leaves of Grass* are outstanding only in their mediocrity in relation to what was to follow. Zweig points out, interestingly, that Whitman was best-known for melodramatic stories – justly forgotten today – about sons who are driven from home, or driven mad, by cruel, indifferent fathers. The persona Whitman created in his poetry was, in contrast, of a loving, caring father.
7. On the transition from liberalism to fascism in national poetry, see Aberbach (2008).
8. Whitman's anti-monarchism is close in tone to that of revolutionary European poets in the 1840s. Petőfi in a proclamation of September 20, 1848, wrote of the deposed Louis Philippe: 'On the French throne there sat a reprobate, rascally king, France gave a great cry and at this cry the throne trembled and collapsed, and the perfidious king fled in terror, and in place of a crown a curse rests on his head' (Petőfi 1974: 268).
9. In 'To a Foil'd European Revolutionaire', Whitman identifies the desire for liberty as the most deeply ingrained instinct, the last to go.
10. 'With this title, Whitman strengthened a correlation between Europe's freedom and that of the United States, illustrating his belief that the European liberation was an echo of American freedom' (Stein 1998: 588). This revolutionary poem retained significance to Whitman. It was one of only two previously published poems which he put in the first edition of *Leaves of Grass* in 1855. The other was 'A Boston Ballad' (1854). See Reynolds (1996: 131).
11. Compare Petőfi's poem '1848': 'We are ashamed for the long night of servitude./ Our anger rises against tyrants./ Our morning prayer is a sacrifice of blood' (Petőfi 1973: 337).
12. In his notebooks, Whitman defines American poetry as poetry of the future: 'The poetry of other lands lies in the past [...] the Poetry of America lies in the future' (Whitman 1984; iv 1435).

13. In *Uncle Tom's Cabin* (1852), Harriet Beecher Stowe points out the irony that Hungarians who escaped Austria after their failed revolt in 1848–9 – a revolt enthusiastically supported in America – were welcomed as heroes by Americans, who were evidently too patriotic to see heroism among escaped Black slaves: 'if any of our readers do, they must do it on their own private responsibility' (ch. 17).
14. One of these 'foreign characters' in 1850–1 was Garibaldi whose attempt with Mazzini to establish an Italian republic in 1848–9 had failed and now lived in temporary exile in New York.
15. The Nation is on Whitman's list of things 'not the Me myself' (*Song of Myself* 4).
16. For Petőfi's disgusted response to the failure of the European revolutions in 1848–49, including the one in Hungary in which he took part (and was ultimately killed), see his poem *Európa csendes, ujra csendes* (Basa 1980: 148), quoted as the epigraph to this chapter.
17. See the Epilogue to *Pan Tadeusz* (1834), quoted p. 251.
18. For examples of political and racial intolerance in Whitman's journalism, see pp. 214, 223 note 31.
19. 'America … perceives that the corpse is slowly borne from the eating and sleeping rooms of the house … that its action has descended to the stalwart and wellshaped heir who approaches' (Whitman 1964: ii 434).
20. Whitman 1984 (i 159). On Whitman's aversion to influence, also see 'Rules of Composition' in his notebooks (*ibid.*, 101). In 'A Backward Glance O'er Travel'd Roads' (1888), too, Whitman openly acknowledges the extent of his reading, much of which in the open air (Whitman 1964: ii 722).
21. Melville's *Moby Dick* (1851), which established, as *Leaves of Grass* was to do, an unmistakably American style, was also written under the influence of 'Young America'.
22. See, for example, Kaplan (1980), Loving (1999) and Morris (2000). Zweig (1984) contrasts the triumphal exuberance of Whitman's 1855 Preface to *Leaves of Grass* with the reality of his home life: 'The weight of illness and approaching death lay upon the house' (240).
23. Whitman's older contemporary, the poet and scholar Henry Wadsworth Longfellow, shared a concern with the Union, drawing on Lönnrot's *Kalevala* in creating a unifying American mythology, but failed to communicate Whitman's complexity and contradictions:

Sail on, O Ship of State!
Sail on, O Union, strong and great!
Humanity with all its fears,
With all the hopes of future years,
Is hanging breathless on thy fate!

('The Building of the Ship' [1849])

All your strength is in your union.
All your danger is in discord;
Therefore be at peace henceforward,
And as brothers live together.

(*The Song of Hiawatha* [1855])

Longfellow's shallowness when compared with Whitman perhaps accounts partly for the fact that although in the 19th century Longfellow was regarded far more than Whitman as an American national poet, his reputation has not stood well the test of time. Still, Whitman's nationalism degenerates shrilly at times into 'a program of democratic cant' (Erkkila 1989: 160).
24. The question of the 'real Me' or 'true self', both individual and national, is central also in Ibsen's *Peer Gynt* (1867).
25. 'Whitman wrote most compellingly out of his search for a lover who was not a mere outline, and out of his inability to find such a person – except, perhaps, in his mother' (Pollak 2000: xxi). He is the poet of the goodbye kiss (Black 1975).
26. On lists of men in Whitman's notebooks, see Whitman (1984: i 146, 226–7). Zweig comments on these lists (1984: 188ff) and on Whitman's 'desperate confession' of his feelings for the streetcar conductor, Peter Doyle, in 'thinly disguised code' in a journal of the late 1860s (*ibid.*, 193–4). Whitman refers to his 'humiliating' pursuit of Peter Doyle as '164', the letter 'P' being the 16th in the alphabet, and 'D' (Doyle) being the 4th. In 'Once I Pass'd through a Populous City', Whitman changes the sex of the love object from male to female, in block letters: 'PURSUE HER NO MORE'. Far from accepting his 'adhesive nature', as he calls it *(ibid.*, 194), Whitman is here clearly repelled by it. Zweig surmises that at some point Whitman had painfully furtive homosexual encounters, inducing him to create a compensatory calm and confident persona, beyond extreme passion, guilt and frustration.
27. For a facsimile and parallel text, see Bowers (1969: v, 64–5). 'Once I Passed through a Populous City' is close in its tone of loss to De Quincey's memory of a prostitute he knew when he was living rough in London, in *Confessions of an English Opium Eater*.
28. In 'Sometimes with One I Love', the poet, similarly, confesses frustrated love as the source of his *Calamus* poems: 'I loved a certain person ardently and my love was not return'd,/ Yet out of that I have written these songs'.
29. After the Civil War, too, Whitman was highly critical of America (Morris 2000: 238ff) and, in *Democratic Vistas*, expressed awareness of the fragility of democracy and its potential failure.
30. Many of the English leaders of the anti-slavery movement were Quakers; and Whitman's Quaker roots are evident in his opposition to slavery.
31. Other threats to America's future are, similarly, not apparent in *Leaves of Grass*. America in the 1850s was in an economic crisis and gripped by one of its periodic bursts of religious mania and xenophobia, especially towards Catholics. The anti-Catholic and anti-German 'Know-Nothings' reached the height of their influence as *Leaves of Grass* came off the press in 1855, and even Whitman shared some of their prejudices, though he did not put them in his poetry (Reynolds 1996: 87).
32. Whitman's support for 'Free Soil' – the belief that territories acquired by the United States in its war with Mexico (1846–47) should be free of slavery – cost him his job as editor of the *Brooklyn Eagle*, the leading newspaper in Brooklyn at the time, whose owner, Isaac Van Anden, sympathized with the slaveowners of the South (Zweig 1984: 27–8).

33. Whitman regarded Blacks as 'sources of dread and emblems of retribution' (Erkkila 1989: 240). On Whitman's racial views, see Klammer (1995) and Folsom (2000). Harriet Beecher Stowe, in the most famous and influential anti-slavery work in American literature, the novel *Uncle Tom's Cabin* (1852), evidently supported the return of Blacks to Africa. The novel ends with a former slave writing to American friends from France of his impending departure for Liberia: 'I have no wish to pass for an American ... As a Christian patriot, as a teacher of Christianity, I go to *my country*'.
34. Elsewhere, too, in his notebooks Whitman identifies with slaves, in lines anticipating *Leaves of Grass* (10): 'I am the hunted slave/ Damnation and despair are close upon me' (Whitman 1984: i 109).
35. For a comparison between Whitman and Tagore, see Sastry (1992).
36. Similar 'secessions' from the Nation may be found among poets as dissimilar as Ibsen, Bialik and Yeats. See pp. 78, 240, 242, and 243.
37. On the influence of mystical literature (e.g., by Swedenborg and Mesmer) on Whitman, see Reynolds (1996: 259ff).
38. Whitman adapted this passage in *Song of Myself*: '... each man and each woman of you I lead upon a knoll,/ My left hand hooking you round the waist,/ My right hand pointing to landscapes of continents and the public road' (46).
39. Parallel confessions of a national poet that the deepest sources of his poetic creativity are personal, and linked with death, are found in Bialik's poems. See Aberbach (1988).
40. On the Quaker background to Whitman's mysticism and his belief in the 'inner light' which puts human beings in touch with God, see Reynolds (2000: 18).
41. Loving (1999) suggests that whereas the poet in the pre-war *Leaves of Grass* was a bachelor, the Civil War was 'a marriage ceremony of sorts – between him and his country' (2). Whitman's 'bride' was the whole country, though his selfless devotion to the wounded men on both sides in his hospital work can also be interpreted as being consistent with his alleged homosexuality.
42. Whitman summed up his view many years afterwards, that the war had been 'about nine hundred and ninety nine parts diarrhea to one part glory' (in Morris 2000: 171).
43. The realism in Whitman's war poems might be contrasted with the chauvinistic romanticism in such poems as George Frederik Root's 'The Battle Cry of Freedom' (1863):

    Yes, we'll rally round the flag, boys,
    we'll rally round again,
    Shouting the battle cry of freedom
    We will rally from the hillside,
    we'll gather from the plain,
    Shouting the battle cry of Freedom.

44. Compare Whitman's declaration of impartial inclusiveness in 'A Backward Glance O'er Travel'd Roads' (1888):

    'I have wish'd to put the complete Union of the States in my songs without any preference or partiality whatever. Henceforth, if they live and are read, it must be just as much South as North – just as much along the Pacific as Atlantic – in the valley of the Mississippi, in Canada, up in Maine, down in Texas, and on the shores of Puget Sound'.

(Whitman 1964: ii 727)

45. For many examples of the role of bereavement in literary creativity, including that of Whitman, see Aberbach (1989). Tennyson, Hardy, D.H. Lawrence and T.S. Eliot are among many poets who produced important poetry after a major adult bereavement.

10 The Artist as Nation-Builder
Yeats and Bialik

> ... *only an aching heart*
> *Conceives a changeless work of art.*
> (Yeats, 'Meditations in Time of Civil War' 1923)

The Hebrew poet C. N. Bialik (1873–1934) and his older contemporary W.B. Yeats (1865–1939) illustrate the enormous power of artists in the creation of modern national culture.[1] Among the Irish and the Jews – as with many other struggling peoples – the cultural nationalism of their great poets was in some ways as important as political nationalism. As national poets, Yeats and Bialik differ greatly from their early 19th century predecessors, such as Petőfi, Mickiewicz and Shevchenko. Their relationship to the nation is more complex and ambivalent. As we have seen, the failure of the widespread European revolutions of 1848–49, the decline of liberal idealism and the growth of totalitarianism shadow their work. Both at times reject national aims, retreating to the private world of the lyric poet, aiming at self-expression and the creation of great art. Yet ultimately both were identified totally with their nation. They were the leading poets of literary movements inspiring and inspired by national revivals. Each spoke for a subject people with glorious and violent ethno-religious memories and legend but threatened by political subjugation and assimilation in powerful empires with dangerously attractive dominant cultures. Though neither was a militant nationalist, both condemned cowardice and extolled heroism – and inspired ultimate independence from Britain: Ireland in 1921 and Israel in 1948. In common with other romantic cultural nationalists, Yeats and Bialik set the artist above the cleric as custodian of national culture. Breaking with failed traditionalism, unsure of political solutions, they fought for the moral regeneration of the nation, a humanist universalist culture, evoking a golden age of collective national memory. As innovators and virtuosos, they married European modernism to indigenous forms and themes. Their poetry belongs to the best in their cultures.

BIALIK AS NATIONAL FIGURE

Together with the Zionist thinker Ahad Ha'am ('One of the People', pen name of Asher Ginsberg [1856–1927]), Bialik helped create modern Jewish national culture. His greatest poetry was written mostly in Odessa in 1901–11. He edited Jewish legends and folklore and wrote the first folk poems in Hebrew and some of the loveliest Hebrew children's poems. He was a founder of the Hebrew national theater (the Habimah) and a leading Hebrew publisher. As poet, editor and publisher, he was dedicated to the concept of *kinnus* (cultural ingathering) by which fragments of Jewish culture from many ages and lands of exile might be 'gathered in' and unified as a modern secular national culture.[2] This concept derived, in part, from the traditional idea of *kinnus galuyot* (the ingathering of the diaspora), the return of the Jewish people to their homeland. In the field of Jewish education, Bialik was regarded as a supreme authority. When he moved to Palestine in 1925, the center of Hebrew literature – previously in Russia and, briefly, in Germany – moved with him. He was on the board of governors of the Hebrew University in Jerusalem and a founder of the Hebrew Writers Union in Tel Aviv and its important journal, *Moznayim*. He served on countless committees and was always ready to advise and help young writers. He was a representative at a number of conferences of the World Zionist Organisation and went on extended lecture tours to raise money for the movement.

Yet, Bialik was no cipher of the national cause. In his poems, essays and letters, he expressed disillusionment and despair with political Zionism at every stage from the foundation of the World Zionist Organization by Theodor Herzl in 1897 until the internal conflicts of the early 1930s.[3]

YEATS AS NATIONAL FIGURE

Yeats, too, was a public nationalist and poetic skeptic. He, too, was a polymath and a self-taught intellectual with no university education. His most lasting 'national' achievement was the Irish National Theatre, which in 1904 became the Abbey Theatre and the center for a school of famous Irish playwrights. But he also founded literary societies, collected and edited Irish folklore, led occultist Celtic societies, wrote nationalist journalism and, briefly, under the influence of the dazzling Maud Gonne whom he loved fruitlessly, dabbled in revolutionary politics. He supported the nascent Irish Arts and Crafts movement and Horace Plunkett's Agricultural Cooperative Society whose aim was to safeguard the economic and social basis of Irish rural society. After Irish independence in 1921, he became for a time a Senator and what he called 'a sixty-year-old smiling public man' ('Among School Children', 1921).

CONFLICT BETWEEN THE PUBLIC AND THE PRIVATE SELVES

The cultural nationalism of Yeats and Bialik was a blood brother of revolutionary political nationalism. Independence confirmed their canonical status. Yet their national role is marked by irony and self-effacement.

Fiercely individualistic, they were suspicious of the very nationalism which unleashed their creativity. They would not have disagreed with Tagore (whose writings Yeats knew well) in the view that nationalism could stifle creativity and encourage selfish materialism.[4] Both poets felt national commitment jostling uneasily with purely private concerns, releasing both originality and guilt.[5] Private trauma, though, mirrored national concerns up to a point. In particular, longing for a woman out of reach – in poems such as Bialik's *Scroll of Fire* (1905) and Yeats' 'No Second Troy' (1908) or 'Words' (1908) – could express collective yearning for national wholeness. Chronic frustration, especially in Bialik, was enlisted in the national cause.[6] Private obsession in each might be viewed as creative mainspring.

Bialik became a national icon almost in spite of himself. His main preoccupations were personal: orphanhood, separation, neglect, suffering, alienation, childlessness, despair.[7] No Hebrew poet has expressed childhood ordeals with such power and lyric beauty, building on biblical and talmudic Hebrew sources. His poems resonate with the yearning of Jews through the ages. His reluctance as national poet was virtually 'proof' of Bialik's authenticity; was not the prophet Jeremiah similarly reluctant? His acclaim as Jewish national poet provoked guilt and a sense of worthlessness and deceit. In his poetry he is the perpetual unloved outsider.

Yeats, too, felt himself an outsider from childhood. He belonged to the 'colonial' Protestant minority which, after the British conquest of Ireland in the 17th century, had supplanted Ireland's Gaelic Catholic aristocracy. In his writings and public role, Yeats hoped to overcome this state of alienation. His English reworking of Ireland's native Gaelic traditions and revival of the legendary heroic pagan Ireland symbolically wedded Protestant 'colonist' and Catholic 'native'. However, what worked in literature did not work in social reality. Yeats' cult of the aristocratic hero was alien to Catholic Ireland, whose populist nationalism was hostile to the 'superior airs' of the Protestant Ascendancy. Yeats' sense of failure as national poet led to his disillusionment with mass democratic values and attraction to eugenics and fascism.

CONTEXTS OF IRISH AND JEWISH NATIONALISM

Bialik was the poet of a Zionist diaspora nationalism which aimed to return the Jews to their ancestral homeland, the Land of Israel. His early readership was mainly Russian Jews under Tsar Nicholas II (1894–1917). Most of these Jews were working class and impoverished and, in various ways, discriminated against and degraded. They had only limited control over the land they inhabited in the Pale of Settlement, the area on the western frontier of the Russian empire to which they were confined by law under Tsarist rule.[8] By the end of the 19th century their numbers reached five million. This was the largest Jewish community at the time.

Yeats dreamed of becoming the poet of the native Irish who wanted autonomy from British imperial rule in their native homeland and a reversal of the land confiscations of the 17th century. He spoke for a rural society still traumatized by the Great Famine of the 1840s which had killed one million and turned Ireland into an emigrant country in rapid demographic decline.

Different though their nationalisms were, Jews and Irish shared common ground as small nations with a long history of religious persecution, subject to a powerful imperial state. They can be categorized as 'chosen peoples', seeing themselves as divinely separated from the world of power by their suffering which uplifted them for a higher, even messianic, purpose. Bialik and Yeats were strongly influenced by this ethno-religious outlook. Each spoke for peoples victimized by imperial power and sure of the moral high ground. Bialik seemed to hold continually in his mind's eye the entire history of Jewish tragedy, above all the destruction of the Temple in Jerusalem by the Romans in 70 CE; while Yeats mourned the destruction of Gaelic aristocratic culture by the English conquest in the 17th century and the failure of Irish revolts.

Still, the cultural nationalism of Yeats and Bialik was as much an inner rebellion against established leaders as a cry against historical wrongs. Each spoke for a generation radicalized by its sense of victimization and destablized by rapid social change. The new moral vision based on a revival of history and culture which they articulated gave direction to radical political activism.

BIALIK AND THE HEBREW REVIVAL

Bialik was the major poet in a wide-ranging Hebrew cultural revival, including Ahad Ha'am and Mendele Mokher Sefarim ('Mendele the Bookpeddler', pen name of S.J. Abramowitz [1835?–1917]), who after 1881 challenged traditional Jewish authority and implicitly rejected the imperial Russian state. The basis of this literature was established mostly in the quarter-century prior to 1881. The liberalizing rule of Tsar Alexander II (1855–1881) had promised civil equality to 'useful' Jews – the tiny minority who were wealthy or professionally trained. Hebrew culture developed during this period as a tool of secular education and enlightenment (Hebrew: Haskalah) which, it was hoped, would improve their lives, acculturate them within Russian society and remove from them the stigma of parasitism. Hebrew literature of the Haskalah also had an important nationalist undercurrent. As the ideas of the Haskalah took root, a Hebrew secular culture flourished and the religious authority of the rabbis was undermined. However, Alexander's liberal program, whose most radical act was the freeing of the serfs in 1861, also threatened the autocratic basis of the imperial state. A wave of Russian nationalism and accompanying anti-Semitism followed, heightened by the failed Polish revolt of 1863 and the Russian-Turkish war of 1877–78. The assassination of Alexander II in 1881 triggered a wave of pogroms which ended the hopes of the Jewish intelligentsia for emancipation under Tsarist rule. It is estimated that from then until the outbreak of World War I in 1914 nearly one third of the Russian Jews emigrated, mostly to America, and relatively large numbers of Jews joined Russian socialist and revolutionary groups. During this period, too, the first organized Zionist movement began: *Hibbat Zion* (Love of Zion) was set up in Odessa in 1881 and brought an estimated 25,000 Jews, mostly from Russia, to Palestine by the time of the creation of the World Zionist Organisation by Theodor Herzl (1860–1904) in 1897. Another 35,000 – the second *aliyah* – came between 1903, when the second wave of Russian pogroms began, and 1914. Modern Jewish nationalism was based largely on an alliance between the disillusioned Russian Jewish intelligentsia and the Jewish lower middle classes.

This nationalism took two forms: (1) political, embodied by Herzl, aiming not at political independence but a mass return of Jews to the Land of Israel as a place of asylum from persecution and (2) cultural, with Ahad Ha'am as chief ideologue, directed at spiritual reformation of the community, the recreation of Jewish identity along secular nationalist lines. The main leaders of political Zionism were westernized educated European Jews whose nationalism was triggered by anti-Semitism and who were relatively unconcerned about the language of the movement, or even the location of the Jewish 'asylum'. (Herzl, for example, not knowing Hebrew, favoured German as the language of Jewish nationalism; and a Jewish national territory did not have to be the land of Israel but any place where Jews could live free of persecution, including Africa or South America.) Cultural Zionists, in contrast, were mostly Eastern European, usually with lifelong immersion in Judaism and Jewish learning, for whom Jewish nationalism was inseparable from the Hebrew language and the land of Israel. From the viewpoint of cultural nationalists such as Ahad Ha'am and Bialik, the language of Zionism had to be Hebrew as it is the most ancient and distinctive source of Jewish identity, the main link of the Jews with their ancestral homeland, the sole language uniting all Jews, in Scripture and prayer. Zionism both political and cultural thrived amid worsening Russian and European anti-Semitism. In Russia, as elsewhere, internal and external crisis provoked Jew-hatred: the war with Japan in 1904–5, social revolutionary unrest in the cities and nationalist insurgence among the non-Russian populations. In these circumstances, Hebrew literature took the gigantic leap from being primarily a didactic tool of the Haskalah to a highly creative vehicle of Jewish nationalism, and Bialik emerged as the Jewish national poet.

YEATS AND IRISH NATIONALISM

Yeats, too, belonged to an extensive cultural nationalist movement, lasting from the 1870s to 1914, which sought to revive Ireland's pre-conquest

Gaelic culture and combat the increasing assimilation of Irish society into industrial Britain. At the same time there was a large-scale constitutional nationalist drive, led by Charles Stewart Parnell (1846–1891), for a Home Rule parliament with limited political autonomy. A catalyst of Irish nationalism was the agrarian crisis of the late 1870s which roused fear of another famine and led to a land war between the Catholic peasantry and Protestant landlords. Irish political nationalism was stimulated further by British democratizing reforms. Expanded educational opportunities opened up the civil service and the professions and devolved local government to the Catholic majority, resulting in a growing native middle class strongly acculturated to British secular liberal ideals but ambitious for leadership of Irish society.[9] Socially mobile Catholics, driven to nationalism by the continued ascendancy of the Protestant minority protected by the British state, allied with the conservative Catholic Church to demand a parliament for the Catholic majority.

After the scandal which wrecked Parnell's life in 1891, a long 'civil war' broke out between secular liberals and clerical nationalists, out of which new forms of Irish cultural nationalism emerged:[10] Anglo-Irish literary and Gaelic revivalism, both with pre-conquest communitarian values. Support for Irish Home Rule was, nevertheless, far greater. However, between 1910 and 1914 the push to Home Rule was weakened by the irreconcilable aims of Irish democratization and the desire of both British Liberals and Conservatives to preserve British imperial dominance; and the outbreak of war in 1914 shelved Home Rule plans in the British government. A faction of the Gaelic revivalists allied with revolutionary nationalists to stage first a rebellion (1916) then a war of independence (1919–21) that overthrew established Irish political leadership and broke the British hold on Ireland.

PERSONAL DILEMMAS AND NATIONAL 'SOLUTIONS'

The nationalism of Bialik and Yeats grew from problems of identity shared by their generation and also from personal trauma. Both poets had an unhappy family history and in early manhood underwent religious crisis. Deracination pushed both to poetry and to the identification with a similarly unhappy national community.

Though his family was from respectable landed stock, Yeats suffered much of his life from status anxiety. When he was a child, his father gave up law for painting. He moved his family from Sligo to London where he joined a pre-Raphaelite community of artists. The young Yeats was swept from a stable rural world into the anonymity of a vast, insecure, alien metropolitan society. Poor, lonely and Irish, he was mocked and humiliated by the English boys at school. He escaped by identifying with his father's cult of the romantic artist as higher being, transcending the material world.[11]

Here is the kernel of Yeats' later perception of the artist as the last aristocrat, struggling for self-mastery and in conflict with society, who by sheer will summons up life-forces that transform the nation. Alienated from English society, Yeats dreamed of leading a viable Irish national community.

Like many young men from similar backgrounds at the *fin-de-siécle*, Yeats went through a religious crisis and a search for personal and collective meaning. Recoiling both from an ossified Christianity and the alternative mechanical scientific ideologies of progress (including his father's Darwinism), he was drawn to mystical and magical cults such as Theosophy and Rosicrucianism. After he and his friend George Russell founded the Dublin Hermetic Society and the Order of the Golden Dawn in the 1890s, he claimed to have rediscovered a cosmic force, ever-present in ancient times but now forgotten except by an esoteric artistic elite. The task of this elite was to revive the ancient wisdom and cast out the deadwood of sectarian Christianity and of industrial materialism. A new millennium of harmony and progress would then come into being.

Abstruse, farfetched, even somewhat ridiculous, this spiritualism yoked to Irish nationalism propelled the young Yeats into missionary zeal for his cause. Already as a young man in London in the 1880s, Yeats (like his father) identified with the Irish peasants in their land war against British imperialism, which he scorned as corrupt. On his family's return to Dublin in 1885, he joined fellow Protestant revivalists on the *ublin University Review*, including the folklorist Douglas Hyde. He studied Standish 'Grady's 'Homeric' *History of Ireland*, celebrating Ireland's legends and heroes. He met the Fenian revolutionary John O'Leary, who became his mentor. O'Leary directed him to the Gaelic myths and legends of the Western Irish peasantry in which he 'discovered' a pre-Christian pagan Druid cosmology, akin to theosophical doctrines. To Yeats, Ireland was a holy land and he was its *magus*. By the end of the 19th century, Yeats had a clear idea of his task as national poet: to give the political struggle a spiritual dimension in the overthrow of a corrupt cosmopolitanism and degenerate European industrial civilization.[12]

How was the enthusiasm of an intellectual coterie transformed into a forceful cultural revival? One answer lay in the fall of Parnell and the disintegration of the Irish political movements in the 1890s, worsening the struggle between religious and secular. To cultural nationalists, this internecine conflict was caused by divorce from Ireland's Gaelic culture and misalliance with Britain. Consequently, Yeats, Eoin MacNeill, Douglas Hyde and George Russell set up institutions to restore Ireland's ancient legendary culture and language: the National Literary and Irish Literary Societies in 1891 and 1892, the Gaelic League in 1893 and the Irish Literary Theatre in 1899. These organizations attracted a rising generation of educated middle class Catholics deeply frustrated in their ambitions for power and status by continued British rule in Ireland and by the control of nationalist politics by an older, 'failed' generation.

BIALIK: THE MAKING OF A NATIONAL POET

Bialik's social and educational background was far removed from that of Yeats, but the pattern of national involvement is comparable. Born in the Ukraine, Bialik lost his father at six and was separated soon after from his mother, unable to support him, and passed into the care of his aged paternal grandparents. His sense of loss, grief and exile, and search for union with the lost motherland, are central in his poetry and resonated with particular force among the Russian Jews.[13] He grew up in the Hasidic tradition which (though he abandoned it) seeded his poetry with religious fervor and mysticism. He went through the main institutions of traditional Jewish learning, the *heder* (the 'room', where children were taught mainly the Pentateuch with Rashi's commentary), the *bet midrash* (house of study, for older students) and the *yeshivah* (rabbinical seminary, for advanced students of the Talmud). As he mastered Hebrew sources, he absorbed the passion for justice of the biblical prophets and love for scriptural exposition and legends of the Talmud. But he also studied in secret the new, prohibited Hebrew literature of the Haskalah (the secular Enlightenment), published with Russian government approval with the somewhat paradoxical aim of promoting Jewish assimilation and breaking down rabbinic authority: after the 1881 pogroms, Hebrew was inevitably allied to the Zionist revival. Bialik simultaneously belonged to the majority and to a minority within it. By his late teens, he was writing Hebrew poetry and was recognized as having exceptional gifts.

At this point, Bialik's ideological direction might be compared with Yeats', as he underwent a crisis of faith from which he emerged a national poet. Neither the quasi-medieval *shtetl* nor tsarist Russia offered a viable future for Eastern European Jews. As we have seen, the great turning point in modern Jewish history was reached when Russian anti-Semitism, stirred up by the Polish Revolt of 1863 and by the chauvinism created by the Russian-Turkish war of 1877–78, became virulent when Alexander II was assassinated in 1881. The pogroms and their socio-economic and psychological consequences dominated Bialik's early life – he was eight when they began in 1881 – effectively ruling out the possibility of Jewish emancipation and civil rights under tsarist rule. These pogroms triggered a large-scale emigration to Palestine; Jews joined longstanding Jewish communities there. Hundreds of Hebrew-speaking groups sprang up in Russia. The Russian-Hebrew intelligentsia unexpectedly found common cause with the Russian lower middle class. The result was a remarkable increase in Hebrew journalism and Hebrew readers whose numbers may have reached 100,000 in the 1880s.[14]

As Yeats found his nationalist mentor in John O'Leary, Bialik found his in Ahad Ha'am. The pogroms of 1903–6 drove him to write a series of 'poems of wrath', expressing angry indignation and despair. *The City of Slaughter*, written after the Kishinev pogrom of 1903, is the most famous and influential modern Hebrew poem. It, more than any other poem, expresses wrath at Jewish cowardice and fatalism. It is an implicit call for action, for emergence from powerlessness. Though it may be that the most authentic poetic voice of both Yeats and Bialik was that of the private lyric poet, the need for action, both personal and national, sparks much of their poetry. Like many late-19th century romantic intellectuals, Yeats and Bialik gloried in and lamented the inward nature of their creative gifts which, they sometimes felt, reduced them to ineffectual passivity from which they longed to escape through masterful action. Both were practical dreamers, their private obsessions not always well-hidden behind the mask of national poet. Ellmann's observation on Yeats applied also to Bialik:

> 'He spent much of his life attempting to understand the deep contradictions within his mind, and was perhaps most alive to that which separated the man of action lost in reverie from the man of reverie who could not quite find himself in action'(1969: 2).

NATIONAL MISSIONS

Yeats and Bialik aimed to overthrow fatalistic stereotypes produced not only by external powers but also self-imposed by their kinsmen. Bialik attacked Jewish passivity enforced both by anti-Semitism and also by Jewish tradition, and Yeats attacked the stage Irish image of the feckless, lovable Paddy propped up by the Church and by the Irish elite kowtowing to British imperial culture. Each sought to make a secular, activist high culture calling up memories and legends of heroism – the Irish chieftain Cuchulain, for example, or the Jewish revolutionary Bar-Kokhba – to stir the young to action.[15] To Yeats as to Shelley, poetry is a great legislative power, the creator of values, a view shared by Bialik, absorbed from the Hebrew Bible. Both Yeats and Bialik saw themselves as teachers of the nation:[16] the poet must write 'the book of the people' ('Coole Park and Balleylee, 1931'), a phrase Yeats took from the blind Irish poet Anthony Raftery (c. 1784–1835). To Yeats as to Bialik, the nation makes possible the individual greatness of a poet: 'You can no more have the greatest poetry without a nation than religion without symbols' (in Ellmann 1968: 15–16).[17]

Yeats was the more programmatic nationalist with a fully worked out *fin-de-siècle* plan for Irish cultural nationalism. He believed that literature was the natural medium for this nationalism. Its roots in the Gaelic bardic oral tradition depicting a golden age of gods and heroes and uniting the community of listeners. This tradition had died with the collapse of native aristocracy. The bard was replaced by the Christian cleric and by the journalist, the apostle of English industrial print culture. Small-scale rural communities were being supplanted by mass urban class societies, driven and fragmented by a lust for power and wealth, exemplified in the rise of empires (*ibid.*, 90).

Ireland, being impoverished and downtrodden, was morally superior to England, corrupted by greed and industry which blackened the countryside and men's hearts: 'Ireland has taken sides for ever with the poor in spirit who shall inherit the earth', Yeats declared on the 100th anniversary of the martyrdom of Wolfe Tone (*ibid.*, 115). Only the solitary romantic artist, Yeats believed, could keep alive the old aristocratic and spiritual ideals. The task of the poet, Yeats wrote memorably in his last poem, 'Under Ben Bulben' (1938), was to recall native history since the English conquest:

> Sing the lords and ladies gay
> That were beaten into clay
> Through seven heroic centuries …

Ireland itself was in danger of 'anglicization' and social division. Yet fragments of Ireland's heroic culture survived in the oral traditions of the Irish-speaking peasantry of the far western counties. This linguistic heritage had evolved a uniquely expressive and imaginative variety of English. Yeats believed that the writer might reconstruct from its folk-fragments Ireland's pagan life-force and stir up latent nationalism among the young English-speaking generation. This was his version of *kinnus*. Remade by a romantic elite, a heroic Ireland based on the land would emerge as a synthesis of English (romantic) culture and the Gaelic heritage, reunited by the cosmology and ethos that preceded the sectarian divisions of Christianity. It was Ireland's mission, once restored, to be an inspiration to a Europe grown weary of materialism and class conflict.

Yeats called for a spiritual and communal 'Anglo-Irish' literature, and he opposed what he saw as the deadening realist forms of contemporary bourgeois England. The poet Samuel Ferguson (1810–1886) gave him a model against which to react. Ferguson's epic poetry, based on Ireland's pagan aristocratic legends, aimed to nationalize Protestant gentry and middle class. Ferguson failed in Yeats' view because his project and its proposed constituency were unnaturally yoked to British culture and politics. Instead, Yeats found his medium in the vibrant Irish-English vernacular, used by Douglas Hyde to catch the authentic idioms of Gaelic oral tradition. Yeats believed in Irish theater, based on Gaelic legends and a new vernacular springing from the allegedly decayed Irish language, as the most effective and influential instrument to stir a new generation of native English-speaking Catholics to nationalism. Theater could be the modern equivalent of the native institutions of oral communal story-telling.

Yeats' drama for the Irish Literary Theatre was also influenced by Wagner and the Bayreuth Theatre. His cycle of plays based on legends of Cuchulain aimed to recapture pre-modern Irish unity as Siegfried embodied German unity in Wagner's remaking of the *Nibelungenlied*. With his chief collaborator Lady Gregory, Yeats hoped for an aristocracy of talent to plumb the Irish national soul.

Bialik, too, yoked his poetic gift to the cultural and political regeneration of ancient traditions, preserved by an intellectual aristocracy. In talmudic folklore and legend, he found heroic life-energies which the Orthodoxy of his time seemed to lack. Much of Yeats' national-culturalism has parallels in Bialik's work: the call for moral regeneration, the pseudo-mysticism and messianism translated into secular form and, above all, the high valuation – perhaps influenced ultimately by Herder – of myth and legend.[18] Like his contemporary revivalists, he was steeped in the classical idioms of Hebrew and its sacred writings. Even when he indulged in mock-heroic satire, he implicitly accepted the power of the Bible and post-biblical Hebrew to inspire. As indicated earlier, one of Bialik major achievements was the editing of the legends in the Talmud and Midrash. To Bialik as to Yeats, the rediscovery of ancient fragments, including those of defeat and exile, was essential in the creation of a new national identity. This was not programmatic activity but a natural consequence of Bialik's esteem for these works as a unique creation of the Jewish people. At the same time, like Yeats, he depicted the poet as a solitary dreamer communing with Nature (e.g., in *The Pool*, 1905), and this, paradoxically, asserted the authenticity of his national role. Nationalism, he felt as Yeats did, freed the purely personal, dammed-up creative urges of the individual.

YEATS' NATIONALIST IMPACT

Yeats' main active period as cultural nationalist was prior to independence, in 1885–1913. Bialik's was throughout his career from the 1890s until his death in 1934. We have seen that in the years just before World War I Yeats helped establish institutions for the creation of an Irish national literature. Both poets inspired their readers by reawakening memories of a golden past but had deeper influence on young nationalists with their fierce attacks on the alleged moral decadence of their people.

Yeats made an early impact through his patriotic plays *Countess Cathleen* (1899) and *Cathleen ni Houlihan* (1902), depicting romantic sacrifice and the ancient personification of Ireland as both mother and beautiful maiden, Cathleen. Even at this early stage, Yeats' pre-Raphaelite interests and Rosicrucianism roused suspicion among traditional nationalists for whom St. Patrick and the Catholic Church – not Gaelic myth – exemplified authentic national values. His theater, too, was controversial from the start. The leading Gaelic League intellectual Eoin MacNeill denounced its cult of aristocratic warriors as elitist and pagan; while James Joyce attacked it as vulgar and provincial: it staged Irish-language plays while neglecting contemporary European drama. Still, Yeats' strident anti-British (and anti-Boer) sentiments brought him the support of romantic militants such as Arthur Griffith. At the end of *Cathleen ni Houlihan*, the young hero abandons his bride to take part in the Irish rebellion of 1798 and offers his life for his country embodied by Cathleen. The lines 'They shall be remembered forever' converted many young Irish to the national cause as similarly banal lines in Bialik's early poems turned young Jews into Zionists, in some cases overnight.

Yeats' Cuchulain plays put onto the stage for the first time the 'ungovernable' warrior hero, who in his battle with fate expressed the Nietzschean will to defy limits. Audiences could recognize in these plays the struggles of revolutionaries such as Patrick Pearse (a Cuchulain devotee), whose heroic individualism led them to scorn the inhibiting checks and balances of democracy. More bitter and provocative were Yeats' satirical verses written when the literary-linguistic revival lost momentum. Poems such as 'September 1913' (1913) spoke of dampened revolutionary ardor in the face of impending Home Rule. Its refrain, 'Romantic Ireland's dead and gone,/ It's with O'Leary in the grave', set the heroic Irish heritage of sacrifice against the decadent reality of a petty bourgeois society governed by greed and hypocritical piety. This was the death of Irish nationalism. Yeats' attack helped drive young cultural nationalists such as Pearse and MacDonagh from constitutional politics to revolutionary activism.[19]

BIALIK AND THE STRUGGLE AGAINST JEWISH POWERLESSNESS

Much of Bialik's poetry reflects the spread of European anti-Jewish hatred and resultant militancy among young Jews of the generation after the anti-Semitic Russian pogroms of 1881–2. In 1899 he wrote a poem which passed the censor only because it was entitled 'Bar-Kokhba', setting it safely at the time of the last Jewish revolt against Rome, in the 2nd century CE:[20]

> Nothing but your fierce hounding
> has turned us into beasts of prey.
> With cruel fury
> we'll drink your blood.
> We'll have no pity
> when the whole nation rises, cries –
> Revenge![21]

After the Kishinev pogrom in 1903, increasing numbers of Jews, outraged by anti-Jewish violence and persecution, and repulsed by the gentile world, turned to Zionism. Bialik's 'poems of wrath', written mostly during the pogroms of 1903–06, reflect a revolutionary change in Jewish consciousness in the process of emerging from powerlessness through nationalism. The poem 'On the Slaughter' was Bialik's gut reaction to the pogrom in Kishinev at Easter 1903:

> If there is justice – let it come now!
> But if it comes after I'm destroyed –
> let its throne be wrecked forever!

let the heavens rot in eternal evil.
Go, wicked men, in violence.
Live on your blood, wash in it.[22]

The degree of victimization of the Jews was, at the time of the pogroms, far greater than the Irish, who were not subjected to systematic government-sponsored legal discrimination and government-tolerated violence.[23] However, like Yeats, Bialik often depicted his people as incapable of national revival. In the direct, forceful style of the ancient prophets he attacked the status quo. He scourged those Jews who remained passive in the face of oppression and denounced those who abandoned their national roots:

'Will dew revive a dead leaf of a tree, or hyssop clinging to rocks, or a broken vine a dry flower? Can trumpet blasts and a raised banner revive the dead?'[24]

This righteous anger was expressed most famously in *The City of Slaughter*, with its attack not on the perpetrators of the Kishinev pogrom but on the unheroic Jews, a small minority, who used the national tragedy to elicit sympathy and funds for themselves:

To the graveyard, beggars!
Dig up the bones of martyred father and brother,
fill your sacks, sling them on backs
and hit the road
to do business at all the fairs;
advertise yourselves at the crossroads so everyone sees,
in the sunshine on filthy rags spread the bones
and sing your hoarse beggar song,
beg the decency of the world!
Beg the pity of *goyim*!
Eternal beggars![25]

As indicated earlier, this poetry illustrates Renan's point that nation-building often involves the distortion of history. Yet, far from being seen as defeatist, Bialik's condemnation inspired the creation of Jewish defense groups in Russia and had lasting effects. Many members of these groups came to Palestine, where they formed the nucleus of the Haganah, the antecedent of the Israeli army.

THE NATION AS MASK

Yeats and Bialik, driven in their nationalism by purely personal experiences and emotions, faced the dilemma of projecting such emotions onto the national cause. The result was added depth and complexity, raising their art far beyond nationalist propaganda.

Yeats' vision of an aristocratic Ireland led by self-sacrificing seers rejecting materialist values can be seen as a reaction of a member of a *declassé* landed family forced for much of his early career to eke out an insecure existence as a journalist in the literary market place. His celebration of romantic, sometimes tragic, individuals who brought high moral ideals to a life of action regardless of mass opinion was derived from his longing for heroism as a shy, insecure intellectual. Yeats made his service to Maud Gonne a metaphor for his thwarted dedication to Ireland. He cast her as heroine queen in his nationalist plays, *Cathleen ni Houlihan* and *Countess Cathleen*, and he used her in his poetry, fusing the dilemmas of nationalist politics with his sexual frustration.

All this is surprisingly close to some of Bialik's poetry, in which the poet's guilt at using national trauma as an outlet for purely personal obsessions (as the beggars do in *The City of Slaughter*) is a major theme.[26] The image of a woman yearned for but emotionally out of reach is an overriding image both for the poet's private failures and for the Jewish people *vis-a-vis* their motherland and the lofty biblical ideals always beyond human reach.

Aware of the irreducibly personal aspect of his verse, Yeats rejected sentimental nationalist propaganda. He particularly disliked the Young Ireland poets, beloved of political nationalists. Their poetry, in his view, seemed to come largely out of external political motives rather than inner passion. Yeats demanded from art an original inner vision welling up from intensely felt experience and expressing communal consciousness. Were private obsessions of the artist compatible with public nationalism?[27] By encouraging writers such as Synge and, later, O'Casey because they were good, Yeats not only subverted his original aristocratic ideal of the artist but also the possibility of a coherent, broad-based cultural movement. By defending the principle of self-expression, Yeats also came into conflict with former supporters such as Arthur Griffith, Maud Gonne and George Russell, who were antagonized by the corrosive satires of Synge and others as they appeared to attack Ireland, Irish institutions, the Irish family and the Church. In 1903, Maud Gonne dashed his romantic hopes by marrying her fellow revolutionary John MacBride. Yeats, 'starved for the bosom of his faery bride' (a pun on 'MacBride'?), pondered deeply thereafter the responsibility of the artist to personal authenticity rather than to a public cause. In 'No Second Troy' (1910), Maud Gonne, transformed into a modern Helen of Troy, shocks the poet with the power of love and beauty to bring violence and destruction. Yeats found greatness in qualities that unsuited him for Maud Gonne, for he was less a man of action than of meditation. Rejected by his muse, he could feel more fully the force of Ireland's defeats and failures.

Bialik was similarly torn between the simultaneous need to defer individuality to the nation and to realize himself as a private lyric poet. His 'national' poems are few, belong to his early period and are not among his best, though they had much influence. It is true that communal bereavement and infertility in his work, conveyed in biblical images of the destruction of the Temple and the loss of Jewish national independence, struck deep chords with his generation who themselves felt orphaned.[28] But they derived partly from a personal sense of loss in early childhood. Bialik chastises his people using the same epithets with which he criticizes himself: they are dry as a tree, withered like grass, rotten from head to foot.[29] Like the beggars in *The City of Slaughter*, the poet uses national trauma for personal ends. A prevailing theme in Jewish liturgy is the yearning for national renewal and for a lost land associated with the nation's childhood. Such yearnings are prominent in Bialik's poetry of his childhood, though he rarely identified the nation's hopes as his own. Early lines dating from 1894 are exceptional:

> I too have power enough.
> In open spaces set free my imprisoned strength!
> A weak nation will blossom,
> My rotten bones will flourish like grass.[30]

Though he revered his nationalist mentor, Ahad Ha'am, Bialik went his own way as a poet. The lacerating guilt that resulted entered his poetry. He remained to the end of his life deeply ambivalent about the degree to which Zionists read into his poems of private trauma a call for national renewal. He was far less a poet of hope than of almost-suicidal despair. A good example is a poem responding to the First Zionist Congress in 1897:

> Do you see who lurks
> behind the door, broom in hand?
> The caretaker of ruined temples –
> Despair![31]

YEATS' RECEPTION AS NATIONAL POET

Yeats and Bialik had very different receptions as national poets. Yeats, longing to be Ireland's national poet, was rejected by the Irish nationalists; Bialik, guiltily ambivalent about his national role, was nevertheless elevated against his will by Zionists into a national institution. These ironic twists of fate affected their creativity.

Why did Yeats in his lifetime fail as a national poet? Yeats hoped to create a sophisticated national culture, open to the world. Ireland, though, had little market for high culture. Her best artists (including Yeats) left for London or Paris. His theater survived through the selfless dedication of writers and actors, financed between 1904 and 1910 by an English patron, Annie Horniman. His cultural nationalism outraged. mainstream Catholic opinion which unfairly perceived his works as a blow for the Protestant Ascendancy.

In fact, Yeats had begun by rejecting his own caste as philistine and unpatriotic and looked to convert the best of the young Catholic middle class to a nonsectarian Irish nationalism. But the new Catholic intelligentsia, many from poorly educated rural backgrounds and imbued with 'memories' of sectarian persecution, remained profoundly ethnocentric and suspicious of secular High Culture. They had little understanding of Yeats' sophisticated neo-pagan vision and felt threatened by Synge's plays championed by Yeats which satirized Catholicism, patriotism and family in the name of freedom. They embraced rather the Gaelic League and its vision of Ireland as a superior rural Irish-speaking peasant community whose golden age was in the Middle Ages. To Irish Catholics, this image of Ireland was an *insula sacra* of Christian values which could prevail against the spread of English materialist values. The campaign of the Gaelic League to revive a culturally separate democratic nation legitimated its drive to overturn the economic, social and political power of the alien Protestant elite and to assume leadership in Ireland.[32] Its leaders denounced Yeats' project as a Protestant ploy to hijack leadership of their cultural revival and divert it towards apolitical aestheticism or, worse, a decadent European neo-paganism.

Some of this criticism was just. Yeats' nationalism had something of the arrogance and ambivalence of the Protestant settler minority, protected by English colonialism, their privileges based on spoliation and religious exclusion. Yet, in common with other Irish Protestants periodically since the 18th century, Yeats turned away from British interests and became an Irish nationalist. Why did these Protestants become Irish nationalists? The answer lies, perhaps, less in their love for Ireland than in disillusionment with England. The condescension shown them by England drove them to identify with aspects of Irish heritage, particularly in the legendary pagan aristocratic period. If in British eyes, they were facsimile aristocrats, in Irish eyes they could be true aristocrats. In his alienation from increasingly urban industrial Britain, Yeats was typical of this Protestant minority. He found his main allies within his own class of reform-minded Anglo-Irish Protestants, such as Lady Gregory, co-founder of the Abbey Theatre; Sir Horace Plunkett, leader of the Irish agricultural co-operative movement; and Sir Hugh Lane, a Plunkett supporter and patron of the arts. Unable to submit to a populist Catholic Irish democratic identity, they pioneered the idea of a new Irish rural nation blending traditions of conqueror and conquered. In the circles of the elite, Yeats somewhat quixotically created from above a heroic Irish nation while asserting the artist's independence from political constraints. Throughout the period 1885–1913, Yeats oscillated between these vexing opposites, dancing on the crossways of the chameleon heart, concerned less with growing into the Nation than in withering into the Truth, breaking with Irish nationalism for the higher responsibility of the artist; leaving Dublin for London, then drawn back to the nationalist fray by crisis in Ireland. All things considered, then, it is not surprising that his reception among Irish Catholics was a damp squib.

BIALIK: PUBLIC SUCCESS, PRIVATE DESPAIR

In Bialik's case, the pressure of anti-Semitism increasingly united the highly diverse international Jewish communities and made possible the idea of a Jewish national poet.[33] However, in Bialik, conflict between the artist and the nationalist was more extreme than in Yeats. Whereas Yeats was attacked for using the nation as a vehicle for self-seeking interests, Bialik seems to have attacked himself in his own poetry – above all in *The Scroll of Fire* – for doing the same. The contrast between his public role as selfless servant of a cause and his consciousness of the private springs of his inspiration filled him with guilt. At times, Bialik expressed this guilt openly: 'When you see me weeping for some wondrous land ... do not mourn or comfort me, my tears are false'.[34]

In 1909 Bialik paid his first visit to Palestine where many Jewish settlers looked to him for inspiration and hope. They did not appreciate that most of his main work came out of private, not national, obsessions. During a public reading in Jaffa from a story of his depicting a sexual liaison between a Jewish boy and a Christian girl, his audience stopped him, demanding national poems instead. In 1923, during the international fanfare which marked his fiftieth birthday, Bialik wrote a poem beginning, 'My spirit is bowed to the dust/ under the yoke of your love', and he compared himself to a coin vulgarly jangling in the national coinbox.

Still, the conflict between Bialik's private concerns as an artist and his public role did not seriously affect his image as national poet. This role, a response to fervent demand, was played effectively by a poet wholeheartedly committed to his cause. Even those who might have questioned Bialik's authority were generally overwhelmed by his dominance as a brilliant cultural figure. Also, from the time Bialik started writing in the early 1890s until his death in 1934, the number of Hebrew speakers and readers grew steadily. The great milestones in the history of Jewish nationalism – the foundation of the World Zionist Organisation by Herzl in 1897 and the Balfour Declaration of 1917 – created an atmosphere of political dynamism and cultural ferment in which Bialik had a highly receptive readership. These market forces ensured Bialik's success as national poet and meant that by the 1920s he could make substantial sums of money from his writing.

YEATS' FAILURE AS NATIONAL POET

Yeats' readership was infinitely larger than Bialik's, but his circumstances as an aspiring national poet were less fortunate. By 1910 the Protestant reform movement, including Yeats' plans for the Irish Theatre, had run to ground for lack of popular support. Even his theatrical *protegés* had subverted his original aristocratic hopes, establishing a largely realist, demotic view of Ireland. To Yeats the last straw was the rejection in 1913 by the Dublin City

Council of Hugh Lane's offer of his priceless collection of paintings on condition that they house it suitably in a separate gallery. Yeats responded with poems such as 'September 1913' declaring his disillusionment with Ireland. He then left for England.

This break marked the end of Yeats' major period as a national-cultural leader and the beginning of his conversion via Ezra Pound to poetic modernism. He used his new stark and direct form of verse to respond to the Easter Rebellion of 1916, 'Easter 1916', praising the rebellion for heroic, even mythical qualities while recoiling from its stony fanaticism: 'too long a sacrifice/ Can make a stone of the heart'. Precisely when Yeats, defeated in public life, turned from activism to immerse himself in his craft, he found a voice whose crystal-sharp tones expressed the psychological transformation of Ireland, anticipating independence:

> I write it out in a verse –
> MacDonagh and MacBride
> And Connolly and Pearse
> Now and in time to be
> Wherever green is worn,
> Are changed, changed utterly:
> A terrible beauty is born.

After independence in 1921, Yeats returned to Ireland where he was made a Senator of the Free State. During the subsequent civil war, he wrote of his despair at internecine strife and his hope for reconciliation. He became involved in several cultural ventures, including a revived Abbey Theatre, and found new controversy defending Sean O'Casey's plays. But the national culture promoted by the new Irish state was oppressively puritanical, populist and Gaelic-Catholic. Large sections of the Protestant community 'returned' to England. Yeats himself retreated to a private Ireland, an idealized conservative Anglo-Irish tradition of Berkeley, Swift, Grattan and Burke. He even flirted with fascism in the 1930s.[35] His last years were spent mostly out of Ireland, and he died in France in 1939.

The great irony of Yeats' career was that his failure as national poet drove him to write some of his finest poetry which was – outside Ireland – universally accepted as the achievement of Ireland's national poet, the first Irish Nobel laureate for literature (1924). His poetry in romantic fashion transforms his public failures into universal triumphs of the human spirit. In 'Coole Park, 1929', for example, he celebrates his cultural efforts and those of his dearest associates, Lady Gregory and John Synge, as the last stand against modernity of the heroic folk tradition starting with Homer. In prose this is blarney; in poetry, sublime. In poems such as 'Sailing to Byzantium' (1926), he elevates his doomed struggles as a metaphor for the eternal battle of the creative imagination against death. And in a sense, Yeats was right: there is no question of victory, but by confronting and defying his fate and recording his struggles in art, the poet can achieve a form of immortality. Yet, the poet's adjuration to the sages of the past to 'gather me/ Into the artifice of eternity' has no mention of Ireland or of his hopes for Ireland. His homeland here is art.

A irony similar to Yeats' is apparent in Bialik's poetry: he made some of his best poetry (e.g., *The Scroll of Fire*) out of the guilty conflict between his collective prophetic identity, the voice of rage and justice, and the soft, private voice of the lyric poet bewailing his losses, of mother and father, of love and youth. In a poem beginning 'The sea of quiet spits secrets' (1901), the poet confesses:

> One world alone is mine –
> The one in my heart.

Bialik's weakest poems included the purely national ones, which date from his early period, pre-1900. Yet, the perception of Bialik was more important than the reality. Political figures as diverse as the moderates Weizmann and Ben-Gurion, the extremists Jabotinsky and Begin and the Zionist Orthodox rabbi Abraham Isaac Kook greeted him as the reincarnation of a biblical prophet and symbol of national resurrection, moving the nation to political action. And so he was. He expressed the rage of the persecuted, the hopes of a people emerging from powerlessness and the sense of a great dislocated past which it was possible, in some form, to recover. Perhaps most important to Bialik's national role, as to Yeats', was the creation of superb language which roused national consciousness and pride even when it did not aim to, and even when it condemned the nation for pettiness, cowardice, passivity and hypocrisy. The act of creation – never mind the content – was part of and stimulated creative, revolutionary nationalism which fed it in turn.

YEATS AND BIALIK: NATIONAL POETS

It is unlikely that either Yeats or Bialik read the other or knew of their lives and circumstances. The value of comparison, though hard to define, is not inconsiderable. Their careers exemplify tensions general to cultural nationalism, between romantic visionaries and 'political' activists. Whereas Bialik and Yeats committed themselves to exploring the individuality of the nation in all its disconcerting complexities, the focus of an Ahad Ha'am and an Arthur Griffith was more on the construction of simpler ideal types (even stereotypes) to create national feeling. The idea of a 'national poet' may be seen as a contradiction in terms.[36] Indeed, prior to Yeats and Bialik, there is no comparable sense of conflict in their literatures – perhaps in any literature – between the solitary artist and the national figure. The poetry of Yeats and Bialik raises complex questions about the relationship between the artist and the nationalist, about the meaning of national art and the constraints imposed as well as the creativity released by nationalism.

Yeats' poetic achievement was greater than Bialik's (and, indeed, virtually all other 20th century poets), though in his lifetime his social and political impact was more modest. Yeats expresses the attraction and pride of belonging to a nation whose legends and culture are powerful tools for overcoming rootlessness and transforming individual concerns into something of wider, more permanent importance. Yet no poet, however gifted, can go against the ethnic grain to construct a nation. Yeats was rejected by the Irish as Bialik never was rejected by the Jews. Still, Yeats chose not to live the life of the cosmopolitan romantic. Repeatedly he came back to Ireland and wrote of it to the end, in 'Under Ben Bulben' (1938), celebrating 'the indomitable Irishry'.

In the long run, though, Yeats had an impact on Irish culture comparable with that of Bialik on Jewish culture. His international recognition as an Irish nationalist and one of the great poets of the 20th century made it impossible for Ireland to ignore him. Since the Gaelic revival failed to produce a vital national culture, Yeats' project to create a distinctive Irish literature in English has appeared increasingly plausible and viable. In particular, the Abbey Theatre has shown through the high quality of its dramatists and the controversies it has excited the potential for Irish cultural nationalism in English. In his reflections on the competing demands of personal conscience and national duty, Yeats was true both to his poetic calling and to his self-constructed national role. His career underscores the contribution of the minority Protestant community to Irish identity. His glorification of pagan Irish heroes of legend denies any single sectarian definition of the nation and has particular value in an island in need of a unifying ideology but wracked by divisions between its different religious and cultural traditions. His individual voice as rebel against disunity and mediocrity in his 'blind bitter land' (and Dublin a 'blind and ignorant town') – a voice originating in the same tradition of prophetic dissent in which Bialik wrote – is the conscience and direction of Irish national culture.

Judging from his poetry, Bialik's life was a failure, full of longing and deprivation, of loss and impotence. His poetic career seems to have been cut short by trauma and ambivalence: after 1911, he practically stopped writing poetry, except for children. Yet as a poet Bialik has a unique place in a moment of unparalleled change in Jewish and world history. He can be read with pleasure by philosophers as well as by children learning Hebrew. Over a hundred of his lyrics have been set to music. His poems of loss and longing, articulated in the powerful symbols and rhetoric of the biblical tradition, resonated with the hopes and fears of his people. His influence on contemporary and subsequent Hebrew poets was enormous. In the history of cultural nationalism he had unparalleled success. A decade and a half after his death, the people whom he lambasted and lamented, who at the time of his birth had no territory of their own nor a political organization to achieve one, created an independent state.

Yeats and Bialik represent a new type of national poet, more complex and ambivalent, which emerged after the failure of the 1848 revolutions and the collapse of liberal hopes in the end of the 19th century. Yet, even their self-doubt as national figures could be seen as a reflection of the multi-faceted, conflicted identity of an evolving nation state. In a nation's struggle for independence, nothing its great poets write can be purely private. The creative powers of national poets can be set free by the national movements of which they are a part. The poet's inner life as well as the nation's history and legends are enlisted in the national struggle for self-determination.

NOTES

* I am grateful to John Hutchinson of the London School of Economics, with whom I collaborated in an article (Hutchinson and Aberbach 1999), which became in changed form the present chapter.
1. On national aspects of Yeats and Bialik in the general context of nationalism, see the Introduction (this volume). There is a vast bibliography on both poets, on Bialik mostly in Hebrew. On Yeats, see Ellmann (1968, 1969), O'Day (1977), Beckett (1976), Hutchinson (1987), Garvin (1987), Howes (1996), Foster (1997, 2003), Regan (2000), Brown (1980, 2010) and Doggett (2006). For a brief account of Bialik's life and selected bibliography in Hebrew and translation, see Aberbach (1988). For a bi-lingual edition of a selection of Bialik's poems, see Bialik (2004). Translations from Bialik in this chapter are by David Aberbach.
2. The Albanian poet de Rada adopted a similar program in the mid-19th century, by which the restoration of folk fragments to unity would unify 'the dispersed nation' (Pipa 1978: 23).
3. On the Jewish national background to Bialik, see Vital (1975). It may be that to the extent that both Bialik and Yeats were disillusioned with national politics, they were prepared to put up with British rule as the lesser of two evils. Bialik shared with Yeats a lack of enthusiasm for the end of British rule and after he moved to Tel Aviv in 1925 tended to support the pro-British Weizmann rather than the militant Jabotinsky. Yeats naturally identified with the Anglo-Irish Protestant landed class, which was mostly loyal to the Empire.
4. On Tagore's views on nationalism, see, pp. 70–1.
5. On private trauma as a motivation in national poetry, see pp. 8–9 and 295–6.
6. The Palestinian Arabic poet Mahmoud Darwish writes similarly of exile in the language of frustrated love: 'You alone are the exile, miserable one./ No woman to hold you to her breast' (Darwish 2003: 141).
7. On the effects of childhood loss in Bialik's poetry, see Aberbach (1982, 1984, 1988, 1989).
8. On the social and historical background to Bialik's poetry, see for example Frankel (1981), Löwe (1993), Klier (1995), Nathans (2002) and Aberbach (2013). On Eastern European anti-Semitism, particularly in Russia, and its role in Zionism, both political and cultural, see Wistrich (2010) and Löwe (2010).
9. For evaluations of the cultural nationalism of Irish Catholics in reaction to British rule, see Garvin (1987) and Hutchinson (1987: ch. 8).
10. The emergence of Irish cultural nationalism is discussed by Hutchinson (1987, chs. 4 and 5), Lyons (1979, chs. 2 and 3) and Kiberd (1995).
11. On Yeats' masks, see Ellmann (1969).

12. On Yeats' study of esoteric literature, see Lyons (1979). On the rediscovery of Ireland's Celtic past, see Sheehy (1980). Yeats' enthusiasm for the Indian poet Tagore evidently had less to do with Tagore's national role as a poet under British imperial rule than with his moralistic outlook representative of Eastern civilization, from which Europe could learn. On Tagore, see pp. 70–1.
13. In his childhood bereavement, Bialik might be compared with other national poets, such as Burns, Solomos and Shevchenko. See the Conclusion (this volume).
14. On Hebrew literature and 19th century Jewish nationalism, see Patterson (1985). On the rapid expansion of Hebrew journalism and the number of Hebrew readers in the late 19th century, see Miron (1987).
15. On mythical and historical heroes similar to Bar Kokhba and Cuchulain in other national poetry, see p. 64.
16. On national poets as educators, see p. 15ff.
17. On the idea that a poet's greatness is linked to national identity, see the Conclusion (this volume).
18. On myth and legend in national poetry, see chapter 2 (this volume).
19. On Pearse's revolutionary nationalism, see Edwards (1977).
20. On censorship as a challenge to national poetry, see p. 73.
21. '*Ein zot ki im rabat tzerartunu*' (Nothing but your fierce hounding, 1899), (Aberbach 1997: 31–2).
22. '*Al ha-Shehitah*' (On the Slaughter, 1903), (Bialik 2004: 78).
23. Though Bialik's 'poems of wrath' of 1903–06 expressed the feelings of a suffering people, it should be remembered that at the time there were still Irish men and women alive who remembered the virtual genocide in Ireland during the potato famine in the 1840s, a far worse catastrophe than anything the Jews experienced from the time of the Black Plague in the 14th century until the Holocaust.
24. '*Akhen Hatzir ha-Am*' (Surely the people is grass, 1897).
25. *Be-Ir ha-haregah* (In the City of Slaughter, 1903), (Bialik 2004: 82).
26. On guilt in Bialik's national poetry, see Aberbach (1988: 63, 107).
27. On the paradox among national poets of being public spokesman and private artist, see p. 293ff.
28. On the interconnection of personal and national grief in Bialik, see Aberbach (1982, 1984).
29. National poets frequently attack their own people, a phenomenon which originates among the biblical prophets. See p. 253ff.
30. '*Iggeret Ketanah*' (A Short Letter, 1894), (Aberbach 1981: 48).
31. 'Al levavkhem she-Shamem' (On your desolate hearts, 1897), (Hutchinson and Aberbach 1999: 515).
32. On the Gaelic League, see Garvin (1987: ch. 5) and Hutchinson (1987: ch. 8).
33. On Jewish resistance to Zionism, see Aberbach (2013: ch. 7).
34. In '*Dimah Ne'emanah*' (Faithful Tear, 1894).
35. On Yeats and fascism, see Cullingford (1981) and O'Brien (1988).
36. On the view of 'national poet' as a contradiction in terms, see pp. 7, 244.

11 Defeat and Independence Struggles in National Poetry

... Lay the proud usurpers low!
Tyrants fall in every foe!
Liberty's in every blow!
  Let us do, or die!

(Robert Burns)

National poetry records not just heroic memories, strengthening the people's sense of unity, distinctiveness, and the resolve not to give up national hopes, but also records defeat, struggle, failure, subjugation, slavery, humiliation and colonialism. Defeat more strongly than victory can call up national feeling, steel national identity and drive national culture to sovereignty. Some peoples – the Armenians, Irish and Jews, for example – have entire histories of defeat, loss of political independence and exile. National poets attack traitors, blaming them for defeat and subjugation, and call for vengeance to overcome the humiliation of defeat.[1] Among many nations, defeat augurs independence:

- in Serbia, defeat by the Turks at the Battle of Kosovo Fields in 1389
- in Greece, defeat by the Turks in 1453
- in Ireland, defeat by Cromwell in 1649 and William of Orange in 1690
- in the Ukraine, defeat by Russia at Poltava in 1709
- in Scotland, defeat by England at Culloden in 1746
- in Poland, defeat and partition by Russia in the late 18th century and the failure of Polish revolts in 1830 and 1863
- in Hungary and elsewhere, defeat in the uprisings of 1848–49
- in India, defeat by England in the Indian Mutiny of 1857
- in Romania, the defeat of the uprising of 1876 against Turkey

To the ardent nationalist crushed by an imperial power, the inversion of Vince Lombardi's famous quote is more than a *bon mot*: Losing isn't everything, it's the only thing.

In the ancient world, the Hebrew Bible (half of which is poetry) contrasted with other civilizations of the first millennium BCE as the creation of a defeated people, aristocrats of the spirit, knowing the bitter taste of exile, poverty, and oppression. Defeat meant not extinction but rebirth as a 'chosen people', intoxicated with its divine mission and national identity. The Jews, defeated by Babylonia and Rome, scattered through the world, were united by trauma. Their history of persecution in Europe was the chief force driving them to rediscover their national identity and reawaken their will for independence.[2] Other ancient peoples – the Assyrians, Babylonians, Moabites, Ammonites, Edomites and Elamites, for example – believed that if they were conquered so were their gods. These peoples vanished from history. In the Hebrew Bible, though, national defeat is not the defeat of God: exile is not the exile of God; conquest by one's enemies is not the end of the nation but a warning to be heeded, a lesson to be learned, a punishment to be expiated, a defeat given meaning by hope of moral revival and return from exile. Empires fall; nations that keep the Bible survive.

Modern national poetry is shadowed by defeat, humiliation, rage and longing to be free, and so poetry gauges the troubled course of modern European nationalism. Much of this poetry was written by men who never saw their countries free: in Greece and Scotland; among Slavs, Poles, Ukrainians and Hungarians, Finns and Norwegians, Bulgarians and Romanians, Indians, Jews, Armenians and Irish; and in newly emerging Islamic countries and former slave societies in Africa, Latin America and the Caribbean. As national poets live their lives on a national-historic timescale, they often think not so much in terms of their limited lifespans but of *la longue durée*, of a time, perhaps in the distant future, perhaps never, when their countries will be free.

Greece was unusual, as the first modern nation, defeated and suppressed by the Ottoman empire, to revolt against its oppressor (1821–29) and win independence.[3] As we have seen, during the revolt, the Greek poet Dionysios Solomos (1798–1857) wrote *Ode to Liberty* (1824), whose opening invocation to ancient Greek heroes became in 1865 the Greek national anthem.[4] Yet, Solomos, a native of Zante (Zakynthos), an Ionian island under British rule until 1864, did not live to see full Greek independence. Even so, Greece was luckier than most subjugated countries, including Scotland whose leading poets of the late 18th and early 19th centuries – Macpherson, Burns and Scott – hoped, futilely, to see Scottish independence in their lifetime. At best they could recall (or invent) the Scottish heroic past, as Scott does in *Marmion* (1808), set against Scotland's defeat by England at 'Flodden's fatal field' in 1513, 'Where shiver'd was fair Scotland's spear,/ And broken was her shield!' The Scots were left with the consolation of a glittering past as an independent monarchy and the hope, however reluctant, of a distinguished (and lucrative) future as part of Great Britain, without losing hope of independence. Other peoples and their poets were less fortunate. As seen in chapter 7, pan-Slavic nationalism led by the poet Jan Kollar was a fiasco. Early 19th century Hungarian poets such as Vorosmarty and Petőfi, who helped create a spirit of opposition to Habsburg rule, did not live to see a free Hungary. Vorosmarty in epics such as *The Flight of Zalan* (1825),

Cserhalom (1825) and *Eger* (1827) revived a lost mythical tradition and the ancient glory of Hungary in war. Petőfi, too, in the failed struggle in the 1840s, caught in his poetry national defiance and hunger for independence: 'I only write/ poems with a bloodstained sword' (1974: 278). Petőfi believed in the power of poets as unacknowledged legislators.[5] Yet, the question posed by Petőfi was unresolved in his lifetime: was Hungary a fallen disintegrated star or a vanished comet that would return?

> The glory of Hungary – a falling star's flight
> swallowed in the night?
> Or a long-ago comet which came
> and went, to come again?[6]

There seemed little hope:

> The sun set. The stars hid.
> The sky is black above
> with just a crack of light
> and for my country, love.[7]

Petőfi's call for action and martyrdom in the war against Russia in 1849 roused Hungarian pride but had little practical effect. Not until several generations afterwards did Hungary actually gain political independence.

Nor did Mickiewicz's poetry do much to bring about Polish independence in his lifetime. Mickiewicz, a Lithuanian Pole born under Russian occupation in the Napoleonic era, was transfixed as a boy at the sight of the French army marching on Moscow in 1812. *Pan Tadeusz* (1834) recalls the futile hope that the French would make a new independent Poland – 'War has come! We shall be Poles once more' – and the empty prediction that with Napoleon's genius and the heroic Polish army led by Poniatowski and Dombrowski, 'we will regain our land' (vi 245–56).[8] Mickiewicz, frustrated by Napoleon's defeat, went on to university study in Vilnius and teaching in Kovno, where he published his first book of poems. In 1824, he was banished to Russia as a member of a secret Polish nationalist group. Five years later, after publishing the anti-Russian epic *Konrad Wallenrod*, he fled to his beloved France. This poem, set against the 14th century war between Lithuania and the Teutonic Knights, thinly disguised Poland's contemporary struggle against Russia. Captives of the Knights, Wallenrod, a gloomy Lithuanian, and the bard Halban keep Lithuanian national hopes alive: Halban in song, Wallenrod by contriving to destroy the Knights. He does this first by becoming their leader, then betraying them – though his guilt over this foul deed drives him to suicide.[9] Some Poles were deeply offended by this slur, as they saw it, against Polish honor: 'I do not want a Poland,' lamented the classicist Kajetan Kozmian, 'obtained at the price of honor!' Yet, the poem electrified a generation raised in bondage – particularly when the Poles revolted in November 1830 (Koropeckyj 2008: 95). Mickiewicz arrived in Poland too late to take part, then he returned to the West for good and wrote *Pan Tadeusz* in Paris. The glory and the sorrow of Poland, hemmed in and divided by powerful empires, subjugated by Russia and defeated in 1830, are poeticized by Mickiewicz in the epilogue to *Pan Tadeusz*. Safely in Paris among a myriad of other Polish exiles, Mickiewicz evoked the 11th century Polish warrior king Boleslaw the Brave and lusted for a Polish victory over Russia which will 'give the world liberty' (*światu swobodę obwieści*):

> ... when Polish eagles take their ancient land by storm
> gorged with corpses, drunk with blood,
> fold their wings as the enemy dies ...[10]

Set in 1812, *Pan Tadeusz* was an idealized portrait of Polish society. The political reality was darker. By the time of Mickiewicz's death in 1855, Poland was in decline, and in 1863 it suffered another major defeat in the uprising against Russia. In the 20th century, Poland gained independence, not by taking up arms but through the collapse of its imperial oppressors.

In Finland, similarly, the *Kalevala*, the great epic of Finnish myth and heroism published in 1835 by the Finnish ethnographer Lönnrot, was ahead of its time.[11] Annexed by Russia in 1809, Finland was unusual in the Russian empire: an autonomous grand duchy with its own four-estate Diet and its own laws, education system, currency and army. Yet, the *Kalevala* more than anything else in Finnish culture planted the idea of an independent Finland, which came thirty-three years after Lönnrot's death, with the fall of Tsarist Russia in 1917.

Shevchenko's book of poems, *The Kobzar* (1840), was, similarly, 'a literary and intellectual declaration of Ukrainian independence' (Subtelny 1988: 234). Though in 1839, the poet recalled a time when 'we ruled ourselves,/ But we shall rule no more' (Shevchenko 1961: 11), he also expressed hope of breaking Russian chains to win Ukrainian liberty.[12] In his 'Testament', dating from Christmas 1845, nearly a century and a half before Ukrainian independence, with the fall of Soviet Russia, Shevchenko prayed that Ukraine would someday be free:

> Bury me, then rise and break
> your heavy chains, water with the blood
> of tyrants your freedom ...[13]

Hebrew poets in Ukraine, including Bialik and Tchernichowsky, had even fewer hopes of an independent Jewish state than the Ukrainians. Neither poet lived to see the establishment of the state of Israel in 1948.[14] In their lifetimes, Jewish nationalism was erratic and uncertain. At the time of Bialik's birth in 1873, few predicted or wanted a Jewish state. Yet, the Jews had the Hebrew Bible as an ever-present testament of hope. The Russian pogroms of 1881–2 crushed hopes of Jewish emancipation under Tsarist rule. Bialik's despair and hope inspired a nation forced into new militancy by genocidal hatred. Influenced by his mentor, the Zionist thinker Ahad Ha'am, Bialik envisaged a form of Jewish nationalism less political than cultural. Both men moved to Tel Aviv in the 1920s, but even then most Jews did not share the enthusiasm for Jewish national revival. Only after Bialik's death in 1934 did the Holocaust convert most Jews – whether they liked it or not – into supporters of Zionism as the Palestinian Jews fought for and won independence from British colonial rule in the immediate post-war years.[15]

Tagore of India was another national poet in the British empire who never saw his country free. India, like Israel, gained independence after the depression of the 1930s and World War II, when Britain could no longer hold onto its colonies. Long before the collapse of the empire, Indian national identity was fed by a sense of British oppression. Tagore attacked Western nationalism as an evil and wrote in *Gitanjali* (1912) of the hope of Indian national awakening based on the spiritual qualities of Hinduism:[16] 'Where the mind is without fear and the head is held high …/ Into that heaven of freedom, my Father, let my country awake' (Tagore 1959: 27–28). A spirit of Indian cultural independence is evident here, long before political independence. Significantly, Tagore's main supporter in the translation and publication of *Gitanjali*, as well as his Nobel Prize for Literature in 1913, was W.B. Yeats, another poet of a nation moving toward independence from the British empire.

A spirit of freedom, from Ottoman Turkish rule, energized the Armenian poetry of Toumanian, described as 'a form of struggle for the survival of his people' (Baliozian 1980: 71). Toumanian's 'The Armenian Grief' defines to many Armenians the survival of national identity under oppressive foreign rule:

> Armenian grief is an endless sea
> a great dark sea of pain–
> and my soul travels that black sea
> with no aim.[17]

The Bulgarian Hristo Botev was another poet of a people under centuries-long Ottoman rule. He, likewise, did not live to see independence, nor did he expect to do so, though he compared the Turkish feudal state to a 'body eaten alive by worms, in terrible agony yet wishing, through the wriggling of the worms, to flutter a little longer' (Topencharov 1982: 68).[18]

Rare are national poets such as Fishta and Yeats who live to see their peoples free. Fishta, a Franciscan monk and educator, changed the language of instruction in northern Albanian schools from Italian to Albanian. Fishta's epic poem *The Highland Lute*, written mostly in 1902–09 in the years before Albanian independence in 1912, was based on centuries-old oral tradition. In loving detail, Fishta recounted traditional customs and beliefs amid the rugged mountains of Albania. He recorded the traditional grievance and hope of independence from Turkish rule associated with the 15th century warrior Skanderbeg. Albania was not a plaything of the Ottomans, a patchwork of territories to be given out like figs among its neighbors, but 'the homeland of our fathers, Motherland of Skanderbeg,/ Motherland of Mois Golemi and of Leka Dukagjini ...' (Mann 1955: 73). Fishta's poem itself did much to crystallize Albanian national identity, which had previously been largely nonexistent.[19] Yeats' poetry, too, agitates for Irish independence in the face of national failure.[20] Yeats more than any other poet – though he wrote in English, not Gaelic – defined Ireland as culturally independent, despite being politically subservient to Britain. After the 1916 Irish revolt, Yeats in 'Easter 1916' best expressed the changed national mood, anticipating political independence, which came in 1921. Both Fishta and Yeats served in the parliaments of their newly created independent states.

ATTACKS ON TRAITORS

In the struggle for independence, national poets – often fired by the example of the Hebrew prophets – rage not only against external oppressors and defeat but also against the nation itself, and the traitors within. The tigers of poetic wrath speak truer than horses of prosaic instruction. There is a *long* list of angry national poets, of whom here are a few:

- Robert Burns (Scotland)
- Ferenc Kölcsey and Daniel Berzsenyi (Hungary)
- Adam Mickiewicz (Poland)
- Henrik Wergeland (Denmark)
- Petar II Petrovic-Njegoš (Serbia/Montenegro)
- Taras Shevchenko (Ukraine)
- Mihail Eminescu (Romania)
- Hristo Botev (Bulgaria)
- Hebrew poets: J.L. Gordon, C.N. Bialik and Saul Tchernichowsky (Tsarist Russia)
- Gjergj Fishta (Albania)
- Tevfik Fikret (Turkey)
- Khalil Gibran (Lebanon)
- Muhammed Iqbal (India/ Pakistan)
- Dun Karm Psaila (Malta)
- Patrick Pearse and W.B. Yeats (Ireland)

Burns, in 'Such a Parcel of Rogues in a Nation,' laid into contemporary Scots 'traitors' who sold their noble hope of freedom for contemptible accommodation with England, while extolling the pure devotion to the Nation of Scottish heroes such as Bruce and Wallace:[21]

> 'O, would, or I had seen the day
> That Treason thus could sell us,
> My auld grey head had lien in clay
> Wi' Bruce and loyal Wallace!
>
> But pith and power, till my last hour
> I'll mak this declaration:–
> 'We've bought and sold for English gold'–
> Such a parcel of rogues in a nation!

In Hungary, Kölcsey, too, invoked the Muse of Blame in *Himnusz* (1823) – adopted in 1844 as the Hungarian national anthem – attacking the Magyars for their defeat by Mongols and Turks. It was Magyar 'crimes' that provoked the enemy attack: 'The Mongol's shaft hissed death./ The Turkish yoke was on our neck'.[22] Kölcsey's contemporary Berzsenyi accused Hungary of following ancient Rome into decay and degeneracy, as 'rotten Rome fell', stirring up heaven-sent revenge and subjugation.[23] Mickiewicz in his poetry lampooned Poles who degrade the nation by assimilating into foreign cultures, neglecting their own. *Pan Tadeusz* mocked the Polish traitor Plutowicz who changed his name and joined the Russian army (IX 133–6; Mickiewicz 1962: 252). Similarly scornful of traitors is the Norwegian poet Wergeland, who provoked law suits in Norway when he raged in print against the Danophile bourgeoisie as blood-suckers, lacking commitment to their own culture. Grief and rage at traitors filled Shevchenko's poetry too. In a poem of 1845, the poet declared that mother Ukraine, crucified by her own children, had suffered even more than Poland:

> In her struggle, our Ukraine
> suffered the extremes of pain,
> worse than anyone, even the Poles.
> Children crucify the mother,
> suck her blood like beer ...[24]

Shevchenko hated the cruel indifference of Ukrainian landlords and the elite – the living dead – sinfully alienated from the nation. Only the idealized memory of the Cossacks, proud, heroic, vengeful, redeemed the defeat, humiliation and corruption of the Ukraine by Russia,[25] with the exception of the mid-17th century Cossack leader Bogdan Chmielnicki who betrayed Ukraine by making a treaty with Russia (Shevchenko 1961: 23–4). Born a serf, Shevchenko was entranced as a child by tales told by his grandfather about the peasant revolt of 1768. Like other national poets – Mickiewicz or Wergeland, for example – Shevchenko denounced contemporary early

Defeat and Independence Struggles in National Poetry 255

19th century cultural 'traitors'. These included those who, like Gogol, went over to the enemy camp and wrote in Russian, which Shevchenko (perhaps with a dig at Gogol's famous story, 'The Overcoat') compared to an ill-fitting coat. Another threat to Ukrainian culture was the widespread Czech Slavophil Movement of Enlightenment led by Kollar, who promoted not the revival of Ukrainian culture but spread 'every Slavic language but your own' (*ibid.*, 253) through eastern Europe in the first half of the 19th century.[26] There is no harm in the study of foreign cultures, Shevchenko writes, but Ukrainian language and literature are sacred:

> Learn, brothers! Think, read,
> to neighbours' gifts pay heed –
> but don't neglect your own:
> for he who forgets his mother
> is punished by God alone.
>
> (*ibid.*, 256)[27]

Njegoš' Serbian epic *The Mountain Wreath* conveyed the homicidal torment felt by many Orthodox Serbs under Muslim rule who felt betrayed by fellow Serbs who converted to Islam: 'the hatred against the Turkish renegades, which was powerful even before, must have assumed extremes of intolerance in Njegoš' time, when the restoration of the state and final liberation from the Turks were set as immediate goals' (Djilas 1966: 316). In *The Mountain Wreath*, Islamic rule over the Serbs was a sign of God's wrath. Converts to the dragon-like Islam were sinners deserving of extermination:

> God is angry at the Serbian people.
> A dragon with seven heads has appeared
> and devoured the entire Serbian nation,
> the slanderers as well as the slander.
>
> (Njegoš 1989: 12)[28]

In Romania, the poet Eminescu denounced corrupt late 19th century Romanian leaders as 'leeches', 'frauds' and 'monsters'. In his poetry, Eminescu also attacked enemies of the nation, chief of which were corrupt Romanian leaders, 'Heirs of the Romans' – 'leeches', 'frauds', 'monsters' ('Third Letter', c. 1881):

> A mob, scum, vermin, our desolation
> now disguised as leaders, rulers of this once great nation ...[29]

In despair, he called on the medieval hero Vlad Tepes (the Impaler) for aid, not against the Turks this time, but against the Romanians: 'Vlad Tepes, come down to us, old prince' (*Cum nu vii Tepeș, doamne*) (Eminescu 1980: 152–3). Vlad will force the corrupt leaders from government and, like the thieves and madmen they are, thrust them into the prison and lunatic asylum where they belong, then burn both houses down: *Să dai foc la puşcărie şi la casa de nebuni!* (*ibid.*, 152). In 'Doina' (1883), Eminescu called on Stefan del Mare, the 15th century Moldavian prince who fought the Turks and other enemies, to rise from the grave, destroy Romania's enemies and regain Romanian independence.

National poets attack the religious establishment for allegedly betraying the moral integrity of the Nation. Prophetic assaults on the Temple priesthood and the religion of mere ritual in the books of Amos and Isaiah have inspired many modern national poets who accuse the clergy for supporting the corrupt status quo instead of leading the people in revolt.[30] The Welsh poet Iolo Morganwg described the late-18th century Church as moribund: 'The Priestcraft religion of Parsons and kings/ Unsanctioned by Liberty's law' ('The Marshfield Shepherd or Parson of Parsons'). Botev, borrowing imagery from Pushkin, attacked corrupt, drunken traitorous Bulgarian priests leading the people like sheep to the slaughter (Botev 1974: 51).[31] In Hebrew poetry, too, the Jewish national revival was strongly anti-clerical. The Russian-Jewish poet J.L. Gordon attacked the rabbis for their stubborn narrow-mindedness, their adherence to the strict letter of the law and their failure to adapt to the modern world. In 1863, Gordon condemned the Jews of his time and their rabbinic leadership as they 'did not learn the art of war' (Gordon 1971: 109).[32] Although Gordon believed that the Russian Jews should assimilate in Tsarist Russia, his attacks on his people inadvertently gave his poetry a national character and contributed to the rise of Jewish nationalism. The alienation and violent revolt against authority and restraints in Gordon's poetry typify national movements (Kedourie 1960: 100–1).

Bialik, Gordon's younger and more influential contemporary, accused the Jewish people, similarly, of apathy and moral rottenness. Bialik's Hebrew poetry served as catharsis for national and personal woes interwoven. Judging from his poetry, Bialik never expected the Jews to be resurrected on their ancestral homeland. Yet, his despairing attacks on his people for failing to act in their interests was crucial in the emergence of Jewish cultural nationalism. After the Kishinev pogrom in 1903, Bialik mocked the Jewish victims as cowards in *The City of Slaughter* (1903), a poem which in its prophetic vitriol goaded Jews to militancy and nationalism. The voice here echoed, ironically, that of the God of Israel in the book of Ezekiel. The reader is taken to the outhouses and pigpens where Jews hid from the murderers:

> Your brothers, your people, descended from the Maccabees,
> from lions – holy martyrs –
> twenty or thirty stuffed in a hole.
> They increased my glory, they made my name holy ...
> They fled like mice. They hid like bugs.
> They died like dogs where they hid ...[33]

The poem ends with Bialik's contemptuous attack on survivors of the pogrom who tried to elicit funds and sympathy for themselves. At the time of first publication, these lines were generally taken, unjustly, as a confession of the shocking and shameful truth about the Jewish people:

> ... To the graveyard, beggars!
> Dig up the bones of martyred father and brother,
> fill your sacks, sling them on backs
> and hit the road
> to do business at all the fairs;
> advertise yourselves at the crossroads so everyone sees,
> in the sunshine on filthy rags spread the bones
> and sing your hoarse beggar song,
> beg the decency of the world!
> beg the pity of *goyim*!
> Eternal beggars!
>
> (Bialik 2004: 173–74)

Bialik condemned not only these allegedly cowardly Jews but also – targets of other poets, such as his fellow Ukrainian Shevchenko – those who preferred assimilation into European culture to their own culture:

> ... as your flesh drips blood
> between the teeth of your destroyers,
> you'll feed them your soul.
> 'This too is the sweeping scourge ...'
>
> (*ibid.*, 211)

Nor did Bialik's Hebrew contemporary Tchernichowsky spare the Jews. In language reminiscent of Gordon, the Jews were atrophied in their 'holy' tradition, 'quacks mummified in body and soul'. In a poem written in Berlin in the early 1920s, Tchernichowsky doubted whether his nation could be resurrected, for it had lost its way, its land of sun had gone:

> Perhaps – – it is no longer, its light is out?
> What God promised us is in doubt – – –[34]

Other poets, too – Fishta, Fikret, Iqbal, Psaila and Gibran, for example – attacked their own people with the aim of cleansing them. In his epic *The Highland Lute*, Fishta spoke in the voice of a spirit which appeared to an Albanian warrior at the time of the Congress of Berlin in 1878 and denounced the Albanians themselves:

> ... today the Albanian people
> Sell their souls for money, *timars*.[35]
> They've denied their faith and bloodline,

And forgotten all their homeland,
And their weapons they make use of
Just to murder one another.
Not to liberate their country,
Not for good and common welfare,
But to choose which foreign ruler
They will call lord of Albania.

(8: 170–79; Fishta 2005: 69)[36]

Turkish poetry of the late 19th and early 20th had similar national self-denunciations. In 'Farewell to Haluk' and 'Free Meal', Fikret depicted Turkey as a once-great empire now an 'old and ailing motherland', crippled by its reactionary clergy, reduced to beggary:

The meal which, gentlemen, trembling waits
To be devoured, is – the life of this nation,
This land of pain, this land of agony!
But gulp it down without hesitation

(Menemencioğlu & Iz, 1978: 169)

In other Muslim countries, too, including Egypt, Morocco and Tunisia, the nationalist 'revolt of Islam' included an attack by their poets against inertia and corruption (Arberry 1964: 378ff.). The Somali poet Sayyid Maḥammad castigated traitors who, in early 20th century conflicts, 'sold me out' by siding with the British 'stinking infidel' against fellow Muslims and kinsmen (Samatar 1982: 151–2). The Indian Muslim poet Iqbal blamed the Indians themselves for their servitude to Britain and Europe. India was no more than a glittering jewel in another's crown, its peasants like corpses on the ground, body and soul in pawn:

It is you who became the willing slave of Europe:
My complaint is against you, it is not against Europe!

(Iqbal 2000: 85)

Gibran, too, exiled at the start of the 20th century, attacked his native Lebanon:

Hypocrisy your religion,
falsehood your life,
nothingness your end; why,
then, are you living?

... I hate you, my countrymen, for
you hate glory and greatness.
I despise you for you despise
yourselves.

(Gibran 1995: 98, 100)

During the famine in Lebanon and Syria in 1916, Gibran was secretary of the Syrian-Mount Lebanon Relief Committee in the United States. Though shocked by the Turkish violation of human rights and the genocide in Armenia, Gibran was outraged too by the apathy of his Arab countrymen in America: '… had I been given the choice of death in Lebanon or life among these creatures I would have chosen death' (Bushrui and Jenkins 1999: 158). Gibran particularly hated the priests. As a freethinker, he was excommunicated by the Lebanese Christian Maronite Church to which he had belonged:

> Your souls freeze in the clutches
> of priests and sorcerers
>
> (Gibran 1995: 97)

His own people, he lamented, ignore his poetry which acts, instead, as inner purgation:

> My tears never reached your
> petrified hearts, but they cleansed
> the darkness from my inner self.
>
> (*ibid.*)

The Maltese poet Dun Karm Psaila – a Catholic priest – attacked the Maltese for their moral failings in abandoning the true faith, in 'To Malta' (1925): 'You were the rose of the world and have become a dunghill' (Arberry and Grech 1961: 91).[37] Irish poets, too, attacked their own people. Patrick Pearse, for example, condemned Irishmen who have, in his view, turned traitor:[38]

> Great my shame:
> My own children that sold their mother.
>
> ('I am Ireland' Pearse 1917: 323)

Yeats, as we have seen,[39] doubted at first that the Irish had the maturity to gain independence. In 'September 1913', he condemned the petty Irish, provincial and clownish ('where motley is worn'), lacking dedication to Ireland, wasting their gifts on other nations. Men who might have led them to independence, such as the Fenian John O'Leary (1830–1907), were gone:

> What need you, being come to sense,
> But fumble in a greasy till
> And add the halfpence to the pence
> And prayer to shivering prayer, until
> You have dried the marrow from the bone?
> For men were born to pray and save:
> Romantic Ireland's dead and gone,
> It's with O'Leary in the grave.

VENGEANCE AGAINST EMPIRES

National defeat and subjugation lead to thoughts of revenge. There was a destructive element in national poetry, even in the more liberal period of the late 18th and early 19th century.[40] Vengeful rage filled the poetry of defeated peoples: the Irish, the Scots, the Greeks, the Poles and the Ukrainians, dominated by powerful, ruthless empires. An anonymous 18th century Irish poet looks forward to the fall of the British empire:

> Time has triumphed, the wind has scattered all,
> Alexander, Caesar, empires, cities are lost,
> Tara and Troy flourished a while and fell
> And even England itself, maybe, will bite the dust
>
> ('Hope' Kennelly 1970: 76)

Macpherson in *Fingal* (1761) worked up a mood of violent defiance from Scotland's distant past to assuage defeat at Culloden a decade and a half previously. At the climax of the poem, the Celts rout the invading Vikings:

> We pursued and slew. As stones that
> Bound from rock to rock; as axes in echoing
> Woods; as thunder rolls from hill to hill,
> In dismal broken peals; so blow succeeded to
> Blow, and death to death, from the hand of
> Oscar and mine.
>
> (I 134–35)

The French Revolution made violent change and independence elsewhere seem possible, even in Scotland. Robert Burns denied Scotland's subjugation in Scots dialect of a violent heroic past, invoking history to assert cultural independence. In 'Robert Bruce's March to Bannockburn' (1793), better known by its opening words, 'Scots wha hae', Burns revived the memory of Robert the Bruce who led Scotland to independence by defeating England at Bannockburn in 1314:

> Scots, wha hae wi' Wallace bled,
> Scots, wham Bruce has aften led,
> Welcome to your gory bed
> Or to victorie!
>
> … Lay the proud usurpers low!
> Tyrants fall in every foe!
> Liberty's in every blow!
> Let us do, or die!

Burns seems at times determined that Scotland would avenge its humiliation:

> Till Revenge, wi' laurell'd head,
> Bring our banish'd hame again,
> And ilk loyal bonie lad
> Cross the seas, and win his ain [own]!
> 'Frae the Friends and Land I Love'

The thirst for vengeance appeared in the writings of Walter Scott, for example *The Lay of the Last Minstrel* (1805):

> Vengeance, deep-brooding o'er the slain,
> Had lock'd the source of softer woe;
> And burning pride and high disdain
> Forbade the rising tear to flow.

In an age of Scots and English fighting side by side against the French, Scott in *Marmion* (1808) aimed at reconciliation. In contrast, some German poets of the period, such as Körner and Kleist, wrote poetry full of hate against the French, rage at the defeat of German territories and lust for revenge. 'Use their corpses to dam the Rhine' (*Dammt den Rhein mit ihren Leichen*) (Leerson 2006: 115, 274), wrote Körner, the corpses being French[41]. Poetry of other defeated and subjugated nations was similarly angry and violent. Aristotle Valaorites' bitter allegory 'The Rock and the Wave' presented Greek vengeance for its long humiliating occupation by Turkey as an inevitable natural process. Turkey was the rock, slowly worn away by its enemy, Greece, the 'wave of drowning':

> Rock, call me revenge. Time has fed me bitter contempt.
> I am raised by pain. Once I was a tear, now a great sea.
> Fall at my feet, worship me. Not seaweed I carry
> but souls, full of loneliness and rage. Wake, hear
> the knock of death ... You made me a bed of death ...
>
> You piled me with corpses, exiled me, poisoned me
> with alms, laughed at my death rattle.
> Give way, rock, let me pass. Calm weather is done.
> I am the wave of drowning, a giant enemy, relentless.[42]

Revenge drove *Pan Tadeusz*: Mickiewicz imagined Poland gorging itself on the blood of its Russian enemies.[43] Revenge at the climax of the poem was no less sweet for being ludicrous. Russian forces in the Napoleonic wars were defeated in gory absurdity when a cheese-house where they were sheltering collapsed on them, and on the ground were 'beams and corpses and the mingling stains/ Of snowy cheese and oozing blood and brains' (IX 877–8, Mickiewicz 1962: 272). Shevchenko's poetry was similarly full of vengeful hate towards Tsarist Russia, with prophetic warnings of a day of judgment to come. Russia, in Shevchenko's view, was 'a prison of nations' (Bilenky 2012: 68). In 'A Dream' (1844), the poet attacked Russia for exploiting and degrading Ukrainians in the mines. There will be a Day of Judgment when the Ukrainian dead will rise and seek justice from their Russian tormentors who enslaved them,

> ... living men, chained, carrying gold from deep mines
> down the greedy throat of tsardom ...
>
> (Shevchenko 1977: 136)

'Testament' and 'The Cold Ravine' (1845) also predicted a day of revenge, when the Ukrainians would break their chains and bless their freedom with the enemy's wicked blood (Shevchenko 1961: 82–3, 85). Shevchenko had good reason to hate the autocratic Tsar Nicholas I, who personally exiled him to Siberia and ordered that the poet should not be allowed to write. In a poem written in 1858 after Shevchenko returned from exile, his health broken, he attacked the Tsar (who had died during his exile) and incited his countrymen to fight for freedom with sledge-hammers and axes (Shevchenko 1977: 270). Shevchenko's contemporary, the Serbian poet Njegoš, used his status as national poet to incite violence against the enemy, the Ottoman Turks who had ruled Serbia since 1389.[44] Njegoš, a Russian Orthodox priest, was especially outraged by the conversion of Balkan Serbs to Islam. In *The Mountain Wreath* (1847), the poet tried to justify genocide of Muslim converts in the name of justice, freedom and self-defense.[45]

Defeat directed against a hated foe, usually an imperial aggressor, underlies violent fantasies in much national poetry. Yet, as seen in chapter 1, the Bible, used by the British and other empires to justify and support imperialism, became a worldwide inspiration for freedom. The next chapter, on national poetry in the British empire, shows that imperial rule, which invariably rouses opposition, can also stimulate conditions for native rule and culture – including highly creative poetry. National poetry in the British empire is exceptional, among other reasons, in that much of it is in English: an inheritance of reviled imperial rule was adopted as a tool of independence.

NOTES

1. On the poetry of former slave societies, see pp. 283–6 and Appendix (e), pp. 311–14. Defeat need not be associated with humiliation and the lust for revenge. Whitman, for example, sees defeat as an inevitable part of life. See p. 23.
2. On Jewish nationalism as a reaction to European anti-Semitism, see Aberbach (2013: ch. 7).
3. On Greek poetry and the War of Independence, See chapter 6 (this volume).
4. On Solomos' *Ode to Liberty*, see p. 155.

Defeat and Independence Struggles in National Poetry 263

5. Petőfi did not underestimate the latent political power of poets such as himself: 'When the people are prominent in poetry, they are very near to power in politics' (Czigany 1984: 191). To Petőfi (1974: 203), poets were the pillar of fire leading the Nation to the Promised Land. See p. 47.
6. Translated by David Aberbach from Petőfi (1973: 124). In a proclamation of 17 March 1848, two days after writing his 'National Song' (*Talpra, magyar*), Petőfi used a similar image in describing the failed revolution in Hungary: 'as the magi gazed at the infant Jesus in the manger, so I gazed with rapt fervor at this new meteor' (1974: 203).
7. Translated by David Aberbach. The Hungarian reads:

   Lement a nap. De csilagok
   Nem jöttenek. Sötét az ég.
   Közel s távolban semmi fény nincs,
   Csak mécsvilágom s honszerelmem ég,
       (in Basa 1980: 68)
   On Petőfi's vision of Hungary, see p. 250.

8. On Poland's struggle for independence in the context of rivalry between the Tsarist and Ottoman empires, see chapter 7 (pp. 176–8).
9. Bialik's poem *In the City of Slaughter* (1903), similarly a poem of suicidal despair set in the past – ostensibly during the Cossack massacres of Polish Jews in the 17th century but actually referring to the Kishinev pogrom in 1903 – was also interpreted (or misinterpreted) by its readers as a poem of national reawakening under Tsarist rule. Both *Konrad Wallenrod* and *In the City of Slaughter*, set in the past, evaded Tsarist censorship. On Bialik's poem, see pp. 238, 256.
10. Translated by David Aberbach (from Mickiewicz 1962: 2). On the Polish 'victory' over Russia in *Pan Tadeusz*, see p. 261.
11. On Finnish myth in the context of the mythologies of other national movements, see chapter 2 (this volume).
12. See for example Shevchenko (1964: 249–50).
13. Поховайте, та вставайте,/ Кайдани порвіте/ І аражою эдою кро'вю/ Водю окропіте (Shevchenko 1977: 198).
14. On Bialik, see chapter 10 (this volume).
15. On Greenberg, the leading Palestinian Hebrew poet of the British mandatory period, see pp. 54–7.
16. On Tagore's anti-nationalism, see pp. 70–1.
17. Translated by David Aberbach (from Tolegian 1979: 159). Armenian folk songs preserved national identity. In Werfel's novel *The Forty Days of Musa Dagh* (1933), these songs are taught to children and sung during the massacres of 1915 (2012: 108, 188–90).
18. On Botev, see p. 173.
19. 'The modern Albanian nationalist myth [is] eagerly promoted to prove a national cohesion historically non-existent' (Ruches 1967: viii). Not until 1911 did Albania seek recognition as a separate state as opposed to the previous categories of Muslim and non-Muslim (Mazower 2000: 98).
20. On Yeats, see chapter 10 and pp. 141–3.
21. On Burns, see p. 271. National self-criticism and self-questioning is prominent, too, in English poetry – though this is poetry of a sovereign power. John of Gaunt's dying speech in Shakespeare's *Richard II* ('This royal throne of kings')

culminates with an attack on English traitors: 'England, that was wont to conquer others,/ Hath made a shameful conquest of itself' (II i 66–7). The love of England in Cowper's 'The Task' ('England, with all thy faults, I love thee still') is similarly tempered by the poet's contempt at the nation's alleged follies and effeminacy:

> ... I can feel
> Thy follies too, and with a just disdain
> Frown at effeminates, whose very looks
> Reflect dishonour on the land I love.

The mood of English national self-questioning continued in the height of the British empire's power, in the poetry of Tennyson and Kipling. See p. 272.

22. Translated by David Aberbach. For a full translation of *Himnusz*, see Kirkconnell (1947: 6).
23. *Ibid.*, 25.
24. Translated by David Aberbach (from Shevchenko 1964: 255).
25. For other examples of heroic models in the nation's cause, see p. 64.
26. On Kollar, see pp. 179–80. In objecting to languages other than Ukrainian, the national language, Shevchenko followed Herder who exhorted French-speaking Germans to spit out 'the slime of the Seine' and speak German instead. See p. 69. Other national poets, such as the Maltese Dun Karm Psaila (who wrote in Italian before turning to Maltese in 1912 when he was over forty), also upbraid their own people for neglecting the national language: 'Why must you discard the Tongue your mother gave you/ and foolishly embrace another foreign Tongue?' (Psaila 1997: xii). Psaila also denounced the Maltese for alleged moral failings and for ignoring the poet and his prophetic message, turning instead after 'greed and frivolity' (Arberry and Grech 1961: 57, 91). See p. 265 note 37. Yet the poet also remembers Malta's external enemies: 'my thoughts go back towards the history/ Of those who committed many crimes against us' (*ibid.*, 83). In *Peer Gynt* (1867), in contrast, Ibsen satirized the cultural nationalists who insisted on a 'pure' language:

> ... foreigners have messed the language up.
> And now they are masters of the land.
> But long ago the orang-utang ruled ...
> then, alas, the foreigners came ...
> Now the voice of the jungle is silenced
>
> (1963: 107–08)

Ibsen's mockery was directed particularly at the influential Norwegian *maelstraevere*, intellectuals of the 1860s who called for a Norwegian language made of local dialects. They condemned literary Norwegian, such as that of Ibsen, as 'Danish', foreign to common Norwegians who live and die – as do Ibsen's orang-utangs – 'uninterpreted', i.e., with no language to preserve their true Norwegian existence. On Ibsen's language, see pp. 77–8.

27. In African poetry, too, cultural 'traitors' are attacked. See p. 313.
28. The imagery might derive from Psalm 74, describing Egypt. See p. 64. A fixture of Serbian culture is Prince Lazar's curse – frequently applied to Serbian converts

Defeat and Independence Struggles in National Poetry 265

to Islam – of those who did not fight at Kosovo in 1389: 'Let him rust away like dripping iron/ Until his name shall be extinguished' (Gorup in Vucinich and Emmert 1991: 114).

29. Spuma asta-nve ninată, ăsta plebe, ăst gunoi
    Să ajun-ga fi stăpînă și pe țară și pe noi!

    (Eminescu 1980: 150)

On Eminescu in the context of conflict between Islam and the West, see p. 103.

30. In *Paradise Lost*, Milton compared the corrupt clergy to wolves:

Wolves shall succeed for teachers, grievous wolves,
Who all the sacred mysteries of heav'n
To their own vile advantage shall turn
Of lucre and ambition, and the truth
With superstitions and traditions taint …

(II 508–12)

Cowper, similarly, wrote: 'When nations are to perish in their sins,/ 'Tis in the church the leprosy begins' ('The Expostulation').

31. On Botev's attacks on the Bulgarian clergy, see p. 173.
32. See p. 176.
33. Translated by David Aberbach (Bialik 1960: 373–4).
34. '*Omrim yeshna eretz* …' (Tchernichowsky 1954: 172).
35. *Timar*: in the Ottoman empire an estate or grant given to obtain exemption from military service.
36. On Fishta's poetry in the context of the conflict of Islam with Christianity, see chapter 3 (this volume).
37. The modernization of Malta under British rule in the 1920s was too much for Psaila. He accused his countrymen in the language of sin, plague, poison, filth, sickness and defilement.He claimed that they had lost their faith and their heritage; their heroes – particularly those who fought the Muslims in the Great Siege of 1565 – were long gone; their monument at the gates of Valletta of Malta at the feet of Jesus was 'a lie' (*ibid*.). Malta is doomed to the same fate as the biblical Babylon ('Fallen, fallen is Babylon') (*ibid*., 93). In a later poem, Psaila continued the attack: '… the multitude blind/ after greed and frivolity/ stopped up their ears,/ turned about their gaze/ so as neither to hear nor to see' (*ibid*., 57).
38. On Pearse, see pp. 191, 237.
39. On Yeats' doubts that the Irish would achieve independence, see p. 143.
40. On the destructive side of national poetry, see p. 4ff.
41. In 1814, the German poet Arndt wrote the popular anthem 'Was ist Des Deutschen Vaterland?' in which Germany was defined as anti-French, 'Wo jeder Franzmann heisset Feind'.
42. Translated by David Aberbach (from Trypanis 1984: 532). On this poem in the context of the Greek struggle for independence, see p. 156.
43. On Mickiewicz's hope for a violent revenge of Poland against its enemies, see p. 251. Unlike their European counterparts, French Canadian found that grievance towards English Canada was not strong enough to goad Quebec to revolt and seek independence. In poems of the 1950s and 1960s, the poet Gaston Miron often echoed European national poetry – 'we will make you, Land

of Quebec/ a bed of resurrections' ('October') – depicting the sense of degradation and humiliation felt by Quebec ('ma terre amere ma terre amande') at being colonized, politically and spiritually, made subservient and allegedly sub-human by English Canada: 'the Goddamn Canuck/ on his knees and with only his knees to speak' (Miron 1984: 35). Yet, in contrast with the grievance felt, say, by Poland toward Russia in Mickiewicz's poetry, or by Serbia towards Ottoman Turkey in Njegoš' poetry, Quebecois grievance toward English Canada, however just, was soothed as Quebec became more self-governing and influential in the Canadian federal government. History and poetry teach the importance of respect for minority cultures; but if respect is forthcoming much of the drive for independence may be lost, and poets cry for freedom in vain.

44. On European national poetry and the medieval Islamic conquests, see chapter 3 (this volume).
45. As this poem became a fixture of the Serbian school curriculum, it contributed to the violent hatred leading to the genocide of the Bosnian Muslims in 1992–95. See p. 183 note 14.

12 The British Empire and Revolutionary National Poetry

... all our pomp of yesterday
Is one with Nineveh and Tyre!

(Kipling)

The British empire, carved by 'trade, need, avarice, a concern to open the world God had given them, like an oyster suspected of a pearl', as Paul Scott puts it in *The Jewel in the Crown* (1984: 132), set off an explosion of national poetry in the British isles and among the many peoples and cultures the empire ruled: including Tagore of India, Shawqi of Egypt, Rusafi of Iraq, Hang Yuehe of China, Yeats of Ireland, Soyinka of Nigeria, Iqbal of Pakistan, 'Banjo' Paterson of Australia, Psaila of Malta, Greenberg of pre-State Israel, Walcott of St. Lucia, p'Bitek of Uganda and hundreds of others. This phenomenon has been almost totally overlooked by historians of nationalism and of the British empire as well as by literary scholars, although the empire no more existed to produce Kipling than the Elizabethan age to give Shakespeare life. Yet poetry harnessed the triumph or guilt of imperial expansion to express Britishness and, in the colonies, the humiliation of defeat, occupation and foreign rule, to define national identity whether as part of independence struggles or, after independence, in confronting and mastering the colonial past.

The British empire, with its relatively free press, greatly increased the number of newspapers, journals and periodicals in many languages, in which poetry was published. Literacy and markets for native poets expanded in the surge to modernity.[1] Liberal British press laws and the tradition of dissent in British culture gave increasingly Westernized poets far greater freedom than under native rule to attack the ruling power, its military repression, economic exploitation, political hubris, religious paternalism and 'orientalist' racism. Rarely convinced that 'empire is a form of international government that can work – and not just for the benefit of the ruling power' (Ferguson 2003: 362) – poets were free to ignore the fact that British rule also created models of good governance and valuable opportunities for the development of sound local government by natives, through the expansion of education at all levels; that particularly in India and Africa, the English language leavened diverse, often conflicting groups into national unity; and that it was possible to believe, as Gandhi (1982) did as a young man, that 'the British Empire existed for the welfare of the world' (287).[2]

Poetry reflected the cruelty of British military expansionism and economic exploitation, which was especially clear in times of famine. In Ireland in 1846–50, a million people starved while the British government argued and dithered, failing in the end not only to send aid as needed but also delaying the repeal of the Corn Laws which prevented the free import of grain to Ireland, leaving the matter to 'the inscrutable will of the great Political Economist in the sky' (Schama 2003: 222). In India in 1877–78, a year or two after Queen Victoria became 'Empress of India' – on the statuary of the Victoria Memorial in Kolkata grateful natives feed at the breast of the Mother Raj – the British shipped millions of tons of Indian grain to bring down British home prices while over seven million Indians died. A famine on an equal scale occurred in 1899–1900 (*ibid.*, 198–9, 268–71).[3] In the generations after these catastrophes, Irish poets such as Yeats (in 'September 1913') sang the 'delirium of the brave' who fought the empire. Indian poets such as Tagore found national unity in the hope of freedom from the empire, 'that heaven of freedom, my Father, let my country awake'.[4]

Broadly, poetry of the British empire demarcates racial and religious prejudice. In the mostly White, English-speaking parts of the empire, signs of nationalism in poetry heralded Dominion status: Canada (1867), Australia (1901), New Zealand (1907) and the Union of South Africa (1910). White poets of the Dominions – such as Charles Mair of Canada, Dorothea Mackellar of Australia or Francis Carey Slater of South Africa – tended to view England as 'home' even if they had never been there. In contrast, non-White national poets throughout the empire – especially in Africa and the Middle East – often attacked the empire in revolutionary and highly popular poems, expressing national identity and a longing to be free.

Yet, the British empire not only galvanized native poetry but also spread the English language and English culture. Much poetry written under British rule was on an artistic level seldom if ever achieved in the modern era before or after independence, and it was radical in abandoning tradition and developing new forms. Major languages, such as Arabic, Hebrew and Hindi, were transformed. Oral traditions in territories under British rule were written down and preserved. Egyptian poetry, for example, underwent revolutionary change under the British occupation (1882–1922). Poets such as Shawqi and Ibrahim, inspired by the Romantic idea of revolt against oppressive rule, hoped to create a more perfect society. (Shawqi's famous lines, 'Red liberty has a gate/ Upon which every blood-soaked hand must knock' [Kadhim 2004: 46], directed against Western imperialism, were inspired by liberal Western ideology and the French Revolution.) Under British rule, their poetry became politically committed in the style of radical European poets such as Milton, Byron, Shevchenko, Petőfi, Hugo and Eminescu. In Iraq, the poet Zahawi was one of many Arabic poets who broke with convention, in part because of the effects of Westernization and the British mandate

(1920–1932). In the introduction to the 1924 Cairo edition of his *Diwan*, Zahawi declared that 'poetry is above all rules'. His poem *Revolt in Hell* (1931) as well as the posthumous *Evil Promptings* represented a fundamental break with the bland ornamentalism which characterized much Arabic poetry prior to British rule (Badawi 1975: 49–50). British influence brought new experimental trends to Indian poetry in the latter half of the 19th century and the early 20th century (Preminger 1993: 597). The Tamil poet Bharati, an early 20th century opponent of British rule in India, was inspired by the ideal of liberty and the political importance of poets and poetry in the writings of Shelley. In Burma, too, a revolution in poetry occurred under British rule. The *Khitsan* (experiment for a new age) movement in the 1930s, stressed 'simplicity, directness, and purity of language' (*ibid.*, 153). Similar transformations occurred elsewhere in the empire – in Africa, Australia and New Zealand for example (*ibid.*, 19, 106–7, 835). British colonial rule was crucial in the revival of Hebrew. The Hebrew press expanded and the number of Hebrew speakers increased dramatically in Palestine in 1917–1948. Modern Hebrew poetry – notably in the work of Shlonsky – sprang from the vernacular for the first time since the time of the Bible (Burnshaw 1965). English scholars, translators and publishers were often among the first to recognize the full significance of native literature and, through translation, make it internationally known. They also stimulated natives to discover their own cultures. Gandhi, for example, first read the Indian classic the *Bhavagad-Gita*, not in India but in London, on the advice of English friends (Gandhi 1982: 76). Tagore's supporters in England won him international fame and the Nobel Prize for Literature in 1913.[5]

Poetry was stimulated by changes leading to independence: by political organizations created under British rule and vital in the establishment of independent states, such as the Congress Party in India, the National Party and Wafd Party in Egypt, the Muslim League in pre-State Pakistan and the Jewish Agency in Palestine. It was stimulated by the many individuals who worked altruistically for the empire and by improved government and economic circumstances created by the empire. It was also stimulated by Christian mission which, although designed to bring colonies into the religious compass of the empire, also provided an education and liberation ideology which facilitated independence. Many aspects of British culture were willingly adopted by subject peoples and preserved long after the British left. The Indian poet Iqbal, fascinated by British culture (he studied at Cambridge and trained as a barrister at Lincoln's Inn) was encouraged by English liberals to write in Urdu and aim for a Muslim territory independent of British rule in India. The work of the Egyptian poet Shukri, too, was influenced by his studies in England. Similarly, the immersion from childhood in English culture by the Bengalese poet Aurobindo Ghose (he went to St. Paul's School for boys in London and to Cambridge University) prepared him to devote much of his life to *swaraj*, the cause of Indian independence.

British rule greatly expanded English poetry, in lands where English had previously been unknown, most strikingly in Africa. Prior to British rule, African poetry was mostly oral. British rule brought a substantial increase in literacy and Western education, contributing to a revolution in African poetry, which was now written and often highly original (Preminger 1993: 19). In Africa, as elsewhere in the empire, colonialism 'incorporated African peoples into the ideological and materialist worlds of Western modernity' (McCaskie 1999: 688), a transformation impossible without the English language. Poets in Kenya, Malawi, Nigeria, Rhodesia (Zimbabwe), South Africa, Uganda, and other territories under British rule, include some of the fiercest critics of British imperialism. Their poetry expressed grievance over slavery, racist humiliation and land expropriation as well as cultural dilemmas posed by colonial rule. At times, poets even grudged the influence of English culture, 'the heart of alien conquest' (Mnthali in Moore & Beier 1998: 173). Yet, much African poetry was published by English presses, establishing internationally African cultures, histories and myths as independent and distinctive, and (as was the case with Lönnrot's *Kalevala* in Finland, whose fame was ensured by translations in dozens of languages) a source of intense national pride.

ANTI-ENGLISH POETRY IN THE BRITISH ISLES

Attacks on British rule and calls for revolt in poetry throughout the empire have many precedents in poetry of the British isles.[6] Poets in Ireland, Scotland and Wales – countrymen of those who created and maintained the empire – often expressed longings for independence similar to those of national poets elsewhere. The British isles took from the Hebrew Bible a tradition of subversive poetry and cultural revolt. The long British history of conflict, compromise and accommodation underlied the relative benevolence of British colonial rule even in hostile circumstances. Poetry of colonial revolt was prefigured in the British isles, in Wales, Ireland and Scotland. This poetry was greatly influenced by the anti-imperialism in the Hebrew Bible, particularly the prophets (Aberbach 1993, 2005). As the British empire adopted the Bible as its missionary blueprint, it could not suppress the dissident power of Scripture as many emerging nations found in it revolutionary inspiration. Many Scottish, Irish and Welsh soldiers and civil servants who served throughout the empire came with a degree of empathy for the struggles of subjugated peoples. For 'Great Britain' was created over a period of centuries through colonization and suppression: 'the forging of this island-nation was itself a reminder of the military, political, and economic processes whose most brutal, and most visibly racist, contemporary [18th century] form was slavery' (Kaul 2000: 3).

National humiliation and angry resentment expressed by poets under British colonial rule are found also among poets of Scotland, Wales and

Ireland. In Scotland, after the resented Treaty of Union of 1707, there was the Scottish defeat and humiliation in the uprising of 1745–46, followed by atrocities of the English army, its continued presence in Scotland, the proscription of Highland customs and the Highland clearances. The best-known Scottish poets of the late 18th and early 19th centuries – Macpherson, Burns and Scott – were at least somewhat anti-English and pro-independence. Macpherson, like Burns, is a poet of Scottish defiance after its defeat by England at Culloden in 1746. Burns imagined Scotland's revenge in language familiar among poets under colonial rule: the world, he wrote, will be a harsh desert 'Till Revenge, wi' laurell'd head,/ Bring our banish'd hame again' ('Frae the Friends and Land I Love'). Walter Scott, too, in *The Lay of the Last Minstrel* (1805) recalls Scots vengeful feelings for these defeats, 'deep-brooding o'er the slain'.

The anti-Englishness of Macpherson and Scott did not stop them from becoming immersed in and identified with British culture and even supporters of the empire.[7] Burns, however, anticipated later anti-British poets such as Shawqi and Greenberg in contrasting the devotion and sacrifice of Scottish heroes such as Bruce and Wallace with contemporary Scots 'traitors' who sell their noble hope of freedom for contemptible accommodation with England: 'We've bought and sold for English gold' ('Such a Parcel of Rogues in a Nation').[8] Scottish poetry also recalls (or invents) a Scottish heroic past, as in Scott's *Marmion* (1808), set against Scotland's defeat by England at Flodden in 1513. Colonial poets often engage in similar reconstruction or invention of a national past, arguing for the distinctiveness of their nation and its spiritual independence.

Among the Welsh, the English were guilty of 'humiliation and patronizing indifference which helped to launch the modern nationalist movement' (Morgan 1982: 3). Welsh humiliation and resentment towards English rule goes back as far as the lament of Gruffudd ab yr Ynad Coch for Llywelyn ap Gruffudd, the last prince of independent Wales, killed by the English in 1282: 'Mine now to rage against Saxons who've wronged me' (Conran 1967: 128). While English poets such as Spenser and Milton treated the Irish as papist barbarians deserving of extermination, Irish poets were outspoken in attacking the English, whom they accused of cruelty and arrogance. After the failed 1798 revolt, for example, William McBurney wrote his bitter, frequently-sung anti-English poem 'The Croppy Boy'. More recently, Patrick Pearse in 'The Rebel' (1915) expressed open hatred of the ruling power: 'ye that have harried and held,/ Ye that have bullied and bribed, tyrants, hypocrites, liars!' (Pearse 1917: 339). After the Irish revolt of Easter 1916, Yeats lauded the martyrs: 'A terrible beauty is born'. Though it failed, the Irish revolt – like the poetry that came out of it – asserted an independent national spirit, bringing political independence a few years later and encouraging similarly violent independence struggles elsewhere in the empire.

English poets, too – including Blake, Coleridge, Clough, Swinburne, the Brownings and T.E. Lawrence – were, at times, highly critical of their own country and its behavior overseas. Blake followed Milton in condemning destructive conquest for its own sake (Wright 2004: 118ff). Coleridge, in 'Fears in Solitude' (1798), written in fear of a French invasion of England, proclaims like a biblical prophet the sins of his own people:

> Like a cloud that travels on,
> Steamed up from Cairo's swamps of pestilence,
> Even so, my countrymen! have we gone forth
> And borne to distant tribes slavery and pangs.
> And, deadlier far, our vices, whose deep taint
> With slow perdition murders the whole man,
> His body and his soul!

Later poets, including Wilfred Scawen Blunt and William Watson, made the same point, that by its own moral standards the empire was lacking. 'The White Man's Burden, Lord', wrote Blunt in *Satan Absolved: A Victorian Mystery* (1899), 'is the burden of his cash' (Brooks and Faulkner 1996: 322). In 'For England' (1904), Watson attacked the empire for neglecting its people at home: the 'starved and stunted human souls/ Are with us more and more' (*ibid.*, 340).

Rudyard Kipling, the poet most widely associated with the power of the British empire and who, to a large extent, expressed and even created its spirit, was also the chief national self-doubter and subverter of the stereotypes of empire. Kipling was a rebel who went beyond British imperialism 'to challenge the very terms and values of conservative England' (Hagiioannu 2003: 183). Kipling recoiled at excessive national pride and was not just a poet of the greatness of the empire but also a prophet of its fall. 'Recessional' (1897), written to commemorate the sixtieth anniversary of Queen Victoria's reign, was a warning against jingoism and overweening national ambition, 'drunk with sight of power', and cast doubt on the future of the empire: 'all our pomp of yesterday/ Is one with Nineveh and Tyre!'[9] In *Something of Myself* (1936), Kipling recalled that the Jubilee celebrations in 1897 had frightened him with their optimism. His poem was, in effect, an antidote against over-confidence, to avert the Evil Eye.[10] Kipling, comparatively un-racist, even at times anti-racist, rejected the idea of Englishness as an exclusive club ('We and They', 1926). Yet, he had practically no idea of the cultural nationalism set off by the British empire and seemed not even to have heard of most of its great non-English poets.

EGYPT

Egyptian poetry of the British occupation (from 1882 to 1922, though British military presence continued until 1952) included some of the foremost voices in modern Arabic poetry: Barudi, Shawqi, Hafiz Ibrahim and

Ghayati, who were also among the best-known public figures in Egypt, and highly politicized. Egyptian poets broke away from the conventions of classical Arabic poetry. Influenced partly by Western poets, including Shakespeare, Byron and Hugo, they struggled to create distinctive original voices of their own. This creativity was 'proof' of the nation's cultural maturity and readiness for independence. The British 'Other' was the catalyst to the remarkable growth of Egyptian poetry. Much of this poetry was subversive as it helped create a modern national identity based on Islam and roused hope for independence. Uniquely in the Arab world, Egyptian nationalism was territorial and non-confessional, based on a long history in which the country even under non-Egyptian rule functioned to a large extent as an autonomous state (Lewis 1998: 102–03). This nationalism was helped by the effective though much hated British administration of Lord Cromer (1883–1907) and by a free press, run mainly by émigrés from Turkish lands (Khouri 1971: 42).[11] By 1913, Egypt had nearly 300 papers and journals in which Egyptian poets published their work (*ibid.*, 42–3). The press became an outlet for a growing sense of Egyptian national unity provoked not only by the revival of historic degradation felt by Muslims at coming under Christian rule but also by the alienation felt by Egyptians toward their leaders, whether Ottoman, British or native (al-Sayyid-Marsot 1999).

The influence of the British free press became apparent as Egyptian poets tested the limits of their freedom. At times they were openly seditious, and in 1909 the press was restricted. For their attacks in poetry on British rule, Ghayati was imprisoned for a year (1910–11) and Shawqi was exiled (1914–19). Ghayati's book of poems *My Patriotism*, influenced by the French Revolution, contained 'the most vehement attacks ever launched by a contemporary poet on both the British and Egyptian authorities' (Khouri 1971: 88). Muhammed Farid, leader of the National Party, contributed an introduction hailing this poetry as 'the approach of the hour of liberation from the Occupation' (*ibid.*, 90).

Egyptian poets attacked European encroachment on Muslim society. They sang the praises of Muslim civilization and mourned historic Muslim defeats by Christian Europeans, culminating first in Napoleon's easy victory in Egypt in July 1798 and then the similarly quick British rout of Egyptian national forces in September 1882. The British occupation of Egypt began as a temporary measure to protect its economic interests in a bankrupt, backward country, particularly the highly profitable sea route to India through the Suez Canal whose security could not be entrusted to natives. As temporary rule dragged on, Egyptian poets rediscovered the Egyptian past. Barudi's poem on the pyramids 'repelling the assault of the ages' was one of many expressing new-found pride in Egyptian history. The poet hoped for the growth of the power of Egypt 'sanctuary of my people'. Yet, infected by tyranny, the country was on a precipice: 'I see swordbearers about to unsheath their swords' (Khoury 1971: 20–23).[12] Barudi's poem 'Damascus', similarly, recalled the glory of militant Islam under the Ummayads, 'high as the sun in its vast domain, in every corner kingship and might' (*ibid.*, 124–5). Shawqi followed Barudi in recreating Egyptian history from Pharaonic times to the present. He quoted Napoleon's speech to his army before the Battle of the Pyramids (1799), '*quarante siècles vous observent*', to emphasize that conquerors and rulers – including by implication the British – come and go but the pyramids are eternal (Shahid 2002: 79–80).

Egyptian poets tended to support and praise the Ottoman empire against the British. In Shakespeare's time, the Ottoman empire had been the most powerful in Europe. By the time of Kipling, it was the weakest. Arabic poets joined in the widespread Muslim outrage at the fragmentation of the Ottoman empire: as Russia conquered the Crimea and Caucasus; Greece, followed by Serbia, Romania and Bulgaria, fought for independence from Turkey; France conquered Algeria and Austria took Bosnia. Now Britain, too, seemed to have joined the pack of Christian jackals as it brought Egypt and Cyprus into its empire. The Turkish empire may have been backward, foreign-dominated, cruel, corrupt and failing. Yet it was Muslim and associated with the historical hope that Muslim power could prevent Muslim countries such as Egypt from being absorbed in the Christian British empire, which at its height ruled over half the world's Muslim population (Robinson 1999). Shawqi's belief, expressed in his poetry, that only the Turks could unify and save the Muslim community, was widely shared. When World War I broke out, Muslims generally approved of the Turkish Sultan's call for a *jihad* against the Entente powers, which were allegedly aiming to destroy Islam (Cleveland 1994: 145).[13]

Egyptian poetry records, as part of the history of British rule in Egypt, a series of humiliations, or perceived humiliations, which made lasting impressions, enhanced Egyptian nationalist feeling and acted in the poetry as anti-British propaganda: notably, the reduced status of the Khedive (1893), the Dinshawai incident (1906) and Lord Cromer's farewell speech in the Cairo Opera House (1907) which, by contrasting British achievements with poor Muslim government, roused Egyptian anger and national feeling.

After 1893, when the nominal Muslim ruler, the Khedive, tried and failed to free himself from British rule, until 1914 when he was deposed, he used Shawqi, official court poet and the leading Egyptian poet of the period, to attack the British. When in 1904, for example, Riad Pasha, a prominent statesman, gave a public speech praising the British, Shawqi replied by calling him a hypocrite and traitor, 'a calamity added to our great misfortunes,/ You praise the occupation while the wound it dealt you bleeds' (Khouri 1971: 63). Other Egyptian poets, too, denounced British rule. In a poem which led to his expulsion from law school, Shukri wrote that the British 'will be defeated by the zeal of the illustrious, the ambition of the valiant, and the determination of the mighty' (*ibid.*, 186).

Smoldering Egyptian resentment against the British broke open in June 1906 with the Dinshawai incident. A small group of British officers shooting pigeons in the Nile Delta became involved in a violent clash with villagers leading to the accidental death of one of the officers. A tribunal set up by Lord Cromer sentenced four villagers to be hanged publicly, eight flogged publicly and others to prison. The British had evidently not expected capital punishments – public hangings had been abolished – and Cromer thought the sentences were a mistake (Owen 2004: 337). The incident triggered immense anti-British feeling in Egypt and a storm of criticism in England. Though Cromer had had nothing to do with the sentencing and was out of the country at the time, it clouded the remaining months of his rule. While many Egyptians saw Dinshawai as symptomatic of a war of Christian infidels against Islam, Cromer in his farewell speech on 4 May 1907 attacked Egyptian misrule by its native leaders: Egypt was as-yet too undeveloped to be independent. Shawqi replied on 9 May with what became the most famous Egyptian poem of the period, his 'Farewell to Cromer', which was often memorized and recited. Identifying himself as a personification of the nation in all its diversity, the poet mocked Cromer as an oppressor, a would-be Pharaoh, 'an incurable disease departing': 'You threatened us with perpetual slavery and humiliation/ And a state allowing no change' (Khouri, 1971: 67, 68). He adds the now-formulaic charge that the British were infidels: '…they have denied God, His deeds and the Nile's blessings' (*ibid.*, 70).

Egyptian poetry, mostly published in widely read newspapers, influenced public opinion and contributed to Cromer's fall – 'Cromer was driven out of Egypt by his critics' – even though it was widely acknowledged that he had ruled Egypt 'with great personal integrity and with a practical concern for the economic well-being of the poorer Egyptians' (Owen 2004: 398, 400). On the first anniversary of the hangings, Shawqi published a poem fiercely attacking the newly retired Cromer: 'Nero, had you lived till the reign of Cromer,/ You would have known how sentences are carried out' (Kadhim 1997: 195).[14] Shawqi inflamed Muslim anti-British feelings by identifying the victims as religious martyrs (*shuhada*'):

> '… their executioners are *kuffar*, infidels engaged in a war against Islam and the Muslims, and the occupation as the rule of *kufr*. It is the religious duty of Muslims as prescribed by the Qur' an not to submit to, but to resist *kufr* and *kuffar*, especially when the latter attempt to impose their will/rule on Muslims'.
>
> (*ibid.*, 200–01)

Ibrahim, similarly, praised the dead Egyptians as martyrs and chastised the British: 'Seek your pleasures far and wide/ And when you weary of the sport/ Shoot the locals dead instead' (Khouri 1971: 85–6).[15]

Cromer left Egypt convinced that Islam was fundamentally intolerant and too prone to hatred and revenge (*ibid.*, 72), a view which roused lasting Egyptian resentment, articulated by Shawqi: 'Whoever curses Islam should know: Mohammed is God's powerful messenger' (*ibid.*, 73). Ghayati went further: 'Does the oppressor believe that we have been humiliated and will not seek vengeance?' (*ibid.*, 96).[16]

INDIA

As in Egypt, Indian poets reacted to British imperial rule with a revolutionary outpouring of poetry in a host of languages, including Assamese, Bengali, Bishnupriya, Dogri, Gujarati, Hindi, Kannada, Kashmiri, Malayalam, Manipuri, Marathi, Nepali, Oriya, Punjabi, Rajashani, Sindhi, Tamil, Telugu and Urdu. The outpouring included Indian poetry in English as well, much of which subverted British rule. At the height of imperial rule, from about 1900–1930, the nationalist movement

> '... included hundreds of popular poets who wrote (or tried to write) rousing poems about Mother India, her glorious, heroic, and ancient past, her present courage in the face of British imperialism, and her determination to win her political and cultural freedom in the near future [and] dozens of more serious poets, most of whom played prominent roles in the freedom movement, both locally and nationally'.
> (Dharwadaker 1999: 187)

Among these poets were Subramania Bharati (Tamil, 1882–1921), Aurobindo Ghose (Bengal, 1872–1950), Rabindranath Tagore (Bengal, 1861–1941) and Mohammed Iqbal (Urdu and Persian, 1877–1938). In the interwar years, overlapping with the nationalist movement, there was also a 'Romantic' phase influenced heavily by the English Romantic poets and their emphasis on the primacy of the individual, contributing 'to the definition of a distinctive modern Indian self' (*ibid.*, 188). Marxist and modernist movements, too, began under British rule in the 1930s. Yet, there was generally a more positive view of the empire among Hindu poets in India than among Muslim poets in Muslim countries under British occupation. The Hindus did not have the same bitter history of war with Christianity as the Muslims did.

Bharati, perhaps India's outstanding patriotic poet, was inspired by Mazzini's oath before the Association of Young Italy to free Italy from alien rule:

> Our dharma will unify the motherland, make it free,
> independent of others, and a republic new!...
> I shall see that the alien rules my land no more.
> (Bharati 1977: 18)

Bharati's main poetic influence in the independence struggle was Shelley, whose name he adopted ('Shelley Dasan') and whose poetry on individual liberty he imitated: 'A nation unlit by freedom,/ Can it be a nation indeed?' (*ibid.*, 58).

Ghose, too, was known for his radical politics and was jailed and exiled. Active in a secret revolutionary society, Ghose was outraged and radicalized by the British partition of Bengal in 1905 and from 1906 to 1908 was at the forefront of the independence movement as leader of the extremist Nationalist Party in Bengal. In an article, 'Towards Swaraj and the Regeneration of India' (1907), he declared:

> 'It is a vain dream to suppose that what other nations have won by struggle and battle, by suffering and tears of blood, we shall be allowed to accomplish easily, without terrible sacrifices, merely by spending the ink of the journalist and petition-frames and the breath of the orator'.
> (Parandjape 1999: 4)

Jailed by the British for a year in May 1908 on suspicion of sedition, Ghose wrote:

> I am the Lord of tempest and mountains,
> I am the spirit of freedom and pride,
> Stark must he be and a kinsman to danger
> Who shares my kingdom and walks at my side.
> (ibid., 288)

Tagore, though less politically active than Bharati and Ghose and repulsed by nationalism, was the poet most closely associated with India's struggle for independence. In 'The Sunset of the Century', written at the end of the 19th century, Tagore prophesied that India could destroy itself through egotistic, materialistic nationalism:

> The crimson glow of light on the horizon
> is not the light of thy dawn of peace,
> my motherland.
>
> It is the glimmer of the funeral pyre
> burning to ashes the vast flesh –
> the self-love of the Nation –
> dead under its own excess.
> (Tagore 1917: 81)

India could save itself only by being true to its Eastern character:

> Thy morning waits behind the patient dark
> of the East, meek and silent.
> (ibid.)

Tagore was rare among poets in using myth to subvert nationalism, retelling the legend of the man who tries to become immortal and is lured to disaster by Indra, Lord of the Immortals:[17]

> 'The West has been striving for centuries after its goal of immortality. Indra has sent her the temptation to try her. It is the gorgeous

temptation of wealth. She has accepted it, and her civilization of humanity has lost its path in the wilderness of machinery'.

(*ibid.*, 78)

Horrified by the national conflicts which led to World War I, Tagore condemned the militancy and materialism of nationalism: 'the spirit of conflict and conquest is at the origin and centre of Western nationalism'; the Nation 'will never heed the voice of truth and goodness' (*ibid.*, 12, 24).[18] Instead, he advocated a form of national awakening influenced by the spiritual qualities of Hinduism in poems such as *Gitanjali* (1912) which can be read as prayers:

> Where the mind is without fear and the head is held high;
> Where knowledge is free;
> Where the world has not been broken up into fragments
>   by narrow domestic walls;
> Where words come out from the depth of truth;
> Where tireless striving stretches its arms towards perfection;
> Where the clear stream of reason has not lost its way
> into the dreary desert sand of dead habit;
> Where the mind is led forward by thee into ever-widening
>   thought and action –
> Into that heaven of freedom, my Father, let my country awake.
>
> (Tagore 1959: 27–28)

Iqbal, too, reacted against destructive Western nationalism and sought a basis for modern Indian nationalism in universal spiritual ideals, mainly in the Koran (Mir 2006: 133–7). The Westernized pro-British Iqbal, with degrees from Cambridge and Munich, observed how Western civilization, especially as represented by the British empire, galvanized Muslim national identity: 'The storm from the West has transformed Muslims into real Muslims' (*ibid.*, 9). Through the prophetic force of his poetry and personality, he 'inspired millions of his fellow-Muslims in India to fight for self-reform and self-realization as a necessary prelude to freedom and independent nationhood' (Arberry 1964: 379). The idea of an independent state of Pakistan is attributed to Iqbal. In his 1930 presidential address to the Muslim League (founded in 1906 under British rule), he called for a loose Muslim federation.[19] After 1947, Iqbal was regarded as the national poet of Pakistan. Yet, as a young man, Iqbal wrote Indian patriotic poetry which inspired Indian nationalists, including Gandhi.[20] In his 'National Song of India' (*Tarana-I-Hindi*, 1904), which opens, 'Our country India is the best in the whole world', Iqbal famously declared the unity of Indians, whatever their religion:

> Religion does not teach mutual discord.
> Strung on a single thread, we are one.
> We are Indians.
>
> (Burney 1987: 8)

Similarly, in 'National Song for Indian Children' he wrote of an India in which Muslims and Hindus live together in peace:

> Its people wise as Moses,
> its mountains grand as Sinai,
> its oceans Noah's anchor,
> its earth a stairway to the skies;
> a breathing paradise on earth.
> This is mine, my native land.
>
> <div align="right">(<i>ibid.</i>, 6)</div>

From the 1920s, Iqbal's patriotic poem 'Our Hindustan' (*Hindustan Hamara*) was sung in Indian schools. The poem, with its refrain *Hindi hai hum* (We are Hindi), again declares Hindustan as the greatest country in the world: 'Hindi' refers to the land, not the religion (Zachariah 2004: 53). Iqbal opposed the separatist political aims (from 1934) of the Muslim League. Iqbal's call to arms was directed not for the creation of a separate Muslim state out of India but, generally, against the West, whose attractions menaced traditional Islam:

> Against Europe I protest
> and the attraction of the West;
> Woe to Europe and her charm,
> swift to capture and disarm!
> Europe's hordes with flame and fire
> desolate the world entire;
> Architect of sanctuaries,
> earth awaits rebuilding: rise![21]

The creation of Pakistan in 1947, nine years after his death, would have horrified Iqbal: partition led to civil war, the murder of perhaps a million people, and the largest forced migration in history, with about 17 million people fleeing across the border in either direction.

IRAQ

As Shawqi and Ghayati attacked British rule in Egypt, and Bharati, Tagore and Iqbal rejected British rule in India, Iraqi poets such as Rusafi undermined British mandatory rule in Iraq which followed the collapse of the Turkish empire in World War I and lasted from 1920 until the Iraqi kingdom gained full independence in 1932. Rusafi also attacked the Arabs for letting themselves be colonized both politically and psychologically: 'Arab people! Where will you be in the end?/ Asleep, even as Destiny opens your eyes?'[22] He also condemned fellow Iraqis who pretended to rule but were in fact puppets of British imperialism. To be ruled by a Christian empire, as the British empire was seen in the Muslim world, was a humiliation which called up the lost glory of medieval Islam. Iraqi poets particularly recalled the age of Rashid, when Baghdad was the proud and magnificent capital of the Islamic world, in contrast with its modern degradation.[23] 'I weep for the splendor of empire', wrote the poet Zirikli (Arberry 1964: 390). In Rusafi's view, the idea of freedom under imperial rule was a mockery: 'If it be said to you: "Your country, folk, will be divided"/ Offer your thanksgivings and gratitude, dance and sing...' (Badawi 1975: 60). Iraqi poets of the British occupation put less blame on the need for internal reform than on Iraqi suffering under the British, as 'a prisoner forced to live in a straightjacket... a theme of which the poets are never weary' (Izzedien 1962: 16, 17). In a poem of 1928, Rusafi blamed the British for obstructing reform: 'How can we hope for progress for Iraq/ When the way of her ruler is not her way?' (*ibid.*, 16). Similarly, to the poet Mallah writing in 1929–30, the British, living in comfort, were robbing Iraq of its resources (particularly oil):

> But it is like a cemetery for its native sons...
> The goods of this country are divided between masters
> like Smith and Cook
>
> (*ibid.*, 16–17)

Another poet, Safi, compared the British to a greedy whale drinking precious water in the desert – 'They have captured Iraq/ We have sacrificed many a soul for it./ Shall our captive land be set free? (*ibid.*, 15). But he also blames Iraqis for the decay of their country, 'for the government is the nation's daughter/ And the nation is an unjust mother' (*ibid.*, 17).

To Basir, ominously, even the prospect of a negotiated independence would not remove the stain of colonial humiliation: 'Suppose the mercy of my jailer should set me free./ The favor would be a burden' (Izzedien 1971: 153). Basir, like Pearse, demanded that independence be won by force. Poetry inspires and compels the nation 'to abandon relative well-being and safety, and sacrifice everything in a desperate bid for freedom' (*ibid.*, 161) – a revolutionary posture which lapsed after the British ceded power to the Iraqi monarchy in 1932.

PALESTINIAN HEBREW POETS

Hebrew poetry under British rule in Mandatory Palestine (1920–48) developed more than at any time since the Bible. The expansion of the Hebrew press, in which much of this poetry was first published, was made possible by British rule, which replaced Turkish rule after the defeat and collapse of the Ottoman empire in World War I. Until 1917, the Russian Pale of Settlement[24] was the center of Hebrew literature, but after the revolution the Bolsheviks banned Hebrew and Jewish culture and expelled Hebrew writers, including the leading Hebrew poets Bialik and Tchernichowsky in 1921–2 (both settled in Tel Aviv). If not for British rule, it is unlikely that vernacular Hebrew would have flourished as it did in the interwar years. By the mid-1920s, Tel Aviv was the new center of Hebrew literature. By 1933 most important Hebrew writers had left Europe and were living under British rule in Palestine. For the first time since the biblical age, Hebrew poets described the landscape of the land of Israel as the setting for actual experience. Shlonsky, a road laborer in the early 1920s, described the transformation of the land in expressionist imagery of prayer:

> My land is wrapped in light like a *talit*.
> Houses stand like *tefillin* boxes.
> Like *tefillin* straps the roads sweep down.
> This is how the lovely town
> Says its morning prayers to its creator.[25]

Lamdan presented the fortress of Masada by the Dead Sea, the last independent Jewish outpost in the revolt against Rome in 66–73 CE, as a symbol of defiant hope:

> How little caressed by God's grace, Masada,
> outcast between desert and sea.
> What will you do, poor mother,
> when your parched fighters come to you,
> their last hope?[26]

By 1936, as the future of the European Jews looked increasingly terrifying, the Arab Revolt broke out in Palestine threatening the future of the Jewish National Home. In that year, Tchernichowsky wrote a poem on King Saul's death on Mount Gilboa (I Samuel 31) calling for a revival of Saul's martial spirit, 'a covenant with the sword', as he went down fighting the enemy:

> Some will remember, some will sing
> the song of Gilboa, the enchantment of En Dor
> for the solitary king, the people's prophet who made
> a covenant with the sword and paid in blood;
> with glorious, generous, humble heart,
> javelin-split, and that of his sons.
> Can a lion betray its stony lair?
> He fell like a lion: he and his men…[27]

Hostility to British control – and to some extent also to Western civilization whose brutal side prepared the ground for the Holocaust – emerged in Hebrew poetry of the 1930s, as fascism and anti-Semitism grew. Among the militant poets were Abraham Stern ('Yair') and Uri Zvi Greenberg. Stern, a classical scholar at the Hebrew University in Jerusalem, was inspired by the ancient Greeks in the belief that anti-Jewish violence must be met with violence. (In this regard, he may have been influenced by Tchernichowsky, translator of *The Iliad* and *The Odyssey* into Hebrew, who believed that Jews must learn revenge from the Greeks to survive in a violent world.) While studying in Florence in 1934, Stern wrote prophetically in Hebrew, quoting Archilochus:

> Yes, I too am a soldier poet;
> Today I write with pen – tomorrow with sword;
> Today with ink, tomorrow with blood;
> Today on paper, tomorrow on human backs;
> The heavens granted the book and the sword,
> Deciding fate: soldier and poet.[28]

Stern, true to his poetry, joined the underground Irgun and, after the British White Paper of 1939 effectively closed Palestine to Jewish refugees during the Holocaust, carried out terrorist attacks with the aim of forcing the British out of Palestine. Captured and killed in 1942, Stern is remembered less as a poet than as a terrorist, but Greenberg towers over most Hebrew poets.[29] Like Stern, Greenberg was in the Irgun during the war, but the torment in his poetry is the fate of the European Jews. Long before the Holocaust, he raged at the gentile world, including the British empire. In a poem addressed to the empire in 1936, Greenberg linked the British, exaggeratedly, with Titus, the Roman general and later emperor, who defeated Jerusalem and destroyed the Temple in 70 CE. He referred to the slogan *Judaea Capta* ('Judea is defeated') inscribed on Roman coins after the fall of the Jewish state:

> British empire, we're your slaves.
> Arabs too lick my honey from your hand.
> We obey your rulers slavishly, our leaders – a traitorous band.
> Like Titus, you gather our exiles, parading them in chains
> in a Hebrew Jerusalem, the torment of a Christian dream.
> A daily *Judaea Capta*, piles of corpses, terror the same,
> the ancient price for us to live in Jerusalem again.[30]

Yet, when war came in 1939, Greenberg saw that the Palestinian Jews had no choice but to support Britain in the war against Hitler. The British victory at El Alamein in 1942 ensured that Germany would not invade and conquer Palestine. To Greenberg, the complicity of Palestinian Arabs led by the Nazi collaborator, the Mufti of Jerusalem, who intended to carry out the Final Solution of the Palestinian Jews, vindicated his belief that the world was divided in two – Jew/Gentile. If the Jews did not learn to defend themselves, they would be totally exterminated. Greenberg became the chief

Hebrew poet of the Holocaust and the Jewish revolt against British rule (1945–47) which followed, culminating in the British withdrawal and the creation of the state of Israel on 14 May 1948. Greenberg's poetry of this period, collected in *Streets of the River* (*Rechovot ha-Nahar*, 1951), was a remarkably complex mixture of grief, violence and love:

> God! I am alive. You gave me strength to live on my grief,
> not be destroyed by it...
> On my people's soil I ask one thing only: Grant me speech,
> from the secret power of the commandments at Sinai,
> I will teach my people:
> You are the inheritors, you replace the martyrs,
> mouths crushed in exile's dust, seas of blood –
> for them the miracle: the enemy did not invade.
> The burden that fell with them as their blood ran
> let us carry with love![31]

NATIONAL POETRY IN FORMER SLAVE SOCIETIES UNDER BRITISH RULE

Some remarkable modern English poets emerged from one-time slave societies that came into the orbit of the British empire. British colonial rule suppressed slavery and encouraged local cultures and national movements leading to independent states. Poets of this national awakening include: Okot p'Bitek of Uganda, Mazisi Kunene of South Africa, M.B. Zimunya of Rhodesia/Zimbabwe, John Mbiti of Kenya, Wole Soyinka of Nigeria and Derek Walcott of St. Lucia.[32] These poets, in common with African cultural nationalists generally, fought to retain their sense of nationality and separate cultural identity. In doing so they found themselves imitating the foreigners with whom they refused to identify themselves, as their native traditions weakened (Plamenatz 1975: 31). Many of these poets, even as they rejected colonial rule, were committed Christians or had a Christian family background and education. They adopted English as their main language of national self-expression, recalling (or constructing) with bitterness and dignity their history and culture. Even when turning away from Western culture and affirming the value of native traditions – for example, p'Bitek in *Song of Lawino* (1966) or Kunene in *Emperor Shaka the Great* (1979) originally written in Lwo and Zulu, respectively – their preferred language is often English.[33] p'Bitek's poem, spoken by an African woman about her husband, gives a bitter indictment of the allegedly unmanning influence of British White culture, 'Like the kituba tree/ That squeezes other trees to death' (p'Bitek 1984: 114). The poem ends with a denunciation of colonial education for crushing African manhood and culture and 'uprooting the pumpkin' of tradition.[34] African oral literature gives a broader picture of widespread tribal warfare, disorder and slavery before the Whites came, making Africa vulnerable to colonialism. The Zulu 'Praises of King Shaka' is a list of Shaka's conquests:

> He felled Nomahlanyana born to the king Zwide,
> He slaughtered Sikhunyana born to Zwide,
> He felled Nqabeni and Mphepha,
> He ate up Dayingubo born to Zwide.
> (Zimunya 1989: 133)

Kunene makes clear in Book 10 of *Emperor Shaka the Great* that Shaka in the early 19th century gave Whites land in exchange for weapons and knowledge of military tactics. In some ways, too, the rule of an imperial Other and the influence of European nationalism encouraged literacy and heightened native appreciation of local history, landscape and traditions, though these are often written in English. Zimunya, in 'The Stone Speaks', affirmed the noble antiquity of the African landscape – 'Older than Moses and Jesus.../ older than all' (Okpewho 1985: 108). So, too, did Mbiti's hymn to the Kenyan landscape, 'Kenya Our Motherland': 'From whose eastern shores/ Ever pounding waves scrub thy rocky ribs;/ In whose northern desert land/ Sand dunes roll over eternal silence' (Okola 1973: 74). Much modern African national poetry cames from oral tradition and local myth. The attachment to the Kenyan landscape in Mbiti's poetry might be linked to the Kenyan folk tale of how the gods on Mount Kenya gave the land to the ancestors of all Kenyans.[35]

The 'scramble for Africa' accelerated with the discovery of diamonds in South Africa in 1867 and of gold nine years later. Increased White immigration and conflict between the British and the Boers led to the creation in 1910 of the Union of South Africa and a renewed native interest in native culture. From the 1920s, the Xhosa poet Krune Mqhayi became a leading figure in the African movement for self-rule. When the Prince of Wales visited in 1925, Mqhayi responded with a condemnation of colonialism:

> She sent us the preacher: she sent us the bottle,
> She sent us the Bible, and barrels of brandy,
> (in Gérard 1970: 61)

Mqhayi believed that African tribes could unite and form a nation as did Western countries such as Britain and Germany. In 1937, Mqhayi's prediction at the missionary college at Healdtown that the Black Africans would one day gain independence made a lasting impression on Nelson Mandela, then a student at the school. The colonial government and the independent Republic of South Africa created in 1961 were White-minority governments which suppressed and persecuted the Black majority. The first free election in the country's history came in 1994, bringing Mandela to power. This history of conflict meant that of all African poetry South African poetry 'is most concerned with subjugation, courage, poverty, prisons, revolt, and the private griefs of public injustice' (Preminger 1993: 19). The poet Denis Brutus was imprisoned for 18 months in the early 1960s for his opposition to apartheid, and he eventually settled in the United States as a political refugee. He wrote of outrage at racial discrimination brought by colonial rule, the land 'scarred with terror... faces split by pain/ the wordless, endless wail/ only the unfree know...' (Brutus 1973: 4, 176). Oswald Mtshali linked South African apartheid laws to the Roman occupation of Judea in the time of Jesus (Moore & Beier 1998: 375–76).[36] Anger at the injustice of apartheid was expressed also in Kunene's Zulu poems, such as 'Thought on June 26': 'Was I wrong when I thought/ The rope of iron holding the neck of young bulls/ Shall be avenged?' (Kunene 1970: 41).[37]

Nigerian poets, too, explored cultural dilemmas created by British colonial rule. In language not unlike that of 19th century national poets under the rule of empires, such as Shevchenko, the Nigerian poet Osadebay asserted a nation's need to control its own destiny. He did not want African culture to be defined by White Europeans:

> Let me play with the whiteman's ways
> Let me work with the blackman's brains
> (Okpewho 1985: 133)[38]

Soyinka, also Nigerian, recalled the humiliations of British colonial racism. In 'Telephone Conversation,' the poet tried to rent an apartment or room from a white woman:

> '**are you dark? or very light?**' Revelation came.
> 'You mean – like plain or milk chocolate?'
> (Moore & Beier 1984: 187)

Derek Walcott, a poet of mixed blood ('poisoned with the blood of both'), a native of the Caribbean island of St. Lucia (a British territory from 1814 until it achieved full independence in 1969) defined his ambivalence as a Black writing English, in 'A Far Cry from Africa':

> I who have cursed
> The drunken officer of British rule, how choose
> Between this African and the English tongue I love?
> (Walcott 1990: 18)[39]

The ruins of a great house built for a slave-owner by his slaves called up ghosts of colonial rule, the Bible taught by missionary Christianity, and Kipling, poet of the death of empires: 'What Kipling heard, the death of a great empire, the abuse/ Of ignorance by Bible and by sword' (Walcott 1990: 20).[40]

Walcott's poetry, like much other poetry in the language of empires, itself contested the change of biblical 'abuse': the chief effect of the Bible was to encourage education, national identity, self-reliance – and creativity such as Walcott's.[41] The poet is reconciled with the former empire through the contemplation of death, the great leveller, uniting slave and master. London, the heart of slave-policy, drew together colonizer and colonized, both enslaved to mortality, to the bell that tolls in Donne's majestic sermon, 'for everything, even in London,/ heart of our history, original sin'.[42]

CONCLUSION

The statue of Oliver Cromwell, sword in right hand, Bible in left hand, in front of the Houses of Parliament is a reminder not just of 'the abuse/ Of ignorance by Bible and by sword', in Walcott's allusion to the evils of British imperial rule, but also of the institutionalized dissidence in British culture whose chief exemplar in poetry is Cromwell's contemporary, Milton in *Paradise Lost*. Milton's Bible-based political ideology – including freedom of expression, the right to overturn repressive government and the creative power of opposition – was the foundation of modern liberal democracy and independence movements whose chief spokesmen included national poets, both in Britain and in the expanding British empire (Kohn 1946). Great Britain, itself a creation of often-warring nationalities with separate literatures, stimulated throughout its empire an immense variety of national poetry in the late 19th and early 20th centuries. Though in some ways repressive and exploitative, the British empire was unusually tolerant of cultural difference and sympathetic to native cultures, and it helped to create conditions for cultural and political independence. Poets – many writing in English – flourished under relatively enlightened British rule with a previously nonexistent free press. No other empire had a comparable impact on the cultures of the ruled. Poetry in India, Egypt, Iraq, Palestine, African colonies and elsewhere reflected the growth of strong national identities under British rule as well as revolutionary desire for independence. Many poets were among the creators of modern literary art in their respective countries and deeply involved in politics and the struggle for independence. However, their poetry was also ideologically imitative of revolutionary poetry within the British isles, of Milton, Burns, Shelley and Yeats, for example, who stress the universal urge for freedom.

NOTES

1. On the spread of literacy in British India, see Joshi (2002). As was the case in much of the empire, the British built many educational institutions, libraries and reading rooms in India and contributed large numbers of English books.

The British Empire and Revolutionary National Poetry 287

The Indian reader had 'relatively complete access to anything printed in Britain' (*ibid.*, 133). Most of India's educated class benefited from English education. Bankimchandra Chattopadhyay, author of *Vande Mataram*, India's 'National Song', was educated at Calcutta University, founded by the British in 1857. The liberal press in the British empire contrasted favorably with censorship in other empires. No poet attacked the British empire as Shevchenko, for example, attacked Tsarist Russia, in 'The Caucasus' (1845), for its censorship laws: 'From the Moldavian to the Finn/ Silence is held in every tongue' (Shevchenko 1961: 71).

2. The Lebanese-born Arabic poet Ahmad Faris Shidyaq (1804–1887), who lived in England (1848–55), took British citizenship and married an Englishwoman, wrote poetry in praise of England and its God-given power warranted by its devotion to doing good and improving the lot of mankind. In a possible echo of the Book of Isaiah (ch. 6), the glory of the English nation fills the earth:

لم يبق من مضرب في الأرض ليس به للإنكليز فخارٌ غيرُ مذكور

(Arberry 1965: 144–5). National poets in other empires – for example Mickiewicz (Poland), Shevchenko (Ukraine) and Lönnrot (Finland) in the Tsarist empire; and Solomos (Greece), Botev (Bulgaria) and Eminescu (Romania) in the Ottoman empire – tend to be hostile toward the dominant culture and prefer to write in their own languages. See chapters 6 and 7 (this volume).

3. Idealists such as Macaulay and Kipling believed in the moral responsibility of the empire (Schama 2003: 200, 201; Gilmour 2003: 247). Humanitarianism was 'a vital component of Britain's national or Imperial identity' (Porter 1999: 198). Yet, there were serious questions about the ethics of the empire, as it was guilty of violent coercion and exploitation as well as neglect. As late as 1943, several million are estimated to have died in a famine in Bengal. Conflicting tendencies were, perhaps, to be expected in an empire that had developed for centuries and at its height was the largest, most powerful and diverse in history: stretching over a quarter of the earth's surface, holding about a quarter of the earth's wealth, with nearly a quarter of the earth's population under its rule. Its character being multifaceted, much depended on who was in office, in the colonies as in Whitehall, when, where, and under what circumstances. As H.G. Wells (1922) put it: 'no single brain had ever comprehended the British Empire as a whole. It was a mixture of growths and accumulations entirely different from anything that has ever been called an empire before' (2006: 329).

4. In *Gitanjali* (Tagore 1959:28). See p. 252.

5. Tagore's main backer was Yeats, who was deeply impressed by the Indian poet for his ambition to restore Indian national self-confidence and assert spiritual superiority in the struggle against British colonial rule (Foster 1997: i 470).

6. On national poetry of the British isles, see chapter 5 (this volume). There were anti-English tendencies in some Dominion poetry too, especially among poets of Irish and Scots origin, but these were diluted as time passed and new local national identities emerged.

7. 'Rule, Britannia' (1740) is by James Thompson, a Scots-born poet. See Kaul (2000).

8. On attacks against traitors in national poetry, see p. 252ff.

9. Tagore shared with Kipling a view of the transience of empires, including that of 'The fierce English/ Radiating their power' which time would sweep away to

'leave not the slightest trace on the constellations' paths' ('They Work', 1941; Tagore 2004: 368, 370). In an earlier poem, 'Change of Era' (1900), Tagore wrote of the dangers of nationalism and of chauvinistic poets such as Kipling: 'The poets' pack cries out, spreading terror' (*ibid.*, 169). Tagore, somewhat unjustly, found in Kipling 'a suggestion of cruelty mingled with the arrogance of power. It makes one feel that from time to time, humankind wishes to tear the fine yet firm fabric woven on the hundred looms of civilization, and plunge into the savagery of its primeval forest-dwelling nature' (*ibid.*, 399).

10. In 'The Islanders' (1901), Kipling attacked the British for their alleged frivolity and laziness, for abandoning the discipline and military preparedness of their ancestors and for jeopardizing the future of the islands:

    Then ye returned to your trinkets; then ye contented your souls
    With the flannelled fools at the wicket or the muddied oafs at the goals.

    Kipling was incensed by the 'venomous, morbid, distorted' imperialism unleashed by the Boer War (Stokes 1972: 92). His warnings were not confined to the empire. In 'Seven Watchmen', written at time of Paris Peace Conference in 1919, Kipling warned the Great Powers of the transience of temporal power and glory: 'the kingdom is within you'.

11. In 1892, the Christian Arabic poet Khalil Mitran left his native Turkish-ruled Lebanon for Egypt partly because, like his fellow émigrés, he preferred to live in a more liberal British-ruled country, rather than under Muslim rule where his criticisms of the government had led to his arrest and nearly cost him his life. By 1914, the Egyptian population expanded under British rule by over 60 percent, from 7.6 million in 1880 to 12.3 million (al-Sayyid-Marsot 1999: 659). Mitran was in the minority among poets in emphasizing the positive side of Westernization in Egypt and the Middle East. For the most part, the achievements of British rule – including economic stability (Egypt became solvent by 1889), expansion of the middle class, human rights, abolition of slavery, establishment of the rule of law, advances in technology and agriculture, better schools, hospitals and medicine, decline of infant mortality, property rights, tax reform and freedom of the press – made little difference in alleviating the sense of Egyptian humiliation and moral injury. Much Arabic poetry of the colonial period supports Said's definition of imperialism in *Colonialism and Imperialism* (1994) as 'an act of geographical violence through which virtually every space in the world is explored, charted, and finally brought under control' (271). Yet strangely, with the exception of Yeats, Said largely overlooks poetry written under British rule – even the great Arabic poets such as Shawqi and Rusafi. He also omits the Hebrew Bible, the chief ideological source of British national identity, of chosenness and of international mission, which many colonized peoples adopted as a charter of liberation. On the positive impact of Western imperialism on Arabic literature, after its centuries-long stagnation under Ottoman rule, see Badawi (1975) and Kadhim (2004).

12. Translation has in some cases been slightly modified. On the role of translation in the creation of world literature (though mostly not poetry), see Casanova (2004).

13. Rusafi, translator of Fikret's Ottoman national anthem into Arabic and later the leading Iraqi poet during the British mandate (1920–1932), responded with popular militant Islamic patriotism to the Ottoman entry into the Great War on the German side on 29 October 1914: 'My kinsmen, the enemies have attacked the homeland,/ So unsheath your swords and defend your families and homes' (Kadhim 2004: 95).

14. For a full translation and discussion of Shawqi's poem on Denshawai as well as his 'Farewell to Cromer', see Kadhim (1997), who also reproduces in full Cromer's farewell speech. Mitran, like Shawqi, alluded to Nero in his poetry, but to express a positive response to Western culture and with more national self-blame along European lines than in Muslim poetry. Mitran was attracted to the humanism of Western culture and wanted to create a liberal democratic political system with equal rights to replace religious adherence (Khouri 1971: 161). His poem 'Nero' suggested that the Egyptians were themselves partly to blame for the British suppression of press freedom in 1909: 'The people who gave victory to Nero are more shameful than he' (*ibid.*, 167). Yet, Mitran dismissed treaties between the British and their Arab subjects as being 'like treaties of wolves with lambs' (Arberry 1965: 166).
15. Ibrahim continued his attacks on the British in Egypt during the uprising of 1919. He satirized a clash between British troops and a group of women protesting the deportation of the nationalist leader Sa'd Zaghlul to Malta:

> Defeated, they scattered in disarray towards their homes.
> So, let the proud army rejoice in its victory and gloat over their defeat.
> Could it be perhaps that among the women
>   there were German soldiers wearing veils,
> A host led by Hindenburg in disguise,
> So the army feared their strength and were alarmed at their cunning?
>   (Badawi 1975: 46)

The Egyptian novelist, Naguib Mahfouz, a child eyewitness of the 1919 revolution, recalled in *Palace Walk* (1956, ch. 56) that this poem was memorized and recited by nationalists.
16. When it came to the defense of Islam, even pro-British Egyptians were roused against Cromer. Ahmad Nasim (1880–1938), an opponent of the Khedive and supporter of British rule – he even praised Cromer for freeing Egypt 'from the chains of tyranny' – attacked Cromer in a 1906 poem for insulting Islam: 'May the dark heavens strike you with a hellish deluge' (Khouri, 1971: 76). The humiliation of British colonialism links much national poetry in the British empire: for example, Pearse in Ireland (Kennelly 1970: 300), Greenberg in Palestine (Greenberg 1990, iii 187), Rusafi in Iraq (Kadhim 2004: 124–5) and Hang Yuehe in China (Yip 1992: 179).
17. In contrast, the radical Indian nationalist B.G. Tilak (1856–1920), who campaigned against the British authorities in 1905 after the partition of Bengal, found in Indian myths, of Krishna and Arjuna for example, harbingers of Indian independence.
18. Critics of Tagore point to the alleged incompatibility of the poet's pacifist universality and hatred of nationalism with his role as Indian national poet: 'Just how could one square passionately debunking the idea of nation and nationalism everywhere and anywhere with support for greater freedom and autonomy for India?' (Regan 2000: 93).
19. Iqbal persuaded Muhammed Ali Jinnah (1876–1948), later the first president of Pakistan (1947–48), to return from England to India and lead the Muslim League (Mir 2006: 14–15).
20. Iqbal also wrote poems on imperial public occasions, such as the coronation of George V in 1910.
21. Revised from Arberry (1964: 381).

22. In Arberry (1965: 167). The Arabic reads:

معشرَ العُرب أين أنتــم من القو   م إذا مــا تمّ انقــلاب الــزمـان

أنيـامٌ والدهـر يـفـتـح فيكـم   مـن جـديـدَيْـه مـقـلـتَـى يقظان

   On Rusafi's anti-colonialism, see Kadhim (2004). Rusafi began as a pan-Islamic supporter of the Ottoman empire and developed a sense of Iraqi national identity under British rule.
23. Arabic poets under French colonial rule were at times as gloomy as those under British rule. The Lebanese poet Nu'aima, for instance, thought the Arabs were in such a bad way that they might just as well bury themselves alive (Arberry 1964: 391).
24. On the Russian Pale of Settlement, see pp. 182, 228.
25. Translated by David Aberbach (Aberbach 2010: 233).
26. Ibid.
27. Ibid.
28. Ibid., 234.
29. On Greenberg as an heir of the Hebrew prophetic tradition, see Aberbach (2005).
30. Translated by David Aberbach (Aberbach 2010: 234).
31. Ibid., 235.
32. On poetry of former slave cultures in Africa, Latin America and the Caribbean, see Appendix (e), p. 311ff.
33. Jeff Opland, who edited the writings of the Xhosa poet S.E.K. Mqhayi (2009) – 'the poet of the whole nation' – described the neglect of Xhosa literature among the Xhosa: in 1976, over 30 years after Mqhayi's death, Opland could find the poet's grave only with difficulty, unmarked and overgrown (2, 12).
34. Though p'Bitek wrote *The Song of Lawino* in his native Lwo, only in its English version – published in 1966, four years after Uganda gained independence from Britain – has it become widely known. Similarly, though Kunene wrote his epic poem *Anthem of the Decades* 'to preserve the varied African literary traditions which too often were denigrated and obscured in the colonial period' (1981: xi), he published this poem first in his own English translation; the Zulu original remained in manuscript. *Emperor Shaka the Great* was neglected as a native oral epic until Kunene translated it into English while living in California. Under French colonial rule, similarly, Black poets such as Senghor and Césaire tended to gain recognition when they wrote in French. See pp. 312–13.
35. For Kenyan myth in the context of myth and nationalism generally, see chapter 2 (this volume).
36. Greenberg, too, linked colonial oppression with Roman imperialism. See p. 282.
37. 26 June 26 1955: the date the Freedom Charter was declared by the African National Congress (ANC) in South Africa.
38. From 'Young Africa's Plea', written between 1930 and 1950. The late-19th century Turkish poet Mehmet Akif Ersoy made a similar plea of the Turks: study Western arts and sciences, for there is no alternative, but 'Let your essential nature be your guide' (Menemencioğlu and Iz 1978: 177).
39. Compare with Senghor, another poet of mixed blood. See p. 314.
40. In this poem ('Ruins of a Great House'), Walcott might have had in mind Kipling's 'Recessional' (1897), though the image of Kipling as spokesman of

imperialism is subverted in this and other poems. See p. 272. Tennyson, the Poet Laureate writing on the occasion of the Queen's Jubilee ten years earlier, included lines of warning:

> Are there thunders moaning in the distance?
> Are there spectres moving in the darkness?
> Trust the Hand of Light will lead her people,
> Till the thunders pass, the spectres vanish,
> And the Light is Victor, and the darkness
> Dawns into the Jubilee of the Ages.
> 'On the Jubilee of Queen Victoria'

For other critiques in African poetry of biblical culture as a tool of colonialism, see the Zimbabwean poet Zhuwarara's 'The encounter' (Zimunya 1989: 110) and Mqhayi's response to the visit of the Prince of Wales to South Africa in 1925 (in Gérard 1970: 61). See p. 284.

41. On the Bible and nationalism, see chapter 2 (this volume).
42. Walcott's description in 'The Bright Field' of slavery as 'heart of our history' (1993: 76) even after independence had a precedent and likely influence in the Hebrew Bible. The story of the Israelite exodus from slavery in Egypt, a chief source of the high valuation of freedom, has inspired much modern nationalism (Walzer 1985). See p. 41.

Conclusion
National Poetry, Morality and Individual Creativity

The land is not ours ...
It owns itself.

(Elizabeth Brewster)

The Hebrew Bible, inspiration of countless religious wars, militant national poets and secular nationalism, envisages the abolition of war and recognition that human ownership is illusory. Biblical poetry and law agree: in song, 'the earth is the Lord's and the fullness thereof'; and in law, the land must not be sold in perpetuity, 'for the land is Mine and you are my strangers and sojourners'.[1] Much national poetry follows this paradox: territorial ownership is conditional upon universal moral values, the truth of which explodes in the prophet's passion, his rage and comfort, reproof and hope, justice, righteousness, truth, loving kindness, mercy. These are the true promised land.

National poetry is a record of constant war, religious conflict and cultural ferment; of unexpected links between widely disparate historical periods and cultures; of ancient texts with attributes of modern national poetry and of modern texts linked to the ancient world, in a huge panorama of cultural history. National striving and creative individualism interlock: the paradox of the best in human creativity joined to bestial destructiveness; moral vision and its betrayal; the repeated spectacle of national struggles in which the individual is lost in his public role but, as a result, finds a new private voice. The torn national poet appears already among the Hebrew prophets, most strikingly when Jeremiah, 'seduced' by God to be a prophet to his wayward nation in its downfall, cries out against his national role:

> You lured me, Lord, and I was lured.
> With your strength you got what you wanted.
> Morning to night I am mocked,
> a laughing-stock to the world. (20: 7)

The prophets, driven by dissenting passion for social justice and moral reform, sought to settle conflicting demands of Self and Nation by joining the two. From the time of Jeremiah, an uneasy balance of private and public defined much national poetry. Particularly in the age of nationalism which sprang from the French Revolution, poets often rejected the limitations of the Nation. They aimed to create, instead, for art's sake, to separate the social creature from the creative individual. Though the Romantic Age burned with nationalism, the dead Byron its greatest symbol, the Romantic emphasis on individual passions seemed paradoxically to leave the Nation out. Poets such as Wordsworth, Schiller and Burns, voices for national freedom and the full exercise of human imagination and ability, stressed universal values. Petőfi, a martyr for Hungary against Russia in the uprising of 1849, saw himself in a struggle for World Liberty:

> When slave nations, sick of the yoke,
> rise up, faces flaming, their red flags
> emblazoned with 'World Liberty'
> and blast it off east to west...
> In the battle against tyrants –
> let me die fighting on the field.[2]

Whitman, responding to the 1848–49 revolts, put the Self, not the Nation, at the heart of *Leaves of Grass*. The Nation had value only if it let individuals fully achieve their wonderful, quirky diversity. To Yeats, too, the instinctive passions of poetry was as heedless of national distinctions as the earth is of borders dividing nations: '...the great passions know nothing of boundaries. As do the great beasts in the forest, they wander without let or hindrance through the universe of God'.[3]

National poets after 1789 were often disenchanted by human depravity, torn between the man who feels and creates out of a unique individual spirit and imagination and the public role directed by collective hopes. If true poetry comes from individual passion, if the poet can speak only for himself, if he must stand apart from the group, how can he speak for a nation? And if his poetry is 'national', can it be any good? Does it not lack the inwardness, the feminine instinctiveness, the connection with a personal, largely subconscious imagination, the irrational, the world of memory and dreams, of unique experience and verbal association? Nationalism for some poets – Ibsen, for example – was an artistic millstone. To Tagore nationalism was a source of corruption when it became more important than the individuals it seeks to benefit.[4] The most overtly national poetry of some poets was often little more than crude jingoism, stirring up a dubious militarism. Their best work explored the self, not the group.

The Risorgimento poet Leopardi, in *The Zibaldone* (1817–1832), was intrigued by the paradox that some national poets enriched their individual voice through their public role. Leopardi conjured up a brooding universal vision, seemingly unconnected with national aspirations, of a cosmos cold and unloving, hostile to joy. Yet he was an ardent Italian patriot and praised the reawakening of the national spirit as a source of individual greatness:

> 'I praise the Italians for turning away from a blind love and imitation of foreign things, and still more for beginning again to use and to value their own; I praise the men who try to reawaken a national spirit, without which there has never been any greatness in the world – not only national greatness, but even individual greatness ...'
> (Leopardi 1966: 83)

Whitman, in 'A Backward Glance O'er Travel'd Roads' (1888), said much the same as Leopardi in recalling Herder's advice to Goethe, 'that really great poetry is always (like the Homeric or Biblical canticles) the result of a national spirit' (Whitman 1964: ii 732).[5] To Yeats, too, the poet's greatness was linked to national identity, part of a collective consciousness:

> 'To the greater poets everything they see has its relation to the national life, and through that to the universal and divine life: nothing is an isolated artistic moment; there is a unity everywhere; everything fulfils a purpose that is not its own; the hailstone is a journeyman of God; the grass blade carries the universe upon its point. But to this universalism, this seeing of unity everywhere, you can only attain through what is near you, your nation, or, if you be no traveller, your village and the cobwebs on your walls. You can no more have the greatest poetry without a nation than religion without symbols. One can only reach out to the universe with a gloved hand – that glove is one's nation, the only thing one knows even a little of'.
> (in Ellmann 1968: 15–16)

The reverse is also true: the poet disclosing his inner world with sensitive honesty can unexpectedly find himself representing the nation. The Senegali poet David Diop wrote, in 'A Contribution to the Debate on National Poetry', 'Let the poet draw from the best that is in him whatever reflects the essential values of his country, and his poetry will be national' (1973: 59). Poets as diverse as Petőfi, Whitman and Bialik wrote of themselves; in doing so, they created a national ideal. Whitman moved naturally from being 'Walt Whitman, a kosmos, of Manhattan the son,/ Turbulent, fleshy, sensual, eating, drinking and breeding' to asserting himself a type of America, national and universal at once:

> I speak the pass-word primeval, I give the sign of democracy,
> By God! I will accept nothing which all cannot have
> their counterpart of on the same terms.
> (*Leaves of Grass* 24)

Yet, why are some poets, and not others, 'national'? What makes the charismatic bond between national poet and nation? Biblical prophets prefigured modern poetry in the intermingling of suffering, personal with national: Hosea's unfaithful wife, symbol of Israel's betrayal of God, her 'husband'; Ezekiel's loss of his wife, an emblem of destruction, of the Temple, Jerusalem and the Judean state in the early 6th century BCE. Escape from mission – as Jonah tries to do – is impossible.

The bonding of prophet and nation, not unlike that of individuals, complex in motives and aims, is nevertheless based on similarity in character, family and social background and experiences: individuals with similar family background or life crises or comparable (often hidden) emotional problems are drawn to one another, even without verbal communication.[6] This principle of homogamy suggests that psychological traits and experiences of the national poet mirrored salient general characteristics of the nation at a given time. The poet's wound was the nation's wound, and vice versa. Among modern national poets, too, the joining of personal and national pain roused creative instinct, wedded to national hopes. Rilke called the propensity to dwell on personal hurts the 'curse of poets'. Yet to the national poet curse could turn to blessing. National poetry can become a vehicle for self-confession. Private disability, grievance and deprivation – of stability, love, health – were sublimated, mastered and overcome through identification with the Nation. Aims such as independence, unity, power and recognition – unlikely or impossible in an individual life – might be realized in the life of the Nation. The national poet in this respect was not unlike political figures such as Robespierre, Gandhi and Kennedy, for whom public and private life were joined, whose struggles for political and inner freedom were one.

Public poets such as Whitman illumined a chief attraction of nationalism: the Nation, as a source of health and immortality, can transcend the weaknesses and corrosion of the Self. The national poet often combats alienation and inner division by becoming one with the nation. To heal the nation the poet heals himself. To make the nation whole, the poet aims to be whole. The wounded Self can be regenerated through the nation. And so, national poets often conveyed not just an image of stable national identity but also its reverse: weak identity giving an edge of desperation to national assertion. As we have seen, poets with a history of severe trauma or disability, such as Burns, Solomos, Kölcsey, Shevchenko, Byron, Leopardi, Fikret, Prešeren or Bialik, were often motivated to revive and heal their wounded, humiliated nation and to rediscover (or invent) lost national unity. Byron found consolation for his own physical and emotional infirmities through hopes for the revival of Jews, Greeks and others whose national state in the early 19th century could be described as crippled. Leopardi drew on his broken physical state in giving conviction and strength to the overcoming of Italian national brokenness. Among some poets, as we have seen, relations with women were symbolic of the nation.[7] National poets may rise from personal despair to the hope for national revival.

To national poets such as the Chilean Pablo Neruda, politics were rooted in the most private drives and hopes. Neruda's 'national' voice, in poems such as *The Heights of Macchu Picchu* (*Alturas de Macchu Picchu*, 1948), came partly in reaction to trauma. His *Memoirs* gave clues to the psychology underlying his fascination with the lost past and the struggle to retrieve it symbolically in his poems: 'I was born on July 12, 1904, and a month later, in August, wasted away by tuberculosis, my mother was gone' (1977: 7–8).[8] *The Heights of Macchu Picchu* traced the rediscovery of the 'mother of stone (*madre de piedre*)' – the fortress of the Inca empire built high in the Peruvian Andes some 3000 years ago, abandoned in the Middle Ages and found virtually intact only in 1912. The poem is 'national' in a limited geographic sense, linking the American present to its troubled past. Yet, it is also national in the figurative sense when the poet climbing the overgrown laddered stone of mountainous jungle to the lost petrified city – symbol of unending human aspiration – echoed God's reply to Job from the whirlwind in lines such as 'Who caught the lightning of the cold (*Quién apresó el relámpago del frío*)' with its consolatory message of angry resignation to the unknowable. The poet recalls the ascent of the human species and the cost of this ascent: suffering, brutality, slavery, (for the city was built by the poet's slave-brothers, *el antiguo ser, servidor*), resurrected in the poem to affirm enduring humanity and culture, in 'the dead kingdom that lives' (*El reino muerto viva todavia*). Neruda, not unlike the prophets, followed a poetic tangent from personal trauma to public affirmation of universal truths.

The Hebrew Bible envisaged a world beyond war and cruelty, a world without nations, united by the love of God, and moral action in the name of God:

> ...and they shall beat their swords into ploughshares,
> and their spears into pruninghooks:
> nation shall not lift up sword against nation,
> neither shall they learn war any more.
>
> (Isaiah 2:4)

To the prophets, nations can overcome their blood-stained failures, their blindness to a higher truth. There is a better world elsewhere, wrote Isaiah, waiting to be found. Nationalism remains a live force, destructive as well as creative, in civilization. Its poetry is vindicated by history, if not in violent upheaval or revenge, then in hope for national renewal, in which politics and morality are one. Poetry remains midwife to nationalism, though rarely with the undiluted violence and idealism of the past.

NOTES

1. Psalms (24: 1), Leviticus (25: 23). Also see Exodus (19:5). On the abolition of war, see Hosea (2: 20).

2. Adapted from Petőfi (1973: 168).
3. W.B. Yeats, 'Nationalism and Literature' (1893), in Pritchard (1972: 36).
4. On Ibsen's disillusionment with Norwegian nationalism, see Meyer (1969: 182). On Ibsen's rejection of a specifically national role, see p. 78. On Tagore's hostility to nationalism, see pp. 70–1.
5. In the 1855 Preface to *Leaves of Grass*, Whitman asserted the link between individual and nation: 'An individual is as superb as a nation when he has the qualities which make a superb nation' (Whitman 1964: ii 458). On Herder's view that national achievement makes individual achievement possible, see p. 68.
6. On attraction and charismatic bonding, even in the absence of communication, see Lieberman *et al.* (1973), Skynner (1976) and Aberbach (1995, 1996).
7. See the Introduction, p. 9.
8. On ways in which childhood loss such as Neruda's can motivate creativity, see Aberbach (1989). For selections from the poetry, see Neruda (1972, 1976).

Appendices

a *Anthems and national poetry*
b *National poetry and Poor Law, from Shakespeare to Wordsworth*
c *Anti-nationalism and nationalism in the poetry of T.S. Eliot*
d *Landscape in national poetry*
e *Poetry of former slave cultures*
f *On Re-reading Bialik: Paradoxes of a 'National Poet'*

a   Anthems and National Poetry

National poetry generally belongs to 'high culture', though there is some overlapping with popular culture. Whereas national poetry can be complex, ironic and ambivalent – even to the point of undermining itself – and often has resonance outside the nation, anthems, though often patriotically stirring, tend to be more straightforward and time-bound. Anthems, integral to modern nationalism, seem not to have existed in the pre-modern age. National poets usually put themselves into their poetry to a greater extent than the authors of anthems and folk songs, many of whom are unknown or forgotten. The Parker and Charles song 'There'll always be an England' illustrates the transient nature of popular nationalist songs. Famous in 1939 when the war broke out, its lyrics can seem hollow outside of its historical context:

> There'll always be an England, while there's a busy street,
> wherever there's a turning wheel, a million marching feet.

Nationalist folk songs tend, similarly, to reflect specific historical events and circumstances. A good example is the Scotman John McEvoy's 'The Wee Magic Stane' which was written after the 1951 expropriation by Scottish nationalists of the Stone of Scone (the possessor of which would, according to tradition, rule Scotland) from Westminster Abbey to Scotland, '*Wi' a too ra li oora li ay*' (Palmer 1988: 267). National anthems are not usually written by national poets, though there are exceptions such as Solomos of Greece ('Ode to Liberty'), Tagore of India ('Janagana') and 'Banjo' Paterson of Australia ('Waltzing Mathilda').[1]

Some deeply nationalistic poems, such as Coleridge's 'Fears in Solitude' (1798), are unsuitable as anthem material as their love for country is too complex. Coleridge, writing as the French were assembling a fleet to invade England, admitted that all that he wrote came out of his love for England. Yet, because of this love, he is driven to attack his countrymen (though he is no pacifist) for thoughtless bloodlust, clamoring for war as for a sport:

> As if the soldier died without a wound;
> As if the fibres of this godlike frame

Were gored without a pang; as if the wretch,
Who fell in battle, doing bloody deeds,
Passed off to Heaven, translated and not killed;
As though he had no wife to pine for him,
No God to judge him! Therefore, evil days
Are coming on us, O my countrymen!

Cavafy's Greek poem 'Thermopylae' is another poem expressive of national identity which is too psychologically complex to be an anthem.[2] Cavafy wrote movingly of the pass at Thermopylae, where in 480 BCE a small band of Greeks held off a large Persian army. He used Thermopylae as a complex symbol of heroically-defended human ideals: justice, truth and generosity. However, the poem ends with the traitor Ephialtis leading the Persians over a mountain path to defeat the Greeks from the rear (Cavafi 1984: 12).

b National Poetry and Poor Law, from Shakespeare to Wordsworth

The link between national poetry and Poor Law has been almost totally ignored. Yet, the evolution of the two main systems of Poor English law in periods of heightened military threat and national consciousness, in the late 16th century and the late 18th/early 19th century, deeply affected the poetry of Shakespeare and Wordsworth, and enhanced its national significance.[3] Both poets wrote with unusual empathy about the poor in times when capitalism came into conflict with the traditional Judaeo-Christian view of the poor, but when national unity – including the impoverished masses – was vital in wartime. Both poets saw the legitimacy of welfare questioned, in opposition to the spirit of Jewish law and Christian love. Both were part of historical debates on state responsibility, Shakespeare at a time when the so-called Old Poor Law evolved and was codified for the first time in secular legislation; Wordsworth, when the Old Poor Law was made obsolete by the Industrial Revolution, ultimately to be replaced by the New Poor Law in 1834.

Both Shakespeare and Wordsworth lived in times of protracted war. In the 1590s as in the 1790s, England faced invasion by Spain in the Elizabethan period and by France in the time of Napoleon after the French Revolution. In between, England faced no comparable threat. Also, between the ages of Shakespeare and Wordsworth (and perhaps before and after as well) hardly any English poetry at its best was as good as theirs. So, the 1590s and 1790s, when Shakespeare and Wordsworth reached creative maturity, were ages of threatened invasion and heightened English nationalism. The urgent need for national unity entered their poetry. War in both cases led to higher taxes. Poverty, already a serious problem, was made worse by crop failure and famine. Shakespeare and Wordsworth were eyewitnesses of worsening conditions in wartime. While many of their contemporaries were repelled by the poor, their sympathy for the poor is striking. Often they recalled biblical passages which, without exception, stress the need to protect the poor. In their poetry – for example, in Shakespeare's *King Lear* and Wordsworth's *Margaret, or The Ruined Cottage* – they go against the current of opinion on the poor.

Nationalism contributed both to a more sympathetic view of the poor and to a determination to improve their lives. It also, through greater awareness of the poor, led to a fear of their power to disrupt society and a consequent determination to control poverty and the poor on a national legislative basis. This was the background to the Poor Laws of 1598 and 1601, passed at the same time when Shakespeare's *Henry V* – the most nationalistic of his plays – was first performed. The Poor Laws of 1598 and 1601 are among the most important and far-reaching achievements in the history of welfare legislation. These laws lasted, in fact, until Wordsworth's time, when the New Poor Act of 1834 replaced them. While Shakespeare's portrayal of the poor reflected conditions of the Elizabethan age leading to new legislation, Wordsworth's portraits of the poor in the 1790s were a radical indictment of Poor Law at the time of the Industrial Revolution and the Napoleonic wars. This poetry was part of a public debate, leading to governmental reform.

The wars against Spain and Ireland were paid for by increasing the tax rate. Harvests failed in 1595–8, and there was famine in the north of England and in parts of the south. Poverty became the main issue in parliament.[4] Shakespeare's audience would have recognized these conditions in Titania's attack on Oberon's evil magic in *A Midsummer Night's Dream*, dating from the late 1590s. Part of the fascination of this play, as well as *King Lear*, was its depiction of aristocrats living rough, as many English poor did. Even though the descent into a state of nature was temporary, it touched on a common human vulnerability of rich and poor, articulated by a magical creature:

> The ox hath therefore stretch't his yoke in vain,
> The ploughman lost his sweat, and the green corn
> Hath rotted, ere his youth attain'd a beard:
> The fold stands empty in the drowned field,
> And crows are fatted with the murrion flock,
> The nine men's morris is fill'd up with mud;
> And the quaint mazes, in the wanton green,
> For lack of tread, are undistinguishable:
> The human mortals want their winter here;
> No night is now with hymn or carol blest ...
>
> (II i 93–102)

In these hard times, the Poor Laws of 1598 and 1601 were an outstanding achievement of Elizabethan social policy. By 1600, London's population reached about 200,000, but the civil parish of rural England consequently became a microcosm of state authority. Legislative recognition of state obligation to the poor was perhaps reflected in *King Lear* (1606), written between the death of Elizabeth in 1601 and the consolidation of the rule of James 1. Lear, made homeless by his cruel daughters, is forced to live like a beggar in the open fields. On the heath, Lear becomes aware for the first time of the 'poor naked wretches', a large part of his kingdom. The king, now no better than they – perhaps worse, being unaccustomed to life as a 'bare, fork'd animal' – enters their lives in his fall to their level. He is a true king, ironically, when he gives up the crown. Lear's fall into poverty makes him feel for the poor, opening the way for his reconciliation with his daughter Cordelia, the embodiment of love. There is implicit irony that Lear, speaking of Christian charity and love to a wholly Christian audience, is a pagan king in a pre-Christian age. His compassionate outpouring is human rather than specifically Christian, with particular resonance in an age when responsibility for the poor was changing from a religious Bible-based privilege of the Church to a secular national legislative problem of the central government:

> Poor naked wretches, whereso'er you are,
> That bide the pelting of this pitiless storm,
> How shall your houseless heads and unfed sides,
> Your loop'd and window's raggedness, defend you
> From seasons such as these? O! I have ta'en
> Too little care of this. Take physic, Pomp;
> Expose thyself to feel what wretches feel,
> That thou mayst shake the superflux to them,
> And show the Heavens mor.e just.
>
> (III iv 28–36)

After the time of *King Lear*, famine in England was rare. It was the Industrial Revolution in the late 18th century, when Wordsworth wrote many of his greatest poems, that revived many of the national issues that the Elizabethan Poor Law was thought to have resolved. It was in Wordsworth's time that the enormous current gap between the rich and the poor worldwide is thought to have begun, around 1800. The young Wordsworth was a radical, inspired by the egalitarian spirit of the French Revolution which he witnessed in 1792–3. Wordsworth championed the poor as the English economy worsened, amid war and inflation. He put the poor, the beggars, the widows and orphaned children, among whom he grew up in the Lake District, at the heart of his poetry, not as objects of pity and charity but as human beings with rich personalities and dignity. He believed that the poor, suffering more than the rich, can teach much about endurance and independence. Wordsworth became a poet of the suffering poor, perhaps the first in Western poetry: the mad mother, the distraught sailor, the old woman who cannot heat her cottage (Goody Blake), the farmer forced to sell his sheep, the poor orphan girl who loses her cloak (Alice Fell), the soldier back from the wars, the old man with swollen ankles (Simon Lee) and other unfortunates and outcasts, forsaken women, convicts and many others.

To Wordsworth, the Industrial Revolution was a form of national suicide. It destroyed the intricate web of English social life that had taken centuries to evolve. He was among the first to write poetry about industry as a cause of family disruption and break-up. He anticipated Marx's attack on factories and their owners for adding social alienation to the woes of the poor, especially the children, universally exploited. To Wordsworth, the rural poor were part of the landscape, part of Nature, part of England; not a problem to be solved or a threat to society.

Wordsworth's poetry reflected growing awareness of poverty as a major national concern. In the century after 1750, the population of England tripled, rising from about 5 million to over 15 million by the time of Wordsworth's death in 1850. It was not clear at the time if productivity could match the population rise. England paid dearly for its wars with France and the American colonies. In the late 1700s when these wars were fought, the cost of poor relief increased five times; and between 1793 and 1813 prices doubled. Wartime shortages led to increases in claims for relief. Taxpayers rebelled and parishes could not cope. At the end of 1796, in 'Ode to the Departing Year', Coleridge, living in the poverty-stricken West Country, wrote of England as a nation that had been cursed.

As the population grew amid economic crisis and hunger in wartime, Thomas Malthus in 1798 published *Essay on Population* arguing that population increase meant an increase in hunger. Malthus' views led to an increasingly harsh view of the poor as a burden on society, to be countered through stringent legislation. The General Enclosures Act of 1801 limited public land to which the poor had access and made their lives harder. As industrial cities grew, hunger forced many off unprofitable rural land and into factories. Families that had worked in a variety of trades at home were now scattered among the mills. It seemed as though a once-free people were now enslaved. Atrocious factory conditions obscured the fact that capital-driven industry could, given time, solve many of the problems it created: those who had worked in the 'dark Satanic mills', as William Blake called them, in the North were better-off than the unemployed poor in the South.

Though England was at war with France, there was a lot of sympathy in England for the ideals of Revolution: freedom, equality, justice. Wordsworth wrote an outraged reply (not published in his lifetime) to the Bishop of Llandaff who in an anti-revolutionary sermon in 1793 argued that the gap between the rich and the poor was natural. Wordsworth, then (age 23) a radical, insisted instead that 'the extremes of poverty and riches have a necessary tendency to corrupt the human heart'. Consequently, Wordsworth wrote, 'a system of universal representation' was needed, 'the suffrage of every individual'. He believed that failure to reduce the gap between rich and poor justified revolution such as that in France. The Revolution, he felt, was for the hunger-bitten children of the world. Here, too, Wordsworth anticipated Marx whose *Kapital* includes a powerful indictment of child labor.

Much English literature in the 1790s was poetry of social protest as England was faced with its worst war crisis since the Spanish Armada. Wordsworth's poems of the 1790s had for their background the rising costs of poor relief, failed harvests and food riots, as well as privation in wartime. This, Wordsworth wrote in his great poem *Margaret or The Ruined Cottage*, was 'a time of trouble', when:

> shoals of artisans
> Were from their daily labour turned away
> To hang for bread on parish charity

To Wordsworth, the small vital daily acts of charity and love in rural England were undermined by legislation. The Poor Laws, in Wordsworth's view, deprived the poor of dignity and the better-off of opportunities to fulfil the biblical ideal of charity. Neither Shakespeare nor Wordsworth were concerned with the religion of the poor, whether they are Catholic or Protestant. To Wordsworth, true charity was expressed in personal relations – not the workhouse or soup-kitchen. He was well-aware of the dark, dirty, crowded conditions of many workhouses as depicted by George Crabbe in his poem *The Village* (1783). Wordsworth, writing about 15 years later, defended the old Cumberland beggar against intrusive legislation and challenged the negative perception of the poor:

> … deem not this Man useless – Statesmen! ye
> Who are so restless in your wisdom, ye
> Who have a broom still ready in your hands
> To rid the world of nuisances; ye proud,
> Heart-swoln, while in your pride ye contemplate
> Your talents, power, or wisdom, deem him not
> A burthen of the earth!

In *The Prelude* (Book X), Wordsworth describes the period 1795–1797, when he lived in the West Country, as the crucial period in his artistic development, when he decided to be a poet. At this time, he began writing his poem on the old Cumberland beggar. The poet watched as poverty became a national problem, as the price of staples, of oats, bread and potatoes, rose dangerously. His letters and his sister Dorothy's journal recorded the wretched poverty and ignorance of the country people who seemed at times to live no better than savages, and his observations enter his poetry. The poem 'The Baker's Cart' described a typical scene: a baker does not stop his cart outside a poor woman's door because he knows she has no money to feed her children. 'The Last of the Flock', also based on an eyewitness incident, depicted the effects of poverty in a time of austerity. The owner of a flock of sheep is forced to sell to provide for his family. This is his situation, in his own words:

> 'Ten children, Sir! Had I to feed,
> Hard labour in a time of need!

> My pride was tamed, and in our grief
> I of the parish ask'd relief.
> They said I was a wealthy man;
> My sheep upon the mountain fed,
> And it was fit that thence I took
> Whereof to buy us bread:'
> 'Do this: how can we give to you,'
> They cried, 'what to the poor is due?'

In 'Goody Blake and Harry Gill', an old woman, poorly clothed and fed, lives alone in her Dorsetshire cottage, unable to afford fuel to warm herself in winter: coal is dear for it must be imported 'by wind and tide'. Goody Blake works long hours in her cottage:

> All day she spun in her poor dwelling,
> And then her three hours' work at night!
> Alas! 'twas hardly worth the telling,
> It would not pay for candle-light.

Yet, Wordsworth understood not just the responsibility of the better-off to the poor but also the need of the poor to give, not merely be objects of charity: 'for this single cause,/ That we have all of us one human heart. This 'one human heart' was, if anything, the single unifying principle of Wordsworth's poems, as it was of Shakespeare's plays – this is what brings both poets so close in spirit to the Hebrew Bible. The feeling of unity with suffering humankind continued in Wordsworth's long poem, *Margaret or The Ruined Cottage*, written around the same time as 'The Old Cumberland Beggar', in 1797. *The Ruined Cottage* showed how a rural family slid inexorably to poverty, as war and famine took their toll, and there was no one to help. The description could apply also to the period when Shakespeare wrote *Julius Caesar* and *Hamlet*, when England, faced with a crisis of invasion, endured crop failures and hunger, compounded by uncertainty over the succession;

> You may remember, now some ten years gone
> Two blighting seasons when the fields were left
> With half a harvest. – It pleased Heaven to add
> A worse affliction in the plague of war,
> A happy land was stricken to the heart.
> A dearth was in the land. They were hard times,
> A wanderer among the cottages
> I with my pack of winter raiment, saw
> What the poor suffered – Many of the rich
> Sunk down as in a dream among the poor
> And of the poor did many cease to be
> And their place knew them not.

The humanity of the poor was stressed here: their embodiment of the divine image, enhanced by an echo of the Book of Job (7:10), 'their place knew them not'. Margaret was loyal to her family and faith, and her story taught us that 'consolation springs from sources far than deepest pain', a lesson not unlike that experienced by Lear on the heath.

Empathy with the poor in Shakespeare and Wordsworth was strikingly at odds with the history of English legislation on the poor, driven (as was legislation in other countries) more by fear of vagrancy, crime and parasitism than by Christian love. The poets embraced the poor; legislators made brooms to sweep the poor away. While not opposing capitalism, both warned of harmful effects of capitalism on the poor. Shakespeare's portrayal of the poor was a powerful, though indirect, indictment of the existing system and a warning, couched in the most diplomatic language (as it had to be), of the threat to England's survival if allowed to continue. And it may be that the sympathy with the poor in Shakespeare's plays reflected and influenced public opinion more than is recognized. From the Poor Law of 1598 and 1601 until the publication of the *Lyrical Ballads* in 1798, England had a relatively effective system of poor relief in which the extremes of poverty were largely banished.

In Wordsworth's time, the Industrial Revolution and the war with France brought extreme poverty back onto the legislative agenda, with an urgency not known since the time of Shakespeare. The Old Poor Law no longer worked. Wordsworth's poetry expressed his revulsion at the Poor Law and his general horror at legislation against the poor. The poet felt this legislation to be degrading, a sign of social failure as the poor were often made to feel more like criminals than the beloved of God in the Judaeo-Christian tradition. Shakespeare and Wordsworth were poets of conscience. In moments when Christian charity was questioned, they returned to the unambiguous sympathy for the poor in the Bible.

c Anti-Nationalism and Nationalism in the Poetry of T.S. Eliot

T.S. Eliot's *The Waste Land* (1921) can be read as a 'Song of Experience' to Whitman's 'Song of Innocence' in *Leaves of Grass* (1855). After World War I, national variety no longer signified health and optimism; rather it meant alienation, breakdown and despair. Yet, World War II triggered a resurgence of English nationalism. Even Eliot, whose poetry is dominated by religion – more precisely the crisis of faith – and who in any case was American until 1927, became something of a national poet at the time of the German attack on Britain in 1940. The heroism in Eliot's poetry was not that of the great epics of national mythology: *The Waste Land* and other poems used fragments of European literature to portray the collapse and fragmentation of Western civilization during and after World War I. Rather, Eliot elevated the flash of spiritual insight, momentary hesitant action, memory and abiding faith. Muted but strong national feeling was expressed in 'Little Gidding' (the last of the *Four Quartets*, published in 1942, and touching on Eliot's English ancestral roots) and in occasional verses written during the war. At this time, Eliot restated the old creative entanglement in his work between national or public events and private experience. In 'A Note on War Poetry' (1942), he defines poetry as '... the abstract conception/ Of private experience at its greatest intensity/ Becoming universal'. Lines in 'Little Gidding' recalled the London Blitz – 'The dove descending breaks the air/ With flame of incandescent terror' – lead to prayer-like reflections on history as the winter light failed in a secluded chapel, 'History is now and England'. 'Defence of the Islands' (1941), written after the British evacuation from Dunkirk in 1940, was a meditation on time and timelessness, on English history and its place in civilization, on the 'memorials of built stone', joined in verse with the memory of the Battle of Britain. Eliot's most complex poetic statement on nationalism and national identity was 'To the Indians who Died in Africa' (1943), written at the time of the North African campaign, as the tide of the war was changing in favour of the allies. Here, Eliot both expressed and retreated from nationalism. When a man dies bravely on foreign soil, as the Indians did in Africa, Eliot writes, 'that soil is his'.

> This was not your land, or ours: but a village in the Midlands,
> And one in the Five Rivers, may have the same graveyard ...

When Eliot wrote in 'national' mode, his language became simpler and easier to understand than his 'modernist' poetry.

d   Landscape in National Poetry

Landscape and morality often go together in national poetry, especially in times of trouble. In Homer, the Greek landscape was associated with justice; in the Bible, the deed to the Promised Land was moral conduct. In crisis, feeling for the land is especially strong. When Jerusalem was threatened by Assyria and, later by Babylonia, the prophets asserted love for the land (e.g., Psalm 48). The English Romantics expressed similar attachment to England during the threat of French invasion in the Napoleonic wars. Coleridge in 'Fears in Solitude' (1798) and Wordsworth in *The Prelude* (1805) wrote of the English landscape as a source of moral good, as did Scott in writing of the wild beauty of Scotland:

> Land of brown heath and shaggy wood,
> Land of the mountains and the flood ...
> (*The Lay of the Last Minstrel* 1805)

The poetry of Whitman before, during and after the Civil War portrayed American landscapes, sprawling and majestic. The land unified the nation, ensuring its survival and regeneration:

> Always Florida's green peninsula – always the priceless
>   delta of Louisiana –
> always the cotton fields of Alabama and Texas,
> Always California's golden hills and hollows, and the silver mountains
>   of New Mexico ...
> ('Our Old Feuillage')

Geography can determine the character of national poetry. Scandinavian poets such as Wergeland, Oehlenschlager and Bjornson expressed gratitude to their countries' natural defenses, protecting them from upheaval and injustice.[5] Their mountains were revered as temples to freedom. Oehlenschlager's national anthem was a paean to the Danish landscape:

> There is a charming land, winding in hills and valleys,
> its wide-branched beech trees facing the salty Baltic.
> Its name: ancient Denmark, Freya's palace.[6]

Bjornson's 'Fatherland Song', Norway's national hymn, was a similarly loving evocation of the country's landscape and history: 'Yes, we love this land, where the wild sea foams,/ wind and weather-beaten ...'[7] The Maltese poet Dun Karm Psaila depicted the island of Malta, '*Fior del Mondo*' (Flower of the World), and the surrounding sea 'blue as indigo, that embraces/ This island of my heart' as source of his poetry:

> from gardens red with orange-trees, from fields
> waving with golden corn from shady valleys,
> white and fragrant with wild narcissi ...
>
> (Arberry and Grech 1961: 55–7, 123)

In the poetry of Saunders Lewis, similarly, the Welsh landscape ('the rugged truth of the land') defined national consciousness, particularly the lake, stream and crag by the house of the poet's father: 'Where else between heaven and earth/ Can I recapture the sound of the folk who gave me birth?' (Elfin and Rowlands 2003: 70). The African landscape, too, was much loved by its poets, as in Mbiti's 'Kenya Our Motherland', a land of flamingoes, deserts and sea, where 'lions sunk in deep, deep slumber/ Awake to the tune of hooting cars' (Okola 1973: 74). Some landscapes, however, inspired complaints. To the short-lived Dutch poet De Genestet, Holland was a miserable 'spongy, porridge-swamp' clotting the arteries with its clammy climate: 'You're fit for clogs alone, O land our forebears plotted/ And, not at my request, extorted from the sea' (Steiner 1966: 83).[8]

e   Poetry of Former Slave Cultures

Despite the ancient history of Africa, Latin America and the Caribbean, defeat, exploitation and humiliation by the colonial powers in the 19th and 20th century was the fulcrum of much poetry in these places.[9] Pre-colonial native history and culture did not generally rouse such powerful feeling or creativity in European languages as the experience of colonialism. In the struggle for independence, poets of former slave cultures, imperial colonies and ex-colonies, such as Senghor, Neruda, Césaire, Diop, Osadebay, Walcott and Soyinka, asserted cultural distinctiveness and universality, national self-awareness and self-criticism, and resistance to the oppressor. They probed psychological wounds left by slavery and colonialism long after independence. Their poetry – usually free verse – proclaimed ideals of freedom, justice, equality and reconciliation, ideals which colonial rule transmitted and, at times, betrayed. This poetry enlivened and competed with the literature of formerly racist-imperialist nations – mainly Britain, France and Spain. It often alluded to violent forces of nature – hurricanes, rivers, volcanoes, tornadoes – as forces of independence, in countries dynamically entangled with their European colonial cultural history. Much of this poetry was in the language of the colonial power, highly critical of foreign rule but enriching its language and competing with its literature. Few wrote with the regret of a Caliban – at taking drunkards for gods and worshipping dull fools.

The Nicaraguan poet Rubén Dario expressed widespread wariness of American influence, pressure and interference in a poem to the American president Theodore Roosevelt in 1905. Roosevelt, renowned as a hunter, could not catch the 'Spanish lion': 'though you have everything, you lack one thing: God!' (Dario 1965: 70). Dario went on to ask in 'The Swans', written before World War I: 'Are we to be overrun by the cruel barbarian?/ Is it our fate that millions of us will speak in English?' (Dario 2005: 19). An answer was given by Neruda in *The Heights of Macchu Picchu* (1948). Macchu Picchu, built by slaves high in the Andes, is a towering monument to the human spirit, which powerful empires cannot crush: 'Let me have back the slave you buried here!' (Neruda 1972: 189).[10] The poet calls the slaves brothers. They worked in all weather, 'swept by the sable whirlwind, charred with rain and night/ stoned with a leaden weight of statuary ...' (*ibid.*, 193). This poetry speaks not just for Chile or Spanish America but for the wretched of the earth.

Angolan poets, too, were in the forefront in the battle against colonial rule. Augustinho Neto, a leader in Angola's struggle for independence from Portugal, recalled slavery in 'the grieved lands of Africa' (Moore & Beier 1998: 6). The French Senegalese poet David Diop portrays African humiliation, the sweat, blood and humiliation of slavery, 'This back that breaks under the weight of humiliation', rather than the idealized '*Afrique des fiers guerriers des savanes ancestrales*' (Diop 1973: 25). To Diop, a paradisical free Africa was destroyed by the White invasion – in fact, the 'irons of slavery' were common in Africa. Long before the relatively brief colonial period, men were enslaved, women corrupted, and children lost their innocence (*ibid.*, 39).

Though poets felt the humiliation of colonialism, some tacitly accepted it as culturally enriching. Hatred of the West, particularly France, was stronger among French African poets than among English African poets.[11] France had higher, more revolutionary ideals, and African disillusionment with France was sharper. Paris, beacon of universal fraternity, became to French African poets such as Césaire of Martinique and Senghor of Senegal, a mire of alienation. They reacted in the 1930s by creating the Negritude movement, to encourage Black pride and self-sufficiency – but generally in the languages of the imperial powers. Césaire's *Cahier d'un retour au pays natal* (*Return to My Native Land*), written in the 1930s then revised twice (1947, 1956), stood out as 'an indictment of Western imperialism and colonialism' (Davis 1997: 178), climaxing in a slave revolt:

> ... the slave-ship breaks apart ...
> It does no good for the captain to hang
> the toughest black from the yard-arm,
> or throw him overboard, or feed him to his dogs.
> The blacks smelling of fried onion
> find the bitter taste of freedom in their spilt blood.[12]

Though hostile to French culture, Césaire wrote *Cahier d'un retour au pays natal* in French rather than Creole, the first language of all Black Martinicans, implicitly acknowledging the dominance of the alien culture which he absorbed and made his own.[13] Ambivalence toward the West among these poets was inherent in the awareness that colonial rule was weakening or coming to an end. Yet Africa remained 'joined by the navel' (*liés par le nombril*) to Europe, as Senghor put it in '*Prière aux Masques*' (Prayer to Masks), written during World War II:

> See how the Africa of empires dies
> in the pitiful agony of a princess,
> Europe too, joined to us at the navel.
> Fix your steely eyes on the children you order about
> giving their lives like a beggar his only coat.
> When the world is reborn, let us cry, 'Present!'[14]

'Que nous répondions présents à la renaissance du Monde ...', Senghor's declaration of African independence and rebirth, was not in Senegalese, his native African language, but in French. The umbilical link with the West was seen in Senghor's use of French, not as an outsider but as one whose sensibility was permeated by French, the poet's first language. Senghor's '*Maître-de-langue*' was Victor Hugo – not an African writer. In *Chants d'Ombre* (1945), Senghor's total assimilation of French culture compromised his African identity, but his African nationalism undermined his identity as a French poet: 'all he has succeeded in doing is to isolate himself both from his own people and white men' (Wake 1965: 15). When Senghor retired as president of Senegal in 1980, he moved back to France where he died in 2001. Similar ironies bedevilled other poets, however enraged against colonial rule: Césaire, mayor of the capital of Martinique, Fort-de-France, aimed not for national independence but to keep the country a *departement* of France! and Augustinho Neto, a leader of the Angolan independence movement against Portugal, ended his days – in Lisbon.

The sense of failure, of grievance and of self-blame among some poets of former slave-cultures was compounded by their use of the language of the colonial masters. At times, these poets attacked both their persecutors and those who ignored or undermined their native culture.[15] With sarcasm reminiscent of Shevchenko's attacks on russified Ukrainians in the 19th century, David Diop mocked kowtowing Africans as ersatz Europeans:

> Poor brother in silk-lined smoking jacket
> Squeaking and droning and strutting in the parlors
>   of condescension
> We pity you
>
> (Diop 1973: 18–19)

Poets of former slave cultures sometimes followed the Hebrew Bible in transforming the legacy of slavery, transforming suffering and hate into a source of collective pride and hope. Noemia de Sousa and Jorge Rebelo fought in the liberation struggle of Mozambique from Portugal and lived in exile for many years. De Sousa declared in language recalling the early 20th century expressionists – the 'mouth torn open in an anguished wound', the body tattooed with wounds from the whips of slavery – the despair, anguish and pride of African identity:

> tortured and magnificent
> proud and mysterious
> Africa from head to foot
>
> (Moore & Beier 1998: 216–17)

Rebelo, known as the 'poet of the Mozambican revolution', wrote with the single purpose of stirring his people to militant opposition to Portuguese rule and ultimate independence. His staccatto language – 'My rifle will break the chains open the prisons kill the tyrants win back our land./ Mother, beauty is to fight for freedom, Justice rings in my every shot' (*ibid.*, 221) – recalled European militants such as Petőfi and Botev.

Much Latin American poetry also came out of slavery, colonialism and the search for national identity.[16] Yet cultural ambivalence was not as sharp and painful in this poetry as in African poetry. Racial integration was more widespread in Latin America than in Africa, as seen in the poetry from the time of the Spanish soldier-poets of the 16th and 17th centuries, notably Alonso de Ercilla, who glorified their Indian enemies as defeated heroes – not victims of western colonialization – and sang the birth of a nation consisting both of Spanish and Indians:

> Of tribes distinguished in the field I sing;
> Of nations who disdain the name of King ...
>
> (Crow 1989: 80)

By the early 19th century, long before most European countries (especially those under Soviet rule), most Latin American countries gained independence from Spain who was weakened by the Napoleonic wars.[17] The poets of the war of independence against Spanish rule, such as Camilo Henriques of Chile, Anastasio de Ochos of Mexico and Vicente Lopez of Argentina, are mostly forgotten. Latin American countries have substantially and unselfconsciously assimilated Western culture, particularly the Spanish language. They benefit, too, from a broader mix of races than in Africa and, economically, from proximity to the United States.

Though angry and bitter, poets of former slave cultures often expressed a mood of reconciliation. The 'language of the oppressors' was also their language of creativity, self-definition and independence. Writing in French in a German prison camp in 1940, Senghor alluded, somewhat ironically in the circumstances, to the brutal maltreatment of Black soldiers in the *French* army in World War II, reviving memories of slavery and colonial oppression: 'Black martyrs, immortal race, let me say the words that forgive' (Senghor 1998: 58). Reconciliation was encouraged by the poet's mixed racial origin:

> Deep inside me I hear the shadowy song of *saudades*.
> Is it the ancient voice, the drop of Portuguese blood rising
> Again from the depth of ages?
>
> (*ibid.*, 144)[18]

NOTES

1. At times, a de facto anthem may be officially disqualified as it is not inclusive enough. This was the case with Chattopadhyay's 'Vande Mataram' (I praise you, Mother India', 1882), which was unacceptable to many Muslims as it comes from a hymn to the Hindu goddess Durga. Instead, it is India's 'National Song' (Kaviraj 2007).

2. On this and other anthems, see Eyck (1995), Csepeli and Orkeny (1997) and Kaul (2000). Thermopylae has inspired national poetry outside Greece. Leopardi, in 'To Italy' (1818), treated the heroism of the Greek soldiers as an inspiration to modern Italy. It must be conceded, however, that the greater the nationalist feeling, the more mediocre national poetry often appears to be. Men appear at times more willing to die for bad poetry than live for good poetry.
3. Appendix (b) is condensed from a talk given at, and published by, The Weatherhead Center for International Affairs, Harvard University (Aberbach 2014). On English Poor Law, see Slack (1988) and Hindle (2000).
4. An underlying factor in the unprecedented parliamentary emphasis on welfare in the later Elizabethan period may have been guilt – guilt over the occasionally cruel treatment of Catholics and perhaps also over the question of monarchic legitimacy – 'the fault/ My father made in compassing the crown' (*Henry V*, IV ii 299–300). This concern with welfare is voiced by Henry V on the eve of Agincourt:

> Five hundred poor I have in yearly pay,
> Who twice a day their wither'd hands hold up
> Toward heaven, to pardon blood ...
>
> (*ibid.*, 304–06)

5. Balkan poets, too, such as Njegoš, expressed love for their country's geography for shielding them from invasion. See p. 169.
6. Adapted from Stork (1947: xv).
7. Adapted from Van Doren (1936: 986).
8. Auden was another poet uncomplimentary about his country: 'England our cow/ Once was a lady – is she now?' (*The Orators*, 1932).
9. Pre-colonial African culture included: the poems, preserved in oral tradition and song, about the legendary 13th century warlord Sunjata Keita, putative founder of the empire of Mali; the poetry of traditionalists such as Bamba Suso and Amadu Jebate of Gambia and Amega Dunyo and Komi Ekpe of Ghana; and the images of the noble antiquity of the African landscape, as described by the Zimbabwean poet M.B. Zimunya (Okpewho 1985: 108). On national poetry deriving from British colonial rule, see chapter 12 (this volume).
10 On Neruda, see p. 296.
11 On African poets writing in English, see pp. 283–6.
12 Translated by David Aberbach. The original reads:

> ... le négrier craque de toute part ...
> En vain pour s'en distraire le capitaine pend
> à sa grand' vergue le négre le plus braillard
> ou le jette à la mer, ou le livre à l'appetit de ses molasses.
> La négraille aux senteurs d'oignon frit
> retrouve dans son sang répondu
> le gout amer de la liberté
>
> (Césaire 1983: 61)

13 Césaire's absorption of foreign cultures while attacking them had many precedents, notably in the Hebrew Bible.
14 Translated by David Aberbach. The original reads:

> Voici que meurt l'Afrique des empires –
> c'est l'agonie d'une princess pitoyable
> Et aussi l'Europe à qui nous sommes liés par le nombril.
> Fixez vos yeux immuables sur vos enfants que l'on commande
> Qui donnent leur vie comme le pauvre son dernier vêtement.
> Que nous répondions présents à la renaissance du Monde ...
>
> (Senghor 1977: 46)

15 On the use of poetry to attack enemies of the nation, both internal and external, see pp. 19, 35, 253ff.
16 On racism and nationalism in Brazilian literature, see Haberly (1983).
17 On 19th century Latin American cultural nationalism, see Castro-Klaren and Chasteen (2003).
18 Compare with Walcott, another poet of mixed blood. See pp. 285–6. Suriname, a South American Dutch colony with a history of slavery, won independence in 1975. Suriname poets such as Rabin Rawalz (1935–) celebrate national diversity: 'There is only one Suriname/ of so many cultures, colors, languages –/ but all are born to Suriname' (see Jyoti 2013: 119).

On Rereading Bialik

Paradoxes of a "National Poet" An Article by David Aberbach in Encounter (1981)

MEN & IDEAS

On Rereading Bialik

Paradoxes of a "National Poet"—By DAVID ABERBACH

> "The rage of Dante against Florence, or Pistoia, or what not, the deep surge of Shakespeare's general cynicism and disillusionment are merely gigantic attempts to metamorphose private failures and disappointments. The great poet, in writing himself, writes his time."
>
> T. S. ELIOT, SHAKESPEARE
> & THE STOICISM OF SENECA

ONE OF THE GREAT, unexplained ironies of modern Jewish history is that Chaim Nachman Bialik (1873–1934), whom Weizmann called a giant of the Zionist movement, and who was hailed in his lifetime and until the present day as the poet laureate of the Jewish national renaissance, had painfully ambivalent feelings about this role to the point of rejecting it.

Instead, he saw himself in the humble role of an artist struggling with his personal agonies. Though he appeared in his poetry to be the virtual reincarnation of a Biblical prophet (Maxim Gorky, who read him in Jabotinsky's Russian translations, called him a "modern Jeremiah"), he was emphatic in dismissing his public role, echoing the prophet Amos: "I am no prophet, no poet,/ But a chopper of wood." His cynicism about writing of Zion is put frankly: "When you see me weeping for some wondrous land ... do not mourn or comfort me, my tears are false." He twice removed the poem containing these lines from his *Collected Poems*.

His friendship with Joseph Klausner, who later became professor of Hebrew Literature at the Hebrew University, was undermined by this ambivalence. "As a poet," Klausner wrote, "Bialik did not take certain nationalist-Zionist obligations as seriously as I thought was right and proper for him."

AT THE TURN OF the century, the growth of Hebrew literature was unavoidably bound up with the rise of Jewish nationalism, so that a Hebrew writer was generally expected to write about national themes. Though in a remarkably short time there would be an eruption of Hebrew talent, in the 1890s (when Bialik began to publish verse) really original Hebrew poetry was scarce. In fact, not long beforehand, Judah Leib Gordon, the best Hebrew poet of his generation, had lamented that he might be the last Hebrew poet. By becoming the first great artist in modern Hebrew, Bialik automatically became a cultural hero, with accompanying responsibilities. The guilt that these responsibilities brought upon him was exacerbated by his close relationship with Ahad Ha'am, the foremost philosopher of cultural Zionism, who exerted a dominant influence upon him, and whom he loved as a father. Ahad Ha'am, worried about the future of Zionism, called upon Hebrew writers to forgo free creativity and to harness their energies to the national cause. Whether Ahad Ha'am's influence stunted Bialik's creative growth is debatable; but after the philosopher moved from Odessa to London in 1906 Bialik's poetry became increasingly overt in its biographical content. His last poem, written shortly before his death, has not a trace of nationalism.

BIALIK HAD NO AMBITIONS to become a national institution, but this is exactly what happened in his lifetime. He shunned the idea of being celebrated by the people, and suffered acute self-reproach over his status as national poet, feeling it to be undeserved. His first visit to Palestine, in 1909, started a wave of Bialik-mania; and to his disgust he was mobbed by crowds of enthusiasts who saw him as their prophet of revival. The Chief Rabbi of Palestine, Abraham Isaac Kook, set the tone for his reception, greeting him rapturously in the name of the people:

"Sing from now, O poet beloved unto us, of the salvation of a people and its God, waken your harp. Be filled with the power and beauty to sing for us a song of the land, a song of rebirth."

To his wife, Bialik wrote from Jaffa, "The people regard me as someone worthy of respect, but I

41

know that I am nothing, a nobody." The international fanfare which went on at the time of his 50th birthday weighed similarly on his conscience. He wrote at that time, "My spirit is bowed to the dust/ Under the yoke of your love"; and he complained, with bitter humour, that he was used as a coin vulgarly jangling in the national coinbox. His view of his poetry as illegitimate offspring, "hybrid children of mixed seed . . . fruit of harlotry", might, among other things, reflect his guilt at writing personal poetry mistakenly thought to be national.

To all appearances, however, Bialik played the role of national poet to the hilt. His best poetry, written mostly in Odessa in the years 1900–1911, was "national" both in its enormous impact upon the Jews and, to some degree, in its intent. His poetic genius and rare knowledge of Hebrew sources, gained through his Talmudic education, thrust him into the vanguard of Jewish writers who believed that if the nation was to be resurrected the language would have to be revived. He was adulated accordingly. The emotional climate which he helped to create was a windfall for political Zionism. Many Jews, raised to believe in the holiness of Israel and the Hebrew language, were as much under his spell as under that of Theodor Herzl.

BIALIK WROTE in an age of tragic social upheaval. The assassination of Czar Alexander II in 1881 had proved disastrous to the Russian Jews. It worsened their confinement in the Pale of Settlement and their severe economic restrictions, and it drove them in vast numbers to escape—to America, to Palestine, or through revolution. With immense poetic energy, unmistakably reminiscent of the style and tone of the Biblical prophets, Bialik seemed to convey not only the desperation which drove millions of Russian Jews to emigrate, but the burden of Jewish suffering in history.

As our voices entreating lift into the
                                darkness—
Whose ear will turn?
As our raw blasphemy streams to heaven—
Over whose crown will it trickle?
Grinding tooth, knuckling ire-veined fists—
On whose scalp will the fury drift?
All will fall   windily
Down the throat of chaos;
No comfort remains, no helping hand,
                                no way out—
And heaven is dumb;
Murdering us with dispassionate eyes,
Bearing its blame in blood-torn silence.

After the murderous Kishinev pogrom in 1903, Bialik was driven to write "The City of Slaughter", the poem which cemented his reputation as national poet. He was barely 30 years old. No other modern Hebrew poem has stirred up such a public outcry in the Jewish world. It is the only poem of Bialik's which, in the aftermath of the Holocaust, has the ring of prophecy Yet for all its power to inspire national outrage, the poem is grotesquely dependent for its artistic success upon Bialik's uniquely personal stress. Moving like a funeral procession, the poem tells, at times with nauseating detail, of a journey into hell, revisiting the scenes of violence, the streets and yards stained with blood, the vandalised houses, the cellars where women were raped and their children murdered. The explosion of sarcasm and bitterness to which this leads at the end of the poem has for its target the cowardly, parasitical survivors who roused Bialik's ire for using this national tragedy to elicit sympathy and funds for themselves:

Away, you beggars, to the charnel-house!
The bones of your father disinter!
Cram them into your knapsacks, bear
Them on your shoulders, and go forth
To do your business with these precious
                                wares
At all the country fairs!

(tr. A. M. Klein)

BIALIK'S chastisement, while it makes for extraordinary poetry—and shook the Jewish people in a way that they needed at the time—does not do justice to the historical facts. Bialik had been sent to Kishinev by Jews in Odessa to find out exactly what had happened, and to write a report. He knew at first hand, therefore, that the pogrom was as severe as it was precisely because some Jews did take up arms and defend themselves; yet in the poem there is no mention of this. The opportunists who so infuriated Bialik were a minority, and their unheroic conduct did not warrant the emphasis which Bialik gives it.

An explanation of these distortions is that Bialik, perhaps unconsciously, identified himself with these *schnorrers* as he does elsewhere: his indignation with them for using national tragedy for personal aims might partly have been a displaced form of self-chastisement for doing the same thing. In one of his poems, God chooses him to be a *schnorrer*-prophet: "Go round from door to door, knapsack on shoulder, go to the doors of generous men, bend down for a scrap of bread."

Even in poetry which appears to express fierce nationalism, the mark of a troubled personality is found. Bialik's central achievement, *The Scroll of Fire*, begins with a spectacular account of the ruin of the Temple in Jerusalem, but abandons national catastrophe to confess the ruin of one man, apparently the poet himself, by the fire of passion.

On Rereading Bialik

THE HEBREW READING PUBLIC tended to overlook the idiosyncratic aspects of Bialik's art. The lopsided view of him was strengthened by his reputation as a political and cultural figure. He was one of the most influential Zionist leaders, frequently attending their congresses, and going on fund-raising missions. He was also an important man in Hebrew publishing, and in the field of Jewish education was looked upon as a pre-eminent authority. He co-edited the legends and folklore of the Talmud in the mammoth *Sefer HaAggadah*, an achievement comparable in its way with what William Butler Yeats did for Irish folk literature and myths. Together with these activities, Bialik produced some of the loveliest children's poems in Hebrew, and over a hundred of his lyrics have been set to music. Bialik, in short, had a charismatic appeal to everyone, from distinguished philosophers to small children learning to read Hebrew, and to everyone he spoke in his own language. Few poets have had such success as spokesman of a nation, the representative of its cultural life and hopes.[1]

To modern Israelis, Bialik is still the national poet *par excellence*, a classic who is highly praised and seldom read carefully. Amos Elon, in his book on *The Israelis* (1971), writes that "None before Bialik nor after has expressed the Jewish will to live in words and rhymes of such beauty and poetic force; he is rightly known today as the national poet of Israel." Clichés such as these are typical of the literature on Bialik. They reflect the popular response to him as the servant of a cause rather than to the content of his work. Jewish nationalists naturally saw in his poetry what was most meaningful to them. The most influential of Bialik's "national" poems, "The City of Slaughter", is known to have inspired the formation of Jewish defence groups in East European towns; but the poem itself is pessimistic to the point of despair. Bialik's mature poetry has little of the "will to live" for which he is commemorated in the traditional stereotype. Quite the opposite is true. In one of his morbid poems, the poet considers ways in which he might die, including suicide:

"... perhaps through my very hunger and thirst for life and its pleasantness, with disgust of soul, braving the fury of the Creator, I will kick at his gift, and cast my life at his feet, like a defiled shoe torn from the foot."

To his friend Ben Ami, Bialik wrote in 1907: "Sometimes I feel like committing suicide—and I am too idle to do this good thing.... What difference if I live?"

BIALIK'S ART, like that of T. S. Eliot, was taken up by a movement which preferred to ignore—or remained ignorant of—the private, psychological reasons for writing, necessarily giving it instead a predominantly socio-political interpretation. Eliot's profession of the need for art to be impersonal did not stop him from disavowing the social import of *The Waste Land* which critics had read into it: "To me it was only the relief of a personal and wholly insignificant grouse against life."

And yet, it is not always undesirable to be misread. Bialik was fascinated, as Eliot was, by the subtleties of revelation, concealment, and deception in language—knowing, as Eliot put it, that "there may be personal causes which make it impossible for a poet to express himself in any but an obscure way." In an essay dealing with "Revelation and

---

[1] The standard, though unfinished, biography is in Hebrew: F. Lachower, *C. N. Bialik: His Life and Work* (Tel Aviv, 1950). A summary in English of Bialik's life and work is contained in the *Encyclopaedia Judaica*.
Translations of Bialik's work are mostly out of date. They include *Aftergrowth and Other Stories*, tr. I. M. Lask (Philadelphia, 1939); *Poetic Works of H. N. Bialik*, ed. Israel Efros (New York, 1948). Selections can be found in *The Modern Hebrew Poem Itself*, ed. Stanley Burnshaw et al. (New York, 1965); and in *Modern Hebrew Poetry*, tr. Ruth Finer-Mintz (Berkeley, 1968).
Articles on Bialik in English include: David Patterson, in *The Foundations of Modern Hebrew Literature* (London, 1960); Mary Catherine Bateson, "A Riddle of Two Worlds: An Interpretation of the Poetry of H. N. Bialik", *Daedalus*, No. 95 (1966); Hayim Greenberg, "A Day with Bialik", in Marie Syrkin, ed., *Hayim Greenberg Anthology* (Detroit, 1968); Robert Alter, "The Kidnapping of Bialik and Tchernichovsky" in *After the Tradition* (New York, 1969); Leon Yudkin, "The Quintessence of H. N. Bialik's Poetry and its Significance", in *Escape into Siege* (London, 1974); David Aberbach, "Screen Memories of Freud, Bialik and Wordsworth", *Midstream*, October 1979.

CHAIM NACHMAN BIALIK

Concealment in Language", Bialik put forward the view that "language in all its forms does not reveal its inner meaning . . . but serves as a partition, hiding it." The persona of national poet was a convenient stay against over-inquisitiveness into his buried life. He writes in a late poem:

> "Therefore he reveals himself, to be invisible and to deceive you. In vain you search the recesses of his verses—these too but cover his hidden thoughts. . . ."

While the excessive veneration for Bialik led him to feel misunderstood, and even perhaps restricted artistically, he might have been thankful at times to hide beneath the protective mantle of National Poet. A British psychiatrist, the late D. W. Winnicott, found the same dilemma in all artists: "the urgent need to communicate and the still more urgent need not to be found. . . ."

The disparity between Bialik's openness as a public man and the hidden burden of his private life—the mainspring of his art—was sensed by a few of his acquaintances. "Bialik seemed always to be publicly revealed like a great open book", wrote the poet Isaac Lamdan shortly after his death.

> "Few sensed that behind this openness gaped the depths upon whose banks the poet walked unseen. Few felt the hidden molten restlessness bubbling and fermenting deep inside this strong-seeming poet. Like foaming bubbles floating on the water which hint at a great tumult within, this restiveness showed in his physical nervousness, his speech, his facial distortions, his occasional heavy silences, the sudden depressed look on his face. . . . Even when he was alive, we hardly knew anything about Bialik's hidden life. What do we know now?"

BIALIK KNEW BETTER THAN anyone that his emotional instability—and the art which issued from it—was largely a product of childhood trauma. Born in the Ukrainian town of Radi, Bialik was the son of a timber merchant whose business failed by the time the future poet was five years old. His mother, to whom he was strongly attached, was known for her wailing at funerals, a highly emotional and pious woman, troubled by the death of her first husband. The family moved to the nearby village of Zhitomir to start a new life, and the father set up as a tavern-owner (Bialik remembered him at this time studying *Mishna* while drunkards staggered in and out). Soon after, he fell ill and died, leaving three children. Bialik was about seven at the time.

Then occurred a blow comparable in its traumatic effect to Dickens' experience in the blacking factory. Bialik's distraught mother, having to go to work, was unable to care for him, so he was taken to live with his grandparents in an outlying suburb Bialik was haunted by this memory to the end of his days, and although his mother was blameless, he could not help but feel betrayed. The death of his father and the forced separation from his mother—far more than the rise of Jewish nationalism—were the motivating forces and the focal points of his later life as an artist. Bialik's unease at being thought a "national poet" can be attributed partly to his awareness of the importance of these personal factors in his creative life.

Bialik was never reconciled to his father's death, and continually felt the ill effects of having missed the benevolent yoke of fatherly discipline and motherly love. At the age of 50 (in a conversation with the Zionist leader Hayim Greenberg), he confessed that he thought of himself as "an orphan who believes that a father does exist and that he might put in an appearance at any moment . . . this stems from weak nerves, from a certain ailment in the nervous system." Many years earlier he had written:

> "If only my father had lived, if only I had grown on his knees . . . he would have educated me in his way, according to my abilities. He would have taught me: this is the way for you to go and I would not have torn into ten pieces, my steps would have been sure on this chosen path, I would have had a settled mind, a man among men, knowing his worth and his place, happy and successful all his days. But because my father died and I was raised by my grandfather, my education was passed into the hands of strangers and my defeat was entire."

Bialik was in a life-long search for a father-substitute, such as Ahad Ha'am, and he projected his feeling of orphanhood on to his generation. In a commemoration of Ahad Ha'am in 1933, Bialik spoke emotionally of the absence of a strong leader (Weizmann, Ben Gurion, and Jabotinsky were then in their prime):

> "The generation which has no man to impose upon it his fearful authority—is an orphaned generation."

Bialik's life with his aged grandparents was restricted and puritanical, duty took the place of creative living, and inspiration was stifled. He was vulnerable to the onslaughts of relatives who had a notion of how to "civilise" the boy. He remembered with especial disgust the torture of religious life which his grandfather imposed upon him, the endless learning equated with virtue, the *Talmud*, *Mishna*, Bible, the Zohar, the prayers each day,

> "a hundred blessings, bundle after bundle of *mitzvot* [commandments], and the minutiae of *mitzvot*, and the minutiae of the minutiae from the day the Lord created the *Chumash* [Pentateuch] until the last book of laws or ethics

was written down. . . . And all this labour the Jew is obliged to undertake, is forced to carry out, is not free to be rid of and escape from, even for one hour."

This side-effect of his family's break-up was secondary to the great tragedy of his adult life—his childlessness—which cannot be ignored in attempting to understand his writing. Whatever the reasons for his infertility (which his poetry constantly hints at), there is no doubt that he dearly wanted a child. The curator of the Bialik Museum in Tel Aviv, a close friend of Bialik toward the end of the poet's life, has told me, "You have no idea how much he wanted children. He was hungry for children. . . ." In one conversation Bialik recalled a 5-year-old girl who had travelled with them on a train (at that time there was talk of his being nominated for a Nobel Prize): "I can't get this girl out of my thoughts . . . if that German woman were to give me little Elsa, I'd gladly renounce all the Nobel Prizes in this world and the hereafter in the next. Let Klausner proclaim someone else as the greatest Hebrew poet. . . ." Of the world from which Bialik came, Maurice Samuel has written: "Childlessness was the great frustration . . . it was a dreadful thing for a Jew to die without leaving behind at least one son to say *Kaddish* for him at the appointed time."

B IALIK'S ORPHANHOOD and separation from his mother are related in various prose fragments, and in the poems "On An Autumn Day", "My Poetry", and *Orphanhood*. "My Poetry" purports to be a confession of the emotional sources of his poetry, particularly the period between his father's death and his removal to his grandfather's house. According to this poem his mother would labour in the market during the day and at home until midnight. At dawn she got up to bake bread: "And my heart knows that her tears fell into the dough. In the morning, when she cut the warm bread, salty with tears, and I swallowed it, her sighs entered my bones. . . ." Bialik never forgot the poverty of this period of his mother's degradation; he indicated that his endeavours for literary success were attempts to ensure that he would never know such poverty again. *Orphanhood*, Bialik's last poem, is the longest and most impassioned account of this troubled period. Comparing himself in his suffering to the fathers of the three main religions, he emphasises the universality of his tragedy: he is not only Isaac on the verge of being sacrificed, but also Ishmael abandoned by his mother, and Christ crucified.

One of the likely effects of his orphanhood was the heightening of his response to the natural world, finding in it some of the attributes of parental love and care, and the paradisal emblem of the lost time before his father's death. There are startling similarities between his poetry of childhood and that of William Wordsworth, who also suffered orphanhood and the complete disruption of his family at the age of seven (and also passed into the care of grandparents with whom he was miserably unhappy). In his semi-biographical prose-poem, *Aftergrowth*, Bialik writes of the language of nature, comparing it to the love which silently radiates from a mother to her child, constituting his bond with external reality:

"There was no speech and no words—only a vision. Such utterance as there was came without words or even sounds. It was a mystic utterance, especially created, from which all sound had evaporated, yet which still remained. Nor did I hear it with my ears, but it entered my soul through another medium. In the same way a mother's tenderness and loving gaze penetrate the soul of her baby, asleep in the cradle, when she stands over him anxious and excited—and he knows nothing." *(tr. David Patterson)*

The same idea is found in Wordsworth's *The Prelude*:

. . . blest the Babe
Nursed in his Mother's arms, who sinks to sleep
Upon his mother's breast; who, with his soul
Drinks in the feelings of his Mother's eye! . . .
Along his infant veins are interfused
The gravitation and the filial bond
Of Nature that connect him with the world.

Separation from the mother or, in Wordsworth's case, her death, seems to have created in both poets the need for a mystic bond with the natural world, a bond so strong that even inanimate objects would appear to have the breath of life:

There exists a silent immanent language, a
secret tongue,
It has no sound, syllable, only shades of hues:
Enchantments, splendid pictures, hosts of visions.
In this tongue God makes himself known to
those his spirit chooses,
It is the language of images revealed
In a strip of blue sky and in its expanse,
In the purity of small silver clouds and in their
dark mass,
In the tremor of golden wheat, in the pride of
mighty cedars,
In the rustle of a dove's pure wing
And in the eagle-wing's sweep . . .
In the roar of light, in the rumble of sea flaming
With sunrises and sunsets.
(tr. Ruth Finer-Mintz)

This language of natural beauty through which God communicates with his chosen ones is remarkably like that of the "sense sublime" in Wordsworth's "Tintern Abbey":

> *And I have felt*
> *A presence that disturbs me with the joy*
> *Of elevated thoughts; a sense sublime*
> *Of something far more deeply interfused,*
> *Whose dwelling is the light of setting suns,*
> *And the round ocean and the living air,*
> *And the blue sky....*

THE BOND with natural objects carried over from the bond with the mother appears to have been an integral factor in the development of the imagination. Bialik writes that as a child he was always imaginatively "entering" objects such as trees or stones. In one such anecdote in which he "enters" the stove mouth, his mother pulls him in. Wordsworth's similar tendencies to incorporate himself within natural objects and his self-confessed need to convince himself of their reality might also be attributed in part to the loss of his mother and the uncertainties aroused by this loss; for as he told Isabella Fenwick,

> "...I was often unable to think of external things as having external existence, and I communed with all that I saw as something not apart from, but inherent in, my own immaterial nature, Many times while going to school have I grasped at a wall or tree to recall myself from this abyss of idealism to the reality. At that time I was afraid of such processes."

In writing of early childhood, though in a somewhat idealised way, both poets were engaged in a form of self-analysis, as if in creative response to the trauma of loss. The poetry of childhood might also have been an expression of a desire for children. After Wordsworth's first legitimate daughter was born, in 1803, he practically stopped writing about childhood; Bialik returned to this theme for the rest of his life. Most of the poetry which he wrote during his last quarter-century was for children, and he poured into this work the love which he wanted to give to children of his own: "I will arise and go to the children, playing innocently by the gate, I will mix in their company, learn their talk and chatter—and become pure from their breath, wash my lips in their cleanliness." But his poetry for children is no escape, for Bialik cannot suppress the themes of longing and deprivation which permeate his other poems. In some children's poems these themes are presented even more starkly:

> *How shall I enter the gates*
> *Of the treasured land,*
> *If my key is broken,*
> *And the door is locked?*

Or, in another poem:

> *In a corner, widower and orphan—*
> *A pale lulav, an ethrog with cut stem.*

> *...My garden is ruined, its stalks crushed,*
> *Its ways untrodden.*

The infertile landscape in Bialik's poetry, as in that of T. S. Eliot, might be the metaphoric landscape of his own infertility: the desert, the dry tree, the ruin, thunder without rain, melancholy in spring, the loss of hope and desire for death which accompany these images and others might reflect the emotional state of being childless In one of Bialik's poems, the theme of "April is the cruellest month" is particularly striking:

> *Spring will sprout once more, and I,*
> *Upon my bough I'll hang in grief—*
> *A sceptre bald, no flower his, nor blossom,*
> *No fruit, no leaf.*

Elsewhere, too, the comparison with a dry tree is found: "... a root of dust, a withered flower ... a single nest of thorns and thistles, an empty shell, at my loins the staff of an oppressor—is this the tree of life?" Bialik's prose and poetry are filled with imagery of this sort. The same imagery—the "dead tree", the tree "crookt and dry", the "withered tree", the "land of barren boughs", the "hollow tree"—is found frequently in the works of T. S. Eliot. *Ash Wednesday* contains the image of being cut off from fertility:

> *...I know I shall not know*
> *The one veritable transitory power*
> *...I cannot drink*
> *There, where trees flower and springs flow ...*

B IALIK'S WRITINGS both illuminate and are illuminated by the works of Eliot. Bialik's constant use of the landscape of ruin and waste land found in Jewish legend and history—the destruction of the Temple (*The Scroll of Fire*); the wanderings of the Israelites in the wilderness (*Aftergrowth*); the impotent Israelite warriors stranded in the desert (*The Dead of the Wilderness*); the quest beginning and ending by a ruin to bring the Messiah ("King David in his Tomb")—may have symbolic significance in the same way as Eliot's use in *The Waste Land* of the story of the impotent Fisher King, the quest for the Holy Grail, and the desert journey to Emmaus with the resurrected Christ: these legends and stories might, on one level, point to the infertility of the poet, and his desire for and failure to achieve sexual rebirth.

Most of the main elements in *The Waste Land* point to an anguished obsession with infertility, and the entire poem revolves around the equation of fertile land with potency. The Fisher King, to take the most notorious example, has suffered a sexual wound which has a homoeopathic effect on the land, making it barren. Eliot's fascination with

Greek drama—the fragment "Sweeney Agonistes" is a brilliant imitation of Aristophanes—seems to have a lot to do with the idea made popular by Cambridge anthropologists such as Jessie Weston and Francis Cornford that the aim of this drama was to promote fertility.

The underlying theme of childlessness breaks into the open only in *The Confidential Clerk*, one of Eliot's late plays, written in the 1950s. Although each of the older characters has had a child, every one is, in a sense, childless. Two of them do not even know that they have children; another has lost his son in battle; yet another has pretended not to be a parent. At the beginning of the play, Sir Claude Mulhammer explains to his retiring clerk, Eggerson, that his new clerk, Colby Simpkins, is to be introduced to his wife, Lady Elizabeth, as "Mr Simpkins", not as "Colby":

SIR CLAUDE: The reason for meeting him as
merely Mr Simpkins,
Is, that she has a strong maternal
instinct....
EGGERSON: I realise that.
SIR CLAUDE: Which has always been thwarted.
EGGERSON: I'm sure its been a grief to both of
you
That you've never had children.

His childlessness has induced in Sir Claude an overwhelming feeling of having failed in life, despite his worldly success. He would have liked to be a potter, and his yearning to create "life itself" out of china or porcelain transparently reveals a desire for children:

... nothing *I* made ever gave me that
contentment—
That state of utter exhaustion and peace
Which comes in dying to give something life....

Valerie Eliot, the poet's second wife, has said that her husband was a naturally paternal man who should have had a large family. In spite of his phenomenal achievement and fame, he was afflicted at the end of his life by a strong sense of failure and disappointment. Precisely the same things have been said about Bialik, with the explanation that his childlessness caused him a massive feeling of inferiority. This attitude is evident in the mood of negation in the writings of both poets. The words "not" or "nothing" are frequent. Bialik, for example, writes that he is "a nothing, a nobody", he is "no prophet, no poet", "I have nothing but a frightened soul"; and Eliot turns away from ordinary life, "I cannot hope to turn again", to the belief that one must "go by a way wherein there is no ecstasy."

BIALIK AND ELIOT are part of a long literary tradition of using imagery of vegetable infertility to symbolise childlessness. The childless man and the dry tree are linked in the Biblical verse, "Neither let the eunuch say: 'Behold I am a dry tree'" (*Isaiah* lvi 3). Macbeth uses similar imagery in speaking of his childlessness: "Upon my head they placed a fruitless crown." D. H. Lawrence, in *Lady Chatterley's Lover*, has the impotent Clifford Chatterley confess the torment of his childlessness in a ruined wood, with "long sawn stumps showing their tops and their grasping roots, lifeless." He says: "I mind more, not having a son, when I come here, than any other time."

Predicate thinking of this sort is found in Bialik's extraordinary sensitivity to images of ruin and infertility, a characteristic which struck the poet Ya'akov Fichman: "Each time that he saw the slightest sign of ruin in the fence or a dry branch on a tree he was extremely troubled by the sight...." He wrote these lines after seeing a broken branch:

Like the twig that falls across the gate,
Sleep comes to me:
My fruit has fallen, what helps me now
My branch or tree?

One source of Eliot's creative impulse was a similar vulnerability to images like these. When he visited Burnt Norton in the 1930s and later wrote a poem with that title, he seems to have been moved specifically by the dry pool, the empty house, and the children playing in the garden—"What might have been and what has been"—as objective correlatives of his childlessness. Imagery such as this, expressed with great pessimistic authority, could be (and often was) taken to reflect the barrenness of a society, urgently in need of change.

AN ANALYSIS of the themes of bereavement and infertility in Bialik's writings, while making clearer his significance as a deeply personal artist of universal interest, does nothing to diminish his stature as a national poet. In fact, his mesmeric national appeal can be attributed partly to this side of his work, which seems, on the surface, to have the least to do with Jewish nationalism. The great blows to Jewish nationhood have traditionally been expressed in imagery of bereavement and infertility, and in a tone of loss remarkably like that in Bialik's poetry. Bialik's longing for his childhood and for his mother (who while still alive was, nevertheless, out of reach) seems to have corresponded with the national longing for Zion, for the imaginary lost paradise of the nation's childhood, for a land which, like the mother, still existed, but seemed equally beyond reach. Partly for this reason, he spoke to his "orphaned generation" with particular conviction.

The personal equivalent of the loss of the national homeland is bereavement, for a bereaved person, especially an orphan deprived of a secure home, knows most intimately the resulting confusions, the instability, and the terrors. Already in the Book of *Ezekiel* the tragedy of the individual and of the nation are symbolic of each other: the death of the prophet's wife both represents and is represented by the destruction of the Temple and the fall of Judah. Not surprisingly, the greatest Hebrew poet of Zion before Bialik, Judah Halevi, also suffered bereavement in early childhood.

The imagery of infertility is also found in traditional depictions of national calamity. In the Bible, the fall of the kingdoms of Israel and Judah is described in images of barren fields and vineyards, rotten fruit, leaves, and roots. In the Book of *Ezekiel*, the fall of Judah is related both in imagery of infertility and bereavement:

> "Your mother was like a vine in a vineyard transplanted by the water.... But the vine was plucked up in fury, cast down to the ground; the east wind dried it up; its fruit was stripped off, its strong stem was withered; the fire consumed it."

Bialik chastens the people, using the same epithets with which he chastises himself: they are dry as a tree, withered like grass, immobile, useless, rotten from head to foot.

One of the persistent themes in Jewish liturgy is the yearning to renew the days gone by, a motif prominent in Bialik's poetry of childhood. The hope for national renewal, for "a new heart and a new spirit", dates from the time of the exile of the Israelite nation by the Babylonians—when it became politically impotent and spiritually an orphan. Bialik occasionally, though not frequently, identified the nation's hopes as his own:

> "My might is that of the nation, I too have power enough! In open spaces set free my imprisoned strength! From the smell of the field the impoverished nation will blossom, and bones that decayed shall flower like grass."

Elsewhere, the poet imagines himself cutting out his heart and hammering it, filling it with new strength. For the most part, a halo of sadness and pain hovers over Bialik's work. The hope for the renewal of the self—as of the nation—is defeated.

MORE CLEARLY THAN most poets, Bialik bears out Lionel Trilling's contention that "the elements of art are not limited to the world of art ... anything we may learn about the artist himself may be enriching and legitimate."

Bialik is the principal subject of his poetry, a Romantic tormented by what he had lost in life and could never regain. In life-long mourning for his childhood, he spoke meaningfully to a people in perpetual mourning for its lost nationhood. The elegiac tone of his poetry is that of the Jewish people in exile. Bialik's private agony mirrored national trauma in such an extraordinary way that the two became intertwined and inextricably linked in the poetry.

Bibliography

Aberbach, David (1981) 'On Re-reading Bialik: Paradoxes of a "National Poet"', *Encounter* 56, 6: 41–8.
Aberbach, David (1982) 'Loss and Separation in Bialik and Wordsworth', *Prooftexts* 2: 197–208.
Aberbach, David (1984) 'Loss and Dreams', *International Review of Psycho-Analysis* II, 4: 383–98.
Aberbach, David (1988) *Bialik*. London: Peter Halban and Weidenfeld & Nicolson. New York: Grove Press.
Aberbach, David (1989) *Surviving Trauma: Loss, Literature and Psychoanalysis*. New Haven and London: Yale University Press.
Aberbach, David (1993) *Imperialism and Biblical Prophecy*. London: Routledge.
Aberbach, David (1994) 'Aggadah and Childhood Imagination in Mendele, Bialik, and Agnon', in *Festschrift* for David Patterson, *Jewish Education and Learning*, Glenda Abramson and Tudor Parfitt (eds.). Chur, Switzerland: Harwood Academic Publishers.
Aberbach, David (1995) 'Charisma and Attachment Theory: A Crossdisciplinary Interpretation', *International Journal of Psycho-Analysis* 76 (4): 845–855.
Aberbach, David (1996) *Charisma in Politics, Religion and the Media*. Basingstoke: Macmillan.
Aberbach, David (1997) 'Hebrew Literature and Jewish Nationalism in Tsarist Russia 1881–1917', *Nations and Nationalism* 3,1 (1997): 25–44.
Aberbach, David (1998) *Revolutionary Hebrew, Empire and Crisis*. Basingstoke: Macmillan.
Aberbach, David (2003) 'The Poetry of Nationalism', *Nations and Nationalism* 9, 3: 255–275.
Aberbach, David (2003a) 'Fanatic Heart: The Poetry of Uri Zvi Greenberg', *CCAR Journal*, Spring issue, 16–32.
Aberbach, David (2005) 'Nationalism and the Hebrew Bible', *Nations and Nationalism*, 11, 2: 223–242.
Aberbach, David (2007) 'Myth, History and Nationalism: Poetry of the British Isles', in *Nationalism and Ethnosymbolism*, A. S. Leoussi and S. Grosby (eds.). Edinburgh: Edinburgh University Press.
Aberbach, David (2008) 'Byron to D'Annunzio: From Liberalism to Fascism in National Poetry 1815–1920', *Nations and Nationalism*, 14 (3): 478–497.
Aberbach, David (2008a) *Jewish Cultural Nationalism: Origins and Influences*. New York and London: Routledge.
Aberbach, David (2010) 'The British Empire and Revolutionary National Poetry', *Nations and Nationalism* 16 (2): 220–239.

Aberbach, David (2012) 'European National Poetry, Islam, and the Defeat of the Medieval Church', *Nations and Nationalism* 18 (4): 603–623.

Aberbach, David (2013) *The European Jews, Patriotism and the Liberal State: A Study of Literature and Social Psychology*. London and New York: Routledge.

Aberbach, David (2013a) 'On Interdisciplinary Approaches to Literature and the Social Sciences', *Times Higher Education Supplement*, August 22, 2013.

Aberbach, David (2014) 'Shakespeare to Wordsworth: The Bible, Capitalism and the English Poor'. The Weatherhead Center, Harvard University.

Aberbach, Moshe, and David Aberbach (2000) *The Roman-Jewish Wars and Hebrew Cultural Nationalism*. Basingstoke: Macmillan.

Abrams, M.H. (1975, orig. 1953) *The Mirror and the Lamp: Romantic Theory and the Critical Tradition*. New York: Oxford University Press.

Akçam, Taner (2006, orig. 1999) *A Shameless Act: The Armenian Genocide and the Question of Turkish Responsibility*. P. Bessemer (tr.). Metropolitan Books, New York: Henry Holt and Company.

Alapuro, Risto (1988) *State and Revolution in Finland*. Berkeley: University of California Press.

Albanis, Elizabeth (2002) *German-Jewish Cultural Identity from 1900 to the Aftermath of the First World War*. Tübingen: Niemeyer.

Alexiou, Margaret (2002, orig. 1974) *The Ritual Lament in Greek Tradition*. 2nd ed. revised by D. Yatromanolakis and P. Roilos. Lanham, Maryland: Rowman & Littlefield.

Alexiou, Margaret (2002a) *After Antiquity: Greek Language, Myth, and Metaphor*. Ithaca and London: Cornell University Press.

Allen, Gay Wilson (1969, orig. 1955) *The Solitary Singer: A Critical Biography of Walt Whitman*. New York: New York University Press.

Alter, Robert (1977) *Defenses of the Imagination: Jewish Writers and Modern Historical Crisis*. Philadelphia, Pennsylvania: Jewish Publication Society of America.

Amichai, Yehuda (1975) *Poems: 1963–1968* (Hebrew). Tel Aviv: Schocken.

Anderson, Benedict (1991, orig. 1983) *Imagined Communities: Reflections on the Origins and Spread of Nationalism*. 2nd ed. Verso: London.

Andrić, Ivo (1977, orig. 1945) *The Bridge on the Drina*. L.F. Edwards (tr.). Chicago: University of Chicago Press.

Arberry, Arthur J. and P. Grech (eds.) (1961) *Dun Karm: Poet of Malta*. Cambridge: Cambridge University Press.

Arberry, Arthur J. (1964) *Aspects of Islamic Civilization*. London: Allen & Unwin.

Arberry, Arthur J. (1965) *Arabic Poetry: A Primer for Students*. Cambridge: Cambridge University Press.

Arberry, Arthur J. (1967) *Modern Arabic Poetry: An Anthology with English Verse Translations*. Cambridge: Cambridge University Press.

Ariosto, Lodovico (1975, orig. 1516, 1532) *Orlando Furioso, Part 1*. B. Reynolds (tr.). Harmondsworth, Middlesex: Penguin Classics.

Armstrong, John (1982) *Nations Before Nationalism*. Chapel Hill: University of North Carolina Press.

Árnason, Jóhann Páal, and Björn Wittrock (eds.) (2012) *Nordic Paths to Modernity*. New York and Oxford: Berghahn Books.

Ashton, Thomas L. (1972) *Byron's Hebrew Melodies*. London: Routledge & Kegan Paul.

Ashtor, Eliyahu (1973, 1979, 1984) *The Jews of Moslem Spain*, 3 vols. A. Klein and J.M. Klein (trs.). Philadelphia: Jewish Publication Society.
Atwan, Robert, and Laurance Wieder (eds.) (2000) *Chapters into Verse: A Selection of Poetry in English Inspired by the Bible from Genesis through Revelation.* Oxford: Oxford University Press.
Augustinos, Olga (1994) *French Odysseys, Greece in French Travel Literature from the Renaissance to the Romantic Era.* Baltimore and London: Johns Hopkins University Press.
Aurobindo, Sri (1942) *Collected Poems and Plays*, 2 vols. Pondicherry: Nolini Kanta Gupta, Sri Aurobindo Ashram.
Avineiri, Shlomo (1976) 'Political and Social Aspects of Israeli and Arab Nationalism' in E. Kamenka (ed.) *Nationalism: The Nature and Evolution of an Idea*, pp. 100–122. London: Edward Arnold.
Badawi. M.M. (1975) *A Critical Introduction to Arabic Poetry*. Cambridge: Cambridge University Press.
Baird, Jay W. (2008) *Hitler's War Poets: Literature and Politics in the Third Reich.* Cambridge: Cambridge University Press.
Baker, David J. (2001) 'Historical Contexts: Britain and Europe' in Andrew Hadfield (ed.) *The Cambridge Companion to Spenser*. Cambridge: Cambridge University Press.
Balakrishnan, Gopal (ed.) (1996) *Mapping the Nation*. London and New York: Verso.
Bancourt, Paul (1982) *Les Musulmans dans les Chansons de Geste du Cycle du Roi.* PhD dissertation. Université de Provence, Aix- en-Provence.
Baron, Salo (1952–) *A Social and Religious History of the Jews*, 18 vols. New York: Columbia University Press.
Bartlett, Robert (1993) *The Making of Europe: Conquest, Colonization and Cultural Change, 950–1350.* London and New York: Allen Lane, The Penguin Press.
Bartok, Bela, and Albert B. Lord (1951) *Serbo-Croatian Folk Songs*. New York: Columbia University Press.
Basa, Enikő Molnár (1980) *Sandór Petőfi*. Boston: Twayne.
Baycroft, Timothy (1998) *Nationalism in Europe, 1789–1945*. Cambridge: Cambridge University Press.
Beckett, Katharine Scarfe (2003) *Anglo-Saxon Perceptions of the Islamic World.* Cambridge: Cambridge University Press.
Bekaryan, Anahit (2004) 'Byron and Armenia: A case of mirrored affinities' in Richard Cardwell (ed.) *The Reception of Byron in Europe*, 2 vols. London and New York: Thoemmes Continuum II 386–405.
Beaton, Roderick, and David Ricks (eds.) (2009) *The Making of Modern Greece: Nationalism, Romanticism, & the Use of the Past.* Farnham, Surrey: Ashgate.
Bede (1968, orig. early 730s CE) *A History of the English Church and People.* L. Sherley-Price (tr.), R. E. Latham (revised). Harmondsworth, Middlesex: Penguin Classics.
Bharati, Subramania (1977) in P. Nandakumar (ed.). *Poems of Subramania Bharati.* New Delhi: Sahitya Akademi.
Bialik, Chaim Nachman (1960) *Shirim* (Poems in Hebrew). Tel Aviv: Dvir.
Bialik, Chaim Nachman (2004) *Bialik: A Bilingual Anthology*. D. Aberbach (ed. and tr.). New York: Overlook Press.

Bisaha, Nancy (2004) *Creating East and West: Renaissance Humanists and the Ottoman Turks*. Philadelphia, Pennsylvania: University of Pennsylvania Press.
Beer, Anna (2008) *Milton: Poet, Pamphleteer and Patriot*. London: Bloomsbury.
Bell, David A. (2007) *The First Total War: Napoleon's Europe and the Birth of Warfare as We Know It*. Boston and New York: Houghton Mifflin Company.
Benjamin, Walter (1999) *Illuminations*. H. Arendt (ed.), H. Zohn (tr.). London: Pimlico.
Bentwich, Norman (ed.) (1952) *Hebrew University Garland*. London: Constellation Books.
Ben Yehuda, Nachman (1995) *The Masada Myth: Collective Memory and Mythology in Israel*. Madison, Wisconsin: University of Wisconsin Press.
Berghaus, Gunter (1995) *The Genesis of Futurism: Marinetti's Early Career and Writings 1899–1909*. Leeds: The Society for Italian Studies.
Berlin, Isaiah (1996) *The Sense of Reality: Studies in Ideas and Their History*. London: Chatto & Windus.
Bharati, Subramania (1977) *Poems of Subramania Bharati*. P. Nandakumar (ed. and tr.). New Delhi: Sahitya Akademi.
Bialik, C.N. (1983, 1990, 2000) *Collected Poems*, 3 vols. D. Miron, et al. (eds.). Dvir & Katz Research Institute for Hebrew Literature: Tel Aviv University.
Bialik, Chaim Nachman, and Joshua Hana Ravnitski (eds.) (1992, orig. 1908–11) *The Book of Legends (Sefer ha-Aggadah)*. W.G. Braude (tr.). New York: Schocken Books.
Bialik, Chaim Nachman (2004) *C.N. Bialik: Selected Poems*. D. Aberbach (ed. and tr.). New York: Overlook Press.
Bieber, Hugo (ed.) (1956) *Heinrich Heine: A Biographical Anthology*. M. Hadas (tr.). Philadelphia: The Jewish Publication Society of America.
Bilenki, Serhiy (2012) *Romantic Nationalism in Eastern Europe: Russian, Polish, and Ukrainian Political Imaginations*. Palo Alto: Stanford University Press.
Black, Stephen A. (1975) *Whitman's Journeys into Chaos: A Psychoanalytic Study of the Poetic Process*. Princeton, New Jersey: Princeton University Press.
Blanning, Tim (2010) *The Romantic Revolution*. London: Weidenfeld & Nicolson.
Bloom, Harold (1969, orig. 1959) *Shelley's Mythmaking*. Ithaca, New York: Cornell University Press.
Bold, Alan (ed.) (1970) *The Penguin Book of Socialist Verse*. Harmondsworth, Middlesex: Penguin Books.
Bosworth, R.J.B. (2002) *Mussolini*. London: Arnold.
Botev, Hristo (1974) *Poems*. T. Atanassova (ed.), K. Ireland (tr.). Sofia Press.
Boulton, W.F. (ed.) (1966) *The English Language: Essays by English & American Men of Letters 1490–1839*. Cambridge: Cambridge University Press.
Bowers, Fredson (ed.) (1969) *Whitman's Manuscripts: Leaves of Grass (1860), A Parallel Text*. Chicago and London: University of Chicago Press.
Bownas, Geoffrey, and Thwaite, Anthony (1998) *The Penguin Book of Japanese Verse*. Harmondsworth, Middlesex: Penguin Books.
Bowra, C.M. (1960) *Poetry and Politics*. Cambridge: Cambridge University Press.
Bowra, C.M. (1965, orig. 1945) *From Virgil to Milton*. London: Macmillan.
Bradford, Ernle (1979, orig. 1961) *The Great Siege: Malta, 1565*. Harmondsworth, Middlesex: Penguin Books.
Brann, Ross (1991) *The Compunctious Poet: Cultural Ambiguity and Hebrew Poetry in Muslim Spain*. Baltimore and London: Johns Hopkins University Press.

Breuilly, John (1993, orig. 1982) *Nationalism and the State*. 2nd ed. Manchester: Manchester University Press.
Brinton, Crane (1966, orig. 1926) *The Political Ideas of the English Romantics*. Ann Arbor, Michigan: University of Michigan Press.
Brooks, Chris, and Peter Faulkner (eds.) (1996) *The White Man's Burdens: An Anthology of British Poetry of the Empire*. Exeter: Exeter University Press.
Brown, Frederick (1996) *Zola: A Life*. London: Macmillan.
Brown, Judith M., Wm. Roger Louis, and Alaine Low (eds.) (1999) *The Oxford History of the British Empire, Vol. IV: The Twentieth Century*. Oxford and New York: Oxford University Press.
Brown, Terence (1981) *Ireland: A Social and Cultural History, 1922–1979*. London: Fontana.
Brown, Terence (2010) 'W.B. Yeats: Biographical Reflections' in E. Larrissey (ed.) *W.B. Yeats*. Dublin and Portland, Oregon: Irish Academic Press, ch. 2.
Brutus, Denis (1973) *A Simple Lust*. New York: Hill & Wang.
Burney, S.M.H. (1987) *Iqbal: Poet-Patriot of India*. S.S. Hameed (tr.). Delhi: Vikas.
Burnshaw, Stanley, Ezra Spicehandler, and T. Carmi (eds.) (1965) *The Modern Hebrew Poem Itself*. New York: Schocken Books.
Bushrui, Suheil and Joe Jenkins (1999) *Kahlil Gibran: Man and Poet*. Oxford: Oneworld.
Butterfield, Ardis (2009) *The Familiar Enemy: Chaucer, Language and Nation in the Hundred Years War*. Oxford: Oxford University Press.
Byron, George Gordon (1977) *Byron's Letters and Journals* Vol. 7. L. Marchand (ed.). London: John Murray.
Calligas, Eleni (2009) 'Radical Nationalism in the British Protectorate of the Ionian Islands (1815–1864)' in R. Beaton and D. Ricks (eds.) *The Making of Modern Greece: Nationalism, Romanticism, & the Use of the Past*. Farnham, Surrey: Ashgate.
Cameron, Norman, and R.H. Stevens (eds.) (1953) *Hitler's Secret Conversations, 1941–1944*. London: Weidenfeld & Nicolson.
Camões, Luis Vaz de (1997, orig. 1572) *The Lusiads*. L. White (tr.). Oxford and New York: Oxford University Press.
Carduner, Jean, Lucian Rosu, and Karl Natanson (eds.) (1986) *Mihai Eminescu: The Evening Star of Romanian Poetry*. Ann Arbor: University of Michigan, Department of Romance Languages.
Cardwell, Richard A. (ed.) (2004) *The Reception of Byron in Europe*. 2 vols. London and New York: Thoemmes Continuum.
Carmi, T. (ed.) (1981) *The Penguin Book of Hebrew Verse*. New York: Viking; Harmondsworth, Middlesex: Penguin Books.
Casanova, Pascale (2004, orig. 1999) *The World Republic of Letters*. M.B. De Bevoise (tr.). Cambridge, Massachusetts and London, England: Harvard University Press.
Castro-Klaren, Sara and John Charles Chasteen (2003) *Beyond Imagined Communities: Reading and Writing the Nation in Nineteenth-Century Latin America*. Baltimore and London: The Johns Hopkins University Press; Washington, D.C.: Woodrow Wilson Center.
Cavafy, C.P. (1984) *Collected Poems*. E. Keeley and P. Sharrard (tr.), G. Savides (ed.). London: The Hogarth Press.
Cell, John W. (1999) 'Colonial Rule' in J. M. Brown, W. R. Louis, and A. Low (eds.) *The Oxford History of the British Empire, Vol. IV: The Twentieth Century*, pp. 232–254. Oxford and New York: Oxford University Press.

Cervantes, Miguel de (1975, orig. 1604) *Don Quixote*. J. M. Cohen (tr.). Harmondsworth, Middlesex: Penguin Classics.
Césaire, Aimé (1969, orig. 1956) *Return to My Native Land (Cahier d'un Retour au Pays Natal)*. J. Berger and A. Bostock (trs.). Harmondsworth, Middlesex: Penguin Books.
Césaire, Aimé (1983, orig. 1956) *Cahier d'un Retour au Pays Natal*. Paris and Dakar: Présence Africaine.
Le Chanson de Roland (1989, orig. c. 1100) G. Moignet (ed. and tr.). Paris: Bordas.
Chaucer, Geoffrey (1972, orig. late 14th century) *The Canterbury Tales*. N. Coghill (tr.). Harmondsworth, Middlesex: Penguin Classics.
Cheney-Coker, Syl (1980) *The Graveyard Also Has Teeth*. London, Ibadan, Nairobi: Heinemann.
Churchill, Winston S. (2002, orig. 1956) *A History of the English-Speaking Peoples: Vol. 2: The New World*. London: Cassell.
Cleveland, William L. (1994) *A History of the Modern Middle East*. Boulder, Colorado: Westview Press.
Clogg, Richard (2002) *A Concise History of Greece*. 2nd ed. Cambridge: Cambridge University Press.
Coleridge, Samuel Taylor (1975, orig. 1817) *Biographia Literaria*. G. Watson (ed.). Everyman edition. London: J.M. Dent.
Colley, Linda (1992) *Britons: Forging the Nation 1707–1837*. New Haven and London: Yale University Press.
Connor, Walker 1994 *Ethno-Nationalism: The Quest for Understanding*. Princeton, New Jersey: Princeton University Press.
Conran, Anthony (ed. and tr.) (1967) *The Penguin Book of Welsh Verse*. Harmondsworth, Middlesex: Penguin Books.
Corse, Sarah M. (1997) *Nationalism and Literature: The Politics of Culture in Canada and the United States*. Cambridge: Cambridge University Press.
Crampton, R.J. (1997) *A Concise History of Bulgaria*. Cambridge: Cambridge University Press.
Crocco, Francesco (2014) *Literature and the Growth of British Nationalism: The Influence of Romantic Poetry and Bardic Criticism*. Jefferson, North Carolina: McFarland & Company.
Crone, Patricia and Michael Cook (1977) *Hagarism: The Making of the Islamic World*. Cambridge: Cambridge University Press.
Crowe, John A. (ed.) (1989) *An Anthology of Spanish Poetry: From the Beginnings to the Present Day*. Baton Rouge and London: Louisiana State University Press.
Cruz, J.A.H.M. (1999) 'Popular Attitudes towards Islam in Medieval Europe' in D.R. Blanks and M. Frassetto (eds.) *Western Views of Islam in Medieval and Early Modern Europe: Perception of Other*. New York: St. Martin's Press.
Crystal, David (2010) *Begat: The King James Bible and the English Language*. Oxford: Oxford University Press.
Csepeli, György, and Antal Örkény (1997) 'The Imagery of National Anthems in Europe', *Canadian Review of Studies in Nationalism* 24, 1–2: 33–41.
Cullingford, Elisabeth (1981) *Yeats, Ireland and Fascism*. London: Macmillan.
Currey, R.N., and R.V. Gibson (eds.) (1946) *Poems from India by Members of the Forces*. London: Oxford University Press.
Czigany, Lorant (1984) *The Oxford History of Hungarian Literature*. Oxford: Clarendon Press.

Daiches, David (1971) *Sir Walter Scott and His World*. London: Thames & Hudson.
Dakin, Douglas (1955) *British and American Philhellenes during the War of Greek Independence 1821–1833*. Thessalonika: Institute for Balkan Studies, Society for Macedonian Studies.
Dakin, Douglas (1973) *The Greek Struggle for Independence 1821–1833*. London: B.T. Batsworth.
Daniel, Norman (1993) *Islam and the West: The Making of an Image*. 2nd ed. Oxford: Oxford University Press.
Daniell, David (2003) *The Bible in English: Its History and Influence*. New Haven and London: Yale University Press.
D'Annunzio, Gabriele (1988, orig. 1903). *Halcyone*. J.G. Nichols (tr.). Manchester: Carcanet.
Dario, Rubén (1965) *Selected Poems*. L. Kemp (tr.). Austin: University of Texas Press.
Dario, Rubén (2005) *Selected Writings*. I. Stavans (ed.), A. Hurley, G. Simon and S.F. White (trs.). New York: Penguin.
Darwish, Mahmoud (2003) *Unfortunately, It Was Paradise*. M. Akash and C. Forché, et al. (eds. and trs.). Los Angeles and London: University of California Press.
Davies, Norman (1996) *Europe: A History*. Oxford: Oxford University Press.
Davis, Gregson (1997) *Aimé Césaire*. Cambridge: Cambridge University Press.
Demata, Massimilianio (2004) 'Byron, Turkey and the Orient' in Richard A. Cardwell (ed.) *The Reception of Byron in Europe*, 2 vols. London and New York: Thoemmes Continuum II 439–452.
Deutsch, Karl (1966) *Nationalism and Social Communication*. New York: MIT Press.
Dharwadaker, Vinay, and A.K. Ramanujan (eds.) (1999) *The Oxford Anthology of Modern Indian Poetry*. New Delhi: Oxford University Press.
Dharwadaker, Vinay (1999) 'Afterword: Modern Indian Poetry and Its Contexts' in V. Dharwadaker and A.K. Ramanujan (eds.) *The Oxford Anthology of Modern Indian Poetry*, pp. 185–206. New Delhi: Oxford University Press.
Diamandoupos, Nikiforos, et al. (eds.) *Hellenism and the First Greek War of Liberation (1821–1830): Continuity and Change*. Thessaloniki: Institute for Balkan Studies.
Dickens, A.G. (1970, orig. 1964) *The English Reformation*. London: Collins, The Fontana Library.
Dickinson, Margaret (ed. and tr.) (1972) *When Bullets Begin to Flower*. Nairobi: East Africa Publishing House.
Dijkstra, C. (1995) *La chanson du croisade: Etude thematique d'un genre ybride*. Amsterdam: Brinkman.
Diop, David Mandessi (1973) *Hammer Blows and Other Writings*. S. Mpondo and F. Jones (eds. and trs.). Bloomington and London: Indiana University Press.
Djilas, Milovan. (1966) *Njegoš: Poet, Prince, Bishop*. Michael B. Petrovich (tr.). New York: Harcourt, Brace & World.
Dodds, Jerrilyn Denise, et al. (2008) *The Arts of Intimacy: Christians, Jews and Muslims in the Making of Castilian Culture*. New Haven, Connecticut: Yale University Press.
Doggett, Rob (2006) *Deep-Rooted Things: Empire and the Nation in the Poetry and Drama of William Butler Yeats*. Notre Dame, Indiana: Notre Dame Press.
Edwards, Ruth Dudley (1977) *Patrick Pearse: The Triumph of Failure*. London: Gollancz.
Eisler, Brenda (1999) *Byron: Child of Passion, Fool of Fame*. London: Hamish Hamilton.

Elfyn, Menna and John Rowlands (eds.) (2003) *The Bloodaxe Book of Modern Welsh Poetry: 20th-century Welsh-Language Poetry in Translation*. Highgreen, Tarset, Northumberland: Bloodaxe Books.
Eliot, T.S. (1970, orig. 1933) *The Use of Poetry and the Use of Criticism*. London: Faber.
Eliot, T.S. (1976, orig. 1951) *Selected Essays*. London: Faber.
Elkins, Caroline (2005) *Imperial Reckoning: The Untold Story of Britain's Gulag in Kenya*. New York: Hanry Holt and Company.
Ellis Davidson, H.R. (1974, orig. 1964) *Gods and Myths of Northern Europe*. Penguin Books: Harmondsworth, Middlesex.
Ellmann, Richard (1969, orig. 1949), *Yeats: The Man and the Masks*, London: Faber.
Ellmann, Richard (1968, orig. 1954) *The Identity of Yeats*. London: Faber.
Elsie, Robert, and Janice Mathie-Heck (eds.) (2004) *Songs of the Frontier Warriors*. Wauconda, Illinois: Bolchazy-Carducci Publishers, Inc.
Elsie, Robert (2005) *Albanian Literature: A Short History*. London and New York: I.B. Tauris.
Elton, G.R. (1971, orig. 1963) *Reformation Europe 1517–1559*. London and Glasgow: Collins.
Eminescu, Mihai (1980) *Poems*. R. MacGregor-Hastie (tr.). Cluj-Napoca: Dacia Publishing House.
Erkkila, Betsy (1989) *Whitman the Political Poet*. New York and Oxford: Oxford University Press.
Erkkila, Betsy (2007) 'Whitman, Marx, and the American 1848' in S. Belasco, E. Folsom, & K.M. Price (eds.), *Leaves of Grass: The Sesquicentennial Essays*. Lincoln and London: University of Nebraska Press.
Eyck, G.G. (1995) *The Voice of Nations: European National Anthems and Their Authors*. Westport, Connecticut: Greenport.
Faiz Ahmed Faiz (1971) *Poems by Faiz*. V.G. Kiernan (tr.). London: Allen & Unwin.
Fanon, Frantz (1983, orig. 1961) *The Wretched of the Earth*. C. Farrington (tr.). Harmondsworth, Middlesex: Penguin.
Farrell, Nicholas (2004) *Mussolini: A New Life*. London: Phoenix.
Felice, Renzo de and Emilio Mariano (eds.) (1971) *Carteggio D'Annunzio-Mussolini (1919–1938)*. Vicenza: Mondadori.
Ferguson, Niall (2003) *Empire: How Britain Made the Modern World*. London: Allen Lane.
Figes, Orlando (2002) *Natasha's Dance: A Cultural History of Russia*. London: Penguin.
Fine, John V.A. Jr. (1987) *The Late Medieval Balkans: A Critical Survey from the Twelfth Century to the Ottoman Conquest*. Ann Arbor, Michigan: University of Michigan Press.
Finley, M.I. (1975) *The Use and Abuse of History*. London: Chatto & Windus.
Fisch, Harold (1964) *Jerusalem and Albion: The Hebraic Factor in Seventeenth-Century Literature*. New York: Schocken Books.
Fishta, Gjergj (2005) *The Highland Lute*. R. Elsie and J. Mathie-Heck (trs.). London and New York: I.B. Tauris.
Fletcher, Richard (2004) *The Cross and the Crescent*. London: Penguin Books
Foley, John Miles (2002) *How to Read an Oral Poem*. Urbana and Chicago: University of Illinois Press.
Folsom, Ed (2000) 'Lucifer and Ethiopia: Whitman, Race, and Poetics before the Civil War and After' in David S. Reynolds (ed.) *A Historical Guide to Walt Whitman*. New York and Oxford: Oxford University Press.

Foster, R.F. (1997, 2003) *W.B. Yeats. A Life.* 2 vols. Oxford: Oxford University Press.
Francis, Emerich (1968) 'The Ethnic Factor in Nation-Building', *Social Forces* 68: 338–46.
Frankel, Jonathan (1981) *Prophecy and Politics: Socialism, Nationalism, and the Jews, 1862–1917.* Cambridge: Cambridge University Press.
Frazee, Charles A. (1969) *The Orthodox Church and Independent Greece 1821–1852.* Cambridge: Cambridge University Press.
Freud, Sigmund (1939) *Moses and Monotheism* in The Standard Edition of the Collected Writings of Sigmund Freud, XXIII, pp. 7–137. J. Strachey (tr.). London: The Hogarth Press.
Frye, Northrop (2000, orig. 1957) *Anatomy of Criticism: Four Essays.* Princeton, New Jersey: Princeton University Press.
Gandhi, M.K. (1982, orig. 1927, 1929) *An Autobiography or The Story of My Experiments with Truth.* M. Desai (tr.). London: Penguin Books.
Garvin, Tom (1987) *Nationalist Revolutionaries in Ireland 1858–1928.* Oxford: Clarendon Press.
Gazi, Effi (2009) 'Revisiting Religion and Nationalism in Nineteenth-Century Greece' in R. Beaton and D. Ricks (eds.) *The Making of Modern Greece: Nationalism, Romanticism, & the Use of the Past.* Farnham, Surrey: Ashgate.
Geanakoplos, Deno J. (1976) 'The Diaspora Greeks: The Genesis of Modern Greek National Consciousness' in N.P. Diamandoupos, *et al.* (eds.) *Hellenism and the First Greek War of Liberation (1821–1830): Continuity and Change.* Thessaloniki: Institute for Balkan Studies.
Gellner, Ernest (1983) *Nations and Nationalism.* Oxford: Blackwell.
Gellner, Ernest (1996) 'Do Nations Have Navels?' *Nations and Nationalism* 2, 3: 366–370.
Gellner, Ernest (1996a) 'The Coming of Nationalism and Its Interpretation: The Myths of Nation and Class' in G. Balakrishnan (ed.) *Mapping the Nation.* London: Verso.
Gerolymatos, Andre (2001) *The Balkan Wars: Myth, Reality, and the Eternal Conflict.* Toronto: Stoddart.
George, Stefan (1958, 1968) *Werke.* 2 vols. Dusseldorf and Munich: Verlag Helmut Kupper vormals Georg Bondi.
Gérard, Albert S. (1970) *Four African Literatures.* Berkeley, Los Angles and London: University of California Ptress.
Gibran, Kahlil (1995) *The Voice of Khalil Gibran: An Anthology.* R. Waterfield (ed. and tr.). Arkana: Penguin Books.
Giddens, Anthony (1985) *The Nation-State and Violence.* Cambridge: Polity Press.
Giffen, Lois Anita (1971) *Theory of Profane Love Among the Arabs: The Development of the Genre*, New York: New York University Press; London: London University Press.
Gilbert, Martin (2010) *In Ishmael's House: A History of Jews in Muslim Lands.* New Haven and London: Yale University Press.
Gillingham, John (1992) 'The Beginnings of English Imperialism', *Journal of Historical Sociology* 5: 392–409.
Gilmour, David (2003, orig. 1994) *Curzon: Imperial Statesman 1859–1925.* London: John Murray.
Glick, Thomas (1979) *Islamic and Christian Spain in the Early Middle Ages*, Princeton, New Jersey: Princeton University Press.

Godman, Peter (1985) *Poetry of the Carolingian Renaissance*. London: Duckworth.
Goldmann, Lucien (1964, orig. 1956) *The Hidden God: A Study of Tragic Vision in the Pensees of Pascal and the Tragedies of Racine*. P. Thody (tr.). London: Routledge & Kegan Paul.
Goldstein, David (ed. and tr.) (1971) *The Jewish Poets of Spain*. Harmondsworth, Middlesex: Penguin Classics.
Goodall, Dominic (ed. and tr.) (1996) *Hindu Scriptures*. London: J.M. Dent.
Gordon, Judah Leib (1973) *Poems* (Hebrew). M. Mahker and D. Niger (eds.). Jerusalem and Tel Aviv: Schocken.
Graham, Colin (1998) *Ideologies of Fire: Nation, Empire and Victorian Epic Poetry*. New York: Manchester University Press.
Greenberg, Uri Zvi (1990–98) *Collected Works: Poems* (Hebrew). 13 vols. D. Miron, et al. (eds.). Jerusalem: Bialik Institute.
Greenfeld, Liah (1992) *Nationalism: Five Roads to Modernity*. Cambridge, Massachusetts: Harvard University Press.
Gregor, A. James (2005) *Mussolini's Intellectuals: Fascist Social and Political Thought*. Princeton New Jersey: Princeton University Press.
Griffin, Dustin (2002) *Patriotism and Poetry in Eighteenth Century Britain*. Cambridge: Cambridge University Press.
Grosby, Steven (1991) 'Religion and Nationality in Antiquity', *European Journal of Sociology* XXXII, pp. 229–65.
Grosby, Steven (1999) 'The Chosen People of Ancient Israel and the Occident: Why Does Nationality Exist and Survive?' *Nations and Nationalism* 5(3): 357–80.
Grunzweig, Walter (2006) "Imperialism" in D.D. Kummings (ed.) *A Companion to Walt Whitman*. Oxford: Blackwell.
Guibernau, Montserrat, and John Hutchinson (eds.) (2004) *History and National Destiny: Ethnosymbolism and Its Critics*. Oxford: Blackwell.
Haberly, David T. (1993) *Three Sad Races: Racial Identity and National Consciousness in Brazilian Literature*. Cambridge: Cambridge University Press.
Hagiioannu, Andrew (2003) *The Man Who Would Be Kipling: The Colonial Fiction and the Frontiers of Exile*. Basingstoke and New York: Palgrave Macmillan.
Hanagid, Shmuel (2000) *Grand Things to Write a Poem on: A Verse Autobiography of Shmuel Hanagid*. H. Halkin (tr. and ed.). Jerusalem and New York: Gefen.
Hastings, Adrian (1997) *The Construction of Nationhood: Ethnicity, Religion and Nationalism*. Cambridge: Cambridge University Press.
Hatzopoulos, Marios (2009) 'From Resurrection to Insurrection: 'Sacred' Myths, Motifs, and Symbols in the Greek War of Independence' in R. Beaton and D. Ricks (eds.) *The Making of Modern Greece: Nationalism, Romanticism, & the Use of the Past*. Farnham, Surrey: Ashgate.
Heine, Heinrich (1961–4) *Werke und Briefe*, 10 vols. H. Kaufmann (ed.). Berlin: Aufbau-Verlag.
Heine, Heinrich (1997, orig. 1844) *Deutschland: A Winter's Tale*. T.J. Reed. (ed. and tr.). London: Angel Books.
Herder, Johann Gottfried (1993) *Against Pure Reason: Writings on Religion, Language, and History*. Marcia Bunge (ed. and tr.). Minneapolis: Fortress Press.
Herder, Johann Gottfried (1997, orig. late 18th century) *On World History: An Anthology*. Hans Adler and Ernest A. Menze (eds.), Ernest A. Menze with Michael Palma (trs.). Armonk, New York and London, England: M.E. Sharpe.

Herzfeld, Michael (2005) *Cultural Intimacy: Social Poetics in the Nation-State*. New York and London: Routledge.
Hill, Christopher (1994) *The English Bible and the Seventeenth-Century Revolution*. Harmondsworth, Middlesex: Penguin Books.
Hillenbrand, Carole (1999) *The Crusades: Islamic Perspectives*. Edinburgh: Edinburgh University Press.
Hindle, Steve (2000) *The State and Social Change in Early Modern England, c. 1550–1640*. Houndmills, Basingstoke: Palgrave.
Hirschi, Caspar (2012) *The Origins of Nationalism: An Alternative History from Ancient Rome to Early Modern Germany*. Cambridge: Cambridge University Press.
Hobsbawm, E.J., and Terence Ranger (eds.) (1983) *The Invention of Tradition*. Cambridge: Cambridge University Press.
Hobsbawm, Eric (2001, orig. 1962) *The Age of Revolution 1789–1848*. London: Abacus.
Hobsbawm, E.J. (1990) *Nations and Nationalism since 1780*. Cambridge: Cambridge University Press.
Holton, David (1991) *Erotokritos*. Bristol Classics Press; New Rochelle: Aristide D. Caratzas.
Holton, David (1996) 'The Function of Myth in Cretan Renaissance Poetry: The Cases of Achelis and Kornaros' in P. Mackridge (ed.), *Ancient Greek Myth in Modern Greek Poetry*. London and Portland, Oregon: Frank Cass.
Hosking, Geoffrey (2001) *Russia and the Russians: A History from Rus to the Russian Federation*. London: Allen Lane, The Penguin Press.
Hourani, Albert (1991) *A History of the Arab Peoples*. London: Faber.
Hovanessian, Diana Der, and Marzbed Margossian (eds. and trs.) (1978) *Anthology of Armenian Poetry*. New York: Columbia University Press.
Howard, Michael, and Wm. Roger Louis (eds.) (1998) *The Oxford History of the Twentieth Century*. Oxford and New York: New York University Press.
Howes, Marjorie (1996) *Yeats's Nations: Gender, Class and Irishness*. Cambridge: Cambridge University Press.
Hroch, Miroslav (1985) *Social Preconditions of National Revival in Europe*. B. Fowkes (tr.). Cambridge: Cambridge University Press.
Hughes-Hallett, Lucy (2013) *The Pike: Gabriele D'Annunzio, Poet, Seducer and Preacher of War*. London: Fourth Estate.
Hutchinson, John (1987) *The Dynamics of Cultural Nationalism*. London: Allen & Unwin.
Hutchinson, John, and David Aberbach (1999) 'The Artist as Nation-Builder: William Butler Yeats and Chaim Nachman Bialik', *Nations and Nationalism* 5 (4): 501–521.
Hutchinson, John (1994) *Modern Nationalism*. London: Fontana.
Hutchinson, John, and Anthony D. Smith (eds.) (2000) *Nationalism: Critical Concepts in Political Science*. 5 vols. London and New York: Routledge.
Hutchinson, John (2005) *Nations as Zones of Conflict*. London: Sage.
Iamartino, Giovanni (2004) 'Translation, Biography, Opera, Film and Literary Criticism: Byron and Italy after 1870' in Richard A. Cardwell (ed.), *The Reception of Byron in Europe*. 2 vols. London and New York: Thoemmes Continuum, I 98–128
Ibsen, Henrik (1963, orig. 1867) *Peer Gynt*. M. Meyer (tr.). New York: Anchor Doubleday.

Iqbal, Muhammad (2000) *Tulip in the Desert*. Mustansir Mir (ed. and tr.). Montreal: McGill-Queen's University Press.
Izzedien, Yousif (1962) *Poetry and Iraqi Society 1900–1945*. Baghdad.
Izzedien, Yousif (1971) *Modern Iraqi Poetry: Social and Political Influences*. Cairo: The Cultural Press.
Jacobson, David C. (1987) *Modern Midrash: The Retelling of Traditional Jewish Narratives by Twentieth-Century Hebrew Writers*. Albany, New York: State University of New York Press.
Jarden, Dov (ed.) (1966) *Divan Shmuel Hanagid* [Hebrew]. Jerusalem: Hebrew Union College Press.
Jarden, Dov (ed.) (1975) *The Secular Poetry of Rabbi Solomon ibn Gabirol* [Hebrew]. Jerusalem: Kiriat Noar.
Jasper, David, and Stephen Prickett (eds.) (1999) *The Bible and Literature: A Reader*. Oxford: Blackwell.
Jeffrey, David Lyle (1992) *A Dictionary of Biblical Tradition in English Literature*. Grand Rapids, Michigan: William Eerdmans Publishing Company.
Jenkins, Romilly (1940) *Dionysius Solomos*. Cambridge: Cambridge University Press.
Jordan, Elaine (1988) *Alfred Tennyson*. Cambridge: Cambridge University Press.
Joshi, Priya (2002) *In Another Country: Colonialism, Culture, and the English Novel in India*. New York: Columbia University Press.
Jyoti, Amar (2013) *Nation, Identity and Diaspora in Surinamese Poetry*. Unistar: Chanddigarh.
Kadare, Ismail (2000) *Three Elegies for Kosovo*. P. Constantine (tr.). London: Harvill.
Kadhim, Hussein N. (1997) 'The Poetics of Postcolonialism: Two Qasidahs by Ahmad Shawqi', *Journal of Arabic Literature* 28: 179–218.
Kadhim, Hussein N. (2004) *The Poetics of Anti-Colonialism in the Arabic QASIDAH*. Leiden: Brill.
Kamenka, Eugene (ed.) (1976) *Nationalism: The Nature and Evolution of an Idea*. London: Edward Arnold.
Kaplan, Justin (1980) *Walt Whitman: A Life*. New York: Simon & Schuster.
Karadžić, Vuk (1997) *Songs of the Serbian People*. M. Holton and V. D. Mihailovich (eds. and tr.). Pittsburgh, Pennsylvania: University of Pittsburgh Press.
Kaufman, Stuart J. (2001) *Modern Hatreds: The Symbolic Politics of Ethnic War*. Ithaca and London: Cornell University Press.
Kaul, Suvir (2000) *Poems of Nation, Anthems of Empire: English Verse in the Long Eighteenth Century*. Charlottesville: The University Press of Virginia.
Kaviraj, Sudipta (2007) 'The Making of a Language of Patriotism in Modern Bengali' in A.S. Leoussi and S. Grosby (eds.) *Nationalism and Ethnosymbolism*. Edinburgh: Edinburgh University Press.
Kedourie, Elie (1960) *Nationalism*. London: Hutchinson.
Kedourie, Elie (ed.) (1971) *Nationalism in Asia and Africa*. London: Weidenfeld.
Kehew, Robert (ed.) (2005) *Lark in the Morning: The Verses of the Troubadours*. Chicago, Illinois, and London: University of Chicago Press.
Kennelly, Brendan (1970) *The Penguin Book of Irish Verse*. Penguin: Harmondsworth, Middlesex.
Kenyatta, Jomo (1938) *Facing Mt. Kenya: The Tribal Life of the Gikuyu*. London: Secker and Warburg.
Kermode, Frank (ed.) (1965) *Spenser*. Oxford: Oxford University Press.

Kershaw, Ian (1998, 2000) *Hitler*. 2 vols. New York: W.W. Norton.
Khouri, Mounah A. (1971) *Poetry and the Making of Modern Egypt (1882–1922)*. Leiden: E.J. Brill.
Kiberd, Declan (1995) *Inventing Ireland: The Literature of the Modern Nation*. London: Cape.
Kidd, Colin (1999) *British Identities before Nationalism: Ethnicity and Nationhood in the Atlantic World, 1600–1800*. Cambridge: Cambridge University Press.
Killham, John (1973) 'Tennyson and Victorian Social Values' in D.J. Palmer (ed.) *Tennyson*, pp. 147–179. London: G. Bell & Sons.
Kipling, Rudyard (1970) *Stories and Poems*. R.L. Green (ed.). Everyman's Library. London: J.M. Dent.
Kipling, Rudyard (1990) *The Letters of Rudyard Kipling: Vol. 1, 1872–89*. T. Pinney (ed.). Iowa City, Iowa: University of Iowa Press.
Kirkconnell, Watson (1947) *A Little Treasury of Hungarian Verse*. Washington: American Hungarian Federation.
Kirschbaum, Stanislav J. (1995) *A History of Slovakia: The Struggle for Survival*. Houndmills, Basingstoke: Macmillan.
Kitromilides, Paschalis (1998) 'On the Intellectual Content of Greek Nationalism: Paparrigopoulos, Byzantium and the Great Idea' in David Ricks and Paul Magdalino (eds.) *Byzantium and the Modern Greek Identity*. Aldershot, Hampshire: Ashgate.
Klammer, Martin (1995) *Whitman, Slavery, and the Emergence of Leaves of Grass*. University Park, Pennsylvania: The Pennsylvania State University Press.
Klier, John (1995) *Imperial Russia's Jewish Question, 1855–1881*. Cambridge: Cambridge University Press.
Kohn, Hans (1946) *The Idea of Nationalism*. New York: Macmillan.
Koliopoulos, John S. (1990) 'Brigandage and Irredentism in Nineteenth-Century Greece' in M. Blinkhorn and T. Veremis (eds.), *Modern Greece: Nationalism and Nationality*. Athens: Sage/ Eliamep.
Koliopoulos, John S. and Thanos M. Veremis (2002) *Greece: The Modern Sequel, From 1831 to the Present*. London: Hurst & Co.
Kook, Abraham Isaac (1978) *The Lights of Holiness, the Moral Principles, Lights of Holiness, Essays, Letters, and Poems*. Ben Zion Bokser (tr.). London: SPCK.
Koropeckyj, Roman (2008) *Adam Mickiewicz: The Life of a Romantic*. Ithaca and London: Cornell University Press.
Kuebrich, David (1989) *Minor Prophecy: Whitman's New American Religion*. Bloomington and Indianapolis: Indiana University Press.
Kunene, Mazisi (1970) *Zulu Poems*. London: Andre Deutsch.
Kunene, Mazisi (1981) *Anthem of the Decades: A Zulu Epic*. London: Heinemann.
Kunene, Mazisi (tr.) (1979) *Emperor Shaka the Great*. London: Heinemann.
Kohn, Hans (1946) *The Idea of Nationalism*. New York: Macmillan.
Lambropoulos, Vassilis (1988) *Literature as National Institution: Studies in the Politics of Modern Greek Criticism*. Princeton, New Jersey: Princeton University Press.
Lamdan, Isaac (1962 [1927]) *Masada* (Hebrew). Tel Aviv: Dvir.
Landsbergis, Algirdas, and Clark Mills (eds.) (1962) *The Green Oak: Selected Lithuanian Poetry*. New York: Voyages Press.
Lebensohn, Abraham Dov (1895, orig. 1842). *Poems* (Hebrew). Vilna: Romm Press.
Ledeen, Michael A. (2002) *D'Annunzio: The First Duce*. New Brunswick and London: Transaction Publishers.

Lee, Sung-Il (1989) *The Wind and the Waves: Four Modern Korean Poets*. Berkeley, California: Asian Humanities Press.
Leerssen, Joep (2006) *National Thought in Europe: A Cultural History*. Amsterdam: Amsterdam University Press.
Leopardi, Giacomo (1966) *Selected Prose and Poetry*. I. Origo and J. Heath-Stubbs (eds. and trs.). London: Oxford University Press.
Leoussi, Athena, and David Aberbach (2002) 'Hellenism and Jewish Nationalism: Ambivalence and Its Ancient Roots', *Ethnic and Racial Studies* 25, 5: 1–23.
Levin, Gabriel (1992) 'Yehuda Halevi and Moshe Ibn Ezra', *Ariel* 87: 35–6.
Lewis, Bernard (1984) *The Jews of Islam*. London: Routledge.
Lewis, Bernard (1993) *Islam and the West*. New York and Oxford: Oxford University Press.
Lewis, Bernard (1995) *The Middle East*. London: Weidenfeld & Nicolson.
Lewis, Bernard (1998) *The Multiple Identities of the Middle East*. London: Phoenix.
Lieberman, M.A., I.D. Yalom and M.B. Miles (1973) *Encounter Groups: First Facts*. New York: Basic Books.
Lieven, Dominic (2000) *Empire: The Russian Empire and Its Rivals*. London: John Murray.
Lindemann, Albert S. and Richard S. Levy (2010) *Antisemitism: A History*. Oxford: Oxford University Press.
Longley, Clifford (2002) *Chosen People: The Big Idea that Shaped England and America*. London: Hodder & Stoughton.
Lönnrot, Elias (1969, orig. 1835) *The Old Kalevala and Certain Antecedents*. Francis Peabody Magoun, Jr. (tr.). Cambridge, Massachusetts: Harvard University Press.
Lönnrot, Elias (1989, orig. 1835, 1849) *The Kalevala*. K. Bosley (tr.). Oxford: Oxford University Press.
Lonsdale, Roger (ed.) (2003) *The New Oxford Book of Eighteenth-Century Verse*. Oxford: Oxford University Press.
Louis, Wm. Roger (1998) 'The European Colonial Empires' in M. Howard and W.R. Louis (eds.), *The Oxford History of the Twentieth Century*. Oxford and New York: New York University Press.
Loving, Jerome (1999) *Walt Whitman: The Song of Himself*. Berkeley, Los Angeles, London: University of California Press.
Löwe, Heinz-Dietrich (1993) *The Tsars and the Jews: Reform, Reaction and Anti-Semitism in Imperial Russia, 1772–1917*. Chur, Switzerland: Harwood Academic Publishers.
Löwe, Heinz-Dietrich (1991) *The Tsars and the Jews: Reform, Reaction and Anti-Semitism in Imperial Russia, 1772–1917*. Chur, Switzerland: Harwood Academic Publishers.
Löwe, Heinz-Dietrich (2010) 'Anti-Semitism in Russia and the Soviet Union' in A.S. Lindemann and R.S. Levy (eds.) *Anti-Semitism: A History*. Oxford: Oxford University Press.
Lycett, Andrew (1999) *Rudyard Kipling*. London: Weidenfeld & Nicolson.
Lyon, Peter (1998) 'The Old Commonwealth: The First Four Dominions' in M. Howard and W.R. Louis (eds.), *The Oxford History of the Twentieth Century*. Oxford and New York: New York University Press.
Lyons, F.S.L. (1979) *Culture and Anarchy in Ireland 1890–1939*. Oxford: Clarendon Press.
MacCulloch, Diarmaid (2004) *Reformation: Europe's House Divided 1490–1700*. London: Penguin.

Macdonald, J.N. (1921) *A Political Escapade*. London: John Murray.
MacCarthy, Fiona (2003) *Byron: Life and Legend*. London: Faber & Faber.
Macdonald, J.N. (1921) *A Political Escapade*. London: John Murray.
MacGregor, Geddes (1968) *A Literary History of the Bible: From the Middle Ages to the Present Day*. Nashville and New York: Abingdon Press.
Mackridge, Peter (1989) *Dionysios Solomos*. Bristol: Bristol Classical Press.
Mackridge, Peter (1998) 'Byzantium and the Greek Language Question in the Nineteenth Century' in David Ricks and Paul Magdalino (eds.) *Byzantium and the Modern Greek Identity*. Aldershot, Hampshire: Ashgate.
Mann, Stuart E. (1955) *Albanian Literature*. London: Bernard Quaritch, Ltd.
Marchand, Leslie (1957) *Life of Byron*. London: John Murray.
Marchand, Lesley (1965) *Byron's Poetry*. London: John Murray.
Marinetti, F.T. (1972) *Selected Writings*. R.W. Flint (ed.), R.W. Flint and A.A. Coppotelli (trs.). New York: Farrar, Straus and Giroux.
Marsland, Elizabeth (1991) *The Nation's Cause: French, English and German Poetry of the First World War*. London and New York: Routledge.
Martí, José (1999) *José Martí Reader: Writings on the Americas*. D. Shnookal and M. Múniz (eds.). Melbourne and New York: Ocean Press.
Martin, F.X. (1976) 'The Evolution of a Myth–the Easter Rising, Dublin 1916' in E. Kamenka (ed.) *Nationalism: The Nature and Evolution of an Idea*. London: Edward Arnold.
Marx, Karl (1972, orig. 1845–46) *The German Ideology*, in *The Marx-Engels Reader*. R.C. Tucker (ed.). New York: W.W. Norton.
Mazower, Mark (2000) *The Balkans*. London: Weidenfeld & Nicolson.
Mbiti, John (1967) *Drum Beat*. Nairobi: East African Publishing House.
McCaskie, T.C. (1999) 'Cultural Encounters: Britain and Africa in the Nineteenth Century' in A. Porter and A. Low (eds.) *The Oxford History of the British Empire, Vol. III: The Nineteenth Century*. New York and Oxford: Oxford University Press.
McFarlane, James Walter and Graham Orton, (eds. and trs.) (1970) *The Oxford Ibsen: Vol. I: Early Plays*. London: Oxford University Press.
McLellan, David (1973) *Karl Marx: His Life and Thought*. Basingstoke BS London: Macmillan.
Mendes-Flohr, Paul R. and Jehuda Reinharz (eds.) (1995) *The Jew in the Modern World: A Documentary History*. 2nd ed. New York and Oxford: Oxford University Press.
Menemencioğlu, Nermin, and Fahir İz (eds. and trs.) (1978) *The Penguin Book of Turkish Verse*. Penguin: Harmondsworth, Middlesex.
Menocal, Maria Rosa (1987) *The Arabic Role in Medieval Literary History: A Forgotten Heritage*. Philadelphia, Pennsylvania: University of Pennsylvania Press.
Merwin, William Stanley (ed.) (1959) *The Poem of The Cid (El Poema Del Mio Cid)*. London: J. M. Dent & Sons.
Meyer, Michael (1985) *Ibsen: a biography*. Harmondsworth, Middlesex: Penguin.
Mickiewicz, Adam (1962, orig. 1834) *Pan Tadeusz*. W. Kirkconnell (tr.). Toronto: University of Toronto Press.
Mickiewicz, Adam (1989, orig. 1828) *Konrad Wallenrod and Krazyna*. I. Suboczewski (tr.). New York: Lanham.
Mickiewicz, Adam (2013, orig. 1834) *Pan Tadeusz*. K.R. Mackenzie (tr.). New York: Hippocrene Books, Inc.
Mir, Mustansir (2006) *Iqbal*. London and New York: I.B. Tauris and Oxford University Press for the Oxford Centre for Islamic Studies.

Miron, Dan (1987) *When Loners Come Together: A Portrait of Hebrew Literature at the Turn of the 20th Century*. Tel Aviv: Am Oved.

Miron, Gaston (1984) *Embers and Earth (Selected Poems)*. D.G. Jones and Marc Plourde (trs.). Montreal: Guernica Editions.

Modrzewska, Moroslawa (2004) 'Pilgrimage or Revolt? The Dilemmas of Polish Byronism' in Richard A. Cardwell (ed.) *The Reception of Byron in Europe*, 2 vols. London and New York: Thoemmes Continuum, II 305–315.

Monroe, James T. (ed.) (1975) *Hispano-Arabic Poetry: A Student Anthology*. Berkeley and Los Angeles: University of California Press.

Moore, Gerald, and Ulli Beier (eds.) (1998), 4th ed. *The Penguin Book of Modern African Poetry*. Penguin: Harmondsworth, Middlesex.

Moore, Robin J. (1999) 'Imperial India, 1858–1914' in A. Porter and A. Low (eds.) *The Oxford History of the British Empire, Vol. III, The Nineteenth Century*. New York and Oxford: Oxford University Press.

Moore, Thomas (ed.) (1932) *The Life, Letters and Journals of Lord Byron*. London: John Murray.

Morgan, Kenneth O. (1982) *Rebirth of a Nation: A History of Modern Wales*. Oxford: Oxford University Press, University of Wales Press

Morris Jr., Roy (2000) *The Better Angel: Walt Whitman in the Civil War*. Oxford: Oxford University Press.

Mosse, George (1973) 'Mass Politics and the Political Liturgy of Nationalism' in E. Kamenka (ed.) *Nationalism: The Nature and Evolution of an Idea*. London: Edward Arnold.

Mqhayi, S.E.K. (2009) *Abantu Besizwe: Historical and Biographical Writings, 1902–1944*. J. Opland (ed. and tr.). Johannesburg: Wits University Press.

Nathans, Benjamin (2002) *Beyond the Pale: The Jewish Encounter with Late Imperial Russia*. Berkeley and Los Angeles: University of California Press.

Neruda, Pablo (1972) *Selected Poems: A Bilingual Edition*. N. Tarn, et al. (trs.). New York: Delta.

Neruda, Pablo (1976) *Residence on Earth (Residencia en la tierra)*. D.D. Walsh (tr.). London: Souvenir Press.

Neruda, Pablo (1977) *Memoirs*. H. St. Martin (tr.). London: Souvenir Press.

Neuhäuser, Rudolf (1974) *Towards the Romantic Age. Essays on Pre-Romantic and Sentimental Literature in Russia*. The Hague: Martinus Nijhoff.

Neuhäuser, Rudolf (1975) *The Romantic Age in Russian Literature: Poetic and Esthetic Norms*. Munich: Otto Sagner.

Newth, Michael (2005) *Heroes of the French Epic: A Selection of Chansons de Geste*. Woodbridge: The Boydell Press.

Njegoš, Petar II Petrovic (1989, orig. 1847). *The Mountain Wreath*. V.D. Mihailovich (tr.). Belgrade: Vajat.

Novak, David (1995) *The Election of Israel: The Idea of the Chosen People*. Cambridge: Cambridge University Press.

O'Brien, Conor Cruise (1988) *Passion and Cunning*. New York: Simon & Schuster.

O'Brien, Edna (2009) *Byron in Love*. London: Weidenfeld & Nicholson.

Okola, Lennard (ed.) (1973, orig. 1967) *Drum Beat*. Nairobi: East Africa Publishing House.

Okpewho, Isidore (ed.) (1985) *The Heritage of African Poetry*. London: Longman.

Okpewho, Isidore (1992) *African Oral Poetry: Backgrounds, Character, and Continuity*. Bloomington and Indianapolis: Indiana University Press.

Owen, Roger (2004) *Lord Cromer: Victorian Imperialist, Edwardian Proconsul*. London: Oxford University Press.
Owen, Wilfred (1967) *Collected Letters*. H. Owen and J. Bell (eds.). London: Oxford University Press.
Pagis, Dan (1970) *Secular Poetry and Poetic Theory: Moses ibn Ezra and His Contemporaries* [Hebrew]. Jerusalem: Mossad Bialik.
Palmer, Roy (1988) *The Sound of History: Songs and Social Comment*. Oxford and New York: Oxford University Press.
Paranjape, Makarand (ed.) (1999) *The Penguin Sri Aurobindo Reader*. New Delhi: Penguin Books.
Parry, Milman (ed.) (1974) *Serbo-Croatian Heroic Songs*. A.B. Lord and D.E. Bynum (trs.). Cambridge, Massachusetts: Harvard University Press.
Patterson, David (1985) 'The Influence of Hebrew Literature on the Growth of Jewish Nationalism in the Nineteenth Century' in R. Sussex and J.C. Eade (eds.) *Culture and Nationalism in Nineteenth-Century Eastern Europe*. Columbus, Ohio: Slavica Publishers.
p'Bitek, Okot (1984, orig. 1966, 1967) *Song of Lawino & Song of Ocol*. London: Heinemann.
Pearse, Padriac H. (1917) *Collected Works*. Dublin and London: Maunsel & Co. Ltd.
Peckham, Robert Shannan (1998) Papadiamantis, Ecumenism and the Theft of Byzantium' in David Ricks and Paul Magdalino (eds.) *Byzantium and the Modern Greek Identity*. Aldershot, Hampshire: Ashgate.
Pennington, Anne, and Peter Levi (trs.) (1984) *Marko the Prince: Serbo-Croat Heroic Songs*. New York: St. Martin's Press.
Perry, Bliss (1969, orig. 1906) *Walt Whitman*. New York: AMS Press.
Petőfi, Sándor (1973) *Works*. J.M. Értavy-Baráth (ed.), A.N. Nyerges (tr.). Buffalo, New York: Hungarian Cultural Foundation.
Petőfi, Sándor (1974) *Rebel or Revolutionary?* B. Köpeczi (ed.), E. Morgan (tr.). Budapest: Corvina Press.
Petrarch, Francesco (2002, orig. 14th century) *Canzoniere*. J. G. Nichols (tr.). New York: Routledge.
Pipa, Arshi (1978) *Albanian Literature: Social Perspectives*. Munich: Rudolf Trofenik.
Plamenatz, John (1976) 'Two Types of Nationalism' in E. Kamenka (ed.) *Nationalism: The Nature and Evolution of an Idea*. London: Edward Arnold.
Pointer, Frank Erik, and Achim Geisenhansluke (2004) 'The Reception of Byron in the German-Speaking Lands' in Richard A. Cardwell (ed.) *The Reception of Byron in Europe*. London and New York: Thoemmes Continuum II 235–268.
Politis, Linos (1973) *A History of Modern Greek Literature*. Oxford: Clarendon Press.
Pollak, Vivian R. (2000) *The Erotic Whitman*. Berkeley, Los Angeles, London: University of California Press.
Porter, Andrew (1999) 'Trusteeship, Anti-Slavery, and Humanitarianism' in A. Porter and A. Low (eds.) *The Oxford History of the British Empire, Vol. III, The Nineteenth Century*. New York and Oxford: Oxford University Press.
Potter, Bernard (2004) *The Absent-Minded Imperialists: Empire, Slavery, and Culture in Britain*. Oxford and New York: Oxford University Press.
Prawer, S.S. (1983) *Heine's Jewish Comedy*. Oxford: Clarendon Press.

Praz, Mario (1970, orig. 1933) *The Romantic Agony*, 2nd ed. A. Davidson (tr.). Oxford: Oxford University Press.
Preminger, Alex, et al. (eds.) (1975) *Princeton Encyclopedia of Poetry and Poetics*. London and Basingstoke: Macmillan.
Preminger, Alex, and Brogan, T.V.F., et al. (eds.) (1993) *The New Princeton Encyclopedia of Poetry and Poetics*. Princeton, New Jersey: Princeton University Press.
Pritchard, James B. (ed.) (1969) *Ancient Near Eastern Texts Relating to the Old Testament*, 3rd. ed. Princeton, New Jersey: Princeton University Press.
Pritchard, William H. (ed.) (1972) *W.B. Yeats: A Critical Anthology*. Harmondsworth, Middlesex: Penguin.
Psaila, Dun Karm (1997) *The Self and Beyond It*. F. Zimmit (tr.). Melbourne: Victoria University.
Pushkin, Alexander (1997) *Selected Poems*. A.D.P. Briggs (ed. and tr.). Everyman edition. London: J.M. Dent.
Quint, David (1992) *Epic and Empire: Politics and Generic Form from Virgil to Milton*. Princeton, New Jersey: Princeton University Press.
Rahman, Fazhur (1979) *Islam*, 2nd ed. Chicago, Illinois: University of Chicago Press.
Ray, Benjamin C. (1976) *African Religions: Symbol, Ritual, Community*. Englewood Cliffs, New Jersey: Prentice Hall, Inc.
Reed, J.D. (2007) *Virgil's Gaze: Nation and Poetry in The Aeneid*. Princeton and Oxford: Princeton University Press.
Regan, Stephen (2000) 'Poetry and Nation: W.B. Yeats' in R. Allen and H. Trivedi (eds.), *Literature and Nation: Britain and India 1800–1990*, ch. 6. London and New York: Routledge and The Open University.
Reif, Stefan (1993) *Judaism and Hebrew Prayer: New Perspectives on Jewish Liturgical History*. Cambridge: Cambridge University Press.
Renan, Ernest (1999, orig. 1882) *Qu'est-ce qu'une nation?* in H. Bhabha (ed.) *Nation and Narration*. London: Routledge.
Reynolds, David S. (1995) 'Political Poetry: Leaves of Grass and the Social Crisis of the 1850s' in E. Greenspan (ed.) *The Cambridge Companion to Walt Whitman*. Cambridge: Cambridge University Press.
Reynolds, David S. (1996) *Walt Whitman's America: A Cultural Biography*. New York: Random House.
Reynolds, David S. (2000) *A Historical Guide to Walt Whitman*. New York and Oxford: Oxford University Press.
Reynolds, Matthew (2001) *The Realms of Verse 1830–1870: English Poetry in a Time of Nation-Building*. Oxford: Oxford University Press.
Rhodes, Anthony (1959) *A Life of Gabriele D'Annunzio*. London: Weidenfeld & Nicolson.
Ricks, David (1989) *The Shade of Homer: A Study of Modern Greek Poetry*. Cambridge: Cambridge University Press.
Ricks, David (1990) *Byzantine Heroic Poetry*. Bristol: Bristol Classical Press (U.K.); New Rochelle, New York: Aristide D. Caratzas (U.S.A.).
Ricks, David and Paul Magdalino (eds.), *Byzantium and the Modern Greek Identity*. Aldershot, Hampshire: Ashgate.
Ridley, Jasper (1997) *Mussolini*. New York: St. Martin's Press.
Riley-Smith, Jonathan (2002) *What Were the Crusades?* Basingstoke: Palgrave Macmillan.

Robinson, Francis (1999) 'The British Empire and the Muslim World' in J.M. Brown, W.R. Louis and A. Low (eds.) *The Oxford History of the British Empire, Vol. IV: The Twentieth Century.* Oxford and New York: Oxford University Press.
Ronsard, Pierre de (2002, orig. 16th century) *Selected Poems.* M. Quainton and E. Vinestock (eds. and trs.). London: Penguin.
Rose, Kenneth (1969) *Superior Person: A Portrait of Curzon and His Circle in late Victorian England.* London: Weidenfeld & Nicolson.
Rosen, Frederick (1992) *Bentham, Byron, and Greece: Constitutionalism, Nationalism, and Early Liberal Political Thought.* Oxford: Clarendon Press.
Rosenberg, Samuel N., et al. (eds.) (1998) *Songs of the Troubadours and Trouvères: An Anthology of Poems and Melodies.* New York and London: Garland.
Roshwald, Aviel (2006) *The Endurance of Nationalism: Ancient Roots and Modern Dilemmas.* Cambridge: Cambridge University Press.
Ruches, Pyrrhus J. (1967) *Albanian Historical Folksongs, 1716–1943.* Chicago: Argunaut Publishers.
Rutebeuf (1989) *Oeuvres Complètes.* 2 vols. M. Zink (ed.) Paris: Garnier.
Sacks, Jonathan (2002) *The Dignity of Difference: How to Avoid the Clash of Civilizations.* London and New York: Continuum.
Said, Edward W. (1994) *Culture and Imperialism.* New York: Vintage.
Sáenz-Badillos, Angel (1993) *A History of the Hebrew Language.* J. Elwolde (tr.). Cambridge: Cambridge University Press.
Salierno, Vito (1988) *D'Annunzio e Mussolini.* Milan: Mursia.
Samatar, Said S. (1982) *Oral Poetry and Somali Nationalism: The Case of Sayyid Maammad 'Abdille asan.* Cambridge: Cambridge University Press.
Santoli, Carlo (1999) *Gabriele D'Annunzio e Arturo Toscanini.* Rome: Bulzoni.
Sastry, C.N. (1992) *Walt Whitman and Rabindranath Tagore: A Study in Comparison.* Delhi: B.R. Publishing Corporation.
al-Sayyid-Marsot, Afaf Lutfi (1999) 'The British Occupation of Egypt from 1882' in A. Porter and A. Low (eds.) *The Oxford History of the British Empire, Vol. III: The Nineteenth Century.* Oxford and New York: Oxford University Press.
Scattergood, V.J. (1971) *Politics and Poetry in the Fifteenth Century.* London: Blandford Press.
Schama, Simon (2003) *A History of Britain 3, 1776–2000: The Fate of Empire.* London: BBC Worldwide Ltd.
Scheindlin, Raymond P. (1986) *Wine, Women, and Death: Medieval Hebrew Poems on the Good Life.* Philadelphia: Jewish Publication Society.
Scheindlin, Raymond P. (1991) *The Gazelle: Medieval Hebrew Poems on Israel, and the Soul.* Philadelphia, New York: Jewish Publication Society.
Schirmann, Chaim (ed.) (1959) *Hebrew Poetry in Spain and Provence* (Hebrew), 2 books in 4 parts. Jerusalem: Mossad Bialik; Tel Aviv: Dvir.
Schiller, Friedrich (1995, orig. 1781) *The Robbers.* R.D. MacDonald (tr.). London: Oberon Books.
Scott, Paul (1984) *The Raj Quartet.* London: Heinemann.
Scott, Sir Walter (1932–7). *The Letters of Sir Walter Scott.* H.J.C. Grierson, et al. (eds.), 8 vols. London: Constable.
Scurr, Ruth (2006) *Fatal Purity: Robespierre and the French Revolution.* London: Chatto & Windus.
Seldman, Naomi (2006) *Faithful Renderings: Jewish- Christian Difference and the Politics of Translation.* Chicago: University of Chicago Press.

Sells, Michael A. (1996) *The Bridge Betrayed: Religion and Genocide in Bosnia.* Berkeley and London: University of California Press.
Senghor, Leopold Sedar (1964) *Selected Poems.* J. Reed and C. Wake (trs.). Oxford: Oxford University Press
Senghor, Leopold Sedar (1976) *Prose and Poetry.* J. Reed and C. Wake (trs.). London: Heinemann.
Senghor, Leopold Sedar (1977) *Selected Poems.* A. Irele (ed.). Cambridge: Cambridge University Press.
Senghor, Leopold Segar (1998, orig. 1964) *The Collected Poetry.* M. Dixon (tr.). Charlottesville and London: University Press of Virginia.
Seton-Watson, Hugh (1977) *Nations and States.* London: Methuen.
Shahid, Irfan (2002) 'The Arabic Mirror' in J.C. Hirsh and R. Severino (eds.) *Napoleon: One Image, Ten Mirrors.* Washington, DC: Georgetown University, Faculty of Languages and Linguistics.
Shaw, M. (1973) 'Tennyson and His Public' in D.J. Palmer (ed.) *Tennyson.* London: G. Bell & Sons.
Sheehy, Jeanne (1980) *The Rediscovery of Ireland's Celtic Past.* London: Thames & Hudson.
Shevchenko, Taras (1961) *Song Out of Darkness: Selected Poems.* Vera Rich (tr.). London: The Mitre Press.
Shevchenko, Taras (1964) *Poetical Works.* C.H. Andrusyshen and W. Kirkconnell (trs.). Ukrainian Canadian Committee: University of Toronto Press.
Shevchenko, Taras (1977) *Selected Poetry.* J. Weir, et al. (trs.). Kiev: Dniepro Publishers.
Shlonsky, Abraham (2002) *Collected Poems* (Hebrew). 6 vols. Tel Aviv: Sifriat Poalim.
Sitwell, Osbert (1950) *Noble Essences or Courteous Revelations.* London: Macmillan.
Skynner, Robin (1976) *One Flesh: Separate Persons: Principles of Family and Marital Psychotherapy.* London: Constable.
Slack, Paul (1988) *Poverty and Policy in Tudor and Stuart England.* London and New York: Longman.
Slater, Joseph L. (1952) 'Byron's Hebrew Melodies', *Studies in Philology* XLIV, pp. 75–94.
Smith, Anthony D. (1979) *Nationalism in the Twentieth Century.* New York: New York University Press.
Smith, Anthony D. (1991) *National Identity.* Harmondsworth, Middlesex: Penguin.
Smith, Anthony D. (1996) 'Nations and their pasts', *Nations and Nationalism* 2, 3: 371–388.
Smith, Anthony D. (1996a) 'Nationalism and the Historians' in G. Balakrishnan (ed.) *Mapping the Nation.* London: Verso.
Smith, Anthony D. (1998) *Nationalism and Modernism.* London: Routledge.
Smith, Anthony D. (1999) *Myths and Memories of the Nation.* Oxford: Oxford University Press.
Smith, Anthony D. (2000) *The Nation in History: Historiographical Debates about Ethnicity and Nationalism.* Cambridge: Polity.
Smith, Anthony D. (2001) *Nationalism.* Cambridge: Polity.
Smith, Anthony D. (2004) *The Antiquity of Nations.* Cambridge: Polity.
Smith, Anthony D. (2008) *The Cultural Foundations of Nations: Hierarchy, Covenant, and Republic.* Oxford: Oxford University Press.

Smith, A.J.M. (ed.) (1943) *The Book of Canadian Poetry*. Chicago: University of Chicago Press.
Smith, Denis Mack (1959) *Italy: A Modern History*. Ann Arbor: The University of Michigan Press.
Smith, Denis Mack (1994) *Mazzini*. New Haven and London: Yale University Press.
Solomos, Dionysios (2000) *The Free Besieged and other poems*. P. Mackridge (ed.), P. Thompson, et al. (trs.). Beeston, Nottingham: Shoestring Press.
The Song of Roland (1990, orig. c. 1100), G.S. Burgess (ed. and tr.). Harmondsworth, Middlesex: Penguin Classics.
Southern, Richard William (1962) *Western Views of Islam in the Middle Ages*. Cambridge, MA: Harvard University Press.
Soutsos, Panagiotis (1828) *Odes d'un Jeune Grec*. Paris: Emler Frères.
Spenser, Edmund (1974, orig. 1590, 1596) *The Fairie Queene*. 2 vols. Everyman edition. London: J.M. Dent.
St. Clair, William (1972) *That Greece Might Still Be Free: The Philhellenes in the War of Independence*. London: Oxford University Press.
Stanton, Robert (2002) *The Culture of Translation in Anglo-Saxon England*. Cambridge: D.S. Brewer.
Stavrianos, Leften Stavros (2000, orig. 1958) *The Balkans since 1453*. New York: Holt, Rinehart and Winston.
Stein, Jennifer J. (1998) 'Revolutions of 1848' in *Walt Whitman: An Encyclopedia*. J.R. LeMaster and D.D. Kummings (eds.). New York and London: Garland Publishing, Inc.
Steiner, George, ed. (1966) *The Penguin Book of Modern Verse Translation*. Harmondsworth, Middlesex: Penguin Books.
Steiner, George (1996) 'A Preface to the Hebrew Bible' in *No Passion Spent: Essays 1978–1996*. London: Faber.
Stern, Abraham ('Yair') (1964) *Poems* (Hebrew). Lehi Publication Committee: Israel.
Stillman, Norman (1979) *The Jews of Arab Lands: A History and Source Book*. Philadelphia: Jewish Publication Society.
Stokes, Eric (1972) 'Kipling's Imperialism' in J. Gross (ed.) *Rudyard Kipling: The Man, His Work and His World*. London: Weidenfeld & Nicolson.
Stork, Charles Wharton (tr.) (1947) *A Second Book of Danish Verse*. Princeton, New Jersey: Princeton University Press.
Stubbs, John (2006) *Donne: The Reformed Soul*. London and New York: Viking Penguin.
Subtelny, Orest (1988) *Ukraine: A History*. Toronto: University of Toronto Press.
Sud, K.N. (1969) *Iqbal and His Poems (A Reappraisal)*. Delhi and Jullundur City: Sterling.
Suetonius (2000), *Lives of the Caesars*. Catharine Edwards (tr.). Oxford: Oxford University Press.
Sutherland, John (1995) *The Life of Walter Scott: A Critical Biography*. Oxford: Blackwell.
Swaab, Peter (1989) *Wordsworth and Patriotism*. D. Phil. Cambridge: University of Cambridge.
Szakaly, Ferenc (1990) 'The Early Ottoman Period, Including Royal Hungary 1526–1606' in Peter F. Sugar, *et al.* (eds.), *A History of Hungary*. London and New York: I.B. Tauris.

Stanislawski, Michael (1988) *'For Whom Do I Toil?' J.L. Gordon and the Crisis of Russian Jewry*. New York: Oxford University Press.
Tagore, Rabindranath (2004) *Selected Poems*. S. Chaudhuri, et al. (eds.). New Delhi and Oxford: Oxford University Press.
Tagore, Rabindranath (1959, orig. 1912) *Gitanjali*. London: Macmillan.
Tagore, Rabindranath (1917) *Nationalism*. London: Macmillan.
Talmon, Jacob (1960) *Political Messianism: The Romantic Phase*. London: Secker & Warburg.
Talmon, Jacob (1967) *Romanticism and Revolt–Europe 1815–1848*. London: Thames & Hudson.
Talmon, Jacob (1986, orig. 1952) *The Origins of Totalitarian Democracy*. Harmondsworth, Middlesex: Penguin Books.
Tasso, Torquato (2009, orig. 1581) *The Liberation of Jerusalem*. M. Wickert (tr.), M. Davie (int. and notes). Oxford: Oxford University Press.
Taylor, Charles (1998) 'Nationalism and Modernity' in John A. Hall (ed.) *The State of the Nation: Ernest Gellner and the Theory of Nationalism*. Cambridge: Cambridge University Press.
Tchernichowsky, Saul (1954) *Poems* (Hebrew). Tel Aviv: Schocken.
Todorova, Maria (2009) *Imagining the Balkans*. Oxford: Oxford University Press.
Toland, John (1977) *Adolf Hitler*. New York: Ballantine Books.
Tolegian, Aram (tr.) (1979) *Armenian Poetry Old and New: A Bilingual Anthology*. Detroit: Wayne State University Press.
Topencharov, Vladimir (1982) *Khristo Botev*. Paris: UNESCO.
Trayiannoudi, Litsa (2004) 'A "very life in… Despair in the land of honourable death": Byron in Greece' in Richard A. Cardwell (ed.) *The Reception of Byron in Europe*. London and New York: Thoemmes Continuum, II 419–38.
Treptow, Kurt (ed.) (1991) *Selected Works of Ion Creanga and Mihai Eminescu*. Boulder, Colorado: East European Monographs.
Trypanis, Constantine A. (ed. and tr.) (1984, orig. 1971) *The Penguin Book of Greek Verse*. Harmondsworth, Middlesex: Penguin Books.
Trypanis, Constantine A. (1981) *Greek Poetry: From Homer to Seferis*. London and Boston: Faber & Faber.
Tucker, Herbert (2008) *Epic: Britain's Heroic Muse, 1790–1910*. Oxford: Oxford University Press.
Tucker, Robert C. (1968) 'The Theory of Charismatic Leadership', *Daedalus* 97, 3:731–56.
Valesi, Paolo (1992) *Gabriele D'Annunzio: The Dark Angel*. Marilyn Migiel (tr.). New Haven and London: Yale University Press.
Van Doren, Mark (ed.) (1936) *An Anthology of World Poetry*. New York: Harcourt, Brace and Company.
Vucinich, Wayne S. and Thomas A. Emmert (eds.) *Kosovo: Legacy of a Medieval Battle*. Minneapolis: University of Minnesota Press.
Virgil (1956) *The Aeneid*. W.F. Jackson Knight (tr.). Penguin Classics: Harmondsworth, Middlesex.
Vital, David (1975) *The Origins of Zionism*. New York and Oxford: Oxford University Press.
Vryonis, Jr., Speros (1976) 'The Greeks under Turkish Rule' in N.P. Diamandoupos, et al. (eds.), *Hellenism and the First Greek War of Liberation (1821–1830): Continuity and Change*. Thessaloniki: Institute for Balkan Studies.

Wachtel, Michael (2004) *The Cambridge Introduction to Russian Poetry*. Cambridge: Cambridge University Press.
Wake, Clive (ed.) (1965) *An Anthology of African and Malagasy Poetry in French*. London: Oxford University Press.
Walcott, Derek (1990) *Collected Poems 1948–1984*. New York: The Noonday Press; Farrar, Straus & Giroux.
Walcott, Derek (1990) *Omeros*. London and Boston: Faber.
Walcott, Derek (1993) *Selected Poetry*. W. Brown (ed.). London: Heinemann.
Walzer, Michael (1985) *Exodus and Revolution*. New York: Basic Books.
Wasserstein, David (1985) *The Rise and Fall of the Party-Kings: Politics and Society in Islamic Spain 1002–1086*. Princeton, New Jersey: Princeton University Press.
Watson, J.R. (2003) *Romanticism and War: A Study of British Romantic Period Writers and the Napoleonic Wars*. New York and Basingstoke: Palgrave Macmillan.
Watt, W. Montgomery (1984, orig. 1974) *The Majesty that Was Islam*. London: Sidgwick & Jackson.
Weber, Max (1961, orig. 1923) *General Economic History*. H.H. Gerth and D. Martingale (eds. and trs.). New York: Free Press.
Wells, H.G. (2006, orig. 1922) *A Short History of the World*. M. Sherborne (ed.). London: Penguin Books.
Werfel, Franz (2012, orig. 1933) *The Forty Days of Musa Dagh*. G. Dunlop and J. Reidel (trs.). Boston: Verba Mundi;
Whitman, Walt (1920) *The Gathering of the Forces*. 2 vols. C. Rodgers and J. Black (eds.). New York and London: G.P. Putnam's Sons, The Knickerbocker Press.
Whitman, Walt (1922) *The Uncollected Poetry and Prose of Walt Whitman*. 2 vols. E. Holloway (ed.). London: William Heinemann.
Whitman, Walt (1932) *I Sit and Look Out: Editorials from the Brooklyn Daily Times by Walt Whitman*. E. Holloway and V. Schwartz (eds.). New York: Columbia University Press.
Whitman, Walt (1949) *Leaves of Grass and Selected Prose*. S. Bradley (ed.). New York: Holt, Rinehart & Winston.
Whitman, Walt (1963) *Early Poems and Fiction*. T.L. Brasher (ed.). New York: New York University Press.
Whitman, Walt (1963–64) *Prose Works 1892*. 2 vols. F. Stovall (ed.). New York: New York University Press.
Whitman, Walt (1978) *The Collected Writings of Walt Whitman, Daybooks and Notebooks*. 3 vols, W. White (ed.). New York: New York University Press.
Whitman, Walt (1982) *Leaves of Grass*. New York: The Library of America.
Whitman, Walt (1984) *Notebooks and Unpublished Prose Manuscripts*. 6 vols. E.F. Grier (ed.). New York: New York University Press.
Whitman, Walt (2003) *The Collected Writings of Walt Whitman. The Journals Vol. II: 1846–1848*. H. Bergman, D.A. Noverr and E.J. Recchia (eds.). New York: Peter Lang.
Wilson, Jean Moorcroft (1999) *Siegfried Sassoon: The Making of a War Poet 1886–1918*. London: Duckworth.
Wilson, William A. (1976) *Folklore and Nationalism in Modern Finland*. Bloomington and London: Indiana University Press.
Wistrich, Robert S. (2010) *A Lethal Obsession: Anti-Semitism from Antiquity to the Global Jihad*. New York: Random House.
Woodhouse, C.M. (1969) *The Philhellenes*. London: Hodder & Stoughton.

Woodhouse, C.M. (1991) *Modern Greece: A Short History*. London: Faber & Faber.
Woodhouse, John (1998) *Gabriele D'Annunzio: Defiant Archangel*. Oxford: Clarendon Press.
Wright, David (2001) 'The Reformation to 1700' in John Rogerson (ed.) *The Oxford Illustrated History of the Bible*. Oxford and New York: Oxford University Press.
Wright, Julia M. (2004) *Blake, Nationalism, and the Politics of Alienation*. Athens: Ohio University Press.
Wright, Roger (ed.) (1991) *Latin and Romance Language in the Early Middle Ages*. London: Routledge.
Yeats, W.B. (1973) *Collected Poems*. London: Macmillan.
Yeh, Michelle (ed. and tr.) (1992) *Anthology of Modern Chinese Poetry*. New Haven and London: Yale University Press.
Yip, Wai-Lim (ed. and tr.) (1992) *Lyrics from Shelters: Modern Chinese Poetry 1930–1950*. New York and London: Garland Publishing Co.
Yoshino, Kosaku (1992) *Cultural Nationalism in Contemporary Japan*. London and New York: Routledge.
Zachariah, Benjamin (2004) *Nehru*. London: Routledge.
Zamoyski, Adam (1999) *Holy Madness: Romantics, Patriots and Revolutionaries 1776–1871*. London: Weidenfeld & Nicolson.
Zimunya, Musaemura (1989) *Birthright: A Selection of Poems from Southern Africa*. Harlow: Longman.
Zweig, Paul (1984) *Walt Whitman: The Making of the Poet*. New York: Viking Penguin.

Index

I Poets and Their Countries

Abu Ishak (11th century), Spain **123**
Achelis, Antonios (16th century), Crete 107 note 29
Albania (independent from Turkey 1912) see Fishta, Frasheri, de Rada, Vasa
Alcuin of York (c. 735–804), England/ France 92, **93**, 105 note 6
America, United States of (independent from Britain 1776) see Eliot, Frost, Longfellow, Root, Whitman
Amichai, Yehuda (1924–2000), Israel 16-7
Angola (independent from Portugal 1975) see Neto, Jacinto
Ardwisson, A.I. (1791–1858), Finland 76
Argentina (independent from Spain 1816), see Lopez
Ariosto, Ludovico (1474–1533), Italy 92, 93, 97, 98, 99, 105 note 6, 107 note 23
Armenia (independent from Soviet Russia 1991), see Servantsediants, Siamanto, Toumanian, Varoujan
Arndt, Ernst Moritz (1769–1860), Germany 187, 200 note 9, 265 note 41
Auden, W.H. (1907–1973), England/ USA 14, 200 note 6, 315 note 8
Australia (federal government from 1901), see Mackellar, Paterson
Austria (united with Hungary 1867–1918, united with Nazi Germany 1938–1945), see Grillparzer

Babylonian Hebrew: see Israel
Baranauskas, Antanas (1835–1902), Lithuania **86 note 34**
Barbour, John (c.1320–1395), Scotland 62 note 28, 135

Barudi, Mahmud Sami Al- (1839–1904), Egypt 15, 272, 273–4
Berzsenyi, Daniel (1776–1836), Hungary 253, 254
Bestuzhev, Alexander (1797–1837), Russia 31 note 53
Bethune, Conon de (c. 1150–c. 1220), France **90**, 92, **94–5**
Bharati, Subramania (1882–1921), India (Tamil) 2, 192, 269, **276**, 277
Bialik, Chaim Nachman (1873–1934), Russian-Hebrew 2, 5, 8, 9, 12, 14, 15, 16, 18, 19, 20, 23, 24, 25, 27 note 10, 28 note 19, 29 notes 24, 25, 27; 30 note 32, 31 note 52, 48, **53–4**, 60 note 17, **63**, 64, 69, 73, 75, **79–80**, 181–2, 184 note 34, 185 note 50, 189, 192, 195, 220, **ch. 10**, 251–2, 256–7, Appendix (f); see Israel
Bjornson, Bjornstjerne (1832–1910), Norway 309–10, 64, 87 note 50
Blake, William (1770–1827) 12, **52**, 54, 71, 143, 201 note 13, 206, 271, 304
Blind Harry (1440?–1492), Scotland 135
Blok, Alexander (1880–1921), Russia 64
Blunt, Wilfred Scawen (1840–1922), England 272
Boiardo, Matteo Maria (1441?–1494), Italy 97, 107 note 23
Botev, Hristo (1849–1876), Bulgaria 4, 6, 7, 18, 20, 27 note 10, 38, 54, 91, 103, 162 note 15, 167, 170, **173**, 182, 191, 207, 252, 253, 256, 287 note 2, 314
Brentano, Clemens (1778–1842), Germany 200 note 9
Brewster, Elizabeth (1922–2012), Canada 292

350 *Index*

Browning, Elizabeth (1806–1861) and Robert (1812–1889), England 7, 62 note 26, 201 note 13, 271
Brutus, Denis (1924–), South Africa 285
Bulgaria (independent from Turkey 1878) see Botev, Chintulov, Rakovski
Burns, Robert (1759–96), Scotland 4, 16, **20**, 26 note 6, 27 note 10, 29 note 27, 51, 63, 64, 137, 139, 187, 192, 200 note 6, 205, 248, 249, **253–4, 260–1**, 271, 286, 293, 295
Byron, George Gordon (1788–1824), England 2, 4, 5, 12, 14, 20, 21, 22, 25, 26 note 4, 29, notes 22, 27; 48, 51–2, 60 note 17, 62 notes 26, 30; 81, 88 note 62, 101, 102, 105 note 6, 135, 139, 145, 147, 149, 150, 151, 154, **156–9**, 160, 161 note 10, **164 note 46**, 171, 172, 182, **186**, 187, **188–90**, 191, **192–3**, 194, 195, 196, 198, 199 note 3, 199 note 4, **200** notes **8, 9**; 201 notes 10, 11, 13, 15, 16, 17; 205, 268, 273, 293, 295

Camões, Luis de (c.1524–1580), Portugal 11, 66, 90, **99**, 105 note 6
Canada (British dominion from 1867), see Brewster, Mair, Miron
Cardenal, Ernesto (1925–), Nicaragua 15
Cavafi, C.P. (1863–1933), Greece 20, 64, 195, **300**
Césaire, Aimé (1913–2006), Martinique 15, 18, 23, 31 note 54, 290 note 34, 311, **312**, 313, 315 notes 12, 13
Chattopadhyay, Bankimchandra (1834–1894), India (Bengali/Sanskrit) 287 note 1, 314 note 1
Chaucer, Geoffrey (1340–1400), England 17, 50, 90, **96–7**, 106 notes 20, 21, 134, 208
Cheney-Coker, Syl (1945–), Sierra Leone 25
Chile (independent from Spain 1818), see Ercilla, Henriques, Neruda
China (republic 1911; Communist rule 1949–), see Mao, Yuehe
Chintulov, Dobri Petrov (1822–1886), Bulgaria 173
Clough, Arthur Hugh (1819–1861), England 62 note 26, 201 note 13, 271–2
Coleridge, Samuel Taylor (1772–1834), England 28 note 18, 51, 136–7, 144 note 6, **271–2, 299–300**, 304, 309

Collins, William (1721–1759), England 134
Cornford, John (1915–1936), England 191
Cowper, William (1731–1800), England 134, 213, 264 note 21, 265 note 30
Crete (united with Greece, 1913), see Achelis, Kornaros
Croatia (independent 1991), Gundulic, Marulik
Cuba (independent from Spain 1898), see Marti
Cynddelw Brydydd Mawr (12th century), Wales **135**

Dante Alighieri (1265–1321), Italy 17, 32 note 57, 96, 106 note 19, 144 note 12, 208
D'Annunzio, Gabriele (1863–1938), Italy 2, 5, 21, 22, 25, **ch. 8**
Dario, Rubén (1867–1916) Nicaragua 311
Darwish, Mahmoud (1941–2008), Palestine 58 note 2, 246 note 6
Defoe, Daniel (1661?–1731), England **134**
Denmark (united with Norway till 1815) see Grundtvig, Oehlenschlager
De Sousa, Noémia (1926–2003), Mozambique 313
Diop, David (1927–1960), Senegal 24, 294, 311, 312, **313**
Donne, John (1572–1631), England 33 note 74, 286
Dunyo, Amega (20th century), Ghana 315 note 9

Egypt (independent from Britain 1922) see Barudi, Khamisi, Hafiz Ibrahim, Mitran, Shawqi, Shukri
Ekpe, Komi (20th century), Ghana 315 note 9
Eliot, T.S. (1888–1965), USA/England 31 note 54, 52, 140, **194–5**, 225 note 45, Appendix (c)
Eminescu, Mihail (1850–1889), Romania 6, 7, 16, 91, 103, 167, 170, **172–3**, 189, 253, **255–6**, 287 note 2
England, see Alcuin, Auden, Blake, Blunt, Browning, Byron, Chaucer, Clough, Coleridge, Collins, Cornford, Cowper, Defoe, Donne, Eliot, Fitchett, Goldsmith, Gray, Grenfell, Hemans, Kipling,

Marlowe, Milton, Owen, Sassoon, Shakespeare, Smart, Spenser, Swinburne, Tennyson, Watson, Watts, Wordsworth, Wyatt
Ercilla, Alonso de (1533–1594), Spain/Chile 86 note 41, 314
Ersoy, Mehmet Akif (1873–1936), Turkey 290 note 38
Eschenbach, Wolfram von (13th century), Germany 90
Ezra, Moses ibn (1055–1135?), Spanish Hebrew 112, **124–5**; see Israel

Ferdowsi, Abolqasim (c. 1000), Persia 11
Ferguson, Samuel (1810–1886), Ireland 142, 235
Figueira, Guillam (early 13th century), France 105 note 7
Fikret, Tevfik (1867–1915), Turkey 29 note 27, 32 note 58, **166**, 253, 257, 258, 295
Finland (independent from Russia 1917) see Arwidsson, Leino, Lönnrot Runeberg
Fishta, Gjergi (1871–1940), Albania 15, 19, 64, 72, 83, 91, 103, 105 note 4, 155, 163 note 39, 165 note 53, 167, 169, 170, 174, 175, 252–3, **257–8**
Fitchett, John (1776–1838), England 144 note 8
France: Alcuin, de Bethune, Figueira, Hugo, Lamartine, Marcabru, de Musset, Ronsard, Rutebeuf; see Lebanon, Martinique, Senegal
Frasheri, Naim (1846–1900), Albania 155, 169, 174
Frost, Robert (1874–1963), USA 75

Gabirol, Solomon ibn (1021/2–56?), Spanish Hebrew 112, **118**, 119, **121–3**, 124, 129
Gambia (independent from Britain 1965) see Jebate, Suso
Genestet, Petrus Augustus de (1829–1861), Holland 310
George, Stefan (1868–1933), Germany 5, 187
Germany (unified 1871) see Arndt, Brentano, von Eschenbach, George, Goethe, Heine, Hölderlin, Kleist, Klopstock, Körner, Lissauer, Möller, Schiller
Ghana (independent from Britain 1957) see Dunyo, Ekpe

Ghose, Aurobindo (1872–1950) India (Bengal) 269, **276–7**
Gibran, Khalil (1883–1931), Lebanon 38, 253, 257, **258–9**
Goethe, Johann Wolfgang (1749–1832), Germany 6, 15, 47, 63, 71, 73, 139, 151, 155, 158, 161 note 12, 194, 199–200 note 4, 294
Gökalp, Ziya (1876–1924), Turkey 16, 27 note 8, 60 note 17, 201 note 19
Goldsmith, Oliver (1730–1774), England 134
Gordon, Judah Leib (1831–1892), Russian-Hebrew 38, 176, 253, 256, 257; see Israel
Gray, Thomas (1716–1771), England 134
Greece (independent from Turkey 1829) see Cavafi, Hesiod, Homer, Kalvos, Pindar, Solomos, Soutsos, Valaorites, Velestinlis
Greenberg, Uri Zvi (1896–1981), Israel 12, 15, 18, 23, 25, **54–7**, 192, 271, **282–3**, 289 note 16
Grenfell, Julian (1888–1915), England 202 note 20
Grillparzer, Franz (1791–1872), Austria 5, 187
Grundtvig, N.F.S. (1783–1872), Denmark 64
Gruffudd ab yr Ynad Coch (13th century), Wales **135**, 271
Guevara, Ernesto Che (1928–1967), Latin America 15
Gundulic, Ivan (1588–1638), Croatia 90, 100, 169, 183 note 10

Hafiz Ibrahim (1871?–1932), Egypt 272, **289 note 15**
Hai Gaon (938?–1038), Babylonian-Hebrew 113; see Israel
Halevi, Judah (c. 1075–1141), Spanish-Hebrew 17, 52, 90, **95–6**, **110–11**, 112, 117, 118, 123, 124, **125–8**, **128–9**, 130 note 1, 132 note 37; see Israel
Hanagid, Samuel (993–1056), Spanish-Hebrew 112, 118, **119–20**, 124, 127, 129; see Israel
Hanka, Václav (1791–1861), Czech 71, 179–80
Hazm, ibn (994–1064), Spain **119**
Heine, Heinrich (1797–1856), Germany 18, 25, **33 note 80**, 71, 139, 189, 213

Hemans, Felicia (1793–1835), England 164 note 47
Henriques, Camilo (1769–1824?), Chile 99, 314
Herder, Johann Gottfried (1744–1803), Germany 4, 15, 16, 17, **67–9**, 85 notes 17, 18, 19; 139, 172, 179, 200 note 9, 201 note 10, 236, 264 note 26, 294
Hesiod (8th century BCE?), Greece 7, 85 note 25, 208
Hölderlin, Friedrich (1770–1843), Germany 161 note 12, 200 note 9
Holland, see Genestet
Homer (8th century BCE?), Greece 5, 7, 9, 29 note 32, 30 note 36, 63, **64–6**, 71, 72, 145, **146–7**, 148, 149, 156, 157, 165 note 48, 181, 215, 243, 294, 309
Hugo, Victor (1802–1885), France 2, 15, 18, 25, 32 note 60, 155, 158, 189, 268, 273, 313
Hungary (united with Austria 1867–1918, independent from Russia 1991) see Berzsenyi, Kölcsey, Petőfi, Vorosmarty, Zrinyi

Ibsen, Henrik (1828–1906), Norway 9, 13, 16, 20, 21, 48, 61 note 24, 71, 77–8, 83, 87 notes 48, 51; 101, 103, 195, 220, 223 note 24, 223 note 36, **264 note 26**, 293; see General Index, 'Peer Gynt'
Iceland (independent from Denmark 1944), see Sturluson
Imber, Naphtali Herz (1856–1909), Russian-Hebrew 2–3; see Israel
Ionian school 14, 102, 150, 155–5, 160 note 1, 163 notes 37, 38; 249; see Greece
India (independent from Britain 1947) see Bharati, Chattopadhyay, Ghose, Iqbal, Tagore
Iqbal, Muhammed (1877–1938), India/Pakistan 15, 21, 22, 23, 32 note 71, **58 note 2**, 253, 257, **258**, 267, 169, 276, **278–9**, 289 notes 19, 20
Iraq (independent from Britain 1932) see Rusafi, Zahawi
Ireland (independent from Britain 1921) see Ferguson, McBurney, Moore, Pearse, Plunkett, Yeats
Israel (independent from Britain 1948): Amichai, Greenberg, Lamdan, Shlonsky, Stern; Hebrew in Babylonia (Iraq): Hai Gaon, Saadia Gaon; Hebrew in Spain: ibn Ezra, Halevi, Gabirol, Hanagid, Saruq, Shaprut; Hebrew in Russia: Bialik, Gordon, Imber, Kook, Lebensohn, Tchernichowsky; see General Index, Bible
Italy (unification 1860) see Dante, Ariosto, Boiardo, D'Annunzio Foscolo, Leopardi, Mameli, Manzoni, Marinetti, Pascoli, Petrarch, Tasso, Ungaretti

Jacinto, Antonio (1924–1991), Angola 15
Jebate, Amadu (1920s–), Gambia 315 note 9

Kalvos, Andreas (1792–1869), Greece 146, 155, **156**
Kemal, Namik (1840–88), Turkey 166
Kenya (independent from Britain 1963) see Mbiti
Key, Francis Scott (1779–1843), USA 1
Kipling, Rudyard (1865–1936), England 2, 5, 21, 32 note 58, 52, **62 notes 26, 31**; **137**, 144 note 8, 191, 201 note 13, 267, 272, 274, 285, 287 notes 3, 9; 288 note 10, 290 note 40
Kleist, Heinrich von (1777–1811), Germany 64, **73**, **86 note 33**, 199 note 3, 200 note 9, 261
Khamisi, 'Abd al-Rahman Al- (1919–1987), Egypt 83
Klopstock, F.G. (1724–1803), Germany 47, 64
Kölcsey, Ferenc (1790–1838), Hungary 29 note 27, 179, 185 note 45, 253, 254, 295
Kollar, Jan (1793–1852), Panslavic 9, 15, 16, 20, 63, 167–8, **179–80**, 189, 249, 255
Kook, Abraham Isaac (1865–1936), Russian-Hebrew 244; see Israel
Kornaros, Vitsentzos (1553–1613?), Crete 107 note 28
Körner, Theodor (1791–1813), Germany 24, 190, 199 note 3, 261
Kotliarevsky, Ivan (1769–1838), Ukraine 16, 179
Krasinski, Sigismund (1812–59), Poland 184 note 33
Kunene, Mazisi (1930–2006), South Africa 82, **283–4**, 285, 290 note 34

Labrat, Dunash ben (?–970) Spanish Hebrew **117–8**
Lamartine, Alphonse de (1790–1869), France 14, 155, 160, 193, 205
Lamdan, Isaac (1900–1955), Israel **81**, **281**
Lebanon (independent from France 1944) see Gibran, Nu'aima, Shidyaq
Lebensohn, Abraham Dov (1794?–1878), Russian Hebrew **176**; see Israel
Leino, Eino (1878–1926), Finland 13
Leopardi, Giacomo (1798–1837), Italy 13, 16, 20, 29 note 27, 64, 192, 215, **293–4**, 295, 315 note 2
Lermontov, Mikhail Yurevich (1814–1841), Russia 32 note 59
Lewis, Saunders (1893–1985), Wales 15, **61 note 26**, 310
Lissauer, Ernst (1882–1937), Germany 33 note 82, 188
Lithuania (independent from Russia 1990) see Baranauskas
Lomonosov, Mikhail (1711–1765), Russia 14, 90, 101, 169
Longfellow, Henry Wadsworth (1807–1882), USA 74–5, 86 note 41, **222–3 note 23**
Lönnrot, Elias (1802–1884), Finland 4, 7, 14, 15, 16, 17, 18, 19, 25, 48, 63, 64, **76–7**, 83, 86 note 45, 166, 167, 178, 189, 207, 222 note 23, 251, 270, 287 note 2
Lopez, Vicente (1818–1903), Argentina 314

Macpherson, James (1736–96), Scotland 16, 18, 71, 74, 86 notes 37, 43; 137, 179, 185 note 48, 200 note 9, 205, 249, **260**, 271
Mair, Charles (1838–1927), Canada 268
Mackellar, Dorothea (1885–1968), Australia 268
Malawi (independent from Britain 1964) see Mnthali
Malta (independent from Britain, 1964) see Psaila
Mameli, Goffredo (1827–1849), Italy 20, 160, 191
Mandelstam, Osip (1891–1939), Russia 18
Manzoni, Allesandro (1785–1873), Italy 15

Mao Zedong (1893–1976), China 15
Marcabru (c. 1150), France 90, 94
Marinetti, Filippo Tommaso (1876–1944), Italy **188**, 196, 199 note 2, 200 note 7
Marlowe, Christopher (1564–1593) 99, **100**
Marti, José (1853–1895), Cuba 5, 15, 20, 38, 191
Martinique (1958– overseas department of France), see Césaire
Marulik, Marko (1450–1524), Croatia 100, 183 note 10
McBurney, William (1844–1890), Ireland 271
Mbiti, John (1931–), Kenya 283, 284, 310
Mexico (independent from Spain 1821) see Ochos
Mickiewicz, Adam (1798–1855), Poland 2, 7, 13, 14, 15, 16, 18, 20, 23, 24, 25, 33 note 81, 38, 47–8, 54, 64, 72, 73, 74, 86 note 38, 160, 167, 168, 174, **176–8**, 182, 184 note 32, 187, 189, 191, 194, 207, 226, **250–1**, 253, 254, 261
Milton, John (1608–1674) 10, 11, 50, 51, 64, 134, 140, 144 note 12, **265 note 30**, 268, 271, 272, 286
Miron, Gaston (1928–1996), Canada (Quebec) **265 note 43**
Mitran, Khalil (1872–1949) Syria/Lebanon/Egypt 83, 288 note 11, 289 note 14
Montenegro (full independence from OttomanTurkey 1878) see Serbia: Njegoš
Mnthali, Felix (1933-), Malawi 37, 270
Möller, Eberhard Wolfgang (1906–1972), Germany 34 note 82
Moore, Thomas (1779–1852), Ireland 200 note 9
Morganwg, Iolo (Edward Williams, 1747–1826), Wales 71, 86 note 37, 144 note 9, 256
Mozambique (independent from Portugal 1975) see De Sousa, Rebelo
Mqhayi, Samuel Edward Krune (1875–1945) South Africa 62 note 31, **284**, 290 note 33, 291 note 40
Mtshali, Oswald (1940–), South Africa 285
Musset, Alfred de (1810–1857), France 7

Neruda, Pablo (1904–1973), Chile 15, 34, 29 note 27, 86 note 41, **296**, **311**
Neto, Augustinho (1922–1979), Angola 15, 18, 312, 313
Nicaragua (independent from Spain 1821) see Cardenal, Dario
Nigeria (independent from Britain 1960) see Osadebay, Soyinka
Njegoš, Petar II Petrovic (1813–1851) Serbia/Montenegro 2, 6, 14, 15, 19, 60 note 17, 63, 64, 91, 92, **100–01**, **102–03**, 105 note 4, 106 note 22, 108 notes 30, 37; 109 note 40, 165 note 53, 167, 168, 170, 171, 253, **255**, 262
Norway (independent from Sweden 1905) see Bjornson, Ibsen, Welhaven, Wergeland
Norwid, Cyprian (1821–1883), Poland 33 note 81
Nu'aima, Mikhail (1889–1988), Lebanon 290 note 23

Ochos, Anastasio de (1783–1833), Mexico 314
Oehlenschlager, Adam (1779–1850), Denmark 87 note 49, 309
Osadebay, Denis Chukudebe (1911-1994), Nigeria 15, 24, **285**, 311
Owen, Wilfred (1893–1918), England 187, 188, 191, 196, 219

Pakistan (independent from Britain 1947), see Iqbal
Palestine (independent from Britain 1948), see Darwish, Greenberg, Lamdan, Shlonsky, Stern
Pascoli, Giovanni (1855–1912), Italy 192
Pasternak, Boris (1890–1960), Russia 18
Paterson, Andrew Barton ('Banjo') (1864–1941), Australia 267, 299
p'Bitek Okot (1931–1982), Uganda 18, 24, 37, 82
Pearse, Patrick (1879–1916), Ireland 18, 20, 25, 38, 70, 143, 191, 237, 243, 253, 259, 271, 280, 289 note 16
Persia, see Ferdowsi
Petőfi, Sandor (1823–1849), Hungary 5, 7, 9, 12, 14, 18, 20, 21, 24, 25, 31 note 49, 38, 47, 54, 64, 83, 107 note 24, 144 note 9, 160, 182, 187, 191, 194, **203**, 207, 221 notes 8, 11; 226, 249, **250**, 263 notes 5, 6, 7; 268, **293**, **294**, 314

Petrarch, Francesco (1304–1374), Italy 96, 105 note 11
Philippines (end of Spanish rule, 1899; independent from USA, 1946) see Rizal
Pindar (518?–438 BCE?), Greece 60 note 19
Plunkett, Joseph (1887–1916), Ireland 38, 191
Poland (independent from Russia, Prussia, Austria 1918–1939; from Russia 1989) see Krasinski, Mickiewicz, Norwid, Slowacki
Portugal (republic 1910), see Camões
Prešeren, France (1800–1849), Slovenia 4, 9, 29 note 27, 295
Psaila, Dun Karm (1871–1961), Malta 17, **107 note 29**, 163 note 39, 253, 257, 259, **264 note 26**, **265 note 37**, 267, **310**
Pushkin, Alexander (1799–1837), Russia 2, 12, 13, 16, 18, 31 notes 50, 53; 32 notes 58, 59; 157, 162 note 15, **166**, **184** notes **32**, **36**; 189, 256

Rakovski, Christian (1873–1941), Bulgaria 173
Rawalz, Rabin (1935–), Suriname 316 note 18
Rebelo, Jorge (1940–), Mozambique 192, 313
de Rada, Jeronim (1814–1903), Albania 17, 63, 169, 173, 181, 183 note 7, 246 note 2
Rizal, Jose (1861–1896), Philippines 201 note 12
Romania (independent from Turkey 1878), see Eminescu
Ronsard, Pierre de (1524?–1585), France 90, 105 note 6, 107 note 27
Root, George Frederik (1820–1895), USA **224 note 43**
Runeberg, Johan Ludvig (1804–77), Finland 64, 86 note 46
Rusafi, Maruf al- (1875–1945), Iraq 6, 15, 23, 25, 31 note 54, 83, **90**, 267, 279–80, **288** notes **11**, **13**; **289 note 16**, 290 note 22
Russia, see Bestuzhev, Blok, Lermontov, Lomonosov, Mandelshtam; Pasternak, Pushkin, Ryleyev; Russian Hebrew: Bialik, Gordon, Imber, Kook, Lebensohn, Tchernichowsky; see Israel

Rutebeuf (c. 1245–1285), France **95**
Ryleyev, Kondrati Fyodorovitch (1795–1826), Russia 166, 191

Saadia Gaon (892?–942), Hebrew 116
St. Lucia (Caribbean, independent from Britain 1979), see Walcott
Saruq, Menahem ibn (c.910-c.970), Spanish Hebrew 117
Sassoon, Siegfried (1886–1967), England 188, 191, 196, 219
Sayyid Maḥammad 'Abdille Ḥasan (1856–1920), Somalia 15, 258
Shawqi, Ahmad (1868–1932), Egypt 2, 6, 16, 23, 25, 83, 192, 267, **268**, 271, 272, 273, **274–5**, 289 note 14
Schiller, Friedrich (1759–1805), Germany 6, **18**, 31 note 47, **63**, 158, 161 note 12, **187**, 200 note 4, 201 note 16, 208, 293
Scotland (union with England, 1707) see Barbour, Blind Harry, Burns, Macpherson, Scott, Smollett, Thomson
Scott, Sir Walter (1771–1832), Scotland 13, **137–40**, 200 note 9, 208, 249, 261, 271, 309
Senegal (independent from France 1960) see Diop, Senghor
Senghor, Leopold Sedar (1906–2001), Senegal 15, 18, 26, 29 note 29, 82, 311, **312–3**, **314**, 316 note 14
Serbia (independent from Turkey 1912) see Njegoš
Servantsediants, Karekin (1840–1892), Armenia 73, 183 note 8
Shakespeare, William (1564–1616), England 99, 134, **136**, **144 note 5**, 215, 263 note 21, 267, 273, 274, **301–03**, 307
Shaprut, Hasdai ibn (c.905–c.970), Spanish Hebrew 117
Shawqi, Ahmed (1868–1932), Egypt 2, 6, 16, 23, 25, 83, 89 note 71, 192, 267, 268, 271, 272, 273, 274–5
Shevchenko, Taras (1814–1861), Ukraine 7, 12, 14, 16, 17, 18, 19, 20, 24, 25, 29 note 27, 31 note 48, 32 notes 59, 62; 38, 47, 60 note 17, 63, 69, 73, 74, 85 note 19, 86 note 39, 100–01, 167, **178–9**, 184 notes 32, 36; 185 note 43, 187, 192, 194, 207, 226, 251, 253, **254–5**, 257, **261–2**, 264 note 26, 268, 285, 287 notes 1, 2; 295, 313

Shidyaq, Ahmad Faris (1804–1887), Lebanon 287 note 2
Shlonsky, Abraham (1900–1973), Israel 55, 269, **281**
Shukri, Abd-al Rahman (1886–1958), Egypt 269, 274
Siamanto (Atom Yarjanian) (1878–1915), Armenia 27 note 10, 109 note 40, 185 note 50
Sierra Leone (independent from Britain 1961) see Cheney-Coker
Slater, Francis Carey (1876–1923), South Africa 268
Slovenia (independent from Yugoslavia 1991) see Prešeren
Slowacki, Julius (1809–49), Poland 184 note 33
Smart, Christopher (1722–1771), England 134
Smollett, Tobias (1721–1771), Scotland 144 note 10
Solomos, Dionysios (1798–1857), Greece 2, 7, 17, 18, 29 notes 27, 32; 83, 91, 102, **145**, 146, 147, 149, 150, 152, **155–6**, 161 note 10, 162 note 14, 163 note 23, 163 notes 38, 39, 40; 166, 170, 172, 182, 187, 192, 249, 287 note 2, 295, 299
Somalia (independent after British and Italian colonial rule 1960), see Sayyid
South Africa (independent after White minority rule 1994) see Brutus, Kunene, Mqhayi, Mtshali, Slater
Soutsos, Alexander (1803–1863), Greece 16, 19, 145, **152–3**, 172
Soutsos, Panagiotis (1805–1868), Greece 160, 162 note 20
Soyinka, Wole (1934–), Nigeria 23, 267, 283, 285, 311
Spain, see Ercilla; also see Argentina, Chile, Cuba, Mexico, Nicaragua
Arabic: Abu Ishak, ibn Hazm, ibn Zaidun Hebrew: ibn Ezra, Halevi, Gabirol, Hanagid, Saruq, Shaprut; see Israel
Spenser, Edmund (1552–1599), England 10, **50–1**, 100, 134, 271
Stern, Abraham (1907–1942) Israel **282**
Sturluson, Snorri (13th century), Iceland 87 note 49
Suriname (Dutch colony, independent 1975), see Rawalz

Suso, Bamba (1900–1974), Gambia 315 note 9
Swinburne, Algernon (1837–1909), England 62 note 26, 201 note 13, 271

Tagore, Rabindranath (1861–1941), India **21–2**, 23, 33 note 73, 63, **70–1**, 83, 201 note 16, 214, 224 note 35, 228, 247 note 12, 252, 267, 268, 269, 276, **277–8**, 287 note 5, **287–8 note 9**; 289 note 18, 293, 299
Tamil: see Tiruvalluvar
Tasso, Torquato (1544–1595), Italy 90, 97, **98–9**, 100, 107 notes 23, 26
Tchernichowsky, Saul (1875–1943) 13, 18, **80–1**, 118, **181**, 253, 257, **281**, 282
Tennyson, Alfred Lord (1809–1892), England 21, 72, **133**, 136, 137, **140–1**, 143, 144 note 13, 189, 208, 225 note 45, **291 note 40**
Thomson, James (1700–1748), Scotland 287 note 7
Tiruvalluvar (1st century BCE?), Tamil 11, 30 note 37
Toumanian, Hovannes (1869–1923), Armenia 18, 30 note 37, 190, **252**
Turkey (republic 1923) see Ersoy, Fikret, Gökalp, Kemal

Uganda (independent from Britain 1963), see p'Bitek
Ukraine (independent from Soviet Russia 1990), see Kotliarevsky, Shevchenko
Ungaretti, Giuseppe (1888–1970), Italy 187

Valaorites, Aristotle (1824–1879), Greece 14, 102, 155, **156**, 160, 161 note 9, 162 note 20, **261**
Varoujan, Daniel (1884–1915), Armenia 109 note 40, 185 note 50
Vasa, Pashko (1825–92), Albania 155, **174**
Velestinlis, Rigas (or Feraios) (1757–1798), Greece 5, 91, 101, 145, 150, 167, 171–2, 190
Virgil (Publius Vergilius Maro, 70–19 BCE), ancient Rome 11, **66**, 84 **note 9**
Vorosmarty, Mihaly (1800–1855), Hungary 14, 249

Walcott, Derek (1930–), St. Lucia 62 note 31, 267, 283, **285–6**, 290 note 40, 291 note 42, 311, 316 note 18
Wales, see Cynddelw Brydydd Mawr, Gruffudd ab yr Ynad Coch, Lewis, Morganwg
Watson, William (1858–1935), England 272
Watts, Isaac (1674–1748), England 51
Welhaven, J.S.C. (1807–1873), Norway 17
Wergeland, Henrik (1808–1845), Norway 15, 17, 63, 194, 253, 254, 309
Whitman, Walt (1819–1891), USA 2, 5, 12, 14, 18, 21, 23, 25, 29 note 23, 31 note 54, 56, 57, 59 note 10, 70, **74–5**, 83, 86 note 41, 89 note 71, 187, 191, ch. 9, 293, **294**, 295, 297 note 5, 309
Wordsworth, William (1770–1850) England 2, 28 note 18, **84 note 13**, 85 note 26, 140, 200 note 8, 293, **301–7**, 309
Wyatt, Thomas 50

Yeats, William Butler (1865–1939), Ireland 5, 7, 9, 12, 13, 14, 15, 16, 18, 20, 23, 25, 28 note 13, 63, 64, 69–70, 75, 83, 135, **141–3**, 189, 195, 198, 215, 220, ch. 10, 252, 253, **259**, 267, 268, 271, 286, 287 note 5, 288 note 11, 293, **294**
Yuehe, Hang (1917–1995), China 267, 289 note 16

Zahawi, Jamil Sidqi al- (1863–1936), Iraq 268=9
Zaidun, ibn (1003–1071) Spain **119**
Zirikli, Khair al-Din al- (1893–1976), Iraq 280
Zrinyi, Nicholas (1616–1664), Hungary 90, 100, 169

II GENERAL INDEX

'A Backward Glance O'er Travel'd Roads' (Whitman) 215, 222 note 20, 224–5 note 44, 294
Abbasid caliphate 111, 113, 114
'Abd ar-Rahman III 114, 117, 130 note 9
Abbey Theatre 227, 241, 243, 245
Abramowitz, S.J. (Mendele) 229
Abu Ishaq 123

Index

Achelous 155
'A Contribution to the Debate on National Poetry' (Diop) 294
Acre 105 note 9
Acropolis 153: see Athens
Actium, battle of (31 BCE) 66
Aeneid (Virgil) 11, 16, 66, 84 note 8
Aeschylus **1**
Afonso Henriques 99
The Age of Bronze (Byron) 190
Agincourt, battle of (1415) 136, 315 note 4
Ahab 40
Ahad Ha'am 54, 226, 229, 230, 233, 240, 244, 252
Aino (*Kalevala*) 61 note 24, 76
Akiba xii, 87 note 55
Alcuin of York 92, 93, 105 note 6
Alcyone (D'Annunzio) 196
Alexander I, Tsar 176, 185 note 43
Alexander II, Tsar 176, 229, 230, 233
Alexandria 91, 96, 149
Alfonso VI 95, 112, 124
Alfonso VII 112
Alfonso d'Este 99
Alfred, King 137, 144 note 8
Ali Pasha 153, 161 note 10, 163 note 27
Alipashiad (Haxhi Shereti) 163 note 27
aliyah 182, 230
Alkalai, Rabbi Yehuda 181
Almohads 112, 125, 127, 128, 130
Almoravids 95, 112, 124, 125, 129
Ambris, Alceste de 197
America: ch. 9; Blacks 75, 213, 214, 219, 222 note 13, 224 note 33; Indians 37, 74, 75, 86 note 41
American Civil War (1861–65) 5, 18, 75, 203, 206, 207, 210, 213, 219–20
American revolution 11–2, 47, 206, 215
Andalusia 112, 114, 115, 118, 121, 123ff., 132 note 37
Andrić, Ivo **67**, 108 note 39, 167, 175
Anthem of the Decades (Kunene) 290 note 34
Antioch 91
anti-Semitism 20, 21, 33 note 80, 53ff., 73, 81, 176, 181–2, 184 note 34, 194, 246 note 8, 229–30, 233, 234, 237, 242, 246 note 8, 281; see Jews, Kishinev, pogroms, Zion
Apollo 181
Arabic poetry 15, 16, 17, 58 note 2, 63, **82f.**, 89 note 71, 89, notes 71, 72; 105 note 9, 106 note 21, 107 note 22, 110, 111, 113, 114, 116ff., 268f., 272f., 287 note 2, 288 note 11, 290 notes 22, 23
Arachova 152
Archilochus 282
'Arditism' 197
Argos 165 note 48
Arjuna 19, 71, 289 note 17
Arminius 64
Arta 152
Arthur, King 19, 72, 84 note 16, 90, 97, 140–1, 143, 144 note 12, 208
Arwidsson, A.I. 76
'As I Ebb'd with the Ocean of Life' (Whitman) **211–12**
Assyria 3, 36, 37, 38, 40, 42, 43, 44, 74, 84 note 6, 249, 309
Astrapogiannos (Valaoritis) 156, 161 note 9
Athens 60 note 19, 102, 147, 149, 151, 152, 154, 158, 159, 162 note 21, 165 note 48, 172: see Acropolis
Augustus 66, 144 note 5

Babylonia 3, 23, 36, 37, 38, 40, 42, 43–5, 74, 249; see Abbasid caliphate
Badis ibn Habbus 123
Baghdad 113, 280
'The Battle Cry of Freedom' (Root) 224 note 43
Bajazeth I, Sultan 100
Balfour Declaration (1917) 242
Baligant, emir of Babylon (*The Song of Roland*) 94
Balkans 2, 19, 63, 67, 92, 101–3, 104, 108 note 35, 109 note 44, 146, 148, 153, 159–60, 160 note 1, 162 note 18, 167, 168–75, 182
Bannockburn, battle of (1314) 62 note 28, 135, 200 note 6, 260
bards: David (Ancient Israel) 14, 40, 50, 54, 64, 93; Halban (Lithuania), 177, 250; Merlin (England) 72, 141, 208; Odin (Germanic) 72; Ossian (Scotland) 86 note 37, 88 note 57, 137, 144 note 9, 179, 200 note 9; Oevin (Norway) 87 note 50
Begin, Menahem 56, 244
Belinsky, Vissarion 13, 17, 179
Bengal 21, 70, 269, 276–7, 287 note 3, 288 note 17
Benjamin, Walter **200 note 7**
Berbers 111, 112, 114, 120, 123, 124, 127, 130 note 7

Berkeley, George 243
Berlin, Congress of 109 note 44, 174, 175, 184 note 24, 257
Berlin, Treaty of 173
bet midrash 233
Bhavagad–Gita 72, 269
Bible: Amos 35, **39–40**, 45, 53, 256; Deuteronomy 9, 40, **41**, 45, 59; Elijah 14, 26 note 6, 40, 72; Exodus **41**, 47, 59 notes 9, 12; 64, 79, 87–8 note 55, 291 note 42, 296 note 1; Ezekiel 9, 17, 18, **45**, 134, 216, 218, 256, 295; Genesis 81, 130 note 1; Numbers **1**; Hosea 9, 12, **44**, 60 note 18, 134, 295, 296 note 1; Isaiah 2, **6**, 18, 19, 35, 42, 45, 46, **60 note 19**, 61 notes 25, 26; 194, 256, 287, 296; Jeremiah 3, 12, 14, 17, 18, 26 note 5, 32 note 60, 35, 37, 38, 40, **42–3**, 45, 54, 60 note 18, 228, **292**, 293; Joel **60 note 16**; Judges **41–2**, 48, 73, 154; Kings 60 note 15; Lamentations 26, **43**, 131 note 11; Micah **40**, 42, 118; Nahum **42**; Psalms **3**, 9, 19, 36, 39, **43–4**, 47, 49–50, 51, 60 notes 17, 19; 61 notes 24, 25; 62 notes 27 28; **64**, 83, 84 note 4, 131 note 24, 264 note 28, 296 note 1, 309; Zachariah 45, 279; Bible, translations of: in Hungarian 47, in Welsh 61 note 26; 3, 9, 10, 11, 12, 16, 19, 36. 39, **46–50**, 51, 52, 57, 61 note 26, 97, 104, 201 note 13, **248–9**; see Coverdale, Five Books of Moses, Geneva Bible, Greek Bible, King James Version, Luther, prophets, Tyndale, Vulgate (Latin)
Bilozerski, Vassily 180
Bismarck, Otto von 14
Black Plague 134, 347 note 23
Boer War (1899–1902) 288 note 10
Borisov brothers 180
Botzaris, Markos 152–3, 153–4
The Bride of Abydos (Byron) 157
Brandeis, Adolf 207
British empire 5, 6, 9, 18, 21, 23, 27 note 10, 30 note 32, 32 note 58, 37, 48f., 56, 62 note 26, 62 note 31, 137, 140ff., 146, 163 note 38, 201 note 13, 213, 226, 234, 246 note 3, 252, 260, 262, 264 note 21, **ch. 12**; see empires
British White Paper of 1939 282
Bruce, Robert 62 note 28, 64, 135, 138, 254, 260, 271

The Bruce (Barbour) 62 note 38, 135
Briullov, Karl 185 note 43
Brooklyn Daily Eagle 205
Brotherhood of Cyril and Methodius 180
Burke, Edmund 243
By Blue Ontario's Shore (Whitman) 83, 203, 207, **208**, **211**, **215**
Byrhtwold **133**
Button Moulder (Ibsen) 78
Byzantine empire 91, 92, 102, 147ff., 161 notes 3, 5, 170

Cairo 2, 113, 269, 272, 274
Calamus (Whitman) 212, 223 note 28
Canterbury 97
The Canterbury Tales (Chaucer) 96
Carnaro Charter (Fiume) 197
Caspian mountains 99
Castile 95, 124
Castriota, George 72, 103: see Skanderbeg
Catherine the Great 148, 170, 176, 190
Cathleen ni Houlihan (Yeats) 236, 239
Cavour, Camillo 14
censorship 43, 73, 177, 184 notes 32, 34; 237, 263 note 9, 287 note 1
Cetinje 2
Cervantes, Miguel de 107 note 28
Ceuta 99
Chaeronea, battle of (338 BCE) 161 note 7
Chansons de Geste 90, 91, **93**, **95f.**, 105–6 note 11, 106 note 15
Chants pour Naëtt (Senghor) 29 note 29
Charlemagne 92, 93–4, 95, 96, 97, 98, 104, 105 note 6, 106 note 19
Charles I 134
Charles V 98, 107 note 27
Charles of Lorraine 100
Charles Martel 93, 103, 171
Chateaubriand, François René 155, 165 note 48
Childe Harold's Pilgrimage (Byron) 139, 157, 158, 190, 191, 200 note 8
Chios 151, 154
Chrétien de Troyes 90
Christianity: see The Church
Christopoulos, Athanasios 151
The Church: Bulgarian 173; English 9, 33 note 74, 49, 50, 51; Greek Orthodox 150, 160, 162 note 15, 159; Maronite 259; Roman Catholic 10, 46, 48, 51, ch. 3, 231, 234, 236, 239; Russian Orthodox 148, 159,

167, 168; Scottish 138; separation from State 12; Serb Orthodoxy 171, 255, 262; Welsh 256; *'Communist Manifesto'*, 221 note 4; 'universal' 10; 'white people's Church' 37; and Bible translation 46ff.; see Jews
The Cid 90, 95, 105 note 43, 208
Claudius 144 note 5
Coburg 202 note 22
colonialism 23, 241, 248, 270, 284, 289 note 16, 290 note 22, 291 note 40, 311ff.; Said on 288 note 11
'Coole Park, 1929' (Yeats) 243
'Coole Park and Balleylee' (Yeats) 234
Commedia (Dante) 96, 106 note 19
Communist Manifesto 204
Congress Party (India) 269
Constantinople (Istanbul) 10, 86 note 39, 92, 97, 98, 100, 101, 102, 106 note 22, 109 note 44, 147, 149, 150, 151, 152, 153, 161 note 10, 169, 170, 183 note 9; Treaty of (1832) 152
Cordoba 112, 114, 115, 117, 118, 120, 125, 127, 130 note 9
Corinth 155, 157, 165 note 48
Corn Laws 268
The Corsair (Byron) 192
Cossacks 24, 73, 74, 81, 101, 178, 254
Council of Trent 98
Countess Cathleen (Yeats) 236, 239
Coverdale, Miles 9, 19, 49
The Cretan (Solomos) 156
Cretan Renaissance 107 note 28, 162 note 14
Crimean War (1853–55) 23, 176, 191
Cromer, Evelyn Baring 273, 274, 275, 289 notes 14, 16
Cromwell, Oliver 23, 50, 51, 62 note 28, 134, 248, 286
'The Croppy Boy' (McBurney) 271
Crusades 5, 10, 24, 90, **92ff.**, 104, 105 notes 6, 9; 107 notes 22, 26; 110, 111, 112, 126, 129–30
Cserhalom (Vorosmarty) 250
Cuchulain 19, 64, 70, 72, 142–3, 234, 235, 237
Culloden, battle of (1746) 137, 193, 200 note 6, 248, 260, 271
Cyprus 40, 92, 96, 147, 274
Czech Slavophil Movement of Enlightenment 179, 255

Danes 133
Darwin, Charles 69, 203, 232

Daughter of Slava (Kollar) 9, 180
David, King 14, 40, 50, 54, 64, 93; see bard
Deborah 13; *Song of Deborah* 41–2
A Defence of Poetry (Shelley) 13, 26
Diakos, Athanasios 160, 162 note 20
Dinshawai 274–5
Diwan (Zahawi) 269
Dohm, Christian Wilhelm von 57
Dombrowski, Jan Henryk 250
Don Juan (Byron) 157, 187, 200 note 8
Donskoy, Dmitri 64
Dred Scott case 213
Druids 232
Dublin Hermetic Society 232
Dundas, Henry 139

'Easter 1916' (Yeats) 75, 143, 191, **243**, 253, 271
Ebbesen, Neils 64
Edward VI 50
Eger (Vorosmarty) 250
Egypt 2, 15, 16, 17, 23, 27 note 10, 37, 38, 40, 41, 42, 47, 48, 59 notes 9, 12; 61 note 23, 62 notes 28, 31; 64, 79, 83, 86 note 36, 87–8 note 55, 89 note 71, 91, 126, 127, 159, 208, 258, 267, 268, 269, 272–5, 288 note 11, 289 notes 14, 15, 16; 291 note 42
Eisteddfod 135
Eleutheria 157
Elijah (prophet) 14, 26 note 6, 40, 72
Elizabeth I 51, 302
Elka's Wedding (Tchernichowsky) 13
Emerson, Ralph Waldo 210, 215
Emmet, Robert 75, 143
Emperor Shaka the Great (Kunene) 82, 89 note 69, 283–4, 290 note 34
empires: see British; Byzantine; Mesopotamian; Ottoman; Roman; Tsarist Russian
English Civil War (1642–49) 11, 50, 51, 133, 134; see Cromwell
Enlightenment, French 194
Epic of Digenes Akrites (Anonymous) 161 note 3
epic poetry 6, 9, 10, 11, 19, 29 note 31, 33 note 81, 62 notes 28, 29; 63, 64ff., 75ff., 100–01, 102, 153, 169, 235
Epidaurus 152
Erasmus 46, 98
Erotokritos (Kornaros) 107 note 28
Eschenbach, Wolfram von 90

Eugene Onegin (Pushkin) 13, 184 note 36
'Europe' ('Resurgemus') (Whitman) **205–6**, 213, 219

'Farewell to Cromer' (Shawqi) 275, 289 note 14
The Fairie Queene (Spenser) 51
Fallmerayer, Jakob Phillip 164 note 47
famine 203, 229, 231, 247 note 23, 259, 268, 287 note 3, 301, 302, 303, 306
Fanon, Frantz 34 note 83, 37
Fasci di Combattimento 198
fascism 5, 21, 22, ch. 8, 228, 243, 281
Fatimid caliphate 111, 113
Fauriel, Claude Charles 151, 162 note 18
'Fears in Solitude' (Coleridge) 136, 144 note 6, **272**, **299–300**, 309
The Feast at Solhaug (Ibsen) 13
Ferdinand and Isabella 95
Ferrara 99, 107 note 23
Fitzgerald, Edward 75, 143
Fiume 21, 22, 186, 195–8, 202 notes 21, 22
Five Books of Moses 30 note 36, 116 note 2
The Flight of Zalan (Vorosmarty) 249
Flodden, battle of (1513) 138, 249, 271
folklore and poetry 15, 16, 31 notes 50, 51; **ch. 2**, 102, 105 note 4, 106 note 22, 108 note 39, 138, 142, **147–8**, 149, 151, **153–5**, 159, 161 notes 6, 9; 156 note 53, 168–9, 173, 174, 179, 181, 189, 227, 232, 235, 236, 243, 263 note 17, 284, 299, 310
forgeries 86 note 37, 137, 144 note 9, 180, 200 note 9
Francis I of France 99
Franco-Prussian war (1870–71) 21
Fratelli d'Italia (Mameli) 191
French Revolution 4, 5, 10, 16, 20, 24, 27 note 12, 31 note 50, 47, 52, 63, 69, 82, **101f.**, 133, 134, 139, 144 note 9, 145, 148, 149, 150, 151, 159, 161 note 10, 166, 171, 172, 179, 187, 188, 193, 194, **199–200 note 4**, 200 note 6, 201 note 15, 204, 205, 206, 260, 268, 273, 293, 301, 303
Freud, Sigmund 58 note 2, 72

Gabriel (angel) 88 note 55
Gaelic 23, 134, 135, 141, 143, 228, 229, 231, 232, 234, 235, 236, 241, 243, 245, 253

Gaelic League 232, 236, 241, 247 note 32
Galicia (Poland) 55
Gama, Vasco da 66, 99
Gandhi, Mohandas 32 note 71, 201 note 12, 268, 269, 278, 295
Garda, Lake 2, 202 note 21
Garibaldi, Giuseppe 47, 188, 191, 202 note 21, 205, 222 note 14
Geneva Bible 50, 61 note 26
genocide: of Armenians 109 note 40, 185 note 50, 190, 201 note 19, 263 note 17; of Bosnian Muslims 109 note 40, 183 note 14, 266 note 45; of Jews 5, 55f., 58 note 2, 81, 89 note 70, 247 note 23, 252, 281f.
George IV 139
George V 289 note 20
Gerusalemme Liberata (Tasso) 97, 99, 105 note 10, 107 note 26
The Giaour (Byron) 157, 158
Gibraltar 124
Gilbert, W.S. 62 note 26, 201 note 13
Gilboa, Mount 81, 281
Gitanjali (Tagore) 252, 278
Goa 66
Godfrey of Bouillon 99, 107 note 27
'God Save the King/Queen' 2, 61 note 25
'Gods' (Whitman) **218**
Gogol, Nikolai 255
Gomel 54
Gonne, Maud 9, 227, 239
Gordon, A.D. 55
Gordon, Judah Leib 38, **176**, 253, 256, 157
Gordon, Thomas 162 note 19
Gouras, John 154
Graetz, Heinrich 162 note 18
Granada 10, 95, 106 note 20
Grattan, Henry 243
Great Boyg (Ibsen) 78
Greek Bible 46, 149, 173
Greek War of Independence (1821–28) 4, 19, 20, 21, 78, 102, 108 note 39, ch. 6, 168, 172, 175; see Ionian islands, Peloponnese, philhellenism
Gregorios, Patriarch of Constantinople 151
Gregory, Lady Augusta 235, 241, 243
Griffith, Arthur 236, 239, 244
Gunpowder Plot (1605) 50
Gutenberg, Johann 46

Habimah 227
Hagar 81, 122

Hadzhi Dimit'r 161 note 9, 173
Hanina ben Teradion 80
Harfleur (*Henry V*) 136
Haskalah (Hebrew Enlightenment movement) 114, 176, 181, **229**, 230, 233
'Hatikva' (Imber) 2
Haxhi Shereti 163 note 27
'The Haydamaks' (Shevchenko) 17, 18, 24, **74**, 86 note 39, **100–01**
Hazm, ibn 119
Hebrew Melodies (Byron) 20, 51, 189, 194
Hebrew: **ch. 1, ch. 4, 229–30**; see Bible; see Index of Poets, s.v. 'Israel'
Hector 65
heder 233
Hegel, Georg Wilhelm Friedrich 161 note 12, 179, 194
The Heights of Macchu Picchu (Neruda) 296, 311
Hellas (Shelley) 151
Hengerdd 135
Henry VIII 46, 48, 49, 50, 99
Herder, Johann Gottfried von 4, 15, 16, 17, 67–9, 85 notes 17, 18, 19; 139, 172, 179, 200 note 9, 201 note 10, 236, 264 note 26, 294
Herkel, Jan 180
Herzl, Theodor 14, 53, 181, 227, 230, 242
Hibbat Zion 230
The Highland Lute (Fishta) 10, 103, 105 note 4, 165 note 53, **174–5**, 184 note 26, 252–3, 257–8
Hitler, Adolf 22, 34 note 82, 73, 85–6 note 32, 198, 202 notes 21, 22; 282
Hobhouse, John 191
Ho Chi Minh 13, 15
The Holocaust 5, 55, 56, 57, 58 note 2, 81, 89 note 70, 247 note 23, 252, 281, 282–3; see Jews, Zion
Holy Grail 141
Holy Land 10, 65, 92–5, 97, 98, 104, 105 notes 6, 7; 110, 123, 124, 125, 126–7, 129
Holy Sepulchre 92, 99
Home Rule (Ireland) 231, 237
Horniman, Annie 240
Hosea 9, 12, 44, 60 note 18, 134, 295, 296 note 1; see prophets
Hoursit Pasha 153
Hrebinka, Yevhen 179
Hundred Years War 97

Hyde, Douglas 141, 232, 235
Hydra 152
Hypsilantis, Alexandros 151, 153

'I am Ireland' (Pearse) 70, 259
Idylls of the King (Tennyson) 72, 140–1, 144 note 13
The Iliad 65, 208, 282
Ilmarinen (*Kalevala*) 76–7
imperialism 14, 31 note 46, 37, 50, 59 note 10, 66, 214, 232, 2612, 268, 270, 272, 276, 279, 288 note 10, 288 note 11, 290–1 note 40, 312; see empires
Indian Mutiny (1857) 248
Indra 277–8
In Memoriam (Tennyson) 141
In the City of Slaughter (Bialik) 19, 53, 73, 75, 184 note 34, 185 note 50, **233–4, 238–9**, 240, **256–7**, 263 note 9
Ionian islands 14, 102, 150, 155–6, 160 note 1, 163 notes 37, 38; 249: see Greek War of Independence
Iorga, Nikolae 162 note 18
Irish civil war (1922–3) 243
Irish language 16, 17, 134, 141, 235, 236: see Gaelic
Irish Literary Theatre 232, 235
Irish potato famine 203, 247 note 23
Irish war of independence (1919–21) 231
Isaiah 2, 6, 18, 19, 35, 42, 45, 46, 60 note 19, 61 notes 25, 26; 194, 256, 287, 296; see prophets
Islam 6, 19, 10, 11, 25, 66, **ch. 3**; conquests 5, 18, 22, 24, 83, 91–2; conversion to 91, 94, 102, 105–06 note 11, 106 note 14, 114, 153, 160, 163 note 23, 168, 171, 255, 262, 264–5 note 28; see Arabic poetry
Istanbul: see Constantinople

Jabotinsky, Vladimir 56, 244, 246 note 3
Jefferson, Thomas 209, 213
Jehoiachin, King 40
Jena, Battle of (1806) 9, 23, 58 note 3, 73, 179, 199 note 3
Jeremiah 3, 12, 14, 17, 18, 26 note 5, 32 note 60, 35, 37, 38, 40, 42, 45, 54, 60 note 18, 228, 292, 293; see prophets
Jerusalem 3, 10, 13, 26 note 5, 42, 43, 44, 45, 51, 52, 54, 55, 56, 57, 58 note 2, 60 notes 16, 18, 19; 64, 71,

73, 80, 81, 91, 92, 93, 94, 95, 96, 98, 99, 105 note 6, 107 note 27, 111, 126, 127, 189, 227, 229, 282, 295, 309
Jesus 96, 99, 191, 204, 263 note 6, 265 note 37, 284, 285
Jewish Agency (Palestine) 269
Jews and Judaism 3, 11, 17, 19, 20, 24, 29 note 32, 30 note 36, ch. 1, 63, 68, 69, 72, 78–81, 84 note 6, 85 note 27, ch. 4, 140, 149, 162 note 18, 175, 176, 180–2, 189–90, 192, ch. 10, 248, 249, 251–2, 256–7, 280–3, 295; see anti-Semitism, Holocaust, Zion, Index of Poets s.v. 'Israel'
Jinnah, Muhammed Ali 289 note 19
John of Gaunt 2, 136, 263–4 note 21
Johnson, Samuel 137
Judith (Marulik) 100, 182 note 10
Julius Caesar 144 note 5
Julius Caesar 306

Kadare, Ismail 28 note 16
The Kalevala (Lönnrot) 4, 14, 17, 31 note 48, 48, 61 note 24, 72, **75–7**, 86 note 45, 87 note 47, 140, 146, 166, 178, 222 note 23, 251, 270
Kalevala Day 4, 178
Kant, Immanuel 6, 57
Karaiskakis, Georgios 152, 153, 154
Karaites 116 note 2
Karavelov, Lyuben 173
Karpenisi 152, 153
Kennedy, John F. 75, 192, 295
Khedive 274, 289 note 16
Kikuyu (Kenya) **82**
King James Bible 48, 49, 61
King, Martin Luther 201 note 12
kinnus 181, 227, 235
Kioutahi Pasha 152, 153
Kisavos, Mount 148
Kishinev pogrom (1903), Bialik's reaction to 19, 53, 73, 75, 184 note 34, 185 note 50, 233–4, **237**– 8, 256
Knights of Malta 107–08 note 29
'Know Nothings' 203, 223 note 31
Knox, John 61 note 26
The Kobzar (Shevchenko) 14, 31 note 48, 86 note 39, 251
Konrad Wallenrod (Mickiewicz) 64, 72, 73, 177, 250, 263 note 9
Korais, Adamantios 149, 151, 162 note 18

The Koran 83, 99, 100, 116, 154, 175, 278
Kosciuszko, Thaddeus (Tadeusz) 86 note 43, 178, 190
Kostomarov, Mikola 180
The Koran 83, 99, 100, 116, 154, 175, 278
Kosovo Fields, battle of (1389) 6, 28 note 16, 64, 84 note 15, 102, 171, 248, 262, 265 note 28
Kotliarevsky, Ivan 16, 179
Kozmian, Kajetan 250
'Kralovedorsky Manuscript' 179–80
Krishna 70–1, 289 note 17
The Lady of the Lake (Scott) 139

lament 9, 26 note 5, 43, 102, 107 note 22, 118, 123, 127, 131 note 11, 135, 147, 169, 171, 271
Lane, Sir Hugh 241
Laon and Cythna (Shelley) 151
Lasker-Schüler, Else 56
Lawrence, D.H. 52, 235 note 45
Lawrence, T.E. 62 note 28, 201 note 13, 271
The Lay of the Last Minstrel (Scott) 13, 139, 261, 271, 309
Laxness, Halldor 29 note 31
Lazar, Prince 108 note 37, 264–5 note 28
League of Nations 28 note 12, 186, 200 note 4
Leaves of Grass (Whitman) 21, **203ff.**
Lemberg (Lvov, Lviv) 55
Lemminkainen (*Kalevala*) 76
Leonidas 149, 150, 152, 162 note 20
Lepanto, battle of (1571) 99, 107 note 28
Leucas 14, 150, 156
liberalism 5, 20–1, ch. 8, 206, 207, 212
Lincoln, Abraham 206, 213, 214
Llywelyn ap Gruffudd 135, 271
Londos, Andreas 157
Louis Philippe I 193, 205, 221 note 8
The Lusiads (Camões) 11, 66, 99, 105 note 6
Luther, Martin 10, 46, 49

Macau 66
Macaulay, Thomas Babbington 287 note 3
Maccabees 19, 53, 64, 81, 256
Machiavelli, Niccolo 12
MacNeill, Eoin 232, 236
Madog ap Maredudd 135
Magyars 179, 254, 263 note 6

Maimonides, Moses 112
Malaga 112
Maldon, battle of (991) 48, 133
Malory, Thomas 140
Malta 91, 147, 253, 259, 264 note 26, 265 note 37, 267, 289 note 15, 310; siege of (1565) 107–08 note 29, 265 note 37
Mandela, Nelson 284
Marathon, battle of (490 BCE) 19, 151, 158
March on Rome 198, 199 note 2, 202 note 22
Margaret or The Ruined Cottage (Wordsworth) 301, **305**, 306, 307
Markish, Peretz 56
Marmion (Scott) 138, 144 note 11, 249, 261, 271
martyrdom 4, 5, 26 note 4, 38, 75, 80–1, 97, 101, 103, 143, 145, 150, 157, 160, 171, 188, 190–2, 235, 250, 256–7, 271, 275, 283, 293, 314
Marx, Karl 11, 30 note 38, 204–05, 221 notes 3, 4, 5, 276, 304
Masada 81, 281
Matthaios, Metropolitan of Myra 148
Mazzini, Giuseppe 190, 222 note 14, 276
McHenry, Fort 1
Mehmet II 97, 147
Melville, Herman 222 note 21
Mendele: see Abramowitz
Merlin 72, 141, 208
Mesopotamian empires 17, 18, 38, 42; see Assyria, Babylonia
Messiah 114
The Messiah (Klopstock) 47
Metternich, Clemens, Fürst von 158, 199 note 4
Micah 40, 42, 118; see prophets
Midrash 16, 69, 79, 89 note 55, 116, 125, 236
Milos Obilic 64
The Minstrelsy of the Scottish Border (Scott) 139
Mircea 103, 169, 173
Miriam (Moses' sister) 59 note 9
Missolonghi 2, 20, 102, 145, 146, 152, 153, 154, 155, 159, 163 note 23, 172, 182, 189, 190, 191
Missouri Compromise 213
Mitchel, John 64
Mohács 98
Mohammed 83, 93, 96, 100–01, 106 note 19, 154, 275

Moldavia 151, 256, 287 note 1
Mongols 105 note 11, 254
monotheism 38, 40, 59 note 12, 93, 113
Morte d'Arthur (Malory) 140
Moses 13, 13 note 36, 51, 58, 59 notes 9, 12; 116, 128, 279, 284
Moscow 148, 177, 250
The Mountain Wreath (Njegoš) 6, 19, 91, 100–01, **102–03**, 108 note 37, 109 note 40, 168, **171**, **255**, 262
Moznayim 227
Mujo-Halil songs 72
Munich Putsch (1923) 22, 34 note 82, 198
Muslim League (Pakistan) 269, 278, 279, 289 note 19
Musset, Alfred de 7
Mussolini, Benito 22, 186, 187, 198, 199 note 2, 202 notes 21, 22
Mustafa Bey 154
Mycenae 165 note 48
My Patriotism (Ghayati) 273
myth: ch. 2; see Arjuna, King Arthur, Cuchulain, Mujo-Halil songs, *Nibelungen*, Odin, Olaf, Skanderbeg, Swerre, Vainamoinen, Wotan; and censorship

Napoleon and the Napoleonic wars 5, 10, 14, 16, 22, 58 note 3, 62 note 29, 69, 73, 101, 133, 134, 138, 139, 145, 148, 151, 160 note 1, 166, 176–7, 187, 192, 193, 194, 196, 199 notes 3, 4; 200 note 8, 201 note 15, 206, 207, 250, 261, 273, 274, 301, 302, 309, 314
Napoleon III 18, 32 note 60, 194
Nasim, Ahmad 289 note 16
Nathan (prophet) 40
nationalism and national poets: in the calendar 4, 26 note 5; and chosenness 10, 11, 18, 35, 36, 38, 39–40, 51, 52, 53, 54, 58 notes 1, 2; 59 note 12, 61 note 22, 74, 102, 104, 106 note 13, 113, 171, 172, 229, 249, 288 note 11; and clergy, attacks on 38, 256, 265 note 29, 173; contradictions 6–7, 29 note 22, 143, 211, 220, 234, 244; cultural 22–3, 28 note 12, 35, 36, 38, 39, 58 note 2, 65, 66, 85 note 27, 141, 148, 168, 172, 174, 183 note 5, 200 note 9, 220, 226ff, 256, 264 note 26, 272, 283, 316 note 17; 'declarations of independence' 14, 31 note 48, 76, 166, 178, 251, 313;

nationalism and national poets *(cont.)*
  and defeat 5, 6, 7, 9, 10, 13, 18, **22–4**, 26, 28 note 16, 33 note 74, 35ff., 39, **42ff.**, 56, 58 note 3, 64, 65, 69, 72, 73, 74, 81, 82, 83, **ch. 3**, 112, 124, 128, 136, 137, 138, 144 notes 9, 10; 146, 147, 151, 153, 156, 161 note 7, 163 note 27, 167, 169, 170, 171, 173, 177, 187, 189, 191, 192–3, 199 note 3, 200 notes 6, 8; 206, 207, 236, 238, 239, 243, 267, 271, 273, 280, 282, 300, 311, 314, **ch. 11**; and the Bible 35–8, 43–4; and education 9, 11, 12, **15ff.**, 19, 26, 47, 101, 102, 104, 142, 148, 150, 166, 187, 201 note 12, 286 note 1; and epic 6, 9, 10, 11, 19, 29 note 31, 33 note 81, 62 notes 28, 29; 63, **64ff.**, 75ff., 100–01, 102, 153, 169, 235; and folklore 15, 16, 31 notes 50, 51; **ch. 2**, 102, 105 note 4, 106 note 22, 108 note 39, 138, 142, 147–8, 149, 151, **153–5**, 159, 161 notes 6, 9; 156 note 53, 168–9, 173, 174, 179, 181, 189, 227, 232, 235, 236, 243, 263 note 17, 284, 299, 310; forgeries 86 note 37, 137, 144 note 9, 180, 200 note 9; and grievance 5, 19, 23, 25, 35, 43–4, 175, 253, 265 note 43, 270, 295, 313; and history, distortion of **71ff.**; and martyrdom 4, 5, 26 note 4, 38, 75, 80–1, 97, 101, 103, 143, 145, 150, 157, 160, 171, 188, 190–2, 235, 250, 256–7, 271, 275, 283, 293, 314; and masks (Yeats) **238–40**; and myth ch. 2; and the 'Other' 5, 11, 18, 38, 92, 105 note 5, 201 note 10, 273; and politics **13–15**; and printing 3, 10, 16, 46, 97, 104; psychology of **8–9, 295–6**; revenge 5, 7, 22, 23, **24–5**, 43–4, 60 note 17, 73, 76, 80–1, 96, 102, 103, 156, 161 note 4, 172–3, 187, 207, 237, 254, 260–2, 271, 275, 282; and totalitarianism 18, 187, 188, 193, 200 note 6, 204, 226; and traitors 20, 38, 75, 178–9, 248, 253–9, 264 note 21, 271; 'unacknowledged legislators of the world' 25–6, 234, 250; and the vernacular 3, 10, 12, 16, 17, 23, 39, 46ff., 57, 61 note 22, 65, 90, 92, 93, 94, 96, 97, 98, 100, 104, 133, 144 note 12, 155; and the wounded self 8, 12, 192, 216, 220, 295, 311; ('see Index of Poets')

National Party (Egypt) 269, 273
Nationalist Party (Bengal) 277
'National Song' (Hungary) 263 note 6, (India) 287 note 1, 314 note 1
'National Song for Indian Children' (Iqbal) 58 note 2, 279
'National Song of India' (Iqbal) 21, 278
Nebuchadrezzar 40
Nero, Emperor 73, 275, 289 note 14
Neue Rheinische Zeitung 221 note 3
New Orleans Crescent 205
Nibelungen 72, 73, 140, 141, 143, 208, 235
Nicholas I, Tsar 18, 166, 176, 184 notes 32, 36; 191, 262
Nicholas II, Tsar 228
Nietzsche, Friedrich 65, 186, 194, 195, 196, 197, 199 note 2, 201 note 19, 202 note 21, 237
Normans 107 note 29, 134, 135; Norman conquest (1066) 10, 48, 133
Novalis (Friedrich von Hardenberg 85 note 26
Navarino, battle of (1827) 152, 159, 172

O'Casey, Sean 239, 243
'*Ode pour la rèsurrection latine*' (D'Annunzio) 195, 200 note 6
Ode to Liberty (Solomos) 102, 147, 149, 152, 155, 166, 172, 249, 299
Odin 72; see 'bards', 'myth'
Odysseus 152, 161 note 4
The Odyssey 161 note 4, 282, 30 note 36, 41, 65
O'Grady, Standish 141, 232
Oisin 142
Olaf 87 note 50
O'Leary, John 141, 232, 233, 237, 259
'Old Chants' (Whitman) 208
Olympus, Mount 85 note 25, 102, 147–8, 153
'Once I Passed through a Populous City' (Whitman) **212**
oral poetry: see folklore and poetry
Order of the Golden Dawn 232
Orlando Furioso (Ariosto) 93, **97- 8**, 105 note 6, 168
Orlando Innamorato (Boiardo) 97
Osnovianenko, Grigorii Kvitka 179
Ossian 86 note 37, 88 note 57, 137, 144 note 9, 179, 200 note 9
Osman (Gundulic) 100, 169
Ottoman empire 4, 5, 6, 10, 18, 19–20, 21, 32 note 58, 60 note 19, 72, 91,

92, 96, 97, 98, 99, 100, 101, 102, 103, 104, 106 note 11, 107 note 28, 108 note 39, **ch. 6**, **ch. 7**, 252–3, 262, 265 note 35, 274, 280, 287 note 2, 288 notes 11, 13; 290 note 22; see empires
Oulalem (Marx) 225 note 5
Ourique, battle of (1139) 99
'Our Old Feuillage' (Whitman) **216**
Out of the Cradle Endlessly Rocking (Whitman) 218

Paine, Thomas 206, 210
Palacky, Frantisek 180
Pale of Settlement (Russia) 182, 228, 280
pan-Slavism 20, 167, 179–80
Paris Peace Conference (1919) 288 note 10
Parnell, Charles Stewart 231, 232
Pharaoh 83, 87 note 55, 275
Pan Tadeusz (Mickiewicz) 13, 18, 24, 33 note 81, 38, **74**, 168, 174, 177–8, **250–1**, 254, 261
Paradise Lost (Milton) 11, 51, 134, **265 note 30**, 286
Patrick, Saint 236
Peacock, Thomas Love 25
Peer Gynt (Ibsen) 21, 61 note 34, 71, **77–8**, 87 note 51, 101, 103, 223 note 24, **264 note 26**
Peloponnese 151: see Greece
Penelope 161 note 4
The Peril of Sziget (Zrinyi) 100
Peter the Great 176, 184 note 32
Peterloo massacre 139
Phanariots 101, 149, 150
philhellenism 101, 150, 151, 158
Philip VI of France 96
Photeinos (Valaoritis) 156
The Pilgrimage of Charlemagne 95, 105 note 6
Pithom 79
Plato 7, 25, 26, 71, 151, 187
Plunkett, Horace 227, 241
pogroms 19, 53–4, 55, 56, 73, 75, 123, 129, 175, 180, 181–2, 184 note 34, 230, 233, 237–8, 251–2, 256–7, 263 note 9
Poltava 16, 248
polytheism 105 note 11, 107 note 25
Poniatowsky, Prince Jozef Anton 250
Poor Law 301ff.
popes, Leo X 98; Pius II 97; Urban 107 note 27

Pouqueville, François 151, 162 note 18
'Prayer of Columbus' (Whitman) 29 note 23, 211, **212**
Prizren, League of 174
prophets in Bible 3, 8, 9, 11, 12, 14, 16, 17, 18, 22, 35, 36, 38, 39, 40, 43, 44, 47, 51, 53, 57, 58 notes 2, 3; 60 note 19, 71, 74; see Amos, Ezekiel, Hosea, Isaiah, Jeremiah, Micah, Zachariah; in postbiblical literature: Mohammed, Jesus
Pyrenees 93, 94

Quakers 223 note 30
Quebec 23, 265–6 note 43

Rabba bar Bar Hanna 79
Rameses 79
Rapallo, Treaty of 197
Ravenna 164 note 46, 190, 195
'Recessional' (Kipling) 372, 290 note 40
Reformation 46, 47, 51, 98, 133, 134, 149, 171, 230
Regensburg 97
Reign of Terror 20, 193, 205, 206; see French Revolution
Reliques of Ancient English Poetry (Percy) 31 note 50, 139
The Renaissance 46, 93, 97, 104, 107 note 23, 149, 171
Renan, Ernest 71, 85 note 21, 238
Revolt in Hell (Zahawi) 269
revolutions: of 1848–49 5, 10, 14, 21, 24, 47, 77, 108 note 35, 170, 203ff., 219, 220, 221 notes 8, 9, 226, 245–6, 263 note 6; English 11, 50, 51, 133, 134; French 4, 5, 10, 16, 20, 24, 27 note 12, 31 note 50, 47, 52, 63, 69, 82, 101, 133, 134, 139, 144 note 9, 145, 148, 149, 150, 151, 159, 161 note 10, 166, 171, 172, 179, 187, 188, 193, 194, 199–200 note 4, 200 note 6, 201 note 15, 204, 205, 206, 260, 268, 273, 293, 301, 303; Russian 13, 168, 175, 280; see wars
Rhodes 92
Riad Pasha 274
Richard II 136
Richard II (Shakespeare) 2, 100, 136, 263 note 21
Richard III (Shakespeare) 144 note 5
Rizopastai 160 note 1
Robespierre, Maximilien 47, 186, 199 note 4, 205, 295

Rodrigo de Vivar: see *The Cid*
Roland: see *The Song of Roland*
Romans and Roman empire 9, 64, 66, 69, 73, 80, 81, 91, 93, 103, 114, 130 note 7, 134, 172, 186, 195, 202 note 21, 229, 255, 282, 285
Romanticism 6, 7, 149, 179, 200 note 7
Romantic School of Athens 102, 149, 152, 162 note 21, 183 note 17
Roncesvalles 93, 208
Rousseau, Jean Jacques 68, 186
Rosicrucianism 232, 236
'Rule, Britannia' (Thomson) 287 note 7
Russell, George 232, 239
Russian Revolution 13, 168, 175, 280
Russification 76, 167, 175, 177, 179, 181, 313; see Tsarist Russian empire
Ruth 59 note 9

Sa'd Zaghlul 289 note 15
Safarik, Pavel Josef 180
Sagrajas 124
'Sailing to Byzantium' (Yeats) 243
Saladin 10, 83, 96, 105 note 9
'Salut Au Monde!' (Whitman) **205, 218**
Sampo (*Kalevala*) 77
Sardinia 91
Sassna Dzerek 73, 183 note 8
Saul, King 61 note 25, 81, 88 note 62, 281
Schelling, Friedrich 6, 161 note 12
Scottish Gaelic 134
'Scots wha hae' (Burns) 200 note 6, **248**, 260
The Scroll of Fire (Bialik) 228, 242, 244
Scythia 21, 99
'September 1913' (Yeats) **75**, 88 note 56, 143, 237, 243, 259, 268
Serb revolt (1804–13)
Seville 112, 117, 121
Shahnameh (Ferdowsi) 11
Shaka, Emperor 82, 283, 284, 290 note 34
Shema 80
Shkodra 154, 174, 183 note 7
shtetl 233
The Siege of Corinth (Byron) 157
Siegfried 235
Sitwell, Osbert 186
Skanderbeg 19, 64, 72, 103, 153, 169, 173, 174, 175, 183 note 7, 253
slavery 18, 21, 23, 24, 36, 37, 38, 47, 51, 75, 101, 150–1, 172, 190, 191, 203, 207, 209, 213–4, 223 notes 30, 32; 224 note 33, 248, 270, 272, 275, 283, 284, 288 note 11, 291 note 42, 296, 311, 312, 313, 314, 316 note 18
Sobiesky, Jan 100–01
sofrim (scribes) 30 note 36
Solveig (Ibsen) 61 note 24, 78
The Song of Lawino (p'Bitek) 283, 290 note 34
Song of Myself (Whitman) 23, **208–10**, 211, **214**, 215, **216, 217, 218**, 220, 222 note 15, 224 note 38
The Song of Roland 10, 19, 29 note 31, **91–4**, 97, 103, 104, 106 note 12, 168, 175
Sorrento 107 note 26
Sparta 149, 150, 158, 159, 162 note 20, 165 note 48
Spartacus 64
The Sphinx 83
Sreznevsky, Izmail 179
'Star Spangled Banner' (Key) 1
Starting from Paumanok (Whitman) 74–5, 209, **217**
Stefan del Mare 256
Stowe, Harriet Beecher **203**, 222 note 13, **224, note 33**
Stratford upon Avon 2
Streets of the River (Greenberg) 56, 57, 283
'Such a Parcel of Rogues in a Nation' (Burns) **253–4**, 271
Suleiman the Magnificent 97, 100
swaraj 269, 277
Swerre 87 note 50
Swift, Jonathan 243
Synge, J.M. 71, 239. 241, 243
Syria 83, 91, 130 note 9, 259

Talmud 16, 69, **79–80**, 116, 130 note 1, 131 note 17, 228, 233, 236
'The Task' (Cowper) 213, 264 note 21
tefillin 55, 181, 281
Tel Aviv 2, 23, 28 note 19, 30 note 32, 227, 246 note 3, 252, 281
Temples in Jerusalem 13, 26 note 5, 38, 39, 43, 45, 52, 64, 73, 80, 105 note 6, 110, 111, 118, 189, 229, 240, 256, 282, 295
theater: Hebrew (*Habimah*) 227; Ireland 227, 232, 235, 241, 242, 243, 245; Norway 77
Themistocles 157
Theosophy 232

Thermopylae, battle of (480 BCE) 19, 64, 150, 151, 158, 162 note 20, 300, 315 note 2 ; see Leonidas
'Thermopylae' (Cavafy) **300**
Thourios (Velestinlis) 150–1
Tilak, B.G. 70–1
Tirukural (Tiruvalluvar) 11
Titus, Roman general and emperor 189, 282
Toledo 112, 124, 125
Tone, Wolfe 64, 75, 143, 235
Toscanini, Arturo 186
traitors 20, 38, 75, 178–9, 248, 253–9, 264 note 21, 271
Treaty of Union (1707) 137, 271
Tricupis, Spiridion 155
Tripolytza, siege of (1821) 155
Tsarist Russian empire 5, 17, 18, 19, 20, 23, 32 note 59, 73, 76, 86 note 34, 166, 175ff., 228, 230, 233, 251, 252, 253, 256, 262, 263 note 9, 287 notes 1, 2; see Pale of Settlement
Turkokratia 150
Tyndale, William 49, 50
tzedakah 45

Umayyad caliphate 111, 112, 118, 119, 120, 123, 129, 130 note 9
Una torpediniera nell'Adriatico (D'Annunzio) 196
'Under Ben Bulben' (Yeats) **235**, 245
United Nations 6, 38 note 13

Vainamoinen (*Kalevala*) 19, 61 note 24, 64, 76–7
Verdi, Giuseppe 14, 48
Vico, Giovanni Battista 72
Valencia 95
Valtetzi 155
Va pensiero (Verdi) **48**
Vendèe 199 note 4
Venice 97, 160 note 1
Versailles, Treaty of 196, 200 note 4
Victoria, Queen 268, 272, 291 note 40
Vienna, Congress of 193
Vienna, 148, 150; sieges: (1529) 97; (1683) 92, 100–01, 104
Vikings 133, 260
Vlad Tepes 103, 169, 173, 255
Vulgate 46

Wafd Party (Egypt) 269
Wagner, Richard 14, 73, 85 notes 26, 32; 143, 235

Wallace, William 64, 138, 254, 260, 271
Wallace (Blind Harry) 135
Wallachia 103, 151, 173
Wallenrod, Konrad 64; see *Konrad Wallenrod* (Mickiewicz)
Waverley (Scott) 139
wars: American Civil War (1861–65) 5, 18, 75, 203, 206, 207, 210, 213, 219–20; Bar-Kokhba (132–35) 19, 54, 64, 234, 237; Boer (1899–1902) 284, 288 note 10; Crimean (1853–55) 23, 176, 191; Crusades 5, 10, 24, 90, **92ff.**, 104, 105 notes 6, 9; 107 notes 22, 26; 110, 111, 112, 126, 129–30 ; English Civil War (1642–49) 11, 50, 51, 133, 134; Franco-Prussian (1870–71) 21; Greek War of Independence (1821–28) 4, 19, 20, 21, 78, 102, 108 note 39, ch. 6, 168, 172, 175; Hundred Years 97; Irish War of Independence (1919–21) 13, 231; Napoleonic 5, 10, 14, 16, 22, 58 note 3, 62 note 29, 69, 73, 101, 133, 134, 138, 139, 145, 148, 151, 160 note 1, 166, 176–7, 187, 192, 193, 194, 196, 199 notes 3, 4; 200 note 8, 201 note 15, 206, 207, 250, 261, 273, 274, 301, 302, 309, 314; Norman conquest (1066) 10, 48, 133; Polish revolts 23, 73, 176, 177, 182 note 2, 190, 229, 233, 248, 250–1, 263 note 8; Prussian- Danish (1864) 21; Roman-Jewish 19, 54, 64, 73, 75, 229, 234, 237, 282; Russian-Japanese (1904–05) 230; Russian-Turkish (1877–78); Spanish Armada 10, 22, 136, 144, 304; Serb revolt (1804–13) 102, 108 note 39, 149, 170; Trojan 65–6 (Homer); Turco-Venetian (1645–69) 107 note 28; War of 1812 1, 215; World War I 3, 5, 13, 21, 22, 23, 28 note 18, 33 note 82, 54, 81, 84 note 15, 101, 102, 160, 166, 168, 170, 174, 175, 185 note 50, 186, 187, 188, 191, 193, 194, 196, 197, 198, 200 note 6, 201 note 19, 202 notes 20, 21; 204, 207, 219, 220, 230, 288 note 13; World War II 4, 184 note 22, 252, 312, 314; see revolutions
Washington, George 47
The Waste Land (Eliot) 28 note 18, 308
Weizmann, Chaim 244, 246 note 3
Wells, H.G. 287 note 3
Welsh language 17, 61 note 26, 86 note 37, 134, 135; *Eisteddfod* 135;

Hengerdd 135; translation of *Song of Roland* 93; see Index of Poets, Wales
Welsh Nationalist Party 15
William of Orange 23, 248
Wilson, Woodrow 200 note 4
Winckelmann, Johann Joachim 161 note 12
'The Wound-Dresser' (Whitman) 219
World War I 3, 5, 13, 21, 22, 23, 28 note 18, 33 note 82, 54, 81, 84 note 15, 101, 102, 160, 166, 168, 170, 174, 175, 185 note 50, 186, 187, 188, 191, 193, 194, 196, 197, 198, 200 note 6, 201 note 19, 202 notes 20, 21; 204, 207, 219, 220, 230, 288 note 13
World War II 4, 184 note 22, 252, 312, 314

World Zionist Organization 53, 227, 230, 242: see Herzl
Wotan 19, 86 note 33
Wright, Francis 210
yeshivah 233

'Young America' 210, 222 note 21
Yugoslavia 196, 197

Zachariah 45, 279; see prophets
Zakynthos (Zante) 2, 145–6, 156, 249
'Zelenohorsky Manuscript' 180
Zhukhovsky, V.A. 185 note 43
The Zibaldone (Leopardi) 293
Zion and Zionism 3, 20, 39, 43–4, 53, 56, 60 note 19, 69, 95–6, 110–1, 113, 117, 118, 123ff., **181–2**, **226ff**, 252
Zionist Congress, First (1897) 240
Zlatarski, Vasil 162 note 18

For Product Safety Concerns and Information please contact our EU
representative GPSR@taylorandfrancis.com
Taylor & Francis Verlag GmbH, Kaufingerstraße 24, 80331 München, Germany

www.ingramcontent.com/pod-product-compliance
Lightning Source LLC
Chambersburg PA
CBHW061422300426
44114CB00014B/1497